Gender Relations in Canada:
Further Explorations

Marlene Mackie

Department of Sociology
The University of Calgary
Calgary, Alberta

Butterworths
Toronto   Vancouver

Gender Relations in Canada
© Butterworths Canada Ltd. 1991

Printed and bound in Canada by John Deyell Company

The Butterworth Group of Companies

Canada	Butterworths Canada Ltd., 75 Clegg Road, MARKHAM, Ontario, L6G 1A1 and 409 Granville St., Ste. 1455, VANCOUVER, B.C., V6C 1T2
Australia	Butterworths Pty Ltd., SYDNEY, MELBOURNE, BRISBANE, ADELAIDE, PERTH, CANBERRA and HOBART
Ireland	Butterworths (Ireland) Ltd., DUBLIN
New Zealand	Butterworths of New Zealand Ltd., WELLINGTON and AUCKLAND
Puerto Rico	Equity de Puerto Rico, Inc., HATO REY
Singapore	Malayan Law Journal Pte. Ltd., SINGAPORE
United Kingdom	Butterworth & Co. (Publishers) Ltd., LONDON and EDINBURGH
United States	Butterworth Legal Publishers, AUSTIN, Texas; BOSTON, Massachusetts; CLEARWATER, Florida (D & S Publishers); ORFORD, New Hampshire (Equity Publishing); ST. PAUL, Minnesota; and SEATTLE, Washington

Canadian Cataloguing in Publication Data

Mackie, Marlene
  Gender relations in Canada

1st ed. published (1983) under title:
Exploring gender relations.
Includes bibliographical references and index.
ISBN 0-409-81159-9

1. Sex role – Canada.   2. Sex differences
(Psychology).   3. Socialization   I. Title.
II. Title: Exploring gender relations.

HQ1075.M32 1991   305.3   C91-093427-4

Sponsoring Editor — Sandra Magico
Editor — Maura Brown
Cover Design — Brant Cowie
Production — Kevin Skinner

To Walter with love

Table of Contents

Tables

Boxes

Preface

As its hybrid title indicates, *Gender Relations in Canada: Further Explorations* is both second editon of *Exploring Gender Relations* (1983) and a brand-new book. The gratifying success of *Exploring Gender Relations* was the reason this recent book came about. Moreover, this volume and its predecessor share the following goals. First, because femininity and masculinity derive their meaning from the relation of one to the other, this book takes as its subject matter the experiences of both sexes. Second, the approach is sociological, rather than interdisciplinary. Although material is drawn from psychology, history, and anthropology, among others, its primary vantage point is sociology. Third, a major objective is to provide an integrated discussion of the Canadian gender literature. This book does make extensive use of important ideas developed elsewhere. However, the reason is to elucidate the meaning of gender in our own society. Finally, this volume tries to maintain demarcation between the sociological study of gender and the feminist convictions that motivate and inform much of this scholarship. Although I write as a feminist, I am convinced that sociologists, qua sociologists, contribute most effectively to the quest for gender equality when they devote their talent and training to scholarship, rather than propaganda.

The material is still organized in much the same way. Chapter 1 introduces the sex/gender distinction. Chapter 2 inquires into female/male similarities and differences. Chapter 3 evaluates various biological explanations of these differences. Chapters 4 through 7 adopt a social-psychological perspective, with Chapter 4 introducing various socialization theories; Chapter 5, 6 and 7 deal in turn with the family, peer group, and secondary and symbolic sources

as agents of socialization. Chapters 8 and 9 analyze gender from a social-structural perspective. Chapter 8 discusses work; Chapter 9, family and aging. Chapter 10 considers movements for gender liberation and prospects for change.

Despite the above similarities, I felt (and Butterworths concurred) that the extensively revised content of this new book warrants a title of its own. Eight years have elapsed between editions. In the intervening years, a rich literature of gender relations has flourished; my own thinking has matured. As a result, every section of every chapter has been rewritten. The new book has two additional chapters. Demographic and policy data have been updated. The social-structural segment of the book has been strengthened. The organization of material in the early chapters has been improved. Previously discussed issues have been re-evaluated. Many new topics have been added, e.g., homosexuality, new reproductive technologies, gender and the military, family violence. The extent to which the sociology of gender has developed in only two decades is truly astonishing.

I acknowledge with gratitude the assistance of many people in the development of this book. Comments made by instructors and students about the content of *Exploring Gender Relations* played an important part. I thank Professor Rick Ponting, the University of Calgary, for his generosity in making available to me his unpublished national data on gender-role attitudes (Chapter 2). I am grateful to Judy Roche and the University of Calgary Office of Institutional Analysis for providing data on faculty enrolments (Chapter 7). University of Calgary support staff Lynda Costello, Thomas Huang, Margaret Koslowski, and Diane Parsons contributed their different talents to this enterprise. Once again, I depended on Cathy

Schissel for library research. This book would not have happened without the technical assistance and encouragement of the Butterworths editors Gloria Vitale, Sandra Magico, Marie Graham, and Maura Brown. Finally, I thank Walter Lindenbach, to whom the book is dedicated, for his love and support.

Marlene Mackie
January, 1991

Acknowledgments

The authors and publishers of the following articles and textbooks have been most generous in giving permission for the reproduction in this text of work already in print. References, of course, appear where necessary and possible in the text. It is convenient for us to list below, for the assistance of the reader, the publishers and the authors for whose courtesy we are most grateful. The following list is organized by author in alphabetical order.

Oxford University Press, Toronto — Nancy Adamson et al., *Feminist Organizing for Change: The Contemporary Women's Movement in Canada* (1988). © Nancy Adamson, Linda Briskin, Margaret McPhail 1988. Reprinted by permission of Oxford University Press Canada.

Macmillan, New York — Margaret L. Andersen, *Thinking About Women: Sociological Perspectives on Sex and Gender* (2nd ed., 1988). Copyright © 1988 by Macmillan Publishing Company. Reprinted by permission.

Fitzhenry and Whiteside, Toronto — Pat Armstrong, "Women's Work: Women's Wages," in Greta Nemiroff (ed.), *Women and Men: Interdisciplinary Readings on Gender* (1987), pp. 354-76.

Canadian Advisory Council on the Status of Women, Ottawa — Pat Armstrong and Hugh Armstrong, *A Working Majority: What Women Must Do for Pay* (1983).

McClelland and Stewart, Toronto — Pat Armstrong and Hugh Armstrong, *The Double Ghetto: Canadian Women and Their Segregated Work* (rev. ed., 1984). Used by permission of the Canadian Publishers, McClelland & Stewart, Toronto.

Fitzhenry and Whiteside, Toronto — Elaine Batcher, "Building the Barriers: Adolescent Girls Delimit the Future," in Greta Nemiroff (ed.), *Women and Men: Interdisciplinary Readings on Gender* (1987), pp. 150-64.

Bantam Books, New York — Jessie Bernard, *The Future of Marriage* (1972).

Indiana University Press, Indiana — Raphaela Best, *We've All Got Scars* (1983).

McClelland and Stewart, Toronto — Naomi Black, "The Second Wave," in Sandra Burt et al. (eds.), *Changing Patterns: Women in Canada* (1988), pp. 80-99. Used by permission of the Canadian Publishers, McClelland & Stewart, Toronto.

Pergamon Press,
New York

Ruth Bleier, *Science and Gender: A Critique of Biology and its Theories on Women* (1984). Reprinted with permission, Pergamon Press PLC.

Jossey-Bass,
San Francisco

Jeanne H. Block, *Sex Role Identity and Ego Development* (1984).

Little, Brown,
Boston

John C. Brigham, *Social Psychology* (1986). Copyright © 1986 by John C. Brigham. Reprinted by permission of HarperCollins Publishers.

Women's Press,
Toronto

Linda Briskin, "Women's Challenge to Organized Labour," in Linda Briskin and Lynda Yanz (eds.), *Union Sisters: Women in the Labour Movement* (1983), pp. 259-71.

Simon and Schuster, Linden Press, New York

Susan Brownmiller, *Femininity* (1984). © 1984 by Susan Brownmiller. Reprinted by permission of Linden Press, a division of Simon and Schuster, Inc.

Supply and Services,
Canada

Lin Buckland, "Education and Training: Equal Opportunities or Barriers to Employment?" in Rosalie Silberman Abella, *Equality in Opportunity: A Royal Commission Report* (1985), pp. 133-56. Reproduced with the permission of the Minister of Supply and Services Canada, 1991.

Calgary Herald

July 28, 1981; May 25, 1987; May 31, 1987; June 7, 1987; October 20, 1987; May 28, 1988; February 3, 1989; October 22, 1989: B5; November 22, 1989: A4; June 2, 1990.

Sage Books,
Newbury Park, CA

CBS Television Network, "Changes in Women's Roles on Television," in Stuart Oskamp (ed.), *Television as a Social Issue* (1988), copyright © 1988. Reprinted by permission of Sage Publications, Inc.

F.E. Peacock Publishers, Inc.
Itasca, Ill.

Janet Chafetz, *Masculine/Feminine or Human?* (1974).

McClelland and Stewart,
Toronto

Lorraine Code, "Feminist Theory," in Lorraine Code and Lindsay Dorney (eds.), *Changing Patterns: Women In Canada* (1988), pp. 18-50.

University of Calgary

Janis Davison-Leong, "Interest Groups and Canadian Broadcasting Regulation: An Examination of Media Watch" (1990). Unpublished Master's Thesis, Communication Studies.

Wm. C. Brown Publishers
Dubuque, Iowa

James A. Doyle, *The Male Experience* (2nd ed., 1989).

Garamond Press,
Toronto

Ann Duffy, Nancy Mandell and Noreen Pupo, *Few Choices: Women, Work and Family* (1989). Reprinted with permission of Garamond Press and the authors.

Lawrence Erlbaum, Associates, Inc.
Hillsdale, N.J.

Alice H. Eagly, *Sex Differences in Social Behavior: A Social-role Interpretation* (1987). Copyright 1987 by Lawrence Erlbaum Associates, Inc. Reprinted by permission.

Doubleday Anchor, Garden City, New York

Barbara Ehrenreich, *The Hearts of Men* (1983). Permission granted by Doubleday a division of Bantam, Doubleday, Dell Publishing Group, Inc.

The Canadian Review of Sociology and Anthropology

Margrit Eichler, "And the Work Never Ends" Volume 22: 5 December, 1985.

Supply and Services, Canada

Margrit Eichler, "The Connection Between Paid and Unpaid Labour and its Implication for Creating Equality for Women in Employment" in Rosalie Silberman Abella, *Equality in Opportunity: A Royal Commission Report* (1985), pp. 537-46. Reproduced with the permission of the Minister of Supply and Services Canada, 1991.

Gage Educational Publishing Company (a division of Canada Publishing Corporation), Toronto

Margrit Eichler, *Families in Canada Today: Recent Changes and Their Policy Consequences* (2nd ed., 1988). Copyright © Gage Educational Publishing Company. Reprinted by permission of the publisher.

Russell Sage Foundation and Yale University Press, New York

Cynthia Epstein, *Deceptive Distinctions: Sex, Gender, and the Social Order* (1988).

McClelland and Stewart, Toronto

Jane Errington, "Pioneers and Suffragists," in Lorraine Code and Lindsay Dorney (eds.), *Changing Patterns: Women in Canada* (1988). Used by permission of the Canadian Publishers, McClelland & Stewart, Toronto.

Prentice-Hall, Englewood Cliffs, N.J.

Robert A. Fine, "Men and Young Children," in Joseph Pleck and Jack Sawyer (eds.), *Men and Masculinity* (1974), pp. 54-62.

Transaction Publishers

Gary Alan Fine, "The Dirty Play of Little Boys" (1986), *Society* 24: 63-67.

Toronto Star

Leslie Truman, "Choosing your baby's sex", January 30, 1987:B5. Reprinted with permission - The Toronto Star Syndicate.

Copp Clark Pitman, Toronto

Jane Gaskell, "The Reproduction of Family Life: Perspectives on Male and Female Adolescents," in Arlene McLaren (ed.), *Gender and Society: Creating a Canadian Women's Sociology* (1988), pp. 146-68.

Butterworths, Toronto

Ellen M. Gee and Meredith M. Kimball, *Women and Aging* (1987).

Journal of Comparative Family Studies	Roger Gibbins et al, "Attitudes and Ideology: Correlates of Liberal Attitudes towards the Role of Women" (1978), 9:19-40.
The Globe and Mail	January 27, 1988; February 25, 1989: D5; December 8, 1989; March 1, 1990.
Kluer Academic Publishers	Erving Goffman, "The Arrangement Between the Sexes" (1977), *Theory and Society* 4: 301-31.© 1977 Kluer Academic Publishers. Printed in the Netherlands. Reprinted by permission of Kluer Academic Publishers.
Prentice-Hall, Scarborough	Edward Grabb, "Conceptual Issues in the Study of Social Inequality," in James Curtis et al. (eds.), *Social Inequality in Canada: Patterns, Problems, Policies* (1988), pp. 1-19.
Fitzhenry and Whiteside, Toronto	Stan Gray, "Sharing the Shop Floor," in Greta Nemiroff (ed.), *Women and Men: Interdisciplinary Readings on Gender* (1987), pp. 377-402.
American Psychological Association	Harry F. Harlow, "The Heterosexual Affectional System in Monkeys" (1962), American Psychologist 17:1-9.
West Publishing, St. Paul, Minn.	Excerpts from pages 171, 179 and 181 reprinted by permission from "Womanspeak and Manspeak: Sex Differences and Sexism in Communication, Verbal and Nonverbal" from *Beyond Sex Roles*, 2nd ed. by Alice Sargent (ed.) by Nancy M. Henley, copyright © 1985 by West Publishing Company. All rights reserved.
John Wiley and Sons, New York	Aletha C. Huston, "Sex-typing," in Paul H. Mussen (ed.), *Handbook of Child Psychology*, vol. 4 (1983), pp. 387-467. Reprinted by permission of John Wiley & Sons, Inc. All rights Reserved.
Plenum, New York	Phillis A. Katz, "The Development of Female Identity," in Claire Kopp (ed.), *Becoming Female: Perspectives on Development* (1979), pp. 3-28.
Oxford University Press, Toronto	Michael Kaufman, "Introduction" (pp. xiii-xix) and "The Construction of Masculinity and the Triad of Men's Violence" (pp. 1-29) in M. Kaufman (ed.), *Beyond Patriarchy: Essays by Men on Pleasure, Power, and Change* (1987).
Canadian Ethnic Studies	Zonia Keywan, (1981) pp. 38-39 in Mary Two Axe Early, Zonia Keywan, and Helen Potrebenko "Ethnicity and Femininity as Determinants of Life Experience" Vol. XIII, No. 1, 1981. 37-42.
McClelland and Stewart, Toronto	Myrna Kostash, *No Kidding: Inside the World of Teenage Girls* (1987). Use by permission of the Canadian Publishers, McClelland & Stewart, Toronto.

Penguin Books	Michele Landsberg, *Women and Children First* (1982). © 1982. Reprinted by permission of Macmillan of Canada, a Division of Canada Publishing Corporation.
W.W. Norton, New York	Christopher Lasch, *The Culture of Narcissism* (1979).
Holt, Rinehart and Winston, New York	Excerpts from *Social Psychology*, Fifth Edition by A. Lindesmith, A. Strauss, and N. Denzin, copyright © 1978 by Holt, Rinehart and Winston, Inc., reprinted by permission of the publisher.
Prentice-Hall, Englewood Cliffs, N.J.	Jean Lipman-Blumen, *Gender Roles and Power* (1984).
American Sociological Association	James W. Loewen and Samuel F. Sampson, "Getting Gender on their Minds: A Classroom Exercise" (1986),Teaching Sociology 14: 185-87.
Garamond Press, Toronto	Meg Luxton and Harriet Rosenberg, *Through the Kitchen Window* (1986). Reprinted with permission of Garamond Press and the authors.
Vintage (Random House), New York	Pat Mainardi, "The Politics of Housework," reprinted with permission from *Sisterhood is Powerful*, edited by Robin Morgan (Vintage); copyright © 1970 by Robin Morgan.
Butterworths, Toronto	Leslie E. Martin, "Women Workers in a Masculine Domain: Jobs and Gender in a Yukon Mine" in Katherine L.P. Lundy and Barbara Warme (eds.), *Work in the Canadian Context: Continuity Despite Change* (2nd ed. 1986).
Penguin Books, Markham	Fredelle Maynard, *The Tree of Life* (1988).
Chatelaine	Rona Maynard, "Father's Rights" (November 1988), pp. 61-63, 140-42.
Calgary Herald	Rosemary McCracken, "Anti-Feminist Backlash" (January 27, 1987), p. A5.
Mentor Books, New York	Margaret Mead, *Sex and Temperament in Three Primitive Societies* (reprint, 1935).
Johns Hopkins University Press, Baltimore, MD.	John Money and A.A. Ehrhardt, *Man and Woman, Boy and Girl: The Differentiation and Dimorphism of Gender Identity from Conception to Maturity* (1972).
Random House, New York	Robin Morgan, *Going Too Far: The Personal Chronicle of a Feminist* (1977).
Pocket Books, New York	Tony Morrison, *The Bluest Eye* (1970).

The University of Chicago Press — Michelle Rosaldo, "The Use and Abuse of Anthropology: Reflections on Feminism and Cross-cultural Understanding" (1980), Signs 5:389-417. © 1980 by The University of Chicago. All rights reserved.

Bantam Books, New York — Rossi, Alice S. (ed.), *The Feminist Papers* (1973).

American Sociological Association, Washington, D.C. — Alice S. Rossi, "Gender and Parenthood" (1984), American Sociological Review 49:1-19.

Information Canada — *Report of the Royal Commission on the Status of Women* (1970).

Harper and Row, New York — Lillian B. Rubin, *Just Friends: The Role of Friendship in Our Lives* (1985). Copyright © 1985 by Lillian B. Rubin. Reprinted by permission of HarperCollins Publishers.

Newsweek — Laura Shapiro, "Guns and Dolls" From *Newsweek* May 28, 1990. Pages 57-58. © 1990. Newsweek, Inc. All rights reserved. Reprinted by permission.

University of Wisconsin Press, Madison — Carolyn Sherif, "Bias in Psychology," in Julia Sherman and Evelyn Beck (eds.), *The Prism of Sex: Essays in the Sociology of Knowledge* (1979), pp. 93-133.

New Star Books, Vancouver — Dorothy E. Smith, *Feminism and Marxism — A Place to Begin, A Way to Go* (1977).

Gage Educational Publishing Company (a division of Canada Publishing Corporation), Toronto — Dorothy E. Smith, "Women, the Family and the Productive Process," In J. Paul Grayson (ed.), *Introduction to Sociology* (1983), pp. 312-44.

Routledge and Kegan Paul, London — Dale Spender, *Man Made Language* (2nd ed., 1985).

University of Alberta Alumni Association, New Trail — Phyllis L. Steele, "My Heart was in Medicine," 41 (Spring), 4-5.

University of Manitoba Press, Winnipeg — Gloria Steinem, "Perspectives on Women in the 1980s: the Baird Poskanzer Memorial Lecture," in Joan Turner and Lois Emery (eds.), *Perspectives on Women in the 1980s*, (1983), pp. 14-27.

Prentice-Hall, Englewood Cliffs, N.J. — Jean Stockard and Miriam Johnson, *Sex Roles: Sex Inequality and Sex Role Development*, © 1980, pp. 188, 206, 209. Reprinted by permission of Prentice-Hall, Inc. Engelwood Cliffs, NJ 07632.

Butterworths, Toronto — Gladys L. Symons. "Careers and Self-Concepts: Managerial Women in French and English Canada" in Katherine L.P. Lundy and Barbara Warme (eds.), *Work in the Canadian Context: Continuity Despite Change* (2nd ed., 1986).

Chapter 1

Introduction

The Canadian pavilion at Vancouver's Expo 86 featured a film entitled "A Day in the Life of Canada." Fast cuts of red and white flags, July 1st birthday cakes, and smiling people communicated the producers' message of pride in country. Suppose the vantage point upon our society were gender, rather than nationalism, and the medium a sociological word portrait, instead of film. What might a day in the life of Canada look like then?

After a hurried breakfast, the husband puts the dishes into the sink, while the wife helps the children into their coats. On their way to work, he drops off one child at the daycare centre, she drives the other to school. An elderly woman sits alone, sipping a cup of tea and staring out the window of a rooming house. Seventeen boys (and three girls) spend their lunch hour immersed in the space-age noises and blue flashing lights of a video arcade. A former air force lieutenant asked to leave the military because she is a lesbian plans to challenge her dismissal in court under the Charter of Rights and Freedoms.

A brother and sister play beside the Christmas tree, he with his GI Joe action figure, she with her Barbie doll. A Pakistani-Canadian university student breaks the news to her boyfriend that her parents plan a trip to the old country to arrange a marriage for her. A single mother dials one telephone number after another, trying to locate a babysitter for her sick child so that she can go to work.

In a school gym, team captains pick their basketball teams. One boy, yet again the last one chosen, stands embarrassed. As a young woman dresses herself, she avoids looking down at her fat belly and "thunder" thighs. The two female students in this year's engineering class insist they really aren't offended by the sexist jokes and cartoons in the engineering student newspaper. A wife gets beat up by her husband because she made red Jell-o instead of green. A bank teller discovers she will soon be replaced by an automated banking machine. An unemployed man sits, head in hands, and contemplates armed robbery. Although the gender implications of these vignettes may not yet be apparent, being female or male has an enormous, and changing, impact upon the lives of Canadians.

The subject of this book is gender in contemporary Canadian society. We focus upon these questions: What does it mean to be female or to be male? How did traditional gender arrangements come about? How are they changing? These matters are approached from the sociological perspective which assumes individuals' experiences of femininity and masculinity to be rooted in the social organization of Canadian society. The women's movement prompted social scientists to ask these questions in the first place. Feminism—"the belief in the full social-political equality of human beings" (Steinem, 1983:15)—motivates and informs our discussion.

SEX AND GENDER

Our first task is to specify basic vocabulary. Although "sex" and "gender" are words laypersons often use interchangeably and idiosyncratically, a consensus has gradually emerged among social scientists to use them in particular ways. *Sex* refers to the biology of maleness and femaleness. The term indicates sexual anatomy (penises, vaginas), sex hormones and chromosomes, secondary sex characteristics (beards, breasts), and coital and reproductive behaviour. *Gender*, on the other hand, is what is socially recognized as femininity or masculinity (Gould and Kern-Daniels, 1977). By "exaggerating both real and imagined aspects of biological sex" (Lipman-Blumen, 1984:2), the cultural norms of a particular society, at a point in time, identify some ways of behaving, feeling, and thinking as appropriate for females, and other ways of behaving, feeling, and thinking as appropriate for males. The emerging convention, then, directs scholars to use "sex" to refer to physiology and "gender" to the sociocultural elaborations upon physiology.

Nevertheless, it is sometimes difficult to determine whether "sex" or "gender" is the appropriate concept (Eichler, 1980:12). The reason? Biology and culture are often inextricably entangled. In other words, such biologically based experiences as pregnancy, menstruation, and erection are influenced by cultural attitudes and values (Lipman-Blumen, 1984:2). For example, turn-of-the-century sex manuals, which warned young Canadians that engaging in masturbation led to such grim consequences as declining health, insanity, and early death (Bliss, 1974) make it clear that this solitary entertainment was a different matter in 1900 than in 1990.

Folk thought dichotomizes sex; biological females and males are viewed as belonging to strictly separate and immutable categories. Most of the time this notion suffices. However, biological sex is more accurately understood "to mean a continuum whereon the reproductive structures, hormones, and physical features range somewhere between two extreme poles" (Doyle, 1985:8). The existence of *hermaphrodites* (people born with the reproductive or genital structures of both females and males) and *transsexuals*, who have had sex-reassignment surgery to alter genitals and secondary sex characteristics, means that for a few individuals, sex is not dichotomous and unchangeable throughout the life cycle.

Laypersons tend to regard gender, as well as sex, as two mutually exclusive, inevitable categories, deeply rooted in human nature (Kessler

and McKenna, 1978). Table 1.1 illustrates this dichotomous thinking that casts the world into categories of "feminine" and "masculine" (Epstein, 1988:232). People expect women to be experts on colour and men on football, women to enter certain occupations and men to be interested in others. These societal suppositions about the essential nature of males and females channel individuals' learning experiences so that such expectations often become self-fulfilling prophecies. These thoughtways stem, in part, from the high degree of congruency between sex and gender. That is, masculinity is usually associated with male sex organs and femininity with female sex organs. Moreover, since sex is determined at conception and is immutable for most people, it seems natural to view gender as similarly constant. Nevertheless, sociologists understand gender to be "a fluid category" (Gerson and Peiss, 1985:317), a continuum of norms and behaviours "socially constructed, socially perpetuated and socially alterable" (Gould and Kern-Daniels, 1977:184).

Gender is *not* an attribute of individuals, like a nose (Stacey and Thorne, 1985). Rather, it is an ancient symbol-system cultures use to understand and to organize both human behaviour and non-human entities (Harding, 1986:17). In Lambert's (1971:2) words, "beliefs about the roles of the sexes are threads running through the fabric of society, having multiple effects upon human institutions and themselves nourished and sustained by these institutions." As we shall see, gender norms are used to evaluate and control individuals. For example, female violators of gender norms are often labelled "bitches" or "dykes," while males thought to break gender norms get called "fags," "sissies," or "wimps" (Schur, 1984).

Although the gender distinction appears to be a cultural universal, the particular expectations based upon anatomy differ among cultures and historical periods. Indeed, within contemporary Canadian society, the content of gender norms varies somewhat by age, region, ethnicity, and social class. Over the past two decades, the women's movement has caused traditional definitions of masculinity and femininity to be critically scrutinized. Nevertheless, this book rests on the thesis that gender, not sex,

TABLE **1.1**

MATCHING EXERCISE

You have five minutes to match each colour (items 1-8) and each football term (items 9-12) with the description that best fits.

Colours

1. puce
2. taupe
3. teal
4. mauve
5. magenta
6. chartreuse
7. ochre
8. sienna

a. brilliant yellow
b. pale light blue
c. pale bluish purple
d. dark mustard yellow
e. brownish gray
f. greenish blue
g. orangish yellow
h. brilliant yellow green
i. deep purplish red
j. brownish purple

Football Terms

9. safety

10. screen

11. curl

12. trap

a. to block by throwing one's body across a player's legs from behind
b. to block out a defensive player from the side after he has crossed the line of scrimmage
c. an offensive player is tackled in or loses the ball out of bounds from his own end zone
d. a pass caught behind the line of scrimmage by an eligible receiver who has two or more blockers in front of him
e. an eligible receiver runs downfield and then circles into an open area against a zone defense

Fields of Concentration

13. Select from the list at right the field that best describes your intended major and postgraduate plans. Enter its letter in the blank at left. Read the entire list before making your selection; if you plan to major in English, for example, and then become a lawyer, select d, not e.

a. social science (anthropology, psychology, sociology, political science, economics, but *not* b, below).
b. helping profession (social work, counselling, education below college level, nursing)
c. business (accounting, management, etc.)
d. law, medicine, other profession
e. humanities (English, foreign language, history, art, music, philosophy, etc.)
f. natural science (physics, chemistry, math, etc.)
g. engineering, architecture, forestry, other building profession

---

SOURCE: Loewen and Sampson (1986).

1j, 2e, 3f, 4c, 5i, 6h, 7g, 8d, 9c, 10d, 11e, 12b.
:ANSWERS

continues to be the fundamental fact of life. Sex (the biological fact) matters a great deal to individuals and to society. However, gender (the cultural embellishment upon anatomy) matters even more. As Ortner and Whitehead (1981:1) put it, the "natural processes of sex and reproduction ... furnish only a suggestive and ambiguous backdrop to the cultural organization of gender and sexuality."

THE IMPORTANCE OF GENDER

Our argument for the importance of gender rests upon three major points that will be further developed throughout the book. First, in Canadian society, as in all human societies, the sexes are differentiated. The biological distinctions between females and males are noted and emphasized. In virtually every culture, human beings use sex differences to identify themselves and other people and to organize social activities. Moreover, the biological distinction between males and females is employed as a gender metaphor to symbolize natural and social events and processes, such as nations, hurricanes, automobiles, and ships, which rarely have anything to do with sex (Harding, 1986:17-18).

Second, the sexes are ranked, and society places more value on males than females. In most, if not all, cultures "whatever is thought of as manly is more highly valued than what is thought of as womanly" (Harding, 1986:18). As a category, males command more prestige, more privileges, and more resources than females.

Third, largely as a result of the different roles and responsibilities society assigns to females and males, and the greater material and symbolic resources enjoyed by the latter, the essential relationship between the sexes is a power relationship. In Lipman-Blumen's (1984:5) words, "power is the infrastructure of the sex-gender system." These three reasons for gender's importance will now be discussed in turn.

Differentiation of the Sexes

From the perspective of the individual, the differentiation of females from males means that the impact of gender begins at the moment of birth and continues until the moment of death. The parents of a newborn infant ask, "Is it a boy or a girl?" Though at this stage the infant is little more than a bundle of tissue with potential, members of society immediately begin to react to it in terms of its sex/gender. For example, a birth announcement in the local newspaper reads: "Rocky move over. In the blue corner, weighing 6 lbs., 15 ozs. born September 14, 1990, Anthony James Paul, a son for proud parents..." Many maternity wards, sensitive to feminist concerns, now wrap newborn babies in white or yellow blankets, instead of pink or blue ones.

Despite some pressure for change, the birth announcement mentioned above illustrates the sex-typed perceptions of their newborn offspring that most parents continue to have. For example, most infants receive names that signal their sex. Aberle and Naegele (1952) reported that fathers expected their daughters to be pretty, fragile, sweet, and delicate, and their sons to be athletic and aggressive. Rubin et al. (1974) interviewed thirty pairs of parents at a Boston hospital within twenty-four hours of the birth of their first child. Fifteen of the couples had daughters and fifteen had sons. Infant girls were described by the parents as "softer," "finer-featured," "littler," and "prettier," and boys as "bigger," "stronger," "firmer," and "more alert." Although males are generally slightly longer and heavier at birth (Barfield, 1976), the hospital records showed that these particular male and female infants did not differ in birth length, weight, or health. From birth onward, parents constantly react to their child as a girl or as a boy.

Moving beyond the perspective of individuals to that of societies, Epstein (1988:6) expresses these important generalizations:

Gender distinctions are basic to the social order in all societies. Like age, gender orders society and is ordered by it. Only by some social arrangement (ordering) between the sexes can societies reproduce, and certainly a concern for reproduction constrains the way in which social groups regard the sexes. Nevertheless, some societies place more emphasis on ordering the sexes than others, although none ignores it.

Throughout life, gender permeates most social relationships and spheres of human activity. There are girls' toys and boys' toys, girls' clothes and boys' clothes. Although Canadian elementary school children now understand that women may participate in traditionally masculine occupations, the girls often fail to apply these beliefs to themselves: "Many of them seemed to be saying, 'Yes, women can become doctors, but I expect to be a nurse'; 'Bank managers can be women as well as men, but I am going to be a teller'..." (Labour Canada, 1986:55). Even when the same occupation is chosen, the male (a physician, for example) has different experiences than his female counterpart. And on it goes. Being a wife, mother, divorcée, widow, or elderly woman is not the same as being a husband, father, divorcé, widower, or elderly man.

Susan Brownmiller's (1984:13) memories about the centrality of gender in her own childish thinking illustrates the impact of sex differentiation:

We had a game in our house called "setting the table" and I was Mother's helper. Forks to the left of the plate, knives and spoons to the right. Placing the cutlery neatly, as I recall, was one of my first duties, and the event was alive with meaning. When a knife or a fork dropped to the floor, that meant a man was unexpectedly coming to dinner. A falling spoon announced the surprise arrival of a female guest. No matter that these visitors never arrived on cue, I had learned a rule of gender identification. Men were straight-edged, sharply pronged and formidable, women were softly curved and held the food in a rounded well. It made perfect sense, like the division of pink and blue that I saw in babies, an orderly way of viewing the world. Daddy, who was gone all day at work and who loved to putter at home with his pipe, tobacco and tool chest, was knife and fork. Mommy and Grandma, with their ample proportions and pots and pans, were grownup soup spoons, large and capacious. And I was a teaspoon, small and slender, easy to hold and just right for pudding, my favorite dessert.

Evaluation of the Sexes

So far, we have established that because the sexes are differentiated, gender is an axis of individual and social experience. If the sexes were equally valued, if society in general shared Maurice Chevalier's sentiment of "Vive la différence!" then the women's liberation movement need never have come into existence. However, in our society, and most others, males are more highly esteemed than females (Lipman-Blumen, 1984:6; Ortner and Whitehead, 1981:16).

The cultural devaluation of females is easily illustrated. Remember the newborn infant that we brought into being a few pages ago? When the parents asked the doctors what sex the baby was, in all likelihood they were hoping for a particular answer. If the baby is their first child or intended to be their only child, parents, especially fathers, tend to prefer a boy (Williamson, 1976). Some people are no longer willing to let nature take its course. Amniocentesis (a method that provides early identification of a fetus's sex) is reportedly used to abort female fetuses in areas of the world, such as China and India, where the preference for boys is especially pronounced (Campbell, 1976). Recently, a Canadian couple paid $2500 to a U.S. clinic which claims to have perfected sex selection technology. The husband, who according to his wife "...was always so mad when we had girls" was " 'desperate' for that boy and was willing to pay dearly for him" (*The Toronto Star*, January 30, 1987:B5).

According to a study of Ottawa kindergarten children, youngsters grasp the social fact of gender inequality early in their lives (Richer, 1983). These children maintained that their school was rife with "girl germs" which threatened boys who came into physical contact with girls. The only way for a boy to ward off girl germs was to enact the purification ritual of crossing his fingers as soon as possible after touching the girl. Richer (1983:118) says, "the fact that the expression 'boy germs' was never used and that in general, the girls made no effort to challenge the girl germs label is indicative of the very early acceptance by both sexes of a hierarchical division between males and females."

Which sex would you yourself prefer to be? Chances are that if you are female, you sometimes wish you were male, and if you are male, you are quite satisfied with your gender status quo. Why do people condone and even admire the masculine behaviour of a twelve-year-old girl and abhor the feminine behaviour of a twelve-year-old boy? Even the labels for these children, "tomboy" and "sissy," communicate societal sentiment. When a teacher asks a sociology class, "How many of you women were tomboys as children?" more than half usually put up their hands. What would happen if the male students were asked, "As children, how many preferred girls' toys and activities?" Similarly, why does feminine high fashion often mimic masculine clothing, while the reverse rarely occurs (Chafetz, 1974:75)? The answer to these questions and many more like them is both simple and not so simple: society values males more highly than females.

Gender as Power System

The momentous impact of gender stems from the direct translation of the greater social prestige enjoyed by males into a monopoly of power at both institutional and interpersonal levels. *Power* is the capacity of individuals or groups to control, influence, or manipulate others' behaviour, whether these others wish to cooperate or not (Kopinak, 1983:405). The sources and ramifications of this inequality are continuing themes of this book.

The causes and consequences of "the near universality of women's subordination to men" (Epstein, 1981:3) will require many chapters of this book to unravel. However, at this point let us introduce what has been described as "the central sociological insight" on gender (Ortner and Whitehead, 1981:8). The critical idea is this: nearly universally, men control the prestigious public domain of economic and political activities, while women are confined to the domestic realm, which is accorded lower value and associated with fewer powers and prerogatives (Rosaldo and Lamphere, 1974:3). So far as the etiology is concerned, we record our major conclusion that contemporary masculine power is really an anachronism, a residue from their historical monopoly of public domain institutions. This monopoly is shored up by the resources, material and symbolic, which it brings.

By "symbolic resources," we mean that a major prerogative and prop of masculine power is their role as the creators and perpetrators of the dominant, authoritative world view. Where alternative perspectives exist, "he who has the bigger stick has the better chance of imposing his definitions of reality" (Berger and Luckmann, 1966:109).

The feminist concept of *patriarchy* emphasizes that the domination of women by men is a pervasive feature of the social organization of all kinds of societies (Smith, 1983:316). It is true that some women are more powerful than some men (e.g., female professionals vis-à-vis their male clients). In addition, some women are dominant over other women (e.g., well-off women who employ immigrant workers in their homes). Nevertheless, if we step back to examine the larger pattern, women are consistently located in strata below men of their own social group (Lipman-Blumen, 1984:48). Males are situated in the highest stratum of every social institution—the economic system, the political and legal systems, the family, the military, the educational and religious systems.

Asymmetrical power has profound consequences for people of both sexes. For instance, at the institutional level, in the majority of Canadian offices, the managers and decision-makers are mostly men, while the typists and cleaning people are mostly women. Despite the appointment or election of women in Canada to such positions as Governor-General, Supreme Court Justice, national political party leader, general, and astronaut, despite the prominence of women journalists, lawyers, and physicians in the mass media, most Canadian women remain segregated into a relatively few, mostly low-skilled, poorly paid occupations (Armstrong and Armstrong, 1984). Moreover, as recent debates in the House of Commons concerning abortion legislation demonstrate, policies concerning women's reproductive capacities continue to be decided by men. O'Connell (1983:46) sums up the situation by labelling poverty the "feminine complaint" and concluding that "the real problem with women in this country is that they are poor."

Gender power is also a significant dimension of face-to-face relations in the micro-world. Family violence is "one of the most hostile expressions of power" (Doyle, 1985:150). Pauline is one of "more than half a million Canadian women who've been kicked, punched, whipped, burned, knifed or shot each year..." (Vallee, 1986:viii).

"He was very cruel to me in the six years that I was married to him," recalls Pauline, who now lives in Ontario. "He beat me quite often, with anything he could get ahold of—a beer bottle, broom handle...his fists, mostly. I was really afraid of him, so I more or less kept my mouth shut unless I was spoken to. I treated him as well as I could. Even with respect...even after the beatings I took and my children took. I always did everything that he wanted me to do because if I didn't, I knew what was going to happen" (Vallee, 1986:14).

Though power is the essence of gender inequality, men's power over women is not the only power differential at issue. Gender politics also involves men's power over men and women's power over men. Pleck (1981:241) argues that "patriarchy is a *dual* system, a system in which men oppress women, and in which men oppress themselves and each other." Men create hierarchies among themselves according to such criteria of masculinity as physical strength, athletic capabilities, ability to make money, and success with women (p. 239).

The division between homosexual and heterosexual men is an especially important aspect of male-male ranking. Antipathy toward and persecution of homosexuals serves to maintain strict boundaries between straight and gay men. "The fear that haunts most straight persons who have gays living or working around them is that they will be 'contaminated' by this association and thereby subvert the world of the straights" (Whitehurst and Booth, 1980:147). According to Pleck,

...this division has a larger symbolic meaning: Our society uses the male heterosexual-homosexual dichotomy as a central symbol for *all* the rankings of masculinity, for the division on *any* grounds between males who are "real men" and have power and males who are not. Any kind of powerlessness or refusal to compete becomes imbued with the imagery of homosexuality (Pleck, 1981:239).

Finally, we emphasize that women are not fully passive victims of male domination. Women resist or subvert masculine power in various ways. At the interpersonal level particularly, females control some resources of their own—sexual favours, charm, fecundity.

The distinction between *macromanipulation* and *micromanipulation* is useful here:

When the dominant group controls the major institutions of a society, it relies on macromanipulation through law, social policy, and military might, when necessary, to impose its will and ensure its rule. The less powerful become adept at micromanipulation, using intelligence, canniness, intuition, interpersonal skill, charm, sexuality, deception, and avoidance to offset the control of the powerful (Lipman-Blumen, 1984:8).

The feminist movement is essentially an attempt to adjust the power balance.

Our objective up to this point has been to introduce some of the key concepts in the sociology of gender relations, especially the sex/gender distinction, and to argue that gender is of immense importance to individuals and to societies. These ideas, intended to provide a framework for future discussion, will be fleshed out in the chapters to come.

THE SOCIOLOGY OF GENDER RELATIONS

The term *gender relations* applies to the study of the causes and consequences of the cultural identification of emotional, attitudinal, intellectual, and behavioural traits as either masculine or feminine. These causes and consequences are examined from the point of view of individuals, groups and society as a whole.[1]

A discipline, or a subfield within a discipline, makes more sense to newcomers if they have some appreciation of its history. Although a detailed history is of interest only to specialists, some general background information places the neophyte in a better position to understand what practitioners are attempting to accomplish, why certain topics are emphasized, and the reasons for shortcomings and gaps in the evidence.

Origin in the Feminist Movement

Gender relations, as a field of study, came into being in 1969, the year that North American sociologists discovered the existence of women. At the 1969 meeting of the American Sociological Association, a women's caucus met to protest discrimination against female sociologists in the profession, discrimination against women in society at large, and the sexist bias in the study of sociology (Bernard, 1973:775). Similar concerns were being expressed by women in the humanities, the other social sciences, and to a limited extent, the physical sciences. The protest of feminist scholars was international, but was particularly vocal in the United States, Great Britain, Australia, and Canada.

In 1970, the Royal Commission on the Status of Women in Canada tabled its report, which contained 167 recommendations in the areas of the economy, education, the family, taxation, poverty, public life, immigration and citizenship, and criminal law. (See Chapter 10.) As Eichler (1985a:620) points out, the background studies for this government report (e.g., Lacasse, 1971; Lambert, 1971) "must be seen as the beginning of a scholarship which is concerned with understanding women's situation in Canada."

In 1971, the Canadian Sociology and Anthropology Association passed a resolution opposing discrimination on the grounds of sex, age, or marital status and encouraging the recruitment of women. In the same year, Robson and Lapointe published a comparison of Canadian academic men's and women's salaries and fringe benefits (one of the background studies for the Royal Commission on the Status of Women mentioned above). This report, as well as a series of studies of women's status in particular Canadian universities, has been analyzed by Hitchman (1974).

The thrust of feminist scholarship in this country has been interdisciplinary in nature. The first university-level credit courses which dealt with women (or sex roles) were probably offered in 1971 (Eichler, 1985a:620). Through the *Canadian Newsletter of Research on Women*, first published in May 1972 under the editorship of Margrit Eichler and Marylee Stephenson, teachers developing these new courses exchanged course outlines and bibliographies. (The newsletter, now titled *Resources for Feminist Research*, continues to communicate information on feminist research and teaching.) The

first two Canadian academic books on women (Henshel, 1973; Stephenson, 1973) also appeared in the early 1970s.

International Women's Year (1975) saw many important scholarly developments in this country. *The Canadian Review of Sociology and Anthropology* devoted its November 1975 issue to women in the Canadian social structure. Inaugural issues of two excellent interdisciplinary journals, *Atlantis* and *Canadian Woman Studies* appeared in 1975 and 1978, respectively. In 1976, Susan Clark and Linda Christiansen-Ruffman organized the first Canadian conference on women and research at Mount Saint Vincent University in Halifax. In the same year, the Canadian Research Institute for the Advancement of Women was founded "to sponsor and assist research into areas of vital interest to Canadian women."

In retrospect, it seems odd that it was the "revival of organized feminism" (Oakley, 1974:1), not their own theories, which alerted professional students of society to the fact that the world contains women as well as men. Be that as it may, realization of the importance of gender did not originate in social science research, but in the cultural ferment occasioned by the re-emergence of the women's movement. (Chapter 10 provides a detailed discussion of feminism.)

The 1960s were marked by protests against the Vietnam War, demands for reallocation of societal power, and for equitable treatment for blacks, native Canadians and Americans, the poor, students and, eventually, women. Universities were prominent among the targets of these social movements. The universities, which monopolize the access to training and credentials required for entry into rewarding occupations and the political elite (Vickers and Adam, 1977:68), were criticized "for not understanding oppressed groups and for not generating public policy that would meet their needs" (Andersen, 1983:12).

The rapidly expanding post-secondary education system in the 1970s, and the increasing numbers of women in academia, also had something to do with gender becoming a political and academic issue in that milieu. By 1981, Canada counted 260 post-secondary institutions. "Women's numbers also rose in the 1970s from 47% to 51% of community college students and from 35% to 45% of university students" (Strong-Boag, 1983:94-95). Unprecedented numbers of students from diverse backgrounds challenged academia to acknowledge in its programs the social reality of nationality, class, race, and gender. One result was the introduction of Canadian Studies, Native Studies, Labour Studies, and Women's Studies into many colleges and universities (Strong-Boag, 1983:95).

The discipline of sociology in Canada was also growing. Only two doctorates in sociology were granted in 1960-61; by 1971-72, thirty-one had been awarded (Hiller, 1979:130). In 1973, there were 648 professional sociologists resident in Canada (Canadian Sociology and Anthropology Association *Bulletin*, October 1974:14). Although the proportion of women (16.4%) was low, in absolute numbers they, along with female graduate students, were becoming a visible, self-conscious minority within the profession. As Epstein (1981:150) suggests, the *number* of advocates very often influences the survival of an idea. Her observation certainly applies to the pivotal importance which gender concerns, formerly overlooked or ignored, came to assume in sociology.

The Sociology of Gender and Women's Studies

In the early 1970s, feminist scholars were divided in their opinions about the best strategy for converting colleges and universities to their way of thinking (Strong-Boag, 1983). The "separatist" strategy considered it prudent to acquire an interdisciplinary institutional base within universities and colleges which was separated from the traditional departments. "Women's studies courses would provide a stronghold from which to campaign and finally convert the academic community. Once conversion was complete, at some unspecified date, Women's Studies could wither away" (Strong-Boag, 1983:98). However, proponents of women's studies believed that partitioning women's experiences into the Sociology of Women, the Psychology of Women, the Literature of Women, the History of Women and so

on would lead to the fragmentation of knowledge.

An "integrationist" strategy, on the other hand, recommended transforming traditional disciplines from within. Exponents of this view concentrated on injecting feminist subject matter into existing courses, developing new courses within their conventional disciplines, putting pressure on their departments to hire women faculty, and encouraging female undergraduate and graduate students (Strong-Boag, 1983:95). Although the integrationists agreed with the supporters of women's studies that no one discipline can completely account for human experience, they argued that depth of study within individual disciplines is equally necessary.

For various reasons, the discipline of sociology seemed particularly amenable to the "boring from within" strategy. The numbers of female faculty and students were growing, and subject matter closely related to gender, such as socialization and the family, already existed in sociology courses and research. Yet impediments did exist. The political activism of women's studies—the conviction that "women's studies must be explicitly political, consciously an academic arm of women's liberation (Boxer, 1982:676)—troubled many sociologists. (See Mackie, 1977.) Finally, as the next section makes clear, sociologists wished to attend to gender, not women. Having said this, it is important to emphasize that a number of sociologists have also been prominent participants in the "separatist" women's studies movement. The energy and ethos of women's studies have been salutary influences upon feminist sociologists, wherever they teach.

Gender Relations: The Study of Both Sexes

The sociology of gender relations includes males as well as females within its purview. Female sociologists, as members of the protesting, disadvantaged sex, tended naturally to confine their early attention to their own situation. However, conceptual issues mentioned above (i.e., the role of power in the perpetuation of gender and the interlocking nature of such female and male roles as wife-husband, girlfriend-boyfriend), made it impossible to ignore men. Moreover, since the feminist movement had happened to men, too, men were reacting to it. One result was the production of a substantial "male sex role" literature during the 1970s.

This attempt to come to grips with masculinity as gender (not generic man) was a novel development in the social sciences. Though most social science before the advent of the feminist movement was indeed about men, early writings that brought *masculinity* into focus were rare. (Hartley, 1959; Komarovsky, 1964 were noteworthy exceptions.)

As later critics pointed out, the "male sex role" literature published by male intellectuals in the 1970s tended to concentrate upon the restrictions and penalties attached to being born male. However, the "essential feminist insight that the overall relationship between men and women is one involving domination or oppression" (Carrigan et al., 1985:552) was evaded. In books such as Goldberg's *The Hazards of Being Male: Surviving the Myth of Masculine Privilege* (1976), the source of the "masculine dilemma" was psychologized. Disregarding the systemic and political nature of gender meant that men could view the sexes as "separate but equal," and the women's movement as a worthy parallel endeavour, rather than a criticism of them. Of course, there were exceptions in the mid-1970s literature (e.g., Harrison, 1978; Komarovsky, 1976; Tolson, 1977), and in more recent analyses of gender from the masculine perspective (Doyle, 1989; Kaufman, 1987a; Lyttelton, 1987; Pleck, 1981). Gay liberation politics, which "have continued to call in question the conventional understanding of what it is to be a man" (Carrigan et al., 1985:551) has had considerable influence upon the sociology of gender relations.

FEMALE SOCIOLOGISTS' COMPLAINTS

Their eyes having been opened by the feminist movement, the women in sociology looked critically at their societies, at their own lives, and at their discipline and put forth three interconnected complaints. First, they were troub-led about the devalued and powerless position of women generally. Second, they protested their own status, both in the profession and in the university. Finally, they charged the field of sociology with gender bias. "Sociology, like political science, economics, philosophy, and psychology, has been blind or biased in its vision of women for decades" (Epstein, 1988:1). Since the first of these concerns constitutes the subject matter of this book, no further comment will be made here. However, their last two complaints—the disadvantaged professional position of women sociologists and the androcentric nature of their field—will be discussed in turn.

The Status of Women in Academia

The disadvantaged position of women in Canadian universities was an early agenda item for sociologists whose consciousness had been raised by the feminist movement. A torrent of newsletters, articles, and books analyzed their situation, and linked the inequitable status of women in the profession to serious flaws in sociological scholarship, especially research on women (Ward and Grant, 1985). See Ambert and Symons Hitchman (1976); A.S.A. (1973); Eichler (1975); Rossi and Calderwood (1973); Smith (1975); Vickers and Adam (1977). By 1978, twenty Anglophone Canadian universities had produced reports on the situation of women within their own institutions (Tancred-Sheriff, 1985:113). The next year, the Association of Universities and Colleges of Canada published an analysis of female-male rank and salary differentials across the country (Boyd, 1979).

The situation of women undergraduate and graduate students was also addressed (Feldman, 1974; Symons, 1978; Vickers and Adam, 1977). In 1969-70, females made up only 36 percent of students enrolled full-time in Canadian universities. Women from working-class backgrounds, from minority ethnic and racial groups, and disadvantaged regions of Canada faced formidable barriers (Vickers and Adam, 1977).

The proportion of women in graduate studies in Canadian universities, 19 percent in 1968-

69, peaked in 1929-30 when 28 percent of the graduate enrolment was comprised of women (Ambert and Symons Hitchman, 1976:138). In 1970-71, only 24 percent of the Master's degrees and 9 percent of the Ph.D.'s were awarded to women.

This analysis concluded that women sociologists, like academic women generally, were few in number, underpaid, concentrated in low ranks and insecure jobs, and absent from positions and bodies with any influence and power within the universities (Vickers and Adam, 1977:99). In 1969-70, only 13 percent of the full-time teachers in Canadian universities were women (Vickers and Adam, 1977:113). The proportion of women dropped drastically as one moved up the status hierarchy. Only 4.8 percent of academic women in Canada were at the full professor level in 1971-72 as compared to 20.5 percent of their male colleagues (Ambert and Symons Hitchman, 1976:117). University boards of governors, senates, department heads, research grant administrators, and graduate thesis advisors were mostly men.

Women academics sat outside the circles of colleagueship. Few in number, they often experienced "the loneliness of the outsider, of the stranger who intrudes upon an alien culture" (Kanter, 1977:207). Bernard (1964:303) coined the term "stag effect" to describe "the easy social contacts possible for men [but not women] at meetings of learned societies and elsewhere." Sociologists of science (Crane, 1969; Mullins, 1973) have shown the importance of informal communications networks for researchers' work. As well, colleagues are a source of professional socialization and professional identity, of friendship and support.

Commentators concluded that women in colleges and universities faced various structural and attitudinal barriers. Structural barriers refer to the fact that academia was organized to suit men, not women. Provision for part-time studies, maternity leaves, daycare centres had not been made. Graduate programs had rigid residence requirements. Attitudinal barriers included gender stereotyping of occupations and cultural definition of science and mathematics as masculine endeavours. As Harding (1986:31) notes, "Women have been more systematically excluded from doing serious science than from performing any other social activity except, perhaps, frontline warfare." Both types of barriers prevented women from getting equal access to higher education in the first place, and made it very difficult for the few who managed to secure training to get fair treatment by Canadian institutions of higher learning. Female academics faced outright discrimination in salaries. They had difficulty attracting mentors and sponsors (Ambert and Symons Hitchman, 1976:142). Hiring often proceeded through "old boy" networks. "It was not unusual for a hiring committee to sit around a table and explore in explicit terms the question, Do we really want a (or another) woman around?" (Vickers, 1976:221). In summary, the evidence indicates that even though women were generally as qualified academically and professionally as men, the academic reward system was characterized by widespread sex-differentiated treatment (Ambert and Symons Hitchman, 1976:117).

What can be said about the situation of university women today? So far as students are concerned, a growing proportion of those receiving degrees are women. In the 1980s, "women received 51% of bachelor's degrees, 40% of master's degrees, and 25% of doctorates. The corresponding percentages in 1971 were 38%, 22%, and 9%" (Statistics Canada, 1985:24). The sex ratio of advanced degrees in sociology appears to be more equal. In 1985-86, women earned 57 percent of the master's degrees and 44 percent of the doctorates in sociology (Herman, 1986-87). Whether by choice or necessity, the part-time undergraduate enrolment is disproportionately female (Statistics Canada, 1985:23). Though significant numbers of women are entering male-dominated fields, most are still concentrated in the type of educational programs that lead to the traditionally lower paid women's occupations (Turrittin et al., 1983). Schooling of males and females is discussed further in Chapter 7.

The social movements of the 1970s motivated universities to seek out women faculty members more actively, and to treat them more fairly. Nevertheless, the timing of women's entry into academia was most unfortunate. In periods when the economy is contracting, the academic sector is *squeezed* as governments cut back their support. The effects of such pressures are more likely to be borne by female [academics] who are generally among the last hired on a full-time basis (Vickers and Adam, 1977:100). The steadily declining number of new positions available in the early 1980s perpetuated lopsided male-female faculty ratios. As a result, women constituted 17 percent of all university faculty in 1985-86 (Guppy, 1989b), up one percent from their 1921 representation (Groarke, 1983:13). Women were more likely to be employed in sociology and anthropology than in other fields (Guppy, 1989b).

Not only are Canadian women faculty "few and isolated, scattered across the country," they "are largely powerless...mainly junior in rank and almost absent from the positions and forums of formal influence" (Tancred-Sheriff, 1985:110). Only 15 percent of women sociologists are at the highest rank of full professors (compared with 31 percent of males) (Guppy, 1989b). For 1971-72, women in sociology earned 87 percent of what their male counterparts earned. By 1985-86, women's salaries had declined to 85 percent of males (Guppy, 1989b). Considering that female sociologists more than hold their own in publishing performance (Mackie, 1986), the discrepancy in status is difficult to justify. According to the Canadian Sociology and Anthropology Association's Directory of Sociologists in this country (Herman, 1986/87), only eight of the 42 sociology departments in Canadian universities were headed by women. Few women are university or college presidents, deans, or editors of mainstream journals. The evidence indicates that "even when women do all the 'right' things, they are rewarded less than men. In study after study, when measures such as scholarly productivity, administrative experiences, degree held, and years of experience are held constant, there is still a gap between women and men" (Simeone, 1987:37). As Guppy (1989a:744) remarks, the fact that this gap in average earnings of academic men and women has narrowed very little since the early 1970s is especially disappointing in view of universities' reputation for enlightened, progressive thinking.

The work experiences of men and women in academia differ significantly. Women are more involved than men in under-valued activities, such as teaching or advising students, rather than research and administration (Simeone, 1987:36). Female teachers are evaluated less favourably than their male counterparts, especially by male students (Simeone, 1987:66). Moreover, the same idea becomes more authoritative when presented by a male rather than a female instructor (Bernard, 1981a:384).

A social science professor remarks: "I feel as if I cannot win in the classroom. If I'm organized and 'professional' students perceive me as cold and rejecting. If I'm open and responsive and warm, I seem to be challenged and taken advantage of, perhaps considered not quite as bright (Martin, 1984:486-87).

Academic women's prospects appear more promising at the beginning of the 1990s. For one thing, more job vacancies are becoming available in this decade as significant numbers of incumbent professors reach retirement age. Also, employment equity programs are being put in place in post-secondary educational institutions, which give preference in hiring, promotion, and admission to members of disadvantaged groups. These selected groups are women, natives, visible minorities, and employable handicapped.

Sociology: An Androcentric Discipline

Feminist sociologists complained that the sociology that had previously been accepted as the science of society was really the male science of the male society (Bernard, 1973:781). Like their colleagues in history, psychology, biology, philosophy, religion, law, political theory, fine arts, the humanities, as well as the more practical applications of these disciplines such as psychotherapy and social work, feminist sociologists found their discipline to be seriously flawed (McCormack, 1989:19). This charge rested upon the following general, inter-related arguments (Millman and Kanter, 1975; Ward and Grant, 1985):

(1) "The selective eye of sociology...has been blind to women for decades" (Epstein, 1981:149). Sociologists in the past neglected women's experiences so that women in socio-

logical writing took the "insubstantial form of ghosts, shadows or stereotyped characters" (Oakley, 1974:1). Sociologists, who were mostly men, either failed to notice women's social behaviour or believed that what women did was trivial and unworthy of serious study (Daniels, 1975:346). As Bart (1971:735) asked, "Who really gives a damn about reading studies...about women, their dilemmas, their problems, their attempts at solutions?" Sociology focussed on male-dominated social institutions, such as the occupational, political, and legal systems. Public, official, upper-echelon behaviours were emphasized, and the unofficial, private spheres of social life were left out (Millman and Kanter, 1975:x). For example, male labour force activity was studied, while housework was ignored (Oakley, 1974). Sociologists advanced rationality as the prime motive for behaviour, and had little to say about emotions. In the pre-feminist era, women's activity became topics for "malestream sociology" (O'Brien, 1979:100) only when it touched on men's lives. For example, the sociology of the family attended to women as wives and mothers, and the sociology of deviance, to women as prostitutes. A few pioneers, such as Helen Hacker (1951), Mirra Komarovsky (1946), and Alice Rossi (1964) somehow managed to produce penetrating analyses of femininity. However, because their writings were not part of a collective cumulative enterprise, they remained anomalies.

(2) Feminist critics argued that the neglect of women's social behaviour by pre-1970s sociology, in combination with the subordinate status of women sociologists, had resulted in the exclusion of the feminine intellectual perspective from the discipline (Smith, 1975; Spender, 1981). Males "held 'normative power': the right to define what was appropriate, legitimate, important..." (Ward and Grant, 1985:143).

This criticism emerged from the *sociology of knowledge perspective*, which plays an important role in feminist thinking about gender.[2] The sociology of knowledge is a branch of sociology concerned with the "social location of ideas" (Berger, 1963:110), the "relation between thought and society" (Coser, 1968:428). A central proposition holds that different locations in

the social structure produce different ways of thinking, or different intellectual orientations toward the world.[3]

The sociology of knowledge proposition that ideas are socially located implies that women dwell "in a female world and men in a male world," which differs "both subjectively and objectively" (Bernard, 1981a:3). These gender-distinctive world views result from differences in female and male productive activities, and in their sexual and reproductive experiences. Different work activities in the home and the labour force lead to men and women having different consciousnesses (Armstrong and Armstrong, 1984:188). In addition, women and men experience reality differently, "just by having 'different' bodies, 'different' physical experiences, to name no others" (Stanley and Wise, 1983:146). In short, *how* one thinks and *what* one thinks are influenced by gender.

According to this position, female and male sociologists do not experience or interpret social reality in the same ways. Therefore, feminist critics inferred that the small numbers and powerlessness of female sociologists have had profound consequences for the discipline. More specifically, "how sociology is thought—its methods, conceptual schemes and theories—has been based on and built up within, the male social universe...." (Smith, 1974:7). This occurred because men attend to and treat as significant only what men say. Therefore, women have been "largely excluded from the work of producing the forms of thought, and the images and symbols in which thought is expressed and ordered" (Smith, 1975). In short, the models of social reality entertained by sociology are not human models, but rather the models of those males who hold power in the profession.

(3) Finally, feminist critics concluded that pre-feminist sociology was bad sociology. How could a sociology which "ignored large chunks of social life," which treated women stereotypically or disregarded them altogether be otherwise? Because women's experiences and intellectual perspective had been missing from sociological thinking, sociological thoughtways were judged to be defective.

Moreover, as McCormack (1989:19) points out, the body of knowledge encompassed by sociology and other learned disciplines justified "a subordinate status for women, a traditional division of labor along gender lines, and labelled as deviant women who chose careers or whose lifestyles, sexual or otherwise, were in any way a departure from these class-based norms."

Feminist sociologists argued that a "Copernican revolution in scholarship" would be required if sociology were to *really* take gender into account. In sociology, "we have envisioned our social universe as if men were in the centre and everything and everybody—women, other men, children, social institutions, etc.—revolved around men" (Eichler, 1984:35). A re-centred sociology, a sociology *for*, rather than *of* women (Smith, 1975:367) would demand a radical shift in thinking. The topics studied by sociologists, the traditional theories of social behaviour, research techniques for gathering data, and the teaching of the discipline—all need revolutionalizing. These areas will be discussed in turn. In each case, we ask: What were the pre-movement criticisms? What progress has been made?

RESEARCH TOPICS

As noted above, topics for study in pre-feminist sociology were male-defined issues, which either omitted women's experiences altogether or misinterpreted those experiences. For example, urban sociology framed "the male at center stage," and overlooked the behaviour of mothers and children in parks, women in beauty parlours, widows in coffee shops (Lofland, 1975). The suburbs were labelled "bedroom communities" because the *men* left during the day. What the women and children were doing was considered unimportant (Richardson, 1981). Although men were not studied in the context of the family, "most did not object to the omission" (Epstein, 1988:22).

Because work is a core area of sociology, it provides a good illustration of what the discipline looked like before and after the "discovery of women." Until recently, books often bore titles such as *Man and His Work* (Ritzer, 1972)

and concentrated on masculine occupations and work problems. For example, analyses of complex organizations overlooked the roles played by female clerks and secretaries. When women's work was mentioned at all, it was confined to a special section (in one book, coyly labelled "A Job of Her Own"). In a chapter on women's occupations, Caplow (1954:232) observed that, "Every skilled trade—including blacksmithing—has a tiny representation of women who indulge a self-conscious eccentricity by following what is regarded as a man's calling." Little was known about nurses, kindergarten teachers, waitresses, typists, or beauticians. Neither housework nor volunteer work were regarded as real work. The most widely used index for measuring socioeconomic status (SES) in Canada (Blishen, 1967; Blishen and McRoberts, 1976) did not consider the SES of female occupations.

Since the early 1970s, an explosion of research has attempted to take into account both women's concerns and the role of gender in such traditional areas as work and social stratification. Scholars have considered the impact of gender upon the labour force (Armstrong and Armstrong, 1984; Connelly, 1978; Marchak, 1977; Peitchinis, 1989); women in management (Colwill, 1982; Kanter 1977; Symons, 1986); women in unions (Baker and Robeson, 1981; White, 1980); part-time work (Weeks, 1984); housework (Eichler, 1977; Lopata, 1971; Luxton, 1980; Luxton and Rosenberg, 1986); the division of labour in the home (Meissner et al., 1975; Lupri and Mills, 1987; Michelson, 1985); women in blue-collar jobs (Martin, 1986); women and micro-electronics (Menzies, 1981). A socioeconomic index based on the labour force characteristics of both sexes was eventually developed (Boyd and McRoberts, 1983; Boyd, 1986). The androcentric state of other traditional topics, such as politics (Kopinak, 1987), deviance (Schur, 1984), the criminal justice system (Baker, 1984), education (Gaskell and McLaren, 1987; Thibault, 1988), sports (Hall and Richardson, 1982), and ethnic relations (Juteau-Lee and Roberts, 1981) has been similarly challenged.

Also of great significance are the many new areas of special import to women that have emerged. Until the women's movement came along, such topics as the following were, for the most part, unstudied: pregnancy, childbirth, and motherhood (Bernard, 1972, 1975; Chodorow, 1978; Oakley, 1980); fatherhood (Horna and Lupri, 1987); voluntary childlessness (Veevers, 1980); involuntary childlessness (Miall, 1986); the emotions (Hochschild, 1975, 1979); wife battering (Macleod, 1980); rape (Brownmiller, 1975); pornography (Malamuth and Donnerstein, 1984); women's medicine (Scully, 1980); women's aging (Abu-Laban, 1980b, 1981; Gee and Kimball, 1987); widowhood (Lopata, 1973, 1979); women's role in cultural production (Tuchman, 1975; Sydie, 1980); gender and language (Spender, 1985); eating disorders (Szekely, 1988) and obesity (Millman, 1980); the ecology of gender (Storrie, 1987). This listing is but a sample of the new topics that have been explored and the researchers active in them.

THEORY

Taking a sociology-of-knowledge stance, feminist scholars argued that sociological theories designed to guide research and to explain social behaviour [4] were grounded in male perception and male experience. This criticism of sociology's abstract conceptual framework is closely related to the problem of androcentric topic choice discussed above. Feminist sociologists eventually concluded that the gaps in topic coverage were not accidental. At least some of these omissions could be attributed to the inadequacy of existing theories which "systematically ignore or erase the significance of women's experiences and the organization of gender" (Stacey and Thorne, 1985:302). Expressed otherwise, sociology's failure to deal meaningfully with half the members of society "throws a harsh light on the theoretical models that have shaped the profession for the past quarter-century" (Epstein, 1981:160). Too often, theoretical "sparks for the sociological imagination" have had to come from outside mainstream academic sociology (Gould, 1980:460).

Theory which omitted or misunderstood women's perspective was judged by feminist sociologists to be defective theory, with limited explanatory power. Such theory emphasized the rational, formal dimensions of social behaviour and overlooked the irrational, emotional, informal dimensions. Because the behaviour of people "out there" involves both dimensions, existing one-sided theories are deficient. Functionalism, the theoretical perspective which dominated sociological discourse on gender in the 1950s and 1960s, failed to appreciate the power and material inequality between men and women (Carrigan et al., 1985:559). Even more disturbing, "scholarly" arguments were used to justify a sexist status quo (Oakley, 1974:28). For example, Talcott Parsons (1955)—the most influential of functional theorists—presented a *Kinder, Kuche, Kirche* view of women's place, as though efficient societal operation demanded that women stay home and play their traditional role. Indeed, sociology's founding fathers have been called "sexists to a man" (Schwendinger and Schwendinger, 1971).

What was to be done to remedy sexism in sociological theorizing? Challenging a stereotypical depiction of women (or men) wherever it occurs represented an obvious step. In some cases, the injection of an appreciation of gender into existing "male-stream" theories has stimulated creativity and improved predictability (e.g., social stratification [Acker, 1973; Nielsen, 1979]).

However, many feminist scholars (e.g., Smith, 1974) conclude that the "add-women-and-stir" solution did not go far enough. Though this approach was valuable for moving women from an invisible to a visible location in social science research, it still accepts male-centred theories as the starting point, and seeks to fit women into them. When women's experience is unlike men's, these traditional models of social life cannot deal with women's situations (Andersen, 1983:13).

For this reason, several critics writing in the optimistic 1970s argued that a proper understanding of gender by sociologists must *radically* affect theory, in the literal sense of producing alterations that go to the very *roots* of the discipline. They talked about "paradigm crises" and the "shattering of old paradigms".[5] Dorothy Smith (1975:367), for example, stated that academic women "are confronted virtually with the problem of reinventing the world of knowledge, of thought, of symbols, and images." In her collection of articles, *The Everyday World as Problematic: A Feminist Sociology* (1987), Smith develops her proposal for an alternative sociology erected upon women's subjective experiences.

Contemporary assessments of the success feminist theory has had in its pursuit of answers to the question, *"And what about the women?"* (Lengermann and Niebrugge-Brantly, 1988:283) are mixed. On the one hand, several commentators (Gould, 1980; Tancred-Sheriff, 1985; Stacey and Thorne, 1985; Ward and Grant, 1985) conclude that mainstream sociological theory has resisted feminist transformation. "Feminist sociology...seems to have been both co-opted and ghettoized, while the discipline as a whole and its dominant paradigms have proceeded relatively unchanged" (Stacey and Thorne, 1985:302). The more pessimistic position argues that the insights of the new scholarship on women have not been incorporated into sociological theory because the feminist challenge has been encapsulated in the specialty areas of the sociology of gender relations and the family, then ignored by mainstream sociology. Women sociologists are left alone, with courses, textbooks, and conferences of their very own. The interdisciplinary focus of feminist sociology has also reduced its impact on sociological thought. Although potentially a salutary influence, the scope of this thinking has been difficult for mainstream sociological theory to "digest." Finally, the politics of knowledge is another important reason why sociological theory has resisted feminist transformation. Because women generally lack power and prestige, "the results of their labours are denigrated through mechanisms of privatization, ridicule and the male-defined aura of insignificance..." (Tancred-Sheriff, 1985:116). Women are on the periphery of central specialty areas in sociology, and play leading roles only in specialties marginal to the discipline. Consequently, they lack "clout" in "what comes to count as scientific knowledge" (Collins, 1983:267).

Although there is truth to the charge that feminist theory has thus far failed to crack the theoretical foundations of the discipline, contrary indications also exist which suggest that the "implications of feminist theory are moving increasingly into the mainstream of the discipline" (Ritzer, 1988:70). A recent volume of sociological theory (Ritzer, 1988) devotes a chapter to the feminist theoretical critique, which it describes as "one of the more impressive examples of sustained intellectual work in recent times" (p. 70). Feminists' theoretical treatments of gender are becoming increasingly sophisticated (see Sydie, 1987). International recognition is being given to the work of Dorothy Smith. A reviewer (Miller, 1989:524) described Smith's *The Everyday World as Problematic: A Feminist Sociology* (1987) as "the most sophisticated attempt on the Canadian scene to fuse prominent themes in contemporary sociological and feminist theorizing into a coherent program of social inquiry." In her overview of feminist scholarship for *The Canadian Review of Sociology and Anthropology's* special issue on the State of the Art and New Directions of Anglophone Canadian Sociology, Margrit Eichler (1985a:634) concluded that since "only a few books which claim general theoretical relevance deal adequately with women, ...by and large mainstream sociology remains sexist." However, ending on a sanguine note, Eichler predicted that Canadian sociology is on the threshold of a move toward non-sexist scholarship. "This involves a vast re-thinking of old premises, and if it is to succeed, it will need the active cooperation of the majority of Canadian sociologists" (p. 634).

METHODOLOGY

Feminist scholars argue that because androcentric logic and research techniques produce data that are necessarily flawed, the linchpin of sexism in sociology remains its methodology (Mackie, 1988; Miles and Finn, 1982; Spender, 1981; Stanley and Wise, 1983; Vickers, 1984). Androcentrism begins with the axioms, the high-order assumptions made about social reality. Although males have only a partial view of total "reality," they are in a position to insist that their views are the *real* views, indeed the *only* views (Spender, 1985:1-2). It continues with the language with which research problems are conceptualized. The syntax of sexism, i.e., the fact that females are ignored in "man-made" language (Spender, 1985) contributes to women's invisibility in research. The methods used to collect information, such as the design of questionnaires and interview schedules, and the subsequent interpretations of those data, they too bear the stamp of the masculine perspective (Eichler, 1984). Obviously, these matters are intimately linked with the difficulties with topic choice and theories discussed above.

The idea of the "machismo factor" in research captures feminists' methodological concerns.[6] Jessie Bernard (1973), following the suggestions of psychologist Carlson (1971, 1972), argued that female and male researchers have distinctive research styles, the agentic mode being preferred by male sociologists, and the communal mode by female sociologists.[7] Note that this statement of preference does *not* imply that *all* women like this sort of methodology, and *all* men that sort.

The *agentic mode* stresses sociology's similarity to the physical sciences; it advocates quantitative methods. "Agentic" research means preference for "hard" statistical data, survey research, laboratory experiments, isolation and control of variables. The agentic mode is infused with *machismo*:

The scientist using this approach creates his own controlled reality. He can manipulate it. He is master. He has power. He can add or subtract or combine variables. He can play with a simulated reality like an Olympian god. He can remain at a distance, safely invisible behind his shield, uninvolved (Bernard, 1973:785).

The communal style, on the other hand, views sociology as a humanistic endeavour. Social science is distanced from physical science, which is regarded as *"the* model in our culture of a supermasculine activity (apart from front-line military duty...)" (Harding, 1986:247, emphasis in original). Agentic research is rejected because it fails to make sense of women's experience.

The *communal mode* involves gathering "soft" data by qualitative methods such as participant observation, informal interviewing, case studies, analysis of autobiographies. It recommends interdisciplinary research, espe-

cially a sense of history. The researcher's own experiences play a prominent role in the research process. One criterion for the plausibility of ideas is their accordance with the researcher's own experiences (Parlee, 1979:130).

Communal research rejects the scientist-subject, "I-them" dichotomy. Instead, the researcher tries to "take the role of the other," to see the world through the eyes of the people being studied. Understanding the experiences of human beings, treated as subjects, not as objects to be manipulated, takes priority over translating "data" into "statistics." Communal research is people-centred, especially woman-centred, and "disavows control, for control spoils the results" (Bernard, 1973:785). In short, feminist critics of the agentic style are convinced that communal mode research is superior research.

Because feminist sociologists have had their consciousness raised by the women's movement, their work is dually motivated: to understand the world and to change it. Benston (1989:59-60), for example, says:

We are feminists because we believe not only that the evidence shows the oppression of women, but, further, that such oppression is wrong. We also believe that society should be changed to end all forms of oppression. Our scholarship is done in that context, but also in the belief that the closer one gets to the truth the better the cause of women will be served.

This combination of intellectual curiosity and value commitment is not, of course, confined to gender relations specialists. All sociologists have values and passions that motivate their work. Most would welcome an end to other forms of injustice, such as race and class oppression. And although this combination complicates academic study (in ways to be discussed shortly), completely impartial or value-free scholarship is neither possible nor desirable. Understandably enough, feminist scholars find open advocacy of their value position immensely preferable to the hidden sexism which masqueraded as value-neutrality in pre-feminist sociology.

Nevertheless, sociologists must specialize in scholarship, not propaganda (Mackie, 1977). Feminist ideological preferences and pronouncements must not be mistaken for social "reality." Facts must not be confused with values. In general, sociology's protection against the retention of faulty generalizations lies in the self-corrective mechanisms of research as a cumulative *social* enterprise. That is, mistakes are usually discovered by the "accumulation of *different* perspectives on the subject matter" (Berger and Luckmann, 1966:10, emphasis added). However, the field of gender relations seems especially vulnerable to the intrusion of bias precisely because specialists share the *same* ideological position, and potentially the same blinders. Therefore, the corrective function of multiple ideological positions is less likely to be in operation.

What has happened since Bernard's (1973) identification of the "machismo factor" in sociological research? On the positive side, among feminists, the search for methods which take gender into account has proceeded vigorously (Vickers, 1984). In approving publication of the pamphlet, *On the Treatment of the Sexes in Research* (Eichler and Lapointe, 1985), and its dissemination to Canadian researchers, the Social Sciences and Humanities Research Council of Canada affirmed the soundness of the feminist critique. As McCormack (1985:7) argues, a separation has developed between feminist politics and feminist scholarship, so that fewer feminists expect sociological research to be the "agit-prop" arm of the women's movement.[8] Scholars' contribution to the goal of gender equality lies in excellence, in doing the calibre of sociological work that simply cannot be ignored.

On the negative side, we reiterate that feminists' ideas about methodology have so far had a "sadly slight impact" on "men's studies" (Vickers, 1984:4). An analysis of journal publications by the author (Mackie, 1985) showed that although women's scholars' use of the communal mode increased between 1967 and 1973, it decreased between 1973 and 1981. Grant et al. (1987:860) found support for "feminist scholars' claims that use of qualitative methods is significantly more common among women than men scholars who publish in major sociological journals." However, quantitative methods were the most common choice for scholars of both sexes. Quantitative meth-

ods, regarded as more scientific and associated with masculinity, carry more prestige than interpretative methods. As Gould (1980:467) indicates, "female sociologists often find themselves torn between wanting to do a sociology of/for women that is challenging and critical, and wanting their work to be seen as legitimate by those who control the discipline." Tough economic times in universities and fierce competition for jobs has underlined the importance of pleasing mostly male gatekeepers, such as journal editors and department heads. Moreover, women scholars remain marginal in the institutions where knowledge is created, preserved and transmitted (Smith, 1984:11). "Even today, women are greatly underrepresented in the prestigious research organizations which conduct much of our research and, where they are represented, they tend to have junior rather than senior level appointments" (Eichler, 1984:19). We conclude that feminists' "rebellious constructions of the mind" (Berger, 1963:133) have so far failed to revolutionize the methodology of mainstream sociology.

TEACHING

Sociology's insensitivity to gender and its consequent neglect of women in both its theory and research inevitably resulted in a curriculum that was incomplete and distorted. Until the women's movement removed blinders, no one noticed that the sociology being taught to students was the sociology of male society.

In retrospect, the sort of sociology taught before the women's movement seems rather odd. Sometimes, male/female was dealt with as a standard demographic variable, a usage that had little to do with gender as we now understand it. For instance, students might learn that the sex ratio is higher in Dawson City than in Ottawa (and the instructor might jokingly remark that "girls" more interested in the MRS. than the B.A. should consider migrating to the Yukon). Sociology-of-the-family courses did consider females, but from the masculine perspective. In general sociology and in social psychology, women turned up once in a while as rather pathetic creatures with low self-esteem, who conformed more than men to pressure, whose attitudes were easily swayed, who concealed their intelligence in order to snare a husband, who feared success and were susceptible to hysterical contagion.

In textbook presentations of that era, women tended to be stereotyped or absent altogether. Gray (1977) describes a statistics text published in 1971 which begins with a story about the author at his office window observing the "splendid displays of beautiful young birds," and delighting in the fact that "with the advent of the mini-skirt, they're becoming even more splendid and more beautiful." The concept of correlation is illustrated in the text by speculation on the relationship between skirt lengths and the rate of traffic accidents. The old days were "when men were men and girls wore flour sack underwear." An easy statistical test is one "even the little old ladies wearing straw hats decorated with flowers can be taught to do."

Types of pictures chosen by authors and editors to illustrate books are often a subtle revelation of social attitudes. Schneider and Hacker (1973:13) report that the pictures contained in twelve of the best-selling sociology introductory texts tended to support their hypothesis of women's relative invisibility. More particularly, content analysis showed that, taking all the books together, 42 percent of the pictures showed only men. The range over the twelve texts was from 25 percent to 63 percent. Comparable figures for pictures showing only women was an overall average of eight percent, with a range of zero to 22 percent.

Today, women's studies have assumed considerably more importance in Canadian institutions of higher learning than was the case fifteen or twenty years ago (Strong-Boag, 1983). A number of textbooks dealing with gender in this country have been written (Ambert, 1976; Mackie, 1987; McLaren, 1988; Nemiroff, 1987; Sydie, 1987; Wilson, 1986). Introductory sociology books now routinely include treatments of gender relations. The *Resources for Feminist Research* and *Canadian Woman's Studies* continue to facilitate the exchange of ideas about women's courses. The journal *Teaching Sociology* regularly publishes gender-related articles (e.g., Blee, 1986). The gender relations and women's studies courses now offered in most Canadian colleges and universities attract many undergraduate students, especially women students. As well, traditional sociology courses (e.g., stratification, deviance) now involve at least some gender content.

Despite some encouraging signs that academia has accepted gender equality, it is appropriate to end this discussion on a sober note. In many cases, faculty members specializing in women's studies often occupy marginal positions in their universities. "Prejudice remains about the worth of research focused on gender. Although there is no doubt that such research is regarded with greater interest than in the past, repeated observation suggests that there is less career payoff for people who choose to work in this area than for those who deal with other topics" (Epstein, 1988:35). Moreover, the students attracted to gender courses tend to be mostly women. As McCormack (1987:289) warns, gender studies still occupy a precarious place in academia. They are endangered externally by a conservative political culture, including reactionary women's organizations like R.E.A.L. Women. They are threatened internally through cutbacks and underfunding by academic institutions that continue to regard "Women's Studies and feminist scholars the way modern medicine regards folk medicine and barefoot doctors."

CONCLUSIONS

The purpose of Chapter 1 has been to introduce the basic concepts "sex" and "gender," to make a case for the importance of sex/gender to both individual and society, and to discuss the emergence of the sociology of gender relations and women's studies in Canadian institutions of higher learning.

A consensus has developed to use the term "sex" to refer to the biology of femaleness and maleness, and "gender" to mean the sociocultural elaborations upon physiology. All societies notice sex distinctions and employ them as a basis of social organization. Moreover, the sexes are ranked. As a category, males command more prestige, privileges, and resources than females. Men have traditionally controlled the prestigious public domain, while women were confined to the domestic realm, which is accorded lower value. Even though large numbers of women are now moving into the public realm, men still command greater material and symbolic resources. Therefore, the essential relationship between the sexes remains a power relationship.

The second wave of the women's movement at the end of the 1960s and the beginning of the 1970s alerted female sociologists to serious flaws in their own discipline. What had been accepted, until then, as the sociology of human behaviour was consequently discovered to be the sociology of male behaviour. Research had been conducted primarily by males (and females who had been socialized to accept the masculine ruling ideas), on topics that interested men, using methods congenial to men. Since sociological theories had also been developed with reference to males alone, women's experiences had been neglected and misrepresented.

Feminist sociologists (e.g., Smith, 1974; 1975) criticized mainstream sociology through the perspective of the sociology of knowledge (Marx and Engels, 1846; Mannheim, 1936). The sociology of knowledge argues that knowledge varies according to the social location of the knower. Therefore, males, who are generally in a socially dominant position, will develop a different view of the social order than women, who are normally in subordinate roles. As a result of this feminist insight, many scholars of both sexes became convinced that it was necessary to bring previously invisible women back into sociological theory, research, and teaching. Perhaps the most important contribution of feminist scholarship and the work it has inspired is that scholars now understand a great deal about the social forces that create the inequality between the sexes. The task of this book is to explicate these social forces.

The content of this volume is divided into ten chapters. The intent of the present chapter was to provide the reader with a general introduction to the field of gender relations. Chapter 2 poses the question: What similarities and differences characterize females and males? Chapter 3 considers the extent to which biology is responsible for gender. Chapters 4 through 7 adopt a social-psychological perspective and inquire into various facets of gender socializa-tion. Chapter 4 focuses on various socialization theories. Chapters 5 and 6 discuss family and peer group as primary agents of gender socialization. Secondary and symbolic (schools, mass media, language) sources of socialization are explored in Chapter 7. Chapters 8 and 9 move to a social-structural level of explanation of work, family, and aging. Finally, Chapter 10 looks both to the past and the future in its overview of the social movements associated with gender.

This book is intended to be an integrated, comprehensive text, appropriate for gender courses in sociology and psychology, as well as social problems and Canadian society courses. Although prior exposure to an introductory level course would be helpful, it is not necessary. The glossary at the end of the book explains the meaning of specialized concepts.

NOTES

1. The reader may still encounter the unsatisfactory, and largely outdated term "the sociology of sex roles" as a label for what we describe as the sociology of gender relations. We emphasize "gender" rather than "sex" because the field's primary focus is *not* sexual relations. The word "role" is equally inappropriate, for two reasons. Firstly, being a girl or boy, or a woman or man is not a social role in the same sense that being a teacher, sister, or friend is a social role. "Gender, like race or age, is deeper, less changeable, and infuses the more specific roles one plays" (Lopata and Thorne, 1978:719). Lopata and Thorne (1978:721) go on to say, "It seems to be that being a woman is not a social role but a pervasive identity and a set of self-feelings which lead to the selection or the assignment by others of social roles and to the performance by women of common roles in some ways differently from men." Secondly, the "sex roles" terminology masked the fundamental status and power distinctions we discussed above. Again quoting Lopata and Thorne (1978:719), "The notion of 'role' has tended to focus attention more on individuals than on social strata, more on socialization than on social structure, and has thereby deflected attention away from historic, economic, and political questions." For this reason, the more inclu-

sive term "relations" has replaced "role" in current definitions.

2. Eichler (1985a:630) remarks that "the most overarching contribution of feminist approaches ...has been in the sociology of knowledge..."(italics deleted).

3. Karl Marx (1904:11) put it this way: "It is not the consciousness of men that determines their existence, but on the contrary, their social existence determines their consciousness."

4. Readers may find helpful the following definitions of *theory* and *theoretical orientation*. According to Shaw and Costanzo (1970:4), a theory is "a set of interrelated hypotheses or propositions concerning a phenomenon or set of phenomena," while an orientation is "a general approach to the analysis and interpretation of behavior" (p. 8). The feminist critique is aimed at both theories and orientations.

5. The meaning of *paradigm* in the context of sociology is somewhat confusing (Eckberg and Hill, 1979). Kuhn (1970), the major authority in these discussions, apparently used the term in twenty-one different ways. However, feminists are referring to Kuhn's metaphysical paradigm, a total world view, gestalt or *Weltanschauung* within a given science (Ritzer, 1975:4). Paradigms are even more general than theoretical orientations (see n. 4).

Paradigm 1 — Normal science — Anomalies — Crisis—Revolution—Paradigm 2

According to Kuhn, major changes take place in any science through revolution rather than through slow, orderly transition. At any particular time, the science is dominated by a specific paradigm. Normal science is a period of accumulation of knowledge, as researchers work under the aegis of the reigning paradigm. Eventually, such work produces anomalies, or things that the existing paradigm cannot explain. If these anomalies are significant a crisis stage occurs, which may end in revolution. The reigning paradigm is discarded and a new one takes its place (Ritzer, 1975:3-4).

Proponents of this viewpoint argue that the effect of the discovery of gender in sociology is sufficient to cause a crisis and a paradigmatic revolution.

6. As McCormack (1987) points out, feminist criticisms of positivistic sociology have been made before. See Blumer (1969). However, the identification of this preferred methodology with superior comprehension of the female world is new.

7. The author's analysis of journal publications documents Bernard's (1973) claim. See Mackie (1985).

8. McCormack (1985:7) elaborates on the growing separation between feminist researchers and feminist activists: "There are, for example some issues like affirmative action where everything that can be said, has been said, and efforts to 'study' the problem should be seen as diversionary, an old strategy to delay implementation. Meanwhile, many of us want to get on with the newer problems which are less immediately political, and to get on with them in a nonpoliticized environment."

Chapter 2

Female/Male Similarities and Differences

"How masculine or feminine are you?" a *Reader's Digest* quiz asked 25 years ago (Pollack, 1967). Give yourself one point for every "A" answer, two points for every "B" answer:

1. Would you rather—(A) work for a pleasant boss; (B) work for yourself?
2. Which do you consider holds the greater hope for the world—(A) religion; (B) science?
3. Which do you like better—(A) music; (B) sports?
4. When buying a new car, which is more important to you—(A) design; (B) engine?
5. Do you prefer—(A) having decisions made for you; (B) to make your own?
6. Men are more successful because of their—(A) appearance; (B) capability?
7. Are your feelings often easily hurt—(A) yes; (B) no?
8. Which do you enjoy more—(A) poetry; (B) detective stories?
9. Have you a great fear of fire—(A) yes; (B) no?
10. Which interests you more—(A) art; (B) politics?
11. Does impolite language annoy you—(A) yes; (B) no?
12. Would you rather be—(A) conventional; (B) startling?
13. Which of these dogs would you rather own—(A) poodle; (B) boxer?
14. Do you like to go to parties and dances—(A) yes; (b) no?
15. Have you ever cried at sad movies—(A) yes; (B) no?
16. Do practical jokes annoy you—(A) yes; (B) no?
17. Which does a woman need more—(A) clothes; (B) intelligence?
18. Do you resent persons using nicknames—(A) yes; (B) no?
19. Would you rather—(A) sell in a store; (B) sell outside?
20. If your lights went out, would you—(A) call the electric company; (B) try to fix them yourself?
21. Do you like to buy antique furniture—(A) yes; (B) no?
22. Do you prefer mingling with people more intelligent than yourself—(A) yes; (B) no?
23. Is it hard for you to get up as soon as you awake—(A) yes; (B) no?
24. Does soiled table linen disgust you—(A) yes; (B) no?
25. Do you feel pity for a drowning bee—(A) yes; (B) no?

As you may have guessed, all "A" answers on this "scientific" test were believed to indicate femininity, and all "B" answers masculinity. Although the contemporary reader will regard many of the items as amusing anachronisms (e.g., #9, #25), others seem quite plausible (#3, #7, #11). Note that masculine traits were considered twice as valuable as feminine ones.

Although the content of "test yourself" quizzes in magazines may be less naive today, these questions continue to be asked there and elsewhere: "How do men and women differ?" "How are they alike?" "Who is superior?" The "battle of the sexes" and the "mating game" stretch back into the mists of prehistory. Therefore, comparative assessments of females and males "change in shape but never in substance across the centuries" (Tavris and Wade, 1984:4). In our century, both laypersons and social scientists have been intrigued by the similarities and differences (especially the differences) between males and females. The issue has been the subject of hot debate since the re-emergence of the women's movement in the 1970s. Feminists have challenged what they consider an inappropriate emphasis upon sex/gender *differences* in our society, as well as the assumption that male traits are the more desirable (Archer and Lloyd, 1985:6).

Chapter 1 introduced the concept of gender differentiation: society makes a huge fuss about the physiological distinctions between females and males. At birth (and sometimes even earlier, through amniocentesis), each individual is placed in one of two categories: female or male. Although at least one person in 200 is hermaphroditic, that is, biologically intersexual (Tresemer, 1975:314), the social assignment into sex categories is completely dichotomous. In everyday thinking, every person should be "'naturally,' 'originally,' 'in the first place,' 'in the beginning,' 'all along,' and 'forever'" one hundred percent male or female (Garfinkel, 1967:116).

The categorization based upon anatomy (sex) is, in turn, linked to cultural definitions of femininity and masculinity (gender). Like sex, gender is dichotomized: people are sorted into two (and only two) categories. Males and females are assigned different roles. They enjoy different rights and privileges; they are subject to different rules of conduct. Each sex is assumed to possess distinctive physical abilities and psychological makeup that both explain and justify the perpetuation of the societal role structure (Spence and Helmreich, 1978). Male dominance is viewed as the inevitable consequence of these fundamental differences. If women are irrational, if they indeed prefer to have decisions made for them and need clothes more than intelligence, as the above quiz suggested, then of course, they must be told what to do by logical, strong, self-confident males.

Gender's close connections with sexuality, identity, and social organization has given it the status of a "moral fact." That is, masculinity and femininity evoke strong feelings in societal members about what *ought* to be, what *must* be. Therefore, gender may be understood as "... a normative system, a pervasive network of interrelated norms and sanctions through which *female (and male) behavior is evaluated and controlled*" (Schur, 1984:11, emphasis added).

Society punishes norm-breakers. Today, punishment for gender deviants usually consists of raised eyebrows, avoidance, mockery, or name-calling. However, history shows that the sanctions meted out to gender deviants were often much more severe. Women were imprisoned, force-fed, subjected to psychiatric ill-treatment and surgical abuse, and executed as witches when they failed to accept prevailing gender norms (Ehrenreich and English, 1978). In Nazi Germany, an estimated 10 000 homosexual males were forced to wear an "effeminate" pink-coloured triangle; many suffered persecution and death in Nazi concentration camps (Lautmann, 1981). Today, anti-gay violence is once again on the rise, fuelled by the public's fear of AIDS (Miller, 1989:9).

Chapter 2 addresses three topics. First, femininity and masculinity in the popular imagination are examined. Of concern here are gender mythology, stereotypes, and societal attitudes about men's and women's roles. Second, the role played by ideology in the scientific study of gender differences is discussed. Third, actual female-male similarities and differences, as they are understood by scientific research in the 1990s, are reviewed. Inquiry into the *source* of sex/gender differences is reserved for subsequent chapters.

FOLK THEORIES ABOUT MALES AND FEMALES

Our world is doubly shaped by symbolic construction. "We perceive 'reality' in terms of the categories we have learned to impose on it, and we actively shape ourselves and others to conform to the images we have created" (Hunter

Collective, 1983:25). Our perceptions of what girls and boys, women and men are like are organized by the myths, stereotypes, and attitudes to which our society subscribes. Quite apart from whatever kernels of truth are captured by them, these folk "theories" often become self-fulfilling prophecies. For example, if females are idealized as childlike and innocent, they will likely be shielded from the sorts of challenging experiences needed to produce competent adults who can stand on their own two feet. Under the circumstances, girls and women almost inevitably come to see themselves as subordinate and weak.

We reiterate an important point made in Chapter 1: males have been the creators and perpetrators of the dominant world view. With few exceptions, men have been the priests, the sculptors, storytellers, writers, artists, and musicians (Tuchman, 1975). Males, as the dominant group, have created the gender imagery for both sexes.

Myths of Women

Beliefs about the powers, motives, and special qualities of women have existed in all cultures, from earliest times. Men's creation of myths about females has provided them with the conviction that they can understand and control woman—the mysterious Other (Williams, 1978). Images from earlier civilizations continue to influence contemporary art, literature, and mass media. "In pentimento fashion, each succeeding civilization paints over the canvas of previous cultures, yet the earlier images of masculinity and femininity bleed through even the most contemporary gender role portraits" (Lipman-Blumen, 1984:69).

The images of women discussed below seem to be universal. However, they are neither exhaustive nor mutually exclusive (Hunter Collective, 1983:28 ff.; Williams, 1978).

WOMAN AS MOTHER NATURE

Woman gives birth, so she is seen to be close to the earth. Like nature, she is powerful and capricious. However, culture (symbolically associated with males) is ultimately superior to nature, for it can transform nature according to its wishes (Ortner, 1974). Author Margaret Atwood (1972:200) tells us that the "nature-as-woman" metaphor permeates Canadian literature. The type of woman portrayed is an "old, cold, forbidding and possibly vicious one."[1] Perhaps because of the impact of Canada's landscape upon our history and mentality, many of the strong and vividly portrayed female characters in Canadian literature are old women. Hagar Shipley in Margaret Laurence's novel, *The Stone Angel* (1964) is a well-known example.

WOMAN AS TERRIFYING ENCHANTRESS

Motivated by evil intent, she uses her beauty and deadly magic to effect man's downfall. Greek mythology contains numerous female monsters, such as Scylla, who squeezes men's bones together and eats them. Female deities, e.g., the Hindu goddess Kali, are evil and dangerous. Folk tales portray witches and sorceresses able to transform men by spells. "In the Western heritage of folk tales, the wicked stepmother has no male counterpart; she is the embodiment of evil—selfish, powerful, and dangerous to men and children alike" (Hunter Collective, 1983:28-29).

WOMAN AS SAINT

Though more frequently portrayed as objects of fear, women are also idealized as objects of love and veneration. The fairy godmother is the counterpart of the wicked witch; the self-sacrificing, pure madonna is the counterpart of the destructive goddess. "The 'good' woman, stripped of her dangerous elements, desires nothing, demands nothing, and receives worship, not equality" (Hunter Collective, 1983:31).

WOMAN AS SEX OBJECT

Images of women as witches or madonnas omit men's interest in women as gratifiers of their sexual needs. This mythological theme acknowledges that women "are literally seen as objects": men perpetually gape at their bodies (Schur, 1984:42, 66). "Men look at women. Women watch themselves being looked at" (Berger, 1977:47). Women's bodies are often reduced to isolated parts: "breasts," "buttocks," "legs." Magazine advertisements use bits and pieces of women, much more often than dismembered men, to peddle contemporary wares.

Woman as Insignificant Non-Person

Woman, who is of no importance in the essential affairs of men, disappears. Said Napoleon Bonaparte: "Nature intended women to be our slaves.... They are our property; we are not theirs. They belong to us, just as a tree that bears fruit belongs to a gardener. What a mad idea to demand equality for women!... Women are nothing but machines for producing children" (McPhee, 1978). Author John Mortimer (1983:245) received from his father this wisdom concerning women:

"Love affairs aren't much of a subject for drama really," he told me at an early age. "Consider this story of a lover, a husband and an unfaithful wife. The wife confesses all to her husband. He sends for her lover. They are closeted in the living-room together. The wife stands outside the door, trembling with fear. She strains her ears to discover what's going on in the room. Some terrible quarrel? A duel or fight to the death perhaps? At last she can stand the suspense no longer. She flings open the door and what does she see? Blood? Broken furniture? One of them stretched out on the carpet? Not at all. The two men are sitting by the fire drinking bottled ale and discussing the best method of pruning apple trees. Naturally, the woman's furious. She packs and leaves for her mother's."

Women like former British Prime Minister Margaret Thatcher who succeed in the public sphere are made into honourary men. Otherwise, like the servant in the classic British mystery story, they are "there," seen, but not heard (Lofland, 1975:144-45).

In general, perceptions of women fall into two categories: idealization and disparagement (Williams, 1978:244):

Woman has been esteemed, worshipped, and protected as often as she has been loathed, ignored, and reviled...Woman is goddess and devil, virgin and whore, sweet madonna and malevolent mom; she can bring a man up to salvation or drag him down with her to hell. On the face of it, the pedestal-gutter syndrome appears to reflect views that are diametrically opposed: woman is good, woman is bad. But in fact these views represent a single attitude: woman is different. After all, whether you are looking up to or stooping down to them, you don't have to look them in the eye (Tavris and Wade, 1984:3).

The last point made by Tavris and Wade is worth repeating. The *pedestal-gutter syndrome* presents females as *other* than human beings on the same level as males.

If men have formulated a mythology of women to provide them with some semblance of prediction and control over these alien beings, it seems reasonable to ask whether women have produced a parallel mythological description of males. Surely women, the less powerful sex, experience a need at least equal to men's to reduce symbolically the other sex to manageable proportions.

It seems likely that characterizations of men have always been part of women's private oral lore ("Men want only one thing"; "Never trust men as far as you can throw one"; "Men are emotionally inadequate creatures who require special pampering like babies"; "Men are violent brutes") (Bernard, 1981a:464). Nevertheless, women have not created a public mythology of men. Since females were excluded from the circle of men who were the philosophers, poets, and great religious figures (Smith, 1974), they have not been in a position to have their versions of the world treated seriously. Prior to the women's movement, women had "no religion or poetry of their own: they still dream[ed] through the dreams of men" (de Beauvoir, 1952:132). However, in recent years, women have discovered a voice of their own to describe both themselves and men (Spender, 1982). Women's views of men are no longer hidden behind kitchen doors and below stairs.

Gender Stereotypes

Suppose you inadvertently eavesdrop on a

conversation and overhear two strangers being described. One is depicted as an adventurous, independent, dominant person, the other as a sentimental, submissive soul. Would you find it easier to picture the first individual as a male, and the second as a female? Probably, since as well-socialized members of society, we all carry "pictures in our heads" (Lippmann, 1922) or stereotypes of the typical woman and the typical man. What is more, cross-cultural research shows that citizens from 30 countries would visualize the first person as male and the second as female (Williams and Best, 1982).

A *stereotype* refers to those folk beliefs about the attributes characterizing a social category on which there is substantial agreement (Mackie, 1973). The term refers to beliefs shared by many individuals, about traits that appropriately describe categories of people, such as ethnic groups, nationalities, occupations and age groupings. *Gender stereotypes* are characteristics consensually assigned to males and females. For the most part, they point to beliefs about female and male "psychological makeup" (Williams and Best, 1982:15).

To social scientists, "stereotype" is not a dirty word. The categorization involved appears to be a necessary aspect of human cognition. Stereotypes compensate for the limitations of human perception and experience.

Each of us lives and works on a small part of the earth's surface, moves in a small circle, and of these acquaintances knows only a few intimately.... Inevitably our opinions cover a bigger space, a longer reach of time, a greater number of things, than we can directly observe (Lippmann, 1922:59).

Instead of trying to decipher the personality of every male or female passing through our lives, we resort to gender stereotypes.

Sometimes, this cultural store of information is helpful; sometimes, it is misleading. As we shall see at the end of this chapter, some traits are false (e.g., that females are more talkative than males). Others are true (e.g., masculine aggressiveness); however, like all generalizations, gender stereotypes do not take into account individual differences in the traits which occur within the sexes, or the degree of overlap between the sexes.

The international study of stereotypes referred to earlier (Williams and Best, 1982) involved samples of equal numbers of male and female university students from 30 countries. The Canadian students were from the University of Lethbridge (Alberta) and St. Francis Xavier University (Nova Scotia). Sample members were asked to indicate which of a list of 300 adjectives were frequently associated with women and which with men. They were requested to report on beliefs current in their cultures, not their own personal convictions. Traits checked by two-thirds or more of the national samples became part of the operationally defined stereotype.

Williams and Best (1982) discovered a remarkable degree of cross-national generality in the psychological characteristics associated with women and men. While one can discern some interesting variations from country to country, these differences are always small relative to the general similarity among countries. These researchers concluded that their findings were consistent with the view that there are general pan-cultural gender stereotypes which are evident in all cultures but which are modified to a degree by specific cultural influences such as religion (Williams and Best, 1982:303-304).

Table 2.1 shows those traits which are part of the gender stereotypes in 19 or more of the 25 countries studied by Williams and Best for whom complete student data are available (1982:77). (The results from their study of children will be discussed briefly in Chapter 4.) The Canadian students who were part of this study subscribed to all the traits shown in Table 2.1. Moreover, 90 percent or more of the Canadian sample added "handsome," "industrious," and "tough" to Canadians' image of males, and "complaining," "confused," "excitable," "frivolous," "fussy," "warm," "whiny," and "worrying" to their female stereotype.

The gender stereotypes of Canadian students were very similar to those of their counterparts in other English-speaking countries (United States, England, New Zealand). However, they still had a great deal in common with the stereotypes of young people from countries as far afield as Pakistan, Japan, Nigeria, and Malaysia. Williams and Best (1982:30) attribute these consensual notions about the

Table 2.1
International Gender Stereotypes

Characteristics Associated with Males or with Females in at Least 19 of 25 Countries (number of countries in parentheses)

Male-Associated Items (N = 49)

Active (23)	Ingenious (19)
Adventurous (25)	Initiative (21)
Aggressive (24)	Inventive (22)
Ambitious (22)	Lazy (21)
Arrogant (20)	Logical (22)
Assertive (20)	Loud (21)
Autocratic (24)	Masculine (25)
Boastful (19)	Obnoxious (19)
Clear-thinking (21)	Opportunistic (20)
Coarse (21)	Progressive (23)
Confident (19)	Rational (20)
Courageous (23)	Realistic (20)
Cruel (21)	Reckless (20)
Daring (24)	Robust (24)
Determined (21)	Rude (23)
Disorderly (21)	Self-confident (21)
Dominant (25)	Serious (20)
Egotistical (21)	Severe (23)
Energetic (22)	Stern (24)
Enterprising (24)	Stolid (20)
Forceful (25)	Strong (25)
Hardheaded (21)	Unemotional (23)
Hardhearted (21)	Unkind (19)
Humorous (19)	Wise (23)
Independent (25)	

Female-Associated Items (N = 25)

Affected (20)	Meek (19)
Affectionate (24)	Mild (21)
Anxious (19)	Pleasant (19)
Attractive (23)	Sensitive (24)
Charming (20)	Sentimental (25)
Curious (21)	Sexy (22)
Dependent (23)	Shy (19)
Dreamy (24)	Softhearted (23)
Emotional (23)	Submissive (25)
Fearful (23)	Superstitious (25)
Feminine (24)	Talkative (20)
Gentle (21)	Weak (23)
Kind (19)	

Source: Williams and Best (1982:77).

distinctive psychological makeup of the sexes to pan-cultural similarities in the social roles of women and men.

The similarity in social roles played by men and women around the globe noted by Williams and Best has been identified by several earlier theorists as the major axis of societal gender arrangements. For example, Bakan (1966) located the essence of feminity in a *communal* orientation, or a concern for the relations between self and others (and contrasted it with the masculine *agentic* orientation). Similarly,

Parsons and Bales (1955) argued that the division of labour in the traditional family required men to be *instrumental* specialists concerned with action in the public domain. Women, on the other hand, were *expressive* specialists, responsible for the emotional well-being of family members. Continuing reference will be made throughout this book to this communal-agentic, expressive-instrumental distinction.

The content of gender stereotypes has two inter-related sources. The traits shown in Table 2.1 spring, first of all, from the societal division of labour. Women are more likely than men to be observed taking care of children (their own and other people's). Men are more likely than women to be seen wielding authority in the workplace. Therefore, observers are apt to conclude that the abilities and personality attributes required for childcare ("softhearted", "kind") and for success in the labour force ("ambitious", "logical") are typical of each sex (Eagly and Steffen, 1984:735). Many of the traits shown in Table 2.1 fall into a feminine warmth-expressiveness cluster ("sensitive," "gentle") and a masculine instrumental-competency cluster ("independent," "rational") (Broverman et al., 1972).[2]

Secondly, gender stereotype content reflects the fact (emphasized in Chapter 1) that every known society esteems males more than females. Male superiority is, of course, an intrinsic aspect of the traditional division of labour. Many of the traits shown in Table 2.1 refer to male dominance ("arrogant," "egotistical," "forceful") and female subordination ("dependent," "meek," "submissive"). Indeed, the gender stereotypes of all 25 nations depict males as "dominant" and "forceful," and females as "submissive" (Williams and Best, 1982:75-76).

Many people regard traditional gender stereotypes as dangerous anachronisms; "dangerous" because as self-fulfilling prophecies, they impede the movement toward equality of the sexes; "anachronisms" because despite two decades of feminist activity, gender stereotyping "continues to be a rather powerful social force" in Canadian society (Edwards and Williams, 1980:218). Stereotypes, functioning as self-fulfilling prophecies, can impede women's fight for equality. If at the outset, women are

assumed to be incompetent in the public sphere, their performance may be judged less successful than it actually is. Or if women are assumed to be less competent, they may be given fewer opportunities to assert themselves (Wrightsman and Deaux, 1981:306). Given the conservative force of gender stereotypes, it is not surprising that males, with their greater stake in the status quo, subscribe to gender stereotypes more than females (Percival and Percival, 1979).

As the above discussion of the source of gender stereotype content suggests, the pictures people carry around in their heads about women and men will not go away until fundamental social change occurs. Specifically, "Gender stereotypes...will not disappear until people divide social roles equally, that is, until child care and household responsibilities are shared equally by women and men and the responsibility to be employed outside the home is borne equally" (Eagly and Steffen, 1984:752).

Gender-role Attitudes

We continue our discussion of gender in the popular imagination by examining the gender-role attitudes held by Canadians. While gender stereotypes refer to shared beliefs about feminine and masculine psychological makeup, *gender-role attitudes*, as the term suggests, point to people's beliefs about the status of the sexes and the appropriate gender division of labour in home and workplace. The gender-role attitudes held by Canadians range from traditional to egalitarian, "from the view that women belong in the home and are responsible for child-rearing, to the view that women and men should have equal access to identical positions and rewards" (Boyd, 1984:3).

Table 2.2 lists six questions which were asked of Canadian national probability samples by researchers Gibbins, Ponting and Symons (1978) and Ponting (1986). The topics covered by these questions illustrate, rather than exhaust, the universe of gender-role attitudes. In other words, particular studies merely sample Canadians' attitudes concerning these matters. (See also Boyd, 1984.) Since four of the six items were asked in 1976 and

TABLE 2.2

CANADIAN GENDER-ROLE ATTITUDES

Attitudinal Item		% Agree	% Disagree	% Undecided/ Neutral**
1. When children are young, a mother's place is in the home.	TOTAL (1986)	64	20	16
	TOTAL (1976)	81	10	9
	Male*	62	19	18
	Female*	65	20	13
	Anglophone*	63	20	16
	Francophone*	62	22	16
2. Although a wife's career may be important, she should give priority to helping her husband advance in his career.	TOTAL (1986)	40	47	13
	TOTAL (1976)	74	21	5
	Male	35	51	13
	Female	44	42	12
	Anglophone	40	47	14
	Francophone	41	47	11
3. In the business world more women should be promoted into senior management positions.	TOTAL (1986)	77	8	14
	TOTAL (1976)	72	14	13
	Male	72	10	18
	Female	82	6	11
	Anglophone	73	9	17
	Francophone	87	4	8
4. A woman should have the sole right to decide whether or not to have an abortion.	TOTAL (1986)	66	26	7
	TOTAL (1976)	56	34	9
	Male	67	24	8
	Female	65	27	6
	Anglophone	65	27	6
	Francophone	70	22	8
5. Overall, the women's movement has had more of a positive effect than a negative effect on Canadian society.	TOTAL (1986)***	73	11	12
	Male	71	12	14
	Female	75	11	10
	Anglophone	73	13	10
	Francophone	71	8	15
6. There should be more laws to get rid of differences in the way women are treated, compared to men.	TOTAL (1986)***	74	13	11
	Male	68	18	13
	Female	80	9	9
	Anglophone	72	15	12
	Francophone	80	9	9

SOURCES: Gibbins, Ponting and Symons (1978) and Ponting (unpublished 1986 data). Used with permission.
* All sex and language group results refer to 1986 data.
** Because of rounding and "don't know" answers or refusals, some totals do not equal 100%.
*** Questions 5 and 6 were not asked in 1976.

again in 1986 by Professor Ponting and his colleagues, these data allow us to draw some conclusions about changes over time.

What conclusions can be drawn from Table 2.2? First of all, Canadians' attitudes concerning gender arrangements in the domestic sphere are more traditional than their public-sphere attitudes. In 1986, 64 percent felt that a mother with young children belongs in the home. (By contrast, 87 percent of a 1982 national Gallup poll felt that a married woman *without children* should take a job outside the home [Boyd, 1984].) Moreover, 40 percent believed that a wife should give her husband's career higher priority than her own.

When questions focus exclusively on the woman in the workplace, i.e., the implications of her work for her family are left unmentioned, Canadians' attitudes become more egalitarian. Seventy-seven percent said more women should be promoted into senior management positions. (Eighty-three percent told Gallup pollsters in 1983 that they thought women could run most businesses as well as men [Boyd, 1984].)

Three-quarters of the sample expressed verbal support for the women's movement (Questions #5 and #6). Finally, two-thirds gave women the right to decide whether or not to have an abortion (Question #4).

Another important conclusion which can be derived from Table 2.2 is that Canadians' gender-role attitudes became more egalitarian between 1976 and 1986. The sensitive domestic issues show especially large shifts over time (Questions #1 and #2). Professor Ponting's findings agree with both Canadian Gallup poll data (Boyd, 1984) and several American studies (Cherlin and Walters, 1981; Thornton, Alwin and Camburn, 1983). This historical change may be attributed to such factors as the growing labour force participation of women, public debate and media attention to gender, higher education, and the declining birth rate.

Some categories of Canadians are more liberal than others. Francophones were significantly more liberal than Anglophones on Questions #3-6; no language group differences emerged for the family-related questions (#1, #2). These findings agree with earlier research (Boyd, 1975; Gibbins, Ponting and Symons, 1978). There is a slight tendency for women to be more liberal than men (Questions #3, #5, #6). However, significantly more men gave the egalitarian response to Question #2; sex differences in replies to Questions #1 and #4 were not significant. Finally, according to data not shown on Table 2.2, people with more formal education tend to hold more egalitarian attitudes.

This section has examined common sense notions about the characteristics and appropriate activities of males and females. Scrutiny of contemporary mythology, gender stereotypes, and gender attitudes shows that the female-male distinction remains salient in the popular imagination. Moreover, male superiority is still assumed. Qualities ascribed to the sexes are supportive of the traditional gender division of labour. The impact of the women's movement on people's thinking about the sexes has been significant, but after analyzing Gallup poll data from 1954 to 1984, Boyd (1984:23) concluded that while enormous change occurred during the period with respect to gender issues, Canadians' gender-role attitudes "also reveal a residue of earlier norms and practices."

IDEOLOGICAL INFLUENCES UPON THE SCIENTIFIC STUDY OF SEX/GENDER DIFFERENCES

The question of how women and men differ and how they are alike has provided subject matter for scientific thought as well as folk thought. "Hot social questions generate hot scientific ones" (Hubbard, 1987:1034). Laypeople have been taught to regard science as an objective, value-free enterprise, uniquely capable of providing accurate answers to the questions that concern them. Certainly, the scientific method is the most effective technique human beings have devised for producing answers to empirical questions. In this respect, science is superior to folklore, intuition, personal experience, revelation, or opinion. Despite its excellent track record, science is fallible. Error can occur.

One reason why experts can be wrong is that "scientists, like everyone else, are born and raised in a particular culture of beliefs, biases, values, and opinions, and to one degree or another, they will be affected in their work by what they hope, believe, want, or need to be true" (Bleier, 1984:3-4). Feminists charge that science has been implicated in the creation and reinforcement of society's myths about the sexes (Lowe and Hubbard, 1983).

From the early decades of this century, the social science of psychology has studied male-female differences. Through the influence of the women's liberation movement, female psychologists became aware of the androcentrism of the "psychology of sex differences" (as this area has traditionally been labelled). In other words, pre-feminist psychology routinely attempted to establish norms and standards for human beings (female as well as male) that were based on male experience alone. Therefore, it ended up being a value-laden activity producing "battle weapons against women" (Bernard, 1976:13). As psychologist Parlee (1975:124) observed, the "knowledge" developed by academic psychologists just "happened (apparently) to support stereotyped beliefs about the abilities and psychological characteristics of women and men, and such beliefs happen to support existing political, legal, and economic inequalities between the sexes."[3]

The question of female-male differences is a sensitive *political* issue, as well as a scientific matter. It is political because answers which enhance the position of one sex at the expense of the other are preferred. In those cases where knowledge has political implications and overtones, people with a stake in the outcome "have usually decided what the facts and their causes are prior to examining the data. Indeed, in many cases *despite* the data" (Weyant, 1979:373, emphasis in original). Prior to the renewed feminist movement, many psychologists (whether consciously or unconsciously) seemed interested in "proving" that (a) any male-female differences demonstrated male superiority, and (b) the differences involved were innate, biological differences.

The Brain Controversy

More than 80 years ago, psychologist Helen Woolley (quoted in Shields, 1975:739) remarked that: "There is perhaps no field aspiring to be scientific where flagrant personal bias, logic martyred in the cause of supporting a prejudice, unfounded assertions, and even sentimental rot and drivel, have run riot to such an extent as the psychology of sex differences."

The brain controversy, which raged between 1900 and 1930, is a famous historical case of this misuse of science (Parlee, 1978; Shields, 1975). At first the debate revolved around the question, "Which sex has the larger brain?" Because it was assumed that both brain size and intelligence increased with movement up the phylogenetic scale, it seemed obvious that the sex with the smaller brain was the inferior sex. (At the time, a similar argument was used to explain alleged intellectual differences between whites and blacks [Epstein, 1988:52].) The brain size of cadavers was measured, and male brains were reported to be larger. However, contemporary critics believe that the finding of male superiority was affected by the fact that the male researchers knew the sex of the corpse before they did their measuring. This information subverted their judgement; they saw what they expected to see.

The second phase of the brain controversy emerged when scientists discovered that various psychological abilities were localized in various parts of the brain. At first, the frontal lobes were viewed as the seat of the intellect. Not surprisingly, "research" showed that men had larger frontal lobes, relative to the parietal lobes, than did women. Later on, the parietal lobes came to be regarded as the source of higher intellectual functions. Scientific opinion reversed itself; studies began to report that men had relatively larger parietal lobes than women. Today scholars agree that neither overall brain size, nor proportions of brain parts, differ by sex.

False Assumptions Underlying Historical Studies of Female-male Differences

Because so much emotion and mystery surround male-female relations, and because until recent years, most of them were men, psychologists entertained a number of biased assumptions about sex/gender differences (Tresemer, 1975; Weisstein, 1971). Deep-seated ideas, which we now know to be mistaken, originated in the cultural context which psychologists share with other societal members.

The example of the brain controversy discussed in the previous section illustrates five important points about the historical study of sex/gender differences. First, the episode exemplifies the conviction, which we saw earlier to be deeply embedded in cultural myths and gender stereotypes, that woman is a different order of being. Second, the scientists involved, as products of their culture, took male superiority for granted. Third, the researchers peering at cadavers' brains assumed that the male-female differences they expected to find were biologically determined. (Chapter 3 explores the validity of biological explanations of the factors which distinguish females from males.)

Fourth, the brain controversy represents one of many attempts in the annals of science to harness the prestige of science in order to buttress the gender status quo. In Williams' (1983:14) words, these early inquiries into sex/gender differences began "with the same old assumptions that woman's lesser cultural contributions to the society and her behavior in the domestic role were part of the natural order of things. The problem was to find the underlying mechanism to account for these at a level that would satisfy the scientific intellect." Findings of difference, then and now, were used to rationalize masculine privilege. Women of "little brain" obviously were capable of handling only menial tasks and responsibilities.

Fifth, the faulty assumptions enumerated above became translated into methodological biases which distorted the design and interpretation of scientists' experiments. That is, the objectivity of scholars can be subverted by their values, a point made in Chapter 1 with reference to sociologists. An even earlier chapter from the history of the scientific study of gender will serve to reiterate our point. An accomplished scientist, van Leeuwenhoek, looked at human sperm under his microscope and asserted that he had *seen* "exceedingly minute forms of men with arms, heads and legs." As feminist biologist Ruth Bleier (1984:3) points out, "one's conceptual framework, a certain state of mind, permits one to see and accommodate certain things but not others." She goes on to argue that van Leeuwenhoek's observations were influenced by "the 20-centuries-long concept and tradition, stemming from Aristotle, that women, as totally passive beings, contribute nothing but an incubator-womb to the developing fetus that springs full-blown, so to speak, from the head of the sperm" (p. 3, emphasis in original deleted).

Contemporary Issues in the Study of Male-female Differences

The traditional "sex differences" approach within the discipline of psychology has functioned to perpetuate some of the outdated thinking discussed above. Although the brain controversy strikes the 1990s reader as a silly affair, "sex differences" research still claims to demonstrate women's inferiority and to justify their low status (Bernard, 1976:13-14).

To illustrate, a finding that a greater proportion of boys than girls exhibit aggressive behavior at early ages is used to explain men's assumption of leadership roles. Yet scientists do not similarly suppose that women ought to become preachers and politicians as girls they usually outperform boys in tests demonstrating verbal ability. Thus, scientists' bias in locating childhood factors for adult performance leads them to selectively highlight the cases supporting stereotypes and underrecognize the cases that might refute them. Such bias also undercuts observation and reporting of non-findings (Epstein, 1988:44).

Feminist psychologists are understandably critical of the "sex differences" approach in their discipline. In the words of psychologist Cheryl Malmo (1984:116-17), the "sex differences" perspective "continues to debate the relevance of minuscule differences in males and females, ... often confuses sex and gender differences, ... typically ignores the fact that average differences between males and females are less significant than variations found within each sex, and... consequently dismisses the vast number of similarities between the sexes—similarities which seem to reflect our common humanness."

Sex/gender differences in aggressiveness provide a good illustration of Malmo's point. As we shall see shortly, the greater aggressiveness of males is well documented. However, this does not mean that *all* males are aggressive or that *all* females are unaggressive. Focussing only on the difference in averages and ignoring the many exceptions is a logical pitfall known as the *fallacy of the average* (Doyle, 1989:68). Research shows that this sex/gender difference, as well as others, can be represented as an overlapping normal curve. Both males and females vary between being highly aggressive and very unaggressive. However, the group average for males is somewhat higher. Nevertheless, a substantial number of females will be as or more aggressive than many males. That is, within-sex differences are frequently more important than between-sex differences.

Feminist reaction to the troublesome issue of sex/gender differences has varied over time. In the 1970s, the feminist social movement pursued its goal of equality with men within a framework of presumed "sameness" with men. Following this lead, feminist scholars minimized sex/gender differences.[4] They objected strenuously to mainstream psychology's emphasis on *differences* because this perspective served the ideological purpose of bolstering traditional social arrangements based on gender inequality. Too often in the past, androcentric thinking had resulted in female difference being interpreted as female inferiority (Allen, 1987). Therefore, the conclusion reached by Maccoby and Jacklin in their prestigious volume, *The Psychology of Sex Differences* (1974), that research supported very few, very slight male-female differences was enthusiastically received by most feminist social scientists at that time. (See Block [1976] for a contrary opinion.)

During the 1980s, a perceptible shift occurred in feminist thinking about sex/gender differences.[5] "Attempts to 'disprove' the existence of sex differences have given way to arguments, both at the scientific and popular level, that differences do exist" (Deaux, 1985:74). Alleged feminine distinctions are now being proclaimed with pride, rather than denied or minimized. Understandably, the sex/gender differences and interpretations of them focussed upon by feminists are those that cast women in a favourable light, rather than those chosen by males to justify traditional gender arrangements. This ideological swing of the pendulum reflects the realization among some contemporary feminists that women's economic and legal interests may be best served by acknowledging crucial gender/sex differences. Child-bearing is an obvious example. Because pregnancy disadvantages women in various ways, special considerations (not needed by men) are required to protect women's position in the labour force (Hewlett, 1986). Two widely acclaimed books written by feminist psychologists during the 1980s— Gilligan, *In A Different Voice* (1982) and Belenky et al., *Women's Ways of Knowing* (1986)—celebrated what their authors feel to be distinctively feminine traits. These controversial works will be discussed in later chapters.

This section has considered the impact of ideology—both the ideology that buttresses male privilege and the ideology of the women's movement—upon the scholarly investigation of the sensitive topic of sex/gender differences. Many people are troubled to learn that politics can influence the directions science takes, and the conclusions it reaches. Some may be comforted by psychologist Alice Eagly's (1987:4-5) conclusion that, while over "the short run, the scientific method may yield incomplete and even misleading descriptions," errors "are generally corrected as tools of analysis are refined and scientists criticize each other's theories and research methods." She goes on to say that "in the long run, maximally valid descriptions of sex differences should follow from the application of the scientific method" (p. 5).

To this point, Chapter 2 has considered these questions: "What do people *think* males and females are like?" "What biases have complicated scientists' study of this problem?" We turn now to the question, "What differences *actually* distinguish females and males?"

ACTUAL FEMALE-MALE DIFFERENCES

This section will consider male-female physiological and psychological differences. Our task is to summarize existing research on such differences. Although some speculative comment about the sources of these distinctions will be offered as we go along, the main discussion of etiology and implications will be reserved for later chapters. The author, being neither biologist nor psychologist, will provide only a brief summary of the enormously complicated research literature. Just how different are the sexes?

Physiological Differences

The biological concept of sex as it pertains to both females and males really involves four highly inter-related aspects (Frieze et al., 1978:83-84):

1. GENETIC SEX (XX OR XY CHROMOSOMES)

Normal human beings have twenty-three pairs of *chromosomes*. Females and males share twenty-two of these pairs. The twenty-third pair determines the genetic sex of the individual. In males, this pair is made up of an X and a Y chromosome, while in females it is composed of two X chromosomes. A person's sex is determined at the moment of conception, when the egg, carrying an X chromosome, is united with the sperm, which carries *either* an X or a Y chromosome. Fertilized eggs with two X chromosomes are females; those with an X and a Y chromosome are males. Normally, XX embryos develop ovaries containing potential eggs, a female reproductive tract, and external genitals consisting of a clitoris and two pairs of skin folds. Embryos with the XY genetic constitution will eventually acquire testes with potential sperm, a male reproductive tract and glands, and external genitals composed of a penis and scrotal sac. Four to five months are required for these sex differences to develop. Until the seventh week after conception, the only distinguishing characteristic is genetic, that is, chromosomal (Barfield, 1976:62-63).[6]

2. HORMONAL SEX (RELATIVE LEVELS OF ESTROGEN AND TESTOSTERONE)

Hormones are chemical substances that the endocrine glands secrete into the bloodstream. All hormones exist in both sexes, though the levels vary between the sexes and within the same individual from time to time (Geer et al., 1984:54). The chief male sex hormone is *testosterone*, which is one of a group of hormones called *androgens*. Until about the seventh week after conception, the fetus retains the potential to develop into either a male or a female. After

this point, embryos with an XY genetic constitution develop testes, and the testes begin to secrete androgens. The androgens cause the male genital development to proceed. The XX embryo does not produce androgens *or* the female sex hormones. In this absence of hormonal stimulation, female genital development takes place (Archer and Lloyd, 1985:71). *Estrogen* and *progesterone* are the primary female sex hormones. As children of both sexes approach puberty, the sex hormone production increases significantly and influences the development of sex glands and organs, and the elaboration of secondary sex characteristics. The release of female hormones is related to the menstrual cycle.

3. GONADAL SEX (OVARIES OR TESTES)

An embryo's genetic sex determines whether its *gonadal cells* become ovaries or testes. The exact means by which this occurs is not yet fully understood. If the embryo carries an X and a Y chromosome, testes are formed approximately seven weeks after conception. These testes then begin to produce male hormones. On the other hand, if the embryo carries two X chromosomes, the gonadal tissue remains undifferentiated until approximately twelve weeks after conception. Two ovaries form from this tissue somewhat later during the gestation period (Schulz, 1984:96).

4. GENITAL SEX (PENIS OR CLITORIS/VAGINA)

As noted above, secretion of the male sex hormones by the embryonic testes results in development of the penis and scrotum. In the XX embryo, it is the absence of hormonal stimulation that produces female development.

As we have seen, the four components of femaleness and maleness are closely inter-related. The genetic sex normally determines the hormonal sex, which in turn determines the gonadal and genital sex. That is, an XY embryo develops into a fetus with testes. The testes secrete male hormones, which in turn trigger the development of male genitals. An XX embryo, on the other hand, develops without hormone production into a fetus having female genitals.

However, on rare occasions, the hormone system goes wrong during fetal development, and produces an *hermaphrodite*, an organism with both male and female tissue (Tavris and Wade, 1984:139 ff.). Hermaphrodites may have one ovary and one testicle. The external genitals may be ambiguous, the individual having what could be a very large clitoris or a very small penis. Some hermaphrodites have external organs in conflict with internal genitalia, for example, ovaries and a penis. The accidents that produce hermaphrodites, tragic as they are for the individuals and families involved, provide researchers with opportunities to explore the relative contributions of nature and nurture to sex/gender. (See Chapter 3.).

Obviously, men and women differ in their reproductive functions. "Only women menstruate, gestate, and lactate. Only men produce semen" (Armstrong and Armstrong, 1978:97). In addition, a number of secondary sex characteristics are apparent, which become more pronounced with puberty (Barfield, 1976:65-70). On the average, males are taller and heavier, and a greater percentage of their total body weight is made up of muscle while a smaller proportion is made up of fat. Females have lighter skeletons, different shoulder and pelvis proportions, different pelvic bone shapes, and different socket shapes at the hip and shoulder. These differences contribute to such feminine characteristics as less strength (particularly in the upper body), less endurance in heavy labour, more difficulty in overarm throwing, and better ability to float.

The average male is stronger than the average female. One reason is the innate difference in skeletal structure and upper-body muscular mass. Another reason is the better athletic training usually provided for males (Tavris and Wade, 1984:44). Once again, we warn against the fallacy of the average. Although the average man is bigger and stronger than the average woman, the variation within the male and female categories may be greater than the male-female difference. For example:

In the annual Boston Marathon, the average man finishes about a half hour ahead of the average woman, but some women finish ahead of most of the superbly conditioned men. Don Schollander's world-record-setting 4 minutes 12.2 seconds in the 400-meter swim at the 1964 Olympic Games would have placed him last against the eight women racing in the 1988 Olympics and a full 8.35 seconds behind winner, Janet Evans (Myers, 1990:180).

In all developed countries, the expectation of life at birth for females exceeds that for males by four to ten years (Nathanson, 1984). In Canada, the average woman outlives the average man by seven years (Statistics Canada, 1985).[7] As is the case in other developed societies, male mortality rates in this country exceed those of females in all age groups. However, differences are most pronounced in the two age groups 15-24 (where male mortality is three times that of females) and 55-64 (where death rates for men are twice those for women) (Nathanson, 1984:193). As Ashley Montagu informed us in *The Natural Superiority of Women* (1952), the fact that males have only one of the important X chromosomes makes them more vulnerable to some 60 genetically transmitted disorders, such as hemophilia and colour blindness. Males are more prone to speech defects, reading disabilities, deafness, and mental defectiveness (Barfield, 1976:68). Males have higher rates of cardiovascular disease and cancer. Males are more often victims of automobile accidents, suicide, and violent crimes. Females have higher rates of milder conditions, including anemia, thyroid problems, arthritis, and difficulties related to pregnancy and reproductive organs (Statistics Canada, 1985).

Although the foregoing discussion has emphasized differences, it is important not to lose sight of the fact that males and females share most physiological characteristics. "Far from falling into two discrete groups, male and female have the same body ground plan, and even the anatomical difference is more apparent than real. Neither the phallus nor the womb are organs of one sex only: the female phallus (the clitoris) is the biological equivalent of the male organ, and men possess a vestigial womb" (Oakley, 1972:18). In short, the "opposite sexes" are not so opposite (Armstrong and Armstrong, 1984:113).

Psychological Differences

So far, we have established that *"biological differences between the sexes are actually minute when compared with the similarities"* (Nicholson, 1984:6, emphasis added). What have social scientists discovered about *psychological* characteristics? This section treats two dimensions of this matter. First, do females and males differ psychologically? Are the popular beliefs which are codified in gender stereotypes valid? For example, are males indeed logical and females intuitive? Are girls and women more emotional, apt to cry at the drop of a pin and like Little Miss Muffet, to cringe when they encounter a spider?

Second, to the extent that the sexes actually do feel, think, and behave differently, how meaningful are these distinctions? Put another way, how adequate are these psychological traits to explain the differences in men's and women's lives? For the most part, discussion of sources of differences is reserved for later chapters.

Our remarks represent a distillation of a rich, but confusing psychological literature. Starting in the late 1970s, psychologists developed a powerful strategy for interpreting what has been described as "an over-researched area littered with contradictory findings" (Nicholson, 1984:3). This strategy, called *meta-analysis*, provides explicit and statistically justified methods of drawing conclusions from a large number of studies that various psychologists have conducted in a given area of gender differences, such as conformity or aggression (Eagly, 1987:35 ff.). "Comparisons of the sexes in virtually every form of behavior imaginable have been reported, and an increasing number of meta-analytic studies have taken advantage of this abundance to make more conclusive statements about the significance of obtained differences" (Deaux, 1985: 51-52). Our consideration of this literature is organized under these headings: Intellectual Abilities; Personality Traits and Social-Psychological Dispositions.

Intellectual Abilities

When the status of women is debated in mixed company, discussion frequently turns to the relative absence of eminent women in history, art, music, literature, and science. On the international scene, Joan of Arc, Marie Curie, the Brontë sisters, and Mother Teresa exhaust most people's mental lists of well-known women. Coming up with Canadian names is an even more challenging parlour game. Laura Secord? Emily Carr? Nellie McClung? Margaret Atwood? Audrey McLaughlin? Gender stereotypes current in our culture hold that women lack the intellectual ability to excel. An analogy is made between soft body and soft mind (Ellmann, 1968:74). *Males* are perceived to be ingenious, inventive, clear-thinking, and logical (Table 2.1). Is this so? What does research have to say on this matter?

IQ

Psychologists (Maccoby and Jacklin, 1974:65; Singleton, 1986:63) conclude that the average scores of males and females do not differ on tests of general intellectual abilities. There is a very good reason for this finding. Most widely used IQ tests have been designed to minimize sex/gender differences (Tavris and Wade, 1984:47). In the construction of these instruments, questions which differentiate between the sexes are eliminated. Specific tasks and abilities at which females succeed are balanced by tasks and abilities at which males succeed. In order to answer our question about intellectual ability, we must examine the components of intelligence reviewed below.

VERBAL ABILITIES

"Women have long been thought to excel at talking—endlessly" (Doyle, 1989:72) For example, women as incessant talkers is a frequent cartoon theme (Mackie, 1990b). In "Blondie," Mr. Dithers describes Mrs. Dithers as having a mouth big enough to catch a frisbee. The "Wizard of Id" turnkey says, "They found a three million-year-old female jawbone." Asks the prisoner, "How do they know it's female?" The answer: "It was still clacking."

For psychologists, verbal abilities include simple measures of articulation, spelling, punctuation, sentence complexity, vocabulary size and fluency, and more sophisticated measures of reading comprehension, creative writing, and use of language in logical reasoning (Tavris and Wade, 1984). Females excel slightly on both simple and higher level verbal tasks (Maccoby and Jacklin, 1974; Hyde, 1981). There is some evidence that girls begin to manifest their verbal superiority in early childhood (Singleton, 1986). Boys talk later than girls, and are more likely to stutter and have reading difficulties. From the age of ten or eleven through high school, female superiority increases. As for which sex talks more, contrary to stereotyped depictions, from preschool onward men talk more. "In fact, males who act more traditional in terms of exhibiting what most would call masculine behaviors are more likely to 'hog' the conversation with others rather than take turns in a dialogue with another" (Doyle, 1989:72-73).

MATHEMATICAL ABILITY

Girls and boys are similar in their early acquisition of quantitative concepts and mastery of arithmetic (Brigham, 1986:330). However, beginning in late childhood, boys score higher than girls on standardized mathematics achievement tests. For example, a nationwide talent search was conducted in the United States to identify students, who before their thirteenth birthday, would score over 700 on the mathematical portion of the Scholastic Aptitude Test (SAT). Males outnumbered females by a ratio of 13 to 1 in the elite group which represented the top one in 10 000 in their age category (Benbow and Stanley, 1983).

Also, males are more likely than females "to engage in a variety of optional activities related to mathematics, from technical hobbies to careers in which math skills play an important role" (Eccles and Jacobs, 1986:367). Only 30 percent of the Canadians who hold a degree or diploma in mathematics or the physical sciences are women (Weston, 1989:5). The male

advantage, which occurs primarily on algebraic items (not arithmetic or geometric problems [Deaux, 1985:56]), is partly, but not entirely, a function of the number of mathematics courses taken. Performance on mathematics tests is also influenced by whether or not people like the subject. According to research, sex/gender "differences in students' attitudes toward mathematics and in plans to continue taking math courses are influenced substantially by their parents' perceptions of the difficulty of mathematics for their child and by their own attitudes about the value of mathematics" (Eccles and Jacobs, 1986:379-80). In summary, while most investigators agree that there is a small but true difference in mathematical performance favouring boys (Feingold, 1988; Henley, 1985:108), research continues into the extent and sources of male quantitative advantage.

SPATIAL SKILLS

Popular thinking also attributes the predominance of men over women in science and mathematics to male superiority in tasks involving spatial skills. Such skills refer to the ability to visually manipulate, locate, or make judgments about the spatial relationships of items located in two- or three-dimensional space. Tests of spatial skills include, for example, embedded figures (locating smaller figures in a larger design), adjusting a bar or rod to a horizontal or vertical position against a tilted background, and body orientation tests. Males do indeed consistently excel in many tasks devised by psychologists to assess space relations. A development trend exists, with young children showing no difference, and a male advantage emerging at the beginning of adolescence and continuing into adulthood (Maccoby and Jacklin, 1974). However, as Tavris and Wade (1984:51) point out, visual-spatial ability depends to a considerable extent on culture. Traditionally, female as well as male Inuit were adept at spotting brown caribou moving across a brown landscape because their culture demanded this skill. In short, spatial skill, like mathematical ability, benefits from practice.

CREATIVITY

Creativity is a highly valued, complex quality (Abra, 1988). The observation that among creative occupations such as painting, sculpture, literature, and music, men far outnumber women, especially within the ranks of the most successful, has stimulated psychologists' interest in possible gender differences in the ability to produce unique ideas (Singleton, 1986:70). Psychologists test creativity by measures such as the Alternative Uses Test, which asks people to list as many uses as they can for common objects, such as a brick. An obvious answer to this is, "You use a brick to build a house." Creative people list unique and almost endless solutions. (One creative soul, quoted by Tavris and Wade [1984:52-53], suggested using a brick as a 'bug-hider.' "You leave it on the ground for a few days, then pick it up and see all the bugs that have been hiding.")

Another test involves showing subjects a picture and requesting them to list all the questions they would need to have answered in order to understand the events in the picture. Such creativity tests tend to have two components, a verbal fluency component and a component involving productivity of unusual ideas. Singleton (1986:70) concludes that according to empirical studies of creativity, "neither males nor females show a consistent superiority in creative thinking ability, although creative tasks which depend more on verbal skills tend to favour females." Girls and women are at least as able as boys and men to generate a variety of hypotheses and produce unusual ideas (Maccoby and Jacklin, 1974:113-14).

In summary, research shows no gender differences in creativity or general intelligence. The logic of IQ construction accounts for the latter no-difference finding. Females excel in verbal abilities and males have the edge in mathematical and visual-spatial skills. It is important to mention again the substantial evidence showing that training significantly improves the performance of both sexes in verbal, spatial, and mathematical skills (Deaux, 1985:56). Finally, we emphasize that for both sexes, intellect is only one factor contributing to eminence. While it is true that men have produced the bulk of the intellectual innovations in art, science, and technology, the reasons are social mechanisms, not women's intellectual inferiority. One broad structural consideration is opportunity to create—appropriate schooling, social support of talent, and so on (Becker, 1981; Cole, 1979; Tuchman, 1975). To ask the rhetorical question, "Why have there been no great women artists?" for example, is "an identification of renown with talent and a refusal to contemplate how much the social organization of training, production, and distribution influences who can become famous" (Tuchman and Fortin, 1984:74).

Personality Traits and Social-psychological Dispositions

Charting the similarities and differences between the sexes becomes increasingly complicated as we move from physiological characteristics to intellectual capacities (reviewed above) and, finally, to personality traits (this section's topic). Because of space limitations, only the most thoroughly studied personality traits are discussed below.

AGGRESSIVENESS

A variety of different types of studies of aggression consistently attest to the truth of the stereotype: males are more likely than females to intentionally hurt others. Starting with hitting and shoving at age two or three, males are more aggressive throughout life (Eagly, 1987; Maccoby and Jacklin, 1974). Sex/gender differences in aggressiveness are found cross-culturally (Whiting and Edwards, 1973). Despite females' reputation for "bitchiness" and "cattiness," research shows males to be both more physically and verbally aggressive than females (Archer and Lloyd, 1985:129). This pattern is more pronounced among children than adults. While adult males are more physically aggressive than adult females, few sex/gender differences exist in psychological aggression (Eagly, 1987). Also, adult men and women think differently about aggression, with women reporting more guilt and anxiety "as a consequence of aggression, more vigilance about the harm that aggression causes its victims, and more concern about the danger that their aggression might bring to themselves" (Eagly, 1987:94). Males are far more likely to be arrested for violent crimes in every society that has kept crime records (Chesney-Lind, 1986; Myers, 1990:181). As we shall see in the next chapter, many attempts have been made to unravel the reasons for the greater male proclivity for aggression. Because of the cross-cultural evidence for a sex/gender difference that begins so early in life, many accounts emphasize biological causation.

Susceptibility to Social Influence

Gender stereotypes describe men as independent and dominant, and women as compliant and submissive. According to the evidence, women are more persuasible than men and are more likely to conform to social pressure in situations involving surveillance by an audience (Eagly and Carli, 1981). Eagly (1987:98) suggests that female influencibility may have something to do firstly, with the higher status positions men ordinarily occupy (i.e., masculine power), and secondly, with women's commitment to preserving group harmony and enhancing positive feelings among group members.

Non-verbal Communication

Male-female differences in many types of body language—use of personal space, touching, gaze, and posture—have been documented (Deaux, 1985:61). In addition, females are more skillful in *understanding* other people's non-verbal communication. Females are especially adept at decoding emotions from facial expressions and voice tones (Hall, 1984). This difference could stem from girls' early training in being sensitive to the wishes of others. Alternatively, females' relative lack of social power might increase the importance of being able to "read" accurately the wishes of more powerful others (Hall, 1978). (We return to this topic in Chapter 7.)

The discussion above has focussed on those

characteristics for which female-male differences have consistently been found. However, many additional traits have received research attention (Maccoby and Jacklin, 1974). We end this overview of personality characteristics with brief comments on two additional traits prominent in gender stereotypes—emotionality and nurturance. With regard to *emotionality*, females appear to be more closely in touch with their feelings and more expressive of them than males (MacKinnon and Keating, 1989). The sexes also differ in which emotions they feel free to express in front of others. For instance, women cry more than men (Ross and Mirowsky, 1984); they are more willing to admit their fears (about spiders, for example [Cornelius and Averill, 1983].) Women smile more. According to analyses of 9000 college yearbook photos (LaFrance, 1985) and 1100 magazine and newspaper photographs, and 1300 people in shopping malls, parks, and streets (Halberstadt and Saitta, 1987), females are more likely than males to smile (Myers, 1990:182). However, despite males' reputation for inexpressiveness, studies show that "anger, disgust, hostility, contempt, and cynicism are just a few of the emotions that men express quite openly in public" (Doyle, 1989:157).

A central dimension of gender stereotypes is the assumption that females are the more *nurturant* sex (Basow, 1986:64). Because only women can bear and nurse children, it seems to follow that women must "naturally" be more qualified to take care of babies, and by extension, others in need of help. There is no evidence that females are consistently more nurturant than males. However, the situation is complicated by the greater likelihood that females will exhibit warm, helpful behaviour when cast into caretaking roles. For example, women show more enthusiasm for unfamiliar infants, being more likely than men to coo and smile at strange babies, and to show distress when they cry (Feldman et al., 1977). Moreover, cross-cultural data (Whiting and Edwards, 1973) show that little girls offer infants and toddlers help and affection, while little boys approach babies to take something away from them (or to get them to do something). Yet it is a cultural expectation that nurturance is supposed to be a feminine quality (Tavris and

Wade, 1984:69-70). In most cultures, girls babysit and care for younger siblings more often than boys. Moreover, males do not always feel free to display nurturance. From their review of the evidence, Maccoby and Jacklin (1974:354) conclude that it is impossible to say whether women are more disposed to behave maternally than men are to behave paternally. For example, the fact that girls more frequently play with dolls has been taken as spontaneous nurturance. However, dolls are presented to girls, not boys, and much doll play is not nurturant. Dolls are hugged and tucked into bed but they are also "scolded, spanked, subjected to surgical operations, and ... even scalped" (Maccoby and Jacklin, 1974:220). "The fact that women are more likely to be in nurturant roles in our society (mothers, nurses, social workers, and so forth) is more a consequence of gender stereotypes than a direct reflection of any fundamental sex difference in nurturing ability" (Basow, 1986:64).

From time to time throughout the book, these and other hypothesized sex/gender differences will receive our attention.

The Magnitude of Gender Differences in Psychological Traits

So far, we have reviewed the evidence for sex/gender differences in selected psychological characteristics, and speculated a bit on reasons for their existence. We turn now to the question of the *significance* or importance of these differences. As mentioned earlier, meta-analysis combines statistically many studies of the same characteristic done by many researchers. The purpose of meta-analysis is twofold: first, to arrive at conclusions about the consistency of the results concerning a given sex/gender difference, and second, to reach statistical judgments on the magnitude of those female-male differences which are found (Glass et al., 1981). Discussion here will be confined to the second objective. The magnitude of the sex/gender difference is expressed by the percentage of variance accounted for.[8] Percentage of variance represents an estimate of the proportion of the range of behaviours that appears to be caused by sex/gender alone. If the researcher could

predict perfectly what a person's behaviour would be, based solely on knowledge of whether that individual is a female or a male, the psychologist would say that sex/gender accounted for 100 percent of the variance for that behaviour. On the other hand, if sex/gender had no influence whatsoever on the behaviour, we would say that it accounted for zero percent of the variance (Brigham, 1986:336). The interested reader might find it worthwhile to pursue the technical interpretation of the "percent of variance accounted for" concept (Eagly, 1987). However, this concept serves our present purpose as a shorthand representation of the importance of sex/gender differences in the psychological characteristics.

Table 2.3 shows the results of meta-analyses of sex/gender differences in some of the intellectual abilities and psychological traits reviewed above. (So far, only a small selection of the characteristics included in gender stereotypes have been subjected to meta-analysis.) According to the table, sex/gender explains a very small amount of the variance: one percent in verbal and mathematical abilities, and susceptibility to social influence; four to six percent in visual/spatial abilities, decoding non-verbal cues, and aggression. Five to six percent appears to represent the upper boundary for the explanatory effect of sex/gender for all psychological traits that have been studied through meta-analytic techniques (Deaux, 1984). This conclusion embraces other traits in addition to those shown in Table 2.3.

This conclusion of slight sex/gender differences deriving from the research of psychologists is at dramatic odds with the chasms dividing male and female experience in the labour force, family, political decision-making bodies. For example, the very small male advantage in mathematics and visual-spatial abilities shown in Table 2.3 cannot possibly explain why men hold more than 80 percent of the jobs in engineering and the natural sciences (Weston, 1989:5). Similarly, the equivocal findings concerning nurturance cannot explain why women around the globe continue to bear most of the responsibility for the young, the old, and the sick.

Although this observation anticipates future chapters, we are reminded of ideas held by

TABLE 2.3

META-ANALYSIS OF PSYCHOLOGICAL CHARACTERISTICS

Characteristic	Sex Showing Higher Levels	Percent of Variance Accounted For
Verbal Abilities	Females better	1
Mathematical Abilities	Males better	1
Visual/Spatial Abilities	Males better	4.5
Aggression	Males greater	6
Decoding Non-verbal Cues	Females better	4
Susceptibility to Social Influence	Females more	1

SOURCE: John Brigham, *Social Psychology*. Boston: Little, Brown & Company, 1986, p. 336.

previous generations about sex/gender differences in swimming ability. During the 1920s and 1930s, fashion dictated that women on North American beaches wear modest bathing costumes that included gloves, stockings, and even corsets. People at that time noted that women didn't like to swim very much, and that they weren't very good at it![9]

CONCLUSIONS

This chapter has discussed female-male differences in the popular imagination and in the work of scientists. Two conclusions are particularly important. First, as a result of the feminist movement, the ease with which value judgments permeate the study of female/male differences is now recognized. As Fausto-Sterling (1985:207) tells us, "there is no such thing as apolitical science. Science is a human activity inseparable from the societal atmosphere of its time and place." Scientific thought, like all types of thinking, is affected by COWDUNG ("the Conventional Wisdom of the Dominant Group") (Waddington, 1977, quoted in Archer and Lloyd, 1985:19). Nevertheless, this "does not mean that science is an idle exercise, a way of doing politics by but another name" (Hubbard, 1987:1034). There really is no alternative "to the slow, painful, and sometimes dull accu-

mulation of quantitative data to show whether the almost infinite variations in the way human beings think, feel, and act are actually linked to gender" (Greeno and Maccoby, 1986:315-16).

Second, a clear contradiction exists between the finely drawn gender distinctions contained in folk myths and stereotypes, on the one hand, and social scientists' general conclusion that the sexes are fundamentally similar, on the other. A core distinction appears between masculine instrumental qualities and feminine expressive qualities in perceptions of the sexes.

Men are said to possess in greater abundance than women self-directing, goal-oriented characteristics such as independence, assertiveness, and decisiveness, qualities that allow them to discharge effectively their role in both familial and extrafamilial settings. Women, on the other hand, are said to possess in greater abundance than men interpersonally oriented, emotive qualities such as kindness, sensitivity to others, emotional responsiveness, and need for affiliation (Spence, Deaux, and Helmreich, 1985:154-55).

Women's allegedly greater expressiveness purportedly explains their affinity for domestic tasks. At the same time, their lesser instrumentality supposedly explains why females are less suited for demanding positions of leadership outside the home (Spence, Deaux, and Helmreich, 1985:155). Yet, according to the evidence reviewed in this chapter, sex/gender differences in characteristics such as aggressiveness and compliance are small in comparison with variability within each sex. How can this be? Are people around the world simply mistaken in their perceptions of sex/gender? The chapters to come, which address the matter of the etiology of gender, should shed some light on these questions.

NOTES

1. Atwood (1972:200) offers as an example of the "nature-as-woman" metaphor E.J. Pratt's personification of the Canadian Shield in *Towards the Last Spike:*
    This folded reptile was asleep or dead:
    So motionless, she seemed stone dead—just seemed:
    She was too old for death, too old for life,
    For as if jealous of all living forms
    She had lain there before bivalves began
    To catacomb their shells on western mountains.
    Somewhere within this life-death zone she sprawled,
    Torpid upon a rock-and-mineral mattress....

2. Although Broverman et al. (1972) and others have emphasized that masculine stereotype traits are valued more highly than feminine ones, Williams and Best (1982:91) conclude that "there is no cross-cultural consistency in the relative favorability of female- and male-associated traits." The male stereotype of their Canadian sample was slightly more favourable. See also Ashmore, Del Boca and Wohlers (1986:83).

3. As psychologist Carolyn Sherif explains, the origin of sex/gender differences research was closely tied to the alleged inferiority of racial groups: "The entire literature on sex differences reflects certain assumptions of its founding father, Sir Francis Galton, who also is responsible for the research tradition comparing racial and national differences. Of course, Galton found that women are inferior, just as he found the British superior to...their subject peoples [of other races]. He was interested in proving the superiority of British males to women and to the colored peoples they ruled, founding a Eugenics Society for the purpose of improving and purifying British blood, even if it had to be contaminated by that of women. Later psychologists improved the research model he developed to make the tests more 'workable,' but it is still the same model with the same assumptions about what a human individual is" (Sherif, 1979:115).

4. A notable exception to the tendency of psychologists, during the first decade of the feminist movement, to minimize male-female differences was the "fear of success" issue. Matina Horner reached the conclusion in her 1968 Ph.D. dissertation that fear of success represented a special problem for women. Horner subsequently published an article in *Psychology Today* (1969) which captured the imagination of social scientists. Her finding of a sex/gender difference was widely accepted as valid. However, subsequent replication studies, summarized in Tresemer (1977), concluded that males equally experience fear of success, so that under-representation of women among high achievers must have other determinants. Nevertheless, many feminist writers outside the social sciences continue to find it hard to relinquish the assumption that fear of success characterizes women (Henley, 1985:106).

5. The growing attraction of *social* psychology and *social* psychological explanations of female-male differences to many feminist psychologists is noteworthy. For example, Carolyn Sherif (1979:121) pointed out the "great need for psychology to extend its cross-disciplinary borrowing beyond the biological disciplines, to which it has continually turned with pride. It needs to learn from the social disciplines and humanities...." Similarly, Alice Eagly (1987:7) proposes a theoretical orientation that "considers sex differences to be a product of the social roles that regulate behavior in adult life." (See O'Leary et al. [1985]; Wilkinson [1986].)

6. This letter to Ann Landers appeared in the May 31, 1987 issue of *The Calgary Herald:* "Dear Ann: It makes me furious that in the year 1987 women are still being made to feel guilty if they give birth to a baby girl and the father wanted a boy. It happens all the time. When the in-laws get into the act, it can be brutal. By now everyone knows that it is the man who determines the sex of the child.... Any woman whose husband is disappointed when a girl arrives should be told, "Don't look at me, Buster, I can only work with what you gave me. It's not my fault you didn't do it right." "Signed Baffled in Canada."

7. In developing nations, males have the mortality advantage, especially in the childhood years (Nathanson, 1984). Interestingly, "the most powerful variable in explaining cross-national sex mortality differentials...is not economic modernization but an index of the status of women" (Nathanson, 1984:203).

8. In order to simplify the discussion of meta-analysis, effect size has been ignored.

9. Source: "Basic Black," CBC A.M. Radio, April 28, 1990.

Chapter 3

Biological Explanations of Female-Male Differences

Chapter 2 established that the distinctions between males and females have been exaggerated in both scientific and folk thought. However, our debunking of pre-feminist overstatement does not imply that all sex/gender differences can be dismissed as traditional nonsense. If men and women are not separate species, neither are they completely identical creatures. Males and females differ in their chromosomes, hormones, primary and secondary sex characteristics, and reproductive functions. Their anatomical dissimilarities are enhanced by fashions in clothing, makeup, and hairstyle. As we saw in Chapter 2, there are some slight sex/gender differences in intellectual abilities and personality traits. Of critical importance to sociologists is the fact that certain assigned roles, soldier and nurse, for example, embody disparate and distinctly "masculine" versus "feminine" norms. Other social roles, which are similar in title and formal outline for either sex, are often played with "masculine" or "feminine" style, depending on the sex of the occupant (e.g., parent). Of enormous significance for all aspects of social life is the fact that the masculinity of men is more highly valued than the femininity of women; males enjoy more power, prestige, and resources than females.

To this point, we have concentrated on enumerating sex/gender differences rather than explaining them. The key question (and the subject matter of this chapter) is this: To what extent does gender have a biological basis? In other words, what are the relative contributions of innate factors, such as hormones and genes, versus learning to female-male differences? Montreal women's studies expert, Greta Nemiroff (1987:xvii) stresses the importance of this intellectual exercise:

Most questions raised by a serious consideration of gender seem ultimately to boil down to "nature versus nurture".... Our conclusions will influence us in deciding how free and powerful we may actually be to effect change in our own lives, in the lives of those we love, and in the world that we inhabit.

All societies provide explanations of the distinctions between the sexes (Epstein, 1988:6). Most feminists prefer interpretations of sex/gender that downplay biology and instead emphasize social structural pressures on males and females, and different socialization lessons learned by the sexes. The major reason is that the "'voice of the natural'...has always been a voice for the *status quo*" (Bleier, 1984:12). Assumptions and "theories" about people's innate nature have been used by conservative thinkers to rationalize and to justify discriminatory treatment of Jews in World War II Europe, blacks in South Africa, and native peoples in our own country. Similarly, biology has been employed as a curse against women. The message has changed little through the centuries: "men are biologically suited to their life of power, pleasure, and privilege, and women must accept subordination, sacrifice, and submission. It's in the genes. Go fight city hall" (Weisstein, 1982:41).

If "anatomy is destiny," then the traditional subordination of females to males is right and proper, and the contemplation of alternatives to the gender status quo makes absolutely no sense. Behaviour patterns that are "wired in" at birth, "God-given or instinct-driven" (Tavris and Wade, 1984:124) remain immutable. However, patterns that are learned are arbitrary and hence replaceable with other sorts of behaviour. To give a concrete example, it would be pointless for Canadian women to push for more power in the political parties and then in the House of Commons, if male leadership and female powerlessness were biologically pre-ordained. Under hypothetical circumstances such as these, femininity would constitute a genetic defect!

This debate concerning the constitutional versus the environmental determination of sex/gender differences is, of course, only one

---

Box 3:1
THE DIMENSIONS OF SEX/GENDER

Taken together, sex and gender involve eight inter-related variables:[1]

1. *Genetic Sex* (XX or XY chromosome). Normal human beings have 23 pairs of chromosomes. Males and females share 22 of these pairs. The 23rd pair determines the genetic sex of the individual. In males, this pair is made up of an X and a Y chromosome, while in females it is composed of two X chromosomes. Genetic sex is determined at the moment of conception.

2. *Hormonal Sex* (relative levels of estrogen and testosterone). Hormones are chemical substances secreted into the bloodstream by the endocrine glands. The chief male hormone is testosterone, one of a group called androgens. Estrogen and progesterone are the primary female sex hormones. Although all hormones exist in both sexes, the levels vary between the sexes and within the same individual from time to time. After the seventh week of conception, androgens cause male genital development to occur. Sex hormone production increases at puberty and influences secondary sex characteristics.

3. *Gonadal Sex* (ovaries or testes). An embryo's genetic sex determines whether its gonadal cells become ovaries or testes.

4. *Genital Sex: External Organs.* Secretion of the male sex hormones by the embryonic testes results in development of the penis and scrotum. In the XX embryo, absence of hormonal stimulation produces development of clitoris and vulva.

5. *Genital Sex: Internal Accessory Organs.* Genital sex may be further differentiated into the prostate and seminal vesicles in the male, and uterus and vagina in the female.

6. *Assigned Gender.* Based on the appearance of the infant's external genitals, assigned gender is the gender the parents and the rest of society believe the child to be. It is the gender in which the child is raised.

7. *Gender Identity.* The person's own conviction of being male or female.

8. *Choice of Sexual Partner.* The person's sexual attraction to members of the same sex, the other sex, or both.

In most cases, and individual is consistently male or female across the above eight variables. That is, an individual with XX chromosomes has an endocrine system that produces a high level of estrogen, as well as internal and external female organs. This person has been designated a female from birth, and believes herself to be female. Finally, she is sexually attracted to males.

Occasionally, however, contradictions exist among these variables. A person whose gender identity contradicts the first six dimensions is called a *transsexual*. A person whose choice of sexual partner is at variance with the other components is called a *homosexual*. A person with contradictions among the biological variables (hormones, chromosome structure, anatomy) is an *hermaphrodite*.

aspect of the antiquated nature-nurture contro-versy, which Bardwick (1972:1) aptly describes as a "phoenix of a cliché that continually experiences vigorous rebirth." Most scientists have abandoned the simplistic dichotomy of nature *versus* nurture. Asking whether femaleness and maleness are *either* biological *or* socio-cultural is like asking if a coin is "really" heads or "really" tails (Kessler and McKenna, 1978:42). Sophisticated models of sex/gender differences are *interactive*, in that they emphasize the interaction between environmental factors (cultural norms, education, parental attitudes) *and* inheritable factors (anatomical and neuro-endocrinological differences), rather than conceptualizing masculinity-femininity in terms of a learned-versus-innate dichotomy. For example, a researcher employing this interactive approach might examine whether the nervous system of the developing child, by virtue of being male or female, facilitates the learning of certain sex-linked behaviours (Archer, 1976:241, 253). For those in favour of interactive models of female-male differences, i.e., those that encompass both biology and social shaping, debate centres on the relative importance of each factor and the mechanisms of interaction between the two (Frieze et al., 1978:72).

Chapter 3 examines the biological foundation of gender. The contributions of socialization and social structure to gender arrangements will be discussed in later chapters. This chapter will present a number of different biologically based viewpoints about the origins of femininity/masculinity. These alternative perspectives came into being because the problem of establishing the contribution of biology to gender has interested scholars from a variety of disciplines. The following topics will be discussed: animal research; the anthropological approach; sociobiology; the psychoanalytic argument; hormone explanations.

SEXUAL DIMORPHISM AMONG THE LOWER ANIMALS

Harlow's Remarkable Monkeys

Three decades ago, Harry Harlow and his asso-ciates carried out a series of experiments on the effects of isolation on rhesus monkeys. The most famous of these studies (Harlow, 1959) involved comparing the importance of the act of nursing with the importance of bodily contact, in engendering the infant monkey's attachment to its mother. Two surrogate "mother" monkeys were constructed. Both were wire cylinders surmounted by wooden heads. One was bare. The wire of the other was cushioned by a terry-cloth sheath. Each "mother" had the nipple of a feeding bottle protruding from its "breast." Eight newborn monkeys were separated from their natural mothers a few hours after birth and placed in individual cages. They were given access to both types of surrogate "mothers." Four monkeys were fed from the wire "mother" and four from the cloth "mother." All the infants developed a strong attachment to the cloth "mother" and little or none to the wire "mother," regardless of which one provided the milk.

Harlow's demonstration of the importance of bodily contact in developing the infant-mother affectional bond is known to every properly educated social science student. A few years later (1962; 1965), Harlow published his less well-known observations on sex differences in monkeys. We will consider Harlow's conclusions at some length in order to illustrate both the rationale for and the shortcomings of animal studies as an approach to the question, "Are human sex differences biologically determined or socially learned?"

In subsequent articles, Professor Harlow described the behaviour of the monkeys who had had surrogate "mothers," when they were placed in special playrooms. The play behaviour was found to be *sexually dimorphic*. That is, males and females displayed rather different types of behaviour. When the monkeys were brought together after two months of isolation, the males, in comparison with the females, were more aggressive, engaged in more rough-and-tumble play, and initiated more games.

Harlow (1965:242, quoted in Tavris and Wade, 1984:131) concluded that sexual dimorphism in the rhesus monkey must be innate:

It is illogical to interpret these sex differences as learned, culturally ordered patterns of behavior because there is no opportunity for acquiring a cultural heritage, let alone a sexually differentiated one, from an inanimate cloth surrogate. When I first saw these data, I was very excited, and told my wife that I believed that we had demonstrated biologically determined sex differences in infants' behavior. She was not impressed and said, "Child psychologists have known that for at least thirty years, and mothers have known it for centuries."

Finally, Harlow (1962) believed that conclusions drawn from his animal research applied to human beings as well.

I am convinced that these data have almost total generality to man. Several months ago I was present at a school picnic attended by twenty-five second-graders and their parents. While the parents sat and the girls stood around or skipped about hand in hand, thirteen boys tackled and wrestled, chased and retreated. No little girl chased any little boy, but some little boys chased some little girls.... .

These secondary sex-behavior differences probably exist throughout the primate order and, moreover, they are innately determined biological differences regardless of any cultural overlap.

However, let us not belittle the female, for they also serve who only stand and wait.

The Logic of Animal Research

The task confronting scientists is to develop explanations for gender arrangements among human beings. There are several alternate strategies for tackling this problem. Each of the available methods offers some advantages and involves some unavoidable difficulties. Such is the case with animal studies. Harlow's work with the neglected little rhesus monkeys provides us with a concrete example of these advantages and disadvantages.

The point to be emphasized is that this type of animal research is motivated by interest in human beings, not in the so-called lower animals themselves. Indeed, the research can be described as "argument by analogy" (Tavris and Wade, 1984:130). Selected features of selected animals are taken as analogs for human features, and comparisons are drawn. Very

often, the creature chosen is one of the primate species. To scientists like Harlow, it seems logical to look to monkeys and apes for answers, because in the primate heritage of our species, "we can find patterns which form similarities and continuities with human behavior, and we can find sharp contrasts which will highlight specializations peculiar to human beings" (Lancaster, 1976:23).

Animals are used to inquire into human sex/gender differences for these reasons:

1. ETHICAL/PRACTICAL RESTRICTIONS

The type and extent of experimental research that can be done with human beings is obviously much more restricted than that done with animals (Armstrong and Armstrong, 1984:109). Harlow's study of the effects of social deprivation is a case in point. Although social scientists have long suspected that an infant's biological potential cannot be actualized without close emotional attachment to at least one adult, no one would dream of deliberately separating a human child from its parents at birth. However, in the 1960s when Harlow was planning his research, ethical considerations did not rule out this strategy with monkeys. (Today, animal rights advocates would very likely take issue with Harlow's ethics.) The rationale for Harlow's linkage between monkey isolation and monkey sexual dimorphism is given below.

2. ALLEGED EASE OF DISTINGUISHING BETWEEN SOCIALLY LEARNED AND BIOLOGICALLY DETERMINED BEHAVIOUR

Another major reason for studying our "evolutionary cousins," the monkeys and apes, relates to the "argument by analogy" mentioned earlier. The assumption is that because these primates are like human beings, but do not undergo the intensive learning that we do, an examination of their behaviour can tell us about our own biological inheritance. As we have seen, Professor Harlow was convinced that any sexual dimorphism observed in his monkeys after two months of isolation was innate. Regardless of whether or not we agree with Harlow's conclusion (and we are not obliged to), research in recent years has increased scientists' respect for the influence of learning, group traditions and ecological patterns of primate behaviour (Lancaster, 1976:24).

3. PRIMATE BEHAVIOUR FORESHADOWS HUMAN EVOLUTIONARY DEVELOPMENT

Interest in female-male differences among monkeys and apes is partially explained by the hints that their behaviour provides about the evolutionary record of human beings (Lancaster, 1976:45). A decade or so ago, more than the present day, feminists from various academic backgrounds were preoccupied with the quest for the origins of sex/gender patterns. They asked "Were things always as they are today?" "When did 'it' start?" (Rosaldo, 1980:391). Primate behaviour provides some scholars with useful conjectures concerning the roots of primordial gender. The anthropological and evolutionary, biosocial approaches will be considered in subsequent sections. Here we simply want to point out the connection with animal studies; evaluation of these approaches will be deferred until later.

4. AVOIDANCE OF RESEARCHER BIAS

As we noted in Chapter 2, social scientists investigating the subject of sex/gender differences are far from immune to the emotionalism surrounding this topic. Until the accumulating evidence began to indicate otherwise, many believed that the use of animal rather than human subjects offered some protection against the intrusion of scientists' value preferences upon their conclusions (in addition to the safeguards generally inherent in the logic of scientific research).

It was hoped that animal studies would avoid the unwitting communication of the experimenters' expectations to the research subjects, and the consequent confounding reactions of the subjects (Armstrong and Armstrong, 1984:108). Unfortunately, the *Rosenthal effect* (as the above has come to be called) can influence studies with animal as well as human

subjects (Middlebrook, 1974:32-33). In a study done by Rosenthal and Fode (1963), a group of university students who were enrolled in an experimental psychology course believed that they were to do an experiment on the rates at which rats of different abilities learned a maze. Half of the students were told that they were to work with "maze-bright" rats, which had been bred to learn mazes easily. Half were told that they had been assigned "maze-dull" rats, which would likely show little evidence of learning. Actually, the rats (which did not differ in ability) had been randomly assigned to the students. Nevertheless, the rats performed as the students expected. Rats identified as "maze-bright" performed significantly better than those identified as "maze-dull." Apparently, without knowing it, the student experimenters had treated their rats differently, and their expectations had produced the expected results.

Critics such as Rosenberg (1976:112) suspect that Harlow's research on monkeys was affected by observer expectations concerning the results. In the North American culture of the 1960s, where a premium was placed on aggressive behaviour and on being male, observers may have *expected* more rough-and-tumble behaviour from the male monkeys.

Other examples of researcher bias, more directly related to sexual dimorphism, clearly indicate that animal studies are not exempt from the intrusion of values. Lancaster (1976:24) points out that early field studies overemphasized the behaviour of adult male primates. Although these males were large and behaved conspicuously, they constituted only 10 percent to 20 percent of the total membership of primate society. However, the social relations of this small minority of adult males were seen as being the social organization of the entire group.

A researcher has considerable discretion in deciding which animal species provides a suitable analog for *homo sapiens*. The decision is important because the choice of species may affect the investigator's conclusions. According to Rosenberg's (1976:111) reading of the evidence, "every imaginable mode of relationship between the sexes exists in different species, from the female lion who does most of the hunting and killing... to the male marmoset who does most of the child care... to the gibbon, very close to humans in the evolutionary sense, among whom there is little if any personality differentiation between the sexes, and males and females are barely distinguishable in their behavior and physical appearance."

Weisstein (1971:79) went one step further when she accused social scientists of citing only those primates that "exhibit exactly the kind of behavior that the proponents of the biological basis of human female behavior wish were true for humans." This perhaps explains the popularity of rhesus monkeys (Harlow's choice), which exhibit some of the most aggressive behaviour found in primates. (Harlow's use of rhesus monkeys has also been criticized [Rosenberg, 1976:113] on the grounds that this species is distant from humans in the evolutionary scheme.)

Some Conclusions about Animal Studies

What can be learned about human sex/gender differences from primate studies? First of all, expert Jane Lancaster (1976:54) concludes that such studies provide "very little real evidence for major unlearned differences in the psychology of male and female primates." In the past, many generalizations were made about primate sex differences in aggressiveness, dominance, maternal behaviour, and so on. However, recent research has made it clear that while there may be major sex differences in certain behaviour patterns in one primate species (e.g., male aggressiveness in rhesus monkeys), these differences may not be apparent in another primate species (e.g., the peaceful gibbon). "It is virtually impossible to generalize about what male primates do or how female primates act.... Each species presents a complex pattern of sexual dimorphisms representing its own specific evolutionary history and current ecological context..." (Lancaster, 1985:5).

A second lesson that deserves particular emphasis here concerns the matter of extrapolation from animals to human beings. By now it should be obvious that Harlow's enthusiasm was misguided; extreme caution must be exercised in making such generalizations. For one

thing, inter-species comparisons are risky. For example, early exposure to the sex hormone testosterone appears to be related to aggressiveness in adult mice and rats. Prenatally androgenized female rhesus monkeys (that is, genetically female monkeys that received a shot of the male hormone, testosterone, before birth) exhibit a high incidence of aggressive play. However, the implications of such findings for masculine-feminine differentiation in humans are unclear. Generalizing from rodents to humans, or from monkeys to humans, is difficult. In addition, as the evolutionary ladder is ascended, the effect of hormones on behaviour becomes less dramatic, and the role of learning more important (Frieze et al., 1978:85-86). Furthermore, as noted above, extrapolation of findings from one primate species to another is often illegitimate. A most extreme position is taken here by Weisstein (1971), who argues that the misuse of animal studies constitutes a flagrant case of observer bias. She rules out all extrapolation because "there are no grounds to assume that anything primates do is necessary, natural, or desirable in humans, *for the simple reason that humans are not non-humans*" [emphasis added] (Weisstein, 1971:77).

Two additional caveats against animal-to-human generalizations should be entered. Often the same label is used for the characteristic in animal behaviour and the characteristic in human behaviour that investigators wish to compare. Nevertheless, the behaviours may not be at all comparable. Take, for instance, the label "aggression." The animal findings refer to aspects of aggression such as threat displays, the latency of initial attack, and the outcome of fights, whereas the human studies of aggression refer to quite different aspects, such as verbal aggression, teachers' ratings of assertiveness, and self-report inventories (Singleton, 1986:5).

A related consideration is that even when the behaviour of two species really is similar, the reasons for that behaviour are not necessarily the same. A fascinating illustration of this point is provided by Tavris and Offir (1977:98). The psychologist Maurice Temerlin and his wife, Jane, reared a chimpanzee named Lucy. Until Lucy reached sexual maturity, she treated

Maurice affectionately and bestowed many wet, exuberant kisses on him. When Lucy began to menstruate, however, the relationship with her "human father" changed. She refused to kiss and hug him and repulsed affection from him. Periods of estrus characteristically mark sexual receptivity, and Lucy offered blatant sexual invitations to men other than Temerlin. Says Temerlin (1975:62), "With any man but me...she would jump into his arms, cover his mouth with hers, and thrust her genitals against his body. This behaviour disconcerted Fuller Brush men, Bible salesmen, and census takers who happened to knock on our door."

Because Lucy's behaviour was so closely related to her hormone-controlled menstrual cycle, Temerlin concluded that chimpanzees may have a biologically based incest taboo. Every human society also has an incest taboo. However, the moral of this anecdote is that Lucy's story *does not tell us whether or not the human incest taboo is biologically based.* Unlike chimpanzees, humans have the ability to create and to communicate norms in order to control their behaviour. Therefore, the pressures in human society to control sex within the family may very well be social rather than biological. In short, humans and animals may demonstrate "identical" behaviour. However, the sources of the behaviour need not be the same.

Do criticisms and cautions such as these mean that animal studies are worthless to students of human sex differences? Not at all. This type of research can open new avenues of thought about human behaviour. For instance, because of the overemphasis on behaviour of adult males, dominance appeared to be the major axis of social organization in primate groups. However, another major theme has been discovered: the mother-infant bond, which over time develops into a *matrifocal* subunit. Some anthropologists (Lancaster, 1976) believe that the role of the mother-infant bond in human societies has not yet been fully appreciated. Research into sexual dimorphism in animals, then, is best viewed as a source of hypotheses, rather than definitive answers, concerning gender patterns in *homo sapiens.* We can safely assume that humans will continue to

"polish an animal mirror to look for ourselves" (Haraway, 1978:37).

THE ANTHROPOLOGICAL APPROACH

Social anthropology provides yet another perspective on the question: To what extent does gender stem from essential human nature? Put another way, are the division of labour and male superiority which characterize contemporary Western societies biologically based? As was the case with other disciplines, the feminist movement alerted anthropologists to the androcentrism of their field. British scholar Evans Pritchard apparently advised young anthropologists setting out to study other cultures to "behave like a gentleman, keep off the women, take quinine daily and play it by ear" (Roberts, 1981:1). Feminist anthropologists came to realize that anthropologists of both sexes had unknowingly been wearing ideological blinders. Male anthropologists, who were in the majority, quite naturally assumed only male activities counted. In their studies of preliterate societies, they generally had access to male informants and male domains. As a result, women were either completely missing from their analyses or were "there in the same way as were the Nuer's cows" (Ardener, 1972:140). Despite this criticism, the contemporary discipline of anthropology has been more amenable to feminist influence than has sociology or psychology (Stacey and Thorne, 1985). One reason anthropology has been more open to feminist ideas is that the topics of kinship and gender lie at the heart of this discipline (Strathern, 1987:278). Their importance has facilitated a fair hearing for feminist discourse about these matters. Another reason has been the "significant female imprint" of pioneers such as Margaret Mead "on the anthropological pavements from the discipline's earliest days" (Stacey and Thorne, 1985:303). See also MacCormack (1981) and Shapiro (1981).

Despite the unevenness in the cultural records caused by anthropology's earlier androcentrism, both feminists and their opponents have found the range of cross-cultural data supplied by anthropology "good to think with" (Strathern: 1987:279). The late Michelle

Rosaldo, an eminent authority on the anthropology of women, gave eloquent expression to the significance of her discipline for scholars of feminist persuasion:

Feminists (and I include myself) have with good reason probed the anthropological record for evidence which appears to tell us whether "human nature" is the sexist and constraining thing that many of us were taught. Anthropology is, for most of us, a monument to human possibilities and constraints, a hall of mirrors wherein...the "anecdotal exception" seems to challenge every would-be law; while at the same time, lurking in the oddest shapes and forms, we find a still familiar picture of ourselves, a promise, that by meditating on New Guinea menstrual huts, West African female traders, ritualists, or queens, we can begin to grasp just what — in universal terms — we "really" are (Rosaldo, 1980:392).

The presence or absence of *cultural universals* in the anthropological record has been taken as evidence for or against a biological explanation of gender. If a certain type of behaviour is found in all cultures, despite other sorts of variation in cultural patterns, that behaviour is assumed to be biologically determined. If, however, cultural comparisons show inconsistency, if social arrangements are sometimes this way and sometimes that, this cross-cultural inconsistency is interpreted as evidence for the social causation of gender arrangements.

We will illustrate the thinking involved in the anthropological approach by describing, first of all, traditional arguments about allegedly universal gender patterns. Secondly, we outline Margaret Mead's (1935) famous argument for cultural conditioning of female-male differences based on her field work in New Guinea. We end this section with a brief overview of the main arguments and conclusions of contemporary feminist anthropologists.

Anthropological Arguments for Biological Causation

The antagonists of feminism maintain that the inegalitarian aspects of gender found in contemporary Western societies are, in fact, characteristic of a broad range of cultures over the course of human history. According to this political stance, existing gender arrangements being "essentially 'natural,'" they *should* stay about what they are: major change would be unsuccessful, or would exact too high a price in emotional strain and consequent illness" (Friedl, 1975:1). Two universals are identified: *a division of labour between the sexes* and *male dominance.*

Advocates of biological causation cite evidence which shows that all societies distinguish between tasks usually performed by men, and those usually performed by women. They point out that men are always the warriors; they have major responsibility for the physical protection of the group from internal and external threats. Men generally exercise control over the significant resources of a society. Those activities in each society which are assigned the greatest value and reap the greatest rewards are in men's hands. Men operate in the public context, and have a wide range of opportunities available to them. By contrast, women's work is limited to the domestic domain. Women almost everywhere are responsible for the care of infants and young children, and for routine cooking. While women may be involved in gathering food, they never have major responsibility for hunting large wild animals, or for butchering large domesticated ones (Friedl, 1975:2). This Man-the-Hunter theory portrays "a small band of fierce-looking, purposeful males carrying weapons and stalking game. If women appear at all, they are at the edge of the picture, placid-looking, holding babies, squatting by the fire, and stirring the contents of a pot" (Bleier, 1984:116).

Male dominance is the second cultural universal claimed by biological determinists. In all known cultures, males are dominant over women of equal age and otherwise similar social status (Frieze et al., 1978:80-82). Men occupy the high-status positions, exercise political power, and generally dominate at the interpersonal level. "Everywhere we find that women are excluded from certain crucial economic or political activities, that their roles as wives and mothers are associated with fewer powers and prerogatives than are the roles of men" (Rosaldo and Lamphere, 1974:3). Moreover, no matter what specific activities men and women engage in, society values the roles played by men more than those played by women. Though women sometimes have a great deal of informal "behind the scenes" influence, women are denied access to areas of public decision-making (Lamphere, 1977:613).

Most anthropologists, feminists as well as critics of feminism, acknowledge the universality of gender division of labour and male dominance. As we shall see, feminists use the anthropological record in such a way that their qualifications and interpretations lead to quite different conclusions than those arrived at by their antagonists. However, the major point of difference between the two positions is the insistence of feminist scholars that social causation be taken into account. Though both sides recognize the importance of human biology, the anti-feminists believe that "nature" alone is sufficient cause for gender arrangements. Accordingly, the latter group has a lot to say about human bodies.

The conservatives emphasize what is truly the most important biological difference between the sexes: women bear children and men do not (Sayers, 1982:7). In earlier societies, the only method of keeping infants alive was breastfeeding. Since women were tied down with pregnancy, birth, and breastfeeding infants, who were dependent for a long period of time, their activities were restricted to a home base. While there, they were responsible for feeding and nurturing family members of all ages, and gathering food available near home. The more geographically mobile men became hunters. Males' larger size and more aggressive nature also made them more suited for the risk-taking involved in hunting, war, and other public activities (Kronenfeld and Whicker, 1986). In sum, biological determinists contend that gender arrangements are the direct outcome of sex differences in reproductive roles and greater male size and strength.

A very specific example of this type of thinking is contained in Steven Goldberg's book, *The Inevitability of Patriarchy* (1973). Here is his rather simplistic line of reasoning. Male bodies contain more of the sex hormone, testosterone, than do female bodies. Because of hormonal differences, males are, on the average, more aggressive than females. Therefore, patriarchy is inevitable, since the male competitive edge

over women allows men always to occupy the high-status, public positions. Again, because of hormone differences, women are better suited for motherhood and homemaking. Goldberg feels that it violates nature for women to seek public leadership. Instead, he suggests that motherhood should be more highly valued. Faced with this "biological reality," societies choose to socialize the sexes so that they do not compete with one another. Females are protected from inevitable failure by being socialized into roles that males either cannot play (childbearing) or do not wish to play (low-status positions) (Frieze et al., 1978:71).

Needless to say, Goldberg's ideas have been challenged by feminists. First of all, research with humans has not demonstrated a clear link between testosterone levels and aggressiveness or competitiveness (Doyle, 1989:60; Fausto-Sterling, 1985). Although male hormones and aggressiveness are related in animals, as we have seen, generalizing from animals to human beings is a risky business. Also, as Chapter 2 emphasized, the sex difference in aggressiveness means that the *average* male is more aggressive than the *average* female. It does not mean that *all* males are more aggressive than *all* females. These average differences cannot explain the pervasiveness of role and status differentiation in our culture (Frieze et al., 1978:81). The response of feminist anthropologists to biological determinism will be dealt with at greater length at the end of this section. First, however, we turn to anthropological pioneer Margaret Mead's well-known challenge to cultural universals.

Sex and Temperament in Three Primitive Societies

In 1931, Margaret Mead set out on a two-year expedition to New Guinea in order to discover to what degree temperamental differences between the sexes were innate and to what extent they were culturally determined. In North American society, females are responsible for the domestic sphere and males for the public sphere. Contrasting psychological qualities are associated with this role division: females are passive, non-competitive and submissive, while males are active, aggressive, and dominant. (These qualities are central to gender stereotypes, at least, if not actual behaviour.) Sixty years ago, as the influence of the Women's Suffrage Movement faded, these sex/gender distinctions certainly seemed quite natural to most people; Mead's skepticism about them is to her credit. Mead tested the universality of female-male differences in temperament among three tribes located within a 100-mile area on the island of New Guinea: the gentle, mountain-dwelling Arapesh, the fierce, cannibalistic Mundugumor, and the head-hunters of Tchambuli.

According to Mead's observations, Arapesh men and women alike displayed an unaggressive, maternal personality that would seem feminine in our society. The mild-mannered Arapesh "see all life as an adventure in growing things, growing children, growing pigs, growing yams and taros and coconuts and sago, faithfully, carefully, observing all of the rules that make things grow" (Mead, 1935:24). An Arapesh boy "grew" his wife. The girl was betrothed when she was seven or eight to a boy about six years older. Although the marriage was not consummated until both reached sexual maturity, the Arapesh male's greatest claim on his wife was that he had contributed the food that became the flesh and bone of her body. Later, both parents participated in childbirth. Conception was believed to require repeated sexual union in order to feed and shape the child in the mother's womb. Both parents lay down to bear the child and observed the birth taboos and rituals (the *couvade*). Mead (1935:42) said that "if one comments upon a middle-aged man as good-looking, the people answer: 'Good-looking, Y-e-s? But you should have seen him before he bore all those children.'" Aggressiveness is eschewed by both sexes. For example, the ideal Arapesh male never provoked a fight, and rape was unknown. Males considered leadership to be an onerous duty.

Mead found that the Mundugumor tribe offered a striking contrast to the Arapesh. Whereas the Arapesh standardized the personality of both men and women in a mould that, out of traditional bias, we would describe as womanly and maternal, the Mundugumor

went to the opposite extreme. The Mundugumor standardized the behaviour of both men and women as actively, indeed pathologically, masculine (p. 131). Members of both sexes were expected to be violent, aggressive, jealous, competitive, and active.

The structure of the Mundugumor family system appeared to be the source of these insecure, aggressive personalities. Here, the social organization was based on a "theory" of natural hostility among members of the same sex. Because father and daughters formed one rival group (called a "rope") and mother and sons another, neither parent welcomed pregnancy. The resulting offspring could abet the forces of the opposing group. The infant, regardless of sex, was not cherished by its mother. For example, weaning consisted of slapping the child. Hostility existed among siblings. All this unpleasantness was intensified by the fact that polygyny (a man having more than one wife at a time) was the ideal. Although wives brought wealth, additional marriages fuelled hostility and jealousy. Sex often took the form of a rough-and-tumble athletic tryst in the bushes. The delights of these bush encounters could be enhanced by copulating in other people's gardens, an act that would spoil their yam crops. The fact that this society was rich was the reason that it managed to exist at all, with so little of its structure based on genuine co-operation.

Among the lake-dwelling Tchambuli, Mead found that the gender roles and the accompanying temperament reversed Western notions of normalcy. The woman was the "dominant, impersonal, managing partner, the man the less responsible and the emotionally dependent person" (p. 205). The Tchambuli derived their greatest satisfaction from art. Economic affairs were relegated to the women, while the men devoted themselves to art and ceremony. Although the system was patrilineal (descent was traced through the male line), it was the women who exercised the real power. The latter worked together in amiable groups and enjoyed the theatricals the men put on, "whereas the lives of the men are one mass of petty bickering, misunderstanding, reconciliation, avowals, disclaimers, and protestations accompanied by gifts, the lives of the women are singularly unclouded with personalities or with quarrelling" (p. 192).

The women were described as "solid, preoccupied, powerful, with shaven unadorned heads" (p. 192) and the men as having "delicately arranged curls," "handsome pubic coverings of flying-fox skin highly ornamented with shells," "mincing steps and self-conscious mien" (p. 186). The women were more "urgently sexed" than the men. And from early childhood, males continued to be emotionally dependent on the women.

From her observations of the three tribes, Mead arrived at the following conclusion. "The material suggests that we may say that many, if not all, of the personality traits which we have called masculine or feminine are as lightly linked to sex as are the clothing, the manners, and the forms of head dress that a society at a given period assigns to either sex... [The] evidence is overwhelmingly in favour of the strength of social conditioning" (p. 206).

During her lifetime, Dr. Mead was never offered a regular faculty appointment at a regular university. Nonetheless, the anthropologist, Francis Hsu (1980:353), in an issue of the *American Anthropologist* celebrating Mead's work, concluded that "...Mead, by her insight into human behaviour and culture, and her ability to address academic and popular audiences alike, is truly the most famous and influential anthropologist in the world."

Contemporary Feminist Anthropologists' Views of Gender

Motivated by the second wave of the women's movement to follow Mead's example, contemporary feminist anthropologists set out: (1) to scrutinize the anthropological record for variability and universality in role specialization and authority within the family; and (2) to examine critically purely biological explanations of these patterns. See Friedl (1975); Leacock (1982); Liebowitz (1983); Martin and Voorhies (1975); Ortner and Whitehead (1981); Rosaldo and Lamphere (1974); Sanday (1981). The issues of division of labour in the tasks of

production and male dominance will be addressed in turn.

DIVISION OF LABOUR

As noted earlier, conservative thinkers maintained that men's near exclusive control of the public domain and women's of the domestic domain sprang from essential human nature. Feminist anthropologists replied that the logic of cultural universals required the proponents of the biological roots of gender to demonstrate that this division of labour prevailed across cultures, from the beginning of history to the present day. Their search of the record showed clearly that this was not so. The division of labour by sex is universal; the sex/gender difference was important to every society examined by anthropologists (Harding, 1986:130). However, considerable cross-cultural variability exists in which sex performs which tasks.

The androcentric Man-the-Hunter theory depicted women as "biological seconds" (Weisstein, 1982:41), passive, subordinate, dependent on men for survival. However, the ethnographic records show the very considerable contribution women make as gatherers of food; they suggest that women's economic activities played a critical role in the evolution of food-sharing, communication, and the invention of containers and tools (Bleier, 1984:121). For example, Aronoff and Crano (1975) used information about 862 societies contained in Murdock's Ethnographic Atlas (1967) to examine the degree to which males and females contribute, differentially, to subsistence economies. The ethnographic record shows that women contribute more than 40 percent to the larder of most of the world's societies. Today, women "form the backbone of African subsistence farming and do an estimated 60-70% of the agricultural work" (Strobel, 1982:110). Our own cultural philosophy that men are the natural providers does not receive universal support.

The way work is organized has a lot to do with a society's level of technology (Friedl, 1975). In hunting and gathering societies, the type of society which prevailed for 98 percent of human history, the sexes are generally full economic partners. Men hunt and provide protein for the group; women gather roots and berries, thereby contributing most of the food supply. The Kung Bushmen of Africa, featured in the movie "The Gods Must Be Crazy," are a contemporary example of this form of social grouping.

Horticultural societies, in which food is cultivated by hoe, emerged in the Middle East about 10 000 years ago, and are found today in sub-Saharan Africa and islands of the Pacific. Here, the amount of subsistence contributed by women is a function of the amount of warfare going on, and environmental conditions. In general, hoe cultivation being compatible with child care, women make the larger economic contribution. Because neither sex automatically controls food, there is considerable flexibility in gender roles. Such was the case with the New Guinea tribes studied by Mead (1935). In hunting and gathering and horticultural societies, relations between the sexes tend to be relatively egalitarian (Basow, 1986:100).

With the rise of agrarian societies in the valleys of the Tigris-Euphrates, Nile, and Indus rivers some five to six thousand years ago, social changes accompanied economic innovation. Because plow cultivation requires fewer workers at sites farther from the home base, men tend to dominate the economy. Women became responsible for domestic chores, such as food preparation, childcare, and care of small animals. When a group begins to increase its food supplies through clearing and plowing land, and by domesticating animals, land becomes property to be owned, defended, and inherited. Concern for paternity increased men's control of women's sexuality. Sociologist Rae Blumberg (1978:33) warns: If you believe in reincarnation, hope that you will never come back as a woman in a traditional agrarian society!

Every one of today's industrialized societies emerged from an agrarian base (Basow, 1986:101). Women's status worsened with the Industrial Revolution which began in England and northwest Europe of the 1800s. Tasks formerly performed in the home were transferred to the factory and taken over by men. Men increasingly assumed dominance of the public sphere. Because factory work is not compatible with childcare, women were viewed as cheap, temporary labour. Women in the higher social classes were discouraged from working. "This pattern of viewing women as cheap temporary labour when a society begins industrializing is strikingly evident in many Third-World countries today..." (Basow, 1986:102). Textile and electronic industries in the export-processing zones in the Third World "have shown an overwhelming preference for female workers who are viewed as a cheap, abundant, and politically docile labor force" (Basow, 1986:102). By the industrial era, the early biologically based gender arrangements had hardened into the stereotypical expectations discussed in Chapter 2.

MALE DOMINANCE

Has male dominance always been characteristic of human society? As our discussion so far has indicated, the cross-cultural record shows decline in women's status from the hunting-gathering and horticultural societies, to agrarian and industrial societies. If we look to the comtemporary scene, we identify women who have become prime ministers in the states of Great Britain, India, Pakistan, Israel, Nicaragua, the Philippines, and Sri Lanka. So much for any argument of "natural" male supremacy! Several Marxian anthropologists (Leacock, 1978; Sacks 1979) hold that some societies were truly egalitarian, but became inegalitarian under the impact of colonialism. Nevertheless, most anthropologists conclude that "masculine dominance appears to be the rule which is at best proved by these possible exceptions" (Harding, 1986:130).

The distinction made in Chapter 1 between macromanipulation and micromanipulation is important to this discussion of male dominance. A survey of human societies shows that positions of authority are almost always occupied by males, and macromanipulation is in their hands. Technically, no evidence exists for matriarchy, or rule by women, Amazonian or otherwise. However, micromanipulation may be exercised by either sex. In preliterate societies, this situation is "illustrated by matrilineal societies [such as the Iroquois], in which senior women assign public offices to males, but may reserve the actual decision-making for themselves" (Martin and Voorhies, 1975:10).

Authority (the social mandate to exercise power) attaches itself to those who *control* the distribution of food or wealth (Martin and Voorhies, 1975:10). The cross-cultural data reviewed above, such as Murdock's Ethnographic Atlas (1967), document women's economic productivity. However, economic contribution alone is not enough. "The road to equality is reached only when women have gained control over their production — that is, have a strong and autonomous position vis-à-vis control of economic resources" (Blumberg, 1978:27).

Authority depends not only on who controls the material means of production, but on who manages the means of symbolic production (Shapiro, 1981:122). Males have generally been the creators of dominant world views accepted by both sexes (Ardener, 1972). This masculine intellectual authority means that no matter what specific activities men and women engage in, society values the roles played by men more than those played by women. For instance, the nurturing behaviour of Woman the Gatherer made possible the survival of human infants that were born with brains still relatively immature, and therefore, requiring long periods of dependency. She invented basketry and digging tools. Nonetheless, hunting and gathering peoples celebrate the rites of hunting not women's childcare or gathering deeds (Rosaldo, 1980:411). Similarly, Tchambuli society, described by Mead (1935), regarded masculine artistic and ritualistic lore as superior to the feminine economic knowledge. Note that the Arapesh wife was the "daughter" of her husband (Rosaldo and Lamphere, 1974:19-20).

Traditional gender arrangements appear to have had their origin in women's reproductive capacities, the long helplessness of the human infant, and the generally greater size and strength of men.[2] Nevertheless, the anthropological past does not reveal a biological imperative for present-day, Western gender relations. As Rosaldo (1980:399) put it, the "'brute' bio-

logical facts have everywhere been shaped by social logics." It is the encrustation of cultural meanings upon biological facts, not biology itself, which is at issue. As human products, ideas are subject to revision (Richardson, 1981:186).

Moreover, twentieth-century technology has altered the significance of differences between female and male bodies. Most jobs no longer require great physical strength. It "permits humans to transcend biology — people can fly although no one was born with wings" (Huber, 1976:2). Birth control technology has had an enormous impact on women's situation (Kronenfeld and Whicker, 1986). Today, the average woman in industrialized nations is pregnant only a few months of her life. Also, such inventions as sterilization of milk, bottle feeding, and daycare centres have made the child-bearing function separable from the child-rearing function. The allocation of domestic tasks to women and public tasks to men can no longer be justified on biological grounds (Richardson, 1981:188). Feminist anthropologists (Ortner and Whitehead, 1981:1) conclude "that natural features of gender, and natural processes of sex and reproduction, furnish only a suggestive and ambiguous backdrop to the cultural organization of gender and sexuality."

THE POINT OF VIEW OF SOCIOBIOLOGY

A biologically deterministic interpretation of sex/gender differences has been advanced by the controversial new field of sociobiology. This perspective first came to public attention with the publication of *Sociobiology: The New Synthesis* (1975), by entomologist Edward O. Wilson. Other volumes (Barash, 1977 and 1979; Dawkins, 1976; van den Berghe, 1975; Wilson, 1978) followed. As we shall see, sociobiology incorporates several lines of reasoning previously encountered in this chapter.

Sociobiology's General Assumptions

Sociobiology has been defined as "the analysis of social behaviour as an outcome of organic evolution" (Boorman and Levitt, 1980). For our purposes, its essential features can be reduced to four:

1. Sociobiology holds that all individuals act so as to maximize their *inclusive fitness*, i.e., the probability of their genes surviving, by promoting their own welfare and that of relatives who share their genes. In other words, behaviour is assumed to be governed by genetic self-interest (Sayers, 1982:51). In his theory of evolution, Charles Darwin (1859) argued that evolution favours particular physical traits, like the ability to walk upright on two legs. Sociobiology extends Darwin's reasoning and assumes that psychological traits persist if they enhance the odds of an individual's passing along his/her genes (Tavris and Wade, 1984:127). Moreover, any behaviour with a genetic component is assumed to be adaptive or functional.

2. The perspective of sociobiology is *evolutionary;* the time scale is very large. Evolutionary arguments are offered for the inevitability of male-female differences. Evolution is believed to have favoured both physical and behavioural dimorphism because of the resulting advantage in attracting mates, producing and caring for offspring, and utilizing resources (Lambert, 1978:98).

3. Sociobiologists look to *cultural universal*s in order to determine whether human behaviour is genetically or environmentally determined (Lowe, 1978:121). Behaviour that is observable in all societies is assumed to be a product of human genetic makeup. Societal division of labour based on sex/gender (discussed above in the anthropology section) is considered by sociobiologists to be one such universal.

4. The behaviour of *lower animals* provides much of sociobiology's data. Extrapolations to human social life are made from these non-human species. For instance, Barash (1979) assumes the behaviour of male mallards, observed mounting females without first going through the courtship rituals normal for ducks, to be equivalent to rape among human beings. Sociobiologists are especially interested in the implications of sexual dimorphism (both anatomical and behavioural) among non-human primates, such as the baboons. The strategies of searching for universals in human behaviour and analyzing animal behaviour are often combined. After a "universal" human behavioural trait has been identified, sociobiologists then attempt to find similar behaviour in non-human primates in order to strengthen the argument that human behaviour has evolved through natural selection (Lowe, 1978:121).

"Parental Investment": A Brief Illustration of Sociobiological Analysis

Sociobiologists stress the "basic asymmetry" of femaleness and maleness (Dawkins, 1976:151). They use evolutionary reasoning to argue that women are biologically programmed to contribute disproportionately to child and home care. Appeals to cultural ubiquity and to the behaviour of other species are incorporated into their argument. They assume that an organism's inclusive fitness depends on producing the greatest possible number of offspring, who themselves survive long enough to reproduce and pass along their genetic code to successive generations. Sociobiologists believe that women and men, of necessity, adopt different strategies to maximize their inclusive fitness (Hubbard, 1983:5-6).

In *The Selfish Gene* (1976), Richard Dawkins locates the source of the traditional domestic division of labour between the sexes in the size differences between the female and male sex cells. From the moment of conception, females invest more in each offspring than do males. Though sperm and eggs contribute equal numbers of genes, the eggs contribute far more in the way of food reserves. Indeed, the sperm, simply concerned with transporting their genes as fast as possible to the egg, make no contribution at all. At the moment of conception, then, the mother is already more deeply committed to the child than is the father. By assuming most of the responsibility for the child's post-natal care, she acts to protect her "start-up costs" (Fausto-Sterling, 1985:184).

In addition, because females cannot produce as many offspring as can males, each child represents a greater investment to women. Women invest nine months in each pregnancy, while men invest only the few minutes heterosexual intercourse requires. Although Hecuba, queen of Troy, was said to have had more than twenty children, in most societies six or seven children is considered a large family. Yet, there is almost no biological limit to the number of children men can produce. A single male ejaculation produces enough sperm to fertilize every woman in North America. Ismail, a seventeenth-century king of Morocco, supposedly fathered 1056 offspring (Barash, 1979:47). Sociobiology finds a biological imperative for the traditional gender division of labour in its assumption that this greater initial investment by the female means she will continue to invest more heavily in her offspring throughout their development.

Biological reasons are also found for the sexual double standard. The male can maximize his chances of leaving surviving offspring by copulating with and abandoning many females, some of whom will raise his offspring (Trivers, 1972:145). In this evolutionarily determined battle of the sexes, the female retaliates against male promiscuity and desertion by trying to dupe another male into providing care for her offspring (Sayers, 1982:54). Feminine coyness pays off in these transactions. By holding back and playing hard to get, the female gains time to identify the male with the best genes and greatest proclivity for domesticity and fidelity. However, males of virtually all animal species have less confidence in their paternity than females have in their maternity (Barash, 1977:300). Therefore, men will try to enforce chastity upon females in order to guarantee that the offspring they acknowledge are genetically theirs (Sayers, 1982:59).

As you might expect, feminist critics have not been very happy with these arguments "to put woman in her (evolutionary) place" (Fausto-Sterling, 1985). They charge that sociobiology's attempt to reduce gender relations to genetic self-interest is based on flawed reasoning. In their view, the assumption that prior parental investment ensures future parental investment in offspring is just that — an assumption.

Evaluating Sociobiology

The controversial ideas of sociobiologists have received wide publicity and catalyzed an enormous critical literature, which varies from partisan enthusiasm to bitter invective. (See the May 1985 issue of *The Canadian Review of Sociology and Anthropology*.) For example, Barash's *The Whisperings Within* (1979), which analyzed the sexual bullying of mallard ducks, angered feminists who interpreted it as an "attempt to establish rape as a widespread natural phenomenon and thus deflect and depoliticize a subject of intense and specific importance to women" (Fausto-Sterling, 1985:162). It is both impossible and unnecessary to address all of the issues involved. Instead, we will concentrate on sociobiology's basic arguments and its account of the etiology of contemporary gender relations.

We begin with a compliment. Sociobiology has exercised a salutary influence on sociology by helping to counteract what van den Berghe (1977:75) calls sociology's "dogmatic environmental determinism" — its refusal, in past years, to recognize any biological component in human social behaviour. "[Sociology's] longstanding opposition to efforts to take biological factors into account in the study of human social systems has become an albatross. If we persist in ignoring or, worse yet, denying the powerful influence of genetic and biochemical factors, we jeopardize sociology's credibility in the scientific community" (Lenski, 1977:73). See also Krohn (1985).

Despite a new open-mindedness to biological possibilities, very few sociologists are impressed with sociobiology's particular brand of wisdom about the body. In her presidential address to the American Sociological Association, Alice Rossi (1984) reminded sociologists "that the subjects of our work are male and female animals with genes, glands, bone and flesh occupying an ecological niche of a particular kind in a tiny fragment of time" (p. 1). Nevertheless, Rossi went on to criticize sociobiologists for their *reductionism:* "they consider properties of society to be determined by intrinsic properties of individual human beings; individuals in turn are expressions of their genes, and genes are self-replicating molecules" (p. 10). Expressed another way, most sociologists hold selfish genes and social arrangements governing female and male behaviour to be distinctive orders of reality.

The most serious criticism of sociobiology is that the "theory is not falsifiable and therefore lacks the most basic qualification for scientific status" (Osler, 1980:121). Sociobiology is simply not vulnerable to empirical test. Gathering evidence for events that occurred eons ago is an impossible task. Attempting to circumvent this formidable problem through arguments about animal behaviour and cultural universals involves logical and empirical difficulties which we reviewed earlier. However, to reiterate, Fausto-Sterling (1985:162) warns against sociobiologists "more than willing to leap from ants to chickens to baboons to humans and back again, with only the most casual glance at the intellectual chasms yawning beneath their feet." So far as universals are concerned, experts tell us that the fact that a custom is widespread does not necessarily imply that it is genetically based. "Certain environmental problems and conditions are common to all human beings, and we might expect to find some common cultural solutions and adjustments that have nothing to do with genetic tendencies" (Tavris and Wade, 1984:130).

The keystone of sociobiology — its assumption that behaviour with some genetic component is adaptive — deserves critical comment. For one thing, grave problems are involved in distinguishing, by empirical means, genetic from environmental effects (Lowe, 1978:119). Even where the role of genetic factors seems established beyond doubt, as in some male-female physical differences, environmental influences can still be quite profound. For example, much of the difference in arm strength between women and men results from society's encouraging the average man to be more active than the average woman (Lowe, 1978:120).

A difficulty related to the previous point (and to cultural universals) also merits our attention. The fact that an observed behavi-

oural trait can be shown to be adaptive cannot be taken as evidence that the behaviour is biologically determined (Lowe, 1978:120). It may well be that the behaviour of "the helpless food-gathering child-breeding-feeding female in the hunting and gathering society who is both protected and victimized by the brute strength of the male" (Boulding, 1976:36) may have been adaptive on evolutionary grounds. However, the causation may be biological or sociocultural or some combination of these factors.

Finally, sociobiology has been criticized for its conservative values and the implications of these values for the formulation of policy. Margaret Osler (1980:123), for instance, charges that, "What is unusual about sociobiology is how crudely and without guile its theorists inject prevailing social values into the body of their science." For instance, sociobiologist Barash (1977:301) says, "women have almost universally found themselves *relegated* to the nursery while men *derive their greatest satisfaction* from their jobs" (emphasis added). Note how Barash's choice of words betrays his prejudices about which kind of work is the more valuable.

We label sociobiology's values "conservative," even "reactionary," on the grounds that its evolutionary approach assumes that social customs exist because they work. This "we're here because we're here" conclusion reflects reasoning that is circular and, therefore, flawed. Moreover, it allows for the fallacious inference that any social practice that has survived must be good (Tavris and Wade, 1984:332).

Feminists seeking to ameliorate the status quo are angered by sociobiologists' endorsation of stability. If survival becomes the ultimate yardstick, then those in power can justify many questionable practices that have had long lives: "not only male supremacy but war, slavery, infanticide, and wholesale imprisonment, oppression, and slaughter of outgroups of every description" (Tavris and Wade, 1984:332). Moreover, if people believe that male-female inequality has a biogenic origin, they are unlikely to support social programs designed to eliminate such inequality. Such attempts to go against "natural law" would be deemed quite futile (Lowe, 1978:123-25). Nevertheless, sociologists cannot afford to misunderstand the biological substratum of gender. In Rossi's (1984:11) words, "Ignorance of biological processes may doom efforts at social change to failure because we misidentify what the targets for change should be, and hence what our means should be to attain the change we desire" (italics in original deleted).

THE PSYCHOANALYTIC ARGUMENT

Overview of Freudian Psychology

Psychoanalytic theory provides yet another perspective on the origins of femininity and masculinity. Both a theory of personality and a system of therapy, psychoanalysis was the brainchild of the Viennese physician, Sigmund Freud (1856-1939). Freud's work, as well as amendments to it made by his disciples and critics, remains highly controversial 50 years after his death. Many of his ideas are an integral part of popular culture. Whether or not they have studied psychoanalytic theory, people speak about rationalizing or repressing unpleasant truths; they search for hidden significance in their dreams and slips of tongue. Freud's views about women provided the first integrated and widely accepted modern theory of feminine psychology (Weyant, 1979:364). Because of the impact of psychoanalytic thought upon Western culture, these views continue to be a basic ingredient in societal conceptions of femininity.

The edifice of psychoanalytic theory rests upon a biological base. (This is the reason for its inclusion in this chapter rather than in the next.) Freud coined the phrase, "anatomy is destiny." He argued that boys' possession of a penis (by far the superior organ) and girls' possession of a clitoris inevitably produced differences in the temperament and personality of adult males and females (Frieze et al., 1978:71). Assumptions about the inherent inferiority of females are embedded in the core of psychoanalytic theory (Lerman, 1987:44). Freud's ideas also shaped the practice of psychotherapy. Therapists, assuming the validity of society's gender

stereotyping, declared their female patients neurotic or even psychotic when they expressed dissatisfaction with the traditional feminine role (Chesler, 1972).

As Williams (1987:29) points out, Freud's attitudes towards women and his beliefs about appropriate relations between the sexes were conditioned by his own personal experiences:

Freud's personal life was conventional and conservative. Martha was a proper Victorian *hausfrau*, loving and subservient to Freud, who was a faithful husband and fond father.... Central European society was strongly patriarchal, distinguishing clearly between the roles of men and women, relegating to men all the duties and privileges of their assignments in the outside world and to women the responsibilities of home and children.

No theorist has been the target of more feminist criticism than Papa Freud. Indeed, a major critique of Freud's theory of female psychology was published in the mid-1920s by Karen Horney, one of Freud's early disciples. She charged that "his ideas about women grew out of masculine narcissism" (Walsh, 1987:19). Many contemporary critics continue the attack. For example, the writer Figes (1970, quoted in Tavris and Wade, 1984:174) believes that, "Of all the factors that have served to perpetuate a male-oriented society, that have hindered the free development of women as human beings in the Western world today, the emergence of Freudian psychoanalysis has been the most serious." Nevertheless, the last 10 to 15 years have seen several attempts to build bridges between psychoanalytic and feminist thought. We will return to the more important of these works at the end of this section. We turn first to a brief description of the psychoanalytic theory of personality.

Key Assumptions

The rich corpus of psychoanalytic theory is based upon these core ideas:
1. The roots of human behaviour lie in the depths of the unconscious. The unconscious is a repository of memories that cannot be re-

called at will. Because these memories represent events that caused emotional pain, they have been repressed, relegated to the unconscious. However, these repressed memories manifest themselves in such everyday experiences as dreams and slips of the tongue, and in neurotic symptoms (Williams, 1987:31).

2. Adult personality is the result of the child's early experiences within the family. This assumption may be expressed in terms of the old saying that the "child is the father of the man" (and "mother of the woman").

3. Freud saw child development as a battle between the family (as agents of society) and the impulsive animal-like nature of the child. Essentially, the parental task is to tame and redirect the inborn urges of the child.

4. Central among these urges is sexuality, which Freud viewed as a primary motive for human functioning. He postulated the existence, from infancy onwards, of a powerful instinct or inborn source of sexual energy which he called *libido*.

Stages of Psychosexual Development

According to Freud (1905), the development of personality parallels the physical maturation of the child. This development from infancy to adulthood proceeds through a fixed sequence of stages, assumed to be universal. The infant is born with an undifferentiated source of sexual energy, the libido. Each stage marks the individual's preoccupation with a different area of the body, called an *erogenous zone*, as the libido becomes attached to this part of the body.

During the first two stages, which occupy approximately the first four years of life, male and female experiences are identical. Indeed, Freud's androcentric bias led him to describe children of both sexes as "little men." In the *oral stage*, which lasts from birth to 18 months, the infant is preoccupied with pleasures associated with the mouth (sucking and biting). The major outcome of this stage is the establishment of a predominant disposition to either trust or mistrust other people.

During the second and third year of life — the *anal stage* — the child develops control over elimination. The anus and buttocks are eroticized as the child derives gratification from emptying the bowels. Toilet training represents the first serious demands made by the parents upon the child for self-control. Out of this conflict emerges the *superego* (conscience) in very amorphous form.

Movement into the *phallic* stage occurs when the child is about four years old. As children substitute masturbation for thumb sucking and begin to be curious about differences in sexual anatomy, erogenous gratification becomes focussed in the genital zone (Chafetz, 1974:14). The *Oedipus complex*, which occurs during this stage, is critical for both the establishment of gender identity and the development of morality. This complex involves the child's craving sexual possession of the opposite-sex parent, while viewing the same-sex parent as the rival who stands in the way of satisfaction of these erotic impulses.

The Oedipal complex is experienced differently by male and female children. Let us describe the male experience first. The boy's feelings of love for his mother become more sexual during the phallic stage. He becomes antagonistic toward his father, who is seen as the competitor for his mother's attention. The male child fears that his father will retaliate against him for his interest in his mother. The feared punishment takes the form of *castration anxiety*. Apprehension centres around the penis because the boy has discovered that females lack this organ. He concludes that girls have had their penises cut off, probably as punishment for some misdeed (Williams, 1987:34). The boy makes a strong connection between females' lack of a penis and their degradation. "The realization of the possibility of castration, the undesirable results (becoming like a woman), and the fear of this possibility lead to the resolution of the boy's Oedipus complex" (Stockard and Johnson, 1980:206). This painful castration anxiety causes the boy's incestuous fantasies to be repressed. Instead, the boy begins to identify with his father, to emulate his gender behaviour, and to internalize the moral inhibitions of this person who possesses both the "bigger and better" penis and the cherished object of the child's fantasies, the mother (Chafetz, 1974:15).

What happens to the female child during the

phallic stage? (Freud, 1925, 1931). She too is sexually curious and pleasured by masturbation. However, Freud regarded the clitoris as an inferior version of the male organ, an "atrophied penis," and wrote of the "momentous discovery which it is the lot of little girls to make. They notice the penis of a brother or playmate, strikingly visible and of large proportions, at once recognize it as the superior counterpart of their own small and inconspicuous organ, and from that time forward fall a victim to *penis-envy*" (Freud, 1925, reprinted in Unger and Denmark, 1975:131). Indeed, Freud referred to woman as "the mutilated creature" and said that the difference between the sexes "corresponds to the difference between a castration that has been carried out and one that has merely been threatened" (Freud, 1925). The male experience of castration anxiety suggested a correlative experience in the female, the experience of horror at the lack of a penis. If the boy fears the loss of his penis, the girl must suffer jealousy from never having had one in the first place (Tauer, 1979:288).

The girl child eventually understands that her possession of a cavity, rather than a penis, is a fate shared with her mother and all other females. Therefore, according to Freud, the girl joins all males in disdaining women. The female blames her mother for her loss of penis. Her penis-envy motivates her to renounce her love for her mother and to turn to her father. Her shift in love for the father derives from her desire to have a (preferably male) child by him which symbolically represents attaining a penis. Some resolution of the Oedipus complex occurs through the girl's later identification with her mother as a symbolic means of possessing the father. She acquires her superego and feminine identity from her mother. However, because the female cannot completely repress her interest in her father (she lacks the powerful motive of castration anxiety), the woman's superego is necessarily weaker than the man's. Thus, reasoned Freud, women's anatomical inferiority led to ethical inferiority.

The phallic stage is followed by the relatively peaceful *latency stage* (which occupies children from six to 12 years). The function of this latter stage is to consolidate the achievements of the preceding three stages. The repression required by the resolution of the Oedipal complex has relegated all sexuality into the unconscious.

With the resurgence of sexual urges brought by puberty, the child enters the *genital stage*. The libido is now directed towards opposite-sex peers, with the boy's erotic focus being the penis and the girl's, the vagina. The feminine identity is established when the wish for a penis is replaced with a wish for a child. Freud dismissed motherhood as "a circuitous route for women to get a penis for themselves" (Stockard and Johnson, 1980:209).

Evaluation of Psychoanaltyic Theory

Psychoanalytic theory has made many important contributions to social science. Freud's highly original views about early family experiences stimulated research on child-rearing practices, especially on cross-cultural variations in these practices. Margaret Mead was one of several anthropologists to be intrigued by his provocative ideas. Freud's solution to the problem of how society gets inside the individual, namely, the identification of children with their parents, was ingenious. As we shall see in Chapter 4, this insight remains important in the formulations of theorists such as Chodorow (1978). His writings about the emotions, sexuality, and the unconscious attend to dimensions of human motivation that were otherwise neglected by social scientific theorizing until fairly recently.

However, as mentioned at the beginning of this section, psychoanalytic theory has drawn more critics than admirers. We begin with several complaints made by social scientists generally. From there, we will move to specifically feminist concerns. First of all, psychoanalytic theory has been repeatedly criticized for over-emphasizing biological causation and minimizing the social context of individual behaviour. Although Freud did highlight the family grouping, he had little to say about culture, political organization, social class, and so on.

A second, related point is that psychoanalytic theory inadequately conceptualizes the role of learning. For example, children's learning about femininity and masculinity involves a whole lot more than an illicit peek at play-mates' or siblings' genitals, as Freud would have it (Chodorow, 1978:146). [3]

Third, much of Freudian theory (like socio-biology) can be criticized for its invulnerability to empirical test (Grunbaum, 1984). For in-stance, how could one prove or disprove that a man with a methodical, frugal accountant-like personality got that way because his toilet-training went awry?

Finally, social scientists concerned with the generalizability of psychoanalytic theory point to its sampling difficulties. Freud's ideas were based on his experiences with middle-class Viennese patients during the Victorian era. Consequently, his notions sometimes do not apply very well to people without psychiatric problems, or to other cultures and historical periods. For example, anthropological findings (Malinowski, 1926) challenge the universality of the patriarchal family structure so necessary to the Oedipus complex. A related shortcoming is that Freud's speculations about children's behaviour were mostly based on his experience with adults, not with children.

For the above reasons, there is significant lack of fit between empirical reality and central psychoanalytic notions about gender. Here are some examples of Freudan ideas that research does not document. Boys' possession of penises and their castration anxiety, and girls' "penis-lessness" and penis-envy are essential to this theory. However, studies of children at the age level of the Oedipal complex find little evi-dence of castration anxiety in boys and even less evidence for female envy of male anatomy (Lee and Hertzberg, 1978:35). You will recall that Freud argued that the female conscience is never as well developed as the male conscience. Research suggests just the opposite (Baron and Byrne, 1977:357). For example, Hoffman (1975) presented children and their parents with a questionnaire asking about such acts as steal-ing, cheating, and hit-and-run driving. Hoffman found that females more than males associated moral transgressions with feelings of guilt. In contrast, the males were more afraid of simply getting caught and being punished. Feminist psychologist Carol Gilligan (1982) argues that females' views about morality are

indeed different from males, but that difference does not imply inferiority. Gilligan's ideas re-ceive further attention in Chapter 6.

Psychoanalysis as therapeutic technique has also come under attack. (Goldberg [1976:24-25]), for example, says psychoanalysts' strat-egy of reconstructing childhood experiences in order to cure adult problems is "a little like treating food poisoning by exploring early eat-ing habits.") Empirical studies demonstrate that clinical therapy based upon psychoana-lytic theory has only limited effectiveness. Eysenck (1952), a severe critic of psychoanaly-sis, reported that of a group of neurotic pa-tients, the improvement rate of those who re-ceived psychoanalysis was 44 percent. How-ever, of the neurotic patients who received no treatment at all, the improvement rate was 72 percent. (See also Eysenck, 1966.)

Many feminists have been outraged by Freud's masculine bias, even misogyny. The attribution to women of penis-envy and weak superego is hardly flattering. The conclusion that their inferior anatomy dooms them to subordinate social roles is unacceptable. Femi-nists suggest that Freud's lack of objectivity becomes obvious when women, rather than men, are given primacy and provide the norm for humanity. Why not assume that the male is biologically inferior and describe his penis as a "bloated clitoris" (Lee and Hertzberg, 1978:34)? Instead of building a theory of gender upon penis-envy, why not dwell upon men's frustration at being unable to bear children, their "breast" and "womb" envy as Karen Horney (1932) did? Anthropologists have found evidence in support of male envy of female biological capabilities in their studies of male initiation rites (Tauer, 1979:290) and the couvade.[4]

Where Freud emphasized biology, his femi-nist critics see cultural conditioning at work. For example, penis-envy, the dynamic that supposedly leads female children to feel infe-rior to males, to desire a submissive role in relation to them (Huston, 1983:400) is not an inevitable result of that organ's superiority. The phallus is valued in male-dominated cul-tures (Stockard and Johnson, 1980:213). In such cultures, females associate the greater power and privileges of males with their conspicuous anatomical characteristic of maleness (Chafetz, 1974:15). Their deprivation of a penis stands for "the deprivation of things that a female as a person truly *should* have: autonomy, freedom, control of her own life...for women are social castrates" (Tauer, 1979:289). Lesbian feminists (Rich, 1980) criticize the assumption of heterosexual arrangements which prevails in psychoanalytic (and other) writings about gender relations.

Despite telling criticisms such as these, a few scholars have urged reconsideration of the utility to feminists of at least some segments of Freudian thought (Chodorow, 1978; Dinnerstein, 1976; Mitchell, 1974; Rubin, 1975). (See Sydie, 1987 for a useful discussion of their work.) Williams (1987:39) notes that "both the followers and the critics of Freud have generally ignored his cautions of the tentative nature of his exploration of femininity, his call for further validation, and his disclaimers of final answers." Dinnerstein (1976:xi) agrees: "Feminist preoccupation with Freud's patriarchal bias, with his failure to jump with alacrity right out of his male Victorian skin, seems to me wildly ungrateful."

These feminist friends of psychoanalytic theory, or "gynocentric theorists" (as Stockard and Johnson, 1980 label them) take as their starting point the Freudian assumption of children's identification or bonding with parents. However, turning Freud on his head, feminist theorists such as Chodorow (1978) focus upon the mother, the enormous power she exerts over young children, and the consequent fear of her experienced by relatively powerless children of both sexes. The dynamics of children's separation from the mother as they strive to become individuals is an especially influential aspect of Chodorow's work. Chapter 5 will consider these ideas in more detail.

A consensus does not now exist among feminists concerning the value of psychoanalytic theory. Although many admire the work of such gynocentric theorists as Chodorow (1978), many more share Lerman's (1987:44) sentiments:

I do not believe that Freud's original theories served women well. I also do not believe that the modern revisions of psychoanalytic theory further the health and well-being of the modern woman. After the initial feminist rejection of Freudian concepts in the early 1970s, some have reaccepted his ideas as having validity and applicability to women. I am not in that group because I see the theory as so fundamentally flawed in its thinking about women that it cannot be repaired, however extensive the tinkering with it.

HORMONAL EXPLANATIONS OF SEX/ GENDER DIFFERENCES

Think of the human body as a hotel switchboard, lit up by a constant stream of room-service orders and complaint calls: "Can you lower the temperature in this room?" "Would you send up a couple of cheeseburgers, please?" The mediators of this ceaseless biological babble — the messengers rushing from cell to cell to satisfy all requests — are powerful molecules called hormones. Named after the Greek word *hormon* (to set in motion), these ubiquitous chemical substances act, in ways still somewhat mysterious, to maintain the exquisite balance of being (Clark et al., 1987:50).

The "exquisite balance of being "governed by some 45 hormones encompasses growth, reproduction, aging, reaction to attack, as well as the experience of moods that range from elation to depression. Hormones also influence sexuality. When hormones flood into the bloodstream at puberty, boys get erections, girls get menstrual periods, and everyone gets acne (Clark et al., 1987:53). As noted in Chapter 2, the prenatal development of male and female forms of internal reproductive structures and external genitalia is controlled by the secretion of male hormones. Without these hormones, the fetus will differentiate as a female, regardless of genetic sex (Williams, 1987:109).

Given the significance of hormones and their connection with sexuality, it is understandable why people sometimes think that body chemistry might also govern gender traits and behaviour. David Reuben of *Everything You Always Wanted to Know About Sex but Were Afraid to Ask* (1969) fame exemplified an over-simplified version of the hormone theory of gender when he wrote that: "Estrogen is responsible for that strange mystical phenomenon, the feminine state of mind." Dr. Reuben got so many of his facts wrong in his book that he and Woody

Allen (star of a movie of the same name) now share equal credibility in the sex education department. Be that as it may, Reuben is not alone in positing hormones as the key to gender. You may recall that anthropologist Steven Goldberg (1973) argues that patriarchical forms of social organization are the inevitable consequence of male hormones. See also Barash (1979:189).

The spectacular growth of endocrinology (the study of hormones) stimulated these questions: Does the higher level of androgens (male hormones) account for the slight superiority of males in mathematical and visual-spatial skills? Does females' lower level of the male hormones explain their alleged deficiencies in these cognitive skills? Is estrogen associated with females' verbal superiority? Do very aggressive men have extraordinarily high levels of testosterone coursing through their bloodstreams? These queries concern individual traits. With regard to social roles, do hormones equip women for lives of baby-tending and sweeping the hearth, and make men natural leaders? Does the volatility of moods associated with premenstrual syndrome disqualify women of childbearing age from responsible positions (Parlee, 1973; 1982)? Taking the argument one step further, we ask: Do biochemical variations among people of the same sex account for variations in sex-typed behaviour? Are macho men loaded with testosterone and dainty women with estrogen? Did homosexuals get that way because of hormonal imbalances? This section will consider briefly some of the enormously complex evidence bearing on these matters. The problem will be approached through appraisal of experimentation with animals; irregularities in hormones and genitalia of humans; and brain lateralization.

Animal Studies Revisited

The hypothesis that hormones cause gender-linked traits and behaviour in human beings has been pursued through studies of animals. The findings of some of this research has supported the hormone hypothesis. For example, when male hormones were administered to pregnant rhesus monkeys, the female offspring showed higher levels of rough-and-tumble play and threatening behaviour than did control monkeys. These masculinized female monkeys also demonstrated male patterns of sexual behaviour, such as attempting to mount normal female monkeys. Prenatal androgens produce similar results in rats (Williams, 1987:110 ff.). Finally, the finding that injections of testosterone increased levels of aggression in certain animals has received widespread attention (Maccoby and Jacklin, 1974:242-43).

However, a comprehensive examination of this hormone work with animals fails to provide convincing support for hormonal etiology of gender in humans. For one thing, the experimental effects of hormones on gender-related behaviour varies widely from species to species (Huston, 1983:416; Williams, 1987:112-13). For example, the evidence that male hormones control aggression in non-human primates ranges from weak to non-existent (Fausto-Sterling, 1985:147). Also, scientists have found evidence for the effects of environment on hormones. For instance, male monkeys whose social position has improved with the removal of dominant group members manifest a change in their testosterone level (Epstein, 1988:57). As you might expect from our discussion of animal research earlier in this chapter, this work has been heavily criticized by gender specialists. Among the complaints is this one: "Endemic to writings on the biology of aggression is the habit of confusing or interchanging social and biological concepts" (Fausto-Sterling, 1985:129). For example, extrapolations are made from the influence of testosterone upon animals' readiness to attack to possible human sex differences in achievement, competition, activity levels, dominance, violent crime, riots, and war. In summary, the data from studies of the consequences of artificially elevated levels of hormones in animals fail to justify the conclusion of hormonal determination of gender in humans.

The Role of Hormones in the Human Experience of Gender-related Emotions

Does the hormone testosterone make men

aggressive, and hence fit for public life? Does the cyclical operation of female hormones create barriers to decision-making posts? (Epstein, 1988:57). These questions are political, as well as technical. As we shall argue at the end of this section, to ask if moods are related to hormones is one thing; to consider that these hormonally influenced mood changes justify status differences between the sexes is quite another.

Authorities disagree about the human connection between testosterone and behaviour (Doyle, 1989:59-60). Lowe (1983:53) states that no connections have been found in humans between levels of testosterone and aggression. Maccoby and Jacklin (1974:243), on the other hand, conclude that aggression "is related to levels of sex hormones, and can be changed by experimental administration of these hormones." Although many studies have found little or no relationship between testosterone levels and various measures of aggression, other researchers continue to pursue a link. The dramatic psychological changes in athletes who have used anaboloic steroids (Taylor, 1985a; 1985b), including hostility, encourages this line of research.

Are women incapacitated by emotional instability during the premenstrual period? Despite the embarrassment in our culture that surrounds menstruation, premenstrual syndrome (PMS) has recently become a topic for television talk shows. Courts in France and England have deemed premenstrual tension to qualify as temporary insanity in criminal cases" (Tavris and Wade, 1984:153). Nevertheless, "half a century's work on the premenstrual syndrome has been flawed by faulty methodology and unfounded interpretations" (Tavris and Wade, 1984:148). Available studies, most clinical and lacking control groups, do *not* establish that mood changes are strongly correlated with phases of the menstrual cycle (Tavris and Wade, 1984:148). Although this does not mean that all menstrual distress is in women's heads, "it would be a mistake to assume that menstruating women are more anxious, tense, or antisocial than the average man" (Tavris and Wade, 1984:153). Women have much lower rates of crime and accidents than do men, whether or not these rates are associated with menstrual periods (Epstein, 1988:58).

So what if premenstrual women are moody and men get more aggressive as their testosterone level rises? Although reliable research fails to underwrite these conclusions, "the question relevant to the genders in society is the *meaning* of differences in hormonal levels" (Epstein, 1988:57). While raging female hormones are widely believed to be detrimental to women's participation in public affairs, no similar hormonal barriers disqualify testosterone-maddened males from sensitive decision-making posts. Having the "right" hormones does not explain masculine advantage; having the "wrong" hormones cannot account for women's lower status. Neither sex can use its hormones as an excuse for antisocial behaviour. Since our society "expects people to manage their moods and assume responsibility for harming others," feminists worry about criminal court decisions that let "women get away with murder — literally — because it's their 'time of the month'" (Tavris and Wade, 1984:154).[5]

Psychosexual Abnormalities in Human Beings

Over the years, John Money and his colleagues at the Johns Hopkins Medical Center have published a series of classic studies on children's psychosexual abnormalities. These errors of nature (and in one case, of physicians) function, up to a certain point, as "natural experiments" that provide some insight into the question of the relative weight of biology and of social forces in the development of gender. Nevertheless, extrapolation from these rather unique individuals to people in general must be made carefully. In addition to atypicalities in hormones and anatomy, the individuals studied by Dr. Money differ from the general public in being part of a clinical population. Their special experiences, including the knowledge of their own abnormalities and the reactions they elicit from therapists and families, constitute intrusive influences upon any conclusions reached.

We turn first to a highly publicized study of genetic females (XX) who had been exposed to heavy dosages of androgens, i.e., male hormones (Money and Ehrhardt, 1972; Ehrhardt and Baker, 1978). This inadvertent exposure that took place before birth occurred either because of their own defective adrenal glands, or because of drugs their mothers took during pregnancy. On the surface, these cases seem to parallel animal experiments discussed earlier. Here, gender specialists had the opportunity to study the effects, if any, of male hormones "on the female human brain and possible ultimate effects of behaviours that are usually seen as gender-lined, as 'masculine' or 'feminine' (Williams, 1987:114). If the human hormone imbalance that resulted in masculinized genitals also produced key psychological effects upon these girls, the case of the biological determinists would be strengthened. We are especially interested in the aggression level of these girls, and their *gender identity*, their conviction of being male or female.

Money and Ehrhardt (1972) interviewed and administered psychological tests to 25 prenatally androgenized girls. They had been born with masculinized genitalia, usually resembling a penis and scrotum closely enough that the girls had been considered to be boys for a time (Bleier, 1984:98). All had received corrective surgery on their genitals so that they were no longer hermaphrodites; all had been raised as girls. The behaviour and attitudes of these girls, now four to 16 years old, were compared with a control group matched for age, IQ, socioeconomic status, and race (but not clinical experience).

Among the findings is the very significant conclusion that all 25 girls defined themselves as female. In other words, their gender identity was congruent with gender of rearing, not with the male hormones they had accidentally received. However, the girls were labelled by their mothers and by themselves as tomboys. Compared with the control group, they preferred boys' sports, outdoor play, and pants to dresses. They were less interested in doll-play or babysitting. More intended to have a career outside the home, or to combine a career with marriage. "Unlike the androgenized female monkeys, however, they were not more aggressive in the sense of being hostile or threatening toward others" (Williams, 1987:114). Although the monkeys had adopted male patterns of sexual behaviour, neither the androgenized girls nor the controls showed much interest in sex. In later life, though heterosexual activity had been delayed, only one of the 25 reported homosexual fantasies and experiences (Baker, 1980:84).

Over and over again, this research is cited by biological determinists, e.g., the sociobiologist Barash (1979:59), to argue that prenatal hormones cause gender behaviour in human beings. Nevertheless, critics disagree. They point out that participation in sports, dress, and career choice are all strongly influenced by culture, and that the girls' tomboyish behaviour was well within the normal range for girls in our society. Further, the fact that their female gender identity was not seriously disrupted by the presence of prenatal androgens is regarded as highly significant. If the research subjects had identified with the male sex, or wished to change their sex, as transsexuals do, or displayed a high level of erotic interest in other girls similar to that of adolescent boys, then the case for hormonal influence on gender would be more impressive (Williams, 1987:115-116). However, such was not the case.

Methodological flaws in this research also undermine any biological interpretation. The scientists made no first-hand observations of the girls' behaviour, but instead relied upon self-reports of the girls and their mothers, whose knowledge about the subjects' medical history likely affected their assessment (Fausto-Sterling, 1985:135).

Paralleling the above research, a small number of studies exist of human infants whose mothers were given synthetic female hormones (estrogen or progesterone) during pregnancy to supplement the very high levels of such hormones which normally accompany pregnancy. The purpose of the synthetic hormones was to avert miscarriage in women with conditions such as diabetes or toxemia. This research provides no evidence of physical abnormalities or of stereotypically feminine personality traits in offspring being associated with these extra doses of female hormones (Huston, 1983:417). Taking all of this work into consideration, we conclude that no reasonable proof exists that gender is caused by prenatal hormones (Bleier, 1984).

The second study to be described reinforces the importance of social assignment in the production of gender. In the 1960s, a couple took their perfectly normal seven-month-old twin boys to a hospital to be circumcised. According to Money and Tucker (1975:91-92).

the physician elected to use an electric cauterizing needle instead of a scalpel to remove the foreskin of the one who chanced to be brought to the operating room first. When this baby's foreskin didn't give on the first try, or on the second, the doctor stepped up the current. On the third try, the surge of heat from the electricity literally cooked the baby's penis. Unable to heal, the penis dried up, and in a few days sloughed off completely, like the stub of an umbilical cord.

Doctors recommended that the boy's sex be reassigned and that female external genitals be surgically constructed. The child's name, clothers and hairstyle were feminized, as the parents made every effort to rear twins — one male and one female. As the following anecdote about the twins at the age of four and a half shows, both the children and parents had successfully developed "sex appropriate" attitudes and behaviour. The mother, talking about the boy, reported, "In the summer time, one time I caught him — he went out and took a leak in my flower garden in the front yard, you know. He was quite happy with himself. And I just didn't say anything. I just couldn't. I started laughing and I told daddy about it."

The mother's corresponding comments about the girl went this way. "I've never had a problem with her. She did once when she was little, she took off her panties and threw them over the fence. And she didn't have no panties on. But I just gave her a little swat on the rear, and I told her that nice little girls didn't do that and she should keep her pants on" (Money and Ehrhardt, 1972:119). For Christmas, the girl wanted dolls, a doll house, and a doll carriage. The boy wanted a toy garage with cars, gas pumps, and tools. Apparently, the twin reassigned as a girl developed into "a healthy young woman" (Schulz, 1984:97).

This oft-cited case, as well as others, suggests that social assignment outweighs biology in determining gender identity and behaviour. So far as the twins involved in the circumcision accident are concerned, the prenatal presence of *appropriate sex hormones* failed to overrule social influences. In the case of the prenatally androgenized girls discussed above (Money and Erhardt, 1972), prenatal exposure to *inappropriate hormones* also failed to overrule social influences.[6] Social labelling seems to be crucial. However, gender reassignment is usually unsuccessful after the age of 18 months (Money and Ehrhardt, 1972). By then, the child has the ability to understand verbal labels for gender and to view the world from a "female" or "male" perspective. Finally, we must point out that the conclusions of psychosexual abnormality research have been criticized because gender reassignment has been supplemented by appropriate surgery and hormone treatment. That is, the individual's biology has been modified to correspond to the assigned gender (Hyde, 1979).

Brain Lateralization

Because sex hormone levels are low in childhood, and similar for girls and boys, researchers have pursued the possibility of hormonal etiology of gender through the examination of apparent differences in the way the brains of adult women and men function (Bryden, 1979; Geschwind, 1979; Goleman, 1978; McGlone, 1980). This research has attempted to tie the slight gender differences in language fluency and visual-spatial abilities to innate sex differences in the brain. The assumption made is that the brain is programmed before birth by sex hormones. Although so far, the scientific verdict on this research is "case not proven" (Nicholson, 1984), popular magazines and books have picked up on this interesting topic (Durdin-Smith and DeSimone, 1983; Maynard, 1984).

The cerebral cortex is divided by a deep groove down the middle into two hemispheres that specialize in different intellectual functions. In about 95 percent of the population, the left hemisphere is primarily responsible for verbal skills, such as understanding other people's speech, learning and remembering verbal material, and reasoning verbally, while the right hemisphere executes visual-spatial skills (e.g., sense of direction, location of objects in space) (Nicholson, 1984). *Lateralization* is the term used to label the specialization in the functioning of each brain hemisphere.

Apparent differences in the brain damage suffered by male and female victims of strokes, accidents, and tumors stimulated the brain lateralization controversy in gender relations. According to this research (Inglis and Lawson, 1981; McGlone and Kertesz, 1973) a male who experiences damage to his left hemisphere suffers impaired verbal skills. He may no longer be able to say what he wants to say in a logical order or understand the meaning of certain words. However, if the damage occurs to his right hemisphere, he is apt to experience loss of visual-spatial abilities, such as his sense of direction. On the other hand, females who suffer damage to either right or left hemisphere experience less severe loss of either verbal or spatial abilities than their male counterparts, Moreover, women (but not men) are reported to have lost some verbal ability through damage to the right hemisphere.

The above findings led some scientists to speculate that female brains are less specialized than male brains, their left and right hemispheres being involved in the performance of both verbal and visual-spatial functions (Levy, 1976). They hypothesize that superior female verbal proclivities stem from their location in two hemispheres. Female spatial abilities are thought to be reduced somewhat because part of the right hemisphere's capacity is taken up with verbal tasks (Nicholson, 1984).

In general, research done up to now has been inconclusive. Whether brain specialization is related to sex hormones, whether the alleged differentiation occurs in childhood or puberty, or indeed, whether gender differences in brain specialization exist at all, remain highly speculative matters. One problem is the lack of match between gender stereotypes and the way skills are divided up between the two halves of the brain:

That is, girls and women are considered to be more verbal (left hemisphere) but less analytical (left hemisphere) and more "intuitive" (right hemisphere) but less visuospatially skilled (right hemisphere); and men are considered to be "naturally" gifted in visual-spatial (right hemisphere) and ana-

lytical (left hemisphere) cognition but not in intuitive, holistic, gestalt thinking (right hemisphere) (Bleier, 1984:92).

Another flaw is the difficulty in establishing the direction of causality which plagues these brain studies. Even if sex differences in brain functioning were unequivocally documented, such brain differences might be the result of distinctive experiences of males and females, rather than the other way around (Lowe, 1983:53). Two final points. First, female and male brains are more alike than they are different. Secondly, even if some differences in specialization occur, the environment enhances or diminishes these potentialities, depending on the sociocultural definitions of femininity and masculinity. See also Epstein (1988:52-56); Fausto-Sterling (1985).

Summary

In this section, the evidence for the endocrinological theory of gender has been appraised. The arguments for it provided by studies of animals treated with other-sex hormones, of the effect of sex hormones on human emotions, of psychosexual abnormalities, and of brain lateralization have been reviewed. We conclude that all these approaches to a biological explanation of gender are unpersuasive.

Compelling evidence for the role of learning in the etiology of human gender and sexuality is provided by the fact that "the most extreme behavioural departures from sex-typed societal norms do not have any known biological basis" (Huston, 1983:413). All human fetuses begin by being female; inputs of male hormones are required to differentiate male characteristics in those fetuses having an XY genetic structure. (See Chapter 2.) Various sorts of sex/gender non-conformity (cross-dressing, homosexuality, transsexualism) appear to be much more common in males than in females. These two factors, taken together, make provocative the hypothesis that prenatal hormone imbalances are linked with postnatal departures from masculinity (Green, 1974:303). Because research techniques of the future might reveal hormonal influences, we should remain openminded about this possibility (Bell, Wein-berg and Hammersmith, 1981; Ross, 1986). Nevertheless, at the present time, there is very little evidence for hormonal (or genetic) abnor-mality in homosexuals or transvestites (Baker, 1980:95; Geer et al., 1984; Huston, 1983), or for transsexuals (Bolin, 1987:42; Ross, 1986).

We began this section by remarking that the centrality of sex hormones in embryonic devel-opment made their linkage with gender an intriguing line of research. Humans come in two sexes, and hormones make a very real difference. We end by observing that gender, unlike sex, is not dimorphic. Studies of humans simply do not support the conclusion "that some behaviours such as competitive sports are 'masculine' and others such as caretaking are 'feminine' and that the brain is pro-grammed before birth to facilitate the appear-ance of one kind and not the other, depending on the sex of the person" (Williams, 1987:115).

CONCLUSIONS

The comic-strip character Adam is a househus-band who stays home to look after the kids while his wife goes out to earn a living. The late child psychologist Bruno Bettelheim consid-ered this role reversal to run "contrary to the laws of nature." According to him, those who go against nature pay a high price. "I'm going to believe in switching roles when the good Lord lets fathers grow breasts so they can nurse the child," said Bettelheim (*Calgary Herald*, June 7, 1987:C6).

Chapter 3 has examined various arguments for the proposition that contemporary gender arrangements reflect "laws of nature." The division of labour and traditional male superi-ority challenged by the "Adam" comic strip are at the heart of these gender stereotypes. We looked at claims about biology and gender contained in animal studies, anthropological and sociobiological approaches, psychoanaly-sis, and hormone research, and asked, "What is the evidence?" Although some conclusions were forthcoming, nearly every section of our discussion of the biological foundations of female-male differences raised more questions than it has answered.

What has been learned so far? First of all, research in biology, anthropology, history, and psychology has converged to make implau-sible the assumption that sex (i.e., biological differences between males and females) deter-mines gender (Harding, 1986:134). Green (1987:385) summarizes this well: "While there may be constitutional differences between the sexes at birth and during the first years, it is baffling to comprehend how they could ex-plain the full range of sex-typed behavioral differences. Innate programming may account for the greater expression of rough-and-tumble play and aggressive behavior by males across species and cultures..., but is there really an area within the brain that makes a dress more attractive than a pair of pants, a truck more attractive than a tea set?" Despite the popular-ity of the position espoused by Bettelheim, no innate reason exists why men should control the public domain, or women should be the caretakers of children. Similarly, the tenuous results from brain lateralization studies on the male visual-spatial advantage cannot account for women's relative absence from engineering and architecture. Remember that sex differ-ences in tests of cognitive skills account for less than four percent of the variance anyway. Though male-female differences in reproduc-tion and in size and strength are indirectly involved in gender arrangements, the cultural interpretation of these differences is what counts.

Secondly, it is folly to search for *either* biol-ogy *or* environmental causation of gender pat-terns. To pose the question as "nature versus nurture" is misleading and simplistic, for the question is a complex one. *Both* nature and nurture are implicated. It makes no sense "to view biology and social experience as separate domains contesting for election as 'primary causes.' Biological processes unfold in a cul-tural context, and are themselves malleable, not stable and inevitable. So too, cultural processes take place within and through the biological organism; they do not take place in a biological vacuum" (Rossi, 1984:10).

Thirdly, this chapter has acknowledged the ideological aspects of science in general, and the search for the etiology of gender, in particu-lar. Feminists have shied away from a biological perspective because it has been used to justify male dominance. The issue is practical, as well as scholarly. If the public believes that male-female social arrangements are rooted in biology and hence immutable, they will lack interest in social programs designed to eliminate inequalities. From the feminists' point of view, the important matters "to address would seem to be not the cause of sex differences, but how much of our collective resources should be devoted to equalizing and in what respects, and how to balance this against other social goals" (Lambert, 1978:116).

NOTES

1. The idea of distinguishing eight variables of sex/gender is taken from Hyde (1979). Apparently, Hyde was influenced by Money and Ehrhardt (1972).
2. Even Margaret Mead, in a later book (1949), acknowledged "that cultural variability in sex roles was founded on 'primary sex differences' conditioned by the reproductive functions and anatomical differences between the sexes" (Sanday, 1980).
3. As symbolic interactionist theorist Cahill (1980) points out, psychoanalytic theory explained gender identity as the product of the child's identification with the same-sex parent, at between three and six years of age, during the phallic stage. However, research consistently demonstrates that the child's gender identity is formed well before this age. "Freud would seem

to have the process of gender development standing on its head. It is because the child has a well-formed gender identity that he or she identifies with the same sexed parent" (Cahill, 1980:130). For a discussion of the development of gender identity, see Chapter 4 of this volume.
4. The *couvade* is a practice among some preliterate tribes in which the father subjects himself to various taboos associated with pregnancy, experiences labour pains, and a long recovery period. He may minimize contact with others, avoid eating certain foods during pregnancy, refrain from performing normal tasks during the postpartum period, etc. Some anthropologists locate the motivation for the *couvade* in the father's practical need to assert his claim to the child in situations where paternity is quite uncertain (Tavris and Wade, 1984:190). It may also be recalled that the *couvade* was practised among the Arapesh (Mead, 1935).
5. Premenstrual tension represents another example of the conflict feminists experience between seeking authoritative acknowledgement of women's differences and being damned for them. To quote Code (1987:202-203): "For if it is acceptable to claim, on the basis of medical evidence and legal precedent, that women are incapacitated by premenstrual tension to the point of being absolved from criminal responsibility, then the judicial decision amounts to a strong affirmation of biological determinism."
6. The evidence considering psychosexual abnormality contradicts Freud's insistence that possession of a penis or a vagina is a necessary or sufficient condition for development of a male or female gender identity (Kessler and McKenna, 1978:57).

Chapter 4

Gender Socialization: The Social-Psychological Perspective on Sex/Gender Differences

What, asks the nursery rhyme, are little girls made of? Double X chromosomes. A vagina, a uterus and, eventually, a bosom. A bit more verbal facility than boys. A bit less independence.

What are little boys made of? An X chromosome. A Y chromosome. A penis and related parts. Later, larger muscles, mustache, beard, or five-o'clock shadow. On the average, slightly more aggressiveness, mathematical, and spatial ability.

Not sugar and spice and everything nice. Not snips and snails and puppy-dog tails. According to our discussion in Chapter 3, this short, prosaic inventory of male-female distinctions captures the essence of sex differences. The list gets longer when consideration is given to matters of fashion (long hair and pants are no longer reliable guides); etiquette and demeanour (who pays for dinner?); and, most particularly, social roles (maternal versus paternal aspirations).

The evidence reviewed in Chapter 3 established the significance of *learning* in the acquisition of femininity and masculinity. Most of the psycho-social characteristics associated with maleness and femaleness in our culture are not inborn, but rather, come about through socialization. Even where biology appears to play a central role, biological and sociocultural influences interact. For example, the average male is bigger and stronger than the average female. Moreover, strength has entered into the traditional definition of masculinity. For these and other reasons, our society has provided more athletic opportunities and facilities for males, thus enhancing their natural advantage. In short, most of the psycho-social differences between the sexes involve learning in one way or another. Chapter 4 is the first of four chapters to examine the socialization process as explanation of how newborn infants become gendered human beings.[1]

THE CASE OF AGNES

These concepts are central to gender socialization: sex; gender assignment; gender identity; and gender expression. In the usual case, the female child is born with XX chromosomes and female genitalia. Eventually, her endocrine glands will secrete estrogen into her bloodstream. At maturity, her reproductive equipment will consist of uterus and ovaries. (See Box 3.1.) *Gender assignment* occurs at birth (Kessler and McKenna, 1978:9). The doctor or midwife inspects the newborn's external genitals, and on this basis, assigns the gender label, in this case, "girl." This classification, which "sticks" for life, sorts the child into one of two varieties of human beings.

The gender socialization experienced as a consequence of this initial gender assignment causes the child eventually to develop a gender identity and to learn appropriate *expressions of gender*. Ordinarily, the individual's gender identity, this personal conviction of being female or male, emerges early and remains unchanged throughout life. Gender identity has an axiomatic, taken-for-granted character which organizes the rest of the person's beliefs about self, others, and the social world (Rokeach, 1968). Usually, the biological female who is assigned the label "girl" at birth comes to view herself as a girl. Experience teaches her how to express femininity, how to behave in ways her culture interprets "as indicative of a normal sexual nature" (Cahill, 1980:130).

Sociologist Harold Garfinkel's (1967:116-85) famous case study of "Agnes" dealt with a situation quite unlike that described above. This departure from the ordinary provides insight into the question of how gender is socially established. Agnes was born with normal penis and scrotum; "her" gender assignment was masculine. However, at age twelve, she began to take secretly her mother's estrogen pills. Eventually, she became completely feminized in her secondary sex characteristics (breasts, absence of body hair, shape of pelvic girdle).

Agnes was a transsexual whose gender identity had, from earliest memory, contradicted her sex and gender assignment. She "regarded herself as a female, albeit a female with a penis.... The penis, she insisted, was a 'mistake' in need of remedy" (West and Zimmerman, 1987:131). Transsexuals resent their own sex organs and "share an intense and insistent desire to transform their bodies into those of the opposite sex, in the conviction that they are victims of nature's mistake" (Restak, 1979:20).

When Professor Garfinkel first encountered her, Agnes had recently moved to California to seek sex-reassignment surgery. Before doctors were willing to take the drastic step of amputating penis and testes, they demanded evidence that the patient has already lived successfully as a member of the other sex. Agnes suddenly faced the requirement to "pass" as a woman, to express femininity convincingly. She did not have the usual long period of gender socialization to learn the details her particular society and historical period associated with femaleness. Instead, she had to suppress evidence of maleness and learn femininity, as she went about portraying herself as a bona fide woman.

Agnes' social accomplishment of femininity depended on the universal assumption that sex and gender are dichotomous: everyone is either male or female. It also depended upon people's willingness to attribute sex/gender on the basis of external cues. The most reliable way to categorize a stranger as male or female, inspection of that person's genitals, would be highly inappropriate under most circumstances. "Except for the moment of gender assignment, genitals play little role in gender attribution. This is largely because in our society genitals are almost always concealed. We expect, for example, that all men have penises under their clothes, but we cannot see them" (Kessler and McKenna, 1978:59). Nevertheless, Agnes took steps to hide her ownership of a penis. She avoided driving a car lest an accident render her unconscious and result in exposure. For the same reason, she avoided solitary dating and drinking.

Agnes was serving a secret apprenticeship to learn the expression of femininity. Like transvestites (who cross-dress for erotic pleasure) and actors impersonating females (such as Dustin Hoffman in his role as "Tootsie"), Agnes consciously created the physical appearance of a woman. Costumes and props available to manipulate this impression include "feminine" make-up (which also conceals facial hair), dress, hairstyles, jewelry, bosom (padded bra, or in Agnes' case, hormone-induced), and high-heeled shoes (Newton, 1972:5). People attempting to contrive the appearance of the other sex and to deny their own tend to overdo it, to go overboard. As Garfinkel put it, Agnes was trying to be 120 percent female, "unquestionably in all ways and at all times feminine" (West and Zimmerman, 1987:134).

Thirty years ago, "acting like a lady" involved mastering cooking, dressmaking, shopping, and home management skills. Equally important, Agnes had to learn to defer to males. She was not to want her own way, offer opinions when she should be retiring, be sharp in manner when she should be sweet, complain instead of taking things as they were, profess sophistication instead of being innocent, or demand services instead of trying to give her male companion pleasure and comfort (Garfinkel, 1967:146-47). In order to pass as a woman, Agnes had also to learn feminine communication patterns and gestures. Vocabulary, voice pitch, and resonance must all be adjusted.

Although scientists continue to study the roots of transsexualism (Walters and Ross, 1986), our present interest lies elsewhere. Two points are important. First, the majority of the population who are not transsexuals must also accomplish gender. However, most people do "naturally" what transsexuals do self-consciously (Kessler and McKenna, 1978:114), and with keen sensitivity to subtle cultural expectations most of us take for granted (Kando, 1973:5). Second, as individuals master the knowledge necessary to behave as gendered persons, they collectively reinforce the "naturalness," the normality, and legitimacy of their society's arrangements about sex/gender (West and Zimmerman, 1987:146).

SOCIALIZATION DEFINED

Socialization is defined as the complex learning process through which individuals develop selfhood and acquire the knowledge, skills, and motivations required for participation in social life. This process is the link between individual and society and may be viewed from each of these two perspectives. From the point of view of the individual, interaction with other people is the means by which human potentialities are actualized. The newborn infant is utterly helpless. Though it has the potential for becoming human, it is not yet human. The infant's experience with other human beings is absolutely crucial for its survival as a physical being and its development as a social being.

Effective socialization is as essential for the society as for the individual. The continuity of Canadian society requires that the thousands of new members born each year eventually learn to think, believe, and behave as Canadians. Each new generation must learn the society's culture. Social order demands self-discipline and control of impulses. However, socialization is also characterized by change. Social circumstances change, and the experiences of the current generation never duplicate those of the previous generation. Socialization

begins with the individual "taking over" the world as it has been constituted by others. However, people rebel and innovate so that "the world, once 'taken over,' *may* be creatively modified or... even re-created" (Berger and Luckmann, 1966:130, emphasis in original).

Gender socialization, a sub-type of general socialization, involves the processes through which individuals learn to become feminine and masculine according to the expectations current in their society. In particular, individuals develop gender identity and learn to express gender norms. Especially important is the the internalization of norms specifying gender inequality and gender division of labour. In Eichler's (1980:20) words, gender socialization "is the systematic teaching of a double standard." Gender socialization has been successful when the double standard seems "natural" to everyone affected by it.

Gender Socialization as Lifelong Learning Process

Socialization is a lifelong process that begins with primary socialization, the basic induction into society that takes place in childhood and adolescence, and continues with secondary socialization. *Primary socialization* involves the development of language and individual identity; the learning of cognitive skills and self-control; the internalization of moral standards and appropriate attitudes and interactions; an understanding of social roles. Both gender identity and the basic understanding of masculinity and femininity are learned during primary socialization.

Primary socialization occurs in a crucible of highly charged emotional relationships with significant others. The family bears the major responsibility for how the child turns out. Our society assumes that if the child develops undesirable qualities, "the practices of the family during the early years — especially parental neglect, indifference, restriction, and absence of joyful and playful interaction — are the major culprits" (Kagan, 1984:242). After all, the family has had jurisdiction over the child during its most malleable years and the strongest of emotional bonds are forged among family members. Therefore, if the child ends up neurotic, unemployed, or a criminal, the family is blamed. Mothers are held especially accountable. Nevertheless, commentators on the modern family (Postman, 1982; Winn, 1983) point out that many obstacles — divorce, reconstituted families, economic necessity for both parents to work outside the home, ubiquitous mass media, availability of drugs—complicate and interfere with the family's performance of its traditional socialization function.

Adult socialization is the social learning that occurs beyond the childhood and adolescent years. Although primary socialization lays the foundation for later learning, it cannot prepare people for the roles and situations that are either unforeseeable at the moment, or that lie far ahead in the future. For one thing, our age-graded society confronts individuals with new expectations as they move through the life cycle. Preparing for an occupation, marrying, bearing children, encountering middle age, and retiring all involve new gender lessons to be learned. Also, society changes, and people must equip themselves to cope with new situations. For example, the women's movement has forced Canadians to deal with new notions about gender. Finally, many individuals meet new particularized situations, such as marital breakdown, chronic illness, geographical and social mobility, and widowhood, which may require further gender socialization. For instance, breast cancer and mastectomy may force a woman to redefine femininity for herself.

Generally speaking, formal organizations, such as universities and corporations, play a more influential role in adult socialization than in primary socialization. As mentioned above, the primary relationships characteristic of the family, babysitting arrangements, and peer groups are critically important in the socialization of children. However, this distinction reflects a tendency rather than a rigid rule. Formal organizations, e.g., schools and churches, can play a key role in primary socialization. On the other hand, friends and family members continue to be important reference persons throughout the life cycle. To complicate matters further, the actual socializing of adults within formal organizations often takes place through the agency of primary relationships. For example, the management of an oil company may decide to fill vacancies in its legal department with female lawyers. The attitudes of longtime employees of the legal department toward this new policy would likely be shaped by the opinions of friends inside and outside the company.

Resocialization occurs when a new role or situation requires that a person replace established patterns of behaviour and thought with new patterns (Campbell, 1975). Old behaviour must be unlearned because it is incompatible, in some way, with new demands. Resocialization is usually more difficult than the original socialization; established habits interfere with new learning. For example, many people are uncomfortable with new, non-sexist language forms such as "Ms." or "chairperson." As this illustration suggests, resocialization is more characteristic of adult socialization than of primary socialization. However, as youngsters mature, they too are expected to discard immature behaviour. A two-year-old boy may cry when he is frightened, but a ten-year-old boy is expected to be manly and brave.

Socialization as Two-way Process

Primary socialization is a reciprocal process that affects socializer as well as socializee. The child is not a "passive victim of socialization." Rather, she or he "resists it, participates in it, collaborates with it in varying degrees" (Berger and Berger, 1975:57). Both child and caregivers are changed by the process. Just as the givers socialize the child, the child socializes the caregivers. In infancy, the child's demands and responses serve to teach the mother and father how to behave as parents. As the child matures, the parents become aware of new facets of mothering and fathering. Over the dinner table, a teenager explains to her parents why k.d. lang, country music star and *Chatelaine* magazine's Woman of the Year for 1988, wears "a sheared-off ducktail, no makeup and no jewelry" and "looks for all God's earth like a cute teenage-boy" (Scott, 1988:54). As this hypothetical conversation about gender-blending entertainers illustrates, teenagers frequently teach their elders the latest nuances of gender.

The next four chapters explore gender socialization in order to understand how girls turn out girlish and boys boyish (Tavris and Wade, 1984:212). The next task of this chapter is to consider the content of the lessons of gender socialization in Canadian society. *What* do youngsters learn so that they become gendered persons? Then discussion turns to theories that psychologists and sociologists have developed over the years, to explain *how* learning occurs. Application of three such theories to gender socialization is treated at the end of Chapter 4.

For the sake of economy of language, sociologists often speak of "society" socializing its constituents. Nevertheless, "society" is not a monolithic entity which operates directly upon the individual. Rather, influence is exerted upon people by the family, the peer group, the school, the mass media, and so on. The next three chapters will analyze how gender socialization is carried out by these agencies. Chapter 5 concentrates on the family, Chapter 6 on the peer group, and Chapter 7 on secondary and symbolic agencies.

THE CONTENT OF GENDER SOCIALIZATION

Each society has developed *scripts* for femininity and masculinity which all societal members are expected eventually to learn (Laws, 1979). These scripts spell out the personality characteristics and behaviours associated with one sex versus the other, the norms governing the interaction of the sexes, and the relative evaluation of females and males. The basis of these scripts is differentiation and evaluation (Chapter 1); they incorporate gender stereotypes and gender role attitudes (Chapter 2). However, the content of gender socialization for all Canadians is not absolutely uniform. The gender scripts receive varying interpretations in different social classes, ethnic groups, and regions of the country. In addition, these scripts are age-graded. That is, the gender norms that pertain

to given individuals change as they move through the life cycle.

The rapid change that characterizes modern societies means that gender scripts are never cast in stone. Like other aspects of socialization content, the socialization lessons pertaining to gender are subject to revision. The social movements of the 1970s and 1980s that challenged traditional gender norms (the women's movement, men's movement, and gay liberation movement) accelerated the pace of change. Nevertheless, because of the great emotionality surrounding sexual and gender matters, gender socialization tends to be more conservatively regarded than other areas, e.g. economic activities.

Gender Socialization goals

Before the second wave of the women's movement, most parents and child-rearing experts alike simply assumed that a sex-typed upbringing was essential for both well-adjusted individuals and smoothly functioning societies. *Sex-typing* is "the prescription of different qualities, activities, and behaviors to females and males in the interest of socializing them for adult roles" (Williams, 1987:191). Sex-typing and gender stereotyping are closely related constructs. Gender stereotypes are commonly held beliefs about the traits characterizing females and males (Chapter 2). Sex-typing, on the other hand, holds that certain traits *should* characterize females and males.

In the mid-1970s, such feminist scholars as Sandra Bem (1974;1976) recommended that androgyny replace sex-typing as the goal of gender socialization. While sex-typing demanded that the individual be *either* masculine or feminine, androgyny advocated being *both* masculine and feminine in relatively equal proportions. *Androgyny* may be defined as the flexible integration of valued feminine (communal) and masculine (instrumental) traits. The androgynous ideal calls for people of both sexes to be, for example, assertive *and* compassionate, ambitious *and* sensitive to others' needs. The androgynous person is able to fire an inept employee, but do so with an appreciation of that person's feelings. On the other hand, a person who is always competitive and aggressive at work, but very dependent and passive off the job, that is, a person who is unable to adjust his/her behaviour to situational requirements, is neither integrated nor flexible (Basow, 1980:297). The term "androgynous" would not apply here. The androgynous person is comfortable exhibiting behaviours associated with either the female or male role, as appropriate to the requirements of the situation.[2]

Feminist discussion of socialization goals received wide media coverage. Some parents, sympathetic to the argument that sex-typing constricts the human potential of both sexes, now advocate androgyny. Others, perhaps most, continue to believe that differential socialization of girls and boys is still required to equip children for the distinctive adult roles they will play. As one journalist put it, the majority of North Americans "are still raising little boys and girls rather than little children" (Treiman, 1988:D10). Some parents who consider themselves to be "liberated" are reluctant to risk socializing their children, especially their boys, to be androgynous. They are loathe to subject their youngsters to ridicule or to render them misfits in a society that remains gender-based. Other parents still think of girls and boys, women and men as opposites. They assume that "what is male is 'not female' and vice versa" (Deaux, 1985:68). Despite these indications of continuing traditionalism in folk thought, it is important not to overstate the conservatism. Some remarkable shifts in thinking have occurred over the last two decades. Recall our earlier discussion of gender-role attitudes (Chapter 2).

A Schema of Gender Socialization Content

Table 4.1 (adapted from the work of Huston, 1983) schematizes the content of gender socialization. The concepts contained in the table represent a distillation of social scientists' research on this topic. An abstract outline of this sort, by necessity, simplifies what actually occurs. However, the table provides us with a systematic way of considering what children must learn in order to become gendered persons. Our discussion of the case of Agnes at the beginning of this chapter incorporated, either explicitly or implicitly, the ideas contained in Table 4.1.

The left-hand column of the table lists five content areas: *Sex/Gender* (the fundamental aspects of maleness and femaleness); *Activities and Interests* (what males and females do); *Personal-social Attributes* (the sorts of persons males and females should be); *Gender-based Social Relationships* (how maleness and femaleness shape relationships with others); *Stylistic and Symbolic Content* (the display of gender through gestures and language).

Each of these five content areas is considered in terms of the four dimensions spelled out across the top of Table 4.1. The first column, *Concepts or Beliefs*, refers to the knowledge a child must acquire about femininity and masculinity. The second column, *Identity*, considers the child's application of this knowledge to herself or himself. *Preferences, Values*, the third column, deals with the evaluative dimension of gender. Children learn to prefer their sex/gender of assignment. They come to value activities and characteristics our society associates with being one sex or the other. The last column, *Gender Expression*, refers to the behavioural enactment of gender norms.

The rest of this section will elaborate on the ideas introduced in these opening paragraphs. Although we'll do the best we can, it will be difficult to capture all the nuances of "real life" child-rearing. As mentioned earlier, gender scripts vary somewhat among ethnic and religious groups, social classes, and regions of the country. Also, since gender socialization is a lifelong process, gender scripts are age-graded. In other words, the content covered by the Table 4.1 labels changes as the individual moves from childhood, through adolescence to adulthood. Finally, the gender scripts guiding child-rearing in individual families range from extremely sex-typed to androgynous. (Refer to n. 2 concerning this last point.)

Sᴇx/Gᴇɴᴅᴇʀ

The very first step in gender socialization for

TABLE 4.1

THE CONTENT OF GENDER SOCIALIZATION

CONTENT AREA	CONCEPTS OR BELIEFS	IDENTITY	PREFERENCES, VALUES (FOR SELF OR OTHERS)	GENDER EXPRESSION
Sex/Gender	Sex/Gender constancy	Gender identity as inner sense of maleness or femaleness.	Wish to be male or female. Greater value attached to one sex/gender versus the other.	Displaying bodily attributes of one sex/gender (clothing, body type, hair, etc.).
Activities and Interests: Toys; Play activities; Household roles; Occupations.	Knowledge of gender-role attitudes, occupational sex types.	Self-perception of interests, abilities.	Preference for toys, games, activities. Attitudes about sex-typed activities by others.	Engaging in games, toy play, activities, occupations, or achievement tasks that are sex-typed.
Personal-social Attributes: Personality characteristics; Social behavior.	Concepts about gender stereotypes or sex-appropriate social behaviour.	Perception of own personality.	Preference or wish to have personal-social attributes or attitudes about others' personality and behaviour.	Displaying sex-typed personal-social behaviour (e.g., aggression, dependence).
Gender-based Social Relationships: Gender of peers, friends, lovers, parents.	Beliefs about sex-typed norms for gender-based social relations.	Self-perception of own patterns of friendship, relationship, or sexual orientation.	Preference for male or female friends, lovers, attachment figures, or attitudes about others' patterns.	Engaging in social or sexual activity with others on the basis of gender (e.g., same-sex peer choice).
Stylistic and Symbolic Content: Non-verbal behaviour; Speech and language patterns; Styles of play.	Awareness of sex-typed symbols or styles.	Self-perception of non-verbal, stylistic characteristics.	Preference for stylistic patterns or attitudes about others' non-verbal and language patterns.	Manifesting sex-typed verbal and non-verbal behaviour.

SOURCE: Adapted from Huston (1983).

the young child involves grasping the elemental idea of femaleness *versus* maleness, of masculinity *versus* femininity. "A child's sex is a biological fact. It is also a social fact" (Maccoby, 1980:203). Table 4.1 labels this axiom of the societal script "sex/gender" to signal that the youngster's conceptualization of biology and sociocultural elaboration are, from the very beginning, intertwined. In short, difference between males and females is the child's most fundamental gender lesson.

Sex-typing by parents, already well indoctrinated in traditional gender scripts, often begins even before the child is born. For example, during the last months of pregnancy, an active fetus that kicks and moves a great deal is often considered to be male. Folk wisdom also relates a child's prenatal position to its sex; boys are supposedly carried high and girls low (Lewis, 1972).

From the moment of their entry into the world, female and male infants are regarded differently. According to an English study (Woollett, White and Lyon, 1982, reported by Lewis, 1986:97), 82 percent of parent's comments within 20 minutes of the baby's birth concerned the infant's sex. Researchers (Seavey, Katz and Zalk, 1975) introduced adults to a seven-month-old infant whose sex was not revealed. When these subjects were interviewed after interacting with the child, all had made up their minds as to what the baby's sex was.

Seventy percent believed the infant to be male (she was not); they based this judgment on the relative lack of hair and the strength of the baby's grip. Those who believed the baby to be a girl based this judgment on cues such as her smiling, round face, and her apparent fragility. The fact that the adults were not very accurate in making infant gender judgments did not stop them from acting on the basis of their beliefs (Katz, 1979:13).

Male and female babies are treated differently from an early age. Girls are cuddled and talked to more, while boys are jostled and played with more roughly (Lewis, 1972). Parents handle girls as if they were more fragile (Minton et al., 1971). Later on, boys are more likely to be punished by spanking and other forms of physical punishment (Maccoby and Jacklin, 1974), and girls by gentle verbal reprimands (Serbin et al., 1973). Boys receive more praise than girls (Huston, 1983:428).

Although these differences in child-rearing techniques may be influenced by the somewhat distinctive behaviour of boy children versus girl children, they also reflect the fact that parents of preschool children have gender-stereotyped expectations for their children. Both parents tend to press achievement and competition more on their sons than their daughters. They also encourage their sons, more than their daughters, to control their emotions, to be independent, and to assume responsibility (Block, 1984:265). As children mature, caregivers pay increasing attention to traits at the core of gender stereotypes; they encourage "appropriate" gender traits and punish "inappropriate" traits (Williams and Best, 1982:18). Socialization becomes more sex-differentiated with the increasing age of the child. The expectation that girls behave like girls, and boys like boys, peaks during the high school years (Block, 1984:95).

Though a child's adult socializers place it in a sex class at birth, it is a few years before the child responds to himself/herself in terms of gender. Eventually, however, as a result of the differential perception and handling described above, the child comes to develop a *gender identity*: a conviction of his/her own masculinity or femininity. As Lewis (1972:56), notes, "what the parent does to the infant, the infant is likely to do back." In other words, the child views herself/himself through the eyes of significant others. Sex/gender, which all along mattered greatly to caregivers, now also matters to the child.

For most people, gender identity is congruent with biological sex. This inner sense of maleness or femaleness begins to be established between the ages of two and three. By the age of three, a child can answer accurately and consistently the question, "Are you a girl or a boy?" (Kessler and McKenna, 1978:101). However, it is not until age five or six, when an understanding of gender constancy develops (see below) that gender identity becomes stabilized (Mussen, 1969:726). This sense of being a person of a given sex does not mean that the child appreciates all the implications. Although the first step is self-labelling, full comprehension of what it means to be female or male comes only gradually (Maccoby, 1980:224). Young children rely heavily on clothing and hair styles as cues to sex/gender. Because genitals are usually concealed, even six year olds are confused about the connections between genitals and gender. Lindesmith et al. (1977) tell the story of a five-year-old acquaintance who attended a party at which children of both sexes bathed in the nude. "When asked how many boys and how many girls were at the party, she answered: "I couldn't tell because they had their clothes off" (p. 374).

As the fourth column of Table 4.1 shows, attitudes accompany gender identity. After children can correctly answer questions about their own sex/gender and understand that they share one of these two categories with other people, they develop *preferences* about being one sex/gender rather than the other. In other words, they adopt an "ethnocentric" view of gender and believe their own is "better" (Losh-Hesselbart, 1987:543). For example, when Zuckerman and Sayre (1982) interviewed children in kindergarten and grades one and two, virtually all these youngsters expressed a preference for their own sex.

Children categorize themselves not only in terms of what they are but in terms of what they are not. If girls are good, then boys must be bad. If girl dolls are pretty, then boy dolls must be ugly. One's own category is viewed in a very positive manner, and girls [of preschool age] appear to be particularly proud and happy about their gender classification (Katz, 1979:14-15).

Later on, the higher value accorded males in our society complicates the evaluative process for little girls (Mussen, 1969:711). A study of the reactions of sixth-grade children to storybook characters reported that children of both sexes would rather be the male characters and do the things the male characters do (Conner and Serbin, 1978).

Another important dimension of gender socialization concerns the *enactment or display of the bodily attributes* — the hairstyle, clothing, and so on considered appropriate in a particular society. (Top right-hand column of Table 4.1[3].) Well before children develop sartorial tastes of their own, their parents are dressing them as girls or boys. Shakin, Shakin and Sternglanz (1985) were able to guess correctly, on the basis of sex-typed clothes, the sex/gender of 88 percent of 48 infants they observed in suburban malls. Infant girls wore pink (75 percent), ruffles, puffed sleeves, and dresses; they carried pink soothers. Infant boys wore blue (79 percent) and/or red. Richardson (1988:43) describes her observations of the children's clothing department:

In a trip through an infant section of any department store, gross imitations of the adult gender-linked styles are easily discernible. On the girls' racks are princess dresses, granny gowns, pink satin pantsuits, and bikinis; on the boys' racks are baseball uniforms, tweed suits with vests and decorative pocket watches, astronaut pajamas, and starched white dress shirts. Often, the differences in style are more subtle; for example, large manufacturers of infant ready-to-wear clothing design male and female variants of the same basic romper. The male variant snaps from left to right, has a pointed collar and a football motif; the female snaps from right to left, has a Peter Pan collar with lace trim and embroi-dered butterflies. (Only diapers and christening dresses seem to be entirely immune to gender typing.)

Through choosing such sex-typed clothing, parents announce their child's sex/gender to the world. Labelling an infant female or male in this way affects people's behaviour toward the child. As sociologist Gregory Stone (1962:105-106) observed, "The world handles the pink-clad child and the blue-clad child differently." The pink-clad child is "darling," "beautiful," "sweet," or "graceful", while the blue-clad child is "handsome," "strong," or "agile."

Before long, the children themselves come to prefer the clothing and hairstyles of their own sex category. However, because of the prestige associated with things masculine, as well as the greater bodily freedom and comfort associated with overalls, pants and flat shoes, females have been more likely than males to rebel against this dress code. The feminist movement encouraged women to wear comfortable, safe, utilitarian clothing (Brownmiller, 1984). Because our society provides females with considerable latitude to dress in a "masculine" fashion, (while stigmatizing males who cross-dress), female transvestites are non-existent in our culture. There are practically no reports of females who experience sexual arousal by wearing men's clothing (Green, 1979:160).

Sex/Gender constancy is the final dimension of the Sex/Gender section of Table 4.1 to be considered. Sex/gender constancy refers to the knowledge that an individual's sex/gender "is a permanent attribute of the person, regardless of changes in the person's hair, clothing, and activities" (Maccoby, 1980:227). Researchers ask children, "Could you be a ____ (other sex/gender) if you wanted to?" Youngsters are also asked what sex/gender they were at birth and will be as adults, and whether they have been or ever could be the other sex/gender (Huston, 1983:402).

Between ages three and seven, children's understanding of sex/gender constancy gradually increases (Huston, 1983:407). They consistently identify themselves as female or male, and prefer sex-typed activities long before they fully appreciate the unchanging nature of sex/gender. We discuss further the development of sex/gender constancy in the context of cognitive-developmental theory later in this chapter.

ACTIVITIES AND INTERESTS

The second row of Table 4.1 takes into consideration the fact that gender norms pertain to what people in our society *do*. These norms define certain activities and interests as being feminine and others as masculine. The application of these norms begins in infancy and childhood, with toys, games, and hobbies viewed as appropriate for one sex or the other. It continues into adolescence and adulthood with gender-based definitions of the situation concerning school subjects, leisure activities, and division of labour in household and labour force. Of significance is the finding that parents and other socialization agents emphasize sex-typed activities and interests more than personal-social attributes (the third row in Table 4.1) (Huston, 1983:407). In other words, parents want their daughters, but certainly not their sons, to play with dolls and miniature tea sets, to sew, and to aspire to be nurses or dancers when they grow up.

The playthings provided by adults channel children's interests and activities. Cultural norms determine which toys are "appropriate" for each sex, and toy manufacturers comply with these norms. The business section of the January 27, 1988 issue of *The Globe and Mail* reported that,

... Mattel plans to introduce a Club California Barbie [doll] this year, complete with convertible, roller skates, high-top sneakers and frisbee, and an Island Fun Barbie, with her own sarong, grass shack and hammock. There will also be a Perfume Party set, where Barbie, provided with scented fashions and jewelry, can preside over the launching of her own fragrance.

Adults supply children with these sex-typed toys. Up to age two, boys and girls receive many of the same toys (teddy bears, blocks, educational toys). However, Rheingold and Cook (1975) inventoried the bedrooms of middle-class children and concluded that parents provided different environments for girls and boys. Boys' rooms contained more vehicles, sports equipment, art material, construction, and military toys. Their rooms contained toys of more categories. Girls's rooms contained more dolls and miniature domestic equipment. If this study were replicated today, (as it well deserves to be), we would expect boys' rooms to contain more computerized playthings.

Children's play helps to create gender differences in taste, ambition, outlook, and experience (Laws, 1979:246-48). As Ambert (1976:71) says, "boys toys... encourage rougher play, activity, creativity, mastery, and curiosity; girls toys, on the other hand, encourage passivity, observation, simple behavior, and solitary play." The toys given to older boys encourage activities away from home, while girls' toys encourage domesticity. Caregivers' activities with children reinforce the same sorts of messages. In the opinion of socialization expert Phyllis Bronstein:

How fathers play with boys — many toss them into the air and do lots of large muscle limb movements — conditions babies to certain things.... I believe fathers who handle infant sons this way — tossing and catching them — are training them to translate fear and risk-taking into fun and pleasure (Treiman, 1988:D10).

Moreover, parents give boys of preschool and elementary school age much more freedom in the physical environment (i.e., freedom from special permission or adult accompaniment) than is the case for girls of the same age (Landy, 1965; Saegert and Hart, 1976).

Gender socialization also encompasses household and occupational roles. Children observe how tasks in the home and in the labour force are divided among male and female adults. Information about the gender division of labour gleaned from observation is augmented by their own experience in helping around the home, as well as the content of books, television, and movies. Parents are guided by their own gender stereotypes in assigning household chores to their children. According to White and Brinkerhoff (1981), children's job opportunities in the home and community are every bit as sex-segregated as their parents' work. Girls babysit and clean house; boys have more and better paying opportunities outside the home doing yard work and manual labour (Greenberger and Steinberg, 1983).

As the above discussion suggests, what youngsters are motivated to learn and have opportunities to learn about work is deeply influenced by notions (their own, their parents', their society's) about the sort of work that lies in store for them in adulthood.

Although *Concepts or Beliefs* about sex-typed activities and interests (the first column of Table 4.1) also refer to other matters, for the sake of space economy our treatment of this topic will be confined to occupational sex-typing. Because work is a central life experience, children's views about occupations constitutes a central dimension of their gender socialization. Many occupations have incumbents who are primarily of one sex or the other; most secretaries are women, and most dentists are men, for example. As we shall see in Chapter 8, this sex-segregated occupational structure is an important reason for the large differences between Canadian men and women with respect to income, job security, and opportunities for advancement.

Occupational sex-typing refers to the tendency to regard sex-segregated occupations as more appropriate for one sex or the other. Elementary school teaching has traditionally been regarded as women's work, while university teaching has been viewed as men's work. Beliefs that men are better suited for certain occupations and women for others are buttressed by reference to gender stereotypes. Thus, women may be considered suited to nursing *because* they are nurturant and men to law *because* they are logical (Williams and Best, 1982).

What are the occupational views of children born since the advent of the women's movement? The Women's Bureau of Labour Canada (1986) asked 700 elementary school children across Canada their beliefs about the sex composition of the labour force when they grew up. Many of the children's ideas remain sex-typed. For instance, they think only women could be nurses and only men could be forest rangers. (When asked why forest rangers had to be men, one child explained that a fire might get so close that the ranger would have to run away.

Women can't run very fast in their high-heeled shoes [p. 26].)

However, according to the Labour Canada (1986) study, these elementary school children predicted that when they become adults, both men and women would be engaged in many of the same occupations. The children found it easier to imagine women entering traditionally masculine professions like dentistry and medicine, than men participating in traditionally feminine occupations such as secretarial work and nursing. Given the low salaries and low prestige associated with much "women's" work, their predictions are probably correct! As we shall see in the next section, this study found the children's own career aspirations to be more traditional than their beliefs about future labour force structure.

The *Identity* column of Table 4.1 considers connections between the self and gendered social scripting of interests and abilities. Obviously, a great deal could be said about this important issue. Our remarks will be confined to two topics: the impact of sex-typed play upon identity; and sex-typed career aspirations.

An article entitled, "The Dirty Play of Little Boys" (Fine, 1986), aptly illustrates our general point that children's play has considerable influence upon gender identity. Aggressive pranks like this one constitute one category of what Fine means by "dirty play":

A group of boys wraps dog feces in a newspaper, lights the newspaper on fire, rings a homeowner's doorbell, and runs away to watch. When the victim comes to the door, he stomps on the flaming package. At that point another boy rings the back doorbell and the man, not thinking, rushes through the house, tracking it with dog excrement (p. 64).

Adults thoroughly disapprove of pre-adolescent pranks such as "mooning" cars (pulling down one's trousers while facing away from the traffic), "egging" cars, and ringing doorbells and running away. However, these activities serve as anticipatory socialization for manhood. Males are supposed to be tough, cool, and aggressive. "There is risk involved in throwing eggs at houses or at moving cars; one could get caught, beaten, grounded, or even arrested" (Fine, 1986:66). Boys gain status within their peer group for behaviour adults regard as troublesome. Such behaviour is the antithesis of "girls' play." In short, boys' identity as males is enhanced by engaging in "dirty play," partly because it is "dirty" play (i.e., it defies adult authority), partly because it is *not* girls' play. (Play and its relevance for the gender identity of adults, as well as children, will receive further attention in Chapter 6.)

Next, we turn to the subject of young people's career aspirations. Our concern is with the extent to which their own ambitions are sex-typed. The Labour Canada (1986) study (see above) also asked the elementary school pupils, "What do you want to be when you grow up?" Two-thirds of the girls mentioned a traditionally masculine occupation. Although almost all these "masculine" choices were learned professions rather than trades, a few girls wanted to be mechanics or truck drivers (p. 43). (One little girl said, "I'd like to become a bus driver when I grow up...But if I can't I want to be the Queen" [p. 28].) Only one percent of the boys chose traditionally feminine careers (office worker, nursery school teacher). The boys looked forward to a wider range of future jobs than did the girls. Boys, but not girls, wanted to be astronomers, air traffic controllers, stockbrokers, machinists, plumbers, mathematicians (p. 43). Many of the girls believed in the equality of the sexes, but did not apply to themselves this general belief.

Many of them seemed to be saying, "Yes, women can become doctors, but I expect to be a nurse," "Bank managers can be women as well as men, but I am going to be a teller," or "Dental assistant is my career goal, although I know that women can be dentists" (p. 55).

Research suggests that youngsters have unrealistic notions about what the future holds. The Labour Canada (1986) study found that almost without exception, the girls expected to marry, to have children, and to assume there would be a husband to provide for the family. "There do not seem to be any unmarried mothers, deserted wives, widows or divorcees among the imaginary women Canadian schoolgirls expect to become" (Women's Bu-

reau, 1986:56). This conclusion is corroborated by Maureen Baker's (1985) national study of the aspirations of adolescents. According to Baker, young Canadian women anticipate both enjoyable work and satisfying family life, but are vague about exactly how this is to be accomplished. A 17-year-old Toronto girl had this to say:

(At age twenty-two) "I'll be owning or managing a clothing store." (At age thirty) "At 6:00 I'll get up and get breakfast for my husband and two kids. One is a baby and one is school-age. I'll drive the one kid to school, feed the baby, and play with it. Then I'll put the baby to bed and watch the soaps..." (Later in the interview — what happened to your store?) "Oh! I forgot about it. I guess someone is looking after it" (Baker, 1985:88).

Over time, young people of both sexes scale down their ambitions. As girls approach the age for actual labour force entry, they lower their aspirations and revise their career goals toward more traditional choices (Miller and Garrison, 1982). As the less-valued sex, females receive less family support to continue their schooling (Turrittin et al., 1983). Obstacles also impede the life course of males. The majority abandon earlier hopes for university education or technical training, presumably for economic reasons (Bibby and Posterski, 1985:161).

Preferences for sex-typed activities in self and others become established early. Studies show that by the time they are three years old, children actively prefer sex-appropriate toys (Kessler and McKenna, 1978:102). Put another way, they do not simply play with the sex-typed toys that caregivers provide. By nursery-school age, boys placed in a situation where many toys are available will choose toy cars, trucks, and airplanes. Girls choose dolls, domestic equipment, and crayons (Maccoby, 1980:212). Same-sex bias is also involved. As noted earlier, Katz (1979) found that little girls invariably preferred girl dolls to boy dolls, and attributed positive characteristics to girl dolls and negative ones to boy dolls. Laws (1979:248-49) cites research that found boys avoided an attractive but "sex-inappropriate" toy to a greater degree than girls did, especially when the experimenter was present, and that boys showed more reluctance to play the role of a girl in a "pretend" telephone conversation.

In general, boys' preference for masculine activities continues to increase with age. Girls' preference for feminine activities also increases up to age five or six. However, during the elementary school years, girls' preference for feminine activities often declines, as they becoming increasingly interested in masculine activities (Huston, 1983:403). For one thing, boys' games enjoy greater prestige. Hyde, Rosenberg and Behrman (1977) tell us that 63 percent of a junior-high sample of girls reported being tomboys, and that 51 percent of an adult women sample reported having been tomboys in their childhood. Can you imagine 60 percent or more of a sample of junior high school boys admitting to being "sissies" or expressing a preference for dresses, sewing, and indoor games?

Children also develop sex-typed attitudes about other people's interests and activities, as well as their own. As the above reference to tomboys implied, boys who deviate from "masculine" standards are likely to run into trouble. Fine (1986:65), in the observational study mentioned earlier, says it is common to hear young boys who have only the foggiest notion of gay sexual behaviour say things like, "You're a faggot," "What a queer." For them, "being gay is synonymous with being a baby and a girl" (p. 65). The use of such rhetoric means that its target has not comported himself in accord with the masculine gender role.

Gender expression considers the extent to which people actually engage in sex-typed activities. Because the purpose of this chapter is to provide an overview of gender socialization, much of our discussion of sex-typed behaviour will be postponed until later chapters. (Chapter 6 provides a detailed consideration of children's play. Sex-typed work in the labour force and home will be dealt with in Chapter 8.) The present treatment of gender-distinctive activity will be confined to children's early manifestation of such behaviour, and to a few observations about rebellion against gender norms.

As you would expect, observational studies report congruence between children's sex-typed toys and activity preferences and their actual play. Even toddlers between one-and-one-half and two years often select and play with same-sex stereotyped toys more than toys typed for the other sex/gender. By age three, they avoid playing with toys stereotyped for the other gender, even when few alternatives exist (Huston, 1983:403). Girls three and four years old engage in dolls and domestic play; boys the same age play more with vehicles (Smith, 1986:123). Much of urban children's pretend play reflects their familiarity with adult roles from television and their own experience. Girls adopt relational roles (such as parent-child; husband-wife) in domestic type episodes, such as "cooking" or "feeding baby." Boys act out fantastic roles involving gross motor activity, such as monsters or spacemen (Fein, 1981).

Not every child conforms to all aspects of the societal script for sex/gender. We mentioned earlier that school-age girls do not have the same attraction to sex-appropriate interests and activities that boys do (Huston, 1983:404). For example, a fictional child knew that, "Adults, older girls, shops, magazines, newspapers, window signs — all the world had agreed that a blue-eyed, yellow-haired, pink-skinned doll was what every girl child treasured" (Morrison, 1970:20). But she was different:

What was I supposed to do with it? Pretend I was its mother? I had no interest in babies or the concept of motherhood. I was interested only in humans my own age and size...I learned quickly, however, what I was supposed to do with the doll: rock it, fabricate storied situations around it, even sleep with it. Picture books were full of little girls sleeping with their dolls. Raggedy Ann dolls usually, but they were out of the question. I was physically revolted by and secretly frightened of those round moronic eyes, the pancake face, and orangeworms hair (Morrison, 1970:20).

Gender rebellion is not confined to storybooks. Not long ago, the Ontario Human Rights Commission ruled that 14-year-old Justine Blainey should be given the opportunity to play on a boys' hockey team. Justine told the inquiry that she preferred the body-checking and slapshots permitted in boys' league play because "it adds a lot more fun" to the game. She also argued that the level of competition is better in the boys' league than in the Ontario Women's Hockey Association (*The Globe and Mail*, December 5, 1987:A7).

As these two examples suggest, young girls are allowed more latitude in cross-sex interests than are boys. Nevertheless, they too are pressured to behave in sex-appropriate ways, especially when they reach adolescence.

PERSONAL-SOCIAL ATTRIBUTES

What sort of people are boys and girls, men and women? In other words, what personality characteristics are associated with each sex? How do females and males manifest these traits in their social behaviour? As pointed out above, caregivers worry less about "appropriate" personality attributes than sex-typed activities. They are more concerned about their boys rocking dolls, than with fostering signs of gentleness or nurturance in the personalities of their boy children.

This section deals with children's learning of gender stereotypes (Chapter 2). Our topic here is the extent to which youngsters come to perceive themselves and others in terms of these cultural prescriptions, and to display gender-stereotyped behaviour.

Rudimentary *knowledge* of sex-appropriate personality characteristics begins to develop between ages two and three, in conjunction with learning about sex-typed activities and development of gender identity (Smith, 1986:119). Children apparently find it easier to master the concept of sex-typed toys and play than personality traits, perhaps because the latter represent abstractions from behaviour rather than concrete, observable activities (Huston, 1983:405). Nevertheless, research shows that children around the world learn about stereotypes surprisingly early (Williams and Best, 1982).

Research assistants gave children across the globe these same instructions:

What I have here are some pictures I would like to show you and some stories that go with each one. I want you to help me by pointing to the person in each

picture that the story is about. Here, I'll show you what I mean (Williams and Best, 1982:154).

The "stories" were 32 very brief, three-sentence representations of gender stereotype traits, 16 for each sex. For example, "One of these people is emotional. They cry when something good happens as well as when everything goes wrong. Which person is the emotional person?" Or, "One of these people is always pushing other people around and getting into fights. Which person gets into fights?" Accompanying these mini-stories were 32 pictures, each composed of a male and female figure in silhouette. After listening to each story, the child pointed to either the male or female figure. When two-thirds or more of the sample of children agreed that a "male-oriented" story belonged with the male figure, or vice-versa, the trait (that is, the adult definition of the concept expressed in the story), was considered to be part of the children's stereotype.

Psychologists Edwards and Williams (1980) carried out the Canadian segment of the Williams and Best (1982) project. The six-year-old and eight-year-old Nova Scotia children they studied (like other children around the world) showed increasing awareness of the adult stereotypes over time. The six-year-old Canadians knew 14 of the 32 adult-defined stereotype items. The older children were aware of 23 of the 32 items. For example, more than 85 percent of the eight-year-olds knew that "appreciative," "gentle," "weak," "soft-hearted," "sentimental," "emotional," "excitable," and "meek, mild" were female traits, and that "aggressive," "strong," "coarse," "cruel," "loud," and "ambitious" described men, not women.

As we move from youngsters' notions of what people in general are like, to their preferences and attitudes about close peers, to their self-perceptions, and then to their actual behaviour, gender stereotypes become less and less important determinants. The *gradient of familiarity* concept seems to explain this generalization: stereotypes operate more powerfully at a distance (Williams and Best, 1982:281). Stereotypes are engaged to describe people in general. They become less important in descriptions of best friends; they become even weaker in self-perceptions. For example, adults respond more stereotypically to strange babies than to their own children. In general, people become more flexible about stereotyping as they grow older. Adolescents are more aware of exceptions to stereotypes than are younger children. They begin to grasp the fact that sex-typed patterns are culturally relative (Huston, 1983:403).

Little systematic work has been carried out on the question of the relationship between *self-perceptions* and gender stereotypes. However, Williams and Best (1982:285) cite research by Davis (1978) into the self-concepts of nine-year-old American children. This study concluded that the self-imagery of the girls was "somewhat female-stereotyped," while that of the boys was more androgynous. Williams and Best (1982:285) speculate that perhaps "children of both sexes receive pro-social messages (be kind, considerate, helpful and so on) that serve to reinforce female characteristics, while the boys, in addition, are encouraged to become masculine (be assertive, independent, adventuresome, and the like)." The fact that parents are less interested in shaping personality traits than activities may also be involved. The author's (Mackie, 1980) study of the extent to which adults incorporate gender stereotypes in their self-descriptions also found the impact of stereotypes to be less than expected.

Display of sex-typed personal-social behaviour (the last column of Table 4.1) has already been considered at length in Chapter 2. Here, we simply reiterate our conclusion that females and males differ slightly in a relatively small number of cognitive traits, such as verbal, spatial-visual, and mathematical proclivities, and personality traits (aggression, dependence). Clearly, gender has more to do with social roles, social status, and power than it does with personality. We turn now to the topic of social relationships.

GENDER-BASED SOCIAL RELATIONSHIPS

This dimension (shown in the penultimate row of Table 4.1) concerns the salience of gender in social relationships. In childhood, it is the sex/ gender of parents, siblings, friends, acquaintances that is at issue. Later on, preferences develop for same-sex or other-sex lovers and mates. Since friendship, courtship, and marriage are topics for Chapter 6, our discussion here will be relatively brief.

An inchoate *understanding* of gender in social relationships begins in infancy. Babies younger than a year are able to discriminate between male and female adults. Voice pitch, odour, handling differences seem to provide cues. As well, infants make gender-specific responses to other babies. Children under two years prefer to gaze at pictures of same-sex infants, although adults cannot differentiate infant sex in the photographs (Losh-Hesselbart, 1987:543). According to Katz (1979:12), "infants apparently acquire rudimentary concepts about gender long before they know much else about the world."

As time goes on, children develop distinctive attachments to their mothers and fathers. In other words, children in most families "have qualitatively different types of relationship with each parent" (Lewis, 1986:98). For example, sons are intrigued with their fathers, who initiate more rough-and-tumble play; and are far more likely to seek out fathers to play. Fathers, more than mothers, tend to encourage sex-typed differences in their children, especially their sons (Lewis, 1986:100). Studies suggest that parents, especially fathers, interact more with same-sex children than with cross-sex children. Parents may feel a greater commonality and a greater responsibility for the socialization of their offspring of their own sex (Huston, 1983:430).

In the third year of life, children show strong preferences for same-sex playmates. In an interesting study, Jacklin and Maccoby (1978) placed previously unacquainted 33-month-old children together in a playroom. Adult observers could not identify the sex of these children, who all wore pants and T-shirts. However, the babies themselves somehow "knew" and directed more social behaviour toward playmates of the same sex. Apparently, very young boys do "something" that makes other babies wary. Other male babies find this "something" exciting and their tendency to withdraw is counterbalanced with positive attraction. The girls, less interested, retreat from male toddlers (Maccoby, 1980:214).

Between ages three and seven, children's preference for same-sex peers deepens (Huston, 1983:407). Throughout childhood, play continues to be sex-segregated (Richer, 1984). Although same-sex friendships remain important at all stages of life, other-sex friendships, both platonic and romantic, take on increasing significance from adolescence onwards.

Beginning in childhood, *identity* is influenced by the gender-based nature of relationships. Psychoanalytic theory, for example, traces the impact upon the ego and superego of relationships with same-sex and other-sex parents (Chapter 3). Throughout life, the sex/gender of peer relationships also shapes identity. Children are defined by others, and define themselves as girls who play with boys; as boys who play with girls (or who never do). As they grow up, they view themselves as someone with a boyfriend or girlfriend (or someone lacking a "relationship"). Whether adults are engaged to be married; wives or husbands; widowed or divorced are matters of great significance for themselves and other people.

Gender and sexuality tend to be fused and confused in people's minds. Past a certain age, same-sex associations are often assumed to be sexually motivated. Whether one is heterosexual or homosexual has enormous importance for self-perception. Many parents consider that homosexuality is one of the worst things that could happen to their offspring. "Before children have the vaguest idea about who or what is a homosexual, they learn that homosexuality is something frightening, horrid and nasty" (Pogrebin, 1983:39). Homosexuals are assumed to have the attributes of the other biological sex (Deaux and Kite, 1987:100). While hatred and fear of homosexuals does not prevent homosexuality, it may discourage androgyny in heterosexual boys. In other words, heterosexual boys may be reluctant to cultivate the sensitive, feminine side of their nature, for fear of being labelled gay. Certainly, homophobia adds "external cruelty to the internal feelings of alienation of homosexual youth" (Pogrebin, 1983:39). Recollections of homosexual men indicate early awareness of having been different

— having no male buddies, playing predominantly with girls, avoiding boys' games, being called sissy (Green, 1987:10-11). During childhood and adolescence, homosexual boys feel overwhelmed and confused by the heterosexuality of their age-mates. Homosexual subcultures are not usually found until they leave home (Brake, 1985:181).

Turning from identity to *Preferences and Values*, we note that attitudes towards self and other are reciprocal. As young people discover who they themselves are, they also develop attitudes about the place of sex/gender in other people's relationships. The celebration of masculinity in our culture means that male, heterosexual definitions prevail. Boys worry about being a "fairy" or a "fag" (Whitehurst and Booth, 1980:64). Gay young people find adolescence an extremely trying time (Herold, 1984:36). According to Bibby and Posterski (1985:84), "...as a group, homosexuals are the number one target of teenage humour." Seventy-four percent of Canadian teenagers feel that sexual relations between individuals of the same sex is wrong (79 percent of the males versus 69 percent of the females) (p. 84).

So far as *Expression of Gender-based Relations* is concerned, sex/gender acts as a major determinant of relationships throughout life. At the same time, involvement in these relationships serves as gender socialization. For example, Firestone (1978:100) wrote that:

It is not uncommon anywhere in Newfoundland to see a pair of boys facing each other with rocks, alternatively throwing and dodging. These duels can themselves be seen as the development of an ability to meet attack with composure and expectation that one's own hostility will be met in the same way.

Just as aggressive play teaches male participants about masculinity, chasing games, one of the most common forms of cross-sex play (Sutton-Smith, 1979), convey gender lessons to those involved. Richer (1984:168) had this to say about the Ontario kids he observed chasing:

The game...involves any number of girls chasing any number of boys. If the boy is caught a kiss can be given by one or several girls. In a variant of this, several boys might themselves catch one of their number and bring the typically wildly resisting boy to the girls to be kissed. Indeed, the boys often assist in this process by holding their peer down so that he can more easily meet his fate. (The image evoked is that of a sacrificial offering.)

The game of the seductive chase reinforces traditional gender patterns. This is so both because it demonstrates the greater desirability of males, and because it suggests implicitly that the main impetus for cross-sex interaction is sexual activity (p. 169).

Later relationships with members of both sexes continue to have gender implications. Especially for boys, peer acceptance is contingent upon acting out, in exaggerated ways, traditional features of male roles, such as being tough and being cool (Doyle, 1989:118). As sociologist Elaine Batcher (1987) discovered, sex/gender is an extremely important ingredient in high school friendship groups. Batcher spent considerable time with groups of Toronto high school students in malls, restaurants, and video-game parlours. She found that these groups centred around the boys; girls were "in" only on good behaviour:

Within the group, acceptable girls assume a range of roles....They are pals who can chum along and be the occasional butt of boys' humour, act as go-fers and remain good sports. They are the trial material on which boys can practise their social-sexual skills and may serve, in turn, as romantic interest ("When the guys in that group break up with one girl, they immediately start going out with another girl in that group"). Girls act as family members, mothers to the patriarchy, with supportive roles ("The girls are just there"). And there are the housekeeping functions of tidying the tables ("There's always such a mess when everybody leaves"), buying or paying for food ("While you're there get me a burger!"), and keeping track of commitments and class schedules ("When did he say that assignment was due?"). In short, while a friendly guy uses his contacts to build a power base, a friendly girl becomes part of someone else's power base. While a friendly boy becomes a wheel, a friendly girl becomes a go-fer (Batcher, 1987:157).

Understandably, these young women looked at themselves through male eyes. Girls attached to popular boys thought highly of themselves. Compliant girls described them-

selves as "muffins" (sweet, kind, caring), "marshmallows" (weak females who let others walk on them). Non-conformist females had to fight such labels as "tomboy," "sleaze bucket" and "slut."

Our intent is not to imply that all high school groups are like the ones Batcher studied. There is no single teen culture. Kostash (1987:55) identifies these varieties that were extant in the late 1980s:

Mods (elsewhere known as New Wavers), arty types who favour The Clash and baggy pants; Punkers, with their celebrated Mohawk-style hairdos, slam-dancing, and self-defined anarchism ("Apathy sucks!"); Headbangers, or aficionados of Heavy Metal bands and very tight jeans, the last of the greasers; Preppies, who are clothes-horses especially fond of Ralph Lauren designs, are fans of Duran Duran...There are also perennially...Brains and Jocks.

Nor do we mean to suggest that every human relationship revolves about sex/gender concerns. Rather, we wish to establish these two points: first, as youngsters are socialized, they learn that relationships are organized in terms of sex/gender (as well as other dimensions, such as age and ethnicity). Second, actual involvement in such relationships serves to reinforce their gender socialization. (This topic will be discussed at length in Chapter 6.)

STYLISTIC AND SYMBOLIC CONTENT

We come to the last of the content of gender socialization categories outlined in Table 4.1. Word choice, voice pitch and intonation, mannerisms, body language, and use of space — all these subtle behaviours enter into our society's definitions of femininity and masculinity. At the beginning of this chapter, we remarked that as Agnes, the transsexual moved from male to female categories, she had to master a higher voice pitch, different gestures and motor patterns, and new conversational tactics. Research shows that adults can use recorded speech samples to identify the sex/gender of hidden speakers with an accuracy far above chance expectation (Sachs, 1975:155). Nevertheless, most people "have few words for" (Haviland

and Malatesta, 1981:183) the barely conscious symbolic content of gender.

Awareness of Sex-typed Symbols. It seems paradoxical that although people often cannot articulate the stylistic aspects of gender, they may, nonetheless, respond strongly to stylistic deviance. For example, "A man who has a high, nasal voice and 'prissy' gestures may encounter considerably more social stigma than one who likes to cook or one who is nurturant" (Huston, 1983:391). Similarly, a woman who crosses her legs by resting her ankle on the opposite knee rather than placing one knee on the other, or who talks "rough and tough" may be as stylistically deviant as the proverbial limp-wristed male. Nevertheless, it is effeminate behaviour in males which arouses the most disapproval because being effeminate (like females) entails loss of status. The parallel situation of females displaying masculine styles is a more complicated double bind. For example, a woman with a sweet, gentle, polite manner of speaking may be seen to lack authority. Although it is fitting that she behave this way, her femininity is devalued. Yet, if she adopts a more masculine speech style or gestures, her behaviour may be interpreted as an aggressive power play, and resented (Sachs, 1975:169). As we shall emphasize in Chapter 7, subtle differences in speech, conversational style, and gestures mirror the relative power positions of the sexes in our society (Henley et al., 1985).

As the last column in Table 4.1 shows, gender socialization involves developing awareness of sex-typed symbols and incorporating them into one's self-perception. Children come to prefer the stylistic patterns associated with their own/sex gender, and to act out these preferred patterns. The neophyte also develops attitudes towards others' behaviours, approving appropriate sex-typed stylistic patterns and disapproving those deemed inappropriate by her/his particular culture. Because it is easier to see and hear other people's symbolic behaviour, we are probably less conscious of our own.

Unfortunately, relatively little is known about the ways in which females and males master the stylistic/symbolic content of gender, or about how its acquisition fits in with the other components of gender shown in Table 4.1

(Thorne and Henley, 1975:23). Expressive aspects of gender are so much a part of everyday life that they seem to be done automatically (Hall, 1984). Nevertheless, we know this content to be socially patterned and socially learned (Goffman, 1979:7). For the most part, the mechanisms of learning are observation and imitation, rather than direct tutelage. Parent-child interaction plays an important role in infancy and early childhood. From middle childhood, through adolescence and adulthood, peer groups exert a strong influence. Because so few studies dealing with actual learning are available, our discussion of the phases of gender socialization content (awareness, self-perception, preferences, and manifestation of verbal and non-verbal behaviour) will be telescoped. Instead, our treatment will follow a developmental logic to emphasize the lifelong nature of gender socialization. Important learning occurs in infancy and early childhood. Symbolic differences are accentuated during the courtship/mating stage of late adolescence and early adulthood. In late adulthood and old age, symbolic differences become muted.

The foundations for distinctive gender expression appear to be established in the sex-specific ways parents handle and communicate with infants. As noted earlier, within the first few months of life boys receive more touching, holding, and rocking than infant girls. In comparison, caregivers spend more time looking at and vocalizing to infant girls (Lewis, 1972). However, by the end of their first year, girls both receive and initiate more touching than do boys (Major, 1981:18).

Language, self, and social awareness are all acquired concurrently. Names form a basis for the development of the self and remain an integral part of social identity, including gender identity. As a first step toward self-awareness, the child learns his or her name. (I am Olivia. I am Oliver.) Even before the child's birth, parental speculations on its sex are often linked with the choice of name (Wolfenstein, 1968:268-69). A given name individualizes the infant and classifies it by sex/gender. Thus, baptizing a child "Tobias William" simultaneously separates this infant from other infants and indicates its maleness. Given names also communicate society's deferential evaluation of the sexes. For example, males are stigmatized by the feminine connotations of bisexual names such as Marion or Beverly. Females often receive male diminutives (Erica, Andrea, Stephanie); the reverse is more rare. Finally, boys are more likely than girls to be named after relatives, and "boys' names are more traditional, less currently fashionable than girls' names" (Rossi, 1965:504).

The complaints of parents who consulted a gender identity clinic tell us a great deal about the gender-related mannerisms and speech styles expected of preschool children (Green, 1974). A mother of a five-year-old boy is concerned about the way he walks, "swinging his hips, and to top it off, he has a slight lisp which drives me crazy" (p. 153). Another complains that her young son's habit of standing with his hands on his hips makes him come "across like a swishy little boy" (p. 266). Others worry because their boys use their hands like a girl, reject rough-and-tumble, boisterous play and messy behaviour, or are scared to death of balls (p. 278). By contrast, the garden variety of tomboyish behaviour in girls tends to be regarded as a passing phase which arouses little parental concern. However, the complaints of the parents of an extremely boyish girl began with her infant expressive behaviour: "From a tiny baby, she was never cuddly, where you could hold her. You would hold her a while, then she would become squirmish and active" (Green, 1974:282). As these clinical data indicate, parents, as socializing agents, hold definite expectations about the stylistic and symbolic content of gender. They become worried when their children's behaviour deviates from the norm.

Observational studies of elementary school children highlight the role played by the peer group in establishing and reinforcing the symbols of gender. In striving to be masculine, boys cultivate dirty talk. Although girls know dirty words too, boys flaunt their knowledge as a way of challenging adult authority (Thorne and Luria, 1986:180). Boys talk about girls in unflattering, sexually explicit terms. Though prepubescent, they try to convince one another that they are "sexually mature, active, and knowledgeable" (Fine, 1986:64). By contrast, the sexually related discourse of girls focusses less on dirty talk than on romantic themes. For example, girls skip to romantic verses, e.g. "first come love, then comes marriage, then along comes Cindy [name of jumper] with a baby carriage" (Thorne and Luria, 1986:184).

Children's non-verbal expressions of gender change as they grow older:

Kindergarten and first-grade boys touch one another frequently and with ease, with arms around shoulders, hugs, and holding hands. By fifth grade, touch among boys becomes more constrained, gradually shifting to mock violence and the use of poking, shoving, and ritual gestures like "giving five" (flat hand slaps) to express bonding (Thorne and Luria, 1986:182).

By contrast, fifth-grade girls often remain physically intimate with one another. They reciprocate cuddly touches, sit close together with arms and shoulders touching, stroke or comb friends' hair. Although girls also poke, shove, and give "high fives," their gestures tend to be more relaxed. In marked contrast to the boys, girls disclose feelings to one another and monitor one another's emotions (Thorne and Luria, 1986:183).

According to journalist Myrna Kostash's (1987) interviews of Edmonton, Vancouver, and Toronto teenage girls, the stylistic content of gender preoccupies adolescents. She tells us that, "a great deal of time is spent in shopping for and buying and applying the accoutrements of femininity — clothes and cosmetics — so that in a very material sense 'leisure' is usefully employed in keeping up with the current codes of femininity and attractiveness" (p. 261). Chapter 7 returns to the topic of symbolic gender socialization.

Our general treatment of the content of gender socialization is now concluded. Next, we turn to various theories of socialization which attempt to explain systematically how this content is learned.

THEORIES OF GENDER SOCIALIZATION

This chapter has approached sex/gender differences as the product of socialization, not biology. However, simply to conclude that these differences are learned still leaves a great deal unsaid. Exactly how does the learning of the gender components outlined in Table 4.1 occur?

Three major theoretical perspectives attempt to explain the detailed processes involved in gender socialization: the *symbolic interactionist, social learning* and *cognitive-developmental* theories.[4] None of these theories was developed to explain gender socialization specifically. Rather, they are all general social psychological theories that are applicable to other aspects of human development, as well as sex-typed behaviour. These perspectives vary in their explanation of how learning occurs and what socialization comprises. Nevertheless, because all have something to contribute to our understanding of gender socialization, it is useful to treat them as complementary rather than competing sets of ideas.

In the pages to follow, the task is *not* comprehensive description of these theoretical perspectives. Rather, the problem is to assess how each theory helps us to understand how people learn the five components of gender content outlined in Table 4.1.

Symbolic Interactionism

Symbolic interactionism began with the American pragmatic philosophers of the late nineteenth and early twentieth centuries — William James, John Dewey, and especially, George Herbert Mead. Sociologists Charles Horton Cooley, W.I. Thomas, and Max Weber were important turn-of-the century contributors. Contemporary refinements in the perspective have been made by many sociologists, notably Herbert Blumer, Manford Kuhn, and Erving Goffman (Stryker, 1981).

Symbolic interactionism embraces a core set of assumptions (Mackie, 1987:110ff.) Interactionists emphasize the distinction between *homo sapiens* and lower animals. To them, distinctively human behaviour is symbolic behaviour. The term *symbol* indicates that people do not typically respond directly to stimuli, but assign meanings to stimuli, and act on the basis of these meanings. These meanings are shared definitions of the situation. Femininity and

masculinity rank high among the important social definitions people learn. These definitions are products of social interaction, especially interaction with significant others. *Significant others* are socialization agents who are emotionally important to the child, e.g., parents. Role-taking is the basic mechanism through which interaction occurs. *Role-taking* (taking the role of the other) means "imaginatively assuming the position or point of view of another person" (Lindesmith and Strauss, 1968:282).

The axioms of symbolic interactionism include a picture of human nature. This theory holds that people are not born human, but become capable of distinctively human thought and conduct only through association with significant others. Human beings are social beings. They are symbol-creating, symbol-using creatures, who have, to a considerable extent, become liberated from biological programming (Turner, 1978:327). Each individual possesses a mind with the rational ability to understand symbols, and the capacity to make moral judgments (Deegan, 1987:4). Each develops a self, which "...is essentially a social structure, and it arises in social experience" (Mead, 1934:140). The formation of self is a crucial aspect of the socialization process (Manis and Meltzer, 1978).[5]

The most useful contribution of symbolic interactionists to the theoretical explanation of gender socialization lies in their systematic attention to the development of the self (Cahill, 1980). For them, gender identity, the inner sense of maleness or femaleness, constitutes one aspect of self. Built upon this conviction of one's own gender, the self-concept eventually incorporates the perception of oneself as possessing various traits (personal-social attributes) that are culturally defined as masculine or feminine. Interactionists assume that language capabilities and self-awareness develop concurrently. Put another way, the stylistic/symbolic content of gender is central to this perspective. Interactionism also acknowledges the importance to socialization of the child's relationships with significant others (parents, peers). For these reasons, we conclude that what symbolic interactionists have to say about gender socialization enhances our understand-

ing of gender identity, gender-based social relationships, and stylistic-symbolic content
(Table 4.1).

Every Canadian child learns society's rules
of correspondence between sex and gender as
they pertain to self, others, and relations between self and others. The fundamentals of
gender socialization are mastered surprisingly
early. Preparatory gender learning begins in
the first weeks and months of life (Cahill,
1980:126). The child's interaction with caregivers begins immediately after birth and
thereafter "every succeeding exchange between [parents and child] can be viewed as an
instance of socialization" (Lindesmith et al.,
1977:313). The groundwork for both gender
identity and language is well established between 18 months and three years (Huston,
1983:407). This is why most authorities regard
the age ceiling for sex/gender reassignment
procedures for hermaphrodites to be three
years (Money and Ehrhardt, 1972:13).[6]

The very young infant has no conception of
what belongs to its body and what does not:

At six or eight months he has certainly formed no
clear notion of himself. He does not even know the
boundaries of his own body. Each hand wandering
over the bedspread for things which can be brought
into the mouth discovers the other hand and each triumphantly lifts the other into his mouth; he draws
his thumb from his mouth to wave it at a stranger,
then cries because the thumb has gone away. He
pulls at his toes until they hurt and does not know
what is wrong (Murphy et al., 1937, quoted in Lindesmith et al., 1977:315-16).

Understanding of "me" and "not me" comes
with the concurrent acquisition of language,
self, and social awareness. Both language and
development of self involve "taking the role of
the other." In order to use language and to
acquire a self, the child must be able to adopt
the perspective of other people toward him-
self/herself.

Language provides names for self, others,
and environmental objects. Names permit the
child both to differentiate self from other objects and to participate in group life. It would be
almost impossible to exaggerate the import of
language. Since the structure and content of
language semantically derogate women

(Schulz, 1975), language itself has a subtle, but
profound effect on the child's eventual comprehension of gender. (See Chapter 7.)

Let's begin at the beginning with an infant
who lacks language. Though experts find it
difficult to establish how the child obtains its
earliest symbols, some "initiative" seems required of the child: "parents imitate the noises
and sounds of their very young children in
greater degree than these children imitate the
noises and sounds of parents" (Stone,
1962:105). Through babbling, the infant accidentally hits on a word-like sound ("ma-ma").
Impressed caregivers imitate the word.
Through repetition, the sound becomes a significant symbol in parent-child interaction.
Gradually, the child learns to imitate adult
sounds and to associate sounds with sensations. The child has made two momentous
discoveries: things have names; *he* or *she* has a
name (Hewitt, 1984:96-97)!

Names form a basis for the development of
the self. Naming a child "Joel" simultaneously
separates this infant from other infants and
signifies its maleness. The "earliest self-identi-
fication with a gender label may be no more
complicated than accepting one's own name"
(Sherif, 1982:378). By repeatedly asking,
"What's that?" What's that?", the child learns
the names of things. Caregivers answer,
"That's a panda bear. That's a car. That's
Grandpa." The capacity to use language allows
the child to learn the meaning of all these
things, including herself or himself. Learning
his/her own name permits differentiation of
self from other objects in the environment. At
some primitive level, the child reasons: "That is
a teddy bear. That is a car. I am Joel." "By
hearing his name repeatedly the child gradually sees himself as a distinct and recurrent
point of reference" (Allport, 1961:115).

As the next step in the genesis of self, children learn not only that "things have names"
but "names have things" (Lindesmith et al.,
1977:289). In other words, children come to
appreciate the characteristics of objects, including themselves. A kitten is a soft, four-legged
creature with a miaow and a tail. A fire is red,
hot, and dangerous. Duncan is a fat, little but-
terball, who hates spinach, whines sometimes,
but is a very good boy. Later on, mastering the

"things of names" also entails learning the meaning of abstract terms, whose meaning cannot be grasped by pointing to an example in the environment (e.g., God, playing fair, being ladylike).

As noted in earlier sections, the child's significant others act differently towards female and male babies. That is, caregivers associate sex-designating labels ("girl," "boy") with gender distinctive interaction with the child. For example, for the first six months or so, male infants are touched more, while female infants are talked to more (Lewis, 1972). Later, the male toddler is tossed into the air ("How's my big boy?"), while the female child is tickled under the chin ("How's my sweet little girl?") (Richmond-Abbott, 1983:102). In short, gender differences in interactional experiences are associated with gender-designating labels (Cahill, 1980).

Children learn to respond to themselves as significant others respond to them. This fundamental observation was established by pioneer symbolic interactionist, Charles Horton Cooley (1902). Cooley used the metaphor of the looking glass to illustrate the idea that children acquire a self through adopting other people's attitudes towards them. The child learns, for example, that he is a boy, that boys are valuable, tough, and so on, and that gender is a matter of consequence in Canadian society. Somewhere between 18 months and three years, this self-categorization as male or female has become a major axis of identity.

In the child's early years, self-development involves taking the role of significant others. Eventually, the child is able to take the role of what Mead (1934) called the generalized other — the generalized standpoint of society as a whole. The *generalized other* "is not a concrete, specific other person, but an abstract other — one's conception of the ideal expectations to which one is subject" (Hewitt, 1984:84). Instead of a child thinking, "Dad says I mustn't cry when I don't get my own way," the more mature youngster can now think, *"They* say boys mustn't cry." However, in a complex society such as Canada, there is not just one generalized other, but many. This means that gender norms represented in the perspective of society as a whole receive different interpretations in

social class, ethnic, religious, and regional subcultures. For example, the societal expectation that females should be more nurturant than males is particularized by many male blue-collar workers to mean that "women belong at home with the kids; " women in the labour force are "robbing male breadwinners of family income..." (Gray, 1987:384).

Symbolic interactionism appeals to many feminist sociologists because it hold out the possibility of a better social world. The perspective makes provision for social change in its thesis "that people are socially created and that people can create new societies in which to live" (Deegan, 1987:3). For one thing, it posits a self that encompasses both a socially defined facet and a spontaneous, creative facet (Mead, 1934). The *Me* represents internalized societal attitudes and expectations. The *I*, on the other hand, is the acting, unique, unfettered self. In other words, the self is composed not only of a pliant "Me," but the non-conforming "I," able to reflect upon and sometimes to reject societal dictates.

A second potential source of change lies in symbolic interactionism's emphasis on the social construction of meaning. In the words of Yoels and Karp (1978:31):

From the interactionist perspective, society exists through the symbolic communication occurring between persons. Since...there is no inherent meaning in an object, it is always possible for persons, through their symbolic activity, to re-define objects in ways that challenge pre-existent definitions of reality.

Take gender as an "object" of symbolic activity. If gender is viewed as social construction, then these definitions of the situation are alterable. Obviously, this theoretical tenet is congruent with the goals of feminism. According to Goffman (1977:302), "the chief consequence of the women's movement is not the direct improvement of the lot of women but the weakening of the doctrinal beliefs that heretofore have underpinned the sexual division of desserts and labor."

Symbolic interactionism, like all theories of gender socialization, has gaps and deficiencies. Other aspects of gender socialization are handled better by other theoretical traditions.

In order to supplement the insights gained thus far, we next consider cognitive-developmental theory.

Cognitive-developmental Theory

Our second theoretical approach to gender socialization is primarily the work of one scholar, Lawrence Kohlberg (1966; Kohlberg & Ullian, 1974). Kohlberg built his ideas about the acquisition of gender upon Jean Piaget's (1928) theory of the systematic changes in children's thought patterns that occur over time. Kohlberg agrees with the symbolic interactionists that self-labelling as girl or boy is the first step in gender socialization. However, the cognitive-developmental approach advances our understanding of gender socialization in several ways. This approach provides a systematic explanation for sex/gender constancy; the greater value attached to own sex/gender; as well as knowledge about and preference for sex-typed personality characteristics, activities/interests, and same-sex relationships (Table 4.1).

At the core of cognitive-developmental theory is the idea that children possess a powerful need to make sense of their world. The child is seen to be *actively* involved in the selection and organization (structuring) of perception, knowledge, and understanding (Mussen, 1969:724). For this reason, cognitive-developmental theory has been described as a "self-socialization"theory (Maccoby and Jacklin, 1974:364).

Nonetheless, the fact that the child is immature means that the reality of the child differs qualitatively from that of the adult. Piaget's observations on the concept of conservation of physical properties provide us with an illustration of this difference. The intellectual operations of the child under six years of age rely heavily on what can be perceived in the here and now. There is difficulty in imagining changed circumstances. If liquid is poured from a short, wide container into a tall, thin container, the child will state that the latter contains more water. Only the higher water level is noticed. If asked to imagine that the contents of the tall container are poured once

again into the short one, the child has difficulty handling this mental reversal. The structure of children's thinking changes in discrete stages until eventually they do show an adult's "accurate" view of the world (Kessler and McKenna, 1978:96).

Kohlberg (1966) argues that children's notions about sex/gender constitute "the child's cognitive organization of the social world in a manner that parallels the cognitive organization of the physical world" (Huston, 1983:397). Their comprehension of gender is a function of their stage of cognitive development. Kohlberg agrees with the symbolic interactionists that gender socialization begins with self-labelling. However, the distinction between male and female is seen by Kohlberg to arise from a judgment of physical reality. Because genitals are usually concealed, children use cues of size, clothing, hair style. In the first two or three years of life, youngsters learn the words "boy" and "girl" and apply them to themselves and to others. Of major importance to this theory is the proposition that self-categorization as "girl" or "boy" serves the child's need to understand the world by organizing incoming information and attitudes (Huston, 1983:397).

Young children are unable to grasp either physical constancy in general, or sex/gender constancy in particular. Until they can understand the concept of conservation despite transformation (described above), they do not have permanent gender identities. Until they understand that the amount of water does not change when poured from one kind of container to another, they also do not grasp that a boy does not become a girl when he abandons trucks for dolls. At the age of five or six, the child develops the concept of conservation, including the idea that gender is invariant. Sex/gender constancy consists of understanding that sex/gender does not change over time ("I am a girl, I will always be a girl"); it is not altered by transformation of observable characteristics ("A woman remains a woman whether she wears a skirt or pants, has long or short hair, is a nurse or a cab driver"); and that gender is not altered by wishing (Huston, 1983:398).

Once constancy has been achieved, the concept of sex/gender becomes considerably more significant as an organizer of the child's understanding of self and environment. This insight motivates behaviour: "I am a boy, and therefore I should act like a boy and do the things that boys do," or "I am a girl and therefore I should act like a girl and do the things girls do."

As children seek actively to understand their social world, they come to "label themselves — call it alpha — and determine that there are alphas and betas in the environment. Given the cognitive-motivational properties of the self, ...the child moves toward other alphas and away from betas. That is, it is the child who realizes which gender he or she is, and in what behaviors he or she should engage" (Lewis and Brooks-Gunn, 1979:270).

Youngsters actively seek further information about the attributes, interests, and activities of people who share their sex/gender. Same-sex adult models are important sources of information. However, children also learn from age mates and the mass media. They value more highly same-sex playmates and activities (and devalue other-sex associations) *after* sex/gender constancy has been acquired.

It is important to understand that children's motive for gender socialization, for the acquisition of sex-typed information and preferences (Table 4.1) is their need for self-consistency and self-esteem. They are strongly motivated to understand what people who share the sex/gender label with them are like. Their self-esteem is enhanced by awarding high value to people and activities similar to themselves (Huston, 1983:398). Bem (1983:601) explains:

In essence, then, cognitive-developmental theory postulates that, because of the child's need for cognitive consistency, self-categorization as female or male motivates her or him to value that which is seen as similar to the self in terms of gender. This gender-based value system, in turn, motivates the child to engage in gender-congruent activities, to strive for gender-congruent attributes, and to prefer gender-congruent peers.

The views of gender held by children six to eight years old tend to be very rigid and moralistic (Maccoby, 1980:237). Playing with dolls or wearing a dress is seen as just as wrong for a boy as breaking a window or stealing from mother's purse. Children in this phase are uncompromisingly stereotypical in their gender attitudes. Maccoby (1980:237) suggests that, "Children may simply be exaggerating sex roles in order to get them cognitively clear." Perhaps cognitive clarity helps them to establish firmly their own gender identity. After this has happened, they can afford to be more flexible. As noted earlier, older children hold gender stereotypes less rigidly.

Cognitive-developmental theorists argue that other theories, such as the social learning and psychoanalytic approaches, have overstressed the socialization role of parents relative to that of peers and the media. Because children positively value the acquisition of sex-related characteristics and behaviour, gender learning occurs with very little direct instruction from parents or anyone else (Brophy, 1977:251). However, cognitive developmentalists do acknowledge that "a family climate of warmth, expressiveness, security...and high social perception" may facilitate gender socialization because it "allows for the explanation and interpretation of the new and problematic" (Kohlberg, 1966:156).

How should the cognitive-developmental theory be judged? Although the approach is not without some problems (which we will get to in a moment), it has provoked enthusiastic appraisals. Empirical support exists for many of Kohlberg's ideas. For example, data demonstrate that the timing of gender learning is closely associated with the timing of cognitive development (Coker, 1984; Leahy & Shirk, 1984). Kohlberg and Zigler (1967) have shown that gender learning is more closely associated with children's general brightness than with chronological age or similarity to the same-sex parent. Children who are cognitively more mature than their age-mates show earlier awareness of gender differences. However, while strong sex-typing is associated with high intelligence in young children, it is associated with low intelligence in adolescents. Therefore, cognitive growth involves acquiring less rigid notions of gender roles (Stockard and Johnson, 1980:196).

Cognitive-developmental theory does present some difficulties. For one thing, many studies find that sex-typed preferences for playmates and toys exist *before* development of gender constancy. Cognitive-developmentalists' contention that this sex-typing becomes more pronounced after gender constancy is grasped has not been consistently supported by empirical research (Basow, 1986:116). Secondly, Kohlberg's work employed male samples; its applicability to females is therefore questionable. Because of the higher prestige males enjoy in our society, the socialization process as described by cognitive-developmental theorists works out more clearly for boys than for girls. It is logically consistent for boys to identify with males who are similar, powerful, and prestigious in our society. However, Kohlberg has trouble explaining why girls should not also identify with men. Finally, neither cognitive-developmental theory nor symbolic interactionism can explain why males are more compulsive about their masculinity than females are about their femininity. Our third approach to gender socialization — social learning theory — complements our understanding by addressing some of these concerns.

Social Learning Theory

The social learning approach to gender socialization extrapolates from the general psychology of learning certain principles about how organisms acquire new responses. "Sex-typed behavior has no special theoretical status; it is learned by the same mechanisms that apply to all kinds of social behavior" (Huston, 1983:396). This perspective explains female-male differences in personality and role behaviour as the product of environmental influences upon the child. Therefore, in comparison with symbolic interactionist and cognitive-developmental theories, social learning theory posits a passive child who is the recipient of one-way influence from socialization agents.

Learning theory adopts the methodological position of *behaviourism*, i.e., the conviction that psychology should deal only with "observables," and that it is unnecessary for the psychologist to speculate about how the organism (rat, pigeon, or human) experiences learning. This focus upon behaviour (rather than on what goes on inside the organism's head),

means that learning theory pertains most to the *gender expression* column of Table 4.1. That is, this approach is more suited to explain why people *display* sex-typed clothing, *engage* in sex-typed games, *associate* with same-sex peers, and *manifest* sex-typed verbal behaviour, than to elucidate people's internalized beliefs or preferences.

Learning theory includes two alternative mechanisms by which sex/gender differences are acquired (Mischel, 1970; Bandura and Walters, 1963). The reinforcement, or direct shaping, approach emphasizes the rewards and punishments children receive for gender-appropriate and gender-inappropriate behaviour. The imitation approach considers the vicarious learning that observation and modelling provides (Bem, 1983:600). These two viewpoints about how learning takes place are not mutually exclusive. Each has supporting evidence. We consider them in turn:

REINFORCEMENT LEARNING

The direct shaping approach considers that parents, teachers, etc. set out deliberately to train children to acquire sex-typed behaviour (Losh-Hesselbart, 1987:544ff.). They reinforce or reward instances of sex-appropriate behaviour, and punish gender-inappropriate behaviour. Rewards are *positive reinforcers:* children are likely to repeat the behaviour that elicited approval, praise, or presents. For example, if a mother rewards her little girl with a smile when she chooses to wear a frilly dress rather than blue jeans, the child is likelier than she otherwise would be to choose a dress in the future. *Reinforcers* are considered to be negative if they have aversive effects on the children's behaviour, so that they will refrain from the behaviour in order to avoid the negative consequences. If a boy's friends call him a "wimp" and a "nerd" for being afraid to challenge adult authority, the boy is more likely the next time to conform to peer expectations.

Common sense suggests (and research shows) that children do learn many of their general socialization lessons through operant conditioning. (Parents positively reinforce desired verbal responses, such as "please" and "thank you." They punish unwanted behaviour such as rude talk, selfishness, or taking candy from stores without paying for it.) However, to be "a viable explanation of sexrole acquisition, it must be demonstrated that parents and other socializers differentially reinforce and punish boys and girls in accordance with sex-role standards (Frieze et al., 1978:107). The role played by direct shaping in inculcating gender socialization lessons has been somewhat controversial (Block, 1984; Maccoby and Jacklin, 1974). All authorities agree that parents do reinforce young children for publicly visible behaviours, such as sex-appropriate clothing, toy choice, and play activities. As discussed earlier, youngsters' contribution to household division of labour is still influenced by sex/gender. Cross-cultural evidence from six societies (Whiting and Edwards (1973) showed that girls are assigned cooking, child-care, and cleaning jobs around the home, while boys are given responsibility for chores that take them away from the home, such as herding animals.

Nevertheless, the evidence concerning shaping of children's personalities according to gender stereotypes is less clear. After reviewing a great deal of research, Maccoby and Jacklin (1974) concluded that beyond encouraging sex-typed clothing and activities, parents apparently did not differentially reinforce such personality traits as dependence in their daughters and aggressiveness in their sons. However, Block (1984) argued that Maccoby and Jacklin's "no difference" conclusion was, in part, the consequence of the fact that the studies they reviewed tended to focus exclusively on *mothers* as socialization agent. Because fathers are generally more concerned about inculcating sex-appropriate behaviour, overlooking their potential influence had been a significant omission. Fathers differentiate more than mothers in their behaviour toward their children, so that paternal shaping may be the more important. For example, girls encouraged by their father to do well more often achieve in school and plan less sex-typed occupational careers (Losh-Hesselbart, 1987:546).

In addition to criticizing earlier research for neglecting the role of fathers, Block (1984) made a strong case for the child's age as an important variable in gender socialization. According to Block, sex/gender differentiation in socialization increases with the age of the child, reaching a maximum during the high school years (p. 85). She points out that Maccoby and Jacklin (1974) arrived at their "no difference" conclusion because earlier research was limited to very young children. Moreover, age and sex of child interact. That is, parental pressures are put on boys and girls at different ages. During childhood, the male role is the more inflexible one and pressures from parents (and peers) are experienced earlier. Socialization agents "are more concerned about 'masculine' behavior in boys than about 'feminine' behaviour in girls" (Losh-Hesselbart, 1987:546). Therefore, "boys receive both more blame, reprimands, and punishment for 'bad' behavior and more praise and encouragement for 'good' behavior than girls" (p. 545). For instance, Lambert, Yackley and Hein (1971) report a consistent tendency for both French-Canadian and English-Canadian parents to be harsher with boys than girls. The authors suggest that "Canadian parents may be reacting to the stereotype that girls are not to be as severely reprimanded as boys, as though the latter were tougher."

By contrast, pressures on girls to act feminine increase in early adolescence, as they become physically mature and capable of becoming pregnant. Bardwick and Douvan (1971:227-28) put it this way:

Since girls are less likely to masturbate, run away from home, or bite and draw blood, their lives are relatively free from crisis until puberty. Before that girls do not have to conform to threatening new criteria of acceptability to anywhere near the extent that boys do. When boys are pressured to give up their childish ways it is because those behaviors are perceived as feminine by parents. Boys have to earn their masculinity early. Until puberty, femininity is a verbal label, a given attribute — something that does not have to be earned.

The above observations help to explain the "compulsive masculinity" of boys.

According to Block's (1984) longitudinal research, school-age girls and boys are indeed differentially socialized according to sex-typed expectations. This shaping encourages, for example, aggressiveness, active play, exploration of the environment, and problem-solving in boys. Such socialization experiences, she suggests, are conducive to the development of "wings" in boys — "which permit leaving the nest, exploring far reaches, and flying alone" (p. 137). By contrast, more circumscribed, more emotional behaviour is encouraged in girls. Their milieu "is more socially interactive, is more structured, provides less feedback, and stresses familial interdependence and respon-sibilities" (p. 138). Such a learning environment is more conducive to the development of "roots" — "roots that anchor, stabilize, and support growth" (p. 138). Block goes on to describe "roots" and "wings" as conjugate legacies:

Wings without roots may eventuate in unfettered, adventurous souls – free spirits who, however, may lack commitment, civility, and relatedness. Roots without wings may issue prudent, dependable, nurturing, but tethered individuals — responsible beings who may lack independence, self-direction, and a sense of adventure. In reviewing the literature on the socialization of female children and adoles-cents, it is difficult to escape the conclusion that, at least until very recently, females in our society are "oversocialized," having been bequeathed roots without wings (Block, 1984:138).

In summary, empirical evidence suggests that reinforcement principles play a substantial role in children's gender display of clothing, activities, and interests, and personality char-acteristics (insofar as the sexes actually differ in personality). However, direct training and administration of rewards and punishments seems to be too simplistic to account, by them-selves, for the richness and complexity of much gender behaviour (Katz, 1979:5). Consider the stylistic/symbolic dimension of gender (Table 4.1). Reinforcement learning is a tedious, trial-and-error process. Much sex-typed behaviour, such as language, is learned far too quickly, is far too pervasive and subtle to be explained by a gradual shaping process (Nielsen, 1978:117). "Besides, most adults are not aware of the many mannerisms, gestures, and speech habits that are part of their [sex/gender repertoire]" (Tavris and Wade, 1984:214). For all of these reasons, the imitation/modelling learning mechanism contributes additional explanatory power to social learning theory.

MODELLING/IMITATION

According to this approach, learning can occur through watching other people's behaviour, observing the consequences of their behaviour, and attending to symbolic material, such as storybooks and television (Bandura, 1977). Large "chunks" of behaviour are acquired this way, rather than the piecemeal behaviours implied by the direct reinforcement approach. The main proposition is that children learn gendered behaviour through imitation of same-sex models.

This version of social learning theory makes an important distinction between the learning and actual performance of behaviours. A reper-toire of potential responses can be acquired through observation (Losh-Hesselbart, 1987:547). Reinforcement (rewards, punish-ments) need not be involved for this learning to occur. The child has usually absorbed more information than is typically revealed in be-haviour (Katz, 1979:5). Actual expression of this behaviour may be delayed indefinitely. Indeed, the evidence suggests that children learn the attitudes and behaviour patterns as-sociated with both sexes. However, they con-fine their performance to that which is associ-ated with their own sex/gender (Hargreaves, 1986:34). Whether behaviours are actually per-formed depends on what happens to the model and what happens to the imitator (Losh-Hesselbart, 1987:548). In short, rewards and punishments play an important part in encour-aging or discouraging overt performance of what people know.

The logic of this approach posits that children's accomplishment of gender socializa-tion depends first and foremost upon their imitation of same-sex parents. Unfortunately, the evidence concerning this key point is am-biguous. Research shows that, other things being equal, children will imitate the more dominant, powerful figure rather than the less dominant, and will imitate the more nurturant rather than the less nurturant model. The diffi-culty is that no compelling theoretical reason is given to explain why the power or nurturance of a model should affect the two sexes differ-ently.[7]

The problem, to restate, is "why children of

the two sexes should learn different things — sex-typed things" (Maccoby and Jacklin, 1974:287). Two possibilities have been put forth: (1) that the same-sex model is more available, and (2) when both same-sex and opposite-sex models are available, children select on the basis of perceived similarity. In neither case are the empirical data persuasive (Maccoby and Jacklin, 1974:286-90). With regard to similarity, Stockard and Johnson (1980:188) point out that while there is some evidence that older children tend to imitate selectively, it is difficult "to see how very young children who have not established a concept of their own sex could know which parent they were more similar to." The vagueness of learning theorists about gender identity — about how and when gender identity is acquired — compounds the problem. Stockard and Johnson (1980:188) go on to point out that,

In fact, correlation studies of parent-child similarities find that children are not especially similar to their own parents, and that it is not at all clear that girls are more like their mothers and boys are more like their fathers. This is true for both young children and young adults, and for both non-sex-typed and sex-typed behavior.

The proposition that girls learn to be feminine by identifying with their mothers and boys learn to be masculine by identifying with their fathers is far too simplistic. One resolution of this dilemma proposes that children grow up observing models of both sexes, but through rewards and punishments, eventually learn the expedience of restricting imitative behaviour to same-sex models. An additional possibility acknowledges the many different, and sometimes conflicting, influences in children's lives (Tavris and Wade, 1984:214).

Both of the above ideas are involved in David Lynn's (1969) attempt to explain the puzzle of "compulsive masculinity." Lynn postulates that because of the greater availability, during early childhood, of the mother (and other female authority figures, such as daycare workers and teachers), as well as relative absence of the father (and other male models) during early childhood, little girls easily develop their gender identity through imitation and positive reinforcement. However, little

boys must shift from their initial identification with the mother to masculine identification. Since male models are scarce (being away at work), boys have greater difficulty than girls in achieving gender indentity. According to Lynn, males must learn by intellectually piecing together the problem of definitions of masculinity. Some of this learning comes from peers and from media presentation of gender stereotypes. Some results from punishment for displays of feminine behaviour. Hartley (1959:457) notes that for boys, "the desired behaviour is rarely defined positively as something the child *should* do, but rather, undesirable behaviour is indicated negatively as something he should *not* do or be [emphasis in original]." As a consequence, males remain anxious about gender throughout life. As adults, they are more hostile toward both the opposite sex and homosexuals than are females. According to one viewpoint (Kessler and McKenna, 1978:100), the higher incidence of "gender disorders," such as transvestism, transsexualism, and paraphelias (preference for unusual sexual practices) among men reflects the precarious nature of male development. Despite his initial confusion about his gender identity, the boy learns to prefer the masculine role to the feminine one. "He is rewarded simply for having been born masculine through countless privileges accorded males but not females" (Lynn, 1969).

This section has reviewed three theoretical approaches to gender learning: symbolic interactionism, cognitive-developmental theory, and social learning theory. As we have seen, all of them contribute to our understanding of gender socialization. Since their individual strengths and weaknesses have been discussed with reference to Table 4.1, there is no need to reiterate them here. However, these theoretical perspectives share certain limitations which merit mention.

First, all these approaches offer more complete and satisfactory explanations for the acquisition of masculinity than for the acquisition of femininity (Kessler and McKenna, 1978:100). Feminist theorists are attempting to rectify this deficiency. For example, Gilligan (1982) has attempted to rethink some cognitive-developmental generalizations about morality so that they apply more accurately to both sexes. Her controversial ideas will be discussed in Chapter 5.

Secondly, all three approaches are very rational in orientation. Unlike Freudian theory (Chapter 3), none really conveys the passion aroused by sex/gender. Indeed, because our male-dominated society defines cognitive activities as superior to sentiment, no sociology of feelings and emotions existed before the resurgence of feminism. Feminist scholars' amendments of symbolic interactionism to include emotionality are valuable contributions (Hochschild, 1975; 1979). After all, gender norms encompass rules about feeling, as well as thinking and behaving. Women are the sentimental sex. They "bear the chief emotional burden of caring for human life from the cradle to the grave..." (Brownmiller, 1984:218). Men, on the other hand, "have the tough mental fiber, the intellectual muscle, to stay in control" (Brownmiller, 1984:208). Because competitive action and physical aggression flow from angry feelings, anger is the exception to male inexpressiveness. However, anger in a woman isn't nice. "An angry woman is hard, mean and nasty; she is unreliably, unprettily out of control" (Brownmiller, 1984:210).

CONCLUSIONS

Chapter 4 is the first of several chapters to treat the development of femininity and masculinity from the social-psychological point of view. In the social-psychological perspective, interest centres simultaneously on the individual and on the social context in which the individual operates. Social, as opposed to biological, influences are emphasized.

Three topics were considered in this chapter: the definitions of general socialization and gender socialization; the content of socialization lessons; and the major theories of gender socialization (symbolic interactionism, cognitive-developmental theory, and social learning). The focus has been on primary socialization, on the childhood and adolescent learning which lays the foundation for subsequent so-

cialization. The chapters to follow will have more to say about the learning which occurs beyond the formative years. This treatment of secondary socialization occurs in the context of discussion of the various socialization agencies.

NOTES

1. This chapter draws upon the author's previous writing on socialization: Mackie (1987; 1990).
2. Androgyny is currently under critical review by feminists (McCormack, 1983; Sedney, 1989). Androgyny has been called a "sexist myth in disguise" (Harris, 1974) because it ends up affirming the prestige and power of masculinity. Since our society rewards and admires masculine behaviour, androgyny benefits women more than men (Pyke, 1980). With the possible exception of a few male pop idols, it is women who do most of the gender-blending. Critics say androgyny really does not eliminate gender stereotypes; it just combines them in new ways (Lott, 1981).
   Some feminists look beyond androgyny (the combination of feminine and masculine traits in the personality), to an ideal state where femininity and masculinity are transcended or superseded as ways of labelling and experiencing psychological traits and being well-adjusted human beings (Bem, 1983; Garnets and Pleck, 1979; Hefner, Rebecca and Oleshansky, 1975). In other words, for many feminist scholars, the goal has moved from *either/or* of sex-typing, to *both* of androgyny, to *neither* of gender transcendence.
3. Goffman (1976:691) refers to the behavioural expression of gender as *gender display*: "If gender be defined as the culturally established correlates of sex (whether in consequence of biology or learning), then gender display refers to conventionalized portrayals of these correlates."
4. The psychoanalytic perspective, which contributes additional insight into the acquisition of gender, was dealt with as a biologically based theory of psychosexual development in Chapter 3.
5. The topic of socialization is the most intensively developed topic among those studied by symbolic interactionists. As Ishwaran (1979:5) wrote: "It is the symbolic interactionists who have provided the main impetus of the sociological enthusiasm with child development or 'development of human nature.'"

6. Some authorities, e.g., Maccoby (1980) argue that sex/gender reassignment can still be effective in hermophrodites older than three years.
7. Recall that psychoanalytic theory posits the identification of the child with same-sex parent as the principal mechanism for sex-typing. In that theory, the motivation for choosing the parent of the same sex is made quite clear. To reiterate, this identification is the result of discovery of genital differences, penis-envy, and castration anxiety, and resolution of Oedipal conflict. See Chapter 3.

Chapter 5

The Family as Primary Agent of Gender Socialization

Chapter 5 continues the discussion of gender socialization begun in the previous chapter. The business of this chapter, as well as the two to follow, is the contribution made by particular *agencies of socialization*. Where do people get their ideas about gender? What influences impinge upon them to shape their attitudes and behaviour in accordance with societal notions of femininity and masculinity? Alternatively, what inspires some individuals to rebel against traditional gender arrangements?

Socialization occurs in many settings and in interaction with many people, organized into groupings of various kinds. Each grouping exerts particular kinds of effects on children and each has more or less distinctive functions in preparing children for social life. Each may therefore be called an agency of socialization (Elkin and Handel, 1984:123).

Although the various agencies of gender socialization tend to reinforce one another's efforts, they have somewhat idiosyncratic interpretations of the definitions of masculinity and femininity current in their particular culture. The purpose of this chapter is to consider the role played by the family in gender socialization.

Sociologists describe the family as a primary agent of socialization. The *primary* versus *secondary* relationship is a long-standing distinction in the discipline. Primary relationships involve frequent close contact and a high degree of personal involvement. They generally take place in small, informal groups. By contrast, secondary relationships involve infrequent and impersonal contact with a low degree of personal involvement, often in large formal organizations (Curtis and Lambert, 1980:106).

Family and peer groups are the prototypical primary groups. There, people are valued and treated as total personalities (not as the segmented selves involved in such secondary relationships as customer-sales clerk or patient-dentist). Primary relationships typically involve deep feelings. For these reasons, both family and peer groups are potent agents of gender socialization. The next chapter deals with peer groups. Discussion of *secondary* group gender socialization agents (such as the school and the church) and of the *symbolic* agents (language, literature, and the mass media) will be reserved for Chapter 7.

THE IMPORTANCE OF THE FAMILY AS GENDER SOCIALIZATION AGENCY

The family's impact upon the child transcends that of all the other agents of socialization. No other agency rivals the family in terms of intensity of emotions aroused or the scope of the power wielded. Learning occurs rapidly during these crucial years of early childhood, during which the family has almost exclusive control. Children are physically dependent on adults, and out of this material dependency develops psychological dependency. Therefore, learning takes place in the context of close emotional bonds. Moreover, the family touches every sphere of the child's existence. The early immersion of the child within the family guarantees that the institution lays the foundation for the later and lesser influences of the other socialization agents, which are considerably more specialized.

There is a second reason for sociologists' assigning primacy to the family. Various characteristics of the family orient the child to specific configurations of experiences, values, and opportunities. By being born into a particular family, the child automatically becomes part of an extended family of grandparents, aunts, uncles, and cousins. Also, the family's social class position means that the child will learn a particular set of values. Moreover, the opportunities of a child born into an upper-middle-class family are considerably different from those of a child born into the working class. The family provides the child with an ethnic background. The role ethnicity plays in socialization varies enormously. Ethnicity means one thing to the visible minority child from Jamaica, another to the recent immigrant from Vietnam, something else again to the fourth-generation Irish-Canadian raised in this country. Finally, the family's geographic location is also the child's. Growing up in Vancouver is a quite different experience from growing up in rural Manitoba. The consequences for gender socialization of the more important orienting characteristics will be considered later in this chapter.

A third reason for the family's importance is its channelling function. In Clausen's (1968:132) words, "the 'widening world of childhood spirals out from the parental home." At first, the child knows only the micro-world of family, babysitter, neighbourhood, and perhaps, daycare centre. However, socialization links the micro-world to the infinitely more complex macro-world beyond (Berger and Berger, 1975:69). Through its channelling function, the family mediates the macro-world for the child. That is, the family has the power to determine the child's exposure to particular schools, churches, and mass media programs, and to interpret for the child the meaning of these secondary influences. Therefore, the efforts of multiple socialization agents tend to reinforce one another.

For the reasons outlined above, all the so-

cialization theories reviewed in previous chapters, except one, acknowledge the pre-eminent influence of the family. (The exception is cognitive-developmental theory, which stresses "self-socialization" and the peer group.) Learning theorists highlight the function of parents as either providing same-sex and complimentary models to their children, or as direct reinforcement agents, meting out rewards and punishments for appropriate gender behaviour. Symbolic interactionists assume fathers and mothers to be the most influential of the "significant others" moulding young people into social beings. (However, peers too play an important part in interactionist theory.) Finally, the dynamics of the more biologically grounded psychoanalytic theory depend upon emotional linkages between parent and child.

In the years since the main ideas of the above socialization theories were worked out, scholars have come to appreciate the extent to which socialization is a reciprocal process, one affecting caregivers as well as children (Ambert, 1990b; LaRossa and LaRossa, 1981). For example, Toronto columnist Michele Landsberg (1982:187) describes how her children taught her to be a parent:

Unsuspectingly, I strolled into the middle of a debate between my 2-year-old son and 3-year-old daughter.

"I say that mummies make the babies," my daughter explained, "but he says daddies do, too."

"Yes, mummies and daddies both," I beamed. I congratulated myself on not telling them more than they wanted to know, and figured our first little step in sex ed. was all wrapped up.

"What do the daddies do?" my daughter pounced. I fought down my surprised laughter and ploughed on with a vivid account of the happy adventures of egg and sperm. All this, I was shakily feeling, was a bit much and a bit soon.

It wasn't over yet. A light dawned on my son's face, a light which I later came to recognize as the spirit of enraptured scientific inquiry. "How does daddy get the sperm to the egg?" he asked sweetly.

And that's how two kids not yet old enough for tricycles taught me to speak straight and true when serious questions were being asked.

The point merits reiteration: socialization is a two-way process.

According to a national poll conducted by

Maclean's magazine (January 5, 1987), 81 percent of Canadians report that the family is becoming "a more important part" of their lives. Nevertheless, we must keep in mind that the concept of "family" means different things to different people. An important reason for this diversity of meanings is the dramatic social and economic changes that Western societies have undergone over the past 50 years. A brief overview of this topic will provide a vantage point for the *fin de siècle* family as gender socialization agent.

THE CHANGING FAMILY[1]

During one hot summer of TV reruns, a nostalgia week on a local channel featured an episode of *Father Knows Best* from the late 1950s. Inside a white, two-storied house, surrounded by green lawns and a picket fence, lived the Andersons: a wise, kind father (clad in a sports jacket with leather patches on the elbows), a charming, slightly less wise mother (in an apron), and three well-mannered, well-groomed children. The story concerned a trophy case that Bud and his father proposed building in the basement to display awards won over the years. The problem? Mrs. Anderson, unlike the other family members, had earned no cups, certificates, or badges to put in the cabinet. After rejecting daughter Kathy's offer to share her award for perfect Sunday School attendance, Mrs. Anderson secretly began taking lessons in fly casting. On the very day of a competition (which she believed she was sure to win), Margaret Anderson fell, broke her leg and, deeply depressed, took to her bed. The title of the program provides the plot resolution; Betty, Bud, and Kathy look to their father for direction and he, of course, didn't let the family down. A celebration of motherhood was held at Mrs. Anderson's bedside. Husband and children presented verbal testimonials to her kindness and self-sacrifice, and then a hand-lettered certificate of motherhood. Being a mother was all that her family (and society) required of her.

A viewer born in the 1960s or 1970s might consider *Father Knows Best* characters to be caught in a *Twilight Zone* time warp. However,

this black-and-white sitcom does convey an important sociological lesson. The lesson is this: Families in general, and gender socialization in particular, must be studied in sociohistorical context. To quote Hayford (1987:10), "In our society the family is the realm of our personal lives, but it is also the realm where we come to grips with powerful social forces that are beyond the control of any individual." Himelfarb and Richardson (1982:381) point out that "change is built into the family, more than in other institutions" of society. They go on to say that, "The family is both a *dependent* and an *independent* variable, having things happen to it, certainly, but also creating and amplifying changes in the wider society" (p. 382). Though the Western family must not be dismissed as passive recipient of the forces of modernization, it has been greatly changed by such trends as industrialization, separation of home and work, urbanization, and secularization. Emphasis has shifted from the family unit to individuals. The collective interests of the family no longer take precedence over individual desires for autonomy, self-realization, and the accumulation of the material goods. Many of these trends have been going on for centuries. Nevertheless, ideological and technological developments have been sufficiently dramatic over the past quarter century to render anachronistic the Anderson family and its problems.

The Anderson family reflects the "classical family of Western nostalgia" (Goode, 1963). Breadwinner father and stay-at-home mother married to each other for twenty-plus years. Three children. (Spot, the dog, and Puff, the cat, were probably off camera in the nostalgia episode.) According to one estimate, only seven percent of the North American population now lives in this once-classic nuclear family unit (*Maclean's*, January 7, 1987:71). The elusiveness of this family model means that gender socialization today is profoundly different from what it was 20 years ago.

In recent years, Canada's birth rate has declined to 1.7 as the result of a variety of factors, including later marriages, postponement of parenthood to later years, a greater proportion of people who never marry, voluntary childlessness, and married women's increasing participation in the labour force. In Quebec where the birth rate is the lowest in Canada, the provincial government provides tax incentives for Quebeckers to raise larger families. The government gives cash bonuses of $500 for a family's first child, $1000 for its second, and $6000 for third and subsequent children (*The Globe and Mail*, April 27, 1990:A3). Gender socialization is a different proposition in the 1990s family of one or two children than it was in larger families of previous decades, such as the TV Anderson family.

Most people who enter marriage "do so by vowing to stay married to each other 'till death does them part'." Despite media statements that "every second or third marriage will end in divorce these days," most Canadians who marry do not dissolve their marriages (Ramu, 1989:12). (See Burch, 1985.) Nonetheless, the number who do so is increasing (Peters, 1989:207). Between 1921 and 1986, the divorce rate in this country soared from 6.4 per 100 000 population to 308.3 (Ambert, 1990a:193). Children were involved in one-third of the divorces obtained in 1986. This means that about 56 000 Canadian children are annually affected by dissolution of their parents' marriages (Peters, 1989:221). In 1986, the wife received custody of the children in 75 percent of the divorces, the husband in 12 percent, with other arrangements, such as joint custody, being made for the rest (Ambert, 1990a:204).

Separation and divorce produce intense emotional reactions from most children at the time of family break-up, and lingering negative effects for a sizeable minority (Bumpass, 1984). The child's developmental stage when parents separate is one of the many variables which affect children's reactions. Preschool children do not understand divorce and often blame themselves for their parents' separation. As Nelson (1985:121) points out, "school-aged children experienced mixed feelings of sadness, anxiety, and anger. Many of these children had conflicts of divided loyalty, wished for their parents to reconcile, and openly expressed anger towards their parents." While younger children often react with disruptive behaviour, older children tend to do so with depression (Nelson, 1985:125). The impact of these events also depends on parents' management of the divorce transition (Spanier and

Furstenberg, 1987:426), and the children's gender. Research "indicates that boys are more adversely affected by parental strife and separation than girls" (Ambert, 1990a:205), in part because more boys are thereby deprived of same-sex models.

Divorce also brings inevitable social and economic changes in children's lives. For example, many learn that when marriages break up, "money is tight for winter coats, babysitters, running shoes and penicillin..." (Maynard, 1984:65). Moves to new neighbourhoods or communities (which often occur) result in loss of friendships and the challenge of establishing new ones. Relations with both custodial and non-resident parents deviate from traditional nuclear-family scripts. Children are likely to find these changes stressful, at least initially. One beloved parent may now be labelled a villain and enemy by the other. A small proportion of fathers become "Mr. Moms" in *Kramer vs. Kramer* custodial father households. Many more join the legion of indulgent "Uncle Dads" (Smith, 1987), with limited opportunities to assume a meaningful role in their children's lives beyond visiting privileges. Many non-custodial parents eventually disappear altogether (Ambert, 1990a:201). Parents' boyfriends or girlfriends who come and go may exercise temporary authority over children of divorce.

Despite the foregoing, it is important to acknowledge that divorce frequently involves positive consequences for children. Many youngsters benefit by escaping the stressful family environment produced by conflict-ridden marriage, and by establishing closer relations with their custodial parents. Though divorce can make children cynical about marriage, they do develop a broader vision of "normal" social arrangements (Whitehurst, 1984:225). Children's response depends on such considerations as their age at the time of divorce, and amount of pre-existing conflict in the home.

As a result of separation, divorce, and births to never-married mothers who keep their offspring, many Canadian children are growing up in one-parent families.[2] More than 80 percent of Canadian lone-parent families are headed by women (Statistics Canada, 1985).

Income is "the key difference between the lone-parent and the two-parent family" (Peters, 1989:224). The income of the average single-parent family headed by a female is less than half that of two-parent families (Davids, 1985). Therefore, families headed by women often experience poverty (Ambert, 1985). In addition, the custodial parent is frequently overwhelmed with responsibility for earning a living, child care, and housework (Michelson, 1985). In such homes, the single parent may treat the child as a pseudo-adult equal, loading the child with many responsibilities of the missing parent, such as cooking, cleaning, caring for younger siblings (Schlesinger, 1983). Pressure may be put on them to act as companion and confidante for their single parent (Schlesinger, 1983).

Because three-quarters of divorced men and two-thirds of divorced women eventually remarry (Ambert, 1990a:205), and half of all remarriages include dependent children (Peters, 1989:226), many offspring of divorced (and never-married parents) eventually find themselves part of reconstituted families. A certain amount of role confusion and ambiguity seems inevitable in complex families involving parents, siblings, step-parents, step-siblings, and an assortment of grandparents, aunts and uncles (Cherlin, 1978). For example, who has authority to discipline children? What kinship terms are to be used? (If a child calls her mother "Mom," what should she call her stepmother?) Does the erstwhile eldest child who has acquired older siblings lose privileges as he descends the pecking order? Although more studies are necessary, American researchers conclude that "the majority of children growing up in stepfamilies appear to develop a reasonably amicable relationship with their step-parents and are not severely handicapped in their social interactions" (Ihlinger-Tallman, 1988:35).[3] Nevertheless, children and adults in reconstituted families must cope with the absence of norms to regulate their family relations (Johnson, 1988).

The economy is another significant influence upon Canadian families, and the socialization of young people. As we shall see in Chapter 8, "the nature of paid work shapes the daily experience of families" (Thorne, 1982:16). For a variety of reasons to be explored in that chapter, only 16 percent of families now consist of couples with one income earner (Armstrong and Armstrong, 1988:163). This means that a majority of Canadian children are now cared for by someone other than a parent during some portion of their day (Eichler, 1983:249). It is extremely difficult to generalize about the socialization consequences of non-familial childcare facilities which range from nannies in residence, to mothers' babysitting cooperatives, licensed child-care centres run by highly trained personnel, unlicensed arrangements in church basements, to the neighbours babysitting in their homes to make a few dollars. We will have more to say about these questions later in this chapter.

The white, Anglo-Saxon, Protestant, American television families presented to 1950s and 1960s viewers seemed to be a prototype of *the* family. Contemporary mass media consumers are more sophisticated. Looking at people in the streets, shops, and schools, as well as on their TV screens, they realize that Canadian families are characterized by increasing racial and ethnic diversity, as well as by religious and social class differences. Over the past three decades, large numbers of people arrived from Asian, Latin American, and Caribbean countries. These newcomers face the dual challenge of conveying something of their culture of origin to their children while their offspring learn to fit into their new society. Often, the new immigrant family protects its members from stress by a "creative schizophrenia," that allows its members to be "modern" at work and "traditional" at home (Berger and Berger, 1984). Both ethnic and class divisions in Canadian society (the latter often related to ethnicity) critically influence socialization, including gender socialization. Demographic variations in gender socialization will be taken up at the end of this chapter.

So far, we have mentioned divorce, lone-parent families, reconstituted families, the dramatic increase in women's labour force participation, and ethnic diversity as contextual factors which influence gender socialization. Numerous additional contrasts could be drawn between the idealized TV family of the 1950s and the actualities of Canadian families in the early 1990s. For one thing, family life has been transformed by scientific and technological innovations. Young people are surrounded by stereos, television sets, computers, and video arcades. Parental authority is challenged by a myriad of sources, including rock video stars and television advertisers. Young people "have become literally attached to the TV, the stereo and the radio... And if you take those away, they go through more loss and despair than if you took away their parents" argues psychologist David Klimek (quoted in Woodward, 1990:60). (See Chapter 7 for further discussion.)

Second, the image of the family as domestic haven, exemplified by *Father Knows Best* has been shattered. We now realize that for many women and children, home is not a safe place. In all likelihood, it never was. Feminists "were among the first to identify family violence as such a pervasive phenomenon that it constituted a 'normal' feature of family life" (Glenn, 1987:363). (See Chapter 9.)

Third, experts intrude increasingly upon the family's authority (Ehrenreich and English, 1978). In the Age of the Expert, educators, psychologists, and pediatricians help, advise, and bully parents in order to protect children from putative parental ignorance. For instance, journalist Lynn Caine (1985:12) writes: "Ever since my children were babies. ..., I've always been afraid of damaging them, of not knowing enough as a mother, of not being good enough, not patient enough, unselfish enough...." By contrast, Mr. and Mrs. Anderson were confident that Princess, Bud, and Kathy were turning out beautifully.

Finally, women's experience in the public domain has made them more independent. Today, they are not quite so likely to depend upon men for either intellectual guidance or financial support. Few television viewers of the 1950s doubted that Father *did* know best. Family life is increasingly influenced by women's definitions of the situation, as well as their activities outside the home.

This general discussion of the changing Canadian family provides a context for our analysis of the role played by that institution in gender socialization. We turn now to this topic.

DO FATHERS AND MOTHERS PARENT DIFFERENTLY?

Biologically speaking, fatherhood means sperm donation, and motherhood provision of the egg, "housing" of the fertilized ovum for nine months, and potentially, breastfeeding. Until the women's movement challenged traditional ideas, parents' gender roles were almost as distinct as their sex roles. Indeed, pre-feminist thinkers regarded this strict (and supposedly natural) division of labour—fathers do this, mothers do that—as a prerequisite for normal, well-adjusted children.

Even today, fatherhood and motherhood carry different connotations:

The meaning of "fatherhood" remains tangential, elusive. To "father" a child suggests above all to beget, to provide the sperm which fertilizes the ovum. To "mother" a child implies a continuing presence, lasting at least nine months, more often for years (Rich, 1976:xiv).

Greeting cards serve as a good illustration of stereotypical notions about parenthood. Mother's Day cards are typically yellow, turquoise, pink, and lavender. They feature roses, daisies, kittens, and swans, and sentimental litanies such as this: "Mom, do you remember midnight squalls, miles of diapers, scrawls on walls, bedtime balks?" (Zwarun, 1984). These cards reflect our culture's idealization of mothers as "all-loving, kind, gentle, and selfless" (Andersen, 1988:165). Mother's Day celebrates the expressive nature of women as children's primary caretakers.

In comparison with the hoopla surrounding Mother's Day, Father's Day sems to be a commercial afterthought. Bill Cosby recalls how he used to shine shoes for a week before Mother's Day to buy his mom a present. "When Father's Day came around, I'd run to the store and buy him (William Cosby, Sr.) two cigarettes —and smoke one on the way home" (*Calgary Herald*, May 28, 1988). Perhaps fathers fare less well because the traditional paternal roles of breadwinner and family authoritarian don't lend themselves to sentimentality. Father's Day cards are maroon, bronze, brown (almost never pastel). The illustrations depict duck decoys, beer tankards, antique pistols, fishing rods, sailing ships, and dogs (hunting dogs, not fluffy poodles) (Zwarun, 1984). In verses nearly as dreadful as those inside Mother's Day cards, most Father's Day cards stress instrumental rather than emotional linkages between progenitor-offspring. For example, "Dad: You've always had what it takes to be a great father — car keys, credit cards, and a full refrigerator."

A few of the Father's Day cards on display in 1988 communicate a new message about androgynous fatherhood. A Hallmark card, done in turquoises and greys, shows a man and a small boy, both barefoot, walking together beside the sea. The message reads:

For My Dad—
who chased away monsters
in the middle of the night
and held by hand at scary movies—
For my dad—who was always there
to catch me at the bottom of the slide—
For my dad — who always helped me
through life's little rough spots—
Even now, when life gets a little scary,
I know there's someone I can always depend on,
and I'll always be very grateful — for my dad.

A parallel shift is occurring in social scientists' thinking about parenting. Before the women's movement, research on parenting focussed almost exclusively on the mother as the crucial socialization agent. A decade or so ago, the label "caregiver" began to appear, presumably to convey the idea that parenting can also be done by fathers and parent surrogates (Rossi, 1985:168). By the beginning of the 1990s, the research literature has become sufficiently rich to permit comparative analysis of mothering and fathering. In the pages to follow we ask: What difference does is make to gender socialization if parenting is done by fathers or mothers? The conclusions reached set the stage for the discussion in subsequent sections of the related question: What gender socialization consequences ensue when children receive "excessive" or "deficient" mothering and/or fathering?

Fathers and mothers following traditional scripts relate differently to their offspring. Mothers are the primary caretakers of young children: feeding them, cleaning them, watching out for their physical safety. By contrast, fathers are more apt to handle children under a year in order to play with them. Since traditional fathers prefer rough-and-tumble play to verbal interaction, they tend to overstimulate their babies and to miss subtle non-verbal communication cues (Coltrane, 1988:1089). Fathers do take more interest as children grow older. However, "their role appears to be the 'fun' one of playing with their children" (Losh-Hesselbart, 1987:546). Mothers cope with youngsters' physical demands, routine problems, and discipline.

As children get older, sex-typed attitudes, particularly those held by fathers, continue to influence parent-child interaction. Parents, especially fathers, interact more with same-sex children than with cross-sex children. In addition, they seem to be more controlling and restrictive with children of their own sex (Huston, 1983:430). For example, the father-daughter relationship is often characterized by more warmth than is the father-son relationship (Block, 1984:74). Fathers are more tolerant of displays of temper and insolence from their daughters than from their sons (Lambert, Yackley and Hein, 1971).

Here is an important research finding: It is the father who plays the more critical role in emphasizing "appropriate sex typing." This is particularly so for sons (Huston, 1983:428). Put another way, fathers more than mothers have been consistently found to treat sons and daughters differently, and to play the more crucial role in encouraging and enforcing sex/gender differences (Block, 1984:8-9). For example, girls encouraged by their fathers to do well more often achieve in school and plan less gender-typed occupational careers (Losh-Hesselbart, 1987:546).

Two factors seem responsible for the more sex-typed response of fathers to their children. First of all, because mothers have traditionally assumed primary responsibility for the socialization of *all* their children, they differentiate less between their male and female offspring (Huston, 1983:428). The greater responsibility of mothers implies more intimate contact with progeny. Mothers observe their children closely; that their verbal and non-verbal communication with them tends to be more effective than their husbands' is well established (Rossi, 1984). As a consequence, mothers are more likely than fathers to perceive and to respond to their offspring as unique little persons, rather than as females or males. The *gradient of familiarity* — the concept that stereotypes operate more powerfully at a distance (Williams and Best, 1982) — explains what is going on here. Traditional fathers tend to react more stereotypically to their own babies than do mothers, in part because they have had less experience than their wives with their offspring (Lewis, 1986:97).

The second reason for fathers' greater contribution to sex-typed socialization may well be a byproduct of the conviction of child-rearing experts in past years that sex-typing was absolutely essential for normal development. Special responsibility to be gender role models was assigned by these authorities to fathers (Pleck, 1987:92). They taught that daughters needed to practise their femininity with fathers. Even more important in this teaching was the argument that healthy, normal boys required male role models. Traditional fathers apparently heeded the experts' advice. "Probably because they are more concerned about 'appropriately' sex-typed behaviour than mothers are..., fathers emit reinforcements and punishments for sex-typed behavior more consistently than mothers do" (Lamb et al., 1986:147). Whether or not this traditional advice was correct is the subject of the next section.

Today, an important avenue of research concludes that the source of the parenting differences between mothers and fathers seems to have more to do with structural opportunities to parent than with the sex/gender of the adults involved. That is, the tasks of providing physical maintenance and psychological nurturance to young children are primarily women's activities, not because women "need" to mother and are biologically equipped to do so, but because of the social organization of work. For example, a study by Risman (1987) compared the parenting behaviours of single fathers, single mothers, traditional mother-at-home families, and two-pay-cheque families. By studying widowed or deserted single fathers

who had not chosen their situation, the researchers bypassed the possibility that they were dealing with extraordinarily keen fathers. If the ability to provide sensitive, effective care to small children were inborn female characteristics, men's care would not be equivalent. If, on the other hand, structural factors are the more influential, "reclassification of the father into the primary caretaker role and the continuing expectations of children to be nurtured will produce mothering by men that is nearly indistinguishable from the behavior of women in the same situation" (Risman, 1987:12). In general, the results supported the structural hypothesis: variation in parenting usually attributed to the biological predispositions or socialization preparation "can be accounted for by the differential situational exigencies and opportunities faced by women and men" (p. 25).

TOO MUCH MOTHERING (AND NOT ENOUGH FATHERING)?

Despite the heavy involvement of women in the labour force, the increasing recognition that fathers as well as mothers are capable of a wide range of parenting skills, and other dramatic changes in family structure described at the beginning of this chapter, the centrality of family roles in women's lives continues to be taken for granted (Lopata, 1987:381). To illustrate, the 1980 movie *Kramer vs. Kramer* presented as remarkable the commitment of a single father (Dustin Hoffman) "who assumes day-to-day responsibility for his child, even to the extent of giving up a lucrative job (and as we all know, making French toast)" (Levine, 1983:28). Mothers who routinely do these things seldom have movies made about them. Equally relevant to this discussion is the anger, contempt, and disgust felt for Meryl Streep as the mother who chose career over custody of her son. These societal scripts for parenthood explain why our treatment of the topics of excessive or deficient parenting by caregivers of both sexes frames the issue in terms of maternal responsibility.

Excessive Mothering of Sons

As industrialization brought increased geographical distance between home and workplace, criticism was voiced about excessive maternal influence, especially on male children (Pleck, 1987). The absence of fathers away fighting World War II intensified this critique. The epithet "Momism" came to refer to obsessive devotion of sons for mothers and mothers for sons, and particularly to the unwillingness of mothers to let their sons develop a sense of masculine independence (Dubbert, 1979:240). Philip Wylie's best-selling popular work, *Generation of Vipers* (1942) argued that such women "raped the men, not sexually, unfortunately [sic] but morally, since neuters come hard by morals."

Maternal power and paternal decline were caricatured in the mass media: "On television, in movies, and in comic strips of the 1940s and '50s, fathers were often made to appear as fumbling incompetents, 'a kind of living fossil, a creature trying to ape some of the manners of a bygone era.' Dagwood Bumstead, for example, blustered and fussed in front of Blondie and the kids, but the reader knew that Dagwood could not control anything, not even the family dogs" (Dubbert, 1979:257-58).

Writers ranging from pop sociologists to social scientists have speculated that the combination of devouring mother and milquetoast (or missing) father produces homosexual sons. "Research within the past two decades has generally not supported the causal importance of early family experiences" (Risman and Schwartz, 1988:127). Indeed, the fact that the American Psychiatric Association in 1973 removed homosexuality from its listing of psychiatric disorders was the outcome of scientific study that had concluded that homosexuality is not a sign of psychological impairment (Macklin, 1987:337).

That early feminist critiques of the traditional housewife role picked up on this theme of the suffocating mother surprises us two decades later. The phenomenon of "Momism" signalled the plight of middle-class women caught in late motherhood with nothing "meaningful" to do. For instance, Pauline Bart (1971) analyzed the Jewish mother, purveyor of unwanted chicken soup and self-sacrificing martyr who 'devoted' her life to her ungrateful children, as an anachronistic caricature of Momism. Similarly, in arguing the need to liberate middle-class women from suburbia, Betty Friedan (1963:265) suggested that women with nothing better to do with their time were harming their sons.

Nancy Chodorow's book, *The Reproduction of Mothering: Psychoanalysis and the Sociology of Gender* (1978) is the best-known contemporary analysis of excessive mothering. Her account is based on psychoanalytic interpretation of clinical case histories (Lorber, 1981:483). Chodorow contends that because traditional societal arrangements leave most of the parenting to women, many mothers "overinvest" in their children and dominate their emotional lives. She (along with other thinkers inspired by Freud) argues that exclusively maternal care encourages a primary feminine identity in male children. Subsequently, boys establish a masculine identity in opposition to women. Chodorow claims that patriarchy, misogyny, and hypermasculinity are all the result of exclusively maternal care (p. 214). Pleck (1981:235) summarizes this line of reasoning:

The male child... perceives his mother and his predominantly female elementary school teachers as dominating and controlling. These relationships *do* in reality contain elements of domination and control, probably exacerbated by the restriction of women's opportunities to exercise power in most other areas. As a result, men feel a lifelong psychological need to free themselves from or prevent their being dominated by women. The argument is, in effect, that men oppress women as adults because they experienced women as oppressing them as children.

As the following anecdotes suggest, adult men fear and resent women's power. A middle-aged executive describes his meeting with three matronly secretaries who are displeased with him as a simultaneous confrontation with his mother, his first-grade teacher, and God. Audiences cheered when Glenn Close, portraying a powerful, if crazy female villain is killed in the 1987 film *Fatal Attraction*. Whatever surface plausibility it may have, this view of the domineering mother can be criticized as an example of "blaming the victim" (Ryan, 1971). In other words, women themselves, not the patriarchal social arrangements which bind them, are held ultimately responsible for their own oppression (Pleck , 1981:236).

Despite women's increasing attention to matters outside the home and strong pressures on fathers to become more involved in child-rearing (see below), other societal forces acting on the family serve to augment women's authority. For instance, Hayford (1987:9) reminds us that "at least one quarter of Canadian women can expect to spend a part of their adult lives as single mothers of young children, either because they have never married or because their marriage has ended." As well, daycare workers, babysitters, nannies, and elementary school teachers are mostly women. In short, women's responsibility for children continues.

What does social science have to say about the impact of predominantly female authority figures upon the gender socialization of children? From the perspective of modelling theories of learning (Chapter 4), children without a parent of each sex will lack an important socializing influence if sex-typing is the socialization goal (Huston, 1983:433). The effect of missing fathers on sons' development has received considerable research attention. For one thing, as noted above, fathers more than mothers treat their sons and daughters differently, and therefore are particularly influential in sex-typing. For another, modelling theory stresses the importance of same-sex modelling.

"Overall, the data support the hypothesis that fathers play an important, though not irreplaceable role in boys' development of masculinity...." (Huston, 1983:433). In particular, young boys in father-absent homes tend to show more feminine patterning of behaviour. For example, six-year old boys in mother-headed divorced families had less masculine preferences for toys and activities (Hetherington, 1979).

The implication that sons are harmed by not enough fathering (and by implication, too much mothering) needs to be put into perspective. Recent well-designed studies have demonstrated that many of the deleterious aspects of "fatherless homes" reported by earlier researchers could be accounted for by the eco-nomic poverty often associated with mother-headed households (Gongla and Thompson, 1987). (See Ambert, 1985). Also, studies must specify the extent to which the absent father is really absent from children's lives. Some divorced fathers remain involved with their kids; others disappear forever. As well, the effects of father absence depend on the age at which the father left. Boys whose fathers left when they were of preschool age show more feminizing effects than those whose fathers left after the preschool period (Huston, 1983:434). Moreover, since children learn through reinforcement as well as modelling, mothers' encouragement of masculine behaviour is important (Hetherington, Cox and Cox, 1978). When lone-parent mothers encouraged independence and exploratory behaviour (rather than being over-protective and apprehensive about sons' independence), and did not hold negative attitudes toward the absent father, disruptions in sons' sex-typed behaviour did not occur (Santrock, 1984: 473). Finally, children are exposed to many models of both sexes. Although parents are of paramount importance, grandparents, uncles, male teachers, friends of all ages, and media figures count, too.

To summarize, well-designed studies that take into consideration all of the variables mentioned above are scarce. However, the weight of available evidence points to the conclusion that "living in a single-parent family does not necessarily harm children" (Gongla and Thompson, 1987:411). The evidence certainly does not establish that strong "emasculating" mothers turn their sons into homosexuals. Indeed, "most boys whose fathers are absent develop normal sex roles,...underscoring the fact that sex-role development is multiply- and over-determined" (Lamb et al., 1986:147).

Lastly, we remind the reader that feminist scholars challenge the premise underlying much of the above research, i.e., the desirability of sex-typing as socialization goal. Bem (1976:49), the psychologist responsible for much of the early work on androgyny, wrote: "My major purpose has always been a feminist one: to help free the human personality from the restricting prison of sex-role stereotyping..."

Excessive Mothering of Daughters

"It is awful and awesome," Alice said, "to think of the power our mothers have over us, no matter how old they are, no matter how old we are. The mother may have been reduced, through age, through time, to a tiny old lady who walks with sticks. But in our hearts, our psyches, she's still the giant shadow mother we saw reflected on the nursery wall. What is equally horrible to contemplate is that I might become, perhaps am already, that kind of figure to my children" (Thomas, 1984:180-81).

The women's movement stimulated considerable discussion of the theretofore neglected subject of mother-daughter relationships (Arcana, 1979; Chodorow, 1978; Dinnerstein, 1976; Friday, 1977; Secunda, 1990). As the passage quoted from Audrey Thomas' novel, *Intertidal Life* indicates, the concept "too much mothering" of daughters continues as a cultural theme. Much of this analysis was based on the psychoanalytic perspective, and emphasized the connection between the mothering they had received and daughters' subsequent unhappiness and failings. For example, Susie Orbach's influential book, *Fat Is A Feminist Issue* (1978), argues that the problem of compulsive eating has a lot to do with daughters' early experiences with their mothers. This literature emphasized that girls have more difficulty liberating themselves from their mothers than do boys. Several books, notably Nancy Friday's bestseller, *My Mother/Myself* (1977), held the all-powerful mother totally responsible for how her daughter turned out. Others (e.g., Judith Arcana's *Our Mothers' Daughters*, 1979), informed by feminist teachings, saw maternal behaviour as "a product of mothers' entrapment within patriarchy rather than a product of evil intentions" (Chodorow and Contratto, 1982:56). Our discussion returns to Chodorow's (1978) version of daughters' experience of excessive mothering because, for the most part, it manages to avoid blaming the victim (Ryan, 1970), and because it represents the most scholarly example of this literature.

Chodorow contends that since our society leaves most of the parenting to women, for "a girl, just as for a boy, there can be too much of mother" (p. 177).[4] Here is her core insight. Being the same sex/gender as their daughters,

and having themselves been girls, mothers of daughters experience their infant daughters as less separate from themselves than their infant sons (Rossi, 1987:265). Chodorow argues that as a consequence of the closer mother-daughter bond, girls develop a less sharply differentiated sense of self than boys. The traumatic experience of separating themselves from their mothers that is required to achieve masculine identity leaves boys with a better established sense of self. According to Chodorow, the consequence of this close bonding is the development in daughters of greater sensitivity to others, greater capacity for empathy. In short, sex-typed personalities in both sexes emerge from interaction with the mother:

Women, as mothers, produce daughters with mothering capacities and the desire to mother. These capacities and needs are built into and grow out of the mother-daughter relationship itself. By contrast, women as mothers (and men as not-mothers) produce sons whose nurturant capacities and needs have been systematically curtailed and repressed (Chodorow, 1978:7).

The psychoanalytic perspective argues that while girls' easier identification with the appropriate parent has rendered their childhood less traumatic than boys', puberty is especially difficult for girls. As Orbach (1978:15) explains, mothers "clip their daughters' wings" in order to prepare them to live in patriarchal society:

...to prepare her daughter for a life of inequality, the mother tries to hold back her child's desires to be a powerful, autonomous, self-directed, energetic and productive human being. From an early age, the young girl is encouraged to accept this rupture in her development and is guided to cope with this loss by putting her energy into taking care of others. Her own needs for emotional support and growth will be satisfied if she can convert them into giving to others.

What does the empirical literature have to say about girls growing up in mother-only homes? Is the mother-daughter bonding posited by Chodorow (1978) accentuated under these circumstances? Because psychologists have assumed that girls are less affected by father absence than boys, girls have been studied less often than boys (Huston, 1983:434). On the whole, the literature shows few effects of father absence on girls' sex-typed self-imagery or activity preferences. However, there is some evidence that working-class teenage girls from father-absent homes lacked experience in interacting comfortably with males (Hetherington, 1972). Just as was the case with boys, maternal encouragement of sex-typed attributes and activities (e.g., adventurous sports), as well as the presence of other male figures in their lives, can compensate for the absence of paternal influence (Huston, 1983:435). The literature does not support effects predicted by Chodorow (1978) such as pathological attachment to their mothers.

INSUFFICIENT MOTHERING

In recent years, the spectre of "Momism" (and father absence) has been joined in the popular imagination by the sad plight of children growing up deprived of adequate mothering. The other side of our culture's idealization of mothers, expressed, for example, in the syrupy stuff of Mother's Day cards, is the conviction that children's development is totally contingent upon the quality of mothering they receive (Glenn, 1987:360). Mothers unable to live up to these images of motherhood from earlier eras are accused of being neglectful and insufficiently loving.[5]

Traditionalists bemoan the fact that familial arrangements of earlier days with "father out coping with the external world, mother at home creating a haven of warmth and comfort within which father can shelter and children grow" (Rapoport and Rapoport, 1977:327) are rapidly becoming obsolete. In fact, this traditional arrangement exists in a very small percentage of Canadian families. Nearly 60 percent of mothers with children under age five hold paying jobs, the vast majority in full-time positions (Statistics Canada, 1987). Many more homes are headed by single parents of either sex, although single fathers who receive custody of their children get a disproportionate share of publicity, considering that custodial fathers are in the minority.

As a consequence of these changes, as well as other social forces reviewed at the beginning of this chapter, motherhood as a full-time vocation is no longer possible (or in the minds of feminists, desirable) for many Canadian families. Yet substitutes are hard to find. In Toronto alone, nearly 43 000 nannies, many of them immigrant women who leave their own children in the care of others, minister to the needs of the children of well-to-do families (*Toronto Life*, April 1988). The federal Task Force on Child Care (1986), chaired by Katie Cooke, concluded that the availability of quality daycare has become an urgent national issue. Its observation that "Canada's child care and parental leave programs lag behind systems operating in most western industrialized countries" (p. 277) raised for governments and laypersons serious issues concerning the provision of accessible, affordable, quality daycare to Canadian families. Such daycare is expensive (up to $6000 per year per child); it is also scarce. According to one estimate, the number of children in need of daycare outnumbers spaces available in licensed centres by more than ten to one (*Maclean's*, November 10, 1986:48).

The ideological, political, and economic issues involved in provision of daycare and possible compensation, perhaps in the form of tax credits, to stay-at-home parents — these complex, controversial matters are beyond the scope of this book. Space limitations require that our focus be the consequences of maternal employment and father-custody homes for gender socialization. However, we do note that a recent review of the research evidence concluded that "no consistent adverse effect of out-of-home child daycare has been found by over a dozen child development investigators" (O'Connell, 1987:374, emphasis deleted). Moreover, studies of the development of bonding between mother and child find little difference among children at home with their mothers, daycare children, and youngsters cared for by babysitters (Gerson et al., 1984:447). Indeed, positive effects accrue from *good* daycare, especially to children from disadvantaged homes (Task Force on Child Care, 1986:209). Nevertheless, the quality of available daycare varies considerably. As noted above, the shortage of affordable first-rate spaces in this country creates serious problems for families. Authorities who believe strongly that young children ought to grow up in their own homes argue that although research finds no obvious harm being done to infants in well-financed, well-managed, non-profit programs, out-of-home child care of this high calibre remains in short supply (White, 1987:362). Providing that parents have the financial freedom to do so, the conservative course of action would be for one of them to remain at home for the first six months of the child's life.

To return to the question of gender socialization, learning theory would lead us to expect the division of labour children experience in their homes to be a critical determinant of their understanding of masculinity and femininity. Children who grow up in homes where the 'father brings home the bacon and the mother cooks it' develop traditional notions about gender. On the other hand, "if sex is unimportant as a basic of role assignment in the family, then children will think in 'modern' or non-differentiated ways" (Lambert, 1971:31).

Children with employed mothers (and lone parents) experience domestic social organization which is, of necessity, less sex-typed than that of the minority of families that continue traditional patterns. Indeed, a substantial literature indicates that children with employed mothers have less stereotyped, "broader concepts of appropriate personality traits, behaviors, activities, occupations, relations with adults, and relations with peers than do sons and daughters of nonemployed women" (Huston, 1983:436). Daughters are particularly influenced by their mothers' employment. In comparison with daughters of full-time housewives, they have higher career aspirations, are more achievement oriented, have higher self-esteem, and more androgynous interests and activities (Huston, 1983:436).

Since an increasing number of mothers are in the labour force, we would expect many Canadian children to be exposed to experiences that may lead to some blurring of gender distinctions. Nevertheless, traditional influences are still at work. Despite predictions of *symmetrical families* that would share household tasks (Young and Willmott, 1973), and "androgynous fathers" anxious for involvement in their children's lives, several Canadian studies (Lupri and Mills, 1987; Meissner et al., 1975)

conclude that when wives go out to work, husbands do *not* substantially increase their share of housework or child care (see Chapter 8). Although couples are more likely to share child care than housework, the father still plays a "minor part" in child care, even when the mother is equally employed full time (Horna and Lupri, 1987). For example, whether she works full-time or part-time, it is still the mother who usually stays home with her sick child (Northcott, 1983). Even when fathers "help out" with the children, mothers do what has to be done, such as feeding and bathing, while fathers' time more often involves play and discipline (Jump and Haas, 1987:99).

In view of the foregoing, it is hardly surprising that many Canadian youngsters continue to be quite sex-typed in their thinking. (See the description of children's perception of occupations [Labour Canada, 1986] in Chapter 4.) Canadian adolescents still regard housework as women's work (Baker, 1985:152). Although the children of professional and divorced mothers entertained more egalitarian ideas about their future occupations, "both sexes seemed to be bound by traditional stereotypes of gender and work" (Baker, 1985:160).

What are the consequences for socialization when fathers *do* take a more active role in childrearing? Studies of increased paternal involvement are "still rare and marred by methodological flaws" (Lamb et al., 1986:142). Nonetheless, several reliable generalizations can be advanced. These conclusions from research discount the popular fear that the personal adjustment and gender identity of children will be seriously disturbed if their fathers assume an extensive role in child care (Lamb et al., 1986:153). Youngsters' gender identity seems neither to be confused nor inappropriately accentuated by greater father influence. Divorcing fathers have difficulty getting custody of their offspring on the grounds that they are incapable of providing primary nurturing care to young children. However, research disproves earlier arguments that infants bond exclusively to their mothers. We now know that infants typically form attachments to both parents at about the same time. (When distressed children have a choice between their parents, they do tend to prefer their mothers

[Lamb et al., 1986:144].) Observational studies report that father-infant and mother-infant interactional patterns share more similarities than differences (Lewis, 1972:167). Moreover, empirical data attest to the supportive, nurturing quality of parent-child relationships in single-father families (Hanson, 1986:182). Finally, studies show that boys and girls develop less traditionally sex-stereotyped self-perceptions and attitudes about female and male roles when their mothers work outside the home and when their fathers are highly involved in child care. Hypotheses about the effects of paternal involvement on personality adjustment have neither been proven nor disproven (Lamb et al., 1986:147-48). We conclude that although more well-designed studies are needed, children who (for one reason or another) do not receive the exclusive attention of their mothers do not suffer deleterious consequences.

NEW AVENUES OF PARENTING

In this section we discuss two important developments in parenting: increased involvement of fathers and new reproductive technologies. Both issues are linked with concerns about women's parental roles raised by the feminist movement.

Enhanced Paternal Responsibility

As discussed above, feminist analysis of the family attributes sex-typed personalities, men's hatred of women, and disturbed mother-daughter relationships to social arrangements in Western cultures that isolate mothers and fail to hold fathers responsible for half the parenting. For instance, Chodorow (1978:213) hypothesizes that mother-daughter relationships in which the mother is supported by a network of women kin and friends, and has meaningful work and healthy self-esteem, will produce daughters with a capacity for nurturance *and* a strong sense of self. Similarly, she argues that men will face inevitable problems so long as parenting is almost exclusively women's jurisdiction: "the very fact of being mothered by a woman generates in men con-

flicts over masculinity, a psychology of male dominance, and a need to be superior to women" (p. 214). If parenting is equally shared, mothers are less likely "to overinvest in and overwhelm" the relationships, and children are better off where love is "not a scarce resource controlled and manipulated by one person only" (p. 217). Men's potential for tender expression will be realized when they assume equal responsibility for child care.

The argument for men's equal participation in parenting, which originated in feminism, was "adopted and highly elaborated as one of the central ideas of the contemporary men's movement, and diffused through the culture more broadly" (Pleck, 1987:94). Robert Fein (1974:62) wrote that the appeal to some men was the promise of fathering experiences as "paths to a man's buried soul."[6] He went on to say:

In a society where it is increasingly possible for a child to grow to adulthood without being given a single opportunity to take care of a live creature (let alone a small human), newly found relationships between men and young children are both valuable in and of themselves and as a means toward larger ends. ...Growing awareness of the 'sandpaper existence' of many [North American] men (the pervasive loneliness, the frantic competition, the prevalence of ulcers and heart attacks, the premature dying) propels some to seek new ways to order the structure and meaning of their daily lives. Relationships between men and young children, long awaited homecomings, may lead toward a more caring society (Fein, 1974:62).

The critique from the men's movement called into question the traditional father, distant, aloof, respected (but feared), who protected and provided for his family (Jump and Haas, 1987:98). It urged fathers to join with mothers as equal partners in child care. The "new father" is present at the birth of his children; he is involved with his children as infants, not just when they are older; he participates in the actual day-to-day work of child care, not just play; he is involved as much with his daughters as his sons (Pleck, 1987:93).

As we shall see in Chapter 10, these concerns have now entered the political arena. For example, Canadian men's groups are lobbying for fathers' rights to custody of their children, and for paternity leave. As yet, the implications of these new interests for women remain unclear. "It is possible to speculate that the increased preoccupation with fathers might be an expression of the move towards women's equality, with men being expected to share child care. Alternatively, it could represent a backlash against women, where men, facing competition from women at work, are attempting to compete with women in the home and to appropriate an area in which women were previously autonomous" (McKee and O'Brien, 1982:5).

Empirical studies, though not as plentiful as one might wish, support several conclusions about parenting. Structural changes, especially women's increased labour force participation, have altered traditional patterns of child care which, in turn, are influencing gender socialization. Though fathers' participation is not equal to mothers', they are more actively involved in their children's upbringing. This is especially the case in dual-career families. In addition, many children are growing up in lone-parent homes. As a consequence, youngsters are experiencing blurred gender distinctions.

Despite the foregoing, it is important to remember that other aspects of the social structure bolster traditional gender arrangements. Society does not really support full involvement of fathers in their children's upbringing; the majority of men still operate under considerable pressure to give their jobs priority over their families. Although particular families may be indifferent about which parent stays home, the wife's status as potential earner of lower wages usually determines that it is she who remains the primary homemaker and caretaker of children.

Though the increasing numbers of fathers pushing babies in strollers may be diminishing the impact of gender stereotypes that label child care as women's work, this imagery still retains considerable legitimacy. The cartoon "Adam," featuring a househusband, illustrates this transitional thinking — even the existence of a comic strip with this plot line in the 1990s attests to men's changing roles. However,

Adam is portrayed as awkward and inept at housework and child care. His wife, Laura, seems guilty about the role reversal. And the outside world doesn't yet understand. In one episode, Clayton comes home from school, miffed because the kids call his stay-at-home father names like "scouring-pad face" and "detergent breath."

Child experts advise that if the parents' goal is to produce children with less sex-typed personalities, two strategies can be adopted. First, the division of labour they model greatly influences youngsters' ideas about masculinity and femininity. If kids see parents sharing babytending, housework, and breadwinning, their own views on who does what are bound to become less sex-typed. Secondly, parents can encourage children to develop their own interests and capabilities, regardless of the gender stereotyping which characterizes popular thinking about these activities. However, as the next two chapters make clear, the contemporary family shares its influence with other powerful agents of gender socialization. Much of this extra-familial influence supports traditional gender arrangements.

A final cautionary note. Several authorities tell us that lone-parent upbringing is probably not the best way to achieve androgynous children. Green (1976), for example, says "two adults involved in the upbringing can counteract each other's more bizarre tendencies and complement each other's talents and blind spots." New family forms, such as co-operatives of same-sex parents, multi-generational families, and reconstituted families may compensate for the experiential and economic deficit of the lone-adult parent. This remark is based on evidence "that any second adult within a household, so long as that adult is committed to the children, can be useful in supporting the children's development" (Weiss, 1982:182).

New Reproductive Technologies

The accentuation of women's lack of power that often accompanies parenthood explains the anti-natalism of the early stage of the renewed feminist movement. The assignment by all industrialized societies of the child-rearing role to women and the economic-provider role to men was seen as the basis for most of the gender structures and their consequences in modern society (Richardson, 1988:197). As McDaniel (1988c:177) puts it, "the generally accepted reason for the secondary social status held by women in Canadian society is our reproductive roles." This is why control of their own sexuality and reproduction remain issues at the very top of feminist movement agendas. Feminist Adrienne Rich (1976:292) wrote: "the repossession by women of our bodies will bring far more essential change to human society than the seizing of the means of production by workers." In earlier days, women's capacity to reproduce was seen "as a handicap, a source of social inferiority (Oakley, 1979). Many feminists argued that freedom and equality required being childless, or celibate, or lesbian.

Over the last several years, feminists have begun to re-evaluate their earlier stance on motherhood, and to consider that it is the patriarchal *institution* of motherhood that is the problem, not the experience itself (Rowland, 1987:513).[7] This revised feminist position acknowledges that while it is true that the motherhood mystique entraps women, giving birth constitutes a primary life experience for women (O'Brien, 1981). Moreover, the best qualities of mothering and maternal thinking "embody the kinds of caring we wish men, too, could express to others" (Rowland, 1987:515). (See also Gilligan, 1982.)

As the second wave of the women's movement emerged in the late 1960s and early 1970s, feminist concern with reproduction revolved about *choice*: women's right to control the conditions under which they became mothers, indeed their right not to become mothers at all. In September 1969, the section of the Criminal Code of Canada outlawing the sale of contraceptives was repealed.

Twenty years ago there was no legal method, short of denial and celibacy, to plan a family. It was considered anathema even to talk about "planning." The overriding assumption was that women were made to have children, and anything else was merely a hobby, between pregnancies, so to speak (Ford, 1989).

Concern about access to contraception and abortion remains alive. For one thing, control over their reproductive systems has yet to be attained by many poor and minority group women in this country and around the globe (McDaniel, 1988c:4). For another, although polls show most Canadians feel abortion should be available with some restrictions (*The Globe and Mail*, September 22, 1989), the right of a woman, her doctor, and perhaps her partner, to choose abortion remains precarious in the new abortion legislation proposed by the Conservative government in 1990.

Nevertheless, reproduction issues are infinitely more complex today than they were two decades ago. Contemporary feminist thinking about the matter must grapple with surrogate motherhood, test-tube fertilization, embryo transfers, freezing of embryos, artificial insemination, Nobel Laureate sperm banks, prenatal sex selection techniques, "harvesting" of unwanted fetuses, artificial wombs, court decisions upholding the rights of the fetus against those of the mother, and much more. The gravity of what has been termed a "reproductive revolution" (Eichler, 1989) is such that the Canadian government, in its April 1989 Speech from the Throne, responded to the lobbying of a coalititon of women's groups and promised to establish a Royal Commission on New Reproductive Technologies. At the time of writing (September 1990), the Commission is travelling across Canada gathering public opinion on these important issues.

While it is true that the new reproductive technologies bring happiness to many infertile couples, their existence stimulates grave concerns. Only a few aspects of this contentious matter can be explored here. Among them are the following: First, the meaning of motherhood and fatherhood has already been irrevocably altered (Eichler, 1989:1). For example, what does parenthood mean when artificial wombs are being developed by which men can be pregnant through the implantation of an embryo in the male abdomen? When women are impregnated from semen which combines donations from their husbands and strangers? When babies conceived through artificial insemination from the husband are carried by surrogate mothers? (McDaniel, 1989).

Second, the existence of these "brave new world" technologies serve to reinforce the motherhood mandate, and perhaps to extend it to fathers. Women's choices about childbearing may actually decrease, as motherhood is glorified and more women are "pressured into seeing themselves primarily as mothers" (McDaniel, 1989:12). As these comments from women interviewed by Charlene Miall (1986) indicate, infertility can be a devastating experience:

[Admitting to reproduction problems was] an admission that you're not a whole person... either sexually or anatomically or both. That there's something wrong ...strikes at the very essence of one's being (p. 272).
It was difficult to tell his family because I know he felt bad because he thought he was failing me and it was also kind of a slap in the eye because of his manhood...(p. 274).

Before the advent of new reproductive technologies, infertile couples could eventually accept their status and get on with their lives. Now, many infertile couples become obsessed with the possibility of a "cure" for their problem, and become willing to undergo heroic efforts. (See Ralston, 1989.)

Third, the costs involved are high. New tech babies cost a lot of money. In Canada, an *in vitro* fertilization costs $30 000 to $40 000 (Eichler, 1989:2). In addition, the new techniques sometimes entail considerable physical pain for women, as well as psychological trauma for both partners. In the end, the success rates of some techniques are exceedingly low. "About 90% of the women who undergo the very stressful treatments associated with [*in vitro* fertilization] walk away at the end of the process without a child" (Eichler, 1989:2).

Lastly, what is *not* new about these technologies is to have the control of reproduction elsewhere than with women. Earlier, childbirth "was taken out of the hands of the traditional experts, midwives and women themselves, and placed firmly under the control of obstetricians who are highly trained medical specialists, usually male" (McDaniel, 1989:7). (See Oakley, 1980.) All these technologies require that the woman become a medical patient,

whether or not the woman is the infertile partner (Achilles, 1988). They therefore increase the chances of female bodies becoming targets for medical manipulation (Arditti et al., 1984). For example, there are documented cases of women undergoing hysterectomies not being told their eggs were being removed for other women's use (Thom, 1988:72). Recent artificial technologies involve a variety of medical specialists, as well as lawyers, judges, and legislators, in the once-intimate experience of baby-making. This loss of privacy and control is enormously troubling.

As Achilles (1988) observes, reproductive technology, old and new, can be viewed either as "hope chest" or "Pandora's box." The Pill and the IUD enhanced women's reproductive freedom. But they cost some women their lives. The new techniques have certainly benefited many couples. (In the United States, more children are born each year through technologically assisted reproduction than are available for traditional adoption [Thom, 1988:70].) However, they also invite caution: "Have we learned anything from experiences like those associated with the pill and the Dalkon Shield? ....Who invented it, who manufactured it, who licensed it, who dispenses it? But who dies from it?" (Rowland, 1987:528).

This brief discussion of reproductive technologies ends our treatment of new avenues of parenting. Out next topic is the role brothers and sisters play in gender socialization.

SIBLINGS AS AGENTS OF GENDER SOCIALIZATION

The household was once described as a "socialization depot" by innovative sociologist Erving Goffman (1977:314), on the ground that "family life ensures that most of what each sex does is done in the full sight of the other sex." Goffman emphasized the role played by siblings in one another's gender socialization: "It is as if society planted a brother with sisters so women could from the beginning learn their place, and a sister with brothers so men could learn their place." Although one-child families are becoming quite common (and little empirical basis exists for the negative picture many people hold about the spoiled, lonely only child [Hernandez, 1986:173]), it is important that our discussion of the family as gender socialization agent include consideration of siblings.

Sibling relationships have three distinctive features (Tesson, 1987:101-102). First, sibling relations are unique in that they share some characteristics of parent-child relations and some of peer relations. Though siblings, like parents, are family members, they do not hold authority over the other children, unless they are much older. Like peers, they are of comparable status. However, as members of the same family, they are usually locked into a lifelong relationship with one another. By contrast, peer relations are entered into voluntarily. If friendship becomes bothersome, it can be ended. This combination results in the special influence of brothers and sisters upon one another.

A second distinctive feature of sibling relations is that unlike friendships which usually proceed free of adult interference, "they are overseen and often significantly controlled by parents" (Tesson, 1987:101). Parents have an interest in how siblings behave toward one another, and may actively police their interaction. The children themselves tend to be very sensitive about their differential treatment by parents. In short, the sibling relationship cannot be understood in isolation; it has to be viewed as part of a system of familial relationships.

Third, although love and warmth may exist between brothers and sisters, a certain amount of tension typically characterizes sibling relations. The primary reason, of course, is the rivalry among siblings for their parents' attention and affection.

Despite contemporary analysts' appreciation of the unique significance of siblings, none of the classical theories of personality development portrayed siblings as important agents of socialization (Lamb and Sutton-Smith 1982:4). Consequently, research has focussed on parent-child relations, and ignored the influence of siblings upon both socialization in general, and gender socialization in particular. That the number, age, and spacing of children are critical dimensions of family structure is common

knowledge. However, little can be said about the relationship of these variables to gender socialization. Unfortunately, we can only speculate about the impact on sibling socialization of such contemporary phenomena as shrinking families (with one or two children), lone-parent or dual-worker families (where considerable sibling interaction may be unmonitored by adults), or blended families (where step-siblings encounter one another midway through their childhood).[8]

Although considerable research will be required before firm generalizations can be stated, such data as do exist suggest that siblings act as surrogate parental models for gender (Weitz, 1977:84). Rosenberg and Sutton-Smith (1968) report that girls with sisters scored significantly higher on the Gough Scale of Psychological Femininity than girls with brothers. Similarly, Brim (1958) found that five- and six-year-old boys with older brothers displayed more of the traits that have traditionally been thought of as masculinity than did boys with older sisters. He also found that girls with older brothers displayed more traditionally masculine traits than girls without older brothers. These girls did not substitute masculine for feminine traits. Instead, their repertoire included characteristics that have traditionally been attributed to both sexes. "One clear difference between one-sex and two-sex families is that the latter households are likely to have both male- and female- stereotyped toys, and children in two-sex families probably also have contact with peers of the other gender who play with their siblings" (Huston, 1983:438).

A number of studies contradict the above conclusion that siblings of one's own gender encourage same-sex stereotyped interests and behaviour through modelling and reinforcement (Huston, 1983:437). This research suggests that same-sex siblings need to establish their identities by developing interests or behaviours that are distinctly different from their same-sex siblings. In her autobiography, author Fredelle Maynard (1988:3) writes that she and her sister Celia moved more and more deeply into different roles: "Celia was the pretty one and I the clever one. How this division became absolute puzzles me still: I was a pleasant-looking child, she was intelligent. But we accepted our separate destinies and even learned to enjoy them."

Sometimes younger children mimic the sex-typed behaviour of their older siblings. Sometimes younger children strive to be different, perhaps to capture the parents' attention, or to carve their own place in the world. If older siblings have already established competence in sex-typed activities, the younger ones may be reluctant to compete. "Parents may also encourage more diverse behavior among their girls if there are no boys, or vice versa" (Huston, 1983:438). Also, parents who have children of both sexes tend to assign household tasks on a sex-typed basis (girls wash dishes; boys take out garbage). When families are all boys or all girls, the tasks assigned to children necessarily become less sex-typed (White and Brinkerhoff, 1981; Brody and Steelman, 1985). In all-girl families, somebody has to take out the trash! It is hoped that future studies will sort out all these possibilities.

DEMOGRAPHIC VARIATIONS IN GENDER SOCIALIZATION

Canada has been characterized as "a pluralist nation comprised of a multitude of historical influences, regional patterns, and ethnic collectivities — a mosaic of histories, religions, cultures, languages, ideologies, and communities" (Driedger, 1987:1). Many cultural elements, such as national holidays, advertisements, comic strips, TV programs, popular sports, name-brand products, and automobiles are widely shared by Canadian families. Nevertheless, one of the most important facts about Canadian society is its heterogeneous nature. This diversity means that children are socialized into particular subcultures which differentially emphasize aspects of the larger culture and have some distinctive ideas and experiences (Elkin and Handel, 1984:80). Though systematic work on how various Canadian subcultures interpret and teach gender relations has barely begun, we do have some preliminary indications of relationship between gender socialization and social class and ethnicity.

Social Class

Canadian society, like all other large societies, is socially stratified. Families' socioeconomic status is usually measured by statistical indices which combine parents' education, income, and occupation. Occupation is the single best indicator of a family's social class position. Social class divisions in Canadian society, frequently interlinked with ethnicity, critically influence socialization. Research shows that children's class origins continue to significantly influence their educational attainment and subsequent occupational success (McRoberts, 1985). Chapter 8 provides extensive treatment of social stratification. Here, we focus our attention on the relationship between social class and gender socialization.

Visualize a large factory which makes electrical equipment. Executives, lawyers, accountants sit in leather chairs, making decisions. Bankers and stockholders are shadowy, behind-the-scene figures. In the office section of the factory, women tap keyboards of word processors and peer at green letters on their monitors. Assembly of electric components is done by hundreds of men on the shop floor. Their positions in the company (and in the outside society) give these categories of people different vantage points on the world, in general, and gender, in particular.

Stan Gray (1987:388) describes the notions about gender shared by male manual workers in a southern Ontario plant that was trying to introduce women onto the factory floor:

Many of the men had resisted the female invasion of the workplace because for them it was the last sanctum of male culture. It was somewhere they would be away from the world of women, away from responsibility and children and the civilised society's cultural restraints. In the plant they could revel in the rough and tumble of a masculine world of physical harshness; of constant swearing and rough behaviour; of half-serious fighting and competition with each other, and more serious fighting with the boss. It was 8 hours full of filth and dirt and grease and grime and sweat — manual labour, a *manly* atmosphere. They could be vulgar and obscene, talk about football and car repairs. Let their hair down. Boys could be boys.

The male workplace culture functions as a form of

rebellion against the discipline of their society. Outside the workplace, the women are the guardians of the community. They raise the kids and enforce some degree of family and collective responsibility. They frequently have to force this upon individualist males. The men would rather go drinking or play baseball or do their own thing while the women mind the kids, wash the family's clothes, attend to problems with the neighbours and in-laws, and so on.

Like rebellious teenage sons escaping mother's control, male wage earners enter the factory gate; there, in their male culture, they feel free of the restraints of these repressive standards (Gray, 1987:388).

As Gray's observations illustrate, members of different social classes, by virtue of experiencing different conditions of life, come to develop different conceptions of social reality (Gecas, 1979; Kohn, 1977). Approaches to socialization also vary by social class. In general, middle-class parents tend to be warmer, more expressive, and less authoritarian in their child rearing than are working-class parents (Gecas, 1976). Kohn (1977) speculates that the parental values apparent in socialization of their children are extensions of modes of behaviour that are functional for them in their occupations. He argues that the white-collar work of the middle class enunciates values of self-direction, such as freedom, individualism, initiative, creativity, and self-actualization. Blue-collar work, on the other hand, is more likely to involve values of conformity to external standards, such as orderliness, neatness and obedience (Gecas, 1976:44-45). These class differences in socialization styles are found in many different societies.

From these general observations, several lines of reasoning about gender can be extrapolated. Working-class parents hold more traditional views of gender than do middle-class parents. Working-class men are more traditional in their thinking than are working-class women (Swatos and McCauley, 1984). Male and female roles are less sharply differentiated in middle-class homes than in working-class homes (Lambert, 1971). Working-class parents are less concerned than their middle-class counterparts about the actualization of female potential. Willingness to experiment with novel forms of family organization, such as stay-at-home fathers, tends to be associated with middle-class origins.

Gaskell's (1988) description of the ideas about gender held by young people from Vancouver working-class neighbourhoods in the last year of high school tells us something about the end products of the socialization process. Though three-quarters of the girls valued paid work over domestic work, they all assumed they would eventually carry primary responsibility for housekeeping and child care. Outside work would not lessen this domestic burden. One young woman said, "I considered engineering pretty seriously [but]...if I'm going to get married that's the most important thing I'm looking forward to" (p. 150). Their views about household division of labour remain traditional:

Sharing the housework would be wonderful. But it is not going to happen. He'd [her boyfriend] never help with the floors or with the dishes. I know him too well. I don't expect him to do it because I know he wouldn't (p. 154).

I don't think men are very good at raising children. From what I have seen of fathers, I don't think they could hack it. I guess that is just the way they were brought up when they were young. Women have a better knack for it than men do (p. 154).

The young men interviewed by Gaskell were even more conservative:

I don't think it should be equal. I think the wife should stay home and clean house and cook, while the male goes out and works (p. 160).

There's a difference between raising kids and looking after them. The woman might spend more time with the kids, but the father has the authority (p. 161).

In most of these young people about to embark on adult life, Gaskell found the passivity that reproduces traditional gender roles. However, in some of the women, she detected the beginnings of discontent that provide the possibility of change. She concludes that information about alternative lives would not be enough to bring about equality for women and men. "Life choices come not merely from some abstract principles of what should happen, but from an assessment of the way the world works, what opportunities are open, what paths are possible" (Gaskell, 1988:166). The topic of gender and stratification will be explored more thoroughly in Chapter 8.

Ethnicity

Canada officially embraces a policy of multiculturalism within a bilingual framework. The primary socialization of Canadians reflects ethnic differences in values, norms, and identity. Ethnicity in this country is further complicated by the fact that "ethnic affiliation is interwoven with the structure of social class" (Blishen, 1973:162).

According to the last census (1981), 40 percent of the population had a British background and 27 percent a French background. The ethnic origins of the remaining 33 percent were extremely diverse. Prior to Canada's revision of its immigration policies in the late 1960s, nine out of ten immigrants arrived in Canada from Europe and the British Isles. By 1984, the leading source countries of immigrants included such non-European countries as Vietnam, Hong Kong, India, Jamaica, and the Philippines (Kalbach, 1987). Moreover, the ethnic composition of the country varies considerably from region to region. For example, the Atlantic provinces are not as ethnically diverse as the Western provinces. Persons of Asian and African descent are found in the largest numbers in provinces with big cities, such as Ontario. Native peoples are more likely to live in the West and the North (Hiller, 1986:18).

To speak about gender socialization in *the* Canadian family certainly represents an abstract oversimplification of reality. Unfortunately, the task of untangling the ways in which gender socialization is influenced by the interacting effects of ethnicity, social class, and region has barely begun. In a special issue of *Canadian Ethnic Studies* on the topic of "Ethnicity and Femininity," editors Juteau-Lee and Roberts (1981:5) observe that in the large social science literature on ethnicity there has been surprisingly little inquiry into the family.

When the histories of ethnic groups in Canada talk about the immigration experience, on an individual level, they talk about men coming over, men working on the railways, or in the mines or on the land.

Women and children are presented as adjuncts, as part of the baggage brought along to support what is presumed to be a male experience...(Juteau-Lee and Roberts, 1981:5).

As a result of the feminist influence on the social sciences, women are now more visible in the ethnic relations literature than they once were. (We will return to immigrant women in Chapter 8.) Nevertheless, home life in which gender socialization takes place remains mostly hidden from researchers.

In order to alert the reader to the impact of ethnicity upon gender socialization in this country, brief illustrations are drawn from Indian/Pakistani, Ukrainian, and French-Canadian ethnic groups. These three groups have been chosen to convey something of the range of ethnic variation. Indian/Pakistani families represent the visible minorities who recently immigrated to Canada from Asia and Africa. The Ukrainians were part of the wave of immigration between 1896 and World War I that came to homestead the prairie provinces. The French-Canadians are, of course, one of Canada's two founding peoples.

Growing Up in Indo-Pakistani Families

Gender socialization in immigrant families partakes of old and new worlds. According to a study of Indian and Pakistani families that came to a western Canadian city in the late 1950s and early 1960s, parents confront difficult decisions regarding adoption of Canadian ways of life versus retention of their own cultural traditions (Wakil et al., 1981). "Most [of the younger generation] feel they are caught up between two cultures with distinct and at times conflicting values and there is no easy way to compromise" (p. 940).

In comparison with "old country" practices, Indo-Pakistani children growing up in Canada are allowed considerable freedom. A noteworthy example: young people are free to determine their own educational goals and future careers. A growing number of parents have begun to encourage their daughters to obtain professional degrees and to take up careers. This parental encouragement "presents a sharp contrast to their conventional images of feminine roles" (p. 934). Parents accept their youngsters' preferences for Canadian food and dress. They tolerate their children's enthusiasm for Western music, movies, and festivals. However, they are saddened by the fact that the second generation is more familiar with Canadian celebrations such as Christmas, Hallowe'en, and Valentine's Day, than with their own religious festivals, such as *Eid, Devali,* and *Gurpurb*. Although parents are delighted with their youngsters' fluency in English, they resent the resulting communication gap between them.

The generations clash over such critical matters as association with people of the other sex/gender and marriage practices. While some parents are willing to let their sons date without supervision, they do not grant the same privilege to their daughters. Females are considered the repository of the *izzet* or honour of the family; they bear special responsibility for the continuity of their family and community. Parents favour arranged marriages through a system of "matchmaking." The traditional idea that "love will grow after marriage" seems more sensible to them than Western romanticism. Though the Canadian-born children were not too happy with these notions at the time Wakil and colleagues conducted their study, the parents' wishes had prevailed; more than two-thirds of all the marriages had been sponsored marriages. However, compromises are occurring. For example, matchmakers seek prospective mates in the old country who have been exposed to Western values. Bridegrooms of Canadian-born brides must be prepared to set aside their traditional authoritarian attitudes and expectations of submissive, stay-at-home wives.

GROWING UP UKRAINIAN

Zonia Keywan (1981) describes growing up female among Ukrainians who came to Canada as "DPs" after World War II. From her account, we learn that the ideas about gender embraced by immigrant women are not necessarily more traditional than those held by Canadian-born women.

As a child growing up in a family of refugees, surrounded by a larger community of refugees, ethnicity was a very central fact of my life. I spoke no English until I went to school; all the people I knew were Ukrainian immigrants and all the activities I participated in were exclusively Ukrainian... .

In Eastern Europe, in the period preceding World War II, it was not at all uncommon for women to engage in such professions as medicine, law, science, etc. Thus, I grew up with the idea that these were perfectly natural things for women to do....The idea that women had as much right as men to careers of some status was further reinforced by my parents' reaction to the very different situation that they found in Canada: they often expressed their amazement at the fact that women in Canada never strove for careers more demanding than that of school-teacher or nurse. Yet another factor in presenting positive role models was that within the Ukrainian organizations to which my parents belonged, women participated on an equal footing with men.

On the negative side: the view of female roles that I picked up at home was in conflict with the realities of the world around me. I learned at rather an early age that to be both ethnic and female was not of great advantage in this country. This I could see from the experience of my own mother who, although she had practised medicine for 10 years in Europe, was not able to pass a sufficient number of exams at the University of Alberta Faculty of Medicine to be able to practise in Canada. Although the attitude towards all immigrants was negative, it was doubly so for women. That my mother's failure was the result of blatant discrimination was not the least bit in doubt — she was told, by one of her examiners, that females do not need to work in professions like medicine because they have husbands to support them.

Seeing my mother's bitterness and unhappiness at the loss of her career did, perhaps, in a strange way have a positive effect on me, in making me realize that to a woman self-fulfillment and autonomy are as important as they are to a man and that she suffers as much as anyone at the loss of these things. But it also made me realize, although I was too young to fully comprehend the situation, that speaking with a foreign accent and being female was not a way of gaining respect (Keywan, 1981:38-39).

FRENCH-CANADIAN GENDER ATTITUDES

Social scientists have paid considerable attention to comparative study of French-Canadian/English-Canadian gender attitudes. The data indicate that French-Canadian attitudes have become increasingly egalitarian over time. In a national study of gender imagery, Lambert (1971) found French-Canadian parents to be more traditional than English-Canadian parents. French-Canadian children, however, had less differentiated views of appropriate gender behaviour than did English-Canadian children. Lambert suggested that the parental difference might be partially attributable to the higher average educational level of his English-speaking sample. This interpretation accords with his finding of greater traditionalism in the working class.

Somewhat later studies showed that although some changes were occurring, French-Canadians remained quite traditional about those aspects of gender relations that pertain to the family. For instance, Boyd's (1975) analysis of Gallup Poll results found that French-Canadians entertained two attitudinal complexes with respect to women. They supported equality between the sexes, but only when the Gallup questions did not evoke maternal or wifely imagery. When these roles did become salient, French-Canadians tended to become more traditional in their attitudes towards women.

As our review of Ponting's (1986) national study of attitudes (Chapter 2) concluded, Francophones are now at least as liberal as Anglophones about gender issues. For example, 80 percent of the Francophone sample (versus 72 percent of the Anglophones) agreed that "There should be more laws to get rid of differences in the way women are treated, compared to men." The language groups now held similar attitudes about gender in the domestic sphere. In 1986, 62 percent of Francophones and 63 percent of Anglophones felt that "When children are young, a mother's place is in the home." When Gibbins et al. had asked this question in 1978, 81 percent of the Francophones and 83 percent of the Anglophones agreed. Hobart's (1981) study of university and technical students across Canada concluded that recent dramatic changes in Quebec families had brought about egalitarianism in formerly sensitive areas such as authority within marriage, childrearing, household management, and women's work outside the home. These changes could, in turn, be traced to such forces as the Quiet Revolution, the diminishing influ-

ence of the Roman Catholic Church, and the worldwide feminist movement (Clio Collective, 1987).

CONCLUSIONS

Chapter 5 is the first of three chapters to discuss the role played by particular socialization agents in teaching young people Canadian society's gender scripts. "The family is the first unit with which children have continuous contact and the first context in which socialization patterns develop. It is a world with which they have nothing to compare and, as such, it is the most important socializing agency" (Elkin and Handel, 1984:127). Moreover, the family is the prototypical primary grouping, characterized by intense emotions and touching all aspects of social existence. In addition, the family achieves its influence through its channelling function as it orients the child to specific configurations of experiences, values, and opportunities.

The chapter began by considering recent important changes in the Canadian family that complicate gender socialization, namely increases in divorce, lone-parent and reconstituted families, and women's labour force participation. Several factors that constrain traditional family authority, such as technological innovation and intrusion of experts, were also pointed out.

Folk thought has held the social roles of father and mother to be as distinctive as the procreative roles of men and women. When this assumption was scrutinized, we found that differences in parenting styles of men and women could be identified. Among them is the important finding that fathers react more stereotypically to their offspring, and therefore make a greater contribution to sex-typed socialization. However, the source of parenting differences between mothers and fathers has less to do with their sex/gender than with structural opportunities to parent (a topic to be pursued in Chapter 9).

Feminist theorists influenced by the psychoanalytic perspective, e.g., Chodorow (1978), suggest that the fact that both boys and girls are raised primarily by women explains sex-typed personalities in both sexes. Excessive mothering is also seen to be the reason for males' hypermasculinity and misogyny. At the same time, the public often blames mothers who also work outside the home for neglecting their children. Although these contradictory criticisms seem plausible, the empirical evidence for both was found to be inconclusive.

Several additional topics were discussed in Chapter 5. New avenues in parenting were described: men's increased involvement in parenting and new reproductive technologies. Although few empirical studies exist, the part played by siblings in one another's gender socialization was considered.

Finally, acknowledging the pluralistic nature of Canadian society, we described briefly some of the social class and ethnic variation in gender socialization.

Two important conclusions flow from this chapter's review of the family as gender socialization agent. First, it would be difficult to overestimate the role played by the family in establishing youngsters' conceptualization of masculinity and femininity. The agencies to be discussed in subsequent chapters (peers, secondary, and symbolic), while influential, are subsidiary to the family. Second, events of this fast-moving world are making necessary considerable rethinking about the family institution — the definition of family, the meaning of parenthood, the reciprocal rights and obligations of mothers, fathers, children. We shall return to the changing social structure of the family in Chapter 9.

NOTES

1. The section on the changing family draws heavily on Mackie (1989).
2. One in ten Canadian single parents has never been married (Davids, 1985:3). Despite the decline in teenage pregnancy, an estimated 80 to 90 percent of all single teenage mothers are keeping their children (Schlesinger, 1985:35).
3. Peters (1989:225) writes: "There is a distinct pattern of courtship and partnership among the divorced. Males are somewhat more likely to remarry. The younger the age at divorce, the greater the likelihood of remarriage. Young divorced women without children often are more

desirable mates in the remarriage market than those who are older and have children. Over 50 percent of the divorced who remarry marry a partner who is also divorced. Remarrying couples are also more heterogeneous in terms of age, race and religion than those who marry for the first time. The age difference between the partners is much larger than commonly found among first married.... Women in the upper economic strata or men in the lower strata are the least likely to remarry. Women in the professions are economically self-sufficient and generally do not wish to rush into another marriage unless non-economic reasons persuade them to do so. Also, many men may have reservations about marrying a successful woman, especially if their own socio-economic status is lower than that of successful divorced women. Lower-class men find it hard to remarry because their limited economic resources bring little in practical terms to a woman seeking economic stability."

4. In her autobiography, *The Tree of Life* (1988), the late Canadian writer Fredelle Maynard describes her strong mother:

My mother was The Competent One. "Mama can do *anything*," my father always said, and that was pretty much the case. She cooked, cleaned, baked, gardened, sewed, nursed, entertained, knitted and embroidered and crocheted, worked in my father's store, all with efficiency and even brilliance. What she needed most, a career outlet of her own, something more significant than painting on silk, more productive of power and regard — that she did not have. So I became my mother's bound delegate, the one to fulfill her dreams. I was The Clever One".... (p. 136).

5. In 1952, Bowlby's writing about "maternal deprivation" received considerable publicity. He argued that mothers who did not devote themselves full time to motherhood were threatened with the possibility that their children would be psychologically or socially maladjusted. Feminists have suggested that the timing of the "maternal deprivation" debate may not have been coincidental. Laws (1979:126-27) writes: "The idea gained currency just at the time when men were being demobilized at the end of World War II, and began to displace women from the jobs they had occupied during the war.... Child care facilities, provided to induce women to enter employment, were disbanded, Women were being pushed out of the paid work force by men, at the same time they were having full

responsibility for child care 'restored' to them. The 'maternal deprivation' thesis provided a convenient rationale for these changes."

6. This concern with fathering expressed in the early years of the men's movement is a good example of the "male sex role" literature of the 1970s which concentrated on the restrictions, disadvantages, and general penalties attached to being male (Carrigan et al., 1985). The feminist critique of the family as an inegalitarian power structure was ignored. Men's problems were "psychologized." See Chapter 9 for a structural analysis of the family.

7. The feminist critique of the family is discussed further in Chapter 9. See Rich, *Of Woman Born, Motherhood as Experience and Institution* (1977), and O'Brien, *The Politics of Reproduction* (1981).

8. Although they have little to say about gender socialization, psychologists Bank and Kahn in *The Sibling Bond* (1982) arrive at several interesting conclusions from their clinical interviews. For example, they advise that "Sibling bonds will become intense and exert a formative influence upon personality when, as children or adolescents, the siblings have had plentiful access and contact *and* have been deprived of reliable parental care. In this situation, siblings will use one another as major influences, or touchstones, in search for personal identity. When other relationships — with parents, children or spouses — are emotionally fulfilling, the sibling bond will be weaker and less important" (p. 19).

Chapter 6

The Peer Group as Primary Agent of Gender Socialization

Chapter 6 continues the discussion of primary group agencies of socialization that was begun with the previous chapter's consideration of the family. It treats the interplay between gender and peer relations in both same-sex and cross-sex friendships across the life cycle.

This chapter shares the previous chapter's interest in the primary socialization that takes place in childhood. Until not so long ago, the prestige of social learning and psychoanalytic theories led social scientists to consider the influence of peers (and other adults) to be inconsequential in comparison with children's relationships with their parents (Peterson and Rollins, 1987:471). However, the waxing of other theoretical approaches, especially symbolic interactionism and cognitive-developmental theory, has led researchers to examine the rich complexity of children's social lives. The influence of age-mates (as well as other adults, both inside and outside the family, such as grandparents, daycare workers, and parents of friends) as socialization agents is now acknowledged. The conditions under which peer influence augments or competes with familial authority in children's lives is a vital, but still insufficiently studied question (Handel, 1990).

A peer group may be defined as "an association of self-selected equals who coalesce around common interests, tastes, preferences, and beliefs" (Bensman and Rosenberg, 1979:80). So far as children are con-

cerned, the term "peer group" designates not a specific group in which a youngster participates, but all his/her membership groups made up of children, to which adults and their concerns are peripheral (Elkin and Handel, 1984:164). For children (but not necessarily for adults), peers are other children of approximately the same age. Peers are particularly important in age-graded societies, such as our own, where people in similar age categories are segregated in schools, neighbourhoods, and various recreational settings. Individuals' peer relationships vary in intensity from casual acquaintances to close friends. This chapter concentrates on the latter.

The peer group is an unquestionably potent socialization agent for both young people and adults. The fact that children do not deliberately set out to socialize is one reason for their influence on one another. As one child said of friends, " 'they never tell you to wash your hands' " (Rubin, 1973, quoted in Thorne and Luria, 1986:180). Nevertheless, from children's need for companionship and approval there results mutual learning of a variety of information, attitudes, and behaviours. "Knowledge" and feelings about sex/gender constitute a sub-set of this peer subculture. Peer relations permit people of all ages "to escape the too close bonds of the family" (Bensman and Lilienfeld, 1979:57). This alternative to the family is especially important for children who, as part of their normal development, must eventually separate themselves from the family's all-encompassing influence and develop other facets of their identity.

The fact that there are some things that can be learned only from equal-status age-mates is another reason why the peer group is influential. Sensitive topics, e.g., sexuality are more easily discussed with peers than with adults. In addition, there are many aspects of the world that matter greatly to children, about which adults are ignorant or indifferent. The fact that much of this peer information might be the wildest misinformation is beside the point. However, peer and adult influences are not necessarily in opposition. Some peer groups are organized around adult values, e.g., those surrounding sports in our society (Elkin and Handel, 1984:167). Peers often augment and, to some extent, reinforce family socialization. According to research (Fasick, 1984), most adolescents maintain warm emotional ties with parents. They can simultaneously participate in youth culture with its transitory concern with clothes, music, and dating, etc. and remain committed to the adult-related values of their parents.

Nostalgia about childhood sometimes leads adults to overlook the unhappy, even destructive side of peer relations. Tesson (1987:103) observes that, "The often-veiled stereotypes of appearance, social class, ethnicity, and gender which form part of adult culture can, when shorn of any pretence, become blunt weapons in the hands of children bent on seeking status advantage in the schoolyard or the street." Fine (1980:315) describes the treatment preadolescent boys mete out to "friends we hate," i.e., not boys who can be ignored as completely beyond the pale, but erstwhile pals who require coercion to force them to obey group norms. According to Fine's observations, these "friends we hate" were victims of pranks, insults, ostentatious silent treatment, and verbal abuse.

Girls, too, practise social cruelty. A four-year old girl at a party turned to the young female host as a strange child approached the pair: "Tell her we don't want to play with

her," she commanded. "Tell her we don't like her" (Shapiro, 1990:58).

PEER GROUPS AND FRIENDSHIP OVER THE LIFE CYCLE

Peers are immensely important to people of all ages.[1] Infants stare at each other with fascination. Toddlers enjoy and benefit from interaction with their age-mates (Vandell and Mueller, 1980).

At 20 months, Percy and Steven are sitting at opposite ends of a rocking boat. Percy screeches. Steven laughs. Percy screeches. Steven laughs. The cycle is repeated several times. Then Steven begins to crawl from the rocking boat. Percy vocalizes, "ah," smiles, and then reaches to Steven and touches his head and shoulders lightly with several pats. Steven walks away (Marvin, 1977, quoted in Vandell and Mueller, 1980:181).

What might reasonably be labelled friendship develops about age three (Bell, 1981:33). Most parents know that companionship with other children is a necessity, not a luxury. They take pains to find "appropriate" companions for their child, and worry if their offspring becomes attracted to "unsuitable" children, or does not seem to make friends at all. Although the very young "often pick up cues from their parents about age peers they should become friendly with," even young children make their own choices (Bell, 1981:32).

By eight or nine, many children are concerned with having one special friend. The best friend "seems to serve a generally felt human need for interpersonal closeness in the preadolescent period..." (Fine, 1980:295). Since popularity is both important and problematic for preadolescents, there is security in the presence of a single friend one can count on (Fine, 1980:316). Intense, exclusive, demanding liaisons with best friends, along with obvious rejection of outsiders, are somewhat more typical of girls than boys (Best, 1983:102). Thorne and Luria (1986:184) observed that, "Compared with boys, girls are more focused on constructing intimacy..." According to these researchers, "girls often talk about who is friends with or 'likes' whom; they continually negotiate parameters of friendships" (p. 182).[2]

Adolescence seems to mark the zenith of peer group influence. A survey of Canadian teenagers reported that 91 percent viewed friendship as "very important" to them, while only 65 percent said the same about family life (Bibby and Posterski, 1985:107). During the junior high and high school years, clique membership carries considerable status (Eder, 1985; Shrum and Cheek, 1987). The teenager's orientation to the companionship, opinions, and tastes of age-mates helps to bridge the gulf between childish dependence on the family and adult autonomy. In the words of Bensman and Lilienfeld (1979:66), "some friendships, especially the friendships of adolescents, are likely to reach considerable depth, intimacy, and mutual involvement. The common vulnerability of adolescents and the lack of sharp barriers to their sense of self enables others who are sympathetic to their aspirations to reach them." Peer relations continue to matter a great deal throughout adulthood, into old age (Matthews, 1986). The actual functions of friendship, however, vary with the participants' position in the life cycle. For example, the friends of adolescence assist the individual to develop a sense of identity; the friendships of old age appear to serve the primary function of protecting the person from loneliness (Bell, 1981:22).

We now turn from this general discussion of the influence exerted by age-mates to consider the relationship between friendship and gender socialization. These questions are addressed: Does the predominant pattern consist of same-sex friendship groups or mixed-sex groups? What evidence exists to support the contention that males' ability to "bond" results in friendships that are superior to female liaisons (Tiger, 1969)? How do cultural definitions of gender influence relationships with the other sex, in adolescence and adulthood? Here, we focus on platonic and romantic relationships. Throughout our discussion the overriding issue is this: What gender-relevant lessons are learned from peers?

PREVALENCE OF SAME-SEX FRIENDSHIPS

The research literature pertaining to the question, "Are people more apt to have same-sex or other-sex friends?" is unequivocal. Throughout the life cycle, same-sex friendships predominate. From ages three or four, children choose playmates of the same sex, regardless of the nature of play activities (Fagot and Patterson, 1969). The same pattern prevails among elementary-school children. A sociometric study[3] of American children in the fourth to sixth grades found that only 5 percent of the friendship choices were cross-sex choices (Hallinan, 1979). Friendship patterns follow same-sex lines through adolescence into adulthood, although cross-sex dating and mating, of course, occur (Frieze et al., 1978:96). Sometimes, mates are also one another's friends!

Why do same-sex friendships completely overshadow cross-sex friendships? One answer is that same-sex friendships flourish because society approves of them. Little Barbara's parents are more comfortable when she plays with Arabella than with Bruce. The three- and four-year-olds who seek same-sex companions are "responsive to the values of their peers, and one of the strongest early values is to associate with one's own sex" (Bell, 1981:35). Kindergarten teacher, Vivian Paley (1984:ix) speaks of "the five-year-old's *passion* for segregation by sex" (emphasis added).

A second consideration comes into play with older people. According to Chafetz (1974:164), "the one way in which neither sex is taught to view the other is as potential friends and peers. Thus in any platonic relationship there is a built-in dynamic encouraging one or both participants to redefine the situation by 'falling in love.' Generally, either both do, in which case TRUE LOVE results, or one alone does, in which case the relationship becomes uncomfortable and is usually abruptly terminated." Though Chafetz's case may be a bit overstated, findings of a *Psychology Today* survey on friendship (Parlee et al., 1979) support her point.

Seventy-three percent of the 40 000 readers who voluntarily mailed in questionnaires felt that friendships with someone of the other sex were different from same-sex friendships. The major reasons given for this position were that sexual tensions complicate the former type, and that society does not encourage them. Almost half these respondents had had a friendship turn into a sexual relationship. This report concerns adults. However, even children are teased about having a "little boyfriend" or "girlfriend" when they play with children of the other sex.

Thirdly, the choice of same-sex friends is a specific case of the well-documented general relationship between interpersonal attraction and similarity (Verbrugge, 1977). People are attracted to people who resemble themselves. Think about your closest friend. How old is that person? What is your friend's eye colour? Ethnicity? Occupation? If a student, what course of studies is he/she involved in? What kind of music and books does he/she prefer? Would you describe this person as religious or not religious? Politically liberal or politically conservative? In all likelihood, many of your friend's characteristics match your own. Research (Berscheid and Walster, 1978) shows that friends are similar in terms of religion, economic background, occupation, education, and political allegiance. (Matching physical features like eye colour and height might indicate the same ethnic background [Rubin, 1973].)

Why similarity? In a well-known proposition (which does have exceptions), George Homans (1950:112) predicted that, "If the frequency of interaction between two or more people increases, their degree of liking for one another will increase." Interaction provides opportunities for rewards. Familiarity with others like ourselves is apt to be particularly rewarding. Similarity provides a basis for shared activities, in this case, doing "boy things" or "girl things." To take the opposite case, it is sometimes difficult to predict how people who differ from us are likely to behave, and this absence of shared frames of reference can be punishing. In

general, then, similarity leads to liking, and liking in turn leads to increased similarity as friends influence one another. Homans's proposition has important implications for gender socialization. As we shall see, young people's same-sex peers tend to reflect the containing culture and to reinforce gender stereotyping (Richer, 1984).

THE QUALITY OF MALE VERSUS FEMALE FRIENDSHIPS

"There is a longstanding myth in our society that the great friendships are between men" (Fasteau, 1975:6). Films and novels have provided numerous portraits of boys' and men's friendships; until recently, they seldom bothered about friendships between females (Wright, 1982:2). "Our culture has traditionally viewed male friendship as embodying the ideals of comradeship and brotherhood. Men have buddies, pals, lifelong ties — bonds of unspoken, unshakeable commitment — the kind of friends for whom one would 'lay down one's life'" (Sherrod, 1987:214-15). The more traditionally masculine the experience — playing on a football team, mastering a Himalayan mountain, surviving a war — the more profound the friendship is supposed to be.

Perhaps the best-known statement of the superiority of male friendship was advanced by Lionel Tiger. In his book, *Men In Groups* (1969), Tiger presented a sociobiological case for *male bonding*, which he defined as "a particular relationship between two or more males such that they react differently to members of their bonding unit as compared to individuals outside of it." According to Tiger, these male bonds generate strong feelings of comradeship and loyalty that differ from the emotional quality of female-female friendships or male-female relationships. This biological propensity for males to bond allegedly resulted from the human evolutionary experience. Men survived early hazards of hunting and warfare through cooperating with one another. Since women did not face these dangers, deep capacity for friendship is genetically transmitted exclusively to men.

As you might suspect, feminist scholars were critical of Tiger's views. They responded that Tiger was vague, even mystical, about the precise nature of this bonding. Indeed, empirical evidence for the existence of a special male bond is lacking (Nielson, 1978:98). However, what about Tiger's reiteration of the longstanding cultural myth that the great friendships in this world are between men?

First, who has more friends, men or women? Sociologists' surveys of people of different ages and occupations, taken together, lead to the firm conclusion that men and women report roughly the same number of friends (Sherrod, 1987:215). For example, in Hallinan's (1979) sociometric study of children's friendships cited earlier, the average child chose about five best friends. According to a California study, the average man named 11 non-kin friends he could call upon for help and advice, while the average woman named ten (Fischer, 1983).

What happens when we go beyond enumerating friendships to examine their content? Both sexes say they desire close friendship. Both describe friends as equally important in their lives (Sherrod, 1987:220). The bonds of male and female friendship appear to be equally strong (Hays, 1985). However, friendship seems to mean different things to men and women. While women look for intimate confidantes, men seek partners to share activities (Caldwell and Peplau, 1982; Sherrod, 1987:217). By "intimacy," men mean the closeness that comes from doing things together; women mean emotional support and revealing disclosure. One man described his relationship with his good friend this way: "We don't act the same way my wife acts with her friends, but it doesn't mean we don't care. It's just different. We express a lot through racquetball" (Sherrod, 1987:236). Men often withhold their personal thoughts and feelings from even their closest friends (Bell, 1981:89). Several studies have documented gender-specific conversational distinctions (Davidson and Duberman, 1982; Morgan, 1976). Men together discuss issues — work, sports, politics, hobbies, movies. Women disclose much more. While they, too, talk about topical issues, they are willing to discuss their personal problems and relationships. Homophobia and fear of sanctions for culturally unacceptable emotional behaviours inhibit men from expressing certain emotions, such as fear or sadness (Swain, 1989:84).

Although, as mentioned above, men tend to *infer* intimacy from shared activities, there are times when they seem to become aware that something is lacking. Needing a friend upon whom they can rely, they may find they have only acquaintances. Quebec sociologist, Bert Young (1987:308), poignantly describes men's "almost total reliance upon women to ward off their basic loneliness and fear of self-revelation." Though Young may exaggerate, empirical studies do find that men at all ages are more likely to report their spouse as their best friend (Andersen, 1988:90). A 42-year-old woman, married 18 years, told a researcher:

Andy says I'm his best friend, and sometimes I feel bad because I don't say the same about him. But I really think the only reason he says it is because he doesn't have any friends himself. He never has had any since we got married.

I don't mean that I don't love him and feel very close to him. I do. But it's different than my relationship with Ginny and what I feel for her. My life is tied to Andy's, so our relationship is very complex and it has a lot of layers. But a best friend, well, that's something else. I go to her for a different kind of sharing and comfort and understanding (Rubin, 1985:65).

Those men who expect marriage to provide their exclusive source of friendship place a tremendous burden on the marriage. One person simply cannot serve all the needs of another.

Many commentators on the quality of female versus male friendships allege that as a consequence of women's competition with one another over men, "each is against the others" (de Beauvoir, 1952:513), and female friendship is "flawed" (Brenton, 1974: 142). André Maurois, for example, claimed that a woman "will always give first place to the man she loves physically, and if he insists, will renounce the most perfect friendship for him."

What do social scientists have to say about folk wisdom that contrasts feminine jealousy and antagonism with jolly masculine camaraderie? The reader will not be surprised to learn that women have greater capacity for friendship than the pejorative myths suggest. At least one study (Gibbs et al., 1980) concludes that it was males who showed greater unfriendliness toward their own sex. Gender specialists point out that *both* sexes compete in the marketplace of love and marriage. Until recently, occupational competition has been mostly a masculine "game": one is reluctant to reveal weakness to a competitor (Chafetz, 1974:182). Also, many men associate (and confuse) male friendship with homosexuality. Gay men repeatedly recount the bitter experience of being abandoned by male friends once they "came out" (Rubin, 1985:102). Moreover, the spectre of homosexuality inhibits demonstrations of tender feelings in male friendships. When such feelings are not choked off completely, they often re-emerge as effusive displays of backslapping and arm punching.

Lastly, we ask: Is there any truth to Maurois's charge that a woman will give *"first place"* to the man she loves and, if he insists, will "renounce the most perfect friendship" for him? Although "perfect" friendships are hard to come by for sociological study, some older studies are available on the effects of marriage on women's friendships. This research concludes that males do dominate the couple's joint friendships: the friends of the husband become the friends of the couple (Babchuk and Bates, 1963; Lopata, 1975). Perhaps the traditional view of women's friendships as unimportant explains, in part, why the husband's friends become *their* friends. However, these less intense couple-friendships exist alongside wives' more intimate same-sex friendships (Bell, 1981:138). Moreover, since women's participation in the public domain is now far greater than when the Babchuk

and Bates (1963) study was carried out, it seems likely that both partners in a relationship are likely to initiate couple-friendships.

In summary, men and women report an equal number of friends. There is no evidence to support the contention that women's friendships are inferior to those of men (Wright, 1982). Nevertheless, the quality of friendship differs by sex, and these differences reflect gender stereotypes. Women's friendships stress expressiveness, while men's stress activity. The adult friendship patterns detailed in this section have their roots in childhood. Socialization influences such as parents, peers, teachers, and the mass media teach boys and girls to adopt different styles of relating to the world and each other (Sherrod, 1987:227). Boys' and girls' different forms of association with one another in childhood play have important implications for their later behaviour. In addition, their peer activities serve to reinforce the notion that males are more important than females. In the pages to follow, we concentrate on the role played by peers in this early socialization process. Finally, we emphasize that statements made about gender differences in friendship are probabilistic generalizations which refer to tendencies, not to absolutes.

EARLY CHILDHOOD PLAY

Socialization theorists such as Jean Piaget (1928; 1932), working from a cognitive-developmental perspective, and George Herbert Mead (1934), from a symbolic interactionist perspective, affirm the importance of play and games for children's social development. In many respects, childhood games are small-scale analogies of society. When children learn about game rules, they are learning, at their level, about societal norms. Similarly, when they learn to play game roles, they are also learning something about playing societal roles. Our interest centres upon the acquisition of gender norms, and the sense of self as a female or male person that arises from childhood play.

For the first two or three years of life, the

play patterns of girls and boys are quite similar (Maccoby, 1980:212-17). Stephen Richer (1984) observed the sex-integrated play of three-year-olds in two Ontario daycare centres. The children "displayed no reluctance whatsoever to play with one another." The boys were found playing "doctor" or "cook" with the girls, just as girls were found playing with blocks and driving trucks and cars. Not once did Professor Richer see sex-based name-calling. These preschoolers "like or dislike one another for what they do, not because of who they are" (Richer, 1984:174). Vivian Paley (1984:x), who has also carried out extensive observations, agrees that "domestic play looks remarkably alike for both sexes at age three." She says that, if asked, a boy will likely say he is Father, but if he were to say "Mother," it would cause little concern.

Four- and five-year-olds have quite different ideas about both play activities and people of the other sex. They now show strong preference for same-sex playmates. Boys engage in much more friendly rough-and-tumble and aggressive play than girls. Struggles for dominance also occur more frequently in boys' play groups (Maccoby, 1980:216). Social play involves negotiation: What shall we play? How shall we play it? Striking sex differences exist in how these negotiations get carried out. Boys shout, quarrel, and make "facial gestures" (heads up, chins thrust out). Girls avoid physical power tactics and resort to exclusion ("You can't play with us!") (Sutton-Smith, 1979:241-42).

The following observations of four-year-old kindergarten children illustrate sex-segregated play:

The four girls in the doll corner have announced who they are: Mother, Sister, Baby, Maid. To begin with, then, there will be cooking and eating, crying and cleaning. Charlotte is the mother because, she tells the others, she is wearing the silver shoes. Leadership often goes to the child who is most confident about the meaning of symbols.

Karen: I'm hungry. Wa-a-ah!
Charlotte: Lie down, baby.
Karen: I'm a baby that sits up.

Charlotte: First you lie down and sister covers you and then I make you cereal and then you sit up.
Karen: Okay.

Abruptly the mood changes. Andrew, Jonathan, Jeremy and Paul rush in, fingers shooting. "We're robbers. Do you got any gold?"

"No," Charlotte says, stirring an empty pot.

Jeremy climbs on the refrigerator and knocks over several cartons of plastic food. "Put up your hands. You're going to jail!"

"We're telling!" The girls stomp out in search of [the kindergarten teacher]. (Paley, 1984:1-2).

Several characteristics of children's play can be distilled from the above episode. We see that the separation by sex/gender of youngsters' activities has become more pronounced. Yet, the children are very interested in what the other sex/gender is up to; the boys visit the doll corner to satisfy their curiosity, to tease. Also notable is the gender stereotypical content of boys' and girls' fantasy play. Obvious as well are different styles of play: the tranquillity of the girls' activities versus the rowdy assertiveness of the boys' play. Lastly, Paley's observations of kindergarten children also hint at gender-specific attitudes towards adult authority. These sweetly compliant little girls seem to harbour ambitions to become teacher's pets. The boys, on the other hand, appear to relish challenging adult authority. This last point is elaborated in the section which follows.

GENDER-SPECIFIC PEER GROUP ATTITUDES IN MIDDLE CHILDHOOD

Gender specialists have long suspected that the peer group of youngsters from about six to 13 years of age exerts a more profound influence on boys than on girls. This thesis has been put forth by psychoanalytically oriented writers, such as Hartley (1959), Lynn (1969), and Chodorow (1978). They argue that as a reaction to the relative absence of fathers and the vagueness of parental expectations, the young boy looks to his peers (and to the mass media) for specific guidance about being masculine. These Freudian-inspired analysts lay stress on the necessity for boys to loosen their identification and emotional ties with mothers and mother surrogates, such as teachers.

In addition to providing tutelage in masculinity, the male peer group functions as a refuge against women's influence (Hartley, 1959). The growing boy faces a conflict between society's insistence that he eschew all things "womanly," and his placement, by the same society, under the almost constant jurisdiction of women. Put another way, the boy who is warned to be strong and to disdain "sissies" "is forced into close contact with the epitome of all sissy-things — women — for most of his day and he is commanded to obey and learn from them." The company of boys his own age provides some protection against the danger of turning out a "sissy," as well as a shield against women's power. In short, the peer group serves to validate masculinity through avoidance of what is feminine.

In contrast, girls of this age need not distance themselves from the feminine worlds of home and school. Although childhood contains challenge and grief for all youngsters, girls, on the whole, do not face the same pressures as boys. Boys begin to pay their dues in the male club early, while girls delay most of the costs of being female until adolescence and adulthood. Our culture makes "inordinate demands on small boys to become instant men, to live up to macho criteria they are as yet unprepared to meet.... They have therefore to seek support from one another" (Best, 1983:5).[4]

The macho code requires boys to be tough:

"It's like my grandaddy says, 'if a boy doesn't have a couple of scars he'll never be a man!'" The very mention of the word "scars" triggered in the third-grade boys an impulse to show off their own scars, those badges of courage that validated their manhood. "I've got a scar here and here," they boasted as they bared arms and legs to provide the best possible view of scars both newly ac-

quired and nearly faded from view (Best, 1983:75).

Boys' scars are evidence of their aggression. However, the girls demonstrate another sort of assertiveness: they like to be "boss," to be in charge. (Charlotte, the "mother" in the kindergarten scene cited above exemplified this desire to control the other children.) According to Best (1983:91), this female brand of assertiveness is part of a package of helpfulness, nurturance, and responsible behaviour shown by preadolescent girls, but not by boys of the same age.

Out of our culture's gender definitions, and the authority exercised over children of both sexes by feminine authority figures (mothers, daycare workers, kindergarten and elementary school teachers) come gender-distinctive attitudes towards adults, age-mates of the other sex, and sexuality. Each of these topics will be treated in turn.

Attitudes towards Adults

The relationships of first-grade children with each other matter far less to them than their individual relationships with adults. Anne and Matthew begin to shove each other away from the puzzle they are putting together. "Anne and Matthew, come here to me," calls Ms. Minor, their teacher. When they stood, circled in her arms, she asked, "Can't you find another way to play?" The children, pleased with the teacher's attention, agree that they certainly can. It is adults, not age-mates who control the rewards. As yet, there are no coalitions of children against the establishment (Best, 1983:10-11).

For boys, the reorientation from teacher to peer group begins in Grade 2. As potential support from peers emerges, more and more boys find it possible to defy the teacher: "Where is your arithmetic paper, Scott?" asked the teacher. "I already gave it to you," replied Scott. The teacher said she didn't remember receiving it. He stood firm. "Well, I gave it to you. If you lost it don't blame me." When the teacher subsequently found his paper crumpled in a ball inside his desk,

Scott looked out the window, humming a little tune to himself. This conduct caused him to be sent from the classroom to sit on the principal's bench. A procession of his peers, on their way to the washroom, risked punishment to visit with Scott on the bench.

For boys, the source of rewards that matter has transferred from teachers to peers. Whenever possible, they escape into the boys' washroom. Although the teacher walks freely in and out of the girls' washroom, she must stand outside the door of the boys' bathroom and call out: "Stop fighting," or "Come out of there immediately." She asks the male principal why the boys are so long in there. He tells her they talk about the other kids in the school and about what they are going to do for the rest of the day. They also use the washroom to see who can urinate highest up the wall (Best, 1983:12-15).

The girls' attitude towards authority contrasts sharply with that of the boys.

...when the boys eagerly ran outside to play, the girls fought among themselves for the "privilege" of staying indoors and helping the teacher. This was the time used by the teachers to tidy up the classroom, and the girls could help. They did such "feminine" tasks as clapping erasers, cleaning the art corner and sinks, and straightening bookcases and cupboards. The teacher rewarded the girls by praising them lavishingly and admitting that she didn't know what she'd do without them (Best, 1983:61).

Sociologists Thorne and Luria (1986), who observed playground behaviour of nine to eleven-year-old children, comment on the greater importance of rule transgression among the boys. For example, dirty words are a focus of rules and rule-breaking in elementary schools. Though both boys and girls know dirty words, flaunting of the words and risking punishment was more frequent in boys' than in girls' groups. Moreover, Thorne and Luria suggest that rule transgression in *public* is exciting to boys in groups. "Boys are visibly excited when they break rules together—they are flushed as they play, they wipe their hands on their jeans, some of them look guilty" (p. 181).

Risk-taking and successfully challenging adult authority result in contagious arousal. "A boy may not have power, but a boys' *group* does" (p. 181). Adults tending children do not often undertake discipline of an entire boys' group. The adults might lose; that outcome cannot be risked. The public nature of these confrontations forges bonds among the boys. The situation of the girls is different. "Girls are more likely to affirm the reasonableness of the rules." When rule transgression does occur, adults experience little trouble in handling the girls. "This may be related to the smaller size of girls' groups and to adults' readiness to use rules on girls who seem to believe in them" (Thorne and Luria, 1986:181).

Attitudes towards the Other Sex

By Grade 2, the macho code forbids boys the company of girls. Because boys who play with girls are regarded as "sissies," to be shunned by other boys, boys distance themselves from girls, and look down on them. According to Best's (1983:90) classroom observations, girls like boys better than boys like girls. Girls are helpful and nurturant towards boys; boys accept this help as their due. The girls revel in the belief that they are in charge.

After youngsters reach age 10 or so, their situation begins to change. Girls' attitudes towards boys remain stable, while boys begin to become more positive about girls. During the sixth and seventh grades, both boys and girls view one another more favourably; the boys' rate of change is the faster. Nevertheless, among children this age, girls' popularity with other girls is affected by their popularity with boys, but boys' status with other boys does not depend on how they stand with girls (Thorne and Luria, 1986:188). Sexual maturation is one important reason why peer groups become less sex-segregated as young people move out of late childhood into puberty (Maccoby and Jacklin, 1974:211). The topic of cross-sex relations in adolescence and adulthood will be taken up later in this chapter.

Sexuality

Despite the fact that parents derive comfort from regarding their children as asexual beings, unmistakable evidence exists of youngsters' intense interest and surprising knowledge about matters sexual (Best, 1983). For example, two children in the lower grades of a Calgary elementary school were in big trouble over a shadow play assigned by their teacher because the plot they devised involved mimicry of the sounds and movements of sexual intercourse.[5] When we think about it, children's precocity is not really surprising. After all, the gender system is organized around the institution of heterosexuality. The web of intricate connections between gender and sexuality comes early to children's attention. Special taboos and tensions surround the language and feelings of sexuality in our culture. These emotionally loaded sexual words and gestures "provide a major resource which children draw upon as they construct and maintain gender segregation" (Thorne and Luria, 1986:185).

The view that sex is exciting, but at the same time, naughty and forbidden, is shared by both sexes. However, boys and girls regard the matter somewhat differently, in part because they receive dissimilar, but equally confusing instructions from adults:

Boys...were taught by mothers and teachers that a gentleman was chivalrous and protective of girls. At the same time, from fathers and the media they learned that machismo called for taking sex when and where they could get it. Girls were taught one basic rule: Don't. Have as little to do with boys as possible. At the same time they were taught that it is important to win boys because being popular and dating are important (Best, 1983:6).

Chapter 4 alluded to the part played by sexual symbolism in gender socialization. As we said earlier, youngsters of both sexes are familiar with the language of sex. However, playground sexuality serves distinctive functions in male and female peer groups. "The preadolescent period is characterized by an extensive discussion of sex, and some action, though by no means as much as the talk would imply" (Fine, 1980:300). Though boys (like girls) discuss sex to pool information, much preadolescent boys' sexual talk is mixed with aggressive imagery (Fine, 1980:301). A function of such "dirty talk" is to taunt and to challenge, to segregate themselves from girls and women. In attempts to shock girls, they thrust their hands into their pants and wiggle fingers through open fly zippers. The charge that a particular boy "likes" a particular girl, especially a pariah, serves as insult and tease (Thorne and Luria, 1986:186). Mutual masturbation groups are apparently one of the initiation rites into manhood (Gagnon, 1972). In sum, dirty talk and dirty play are integral parts of boys' public rule-breaking (Fine, 1986).

If preadolescent boys are trying to put distance between themselves and the female world, and to earn "jock points" from their peers, girls this age look ahead to romance and domesticity. Girls' language elevates the emotional and romantic above the explicitly sexual. They use dirty words much less often than boys. They talk privately about which boys are "cute," and about which girls have "crushes" on which boys (Thorne and Luria, 1986:184). Best (1983:117) says, "Third-grade girls spent endless amounts of time fantasizing about 'boyfriends' and marriage. Any gesture of appreciation shown to them by boys—the lending of a pencil or an eraser—was viewed as a display of personal interest and would be eagerly discussed with the other girls." As noted in Chapter 4, these asymmetrical attitudes are responsible for chasing games, one way in which children's sex segregation is regularly broken (Richer, 1984; Sutton-Smith, 1979).

Let us stop for a moment to reflect upon peer relations in middle childhood. Gary Alan Fine (1980:303) argues that for preadolescent boys in many cultures, "the friendship tie provides the support necessary for breaking the normative rules of adult society..." Elsewhere, (1986:63) he remarks that "boys are 'boys' only when they are with their peers." Although this accentuation of gender in the company of age-mates likely does not hold to the same extent for preteen girls, the centrality of peer influence in the gender socialization of both sexes is beyond dispute. Peer interaction, especially that segment carried on outside the sight and hearing of adults, reinforces traditional gender norms. The segregation of the sexes accentuates differences. The gender stereotypical content of peer relations—male competition and rowdiness, female nurturance and domesticity—provides early practice in being little men and little women. Children are relatively unsophisticated, so their enactments of gender are apt to be caricatures, oversimplified and overemphasized. Of paramount importance are the non-egalitarian patterns of perceiving and dealing with the other sex that are being established. Both "boys and girls evaluate boys' activities and boys in general more positively than they do girls and girls' activities" (Richer, 1988:265).

The present section has concentrated on very general themes. Its purpose has been to communicate to the reader something of the ambience of children's peer groups. More detailed comparisons of girls' and boys' friendships and games are offered in the next section.

FEMALE-MALE DIFFERENCES IN PRE-ADOLESCENT CHILDREN'S PLAY

Some leisure pastimes, e.g., watching videos, reading, are shared by children of both sexes. However, boys and girls are characterized by somewhat distinctive patterns of affiliation and forms of play. As a consequence, distinctive social skills are acquired that may very well have consequences for their behaviour in adulthood.

Despite indications that sex differences are lessening, the sex-segregated play of girls and boys still takes different forms (Eder and Hallinan, 1978; Lever, 1976, 1978).

Girls play indoors more than boys. Girls' activities tend to be more private (played behind closed doors), while those of boys are more public. Girls' indoor play is quieter and more restricted in body movement. A sex difference exists in the size of children's play groups (Eder and Hallinan, 1978). Girls tend to play in small groups, especially the *dyad* (two-person group). Boys, on the other hand, prefer to congregate in larger groups. The size of the group is explained by the type of game preferred, as well as the indoor versus outdoor setting. Girls prefer activities such as skipping, hopscotch, Barbie dolls, and conversation. [6] Boys, however, are more likely to participate in team sports.

Differing group size entails several considerations. First, liking one's playmates matters more to girls. Their play often involves intensive interaction with one or two "best friends." However, "for much of the interaction that occurs in boys' play groups, liking and disliking one's playmates is essentially irrelevant" (Maccoby and Jacklin, 1974:207). Since the game is what matters, the choice of participants is likely to be made on the basis of game skills. Every Saturday, a 12-year-old boy complained about two of the boys with whom he played weekly football. His sister asked, "If you don't like them why do you play with them?" The brother's response was, "You've got to be crazy. We need eleven for the team" (Sutton-Smith, 1979:253).

The relative exclusiveness of play groups is yet another concomitant of size. The larger number of participants required for masculine games encourages male dyads to expand. There is no similar pressure on female dyads. The girls, who tend to engage in more intimate behaviour than boys (telling secrets, for example), protect their exclusive groups against the advances of newcomers. Not realizing the social forces at work, little girls may blame themselves for the greater trouble they sometimes have in making friends, i.e., in penetrating existing cliques.

A third factor is the age-homogeneity of groups. Girls' play groups tend to involve youngsters of the same age. The reason? For girls, only age-mates can be best friends. By contrast, age-homogeneity is less important to boys. Their games require many participants to fill designated roles. When age peers are scarce, younger children are allowed to join in. "You're better off with a little kid in the outfield than no one at all" (Lever, 1976:480).

In general, girls engage in more unstructured play and fantasy play, while boys engage in more competitive games, involving teams of interdependent players with definite and differing roles and specific rules. Hockey is a good example. Such games require coordination of effort and continuous negotiation of rules. One player is not equal to another: there is hierarchy and dominance behaviour. In comparison, girls' games provide fewer opportunities for dispute. When a quarrel does break out, girls rarely fight over rule interpretation, as boys do. Instead, the game breaks up and the girls go home.

Girls prefer cooperative play or turn-taking activities, where each girl skips or bounces a ball. In the latter, girls spend considerable time as an audience watching the performer. In contrast, boys all tend to play at the same time (Sutton-Smith, 1979:244). Girls' activities involve competition that is subtle and indirect. In traditional games such as skipping, one person's success does not necessarily signify another's failure (Gilligan, 1982:10). Indeed, girls are less likely to compete at all. Girls prefer to ride bikes, boys to race them. Bodily strength and bodily contact are irrelevant in girls' games (Lever, 1976).

Girls participate in predominantly male games more than boys play in girls' games. Boys are likely to need an extra team member from time to time. Also, girls gain prestige from associating with the more highly valued male activities. Boys, on the other hand, are punished for "sissy" behaviour. Consequently, when boys do play girls' games, they often display *role distance* (Goffman, 1961). They are there, not as serious role players, but as buffoons or teases, to annoy the girls. However, girls playing boys' games do so as serious participants (Lever, 1976:481).

Finally, a point established earlier warrants reiteration: differences exist in the ambience of boys' and girls' play. Boys impose a *machismo* code on one another (Best, 1983:22). Be first. Be tough. Defy authority. Don't be a sissy or crybaby. Keep your distance from females of all ages. Raphaela Best (1983:88), after years of observing elementary school children, concluded that, "After the almost painful picture of the boys' world and its impact on the rejected boys, entering the girls' world was like moving from a dark and fearful forest into a sunny valley."

THE ADULT IMPORT OF CHILDHOOD GAMES

Boys and girls derive different sorts of social skills from their childhood games that social scientists believe prepare the way for gendered behaviour in adulthood. The very general lesson children of both sexes learn from their peers is this: males and masculine activities are more valuable than females and feminine activities. This exceedingly strong impression of the gender hierarchy conveyed by other socialization agencies, as well as age-mates, becomes an axiom of life experience.

Boys' games, particularly team sports, provide a learning environment for the cultivation of the kinds of skills later demanded by the complex organizations characteristic of the public domain in modern societies. In principle, boys learn to deal with a diversity of roles, to coordinate their actions, to cope with impersonal rules, to work for collective as well as personal goals, to associate with people they don't particularly like. Sports provide experience in leading and following, and in handling criticism. Being able to depersonalize attacks, and to maintain self-control in the face of criticism, is an especially valuable aptitude (Lever, 1978:480-81).

Girls' spontaneous, imaginative, mostly rule-free play teaches quite different, but on the face of it, equally valuable skills. Since activities such as skipping rope often have no explicit goals, girls experience less interpersonal competition. Leadership is less relevant. Girls often prefer to talk rather than to play formal games, and thereby develop the ability to converse and to empathize with others (Lever, 1978:481). Girls get to know their best friend and her moods so well that "through non-verbal cues alone, a girl understands whether her playmate is hurt, sad, happy, bored..." (Lever, 1976:484). They become experienced in non-hierarchical settings without acknowledged leadership. Finally, girls learn to be an appreciative audience for males who have learned to take centre stage.

It is reasonable to suppose that this childhood learning serves as anticipatory socialization for the gendered roles of adult life. Basically, childhood play equips adult females to operate successfully in primary group settings, such as the family, but not in secondary group settings where power is wielded and the business of the world is conducted (Lever, 1978:482). Boys' games, particularly team sports, provide a learning environment for the cultivation of skills later demanded by bureaucratic work organizations. Note that the existence of causal linkages between children's play and adult skills is being inferred. Although these hypotheses do seem plausible, longitudinal research is needed to establish firm linkages between gender-related childhood play and success in adult endeavours. Organizational skills can, of course, be learned in other places besides competitive team sports. Though primary socialization has more impact than that experienced later in life, business administration schools and on-the-job training manage effective socialization of adults.

Anyone walking past a video arcade, with its eerie blue lights and space-age noises, or a schoolyard, filled with shouting girls playing soccer, would realize that youngsters' leisure activities today are not what they were twenty years ago. Not only is more time spent with electronic entertainment, especially by boys (Panelas, 1983; Turkle, 1984), but outdoor activities are changing, too.

It is girls' outdoor play preferences, not boys', that are changing (Huston, 1983:104).

Cosbey (1980:56) observes, "I have noticed in the elementary schoolyards of Regina not only that baseball games frequently include as many girls as boys, but that the girls frequently seem to be pitching, catching, and running as well as the boys." Our society now endorses physical activity for people of both sexes and all ages. Relatedly, adult encouragement of organized, competitive team play has significantly influenced children's recreation. However, shifting gender norms also contribute to changing play patterns. Because traditionally male games both carry the prestigious cachet of masculinity and are intrinsically interesting, girls adhere less rigidly to sex-typed interests than do boys. Girls take up baseball, but boys do *not* take up skipping (Eder and Hallinan, 1978). According to one observer (Cosbey, 1980:56), "as girls move into previously boys-only games, the play-preferences of boys become more and more restricted to the most 'masculine' games, as if to preserve their sense of masculinity."

MORAL DEVELOPMENT AS OUTCOME OF CHILDHOOD GENDER SOCIALIZATION EXPERIENCES

In 1982, Carol Gilligan published a much-admired and much-criticized book, *In A Different Voice*, which argued that women and men follow different paths to moral development. Gilligan appeared on the January 1984 cover of *Ms.* magazine as their Woman of the Year. For the next few years, the very name "Gilligan" was a buzzword in feminist and educational circles (Tronto, 1987:646).

The initial stimulus for Gilligan's ideas was the assessment made by cognitive-developmental theorist, Kohlberg (1963, 1981) (and by Freud, before him) that women are less morally advanced than men. In Gilligan's mind, this constituted yet another example of a theoretical model derived from male samples being applied to both sexes, and female deviation from the male standard being labelled inferior. Gilligan's own work on moral development builds upon conclusions reached by Lever (1976) and others (see above) concerning sex/gender differences in children's play.

Especially significant were female-male differences in attitudes towards rules. Girls tended to be more tolerant about rules, more willing to make exceptions to maintain relationships with others. Boys focussed more on protecting and elaborating on the rules of the game, than on their relations with other players. "In fact, it seemed that the boys enjoyed the legal debates [over rules] as much as they did the game itself... In contrast, the eruption of disputes among girls tended to end the game" (Gilligan, 1982:9).

From these data concerning children's play (and from her own study of perceptions of abortion), Gilligan extrapolated several generalizations about moral development. She concluded that connectedness with others is of supreme importance to girls and women. Ruptured relationships, power, and aggression all deeply threaten them. Males, on the other hand, see the world in terms of autonomy, hierarchy, and conflict. They are threatened by intimacy. Gilligan hypothesizes a different type of morality for each sex. According to her, female morality is the morality of the "web," that is, a morality that emphasizes fulfillment of responsibilities of individuals connecting with one another. Theirs is an *ethic of care*. In comparison, masculine morality is analogous to a "ladder," in which morality consists of a hierarchy of fundamental rights and freedoms that regulate the behaviour of independent, competitive individuals. The masculine morality she termed an *ethic of justice*. Females, then, have different, but not less mature, constructions of moral problems.

Gilligan's thinking was also influenced by the work of Chodorow (1978) (discussed in Chapter 5). The hypothesized sex differences in moral thought arise out of children's early experiences with female caretakers. Girls learn femininity through attachment to the mother, the primary care giver and model in childhood. Boys, however, learn masculinity through separation from the mother figure. Boys develop "a self defined through separation"; girls "a self delineated through connection" (p. 35). Throughout

life, "male gender identity is threatened by intimacy while female gender identity is threatened by separation" (Gilligan, 1982:8).

Gilligan's challenge to masculine theoretical models has been enormously influential. Her bold arguments in support of the proposition that the feminine ethic of care is a *different*, not an inferior mode of thought have captured the imagination of social scientists and laypersons alike. Recently, however, this enthusiastic reception of her work has been tempered by sober evaluation. Empirical tests of Gilligan's ideas about sex/gender differences in moral thought are inconclusive (Walker, 1984). In addition, her primary research into concerns about abortion, on which the book rests, has been challenged because it deals with women—and only women (Kerber, 1986:305). How can one arrive at comparative statements about the sexes when only one sex is sampled? In attempting to secure the higher moral ground for the feminine brand of virtue,[7] and speaking about "two voices" of morality, Gilligan strongly implies sexually dimorphic psychological differences. All females are this way; all males are that way.[8] Though her invocation of socialization research argues that morality is learned, her study at times also suggests a biological basis for virtue (Risman, 1987). Recall that the psychological literature provides little support for the proposition that females are more altruistic or caring (Colby and Damon, 1987). And, it provides *no* support for dichotomized female-male gender distinctions. In short, Gilligan's emphasis on natural female virtue contrasts sharply with the thinking of feminist psychologists of the 1970s (Stacey, 1983) (see Chapter 2). Finally, Gilligan has been accused of romantic oversimplification. "If women can be counted on to care for others, how are we to deal with self-interest, selfishness, and meanness of spirit which women surely display as much as do men?" (Kerber, 1986:309).

CROSS-SEX RELATIONSHIPS

These questions are addressed in this section: How are primary relations that involve females and males influenced by society's gender scripts? What role do cross-sex relationships play in gender socialization? The main premise is that a dual influence is at work. Cross-sex friendships are shaped by societal definitions of masculinity and femininity. Moreover, the way that such relationships are played out serves to reinforce gender norms.

As noted above, people prefer same-sex relationships. "Most people spend the greater part of their social and working lives with other people of the same sex. Friendships, kinship contacts, and informal networks at work consist predominantly of same-sex relationships" (Woolsey, 1987a:116). The pages to follow underline the fact that cross-sex friendships are less common than same-sex friendships; in adulthood, such relationships tend either to turn into love affairs or to dissipate. We examine, first, platonic or non-erotic relationships, then romantic relationships.

Platonic Friendships

In comparison with same-sex friendships, close friendships between women and men are few and far between. Those platonic relationships which get started at all are apt to be tentative, unstable, short-lived. Why should this be? Four inter-related factors seem to be responsible. All of them boil down to one basic reason: constricted cultural specifications concerning the ways females and males *ought* to relate to one another.

Adult friendship involves intimacy, trust, and mutuality, rather than exploitation. In other words, mature friendship is fundamentally a relationship between equals. Therefore, our society's traditional assumption of male superiority has been the first and most basic barrier to friendship between the sexes. One consequence of this differential evaluation of the sexes is the folk wisdom, discussed earlier, which holds that women are inherently less capable than men of developing significant friendships. As

one chap put it, "Life really is very simple: men are for friendships and women are for f——g" (Bell, 1981:104). The feminine counterpart of this folklore advises that men are exploiters "after only one thing." Obviously, these notions mitigate against establishing close cross-sex relationships without sexual overtones (Bell, 1981:95).

Secondly, our culture encourages people to regard love as a zero-sum game, to assume that each person has only a finite quantity of that emotion available to give (Chafetz, 1974:162). If either person in the cross-sex friendship pair has romantic attachments to a third person, the third party may feel threatened, and discourage the friendship. Our reasoning often goes like this: If Person A loves Friend B, then Person A has less love to give to Lover C. Indeed, *Roget's Thesaurus* lists "jealous" among the synonyms for "loving," and Webster's *Third New International Dictionary* offers this Freudian-tinged definition of "platonic love": *A close relationship between two usually opposite-sexed persons in which an element of sexual attractiveness or libidinal desire has been either so suppressed or so sublimated that it is generally believed to be absent.* The tendency for the friendship to turn romantic is clearly implied.

Male jealousy has long been acknowledged in literature and law. Wives have been viewed as husbands' property, and trespass upon this property (adultery) has been grounds for divorce. Daughters have been defined as fathers' property, and their defilement grounds for damages. Accusing a man of being a cuckold is a supreme insult in most societies (Chafetz, 1974:164). While no sex differences exist in reported levels of jealousy (White, 1981), there are sex differences in manifestations of this nasty emotion, which the Bible describes as "cruel as the grave" (Solomon 8:6). Males are more likely to become angry and preoccupied with their rival (the *rooster effect*), while females experience more depression and self-blame (Thompson and Richardson, 1983).

A third cultural reason explains why adult platonic relationships rarely develop in the first place and why they tend to be fragile if they do. The third reason is closely related to our second point. The popular image of cross-sex relationships is limited to sexuality, perhaps romance, but does not extend to friendship (Matthews, 1986:111). While it is commonly assumed that men and women may develop a sexual relationship without any degree of friendship, many regard as debatable the possibility of friendship without sexual overtones (Bell, 1981: 105). "Females are taught to view males primarily as potential mates or husbands, namely, the objects of TRUE LOVE. Males learn to view females primarily as sex objects to be exploited if possible, married if necessary" (Chafetz, 1974:164). Given these stereotypical views, "every encounter between a woman and a man then becomes heavy with unspoken demands: confirm that I'm desirable, acknowledge my virility, my orgasmic capacity, prove to me that I'm a sexual being—that's your role, that's your job" (Brenton, 1974:15). Although these views may be exaggerated, they do make the point that men and women have not been taught to regard one another as peers. This brings us to the fourth reason.

We noted earlier that similarity of important attributes predicts interpersonal attraction and friendship. There seems to be "a sense of identifying with, sharing common experiences, and having some advantages and disadvantages in common with other members of one's own sex" (Woolsey, 1987a:117). Both men and women prefer same-sex to cross-sex friendships (Rose, 1985), and speak of the "special tie" that exists in the former (Woolsey, 1987b:129). Most respondents to an empirical study of friendship "felt there is a basic difference between men and women that precludes friendship" (Matthews, 1986:96). As Whitehurst and Booth (1980:63) point out, the separation of boys and girls during pre-adolescent play serves to create ignorance and mistrust about the other sex's motives and capacities. From her interviews with Canadian teenage girls, Myrna Kostash (1987:93) learned that, "There is not, at this stage of life, much of a sense that boys are on your side." A nineteen-year-old told her:

"With boys you have to make a special effort. You can't talk to them the way you talk to girls. They have different interests, they're easily distracted, you never know what's going to upset them" (Kostash, 1987:93). Male respondents would undoubtedly tell the same tale.

We conclude that in comparison with same-sex friendships and romantic attachments, friendship between the sexes remains the exception rather than the rule. However, sociologists have arrived at some generalizations about the likelihood of cross-sex friendship. In terms of life cycle, developing friendship with the other sex is most probable in late adolescence and early adulthood (when people are unmarried). At this age, young men and women are testing "their emerging maleness and femaleness against each other" in a "safe" (nonsexual) environment (Brenton, 1974:163). A female friend can be particularly useful to the male. Since male competitiveness discourages disclosure of anxieties and weaknesses to other males, female friends can serve as safe confidantes (Chafetz, 1974:165; Komarovsky, 1973).

The potential for cross-sex friendship rises again in late adulthood and old age, when divorce and widowhood leave many people open to, and needy of, friendship (Matthews, 1986:91-92). Because women live longer, more of them are available as friends to a decreasing number of older men (Bell, 1981:102). One woman describes how she acquired her "male escort," the widowed husband of an acquaintance. He happened to be in line behind her in the grocery store.

So, I said, "How is your wife?" because I knew that she had been ill and living in a nursing home. And he said, "Oh, she died about two years ago." And I said, "I am terribly sorry. I didn't know that." And he knew that my husband had died. And he said, "Well, I'll call you;" and I said, "Well that would be nice. We can go for a walk or something." So he did and he has been my friend ever since. And I'm not interested in romance (Matthews, 1986:94).

The stereotype of older people as asexual

facilitates the sort of platonic relationship described in the above quotation. Nevertheless, many older people do, in fact, remain sexually active.

Cross-sex friendships occur more frequently among well-educated middle-class professionals, than blue-collar workers (Bell, 1981:102; Booth and Hess, 1974). For one thing, the middle-class entertain less traditional ideas about gender. In contrast, 'machismo' values held by many working-class males devalue women, so that association with women on the job is demeaning, and friendship with them unthinkable. Consequently, women workers moving into non-traditional blue-collar work often encounter sexual harassment (Gruber and Bjorn, 1982; O'Farrell and Harlan, 1982). Second, white-collar work environments, being less sex-segregated, provide more opportunities for friendship.

Although middle-class work settings are more conducive than their blue-collar counterparts to the development of egalitarian relationships, opportunities for platonic friendships still remain constricted. One reason is that women's work across social classes remains strongly sex-segregated. Women in the traditional feminine professions—elementary school teachers, nurses—work mainly with other women. Also, jobs that are done by both sexes, such as computer programmer, retail sales clerk are segregated by industry and firm so that few companies employ both men and women to do the same work (Ferree, 1987:325). Equally important is the subordination of many women, for example clerical workers, to male bosses. We reiterate that friendship is a relationship between equals. Finally, men have traditionally used their organizational relationships to advance their careers. Women in male-dominated professions have been left out of these networks, partly because of their female status, partly because their lack of resources renders them unattractive network participants (Kanter, 1977). For pragmatic reasons, researchers have attended to the gender implications of networks, mentors, sponsors, and role models. (See Auster, 1984; Speizer, 1981;

Symons, 1978). In comparison, little research has been done on the topics of cross-sex friendship, colleagueship, or sexual relationships in work settings.

Romantic Relationships

Romantic love and intense liking are not simply different gradations of the same emotion. Compared with deep friendship, romantic love has a swifter onset, stimulates more fantasies, is more fragile and short-lived, and causes more suffering and frustration (Berscheid, 1985:435). Liking "seems consistently associated with good thought and feelings, but passionate love is often associated with conflicting emotions, as shown by teenagers' frequent question of whether it's possible to love and hate someone at the same time" (Brigham, 1986:200). Liking appears to be based primarily on affection and respect, while the dimensions underlying loving are attachment, caring for the welfare of the other, and intimacy (willingness to disclose the self to the other) (Rubin, 1973). The ideology of romantic love underlies the mate-selection process in Western societies, such as Canada, where nearly everyone expects to fall in love eventually (Goode, 1959).

In societies subscribing to this ideology, physical sensations—light-headedness, rapid heartbeat, queasy stomach, inability to concentrate—when experienced in a context in which their cause can be attributed to another person, are defined as "love." An interesting experiment carried out by Dutton and Aron (1974), and described in Alcock et al. (1988:266-67) demonstrates that the source of emotional arousal can sometimes be misattributed. These researchers asked male subjects to walk across the shaky Capilano suspension bridge which crosses a deep gorge in Vancouver. An attractive female confederate met them on the other side. In comparison with subjects who encountered her after crossing a solid, concrete bridge, those who met her while in an aroused state included more sexual imagery in a projective test and were more likely to

TABLE 6.1

A LIST OF 25 RELATIONSHIPS

1.   Verbal and physical flirting at a party, without follow-up.
2.   A boy/girlfriend living together for a period after several months of dating.
3.   A de facto relationship between two previously married people.
4.   A young marriage after an unwanted pregnancy.
5.   A permanent but nonsexual relationship between two young religious people.
6.   A "going steady" relationship maintained mainly to impress peers.
7.   A long-lasting, close platonic relationship.
8.   A steady relationship where each person goes out with other members of the opposite sex.
9.   Widowers remarried in middle age, after several years of living alone.
10. A one-night sexual encounter.
11. A marriage of twenty-five years.
12. A mainly physical relationship with an older and more experienced person.
13. A school affair between teacher and pupil.
14. Brief, fluctuating relationships among members of a permanent social group.
15. A young marriage after a long, involved courtship.
16. A relationship in which only one of the partners is deeply involved.
17. Having an affair with a married person.
18. A short, mainly sexual affair between two students.
19. An irregular, occasional dating relationship for mutual entertainment between two young people.
20. The continuation of a once personal relationship by letters and telephone calls from overseas.
21. A short, emotional holiday affair.
22. A long, involved "going steady" relationship at school.
23. "Love at first sight," followed by engagement, after a brief but intense relationship.
24. A short, mutual first love.
25. The recommencement of an old flame, that didn't work out before.

Source: Forgas and Dobosz (1980)

telephone her later. In short, somatic sensations of fear were misinterpreted as physical attraction!

Just as individuals interpret their emotional symptoms according to cultural scripts, they define their emerging contacts with others in terms of the repertoire of relationships provided by their culture. "Falling in love," "being engaged," "getting married" and "extramarital affairs" are venerable ways of pigeon-holding romantic involvement. "One-night stands" and "living together" are more recent relationship categories. Table 6.1 shows that many other sorts of romantic relationships emerged when sociologists asked university students to describe in detail their own or familiar others' relationships (Forgas and Dobosz, 1980). Can you add to this list?

Close scrutiny of romantic relationships provides considerable insight into the workings of gender. During dating and courtship rituals, females are apt to be especially femi-nine, males especially masculine. In the passage which follows, Goffman (1977:323) describes playful "gender displays:"

Thus between males one finds various forms of horseplay—shoving, pushing, punching, withholding—along with mock contests such as Indian wrestling, spur of the moment races, handsqueeze trials, and the like. Across sex, males engage in lift-off bear hugs, mock chasing after, coercive holding in one position, grasping of the two small wrists in one big hand, playful rocking of the boat, dunking, throwing or pushing into the water, spraying with water, making as if to push off a cliff, throwing small stones at the body, approaching with snake, dead rat, squid, and other loathsome objects, threatening with electrical shocks of an order they themselves can bear, and other delights. Observe that by unseriously introducing just those threats and pains that he might protect a woman from, a male can encourage her to provide a full-voiced rendition of the plight to which her sex is presumably prone. And, of course, she herself can create the unserious circumstances in which her display of gender will be possible, as when she pummels he who holds her, as if out of hopelessness at having any effect upon the giant that has captured her, or hides her eyes from the terrible things that are being shown on the silver screen while he laughingly watches on, … or unsuccessfully attempts to open a jar with a play at straining all her muscular reserve...

Our discussion focusses on romantic relationships among the young. Although falling in and out of love is not limited to individuals in their teens and twenties, people this age are both more constrained by pressures for gender-appropriate behaviour, and impressed by the lessons of gender socialization. The gender displays detailed by Goffman (1977) seem less appropriate for older people.

As teenagers strive to disentangle themselves from the parental nest (Zellman and Goodchilds, 1983:50), peers become increasingly important definers of self and the world. Though this section concentrates on heterosexual relations, we do not want to lose sight of the powerful influence wielded by same-sex peers. This influence operates differently for females and males. The female peer group approves good looks, clothes, and popularity with the boys. According to Greenglass (1982:73), "while pressure on girls for early marriage is now decreasing, there is still considerably more pressure on adolescent girls to establish heterosexual relationships than to pursue a career." The male peer group, on the other hand, emphasizes sports, future job or career preparation, and girls as the means to explore their sexuality (Greenglass, 1982:74).

On the basis of six months' observations of teenagers in middle-class Toronto malls, Elaine Batcher (1987:151) concludes that,

We tend to see young women as very free, but observations of individuals and groups have shown that sex, drugs and rock music, specifics of the teen culture, are not advancements in young women's freedom, but further pathways of their control by the social group, within which girls play very conventional roles. A girl may be planning a future of accomplishment, but in giving up individuality in favour of acceptance she is throwing her destiny into the hands of others. The

message is an old one, but the details are ever fresh.

In the pages to follow, a series of questions are raised about heterosexual romantic relationships. Where possible, reference will also be made to homosexual relations.

What Do Males and Females Want in Relationships?

Cultural expectations, prodded by biological urges, lead most people past puberty to want a romantic relationship. Farrell (1986:120) says young adolescents of both sexes have in common the desire for attention. However, they want attention for different reasons. "Girls want male attention to lead to 'dates,' going steady, a gold bracelet, or other symbols of her primary fantasy. Boys want the attractive girl's attention for a different reason — physical intimacy." During this immature stage, the goal for both really amounts to a "trophy" to show off to their peers.

As they grow older, young women and men develop some agreement about relationship goals (Peplau and Gordon, 1985:259 ff.) Both look for closeness with a special person; marriage is a major goal for 95 percent or more of heterosexual college students. When asked what they want out of long-term relationships, both sexes emphasize affection and companionship. However, intimacy and verbal self-disclosure are more important to women, and shared activities, especially sex, matter slightly more to men. Because most people choose mates from similar social class and ethnic backgrounds (Baker, 1990b:46), considerable consensus exists in young people's expectations about their love relationships. For example, traditionalists about gender arrangements are usually matched with traditionalists, and feminists with feminists. However, there is likely "to be a small but consistent difference in the relative traditionalism of partners, with women being more pro-feminist than their male partners" (Peplau and Gordon, 1985:259).

A questionnaire study of heterosexual and homosexual relationships concluded that gender exerts greater influence on relationships than does sexual orientation (Peplau, 1981). Men's goals in intimate relationships are similar, whether the partner is female or male. The same is true for women. Only one major difference was reported:

Heterosexual couples — whether they are dating casually, living together, or married — are powerfully influenced by the model of traditional marriage, a social institution that prescribes very different roles for men and women. In contrast, most homosexual couples reject husband/wife roles as a basic for love relationships. Instead, gay relationships resemble "best friendships," with the added component of romantic and erotic attraction (Peplau, 1981:20).

Chapter 9 returns to the topic of marriage as gendered social structure.

What Traits Do They Seek in Partners?

There is much commonality in the qualities desired by women and men (Peplau and Gordon, 1985:261). Both seek a partner who is affectionate, understanding, and has a "good personality." However, beyond this agreement, our culture encourages certain sex-linked asymmetries in the characteristics of dating and marriage partners. The traditional bargain has involved women trading their beauty, sexual favours, and fecundity for the male-controlled resources of money, status, and protection. Women have been taught to seek a partner who is taller, older, more experienced, more occupationally successful. Sociologists refer to women's tendency to marry "up" as the *marriage gradient* (Bernard, 1972). They emphasize that since men with these characteristics have more power and resources than their brides, the marriage gradient contributes to the non-egalitarian nature of marriages (Baker and Bakker, 1980:554). For their part, men have traditionally sought a woman with the potential to be an attractive companion, and a good homemaker and mother.

Societal changes such as women's increased labour force participation and feminist ideology have altered the traditional bargain. Nevertheless, women still emphasize occupational attainment and intelligence, while men seek physical attractiveness and sex appeal in their ideal partner (Peplau and Gordon, 1985:261). Personal advertisements in newspapers provide good illustrations of these generalizations.

Across cultures and centuries, females have been encouraged (or obliged) to reconstruct their bodies to conform to male erotic expectations (Hunter Collective, 1983:33): in the East, the bound feet of the Chinese, the Burmese neck ring, the Japanese obi; in the West, the steel-ribbed corset and whalebone stays. Today, the obligation to be beautiful is felt by both sexes, but especially by women: they totter about on stiletto heels, pierce their ears, undergo silicone injections in breasts "too small" or reduction surgery in breasts "too large," and submit bodies they loathe to Weight Watchers, Diet Centres, hypnosis, liposuction, and stomach stapling. Although the women's movement stimulated some appreciation of the energy, money, and pain produced by our society's emphasis on looking good and staying young, it "does not seem to have had much real impact on cultural standards of beauty and the industries which feed on these" (Laws and Schwartz, 1977:45).

A study of American heterosexual and homosexual couples found that only lesbians were free of the tyranny of beauty (Blumstein and Schwartz, 1983:246). Physical appearance was an important factor in bringing together heterosexual and gay male couples; it continued to have an impact on established relationships. Indications are that male physical attractiveness may be becoming an increasingly important factor in opposite-sex attraction (Berscheid, 1985:455). For example, short males suffer from "heightism." One study (Gillis and Avis, 1980) reported that among 720 couples, in only one case was the male the shorter partner. Ten percent of males in their teens, 20 percent in their twenties, and so on show obvious hair loss in a society where a full head of hair implies youth, confidence, vitality, and virility. No wonder that researchers testing the experimental drug minoxidil, reputed to grow hair on balding heads, were flooded with volunteers (Castleman, 1986:51). Such contemporary phenomena as fashion magazines aimed at men, male strip shows, and "buns" calendars suggest that males, too, are becoming sex objects. The physical fitness craze puts pressure on both sexes to develop strong, attractive bodies.

Though most of us dream about dating and mating with someone gorgeous, we tend to be sufficiently realistic to settle for an individual reasonably close to our own level of attractiveness. It is just as well that we do. Blumstein and Schwartz (1983:265) tell us that "a couple is more likely to prosper if both partners are equally attractive than if one partner is far more alluring." Here, gay couples face the biggest problems, since both partners may be judged according to the same standards of physical attractiveness. As well, couples match up on mental health, physical health, popularity, intelligence, warmth, dependability of character, family background (race, religion, parents' educational level, income), and so on. The tendency noted at the beginning of this chapter for similar people to be drawn together is termed *homogamy* (Walster and Walster, 1978:139).

WHO TAKES THE INITIATIVE?

Males generally take the *direct* initiative in initiating cross-sex relationships. With experience, they are drawn to women who are both desirable to them *and* likely to accept their overtures (Huston and Ashmore, 1986:189). Since rebuffs are painful, males prefer females who are interested in them, rather than females who play "hard to get" (Walster et al., 1973). While the traditional masculine role requires him to make the verbal overtures, the feminine part in the mating dance involves making herself at-

tractive and signalling availability through body language and eye contact. "Drink to Me Only with Thine Eyes"—making mutual eye contact—marks the beginning of conversation between previously unknown individuals (Deaux and Wrightsman, 1988:132). As we would expect, attractive people are more likely to find themselves locked in mutual eye contact with strangers (Exline, 1971). (Later, couples in love express their intimacy by spending more time gazing at one another than do less passionate couples [Rubin, 1970].)

The early stages of the traditional courtship ritual often prove traumatic for both sexes. She has to bide her time until he chooses to take the initiative (if he ever does). He has to risk rejection. Kostash (1987:93) describes the young woman's point of view: "Learning love and loss. It begins with flirting in the cafeteria—a sidelong glance from under half-raised eyelids, a smile, an embarrassed giggle—and it ends with a broken heart and a vow never to be so vulnerable again." Farrell (1986:132-33) expresses the male's perspective: "It hurts a lot less to be rejected by a sex object than it does to be rejected by a full human being. So if a male can turn women into objects and sex into a game (and call it 'scoring'), he will be able to treat rejection less seriously. He will hurt less" (emphases deleted).

Norms of the dating/mating game seem to be changing. Anecdotes about attractive high school boys being bombarded with telephone calls from girls, and the initiatives taken by middle-aged, previously married women at singles dances suggest that this may be so. However, in the context of traditional norms which specify that men ask and women say "yes" or "no," even today, a woman who strongly signals her interest may be viewed as "on the make," or "an easy lay" by her male target (Huston and Ashmore, 1986:190). At least one study (Abbey, 1982) demonstrates that men "see" much more sexual interest or invitation in women's behaviour than women actually intend. More research is required to explore these interesting avenues.

Is FALLING IN LOVE DIFFERENT FOR FEMALES AND MALES?

Which sex is the more romantic sex? If we focus upon beliefs about love, we get one answer.

The romantic person believes that true love lasts forever, comes but once, is strange and incomprehensible, and conquers barriers of custom or social class. The pragmatic person rejects these ideals, knowing that we can each love many people, that economic security is more important than passion, and that some disillusionment surely accompanies marriage (Peplau and Gordon, 1985:263).

By these criteria, young women are slightly, but consistently, less romantic than young men. Since choice of mate has traditionally determined women's fate (they are choosing both a companion and a standard of living), they apparently cannot afford to be frivolous about romance (Peplau and Gordon, 1985:264).

If we inquire into the *experience* of love, our conclusions are different. First, the sexes do not differ in the intensity of their love for one another (Rubin, 1973). (Nor have differences been found in the depth of love felt by lesbian, gay male, or heterosexual couples [Peplau, 1981:34].) However, women are more likely than men to report various emotional symptoms of love: "floating on a cloud," "wanting to run, jump or scream," "feeling giddy and carefree," and experiencing "trouble concentrating" (Kanin et al., 1970). Whether these results represent actual differences in experience of love or whether women are simply more willing to disclose their euphoria is unclear. Finally, men report falling in love earlier in the development of the relationship (Peplau and Gordon, 1985:264-65). There are several reasons why men fall in love more quickly (Huston and Ashmore, 1986:191). If the man has been the initiator, he is already more attracted. Since he usually exerts greater influence on the couple's recreational activities, he may be enjoying their dates more. Lastly, he may be more eager to fall in love because being in love increases the likelihood that the relationship will become a sexual one.

Finally, women and men prefer different *styles* of love which are consistent with gender definitions (Cancian, 1985;1986). By "love," women mean emotional closeness and verbal expression of their feelings. Men mean sharing activities, especially sex, and helping their partners, e.g., fixing flat tires. Since women are allowed dominion over expressive matters, only their style of love is recognized as "love" in our society (Cancian, 1985).

Is SEX DIFFERENT FOR FEMALES AND MALES?

It goes without saying: sex and romance go together, in thought if not in deed. Eighty percent of Canadian adolescents hold that premarital sex is acceptable if the couple love one another. Fifty percent think intercourse is all right within a few dates when the couple *like* each other (Bibby and Posterski, 1985:77). When Bibby and Posterski were conducting their survey, few young people understood the dangers of sexually transmitted diseases, such as AIDS and herpes. Recent research suggests that although young people now possess high levels of knowledge about AIDS transmission and prevention, most think the disease is unlikely to affect them personally (Maticka-Tyndale, 1989).

There are few absolute differences between male and female sexuality. Biological sex is constrained and directed by the roles society offers men and women (Blumstein and Schwartz, 1989). Sexuality carries different connotations for males and females (Mackie, 1987:151 ff.). Young Canadian females are more likely to require a love relationship as a prerequisite for premarital sex. Young males, on the other hand, tend to be interested in sex solely for physical pleasure (Herold, 1984:11). Whitehurst and Booth (1980:64-65) describe the male adolescent's perspective:

Male sexuality is almost never learned as something to do which adds to his stock of humanness, but something that is done to prove he is not a "fairy," "fag," or homosexual, to prove that he can get young women to "lay," giving him what he wants. Male sex expresses power, exploitation, and anti-feminine attributes; it is rarely an expression of his sense of human tenderness in love and emotional bonding. Even when this happens boys are not easily able to communicate such feelings, especially to a male peer group—for this might prove that he has lost control and is not acting according to the dominant norms of the group, which are generally the opposite.

Whitehurst and Booth (1980:65) go on to point out that as a result of cultural conditioning, adolescents end up acting "much more sexual than they often feel (girls fending off—whether they want to or not because that's what they're supposed to do; boys fighting for sex—whether or not they are in fact really very interested)."

Adult sexuality continues to be strongly influenced by traditional gender patterns. Women seek a relationship first, while men more frequently look for sex for its own sake (Blumstein and Schwartz, 1989:124). Heterosexuals often misunderstand what sex means to their partners. Take the possibility of outside sex, for example. The male partner frequently has a casual view of [his] sex outside the relationship, while the female partner may be devastated (Blumstein and Schwartz, 1983:266). Gay sexuality is also influenced by gender norms. "Husbands and male cohabitors are more like gay men than they are like wives or female cohabitors. Lesbians are more like heterosexual women than either is like gay or heterosexual men" (Blumstein and Schwartz, 1983: 303). For instance, both male homosexual partners may claim the right to initiate sex in order to confirm male identities. Both partners in a lesbian relationship may have inhibitions about taking the initiative. In summary, male-female differences in sexuality are socially constructed.

WHO CONTROLS THE BALANCE OF POWER?

What factors tip the balance of power in favour of one partner rather than the other? Three factors seem important (Peplau and Gordon, 1985:273; Sprecher, 1985). First,

social convention has long given Canadian males greater status and authority in heterosexual relations. The belief that the boyfriend has the right to be the "leader," or that the husband ought to be "head" of the family often gives the male partner the advantage in a particular relationship.

Second, the balance of power is affected by the relative resources of the partners. Men are more likely to control money, status, and brute force, and women, sex. The woman's educational and career goals can be an important predictor of power in university student relationships. According to an American study (Peplau and Campbell, 1989:128), if the girlfriend aspired to a bachelor's degree or less, 87 percent of the students reported that the male had greater power. However, if the girlfriend planned an advanced degree, only 30 percent reported that the man had greater power. This finding is consistent with research which shows that paid employment increases wives' power in marriages (see Chapter 9).

Third, power in dyads resides in one partner's involvement or dependence upon the other. This dependence may be financial or emotional. It hinges, to some extent, on the existence of alternatives to this particular relationship. The *principle of less interest* (Waller, 1937; Turner, 1970) holds here. According to this concept, the partner who cares less about the quality of the relationship, or whether the relationship continues at all, enjoys an advantage over the other. "Because women tend to value relationships more highly than men, work more to sustain them, and feel more responsible for their outcomes, women are likely to care more about having and preserving a relationship than men are" (Richardson, 1989:110). However, the interplay of the principle of less interest with gender varies over the life cycle. Generally speaking, females are at the peak of their power during dating and courtship. Because traditional gender arrangements put wives at a power disadvantage, and aging diminishes feminine resources, women never again feel so cherished. A wealthy, divorced man in his late forties mused about his changing social fortune: "In light of my experiences now, I can hardly believe that when I was a high school student, I had to *beg* girls to go out with me."

Another facet of power in close relations concerns the tactics that individuals use to try to influence each other (Peplau and Gordon, 1985:274). As a result of prior socialization, the sexes learn somewhat different strategies. For example, college men are more likely to report using direct approaches to their objectives, such as bargaining or logical arguments. By contrast, more women admit using indirect approaches, such as becoming silent, pouting, or using tears (Falbo and Peplau, 1980). Though social desirability may interfere with who is willing to admit what, micromanipulative strategies are the resource of the less powerful (see Chapter 2). The masculine style of rationality, "keeping cool," "stone-walling it" communicates a sense of "rightness" to male decisions and is, therefore, an effective means of keeping the upper hand. In one of the last interviews before his death, actor John Wayne talked about his calculated inexpressiveness (Sattel, 1976):

Another thing I learned—if you cry, the audience won't. A man can cry for his horse, for his dog, for another man, but he cannot cry for a woman. A strange thing. He can cry at the death of a friend or a pet. But where he's supposed to be boss, with his child or wife, something like that, he better hold 'em back and let them cry.

Social scientists are beginning to realize the extent to which physical coercion is employed as a power tactic in heterosexual relationships. An estimated one million women in Canada are battered every year (MacLeod, 1987). Men, too, are victims of spousal abuse, though the injuries women incur far exceed what men experience (Brinkerhoff and Lupri, 1988; Strauss et al., 1980).

A growing body of research on violence in dating relationships reveals that dating violence is as extensive as marital violence, and that women are most often on the receiving end. At the most abstract level, this violence may be understood in the context of societal male supremacy where men have traditionally been given the right to control women through physical force. More specifically, researchers conclude that dating violence occurs when women challenge their partner's right to control them and men respond with violence (Stets and Pirog-Good, 1987). Violence occurs most often, not in casual dating, but in more serious relationships where partners are more emotionally dependent on one another, and issues of control arise because more is at stake (De-Keseredy, 1989). In sum, power tactics reflect the general power structure of heterosexual relations in our society (Peplau and Gordon, 1985).

According to Gloria Steinem (1983:22-23), untangling violence from gender and from sexuality is one of the crucial worldwide tasks of feminism. She says:

When you tell one group of people — men — that they are superior and tell another group — women — that they are inferior, it is a lie. It can only be maintained by violence.... Many men, through no fault of the individual man, but rather a fault of the culture, have been convinced that they are not real men unless they are dominant over women. It is like a drug. Without this sense of dominance over women, some men feel that they are nothing; they are not real men or real persons.

THE END OF PASSION

Eventually, the day comes when passion flags, stomach butterflies settle down, and euphoria dissipates. Sometimes the couple part company. Same-sex relationships are generally briefer than their heterosexual counterparts, likely because gay relationships do not receive the societal support heterosexual relationships do. Therefore "gays encounter fewer barriers to calling it quits" (Peplau, 1981:34). When the break-up of a heterosexual pair does not come about through mutual decision, the woman is more likely to have initiated the split (Rubin, Peplau and Hill, 1981). Perhaps as a consequence, men are more depressed and lonely than women afterwards, and experience more difficulty accepting the end of the relationship (Hill, Rubin and Peplau, 1976). Contrary to folk wisdom, "men tend to fall in love more readily than women, and women fall out of love more readily than men" (Deaux and Wrightsman, 1988:266). After it ends, couples rarely agree on what caused the breakup (Rubin, Peplau and Hill, 1981).

Sometimes, passionate relationships ripen into compassionate love with its shared understandings, habits, and attachment. As the passionate flame becomes a warm "afterglow" (Reik, 1972), these couples "find, happily, that a friend is really what they needed all along" (Walster and Walster, 1978:125). Indeed, when couples married 15 years or more were asked what kept them together, the top reason volunteered separately by both was, "My spouse is my best friend" (Lauer and Lauer, 1985).

The pre-feminist sociological literature portrayed the marriage as an arrangement of love between equals or near equals, using terms such as "companionate marriages," and "symmetrical marriages." As we shall see in Chapter 9, feminists and other critics of the family have drawn a different picture of marriage. Instead of love and friendship, they have emphasized patterns of inequality and conflict. Their analysis of the family asks, "What is the source of husbands' power and wives' subordination?" (Thorne, 1982:13).

Falling in and out of love, like platonic friendship and marriage, is guided by cultural and subcultural patterns. Despite more liberal gender and sexual norms, the "politics of courtship may be especially resistant to change because couples beginning to court often engage in posing—the tendency to fall back on those gender roles that are stereotypically appropriate or safe..." (McCormick and Jesser, 1983:71). Dating and courtship tend to reinforce the sex-typed socialization of earlier years. The first important romantic relationship may represent the crossroad where the young woman volunteers for "second place" and accepts masculine definitions of her situation. Cohabitation, marriage, and most particularly, parenthood all tend to be conducted accord-

ing to inegalitarian gender norms. Chapter 9 will return to this topic.

CONCLUSIONS

Chapter 6 continued the discussion of gender from the social-psychological perspective. It addressed, once again, the central question: How do people learn femininity and masculinity? The focus of this chapter has been the peer group as primary group agent of socialization. Same-sex and other-sex friendships, platonic relationships, and romantic relationships were scrutinized.

The interplay of gender and peer relations is twofold. First, society's gender scripts shape the structure of peer relations. For example, sexuality is assumed to be the raison d'être for cross-sex relationships. Skepticism about the possibility of platonic relationships was the theme of the 1989 movie, *When Harry Met Sally*. Billy Crystal as Harry believes men and women cannot be friends. "The sex part always gets in the way." Children's play groups provide another illustration of the first point. Girls' preference for indoor play, involving a small number of participants in quiet conversation, contrasts sharply with boys' proclivity for organized team competition. These traditional activities are congruent with gender stereotypes.

Second, peer activities serve to convey gender socialization lessons. From participation in play groups in middle childhood, girls learn the communicative skills and emotional expressiveness called for in the nurturant roles that lie ahead of them. Boys, on the other hand, learn the skills demanded by complex organizations in the public domain, such as teamwork, competition, accepting criticism. From childhood on, both same-sex and cross-sex relations teach attitudes towards the other sex. Boys learn emotional distance from females and disdain for everything feminine. Girls learn to accept second place. In Richer's (1988:106) opinion, this "rigid association between sex and play activity is the harbinger of both domestic and labour market inequality."

The next chapter will conclude our discussion of gender socialization with an analysis of secondary and symbolic socialization agents.

NOTES

1. Selman and Selman (1979) describe how children's perceptions of friendship develop from ages three to twelve.
2. Bigelow and LaGaipa (1980:39) remark that a major reason why children's friendships are fragile is that youngsters "lack the cognitive foundation necessary for appreciating and understanding the meaning of friendship."
3. *Sociometry* is a research technique for measuring the attraction and repulsion patterns in small groups. Subjects are asked to designate a small number of people they would prefer to associate with, usually for specific work and play activities. Sometimes they are also asked to name people they would prefer not to associate with.
4. This news report from Fort Worth, Texas, illustrates the pressure on small boys to be "instant men." "A 5-year-old boy who drank a third of a litre of bourbon after an adult prompted him to do it 'like a man' died yesterday morning. Police said Thomas Griffin was given the bourbon at a party Friday night. A third of a litre is equivalent to about seven normal drinks. Anthony Jimerson, 21, was charged with injury to a child." (*The Globe and Mail*, March 1, 1990).
5. Personal communication from Janet Evans, a Calgary elementary school teacher.
6. Margaret Atwood's novel, *Cat's Eye* (1988:52 ff.) contains a wonderful description of the play of preadolescent girls in the late 1940s.
7. The tone of moral superiority in works such as Gilligan (1982) and Belenky et al. (1986) provokes cautious skepticism in the minds of some critics. Turn-of-the-century suffragist feminism also adopted the higher moral ground. Suffragists "maintained that women were more law-abiding, more peace-loving, more charitable than men. Give women the vote, the argument went, and the streets would be clean, child labour would be eliminated, war would end" (Kerber, 1986:308-309).
8. Although Gilligan (1982) talks about feminine and masculine "voices," she does not claim that these modes of thought are sexually dimorphic. She cautions the reader that "this association is not absolute, and the contrasts between male and female voices are presented ... to highlight a distinction between the two modes of thought and to focus a problem of interpretation rather than to represent a generalization about either sex" (p. 2).

Chapter 7

Secondary and Symbolic Sources of Gender Socialization

Chapter 7 is the last of four chapters to consider the acquisition and reinforcement of gender from the social-psychological perspective. To reiterate, our problem is to explain how people develop masculine or feminine identities, personality traits, attitudes, and behaviours. Our approach is social-psychological; that is, we explore how the social environment impinges upon the individual. Our main concern is *not* with biology, psychology, or social structure, but with the influence of various *secondary* and *symbolic* agencies of socialization. Attention will be given to the school and the church (as examples of secondary agents), and to the mass media, language, and non-verbal communication (as symbolic sources). The nature of secondary and symbolic socialization agencies may be best understood by comparing them with the primary agents discussed in Chapters 5 and 6.[1]

First of all, family and peer relationships have greater potential to arouse intense emotions than the more impersonal secondary agencies. Throughout life, primary bonds to relatives and friends are stronger than secondary ties to schools, churches, clubs, business offices, unions, etc. For instance, Lightfoot (1977), who contrasts the primary relationship of parents with their children with the more secondary relationship of teachers with their pupils, says "chaotic fluctuation of emotions, indulgence, and impulsivity" found in the association of parents and children does *not* characterize teacher-pupil relations (p. 396). "Even those teachers who speak of 'loving' their chil-

dren do not really mean the boundless, all-encompassing love of mothers and fathers, but a very measured and time-limited love that allows for withdrawal" (Lightfoot, 1977:396). The fact that this idealistic description of parental love does not apply to all families does not undermine our main point: intense affectivity bespeaks influence.

Another way of saying all this is that parents have *particularistic* expectations for their children (and friends for their friends), while teachers (and preachers) have *universalistic* expectations (Lightfoot, 1977:396). Parents and friends attend to individual qualities and needs. Parents dream of unique futures for their offspring. In contrast, teachers and preachers try to judge everyone by the same objective standards; they hold out generalized goals for all children.

A second fundamental distinction between primary and secondary agencies concerns the timing of their influence. Children encounter primary socialization agents very early in life when they are most impressionable, before they move beyond the intimate circle of family, playmates, babysitters, neighbours to confront the more formal school. Many youngsters also participate in Sunday school, hockey teams, Brownies, Beavers, and so on. The recent invention of the daycare centre has made this biographical distinction less sharp than it once was. Nonetheless, research evidence shows that timing is important, that gender identity, for example, is "very solidly entrenched before children even enter public school" (Richer, 1979:198).

Third, the primary agents are particularly important because they determine the child's exposure to subsequent agents and interpret the meaning of these secondary influences. The family's "chanelling function" was mentioned in Chapter 5. The family determines which school and which church (if any) the child will attend. It has the authority to decide which television programs the child may watch, which videos may be rented. Here is a gender-related example of this point. The Mennonite Brethren Church advocates a conservative Christian interpretation of femininity and masculinity. Teenage members of Mennonite Brethren congregations receive parental and peer support for adherence to these gender norms.

Leaving primary agencies aside for the moment, we note that symbolic and secondary sources are characterized by some important differences. An obvious distinction is that secondary agencies involve direct personal interaction while the impact of symbolic sources is less tangible. Also, school, church (and family) deliberately set out to equip children with the knowledge required to fit into adult society. Admittedly, much of the impact that these agencies have upon children's gender socialization is unintentional. The school's "hidden curriculum" conveys important attitudes and values which educational authorities do not intend, or even recognize. Nevertheless, the socialization aims of secondary agents are more clearly articulated than those of the symbolic agencies. The mass media—television, audiotapes, videotapes, movies, records, radio, newspapers, magazines, books—are impersonal communication sources that exist to entertain, to inform, to sell products to large audiences. For most people, the fact that the media are also in the business of gender socialization is beside the point.

In contrast with secondary agencies, the part played in gender socialization by language and non-verbal communication is more subtle, yet more profound. Language is the major means by which all socialization agencies socialize. Nevertheless, language constitutes more than a conduit or vehicle of influence. We assume, along with many other scholars (Sapir, 1933; Whorf, 1949; Berger and Luckmann, 1966; Schutz, 1967) that "reality" is constructed and

perpetuated through symbols, and through language as a specific set of symbols. Indeed, gender really amounts to a complex of symbols built upon biological sex, that specify attributes, normative behaviour, rights and duties, and relative prestige of females and males in Canadian society. Thus, to a considerable extent, what people think and know and do is determined by the language categories at their disposal. Since language and sex/gender are linked in many complex ways, children's linguistic lessons are also lessons in gender relations. Women have been excluded historically from the production of culture, so that the English language has been literally "man made" (Spender, 1985). The English language, among others, denigrates women while it asserts male superiority. Therefore, experience with the language teaches the "semantic derogation of women" (Schulz, 1975:65).

Non-verbal communication—gestures, facial expressions, use of physical space—also serves to reinforce traditional gender norms. Feminists have been alert to these messages. For example, at the kickoff of the 1984 federal election campaign in Edmonton, Prime Minister and Liberal Party leader John Turner patted the bottom of Liberal Party president Iona Campagnolo; she let Turner (and the Canadian public) know his gesture was not appreciated:

Standing on stage before the cheering throng [Turner] leaned over to party president Iona Campagnolo, gave her a kiss on the cheek and patted her bum. The ardent feminist spotted a CTV camera in her peripheral vision and tried to defuse the incident by swatting the prime ministerial posterior five times in return. Both of them smiled for the cameras as he leaned forward and said something to her which included the words "a perfect ass." "What was I supposed to do?" Campagnolo said later. "Do nothing and let Canadian women think I think that sort of behaviour is okay?..." (Weston, 1988:81-82).

In short, the symbolic agents are ubiquitous socializers, which also serve as vehicles for primary and secondary gender socialization.

THE SCHOOL

Education is a pivotal social institution in modern societies "mediating between ascriptive factors given at birth, namely social class and gender, and ultimate position in society" (Russell, 1987:229). Gilbert and Gomme (1987:199) suggest that one clue to the salience of education in our society is the numbers of people involved in this enterprise. According to these sociologists, one-third of all Canadians are students, teachers, or administrators. Another clue to education's importance is its cost to Canadian taxpayers. In the mid-1980s, education cost $33.3 billion, the second highest government expenditure (after social security) (Gilbert and Gomme, 1987:200).

Especially relevant to the present task is the major role that industrialized nations, such as Canada, assign to the school in preparing children for adulthood. "From kindergarten to high school graduate, the average young Canadian currently spends about 17 000 hours in the school" (Lennards, 1990:399). A substantial segment pursues additional education at the post-secondary level. The knowledge and skills required to function effectively in urbanized, industrialized societies are far too extensive and complex for parents to convey to their children. Schools channel people through programs of occupational preparation into positions in the socioeconomic structure.[2] In addition to its technical function, the school necessarily reflects the culture of which it is part and transmits to the young an ethos and a world view (Parsons, 1959).

Education and the Liberal Reform Tradition

Liberal social reformers, including activist sociologists, have long appreciated the crucial role of education in modern societies (Thibault, 1988). On the one hand, they criticize the part education plays in preserving and justifying the status quo. The reader may recall our comments in Chapter 1 concerning male-authored theoretical tradition in sociology as bolsterer of the gender status quo. On the other hand, social movement advocates remain perpetually optimistic "that educational change and reform can bring about social change and reform" (Himelfarb and Richardson, 1982:289).

In view of the foregoing, the hopes and concerns about education expressed by feminists, whose lineage extends back to Mary Wollstonecraft in the 18th century, make sense. (See Virginia Woolf, *Three Guineas* [1938].) Less than a century ago, women were "almost completely denied access to any form of higher education beyond the skills of reading and writing" (Smith, 1987:26). Therefore, educational opportunity for women was a focus of the suffrage movement in both Europe and North America. Advocates of equal rights for women argue that,

Education is a radicalizing force. Beginning with its most basic ingredient, literacy, education fosters radicalism by enabling the less powerful to read and spread dissent. Education thus threatens the power establishment, whose power is enhanced by its control over knowledge.... Education, the potential equalizer and radicalizer, everywhere has been less available to women (Lipman-Blumen, 1984:134-35).

So far as Canada is concerned, the specific nature of feminist complaints about the education system has changed over the years. Early feminists fought against the exclusion of Canadian females from formal schooling. For example, an 1866 regulation in Upper Canada proposed to count a girl as half a boy for administrative purposes. Efforts were made to exclude girls from classical courses, such as Latin, which were necessary for admission to universities and the professions (Prentice, 1977, cited by Guppy et al., 1987). As Strong-Boag (1979: 110) writes, "In the nineteenth century neither Canadian universities nor professions were wholly happy with the prospect of female recruits. Opponents of higher education for women were legion." For instance, the President of the University of Toronto insisted, in 1884, that the "college buildings had been planned 'so entirely in anticipation of their exclusive use by male students' that 'extensive and costly additions' would be required to accommodate an experiment 'condemned by so many experienced educators'" (Buckland, 1985:137). Opponents of higher education for women argued that the experience would damage women's delicate health and reproductive capacities. Therefore, female intellectual development would be necessarily bought "at the price of a puny, enfeebled race" (Sayers, 1982:18).

By 1970, when the Royal Commission on the Status of Women delivered its report, equality of educational opportunity for both sexes meant a good deal more than formally equal access (Gaskell and McLaren, 1987:106). The Commission began its discussion of education with what has become almost a ritualistic statement of faith in the power of education to reform society: "Changes in education could bring dramatic improvements in the social and economic position of women in an astonishingly short time" (p. 161). The 32 far-reaching recommendations made by the Commission dealt with such concerns as adoption of textbooks that portray both sexes in diversified roles and occupations; provision of career information about the broad field of occupational choice for girls; improved availability of sports programs for both sexes; development of educational programs to meet the special needs of rural and immigrant women, and of Indian and Inuit girls and young women; and the continuing education of women with family responsibilities.

Although the Royal Commission on the Status of Women had identified some important structural issues, the thrust of the 1970s feminist critique of education was nonetheless against false ideas and consequent misguided behaviour (Armstrong and Armstrong, 1984). The main targets were gender stereotyping in curricula and textbooks; teachers' sex-typed treatment of girls and boys; girls' fear of mathematics; lack of adequate career information for girls.

This section considers the educational institution, as it extends from kindergarten to university, as agent of gender socialization. In the interval since the Royal Commission on the Status of Women Report (1970), our understanding of the role of the school in reinforcing traditional gender norms has become more sophisticated. The influx of vocal adult women students into community colleges and universities, particularly into women's studies courses, has contributed immensely to social scientists' understanding of the impact of schools upon females. Gaskell and McLaren (1987) and Gaskell, McLaren and Novogrodsky (1989) present useful accounts of the Canadian school as gender socialization agent.

Teacher Interaction with Children

The feminist critique of the 1970s opened people's eyes to the conventional understandings of gender which often guide teachers' classroom behaviour. For example, Dr. Penny Codding, now a University of Calgary chemistry professor, says, "I was actively discouraged when I was 18 years old by my first year chemistry teacher who told me girls couldn't be chemists" (Heinemann, 1988:5). Since then, many teachers have had their own consciousness raised, and work toward gender equality. Nevertheless, observational studies of classroom behaviour indicate that teachers often emphasize sex/gender differences in their dealings with students, that they evaluate male and female academic abilities differently, and that through focussing greater attention on boys, they contribute to male dominance of classrooms. Together, these attitudes and practices serve to devalue girls and render them invisible in the classroom (Russell, 1987:239).

Cognitive-development theory proposes that the child learns early that girls and boys belong in different and invariant categories (see Chapter 4). Teachers provide cues that encourage children to notice and emphasize female-male differences. According to Richer's (1979) two-month observational study of a kindergarten class in an Ontario urban school, the teacher found sex/gender to be a practical basis on which to organize the children. For example, children lined up by sex to move from one activity to another—going to the library or the gymnasium, retrieving food from their lockers, preparing to go home. Also, sex was used to motivate participation in activities—"The girls are ready, the boys are not" or "Who can do it the fastest, the boys or the girls?" Richer (1979:201) cites this illustration of organization and motivation:

[In] the coordination exercises, where the children were asked to respond quickly to changes in directions regarding hand movements, the commands were invariably given by sex: "Boys, put your fingers on your nose; girls, put your hands in your laps; boys, touch your toes, etc." When someone slipped up here, the teacher's admonishment sometimes took the following form, "Are you a girl? I thought all along you were a boy." This kind of reference, which in this case left a child squirming a little in embarrassment, served not only to accentuate further the sex differences in the class, but also to put a negative value on behaviour inconsistent with one's own sex.

Parenthetically, we ask whether the embarrassment described in the quotation above stemmed from sex inconsistency per se, or from loss of status associated with the "demotion" from girl to boy? Be that as it may, this sex segregation reinforces the gender stereotyping children have begun long before they entered school.

Teacher behaviours communicate gender attitudes to children in other ways. Especially in the elementary grades, teachers tend to reward children of both sexes for feminine behaviour (Fagot, 1981; Fagot and Paterson, 1969). Stereotypically feminine behaviour—being quiet, obedient, dependent, neat and sober-minded—has been more acceptable to teachers than masculine "bouncing about, questioning, being curious or aggressive" (Howe, 1974:124). In both preschool and elementary school classes, boys receive more disapproval, scolding, and other forms of negative attention than do girls (Huston, 1983:439). However, boys receive more attention and praise from teachers, as well as more punishment (Basow, 1986:126).

Paradoxically, teachers find compliant, nondisruptive feminine patterns of behaviour easier to deal with, but at the same time, express a preference for teaching boys over girls (Schneider and Coutts, 1979). "The 'overachievement' of girls in the lower grades is, according to several teachers, a result of their docility and conscientiousness" (Russell, 1987:241). A high school teacher said: "The fellows I prefer to teach, more than the girls, because they don't get as up-tight about little things. Like I find in my Grade 10s they don't hold grudges and they're fun, while the girls are taking themselves far more seriously" (Russell, 1987:240). This subtle devaluation of femininity, along with the fact that boys get more attention, and are permitted to dominate classroom interaction at all grade levels reinforces the societal message that boys matter more than girls.

According to an American study (Sadker and Sadker, 1987:144)

Teachers behave differently, depending on whether boys or girls call out answers during discussions. When boys call out comments without raising their hands, teachers accept their answers. However, when girls call out, teachers reprimand this "inappropriate" behaviour with messages such as, "In this class we don't shout out answers, we raise our hands." The message is subtle but powerful. Boys should be academically assertive and grab teacher attention; girls should act like ladies and keep quiet.

These authors point out that education is not a spectator sport. When students participate in classroom discussion, they end up with more positive attitudes towards school and learning.

Despite all the attention they receive, boys are less likely than girls to feel at home in the classroom (Sadker and Sadker, 1987). In order to counter teachers' influence and thus maintain their masculinity and their independence, they turn to their male peers. Richer (1984) says that, "...as school progresses, boys are increasingly forced to *confront* the school as a group; the boys thereby differentiate themselves both from the school and from the girls, who exhibit considerably greater compatibility with the social demands of public education" (p. 177, emphasis in original).

Critics have worried about the unfortunate consequences for boys of the "feminine bias" of elementary teachers, who tend to be disproportionately female. Some feared that the "feminized" school environment would "feminize" boys. Others have linked this environment with boys' difficulty with academic subjects, such as reading (Best, 1983). Less often recognized is the possibility that this "feminine bias" may harm girls, too. Girls perform at least as well as boys in terms of school grades and years of education (they do less well if criteria are standardized test scores and enrollment in mathematics and science courses) (Gaskell et al., 1989:18). However, "the cultivation of passive obedience in school may have long-term deleterious effects on girls' independence and self-esteem" Huston (1983:439). Certainly, girls derive less eventual payoff from their education than boys.

Equality of Opportunity: Access to Material and Activities

Phyllis Steele (1987) was one of two women admitted to the University of Alberta Faculty of Medicine in 1928. Because university authorities felt the subject of male genitalia was too embarrassing for women to study, the two female med students were forbidden to attend classes on these subjects. Steele was nevertheless required to pass an oral examination set by the Professor of Urinary Diseases:

I appeared for my oral examination. I was alone with the professor. He sat at his desk, with me squarely in front of him. He looked up with a scowl:

"Miss Steele."
"Yes."
"You're up for your final today?"
"Yes, Sir."

He spent some time, I think looking over my past records and marks, while I became more and more nervous. Finally, he said, "I have just one question for you. How much cinnamon do you put in an apple pie?"

I was aghast at this question, but I didn't dare protest in fear that he would throw me out. So I stuttered, "A teaspoonful, Sir."

He banged my record book down and said, "That's all a woman needs to know." He pointed to the door. "You can get out now."

Although the pioneer women physicians were certified to practise medicine, they did not receive training equivalent to that given their male classmates (who were not thought to need protection from embarrassing study of female anatomy and physiology).

Even today, gender-differentiated experiences with school materials and activities begin with selection of toys and games in preschool play, and continue into course and program enrollment in high school and university. In the past, segregating girls into home economics and typing courses and boys into shop classes reinforced traditional notions about gender. Moreover, different educational experiences served to channel the sexes into different occupations. As many of the barriers erected by

educational institutions have disappeared during the past decade, attention has shifted from formal exclusion to the tendency of one sex or the other to disqualify itself from worthwhile experiences because of attitudes derived from previous socialization experiences. Because of space limitations, only a few important examples can be developed here.

Schools (and other community agencies) have come under severe criticism for providing separate sports activities for boys that are more varied, extensive, and better funded than those available to girls. According to the Canadian Association for Health, Physical Education and Recreation, significantly fewer girls than boys are physically fit at each age level. The activity level of girls begins a decline at age 13, so that only 24 percent of girls 15-19 years achieve a recommended level of fitness, in comparison with 50 percent of boys the same age (Smith, 1988:A16). Performances by top female athletes make sex-segregated school programs appear strangely anachronistic. For instance, in 1988, Vicki Keith became the first person to swim all five Great Lakes; synchronized swimmers Carolyn Waldo and Michelle Cameron earned two of the three gold medals earned by Canada at the Seoul Summer Olympics.

Athletic programs and facilities have also come under harsh criticism from gender relations experts. Critics have charged that early patterns of gender-differentiated play are replicated in the labour market in the form of occupational segmentation (Richer, 1988:98). Sport has been described as "one of the 'last bastions' of male power and superiority" (Messner, 1987:54). More particularly, these patterns are considered detrimental because of their linkages with skills and attitudes. As we pointed out in Chapter 6, girls have not had the same opportunity as boys to develop team or competitive skills which appear to be tied to success in adult organizations. Gender experts also criticize traditional school sports programs from the boys' point of view. They suggest that unrelenting emphasis on competition and success in sports can be detrimental to boys, especially for the many without athletic talent (Messner, 1987).

Considerable concern has also been expressed about sex-differentiated participation in mathematics and science courses (Gaskell et al., 1989:25). After about the age of 14, males perform better in standardized mathematics tests and take more elective mathematics courses in high school. When science and mathematics courses become optional, females are more likely than males to avoid them (Scott, 1981). Women's lower participation in the scientific professions is, in part, the consequence of girls' being "filtered out" of high school math courses (Mura et al., 1987). As we noted in Chapter 2, the actual male advantage in mathematical and visual-spatial abilities established by psychologists is much too small to explain the fact that few female students become scientists, engineers, and architects. The issue is the way schools treat female-male differences. An American educator charges:

Boys learn to read more slowly than girls, for instance, and suffer more reading disabilities such as dyslexia, while girls fall behind in math when they get to high school. Society can amplify differences like these or cover them up....We rush in reading teachers to do remedial reading, and their classes are almost all boys. We don't talk about it, we just scurry around getting them to catch up to the girls. But where are the remedial math teachers? Girls are *supposed* to be less good at math, so that difference is incorporated into the way we live (Shapiro, 1990:57).

In the same vein "many girls show disinterest or even marked dislike for what computers do" (Van Gelder, 1985:91, emphasis deleted). Again, the point is not formal exclusion of girls from courses, but rather factors that diminish interest and self-confidence. Modern life increasingly demands computer literacy. Women conditioned to doubt their aptitude for mathematics and computing science will pay a large price: "Computer technology is increasing employment opportunities in the occupations where women are least represented; on the other hand, it is diminishing employment opportunities in the clerical occupations and in the related administrative and supervisory positions which women were using as career ladders" (Menzies, 1984:292).(*Sex Roles*, Vol. 13, #3-4, 1985 focusses on "Women, Girls, and Computers.")

Educators and professional scientists are now attempting to relay a new message: girls *can* do math and science; they *can* aspire to careers in science and technology. We have space for only a few examples. The National Film Board prepared *I Want to be an Engineer* which features three women engineers talking about their careers. The NFB also made *She's A Railroader* and *Louise Drouin, Veterinarian*, which profile women working in stereotypically masculine occupations. Organizations such as the Canadian Association for Women in Science and Women in Scholarship, Engineering Science and Technology sponsor conferences on topics such as "Confronting Technophobia" and "Rewarding Science Programs" in an attempt to reach into secondary schools where career decisions are made (Armour, 1988). Most of the effort to combat occupational sex-typing is directed at attracting girls into better-paid "masculine" occupations, rather than boys into "feminine" work. However, some schools have relabelled their typing courses as "keyboarding." Apparently, many male computer enthusiasts, realizing the usefulness of typing, are enrolling in unisex keyboarding courses. More ambitious attempts to break down masculine stereotypes are also being made. For example, "Boys for Babies," a brief course for Grade 5-6 boys offered in Toronto area schools, gives boys an opportunity to care for infants who are brought in from the community (Gaskell et al., 1989:56-57).

Textbook Depiction of Gender

Sociologists' long-time concern about school texts (Pratt, 1975), particularly those used in the early grades, is explained, in part, by the nature of young readers. Many children read little besides the books they encounter at school, and they carry the cachet of authority. One of the observations of cognitive-developmental theorist Jean Piaget is that children do not develop the intellectual ability to be critical about what they read until their later school years. Therefore, for better or worse, texts have considerable potential for conveying social attitudes along with factual material. The current interest in textbook treatment of gender parallels an earlier concern with the treatment of racial groups.

The Report of the Royal Commission on the Status of Women in Canada (1970) analyzed the gender imagery in a representative selection of Anglophone and Francophone elementary school texts. Versatile characters who had adventures were invariably males. In French-language textbooks, the girls "are preparing to be only mothers and housekeepers, and are portrayed as passive, self-sacrificing and submissive" (p. 175). A series of readers used in Ontario featured a stereotyped family. The kind, understanding father took his children on interesting expeditions, while the mother stayed home to prepare meals and to tell the children "what is best for them." Even the arithmetic books were sex-typed, with children being presented with such problems as: "A girl can type about 48 words per minute. She has to type 2468 words. Can she do this in 45 minutes?" (p. 175).

Over the next decade, a great many studies (e.g., Pyke, 1975) concluded that the illustrations, language, and depiction of roles in texts were providing children with clearly differentiated gender imagery. "Little nurturance or social and emotional complexity are associated with men and boys in these materials, and little strength, skill, or capacity for making decisions with women and girls" (Minuchin and Shapiro, 1983:243). Occupational roles were more salient and varied for men than for women, who tended to be depicted as homemakers or as involved in conventional "female" jobs. Women were seldom shown as both working outside the home and raising families, a serious lag between educational material and reality. This research, combined with political lobbying, produced results. "Under pressure from women's groups, publishers and ministries of education across the country appointed advisory groups on sexism and began to issue new guidelines for non-sexist materials" (Gaskell and McLaren, 1987:8).

Considerable effort has been devoted to improving the quality of teaching materials. Gaskell et al. (1989:56) conclude that while "Canadian materials are not as abundant as American sources... the long drought of materials portraying women's experiences in all facets of life is mercifully coming to an end."

Although most studies of gender socialization in the schools have focussed on elementary-school texts (and rightly so, considering the impressionable nature of beginning students), high school and university texts have not been completely ignored. With regard to university texts, Adam (1986:399) argues, "They constitute the 'front lines' in the transmission of scholarly knowledge and present the 'first face' of a discipline to the uninitiated." For instance, critics have complained that in senior literature and history texts, women are either given tiny roles as mothers, wives, daughters, or lovers, or are totally invisible. "Men's lives, at least in literature and history, *seem* more interesting than women's" (Howe, 1974:127). The treatment of gender in sociology texts has also been a continuing concern (Schneider and Hacker, 1973; Nett, 1979). Adam (1986:406) concluded: "A survey of Canadian sociology textbooks shows weak coverage of lesbian and gay communities in Canada. Despite almost universally 'liberal' rhetoric, a closer reading of the texts reveals profound ambivalence in sociological treatments of homosexuality." Now, many teachers at all levels, and administrators and writers of classroom material are at least aware of such biases. The interested reader is referred to our Chapter 1 discussion of women's studies, as well as to Andersen (1987) and Nemiroff (1989).

Role Models in School

Relatively few men teach other people's children. In 1986, women constituted 72 percent of Canada's elementary school teachers, but only 35 percent of secondary teachers, and 17 percent of university teachers. As Dorothy Smith (1987) argues, "more advanced training for older students has a higher status than education for younger and less advanced students. This status structure has little to do with the skills required or the social importance of the work itself and a great deal to do with control over the standards and substance of education." Indeed, very few women make policy decisions about education (Gaskell and McLaren, 1987:22-23). In no Canadian province does the employment of women as high school principals rise above 12 percent (*The Globe and Mail*, May 5, 1990:A6).

Those in control decide what will be taught and how it will be taught. They also provide children with role models. Children's observations of their school environment teach them about the distribution of power in the adult world. In other words, the experts and authorities whom youngsters encounter at school are living examples of what males and females can be and do in this society.

Kindergarten and elementary school are both places where women rule. As mentioned earlier, many educators emphasized the advantage to girls of having a same-sex teacher, and worried that the "feminized" school atmosphere might turn boys into sissies. In the observational study referred to above, Richer (1979) discovered that pupils' identification with their kindergarten teacher occurred in three stages. During the first stage, the girls (but not the boys) were actively engaged in creating an *affective* bond between themselves and the teacher. The girls sat closer to the teacher and initiated physical contact with her, such s hand-holding, caressing and leg-hugging. This behaviour began on the first day of school. About three weeks later the second stage, teacher *imitation*, began. Once again the behaviour was limited to the girls. The performance went this way: one of the little girls sat on the piano stool (the teacher's territory), book in hand, and pretended to read to an imaginary class of children. Gradually, this drama of the surrogate teacher moved on to the third, or *identification*, stage, as the child adopted the teacher's attitudes and behaviour, and other children formed a real audience. For example, the "teacher" would realistically portray anger over acts of "deviance" detected in her audience. This drama was observed at least 19 times. Richer concludes that through this identification "which occurs because of shared sex", the girls' gender identity is reinforced, and appropriate behaviour and attitudes towards school are learned.

Association with female authority figures undoubtedly helps little girls in the primary grades to feel at home at school. As noted earlier, boys tend to reject female role models and to turn to their peer group. For young

children of both sexes, the few males they encounter at school may be especially important sources of information about male gender roles, because young children have limited opportunities to observe and interact with adult males (Basow, 1986:127). Later on, older children soon learn that women teach the "babies," while men teach the "bigger kids." These observations, as well as distinctions in status between male principals and female teachers, serve to reinforce the traditional gender division of labour in the home and other institutions.

In colleges and universities, instructors serve as role models and mentors for career decisions. "The lack of women role models in professorial and high administrative positions in medical, law, and business schools, as well as in university math and science departments, creates a dearth of live examples whom female students might emulate" (Lipman-Blumen, 1984:149). In addition, male students lack live models to encourage them to move into stereotypically feminine occupational areas. Although changes in higher education are taking place slowly, the unbalanced sex ratios of role models which are available help to perpetuate the gender status quo.

Midwife-Teachers and Banker-Teachers

The style of university-level teaching has come under attack from feminists. In the highly acclaimed book, *Women's Ways of Knowing* (1986), Belenky et al. argue that up until now, higher education has been organized according to the masculine agentic style. Borrowing the metaphor from Freire (1971), they term males who teach according to this style "banker-teachers." By contrast, instructors who employ the communal feminine style are labelled "midwife-teachers." "Midwife-teachers are the opposite of banker-teachers. While the bankers deposit knowledge in the learner's head, the midwives draw it out" (Belenky et al., 1986:217).

Hierarchy, role specialization, and adversarial style of discourse characterize university classrooms presided over by banker-teachers. The masculine pedagogical tradition stresses distance between competent, powerful professors who know, and powerless students who arrive knowing nothing of consequence. The banker-teacher's role is "to 'fill' the students by making deposits of information which the teacher considers to constitute true knowledge" (Freire, 1971:63). The students' task is merely to "store the deposits" in their notebooks (Belenky et al., 1986:214). Finally, the masculine agentic style assumes that conflict and challenge foster learning. Positions are attacked and defended. Ideas must stand up under a barrage of skepticism and doubt.

Midwife-teaching, which Belenky and colleagues say women university students find more congenial, operates on the basis of entirely different assumptions. Here, both teacher and students engage in the process of thinking in a public dialogue. The midwife-teacher is not just another student, however; she has authority based on her greater experience, not on subordination of students. There is no need for the teacher to pretend she knows everything, to present only polished final products to her students. Nor are the students merely empty containers waiting to be filled with the teacher's superior knowledge. Ideally, teachers and students are connected together in a caring relationship as together they seek knowledge. Finally, cooperative construction of knowledge replaces adversarial doubting. According to Belenky et al. (1986:227), women find "the experience of being doubted debilitating rather than energizing." "Because so many women are already consumed with self-doubt, doubts imposed from outside seem at best redundant and at worst destructive, confirming the women's own sense of themselves as inadequate knowers" (p. 228).

Women's Ways of Knowing (Belenky et al., 1986) is not without difficulties (Ostrander, 1988). [3] Nevertheless, their argument that university students of both sexes would thrive under the tutelage of midwife-teachers merits consideration.

Current Assessment of Schools' Role in Gender Socialization

What progress has been made? As indicated above, the criticism of faulty educational mate-rials and attitudes that began in the early 1970s has produced an impressive amount of remedial action (Gaskell et al., 1989). At least some provincial departments of education have tried to discourage gender stereotyping, produce new curricula, and encourage women to apply for positions of responsibility. For example, in response to pressure from the Ontario Ministry of Education, one Ottawa elementary school named a "positive action committee" which, "provided staff with consciousness-raising reading material on gender; showed films on sex-role stereotyping to both staff and students; increased the number of library holdings on the contribution of women to Canadian society; and organized several seminar sessions on pedagogical practice" (Richer, 1988:100). As suggested earlier, this agenda of remedial action is far from complete. However, the majority of educators should now at least be aware of the possibility of sex-typing and gender stereotyping.

Several different lines of research shed light on the comparative significance of school as socialization agent. For example, Richer (1988) compared drawings made by pupils in grades one through six in an Ottawa elementary school before and after a seven-year consciousness-raising program in their school. In 1979, children were asked to draw a picture of themselves engaged in their favourite sport, game, or activity. In 1986, Richer returned to the same school and made the same request of a different cohort of youngsters. Despite the efforts made in the intervening years to sensitize school personnel to gender inequality, the analysis of activity type drawn by children revealed that there was "virtually no cross-over by either sex into the spheres traditionally dominated by the other" (p. 104). In 1986, 97 percent of the boys' drawings and 89 percent of the girls' drawings were still sex-segregated.

The school is one socialization agency among many. Richer (1988) concludes that the school, as a secondary socialization agent, reinforces and elaborates basic ideas acquired by the child from primary sources such as the family. The role of children themselves as a force of conservatism (discussed in Chapter 6) warrants reiteration in this context.

Other social scientists, employing other

TABLE 7.1

UNIVERSITY OF CALGARY FULL-TIME UNDERGRADUATE ENROLMENT BY SEX/GENDER*

FACULTY	FALL 1976		FALL 1989	
	N	**%**	**N**	**%**
EDUCATION				
Male	538	26.6	277	24.3
Female	1483	73.4	864	75.7
ENGINEERING				
Male	846	95.6	1184	88.8
Female	39	4.4	150	11.2
FINE ARTS				
Male	160	42.1	199	37.1
Female	220	57.9	338	62.9
GENERAL STUDIES				
Male	1273	58.0	2721	48.4
Female	920	42.0	2904	51.6
HUMANITIES				
Male	72	47.7	186	34.8
Female	79	52.3	349	65.2
LAW				
Male	40	65.6	91	44.4
Female	21	34.4	114	55.6
MANAGEMENT				
Male	874	76.0	480	59.2
Female	276	24.0	331	40.8
MEDICINE				
Male	254	70.9	346	59.7
Female	104	29.1	234	40.3
NURSING				
Male	—	—	9	2.9
Female	194	100.0	304	97.1
PHYSICAL EDUCATION				
Male	196	54.1	315	56.6
Female	166	45.9	242	43.4
SCIENCE				
Male	631	71.2	771	62.0
Female	255	28.8	472	38.0
SOCIAL SCIENCES				
Male	608	61.4	1184	49.7
Female	383	38.6	1199	50.3
SOCIAL WORK				
Male	78	26.6	62	20.0
Female	215	73.4	248	80.0
TOTAL UNDERGRADUATE**				
Male	5570	56.1	7830	50.0
Female	4355	43.9	7830	50.0

*   These data were compiled by the Office of Institutional Analysis, University of Calgary and are used with their permission.
** Since several Faculty categories of little interest to readers of this book have been omitted, the Faculty totals do not sum to the total undergraduate enrollment.

sorts of data and reasoning, also "speak to the futility of attempting change [in gender inequality] (a) through discourse alone and (b) by using the school as the central change agent" (Richer, 1988:104). Indeed, an American researcher argues that "despite some conspicuous problems, females are probably treated in a more egalitarian way in schools than in other institutions" (Sexton, 1976).

For two decades, optimistic social reformers have looked to the education system to right gender wrongs. Undoubtedly, the best gauge of the school's efficacy is the long-term "payoff" for females. Females and males begin with equal intellectual potential. Similar achievement motivation exists throughout the school years (Maccoby and Jacklin, 1974:164). "Girls fail fewer grades and obtain higher marks than boys" (Gilbert and Gomme, 1987:211). In elementary school, at least, the so-called "feminized" atmosphere makes school a more congenial place for girls. Yet somewhere in the sequence of movements from elementary school into the labour force, the early success of females is reversed, and they lose their initial advantage.

Both sexes are equally likely to complete high school. Since the mid-1960s, women's enrollment in colleges and universities has increased steadily, so they now earn half the undergraduate degrees and outnumber males in community colleges (Buckland, 1985:137). Indeed, the attendance of both sexes has mushroomed, partly as a consequence of attempts by the Canadian government to facilitate equality of educational opportunity to all its citizens by provision of student loan programs and expansion of community colleges and universities. Despite improvement in female enrollment in post-graduate programs, women are earning fewer advanced degrees. In 1984-85 men were awarded 60 percent of all Master's degrees and 75 percent of Ph.D. degrees (Gilbert and Guppy, 1988:164). Women's participation in the better-paying professions, such as law and medicine, has increased. Between 1971 and 1981, female representation in male-dominated professions grew from 11 percent to 19 percent (Marshall, 1987). But despite these significant changes, sociologists point to the continuing

gender-tracking in the fields of study men and women pursue (Gilbert and Guppy, 1988:165). (see Table 7.1). Women still obtain their occupational qualifications in a narrow range of poorly paid occupations. Therefore, the 1985 Royal Commission on Equality in Employment stated that,

Women experience great economic disadvantage in our society: they have lower average incomes; they are employed predominantly in sectors and jobs that are the lowest paid; they do not earn the same amount as their male counterparts in performing the same job or one of similar value. Therefore, women are heavily represented among all low-income groups, the "working (i.e. employed) poor" as well as the low-income group on social assistance (Buckland, 1985:144).

Many feminists have become disillusioned with the "glacially slow" movement of education towards remedying women's status in society (Gaskell and McLaren, 1987:393). Speaking more generally, Schecter (1988:171) argues,

The use of education as a means to overcome inequality has proved to be false on nearly all counts. Despite the association between education, income, and occupation, very little of future economic success is actually explained by school attainment; and very little of what schools do seems to affect the latter.

Therefore, feminist analysis of gender inequality in Canadian education has shifted away from the socialization issues discussed in this chapter to address more structural concerns. Treatment of the structural approach must wait until Chapter 8. However, we emphasize here that one aspect is increasing attention to the fact that people's educational experiences are affected by other characteristics besides their gender, notably social class, race, ethnicity, and education (Gaskell and McLaren, 1987:395). The "handicaps of gender and class co-exist" (Turrittin et al., 1983:416). As Pike (1988:177) points out, despite the expansion of Canadian post-secondary education during the past 25 years, universities remain "disproportionately the preserve of the middle and upper-middle classes."

RELIGION

This section considers the gender socialization role played by the church, our second example of an institution that deliberately sets out to socialize. The church, like the school, is a secondary socialization agent in the sense that its influence is mediated by family and peers, and exposure to it occurs later in the child's life. However, the church has several unique features that amplify its socialization effects. For one thing, religion is a pervasive social institution, active in education, social services, child welfare, the mass media, and political action. For another, the church "carries with it *moral authority* and frequently, threatens sanctions beyond the here-and-now on into eternity" (Richardson, 1981:97, emphases in original). Where the church is powerful, people who challenge its teachings about gender (or other issues) risk censure and ostracism from the community of believers in this life, and eternal damnation in the next.

Our discussion of religious gender socialization will, of necessity, be two-pronged. This dual approach reflects the fact that the church accomplishes gender socialization both directly, through the efforts of human agents in its service, and indirectly, through the permeation of the culture by its ideas. Although not everyone is exposed to direct religious conditioning in childhood, each of us has been influenced by religious traditions in the take-it-for-granted culture. This discussion of the content of religious thought anticipates, to some extent, our discussion of symbolic sources of gender socialization at the end of this chapter.

Some idea of the importance of gender socialization within the religious context may be gained from data on the prevalence of religiosity in this country. According to national surveys carried out by sociologist Reginald Bibby (1987), 89 percent of Canadians maintain ties to established religious groups, 77 percent say they pray, and 66 percent believe in a personal God (p. 82). Only 7 percent acknowledge being agnostics and 4 percent atheists (p. 64). Most people continue to look to the church for ritualistic help when the time comes to marry or to die. Moreover, the churches speak out officially on many matters. Despite this evidence of the importance of religion, Bibby concludes that Canadians "appear to be moving away from Christianity or other religions as meaning systems addressing all of life" (p. 80). Attendance at services has declined drastically. Church life is cited as the source of a "great deal of enjoyment" by only 16 percent of adults, and 8 percent of teenagers (p. 209). According to many social scientists, "the once pervasive and controlling influence of the Christian churches over all aspects of social and political behavior shrunk in the last two centuries to the role of guardian of marriage, family, and the home" (Briggs, 1987:408). Though circumscribed in comparison with past authority, these areas of social life and public policy continue to be the focus of gender analysis.

Two questions concern us in the pages to follow. First, what contribution do religious traditions make to definitions of femininity and masculinity? Second, are the rewards of organizational experience equally available to both sexes? This section will consider religious influences upon gender socialization under these major headings: the content of religious teaching: religious social organization; the feminist critique of the religious institution. Many religious traditions speak to gender. Unfortunately, space limitations require that we confine our observations to the Judeo-Christian tradition, the dominant religious influence in Canadian society.

Gender in Religious Teachings

Since the end of the sixties, the renewed women's movement has had a great deal to say about traditional religion. In particular, feminists have expressed concern about the manner in which Judaism and Christianity interpret and present gender to young people in their teachings. (Briggs, 1987). Ruether (1974:9), for example, claims (perhaps extravagantly) that religion is "undoubtedly the single most important shaper and enforcer of the image and role of women." A traditional perspective on gender relations and the status of women appears to be deeply rooted in Western religious thought. While it is true that our religious heritage does contain material supportive of equality between the sexes, "there can be little doubt that the parables, stories, teachings, and gospels of the Judeo-Christian tradition that our culture has chosen to emphasize are those that perpetuate gender-stereotyping" (Richardson, 1981:100, emphasis in original deleted). These religious traditions developed historically in the context of patriarchal societies. For centuries, women were excluded from leadership roles and eliminated "as shapers of the official theological culture" (Ruether, 1981:53). Therefore, the church has provided divine sanction for the denigration of females and for traditional gender patterns.

Children seem especially vulnerable to religious teaching. One scholar argues that:

In the first place, the doctrines of a religion are usually learned at an early age....Socialization of the young is etched deeply. The messages of religion are carved into vivid scenes by the child's literal interpretations of Heaven and Hell, God and Satan, Good and Evil. The childhood literalness may be finally rejected by the adult, but the feelings and imagery initially associated with those learnings tend to linger. Questioning the moral authority of the church or its spokesperson, therefore, raises the deep-seated childhood images and fears of the transcendental, as well as whatever concerns about the transcendental the adult carries (Richardson, 1981:100).

The impact of early religious training is enhanced by the fact that the child is not confronted by a disembodied set of religious teachings. Religious ideas are typically sponsored by family, relatives, and friends, and hence carry the primary group's "stamp of approval."

A brief survey of Judeo-Christian theology demonstrates why troubled feminists feel that many Sunday school lessons are not fit for little children. The male image of God and the fact that Jesus Christ is his son, not his daughter, buttress male supremacy on earth. In the words of feminist theologian Mary Daly (1975:156), "If God in 'his' heaven is a father ruling 'his' people, then it is in the 'nature' of things and according to divine plan and the order of the universe that society be male-dominated." Critics (e.g., Miller and Swift, 1977:64) are not reassured by the counter-argument that sacred metaphors must not be taken literally, that the symbolization of a masculine godhead does

not mean that God really *is* male. If God is always presented as father, judge, shepherd, king, how can women (never mind children) believe that God is both male and female and yet transcends sex/gender differentiation (Squire, 1980:35)?

The depth of this masculine image of God is shown by research carried out by Diamond for his doctoral dissertation (described in Richardson, 1981:112). Using charades as a research vehicle, Diamond requested his subjects to act out the word "God." He reports that "male characters tend to take on Godlike qualities (such as puffing out their chests, looking stern and pointing a mighty finger down from on high) whereas female characters assume the supplicant role by kneeling before and praying to God." The male actors can imagine themselves as God, but the female actors cannot.

Giving Jesus a human mother does not solve the problem. No matter how revered she is, the Virgin Mary remains human and, as such, subordinate to the masculine Trinity. In addition, she symbolizes women's inferiority. She incubates and brings forth a God, infinitely superior to her, just as other women incubate and bring forth males superior to themselves (Poelzer, 1980:37).

Some attempts have been made to eliminate patriarchal imagery from religious language. Following her call for "the death of god the Father," Daly's acclaimed book, *Gyn/Ecology* (1978), did not use the word "God" at all. However, according to University of Ottawa professor of religion Naomi Goldenberg (1978), a fundamental dilemma is involved. While feminists are right in their conviction that female equality is not possible in religions that maintain an exclusively male image of God, she argues that altering such imagery might spell the end of Judaism and Christianity. More specifically, Goldenberg believes that replacing the masculine image of God with either a feminine image of the divinity or with an "impersonal, shadowy, and abstract principle" would destroy the psychological impact of these religions (as interpreted by Freud and Jung).

The Book of Genesis contains two versions of the story of creation. The fact that the church has downplayed the non-sexist version has provided scriptural justification for the inferiority of women. "And God said, Let us make man in our image, after our likeness: and let them have dominion...over all the earth ...." "so God created man in his *own* image, in the image of God created he him; male and female created he them" (Genesis 1:26-27). This latter version of the creation of humankind emphasizes that male and female were created simultaneously, and that God is either simultaneously male and female, or neither (Walum, 1977:127).

At any rate, it is the creation story quoted below that is usually taught to children. (Some religionists interpret it as simply an elaboration on the one discussed above.)

And the Lord God formed man of dust of the ground, and breathed into his nostrils the breath of life; and man became a living soul....

And the Lord God said, It is not good that the man should be alone; I will make him an help meet for him.

And out of the ground the Lord God formed every beast of the field, and every fowl of the air, and brought them unto Adam to see what he would call them....

And Adam gave names to all cattle, and to the fowl of the air, and to every beast of the field; but for Adam there was not found an help meet for him.

And the Lord God caused a deep sleep to fall upon Adam, and he slept; and he took one of his ribs, and closed up the flesh instead thereof;

And the rib, which the Lord God had taken from man, made he a woman, and brought her unto the man.

And Adam said, This is now bone of my bones, and flesh of my flesh; she shall be called woman, because she was taken out of man. [Genesis 2:7, 18-23]

Tradition depicts Woman as a creature made to assuage Man's loneliness, to serve him. God created her when the animals, created first, failed to be adequate company for Man. Some churches have used the sequencing of creation—the "fact" that Eve was made *after* Adam—to justify women's subordination. (A feminist commentator replied dryly, "If it's a matter of orderly progression then man ought to be subject to monkeys!" [Wallace, 1976:118].) The trajectory of her career thus established, Eve went on to become the "first sinner" and responsible for the couple's eviction from the Garden of Eden.

Ancient Judaic tradition includes stories of Lilith, Adam's first wife. Although her name does not now appear in Genesis, some scholars (Rivlin, 1972; Weiner, 1979) believe that the first creation story refers to Lilith. Mythology has it that when Lilith demanded equality with Adam (and objected to lying beneath him during intercourse), she left Eden rather than accept second place. She became a vampire-like demon, a whore and a killer of children. The moral of Lilith's story: banishment from paradise was the price of asking for equality.

Attitudes towards women expressed in the Old Testament are not totally consistent, for it was written over a period of many centuries. The Book of Proverbs depicts women as sources of great wisdom. However, "the overall effect is clearly that women have a subordinate position" (Roberts, 1984:351). Historically, the Christian tradition represents a synthesis of Hebrew and Greek world views; male supremacy is celebrated and women are denigrated. Portions of the scriptures were written exclusively for men (Roberts, 1984:350). For example, the Ten Commandments teach that "Thou shall not covet thy neighbor's *wife*." During the exodus, the Israelis made a pact with God, which required *circumcision* (Walum, 1977:130). "...I thank thee, Lord, that thou has not created me a woman" (Orthodox Jewish prayer). When women are addressed, the message often serves to remind them of their inferiority (Roberts, 1984:351). For example, the bodily processes of women (but not men) are associated with contamination. "If a woman have conceived seed, and born a man child, then she shall be unclean seven days; ... But if she bear a maid child, then she shall be unclean two weeks..." (Leviticus 12:2, 5).

The New Testament gospels present a considerably more positive view of women (Ruether, 1975). Even though Jesus was the son of God and his apostles were all male, feminists acknowledge that his attitudes toward women were unusually egalitarian for his time and culture. Jesus "violated Judaic law by touching menstruating women, by speaking alone with a woman not his wife, by allowing women to witness and to testify to his resurrection" (Walum, 1977:129). He reminded men, eager to stone an adulterous woman, of their own shortcomings. Jesus and his disciples were "men of emotion—they cry, fear, and agonize; they are able to be weak... and to demonstrate compassion... and humility" (Walum, 1977:129).

Nevertheless, despite the living example of Jesus, "Christian ideology has contributed no little to the oppression of woman.... Through St. Paul the Jewish tradition, savagely antifeminist, was affirmed" (de Beauvoir, 1952:89-90):

Wives, submit yourselves unto your own husbands, as unto the Lord. For the husband is head of the wife, even as Christ is the head of the church...[The Epistle of Paul to the Ephesians 5:22-23]

As feminist theologians have pointed out, the Christian tradition emphasizes two major images of women, both of which are "symbolic representations of male ideas about sex": "the sexual purity of the virgin, the sexual procreativity of the mother"—Mary—and the "sexual evilness of the temptress"—Eve (Hole and Levine, 1971:380-81). Neither the "virgin mother" nor the "sinner" has any resonance in the experience of contemporary women. Equally important, holding Eve responsible for the eviction from the Garden of Eden, for original sin, has provided religious justification for misogyny (Roberts, 1984:354).

While it is true that the symbolism and mythology of the Bible are rooted in a patriarchal time, modern translations and sermonizing have emphasized male-centred religious imagery and minimized egalitarian aspects of biblical teachings. The central point is that the Judeo-Christian tradition has fostered the doctrine of feminine inferiority and reinforced traditional roles.

The Social Structure of Religion

The content of religious teaching about gender, discussed above, reflects the historic exclusion of women from religious leadership in Christi-

anity and Judaism. (Ruether, 1981). Most of the major prophets and shapers of official theology have been men. With a few exceptions, men have been the authority figures—deacons, priests, clergymen, bishops, cardinals, popes. Men's ideas "of what a properly religious woman should do and be" (McGuire, 1987:98) have prevailed. Ceremonial ties with the deities were maintained by men. When women were permitted a role beyond that of member of the congregation, it was usually a service role. For example, in the Roman Catholic church, the nuns teach and nurse, while the priests celebrate Mass, perform marriage ceremonies, and ordain other priests. Women's place in Conservative and Orthodox Judaism was to run a pious home. "Ever subordinate to men, whose highest calling was to study Torah, women have been honored as those who care for domestic practicalities..." (Carmody, 1979:276). Women's religious functions were limited to such matters as baking the ritual bread and lighting the Sabbath candles.

How has the exclusion of women from church leadership positions been justified? As we might expect, scriptures and tradition offer authority for confining women to passive, secondary roles (Ruether, 1981). For example, the New Testament reads: "But I suffer not a woman to teach, nor to usurp authority over the man, but to be in silence (1 Timothy 2:12). The comparable statement in Rabbinic Judaism reads, "Cursed be the man who teaches his daughter Torah." In forbidding the ordination of women as priests, Catholicism has cited Thomas Aquinas's definition of woman as a "misbegotten male," lacking full moral self-control and capacity for rational activity. "If one were to ordain a woman it, quite literally, would not 'take,' any more than if one were to ordain a monkey or an ox" (Ruether, 1981:54). Women's exclusion has also been justified as an expression of woman's greater proclivity for sin (woman are "second in creation but first in sin" [1 Timothy 2, 13-14]). The Christian churches have argued that Christ intended leadership to be male, and that "the ministerial representation of Christ requires physical masculinity" because Christ himself was male (Walum, 1977:132).

In taking official positions on controversial matters such as the ordination of women or homosexuals, churches must also be cognizant of their survival as organizations. To remain viable, religious organizations must maintain a sizeable membership base capable of providing financial and other types of resources. Recent history shows that adopting an innovative stance on gender issues risks a potentially divisive response. For example, the ordination of women has been described as "a subject which has been more divisive than any controversy the Anglican Church has faced this century." According to some church leaders, the proposal to ordain women in the British Church of England "could lead to a permanent split among 70 million Anglicans in 164 countries" (Baum, 1988). Similarly, the 1988 decision by the national General Council of the United Church of Canada to open the door to ordination of practising lesbian and gay persons has divided the country's largest Protestant church (Riordon, 1990). A number of individual congregations registered their protest by withholding financial support to the church's head office. As a result, the church fell $3 million short of its objective for 1988 (*The Globe and Mail*, February 3, 1989:A11). On the other hand, the issue of organizational survival occasionally motivates churches to make gender-inclusive decisions. Churches already in serious trouble, with declining enrollment and dwindling financial resources, sometimes have little to lose in accepting female priests (Roberts, 1984:363). Witness this headline: "Anglican bishops pointed to a desperate shortage of ministers in Africa as a strong reason for accepting women priests" (*Calgary Herald*, August 6, 1988:H8).

Some segments of organized religion are now receptive to women's interests. Lois Wilson became in 1980 the first female moderator of the United Church of Canada. Many of the large Protestant denominations now ordain women. This decision was taken by the United Church in 1936, the Presbyterian Church in 1965, and the Anglican Church in 1976. The Lutherans and some Baptist conventions also ordain women (Orwen, 1983). However, as McGuire (1987:101) points out, "Acceptance of changes in religious roles for women fre-

quently hinges upon whether a group accepts religious traditions as literal truths and divinely ordained." Thus, fundamentalist Protestantism, Roman Catholicism, Orthodox Judaism, Eastern Orthodoxy, and orthodox Islam generally oppose changing women's traditional roles. As recently as October 1988, Pope John Paul II ruled out the priesthood for women in an apostolic letter which concluded that women, though equal to men, are formed by maternal qualities.

So far, the number of women clergy is small. Often, female clergy remain underpaid, underemployed, marginal professionals and are deflected from ministerial roles into teaching (McGuire, 1987:102). A female United Church minister said, "There wasn't anything I could put my finger on.... It was just clear that I was some kind of an assistant rather than a full minister. I wasn't given any responsibility" (Orwen, 1983).

Assessment of Church's Role in Gender Socialization

Religious socialization augments and reinforces the influence of other gender socialization agencies. The socialization effects of the church are both direct (as an organizational agent) and indirect (as a contributor to Canadian culture). This dichotomy oversimplifies because it ignores the interaction between organization and culture. It is useful, nevertheless, to consider separately the gender implications of church organization and church teaching.

Few generalizations that embrace women's status in Protestant, Roman Catholic, and Jewish church organization can be made. It seems fair to say that today all branches find it necessary to deal, in some way, with the "women question." The accommodation made by some (Orthodox Judaism, ultra-conservative Protestantism) is minuscule. Others (e.g., Roman Catholicism), while continuing to exclude women from decision-making and clergy, struggle with feminist pressure within their ranks. In mainline Protestant churches, women are taking clerical and decision-making roles. Where women's position in religion remains marginal, there are serious consequences, direct and indirect, for religious socialization. Few children encounter female clergy. Most youngsters who go to church or see preachers on television experience only males making ceremonial contact with the deity. Once again, they learn that important social roles are the prerogative of males. Experiencing the separation of females from males in traditional Jewish (and Muslim) religious practice provides children with more evidence of the bifurcation of gender.

We come now to the impact upon religious teachings of reserving secondary roles for women (relegating them to the pews in the back of the church, while men preside over the altars and legislative chambers). These socialization consequences, while more roundabout than the role-modelling effects discussed above, are yet more insidious. We say this because religious teachings move outside church boundaries into the general culture. So long as women remain outside the churches' inner circle, the feminine intellectual perspective is missing (Ambert, 1976:107). This means that male-constructed religious doctrine goes unchallenged. It also means that churches ignore women's point of view on matters of concern to them. To illustrate, from 1918, (when Canadian women were given the right to vote federally, until it lost the battle in 1940, the Roman Catholic church fought to keep Quebec women from gaining the right to vote. [4] Today, the Vatican still staunchly opposes birth control and abortion. A succinct statement of traditional church teachings is that the "resounding message of the Bible—Old and New Testaments alike—is the necessity of an unquestioning patriarchal order between the sexes" (Lipman-Blumen, 1984:74).

The feminist movement has sought to enlarge women's participation in many (but of course, not all) religious traditions. Women demand a place in divinity schools, in pulpits, in bishoprics. These organizational ambitions are accompanied by re-examination of religious traditions. "Can Torah, [the] New Testament or the Koran be read in such a way that they become sources and symbols for women's power and full participation in the religious life of their communities?" (O'Connor, 1989:102). Both the attempt to enlarge women's participa-

tion in the churches and to reconceive women in the religious traditions carry important implications for gender socialization.

THE MASS MEDIA

The mass media, impersonal communication sources that reach vast audiences, are immensely important symbolic socialization agents in Canadian society. Because the media keep people in touch with what is happening in the world, and coordinate other societal institutions, they have been described as the "cement of modern social life" (Tuchman, 1978). In part, this cementing functioning takes place as the media constitute individuals into a *community of discourse*. To quote Tuchman (1979:540), "a community of discourse is comparable to a language: it integrates and controls; it provides common elements for strangers to use when they meet and creates strictures for what can be noticed or said." Canadians of various ages, social classes, regions, and political predilections are able to identify and discuss Pierre Berton, Madonna, Ann Landers, and Dagwood Bumstead. Weekday evenings at 10:00 p.m., millions tune into the CBC "National" newscast. When talk show host Oprah Winfrey shed 70 pounds, nearly everyone had something to say about it (and 200 000 viewers telephoned to inquire about her crash-diet regimen) (*Time*, November 28, 1988:55). Children's participation in this community of discourse is a vital aspect of peer socialization. Being television-wise brings them prestige on the playground (Ellis, 1983). Children discuss what they have seen on TV and enact the roles of television characters in their fantasy play (Fouts, 1980). Boys watch World Cup soccer on TV and practise fancy kicking on suburban streets. Adolescents relate to one another through rock music tapes and videos.

Women's groups have long been cognizant of the power of the media in shaping attitudes. Although exceptions certainly exist within and among media, mass communication sources convey traditional, often sexist, messages about gender relations. (The media exaggerate the dividing line between females and males. Their caricatured portraits rely on gender stereotypes.) Women (and to some extent, men)

sex objects

are objectified as sexual beings. Females' devaluated status is perpetuated.

Two main factors lie behind these charges. First, despite some improvement over the past two decades, relatively few women hold positions of authority in media industries. Indeed, feminist critics have accused both Canadian and American media of "widespread discrimination against women in broadcast industry employment practices" (Cantor, 1988:76). See the Canadian Task Force on Sex-role Stereotyping in the Broadcast Media (CRTC, 1982:5). Moreover, it is hard for those few women who are employed in the media to resist ideas and attitudes that disparage women. As we have noted before, successful female professionals are usually those who satisfy the criteria of male gatekeepers (Smith, 1975:367).

Take the press. Only six percent of publishers in Canada are women. Nine percent of editors-in-chief and six percent of managing editors are women (Smith, 1990:D8). Yet more than half the students in Canadian journalism classes are now women:

They are joining the ranks of senior reporters, bureau chiefs, columnists, editorial writers and top newsroom managers across the country. Their influence is felt… in redefining what is news. However, change has come hard in a traditionally male-dominated workplace. Women have had to do all the pushing so far and the pace of change has been glacial (V. Smith, 1990:D8).

Second, the media are sexist because they mirror cultural notions about gender—they take and accentuate societal images of gender and sexuality—and, in turn, shape and strengthen these views. To be acceptable, media content must contain dominant social beliefs and images. Bogart (1988) says of television advertising: "Commercial producers appear to be self-consciously peopling their world with characters to whom anyone in the audience might relate without any jarring sense of social incongruity." Then, as learning theory hypothesizes (Chapter 4), the presence of sexist images in the media (and the relative absence of egalitarian gender images) encourages role-modelling (Andersen, 1988:30). These general points will receive amplification in the pages to follow.

As early as 1951, women registered official complaints about the portrayal of women in the media.[5] In 1970, the Royal Commission on the Status of Women in Canada accused the media of perpetuating stereotypes of *both* sexes. The Commission was especially critical of the "degrading, moronic" depiction of women in advertisements. It argued that while men, too, are stereotyped, "the results may be more damaging for women since advertising encourages feminine dependency by urging women not to act but to be passive, not to really achieve but to live out their aspirations in the imagination and in dreams."

More than a decade later, the Task Force on Sex-role Stereotyping in the Broadcast Media of the Canadian Radio-television and Telecommunications Commission (CRTC, 1982) had this to say in its report, *Images of Women*: "Stereotyped images of women and girls are reinforced and perpetuated, and to some extent even seemingly legitimized, by the mass dissemination of these images in broadcasting. Such images constitute a limiting or narrowing of women's, men's, and children's perceptions of themselves and their roles in society" (CRCT, 1982:3). In short, the "media do not portray women and men as equal, and equally capable human beings" (p. 4).

The CRTC recommended that the broadcasting and advertising industries address the issues raised in the above report through industry self-regulation for a trial period of two years, 1982 to 1984. During this time, the CRTC undertook to monitor the content of TV and radio, to assess the effectiveness of self-regulation in reducing gender stereotyping in broadcasting. MediaWatch, a national voluntary women's organization formed in response to the Task Force set out to educate Canadians on issues of gender stereotyping in broadcasting. Their goal included suggesting how the public could register criticisms with broadcasting and advertising industries. To facilitate this communication, MediaWatch established a complaint system so the public could voice its concern (Davison-Leong, 1990:128).

In 1986, CRTC public hearings were held.

All of the industry members who presented at public hearings thought that the period of self-regulation had been successful for there was now an awareness of sex-role stereotyping. In contrast, the public which was composed of citizen's groups, individuals, and MediaWatch felt that industry self-regulation had not succeeded in reducing sex-role stereotyping. In the CRTC's opinion self-regulation had only been partially successful and further action was considered necessary (Davison-Leong, 1990:5).

This new policy imposes a condition of licence on all broadcasters. (See CRTC, 1986). To date, there have been no suspensions of broadcasters' licences. As Davison-Leong (1990:219) observes, "it would be naive to conclude that since the CRTC's policy statement on sex-role stereotyping adopted a condition of license for the broadcasting industry that this issue has been resolved."

By the 1990s, the media (which include more than the broadcasting media discussed above) have become well aware of feminist concerns and, on occasion, responsive to feminist criticism. A brief discussion of individual media as gender socialization agents follows. As we shall see, the more a communication source must appeal to the masses, the more traditional the gender imagery tends to be. *Mass* media represent conservative interests. Large audiences are needed to make profits. These mass audiences respond to contemporary, but familiar images. Therefore, "content cannot 'move ahead of' public opinion" (Wilson, 1981:242). There is cause for feminist critics to remain troubled about the impressions of masculinity and femininity conveyed by these powerful, ubiqitous symbolic socialization agencies.

Television

Child development experts have been especially concerned about the socialization effects of television, which occupies Canadian youngsters an average of 21 hours per week (Singer, 1986). Television has been called the "plug-in drug" (Winn, 1977), the Phantom Babysitter, and the Great Leveller, "mowing down all the bright young minds to the same stunted level" (Landsberg, 1982). Many children are zombie viewers, who watch anything and everything, "silent, immobile, mesmerized" (Goldsen, 1979). TV has also been labelled the Total Dis-

closure Medium because information and imagery intended for adults are readily accessible to children. Youngsters tune in to "incest, promiscuity, homosexuality, sadomasochism, terminal illness, and other secrets of adult life" (Postman, 1982).

The gender-relevant content of television has undergone many changes since the Royal Commission on the Status of Women (1970) brought the matter to Canadians' attention. These changes can be attributed to the major demographic, economic, and political shifts that occurred over the past decade(s), as well as the pressure of women's organizations (Cantor, 1988:80). All kinds of females now show up on the television screen: expert women (Barbara Frum, Dr. Ruth), funny women (Carol Burnett), angry women (Cagney and Lacey), traditional women (Marge Simpson, Tammy Baker), strong women (Jane Fonda), vacuous women (Vanna White). Women newscasters, business commentators, talk show hosts, and disc jockeys are present in significant, if not representative, numbers.

Continuing with the theme of TV innovation, we note that this medium (along with others) has publicized some new gender notions over the past two decades. Certain segments of the public have followed debate about the evolving roles of men and women in educational programming on the CBC and public broadcasting channels, e.g., TV Ontario, ACCESS Alberta. Perhaps more consequential have been the challenges to tradition conveyed by situation comedies that attract large audiences. Here is a conversation from *All In the Family*, a comedy hit of the 1970s (CBS Television Network, 1988:115):

Edith Bunker: Do you think that the work I do here in the house, the cookin' and the washin' and the cleanin' and the shoppin', is worth a dollar a week?
Archie: About.
Edith: Well I figured it all out, see. A dollar a week for 52 weeks, cause there's 52 weeks in a year, comes to $52 a year.
Archie: Well, that's close, yeah.
Edith: And we've been married 30 years, right? That's ten three's. And ten 52s is $520, and three $520s comes to $1560, which you owe me.
Archie: Hold, hold, hold, hold it!
Edith: Let's make a deal. If you pay me right now

$500, I'll let you keep the $1060 that's left.

Archie: What do you mean keep? When the hell did I ever have it?

Edith: When you didn't pay it to me.

Archie: But I don't see it nowheres. What did I do with it?

Edith: Well, how should I know? See? You don't have to tell *me* every time you spend your money. Why should I tell you?

As mentioned in the introduction to this section, the media reflect their societal context. Over time, sitcom messages contradicting long-standing gender assumptions have grown stronger. Roles are reversed in *Who's The Boss?* Mrs. Huxtable on *The Cosby Show* is a lawyer; Mrs. Keaton on *Family Ties* is an architect. *Baby Boom* satirizes "motherhood in the fast lane" by portraying a "yuppie trying to juggle a baby and a high-pressure corporate job" (*Time*, October 17, 1988:67). The four "Golden Girls" challenge the notion that only young women belong on television. In the TV world of strikingly beautiful women, 211-pound Roseanne breaks the sitcom rule of dedicated, selfless motherhood. Says Roseanne: "I figure when my husband comes home at night, if the kids are still alive, then I've done my job" (Collins, 1989:34).

Despite these very changes, systematic analysis of television content shows the traditional patterns to be there still. First of all, there continues to be substantial underrepresentation of women in TV entertainment. Older women and minority group women are special victims of this "symbolic annihilation" (Tuchman, 1978). Over the past three decades, in both adult prime-time programming and children's Saturday morning cartooning, males outnumber females by a ratio of about 3:1 (Greenberg, 1988). (One might ask why *Sesame Street* characters Big Bird, Cookie Monster, and Grover have to be identified as male.) This sex ratio varies by type of programming, from the high of 6:1 in action-adventure shows, to equivalent 1:1 in afternoon soap operas. With regard to broadcasting journalism, women are a fashion-conscious part of male-female news teams, reading "soft" news and local news. The authoritative voices conveying national and international news (the Lloyd Robertsons and Peter Mansbridges) are still mostly male. In summary, counting fewer women conveys the message that they count less (Greenberg, 1988:89).

Second, there is substantial evidence that women's TV roles continue to be more constrained by traditional gender norms than men's (Greenberg, 1988). Take the highly competitive world of local newscasting. Although appearance on the air is important to both men and women who appear in front of the camera, Calgary CBC anchor Kathy Daley, who spends $2000 a year on clothes, says, "For women, it's brutal. If you just consider what professional women have to go through compared with men in any job, it's amplified in television because everybody sees it" *Calgary Herald*, October 22, 1989:B5).

As another example of traditional constraints impinging more on females, sitcom women are still more likely to focus on domestic matters. Even women who hold professional jobs give priority to home and family. (Though both Cosby show parents have an amazing amount of time to spend at home, we do see Dr. Huxtable involved in medical matters much more often than Mrs. Huxtable in her law office.) Despite departures from stereotypical depiction, the men are apt to be autonomous and aggressive, the women nurturant, emotional, dominated by others, and defined by their relationship to males (Durkin, 1986). Women appear less in control of events in their lives (Greenberg, 1988). Middle-aged and older men are commonplace, but women are still typically young and attractive. Moreover, the few older women who do turn up (Joan Collins, the "Golden Girls") are expensively groomed and attractive, not grandmotherly figures.

Finally, television remains obsessed with sexuality and violence. In a plug for *Dear John* and *Night Court*, "the stars of the two television shows were sharing their thoughts of women: 'Chicks' said one. 'Babes,' offered the other. 'Foxes. Skirts. Sweet Cheeks. Bimbos. Lustbuckets,' they exchanged" (*Calgary Herald*, June 2, 1990:C10). A high proportion of the victims of violence on television are female. An estimated 90 percent of the victims of sadistic TV violence are female, usually young, achieving, independent, sexual women. "What are we being told here?" asks Gloria Steinem (1988:15).

Media Advertising

National consumer product advertising has become one of "the great vehicles of social communication" (Leiss et al., 1986:3). "A powerful force affecting all groups in society, advertising is of special significance for children, since their values, identity, and behavior patterns are just developing" (Singer, 1986:78). As noted earlier, advertising's one-dimensional presentation of the sexes has provoked two decades of vigorous protest from feminists. Women have been depicted as sex objects preoccupied with their fingernails and hair, as housewives weeping over waxy build-up on their floors, as mothers ecstatic to find a cereal their family likes. Women are shown as immature, emotional, seductive, and lacking in intellectual authority. The vast majority of female models are young. That middle-aged women are unattractive and undesirable is assumed by beauty care product ads that feature middle-aged models only because they do *not* look their age. (The campaign for Oil of Olay lotion proclaims: "I don't intend to grow old gracefully. I intend to fight it every step of the way.") By contrast, middle-aged men posed with young women are commonplace (Umiker-Sebeok (1981). Although the numbers of visible minority group members have been growing, "visible minority women remain close to invisible" in advertising run in *Maclean's*, "one of Canada's most important and widely circulated magazines" (MacGregor, 1989:139).

Advertising glorifies consumer culture; both sexes are shown satisfying their needs and desires "by buying mass produced, standardized, nationally advertised consumer products" (Schudson, 1984:147). Given this premise, the males and females inhabiting the make-believe worlds of advertising still have distinctive roles to play. The competent, knowledgeable people with public lives which transcend choices about bathroom bowl cleaners and products to prevent underarm "wetness" have been males. For example, a content analysis of Canadian television ads reported that men were shown in the home 27 percent of the time (versus 52 percent of the time for women), that 94 percent of the voice-overs were male, that women's competence tended to be confined to

personal-care products (versus "big-ticket" items) (Haspiel, 1981). While it is true that the male image is the more flattering, both sexes are nonetheless being stereotyped. Masculinity means being knowledgeable, in control, active, aggressive in the fantasies created by advertising agencies. The macho cowboy with the cigarette hanging out of his grim face in the Marlboro ads is tough and unemotional ("Real males don't smile" [Posner, 1987:182]).

Gender is "the social resource that is used most by advertisers" (Jhally, 1987:135). One obvious reason: advertising containing gender imagery pays off. Gender, "one of our deepest and most important traits as human beings... reaches into our very core of our definition as human beings" (Jhally, 1987:136). Given the nature of our society, it is important for people of all ages to understand themselves as either male or female. Therefore, viewers attend to ads linking products with gender and sexuality. We agree that sex/gender is fascinating. But why does advertising deal in stereotypes, in simplistic, narrow depiction of the sexes? Advertising caricatures the sexes more than either the programming on television (Greenberg, 1988) or than features in magazines. Why is this so? The reason is the need of advertisements to communicate telegraphically—to get their story across in very little time or space (Singer, 1986:114). To manage this, advertising draws upon the taken-for-granted nature of gender: "Advertising...surrounds us and enters into us, so that when we speak we may speak in or with reference to the language of advertising and when we see we may see through schemata that advertising has made salient for us" (Schudson, 1984:210). In other words, advertising contributes to the "community of discourse." Children at play chant slogans and jingles. University classes happily accept invitations to talk about ads they have enjoyed (Wendy's "Where's the beef?"; Alka Selzer's "I can't believe I ate the whole thing"); and those they've hated ("Sucrets' 'Barbara, Barbara... you up?'; the ring-around-the-collar commercial that holds wives responsible for husbands' unwashed necks).

In *Gender Advertisements* (1979), Erving Goffman assembled print ads according to "themes of genderism" in order to demonstrate how gender is constructed. Series of pictures are grouped to concentrate on how gender is depicted through minute physical expression and postures. These ritual displays of gender take advantage of, and then accentuate, cultural norms about how women and men are supposed to look, act, and relate to each other (Leiss et al., 1986:166).

Here are some of Goffman's conclusions about advertising's hyper-ritualization of gender (Goffman, 1979:84). Goffman's fundamental point is that men equate females with children and consider both subordinate to themselves. In advertising, a woman is taller than a man only when the man is her social inferior. When a photograph of men and women illustrates instruction of some sort, the man is always instructing the woman (and male children instruct female children). When an ad requires someone to sit or lie on the floor, that someone is hardly ever a man. Goffman (1979:41) tells us that "floors are associated with the less clean, the less pure, less exalted parts of the room," and that "lying on the floor... seems also to be a conventionalized expression of sexual availability." There is repeated usage in advertisements of "women posed as children, acting like children, looking like children: utterly devoid of the natural sobriety which one associates with adult mien" (Gornick, 1976:viii). Women often have their fingers in their mouths. They stare vacantly into space. They show dependency by snuggling and leaning against men for protection. By contrast, men are depicted as grownups, alert, erect, fully clothed, in control. In short, ads use subtle non-verbal communication to sell traditional "genderism."

While advertising is fundamentally conservative, tied to the prevailing ideology of the culture, its content shifts somewhat with changing social currents (Umiker-Sebeok, 1981). Several recent trends may be identified. One prominent feature has been the increasingly sexually explicit content of ads (Jhally, 1987:135 ff.; Soley and Kurzbard, 1986). Televized sporting events run huge numbers of beer ads "that stick women in stereotyped roles of shapely objects to be enjoyed with a cold one" (Strauss, 1990). As Posner (1987) emphasizes, men as well as women are being sexually exploited in contemporary ads. For example, raunchy ad campaigns for Calvin Klein and Guess designer jeans, and for Obsession perfume feature nude people ready for mysterious erotic activities. Beer ads teach that women exist to gratify male sex urges. A 1990 television ad for Molson Canadian beer showed "the rare long-haired fox" being hunted by a moose, loon, and wolf. The camera pans up the shapely, bikinied body of the woman referred to as the fox. The animals chasing her, men of various shapes and sizes, include an overweight "moose." Magazine ads for More cigarettes suggest an analogy between this brand of cigarette and penises. The woman yanking the man by his tie and holding her cigarette at a suggestive angle ask rhetorically, "Why such a long cigarette? I like to stretch things out."

The woman's aggressiveness in this More ad suggests a second recent trend: the impact of feminism and changes in women's status upon advertising. One manifestation of this influence is current ads that make men look just as silly as they have usually shown women.

A commercial for Drano shows a young hunk bathing alone at dusk to the tune of "Splish Splash." His energetic rub-a-dubbing is stopped by a clog, but he hops out, pours in the Drano, and is so happy to be having germ-free fun on a Saturday night that he kisses a bathroom pipe (Lippert, 1988:414).

However, other ads convey more genuinely enlightened messages about gender relations. Advertisements featuring men with babies are a noteworthy example. A magazine ad for Omega watches shows a man seated at a piano, hugging a toddler against his body as he picks out a one-handed tune. The slices of life in a series of liquor ads show female friends exchanging confidences: "He's crazy about my kid. *And* he drinks Johnnie Walker." "He thinks it's fine for me to make more than he does. *And* he drinks Johnnie Walker." Naturally, ads such as these are attempts to appeal to women who now have disposable income and social status of their own. Whatever the motive, new images of masculinity and femininity are being communicated. The Metropolitan Life campaign makes enlightened use of the female *Peanuts* characters to show females as responsible, competent beings. AT&T ads promoting long-distance telephone calls employ people very different from the strikingly beautiful, youthful models of predominantly northern European origins who people most ads (Bogart, 1988). A handsome silver-haired couple eye one another fondly. The caption reads: "Flirt with her again. Call the U.K. She was your childhood sweetheart. The girl you always planned to marry. And even though so much has happened since you left London, since you left her side, you still carry a torch for her. Why not give her a call and tell her?" A content analysis of women's role portrayals in magazine advertising between 1958 and 1983 (Sullivan and O'Connor, 1988) concluded that current ads more accurately reflect the true diversity of women's social and occupational roles than do those of earlier generations.

Despite the genuine change described above, in many, perhaps most ads the "underlying ideological foundation remains untouched" (Umiker-Sebeok, 1981:210). The Virginia Slims slogan, "You've come a long way, baby" twists feminist ideas to sell explicitly the harmful habit of tobacco smoking (and, implicitly, the equally dangerous notion that women cannot be too thin). Superwoman ads portray a woman as a physician or an executive. However, her facial expression, hair, makeup, posture define her as out of place, merely playing at being a professional. Offices frequently contain organdy curtains, mirrors, and houseplants, which make the workplace look much like a suburban home (Umiker-Sebeok, 1981). During the 1988 Christmas season, the *New Yorker* ran this jewelry ad: "When the score is love, suggest he serve diamonds. Ask him to look at these elegant, shimmering diamond tennis bracelets starting at around $3000. He's always offering to help improve your backhand. Take him up on it."

It seems that the more people see an ad, the more gender traditional its content is likely to be. High-circulation magazines (*Playboy*, *Penthouse* for men, *Good Housekeeping*, *Family Circle* for women) specialize in ads portraying macho males and gorgeous females (Farrell, 1986). Guidelines and recommendations for non-sexist advertising proliferate, while enforcement seems nobody's responsibility.

Magazines

If you were designing a comparative study of media presentation of gender, would you expect magazines to be more or less "liberated" than television? There is a basic difference between these media that supports the latter prediction. Commercial television is a monolith, whose messages must appeal to the lowest common denominator. Also, the cost of television time encourages conservatism among advertisers and producers. In contrast, notice the variety of magazines available on the newsstand! A *New Yorker* cartoon depicts a bewildered gentleman standing in front of a newsstand displaying these magazines: *People, Ordinary People, Talented People, Healthy People, Old People, Night People, City People, Cat People, Left-Handed People, Alienated People, Rich People.* Though the cartoon exaggerates, magazines are designed to appeal to particular segments of the population. Advertising congruent with reader characteristics is solicited. This advertising, and not the price paid by individual purchasers of the magazine, underwrites the costs of publication. While high-circulation magazines cannot afford to be whimsical about changing their formats, magazines must nevertheless keep pace with readers' changing interests. "To sell, magazines must reflect the dominant contemporary ethos" (Geise, 1979:52).

Newsstand browsers will have observed changes in the magazines offered for sale. Consider women's magazines (the type on which researchers have focussed). *Seventeen* appeals to teenagers, *Chatelaine, McCall's, Ladies' Home Journal,* and *Good Housekeeping* to middle-class homemakers; and *Family Circle, Woman's Day,* and perhaps, *National Enquirer* to working-class women. Until recently, publishers and advertisers viewed women as a much more homogeneous, easy-to-reach mass market than men. Magazines for men covered a gamut of interests: *Sports Illustrated, Popular Mechanics, Fortune, Car and Driver, Esquire,* and *Playboy* (Phillips, 1978:117). Women were homemakers (and homemakers-to-be), period. This statement by a former *Life* magazine editor carries implications for both sexes: "The most financially successful magazines of the past ten years have been designed to appeal to highly particularized intellectual, vocational, and avocational interests and are run by editors who know precisely what they are saying and to whom they are saying it" (Phillips, 1978:117). The existence of "men's" magazines displayed together in one place on store racks and "women's" magazines in another continues to reinforce the social reality of gender. The fact that computer, consumer education, and news magazines are usually grouped with *Esquire* and *Gentleman's Quarterly* does not prevent women from buying them.

Moreover, the fact that women's magazines no longer target an exclusive audience of home-makers (or would-be homemakers) now communicates the message that there are different kinds of women as well as different kinds of men. In 1965, Helen Gurley Brown created *Cosmopolitan*, a women's magazine that would go beyond homemaking hints and beauty advice to help contemporary women "get through the night" (in the words of its editor). Since then, *Ms., Playgirl, Self, New Woman, Shape, Working Woman,* and *Working Mother* have appeared to address and to capitalize on the changing roles of women. *Ms.,* the most political of the magazines, was founded in 1972 by Gloria Steinem and friends, and chronicled issues related to the women's movement. *New Woman* preaches that any determined woman can become an economically successful "gray-suited upwardly mobile corporate woman" (and, according to critic Ehrenreich [quoted in Tuchman, 1979:537], thereby undermines feminist criticism of the status quo). *Shape* caters to women's interest in the body beautiful. Then there are magazines connected more specifically with the "fashion-food-home mold" of women's interests (Phillips, 1978:117), e.g., *Glamour, Vogue, Gourmet.*

Magazine research (considerably less extensive than television research) has concentrated on variations upon one central theme: the portrayal of the female role in magazines with high female readership such as *Redbook* and *Ladies' Home Journal*. The assumption is made that magazines transmit cultural prescriptions of female role performance and, at least by implication, of male role performance (Ferguson,

1978:98). Content analyses of non-fiction in high-circulation women's magazines conclude that today's magazines are not so much rejecting traditional gender patterns as giving flexible consideration to non-traditional alternatives (Geise, 1979). Women's magazines are now interested in women's work, government policy affecting women's issues, and so on. However, they continue to devote disproportionate content to children, health, home, food, and beauty (Robinson, 1983). Moreover, magazine fiction, though changing over the years to acknowledge women's outside work and more liberated sexuality, tends to be more gender traditional than non-fiction. In stories run in women's magazines (as well as Harlequin-type romance novels and soap operas):

Women are usually depicted as subordinate to men and passive-dependent, but even when presented as relatively independent the basic message is that sexual relationships are central and all-important in women's lives—more important than family, children, and career at the individual level, and, of course, more important than politics, the economy, or war and peace at the societal level (Cantor, 1987:190).

To summarize, research shows that magazines have been more responsive to change than television. The variety of publications available means that magazines vary in the role models presented to their readers. Even high-circulation magazines such as *McCall's* show a "gentle support" for the women's movement (Tuchman, 1979). (*Family Circle* women exchange household hints and recipes. *Vogue* women sell elegance. *Shape* women seek muscle definition. *Working Women* are economically productive. *Chatelaine* women attempt to be all of these things, and politically engaged, too.) However, the sheer diversity of magazines and the distinctions among fiction, non-fiction, and advertising (discussed earlier) mean that any generalizations must be cautiously put.

Finally, we emphasize the importance of advertising dollars on the gender-related content, indeed the very existence of magazines. *Ms.* magazine provides an excellent illustration of this point. *Ms.,* whose advocacy journalism either ruled out or alienated big-budget advertisers, was forced to suspend publication in November 1989. Its attempt over the years to woo advertisers by diluting its feminist content had turned off many of its original fans. Six months later, its feminist convictions re-kindled, *Ms.* attempted a come-back. Since the new *Ms.* carries a hefty newsstand price-tag, but absolutely no advertising, founding editor, Gloria Steinem (1990) was free to comment publicly on advertising's impact on the editorial content of women's magazines:

Food advertisers have always demanded that women's magazines publish recipes and articles on entertaining (preferably ones that name their products) in return for their ads; clothing advertisers expect to be surrounded by fashion spreads (especially ones that credit their designers); and shampoo, fragrance, and beauty products in general usually insist on positive editorial coverage of beauty subjects, plus photo credits besides. That's why women's magazines look the way they do. (p. 19)

Time will decide whether readers will support the resurrected *Ms.*

Conclusions About the Media as Gender Socialization Agents

Three conclusions emerge from consideration of the large body of research concerning the media's role in gender socialization. First, popular culture currently comprises both traditional and non-traditional gender imagery. Second, some media content matters more than others. Third, the media contribute significantly to children's development of traditional views about gender relations. Each of these points requires elaboration.

First, the media are not monolithic. Although contemporary mass sources continue to convey traditional ideas about gender, they also promote "the rise of a consciousness of feminist concerns in the public discourse" (Press, 1986:313). Take movies for example. The last five years saw a number of films released that involved women with complex and active roles, both on screen and behind the scenes. *The Handmaid's Tale*, based on Margaret Atwood's feminist novel, filmed themes of religious fundamentalist repression and takeover of

women's fertility. The fantasy *Willow* features a baby *girl* destined to save the world and a *female* wizard. *The Accused* breaks new ground for Hollywood by convincing viewers that no woman, regardless of provocative dress, suggestive behaviour, or unsavoury reputation, deserves to be raped. *Blue Steel* explores the darker side of masculinity. Jamie Lee Curtis, asked why she wants to become a policewoman, snaps: "Because I wanna shoot people. Because I like to slam people's heads up against the wall" (Huffhines, 1990). Curtis' violent character, while troubling in other respects, does break the gender mold.

Nevertheless, many more recent movies conveyed gender traditionalism and/or misogyny. *Pretty Woman,* which featured a hooker who earned a new wardrobe and a new life by connecting with the right man, was a 1990 update of the Cinderella Fairy tale. The 1988 box office hit *Fatal Attraction* is about men's fear of women and the career woman as monster (*Time,* November 16, 1987). Molly Haskell (1988:87) says of *Three Men and a Baby:* "In a society in which 88 percent of single-parent households with children are run by women [the U.S.A.], and by women often impoverished by divorce, the most successful movie of the year featured a 'single-parent' household run by men, and upscale men at that." Released in the same year were *Dead Ringers* (featuring women subjected to torture by a mad gynecologist equipped with medieval medical instruments); *Slumber Party Massacre* (female victims of slashing); and *Rambo III* (vicious masculine camaraderie). The box office and video store hits at the beginning of the 1990s are supercop films (*Lethal Weapon, Miami Blues, Dick Tracy*) where masculine models are emotionally controlled killers and female models are either glamourous props or victims of violence.

Still on the first point, storybooks for children also make available some non-traditional gender imagery. Robert Munsch's *The Paper Bag Princess* was popular with Canadian youngsters in the 1980s. In this book, the heroine rescues Prince Ronald from the dragon "only to discover that he is a hypercritical dandy who objects to her singed clothes and battle scars" (Ross, 1983:44). In the end, she calls him a "bum" and they don't get married.

However, a beautifully illustrated version of Hans Christian Andersen's *The Little Mermaid*—another tale of princes and princesses—also sold well in the same time period: "In Andersen's story, the little mermaid falls in love with a prince and exchanges her voice for human legs, only to stand mutely by as the prince jilts her for a human princess. In desperation, the land-bound mermaid throws herself into the sea and turns to foam" (Tousley, 1985).

Comic strip pages in daily newspapers also send contradictory gender messages. Several new strips humorously convey engaging examples of enlightened gender imagery. There is "Adam," the couch-potato househusband who spoons pablum into the baby, while Laura, his business-suited wife accumulates frequent-flyer points. The didactic strip, "Sally Forth" lectures on the justice of shared housework and shared parenting when both partners are in the labour force. "Cathy" worries about being single in the 1990s. Nevertheless, many strips continue to assume and reinforce the traditional, asymmetrical gender division of labour, and gender stereotypes. For example, "Blondie" keeps house, shops, and talks on the phone (but never reads anything [Brabant and Mooney, 1986]). Rex Morgan is the wise physician, June his supportive "office wife." General Halftrack in "Beetle Bailey" denigrates his middle-aged wife, as he lusts after the shapely young secretary. Sarge in the same comic strip disciplines Beetle Bailey daily by beating him.

Popular music also offers a variety of gender imagery. Golden Oldies often idealize women ("Earth An-gel, Earth An-gel, will you be mine?"). Country ballads sing about strong cowboys falling into unrequited love with bad women. Rock music (the favourite music of more than three-quarters of Canadian teenagers [Bibby and Posterski, 1985:36]) has been criticized for its misogyny (Harding and Nett, 1984). The reviewer of a Mötley Crüe concert wrote: "The entire concert was a sermon in egotistic sexuality that makes lust, not love or even caring, the only form of expression between men and women" (*Calgary Herald,* October 20, 1987). Indeed, a member of Kiss ("Burn Bitch Burn") boasts about having "bedded down" 3000 women during his rock band trav-

els (*Herald Sunday Magazine,* September 4, 1988). The message of the rap group 2 Live Crew album "As Nasty As They Wanna Be" "...is one of menacing studhood that expects every woman to lie down and submit in silence" (*Time,* May 7, 1990:62).

Countervailing influences also were heard. A few women—Cindy Lauper, Madonna, Tina Turner—had rock hits on the charts in the 1980s. Although their presence did little to mitigate the "kneejerk" misogyny of the rock scene, the Eurythmics told the world that "Sisters Are Doing It for Themselves." k.d. lang's strategy of parodying country music through "on-stage antics, choice of costume, refusal to wear makeup, and powerful renditions of country classics" also demonstrated how women can challenge the musical mainstream (Sawchuck, 1989:54). Additional examples of contradictory gender messages in the media could be cited. However, we consider the point made and move on to our next generalization.

We come now to our second generalization regarding the part played by the media in gender socialization. Despite the recent availability of liberated gender messages in most media, the truth is that not all sources of gender imagery are equally powerful. For one thing, some media are more influential than others. This differential impact may be labelled the *drench effect* (Greenberg, 1988). The impact of television has been amply established (Liebert and Sprafkin, 1988; Oskamp, 1988). For this reason, it is safe to assume that more children have been exposed to father-knows-best slices of life on television's *The Cosby Show,* than to the iconoclastic *Paper Bag Princess.* Moreover, within the same medium, some imagery may have unusually strong impact, while other gender portrayals have little appeal. Speaking of television, Greenberg (1988:97) says, "Some characters in some series, or mini-series, or single programs may be so forceful as to account for a significant portion of the role images we maintain" (p. 97).

Novels published in the 1980s provide another illustration of our point that presentations of gender do not have equal impact. In *No Fixed Address* (1987), Aritha Van Herk's sexually adventurous female character, Arachne, takes to the road, as a pedlar of ladies' underwear. Janette Turner Hospital's *The Ivory Swing* (1982) depicts the non-person status of a young widow in India. Jane Rule's *Memory Board* (1987) tells the story of two aging lesbians nurturing one another after decades together in a committed relationship. More highly publicized than the above books, Margaret Atwood's *The Handmaid's Tale* (1985) is a feminist warning of a futuristic totalitarian society. These books challenge their readers to reconsider their ideas about gender. Yet, much more likely than "Canlit" to "drench" the gender imagery of women are Harelequin novels (Modleski, 1982) or best-selling romances by authors such as Danielle Steel. Similarly, we hypothesize that men's gender imagery is drenched by spy thrillers (Len Deighton, John LeCarré) or crime novels (Lawrence Sanders, Joseph Wambaugh), where men are adventurous heroes, and women are murder victims, rewarding tidbits enjoyed after a hard day's work, or absent altogether.[6]

Our final point: the media play a significant part in teaching and reinforcing traditional ideas about gender. The effectiveness of the mass media as gender socialization agencies has been well established. Roberts and Maccoby (1985:579), writing in the prestigious *Handbook of Social Psychology* conclude that "there is solid evidence that the way sex roles are portrayed in the mass media can affect children's and adolescents' attitudes and perceptions of what is and is not appropriate for the two sexes." Excellent studies document the cumulative effects of television on youngsters' gender attitudes. Research concludes that "children model themselves after the characters portrayed in programming and advertising" (Courtney and Whipple, 1983:58). Moreover, studies show that children who watch a great deal of TV hold more traditional gender attitudes than do light viewers (Beuf, 1974; Butler and Paisley, 1980).

Especially pertinent is a quasi-experimental study of a British Columbia community before and after the introduction of television (Williams, 1986). Because of geographic barriers, this town could not receive TV signals until 1973. A team of University of British Columbia researchers concluded that: "Children's sex-role attitudes, that is, beliefs about appropriate

and typical behaviour for girls and boys, were more strongly sex typed in the presence than in the absence of television" (Williams, 1986:400). Team researcher Meredith Kimball makes the point that media messages corroborate traditional information children receive from other sources. However, she goes on to say that "...since parents, peers, schools, books, and other media also usually present traditional models and messages, it is noteworthy that the introduction of television" into this community "added enough to these messages to produce an increase in sex typing" (Kimball, 1986:289).

In summary, then, children's incidental learning from the mass media about femininity and masculinity corroborates gender presentations by other socialization agencies.

VERBAL AND NON-VERBAL COMMUNICATION

Language and non-lingual communication forms make up the last gender socialization source to be discussed in this chapter. It would be almost impossible to exaggerate the importance of language in human affairs. According to Berger and Berger (1975:75), language provides society's most powerful hold over us. A language-less human being is an oxymoron: the utilization, interpretation, and creation of high-order signs distinguish humans from the lower animals and give them characteristically human qualities (Lindesmith and Strauss, 1956:131 ff.).

Language helps form the limits of our reality. It is our means of ordering, classifying and manipulating the world. It is through language that we become members of a human community, that the world becomes comprehensible and meaningful, that we bring into existence the world in which we live (Spender, 1985:3).

Scholars also emphasize the significance of non-linguistic communication. Ogling, smiling, and grimacing, as well as limb arrangements and amount of personal space commanded—all constitute rich sources of information. Many types of non-linguistic messages are relevant to gender socialization.

In the 1970s, feminist scholars began to identify the role of language and non-verbal communication in the social construction of gender (Henley, 1977; Thorne and Henley, 1975). They argued that the English language (among others) denigrates females, while it asserts male superiority. Women's historic exclusion from the public arena meant their exclusion from the production of language and culture (Smith, 1987). As a result, language both ignores and derogates women. "Men control language and language controls us" (Cameron, 1985:34). According to Spender (1985:18), "all words—regardless of their origin—which are associated with females acquire negative connotations, because this is a fundamental semantic 'rule' in a society which constructs male supremacy." This "semantic derogation of women" (Schulz, 1975) constructs and confirms female inferiority.

Feminists also argued the related point that male-constructed language is inadequate for expressing uniquely female experience. "We speak the language of patriarchy, we translate our experiences in a form foreign and deprecative to us" (Martel and Peterat, 1984:44). Their conclusion: women's understanding of themselves is seriously disadvantaged. For example, since males have had the "power to name," women's own sexual experience is often described in a misogynous language of dirty jokes and offensive expressions for women (slut, piece of ass, pig, pussy). Women lack their own colloquial words for vagina, for clitoris, for orgasm (Bernard, 1981a:376 ff.).

This section will treat symbolic forms of gender socialization under these headings: gender differences in the structure and content of language; female/male linguistic usage and conversational style; non-verbal communication; socio-linguistic gender subcultures; prospects for change. The subtext of this discussion is children's developing conceptions of gender as they learn our society's communication forms. Our major premise is captured by Davy's (1978:47) comment: "Since language categories are internalized at an early age, we tend to think of them as 'given' and truly representative of the order of things in the objective or natural world."

Gender Differences in Language Structure and Content

A pervasive theme of the English language is that males are more important than females; indeed, that "all people are male until proven female" (Eakins and Eakins, 1978:111). As children learn language, then, they unconsciously learn something about the relative value of the sexes.

DEFINITION BY GENDER

Words label. Speaking of women as "the opposite sex" exaggerates male-female differences. In addition to naming, these labels often imply hidden messages about their referents. (A father nicknames his small son "Tiger," and his daughter "Dolly.") Emotionally charged verbal labels also serve to control behaviour. Male children are effectively chastised by being called "fags" or "girls." (A basketball coach yells at a boy who isn't playing well, "Where's your purse, Mrs.—?"). Similarly, the expletive "bitch" carries the connotation that the woman has failed to observe traditional gender standards.

Terms of address also arouse feminist ire. For one thing, people feel free to be more familiar semantically with women. In the 1990 Liberal Party leadership contest, the frontrunners were "Chretien," "Martin," and "Sheila." Observations of males and females in parallel positions in various companies and public places showed that women were more often addressed by first names or nicknames, while men were generally dealt with more formally, by title or last name (Eakins and Eakins, 1978:116). Usually men are at the top of work hierarchies and women are at the bottom. Men call the women by their first names, and the women address the men by last name plus title (Thorne and Henley, 1975:16).

Also, despite innovations such as hypenated surnames, most women continue to lose their surname upon marriage. Men, however, not only keep their last name for life, but pass it on intact to sons. In general, women are labelled in terms of the men with whom they are associated—"Mrs. Jones," "Harvey Hart's daughter." (When Margaret Kemper, ex-wife of former Prime Minister Pierre Elliot Trudeau gave birth to her fifth child, the newspaper headline read, "PET's ex has a girl" [*Calgary Herald*, February 3, 1989]). The significance of the now widely accepted neologism, "Ms." has been described as follows: "First, it separated women from their relationships to men both as daughters and as wives, and established 'women' as a linguistic category in its own right. The new privacy regarding marital status symbolically elevated women to personhood from their previous commodity status in the marriage market where 'Miss' meant 'for sale,' and 'Mrs.' meant 'sold'" (Davy, 1978:47).

LANGUAGE'S EVALUATION BY SEX

The English language also appraises the sexes. For example, *masculine connotations* tend to be strong and positive, while *feminine connotations* tend to be negative, weak, or trivial. All references to God are masculine: Father, Lord, King. Mother Earth (the land to be cultivated, used) is feminine. The negative connotations attached to the word "woman" become obvious when we compare taking defeat "like a man" and taking defeat "like a woman." The *order* of word usage also communicates differential evaluation: "men and women," "boys and girls," "males and females," "husbands and wives." Henley et al. (1985:171) argue that "this order is not coincidental, but was urged in the sixteenth century as the proper way of putting the worthier party first." Another illustration of this phenomenon is *reverse devaluation*. Here, what is admirable in one sex is disdained in the other. Probably men fare worse in this trade-off of stereotyped traits. Labelling a woman "mannish" is less insulting than labelling a man "womanish." Indeed, "there are surely overtones of praise in telling a female she runs, talks, or, most especially, *thinks* 'like a man.'" Then there are *praise him/blame her* pairs of words. He is a "bachelor" (romantic, eligible, free), she is an "old maid" (poor thing!). He is a "chef" and expert, while she is merely a "cook." He is "master" of all he surveys, she is a "mistress," a kept woman. She "chattered," he "discussed." She "nagged," he "reminded." She

"bitched," he "complained." She is "scatterbrained," he is "forgetful." She was "wrinkles," he has "character lines." Finally, there are *euphemisms*, which substitute a soft term for an offensive term. "Woman" apparently carries implications of sexuality and maturity that need to be toned down. "Lady" connotes the expectations of propriety and politeness which control females from childhood. "Girl" carries not only connotations of youth, but implications of immaturity and irresponsibility. The office "girl" may be eighteen, thirty-eight or fifty-eight years old (Eakins and Eakins, 1978:125-34).

LANGUAGE'S EXCLUSION OF WOMEN

Feminists have been battling the "he/man" problem, yet another way in which the English language fails to speak clearly and fairly of both sexes (Martyna, 1980). Here, language excludes and subsumes women through generic masculine terms that are supposed to refer to people in general: "he" "mankind," "man, the social animal," "man of good will." (Or even, "Man, being a mammal, breast-feeds his young" [Martyna, 1980:489]). The grammarians' claim that the generic masculine implies the female, that "man embraces woman," is countered by the feminists' claim that the generic masculine is both ambiguous and discriminatory. Empirical evidence shows that people of both sexes interpret generic masculine terms as *exclusively* male. For example, Schneider and Hacker (1973) showed college students pictures that were to fit under chapter headings for a hypothetical sociology text, headings such as "Social Man," "Industrial Man," "Political Man." Analysis of the pictures selected revealed that these chapter titles invoked images of males only, thus "filtering out recognition of women's participation in these major areas of life" (Miller and Swift, 1977:19).

The evaluation implied by generic masculine language is nicely illustrated by Spender (1985:23): "It is all right, for example, to call a mixed sex group 'guys' or 'men' but it is a mistake—and an insult—to refer to a group which contains even one male as 'gals' or 'women.'"

While individual examples of sexism in language may seem trivial, their combined impact is profound when we remember that people's perceptions of the world are linked closely to their language. As children learn a language, they learn something about women's place and men's place.

Female-male Linguistic Usage and Conversational Style

As emphasized above, the sexes do not stand in the same relationship to language (Philips, 1980). Most obvious are distinctions in speech content. Females sprinkle their conversation with words like "PMS," "moisturizer," "casserole," and "robins' egg-blue" garments. Men talk about solenoids, hat tricks, and drill bits (Frisbie, 1985:56). In narrating an experience, young women use "go" instead of "say": "I saw Jane at the mall," one will say. "And I go,' What are you doing here?' And she goes, "Spending money." And I go, "Where'd you get it?' And she goes, "From dad'" (Kostash, 1987).

Their interactual styles also differ: "Men put a greater emphasis on hierarchical organization, on interactions that assert direction and dominance, whereas women engage in more egalitarian, cooperative participation, and more expressive, receptive, encouraging, and supportive interactions" (Aries, 1987:155). Women's supportive, collaborative language use and conversational style versus men's competitive, challenging orientation simultaneously express and contribute to the maintenance of gender dichotomy and male dominance.

It is important, nevertheless, to keep in mind that the gender differences isolated are matters of degree, not absolute distinctions. Some years ago, the proposition that males and females speak in separate languages or "dialects" (Lakoff, 1975) intrigued social scientists. However, subsequent research failed to support this once popular notion. For one thing, males and females, as members of the same species, have most characteristics in common. For another, speech style is affected by numerous variables besides sex/gender, such as socioeconomic status, education, occupation, age, geographi-cal region, and ethnic background (Haas, 1979:624). Finally, as we shall see later on, the salience of gender's impact upon conversational style is affected by the context of interaction.

Studies of spontaneous interaction between the sexes in such natural settings as homes, university coffee shops, and doctors' waiting rooms produced several important generalizations. First, women tend to do more of the interaction work than men; that is, they assume a disproportionate share of the responsibility for keeping conversations going. Nevertheless, decisions about what is appropriate conversation remain the males' prerogative (Fishman, 1978). Men more often display minimal responses ("Mm hm") as a lazy way of filling a turn, and indicating lack of interest. In Fishman's (1978) taped conversations of three couples in their homes, the male partners produced more than twice as many statements as the female partners, and they almost always got a response. Many times, one or another of a couple read aloud or commented on a passage from a newspaper or book. "The man's comments often engendered a lengthy exchange, the woman's comments seldom did" (p. 402). Similarly, Derber (in Kohn, 1988:65) found that "the wife gave more active encouragement to her husband's talk about himself, while the husband listened less well and was less likely to actively 'bring her out' about herself and her own topics."

Second, researchers report that women sustain conversations by asking a great many questions. Fishman (1978) found that women asked two and a half times as many questions as men. Women used some version of the conversational opening, "D'ya know what?" twice as often as men. (Children use this strategy to insure their right to speak). Also, women more frequently turn declarative statements into tag questions (Eakins and Eakins, 1978). (It's nice out, isn't it?") These female questions seem to reflect gender in several ways. As Aries (1987:156) points out, questions may "express a degree of solidarity toward the addressee by facilitating the addressee's contribution to discourse, or may express politeness by attenuating the force of a speech act..." Other commentators have interpreted questions, especially tag questions, as indicative of women's uncertainty and, hence, of their subordinate position (Lakoff, 1975).

Third, according to these studies, men interrupt women considerably more than women interrupt men (Kollock et al., 1985). From their analysis of spontaneous talk in university settings, West and Zimmerman (1977) discovered that males interrupt females much more often than they interrupt other males, and more often than females interrupt people of either sex. Interruptions serve "as a projection on the speaker's part that he or she is worthy of more attention — has more of value to say and less to learn — than the other party (Kollock et al., 1985:35). The fact that similar patterns of interruption characterize interaction between adults and children, and between doctors and patients (West and Zimmerman, 1977) suggests the centrality of status/power. Indeed, Grief (1980) tells us that American fathers and mothers interrupt their two to five year old daughters more than their sons.

Fourth, stereotyped portrayals of women as talkative are inaccurate. Conventional wisdom holds that women are verbose; they natter about trivialities (Spender, 1985). Nevertheless, study after study reports that men speak more often and at greater length than women (Henley et al., 1985; Kollock et al., 1985:35). Moreover, women do not gossip more than men (Levin and Arluke, 1985).

Fifth, Women's speech is more polite than that of men. Men engage in more profanity, verbal duelling, and joking (Thorne and Henley, 1975).

> The woman: "Oh dear, you've put the peanut butter in the refrigerator again, haven't you?"
> The man: "Shit, you've put the damn peanut butter in the fridge again" (Lakoff, 1975).

"Oh, fudge! My hair is on fire!" is a recognizable caricature of women's speech. Though the social class and education of speakers and auditors also enter into the matter (Philips, 1980:535), society expects more circumspect speech from females, who even today are more likely than males to be criticized for profanity or vulgarity. Many feminists argue that females' more circumspect speech patterns, their

willingness to listen and to respond in non-combative fashion, signal their subordination. Inferiors *should* be quiet and polite. However, the social-role interpretation of gender differences also seems plausible (Aries, 1987). That is, women's more receptive, encouraging speech patterns fit in with their traditional socio-emotional role specialization.

Finally, we underline the point that sex/gender differences in language usage and conversation are affected by other factors (Aries, 1987). For example, one study found that the participation of wives in the women's movement affects spousal couples' conversational patterns. Husbands spoke longer than wives where wives were not active in the movement; however, when wives were active feminists, they had more to say than their husbands (Hersley and Werner, 1975). Also, female-male differences discussed above earlier were greatly reduced when couples' interaction was formal and public rather than informal and private. In public settings, talk has more to do with information than expressivity. The greatest differences occur when couples are out of public view in intimate settings (Aries, 1987:159).

Another important situational factor which has an impact on gender differences in communication is the sex composition of the group. All-male groups emphasize the establishment and maintenance of stable dominance hierarchies. In comparison, all-female groups show considerably less interest in dominance. For instance, female speakers sometimes express discomfort with leadership positions and make an effort to draw out more silent members (Aries, 1987). Here, an interesting finding reported by many studies: men in mixed-sex groups display less hierarchical behaviour than do men in single-sex groups. Although men in mixed-sex groups still do more of the talking, male communication behaviour does come closer to the female pattern. That is, the presence of women increases the frequency of men's supportive interaction, such as speaking with individuals rather than addressing the group as a whole, their willingness to talk about personal problems, and decreases their combativeness (Aries, 1987:160).

Finally, a study that compared natural conversations among cross-sex couples and female and male same-sex couples with more or less power concludes that it is power differences, not sex as a quality of persons, that accounts for the division of labour in conversation. Though sex/gender by itself has little to do with the conversational division of labour, sex/gender and power are generally closely tied in heterosexual couples (Kollock et al., 1985).

Non-verbal Communication

There are other ways of sending messages besides language. Staring, winking, smiling, shrugging are all well-recognized means of "speaking." Indeed, non-verbal communication carries four times the "conversational" weight of verbal messages when both are used in communication (Argyle et al., 1970).

Though females and males are more alike than different in their non-verbal behaviour (Birdwhistell, 1970), those learned gender differences that do exist appear to serve three inter-related functions. First, non-verbal messages communicate "I am female" or "I am male." In other words, they *display* gender (Goffman, 1976). Because of the innate similarity of the sexes, elaborate codes have developed which allow others to determine people's sex/gender without inspecting their genitals. Differences in walking, arrangement of limbs while seated, smoking cigarettes, inspecting fingernails, etc. make gender visible and salient (Pearson, 1985:265).

Second, non-verbal cues, like language, indicate status and power (Henley, 1977). Henley et al. (1985:179) argue that the subtle nature of non-verbal communication, compared with speech, renders it "a perfect avenue for the unconscious manipulation of others." They go on to say:

Nonverbal behavior is of particular importance for women, because their socialization to docility and passivity makes them likely targets for subtle forms of social control, and their close contact with men—for example as wives and secretaries—entails frequent verbal and nonverbal interaction with those in power. Additionally, women have been found to be more sensitive than men to nonverbal cues, perhaps

because their survival depends upon it (Henley et al., 1985:179).

A third, and overlapping interpretation (which we also encountered earlier in explanation of linguistic differences) stresses that gender distinctive non-verbal behaviours are imbedded in social roles (Eagly, 1987). Since women have been disproportionately involved in domestic roles and men in agentic roles, each sex has acquired somewhat different skills to carry out social interaction. For example, as Henley et al. (1985:179) mention above, women are better than men at decoding non-verbal messages. They are also more adept in encoding (sending) non-verbal signals, especially via the face. According to Eagly (1987:106), "...the idea that the female gender role fosters communal qualities and thereby encourages women to be pleasant, interpersonally oriented, expressive, and socially sensitive provides an interpretation of most of these nonverbal sex differences."

Below we focus upon the major gender differences in non-verbal behaviour that have been established by researchers (Hall, 1984). Once again, the point to be emphasized is that children, in learning the subtle canons of body language, have their notions about the traditional gender division of labour and power/status asymmetries reinforced.

Gaze

Women gaze at other people more than men do (Eagly, 1987:103). This gender difference in gazing serves the power function of communication discussed in the previous section. In status-differentiated groups, the high-status person typically receives the most visual attention. Why? The low-status person "looks at" the high status person for direction or approval (Lamb, 1981). Also, people do more looking when they are listening to another speak. As noted earlier, men in mixed-sex groups do more talking than women. Nonetheless, the social-role interpretation also applies. Looking at people (along with the nodding, also more characteristic of females) communicates social sensitivity, as well as deference.

Women are stared at more than men (Eagly, 1987:103). Staring (intense gazing) communicates aggressiveness and sexual invitation. Men signal dominance and sexuality more blatantly than do women (Haviland and Malatesta, 1981).

SMILING

Women smile and laugh more in social situations than do men (Hall, 1984). The social-role interpretation again seems plausible. Since traditional femininity emphasizes affiliation, women's smiling meets their social obligations. However, feminists have also stressed the power function (Firestone, 1971). A journalist argues that,

Just as baby horses grin insanely at their elders, begging them not to bite poor, wee me, disadvantaged human groups smile at those in power. Women smile more than men because they have to appease men. The pasted on smile makes us more manageable, reassures men we're no threat to them (Zwarun, 1989:A3).

DEMEANOUR

Goffman (1967:77) defines *demeanour* as "that element of the individual's ceremonial behaviour typically conveyed through deportment, dress and bearing." Females show more circumspection in their demeanour, a less casual posture and bearing than do males (Eakins and Eakins, 1978:159 ff.). Men tend to keep their legs apart at a ten-to-fifteen-degree angle; women keep their knees together. Women more often than men hold their arms with elbows close to their sides. The torso lean of the male in conversation is farther back and more relaxed. By forward leaning, women indicate more involvement. In general, women's bodily demeanour is more restrained and restricted than men's. The status explanation seems appropriate here: "Among nonequals in status, superordinates can indulge in a casualness and relative unconcern with body comportment that subordinates are not permitted" (Eakins and Eakins, 1978:159). Females have to strike a delicate balance between communicating the

responsiveness required by their socio-emotional specialization, and signalling blatant sexual availability.

TOUCHING

Research findings regarding gender differences in touching behaviour are less well established than those treated above. The fact that "touch has many variants (e.g., handshakes, pushes, strokes, pats, hugs, kisses) and conveys many meanings" which vary depending on social context, makes this a complex research issue (Eagly, 1987:105). Studies (Stier and Hall, 1984) confirm the tendency for females to engage in more same-sex touching than males. Apart from formal handshaking and locker-room swatting, male touching of other males often carries homosexual connotations (Deaux, 1976:65).

Whether males touch females more than females touch males remains a controversial question. A decade ago, proponents of the power/status function had believed this to be true. They pointed out that touching is the nonverbal equivalent to first-naming. When both are used reciprocally, they indicate solidarity or intimacy; when used non-reciprocally, they indicate status (Henley, 1985:194). "Just as the boss can put a hand on the worker, the master on the servant, the teacher on the student, the business executive on the secretary, so men more frequently put their hands on women, despite folk mythology to the contrary" (Henley et al., 1985:181). Sexual harassment legislation now exists to protect subordinates from unwelcome advances of their superiors.

PERSONAL SPACE

Men, in comparison with women, command more personal space. Men prefer greater standing and sitting distances between themselves than do women. They expansively dominate the space around them—they sprawl, they sit with legs spread out, they pace a room, they gesture extravagantly. In contrast, women condense or compress. They keep legs crossed, elbows at sides, move around the room or stage less when speaking in public, maintain a more erect posture, and seem to be trying to take up as little space as possible (Henley, 1977). Gender differences in space communicate dominance and submission. Higher status people command more space. They have larger houses, cars, offices, desks. Inferiors own less space, and their personal space is more readily breached by others (Eakins and Eakins, 1978:169-71). People of both sexes are more willing to intrude upon a woman than upon a man (Unger, 1978:477). Sometimes space use is tied to social roles. Allowing people "to approach closely can help women develop rapport with others in benign and friendly social contexts" (Eagly, 1987:106).

In sum, important gender socialization lessons are conveyed by the "silent language" (Hall, 1959). This is so for the simple reason that many, perhaps most, of these lessons remain below the level of conscious awareness.

Sociolinguistic Gender Subcultures

In the preceding discussion, two explanations of gender differences in verbal and non-verbal communication were developed. The *micropolitical explanation* argues that the superior power of males structures communication. Males' historical control over cultural institutions has resulted in the semantic derogation of females. Also, power structures interpersonal exchanges between the sexes. Males successfully take control of conversation, decide which topics will be pursued and which dropped, and interrupt female speakers. Men learn that power lies with those who do not disclose their vulnerability. Therefore, they try to gain and to keep the upper hand over women by refraining from self-revelation or emotional displays (Spender, 1985:46-47). Women, on the other hand, become adept at techniques required of the powerless in intimate relationships (Lipman-Blumen, 1984:30-31). They acquiesce, even cooperate, with aggressive, masculine communication tactics. They become well versed in interpreting the body language and emotional states of the dominant males. Because many (not all) lack authority in the public world, they (along with other low-status categories like children and minority ethnics) rely on manipulative, indirect, coy methods of dealing with the dominant group—charm, deceit, teasing, tears. These strategies are often denigrated by males, if and when they become aware of them.

The second, but closely connected, *role explanation* argues that gender differences in communication result from the traditional division of labour. Despite considerable change in gender norms, "certain work, activities, privileges, and responsibilities are still assigned to individuals on the basis of sex" (Aries, 1987:167). Women's verbal and non-verbal communication centres around relationships and the interpersonal sphere; men's reflects the agentic concerns of the public sphere.

An interesting thesis put forth by Maltz and Borker (1982) incorporates both these explanations. These researchers argue that children learn the rules for gender-distinctive communication during interaction with their peers (Chapter 6). The period from five to 15 years, when youngsters interact primarily in single-sex groups, is especially important (Aries, 1987:168). "Members of each sex are learning self-consciously to differentiate their behavior from that of the other sex and to exaggerate these differences" (Maltz and Borker, 1982:203). During the preadolescent years, the "girls' world" consists of small groups, often pairs, based on supportive talk. Direct criticism is usually avoided. "The world of boys, by contrast, is more hierarchical, marked by the constant manipulation of relative status, and filled with posturing and counterposturing to assert dominance, attract an audience, and assert oneself when other speakers have the floor. Verbal challenge is a hallmark of boys' interactions" (Hall, 1987:188).

Communication differences continue into adult life, with females' style emphasizing affiliation and egalitarianism in comparison with male competitiveness. As a consequence of growing up in somewhat (but not totally) separate sociolinguistic communities, each sex often wrongly interprets the other's communication. For example, women may see questions as conversation maintenance; men see questions as requests for information. Women may share experience and problems, and respond by offering reassurance; men often interpret presentation of problems as requests for solution, and "respond by giving advice, lecturing, acting as experts" (Aries, 1987:168). Women formulating ideas may expect partners to listen and to encourage. When male partners respond by challenge and debate, confusion and hurt often result (Surrey 1985). As Reik (1954:15) remarked long ago, men and women may be sending different messages "even when they use the same words. The misunderstanding between men and women is thus much less a result of linguistic and semantic differences, but of the emotional divergencies when the two sexes use identical expressions."

Changing Sexist Forms of Communication

The relationship between language and society is dialectical. That is, language reflects social reality; language also shapes social reality (Berger and Berger, 1984:52).

A twofold lesson may be drawn from this well-established generalization. Firstly, as social structural change results in more egalitarian relationships between the sexes, sexist language will diminish and communication styles will become more homogeneous. Events of the last two decades have shown this to be so. For instance, not too long ago, gender-inclusive language was openly ridiculed. *Time* magazine called the language issue "ms.guided." *TV Guide* wondered about the "women's lib redhots" with their "nutty pronouns" (Martyna, 1980:484). Today, gender-neutral terms are routinely employed by the CBC, *The Globe and Mail*, the *New York Times*. In addition, many people of both sexes are now aware of masculine non-verbal power plays (interrupting or monopolizing conversation) and feminine manipulative tactics (tears, flattery). These micropolitical communication forms no longer operate as a matter of course. Nevertheless, utopia has not yet arrived. Though the sexes are more equal than they once were, our society remains patriarchal. Therefore, the tendency to denigrate communication forms simply because of their association with females remains.[7]

The dualistic relationship between language and society also implies the power of non-sexist communication to alter the gender status quo. Many feminists have advocated taking active steps to eliminate sexist language. Language has been recognized as ideology:

Language subtly legitimates patriarchy through sexism. It weaves sexism into a complex web of myths, religions, practices and beliefs which exclude women or pejoratively label them. Furthermore, these labels are part of a language we learn and use; they mold our vision of ourselves and of the world. Just like the slave who confesses to being "no good" because she or he has learned to gauge personal worth according to the master's (seldom mistress') definition of a "good slave," we use a language which constantly judges our second rate worth—or worthlessness (Martel and Peterat (1984:49).

Leaving this ideology unchallenged perpetuates patriarchy. On the other hand, "changing the usage and structures of language constitutes at least a first step toward changing societal practices, if only by increasing the awareness of the existence of sexism in conventional language and/or by indicating a nonacceptance of such sexist usage" (Blaubergs, 1978:245).

In addition to pressing for elimination of sexist forms, feminists have addressed the question (mentioned earlier) of the inauthenticity for women of existing language. In this connection, Smith (1987:58) describes women's experience "as yet unformulated and unformed; lacking means of expression; lacking symbolic forms, images, concepts, conceptual frameworks, methods of analysis; more straightforwardly, lacking self-information and self-knowledge." Therefore, as we mentioned at the beginning of this discussion, investing language with women's own different and positive meanings has become a priority for feminists. Witness the attempts of women writers such as Margaret Atwood (*The Handmaid's Tale* [1985], *Cat's Eye* [1988]) to create new language or to use language in new ways specifically calculated to encode the female experience (Thorne, Kramarae, and Henley, 1983:19). As well, women's studies courses have helped women "translate their ideas from the darkness of private experience into a shared public language" (Belenky et al., 1986:203). Chapter 10 returns to the question of feminist strategies.

CONCLUSIONS

Chapter 7 has examined the part played by these secondary and symbolic agents of gender socialization: the school, the church, the mass media, linguistic and non-verbal communication. Two major conclusions emerge from our discussion. First of all, the secondary agents augment and elaborate upon family and peer group definitions of gender. Although further documentation is required of the linkages between primary and secondary agencies (and the connection of both to the pervasive influence of language), the emphasis placed on the family by gender socialization theorists seems to be appropriate. Secondly, the influence of all these gender socialization agencies upon the child appears to be consistent and cumulative in impact.

Many Canadian parents, teachers, and policymakers have come to appreciate the arbitrary and damaging nature of traditional gender stereotypes. Although the difficulties inherent in altering cultural values and familial behaviour cannot be underestimated, thought is being given to healthier definitions of femininity and masculinity, and to the possibility that adult gender identities are not immutable. The general assumption is that if gender differences are socially induced, they can be socially altered. Nevertheless, the ambiguity surrounding proper feminine and masculine behaviour is bound to produce confusion in gender socialization patterns well into the future.

Up to this point, gender has been considered from a biological perspective and from a social-psychological perspective. We turn next to a social-structural analysis of the problem.

NOTES

1. Since space limitations make it impossible to discuss *all* sources of gender socialization in the body of the book, the reader may find this more complex enumeration helpful. It is based on Lippitt (1968:335).

a. The formal education system, public and private.
b. The churches, with their programs for children and youth.
c. The leisure-time agencies, with their recreational, cultural, and character education programs.
d. The social control and protection agencies such as the police, courts, traffic-safety agents, etc.
e. The therapeutic, special correction and resocialization services such as counsellors, remedial clinics, and programs for the handicapped.
f. Employment offices and work supervisors who hire the young and supervise them on their paid jobs.
g. Political leaders who have an interest in involving the young in political activities.

The seven sources listed above offer more or less articulated programs and have professional socialization agents. They are the *secondary* socialization agencies. The next two sources, the *primary* ones, are considerably more informal in their efforts, but they still involve direct agents:

h. The family.
i. The peer group.

The remaining two sources of socialization, the *symbolic* sources, lack direct agents:

j. The mass media.
k. Verbal and non-verbal forms of communication.

2. Although education directly affects occupational attainment, its role in intergenerational occupational mobility in Canada is a matter of considerable debate. The question is whether the school can remedy prior inequalities of income, power, prestige or whether, as conflict theorists hold, the school perpetuates and extends such inequalities (Pike, 1988). See Russell (1987) for a discussion of the ramifications of this controversy for the perpetuation of gender inequality.

3. Ostrander (1988:745) has this to say about Belenky et al. *Women's Ways of Knowing* (1986): "The premises of the book rest on acceptance of an essentialist and a historical approach to sex differences. The argument that women may see the world differently from men because women occupy different and equal positions in a stratified gender structure (as advocates of a feminist standpoint do) is entirely different from the perspective taken here, where women are seen 'naturally' or as a consequence of mothering to have qualities other than those of men. And to suggest that the qualities of these ways of knowing are characteristics that women have in com-

mon subsumes analytic categories other than gender, even when the sample is diverse in race, class, and ethnicity."

4. Quebec's Roman Catholic Church issued a formal apology to the women of Quebec for having fought to keep them from gaining the right to vote. The apology came at a ceremony to mark the fiftieth anniversary of Quebec women being given the federal franchise (*Calgary Herald*, April 28, 1990:E5).

5. "As early as 1951, women's groups protested the portrayal of women in Canadian broadcasting. Nineteen women's groups brought their demands to the Royal Commission on Arts, Letters and Sciences, also known as the Massey Commission" (Davison-Leong, 1990:6).

6. Grayson (1983) concludes "From an examination of English Canadian novels over a 200-year period, it is clear that the English Canadian novel is a vehicle for the perpetuation of male hegemony. Over the time period in question, the vast majority of novels embodied an acceptance of women's subordination. Only a few have either questioned or rejected women's inferior position. Moreover, the latter sentiment has only become manifest in recent years."

7. Spender (1985:30) speaks to this point: "Some attempts have been made to modify sexist words and there are signs that this on its own is insufficient to reduce sexism in language. Words such as police *officer* and chair*person* have been an attempt to break away from the negative value which female words acquire by the creation of sex-neutral terms. But sex-neutrality is not a meaningful category in our society, and while the world is obsessively divided into masculine and feminine, people have a genuine need to know whether the chairperson or the police officer is a man or a women: only then are they able to decide whether the appropriate classification is positive or negative. It is not idle curiosity which prompts them, but necessity, in a patriarchal order, for if we are to make sense of the world we inhabit the distinction between masculine and feminine is a crucial one."

Chapter 8

The Social-Structural Approach To Gender Relations: Work

Chapters 8 and 9 adopt a social-structural perspective, as the final theoretical link in a comprehensive explanation of gender relations. Chapter 8 deals with stratification and work, Chapter 9 with family and aging. This macrosociological analysis complements and builds upon the material presented in previous chapters. The content of this chapter and the next one should be considered to supplement and extend, not compete with, discussions of the biological and social-psychological foundations of gender in earlier chapters. According to the structural perspective, the most important observations about gender relations concern the fact that males usually occupy the more privileged positions in society's key social organizations, such as the institutions of work and family. Therefore, interest centres on the social location of females and males, rather than the sexes' physiological or psychological differences, or their learning of distinctive gender roles. The tasks of Chapter 8 are as follows: (1) to introduce the concept of social structure (2) to discuss social stratification and gender stratification and (3) to explore the organization of paid and unpaid work.

THE MEANING OF SOCIAL STRUCTURE

Social structure, the most fundamental of all sociological concepts, refers to routine ways of thinking and doing among societal members that remain relatively constant over time (Berger and Berger, 1975:6). "Despite the hu-

man capacity for flexible and creative action, there is an underlying regularity, or pattern, to social behavior in any society" (Robertson, 1981:80). Some patterns govern the immediate transactions among individuals. For instance, familial behaviour is guided by shared ideas concerning the rights and obligations of wives/mothers, husbands/fathers, children, and extended family. Other patterns, concomitants of face-to-face interaction, concern large numbers of people, most of whom will never meet. These complex social forces are the focus of this chapter. Major structural concepts to be discussed later on include societal division of labour, class structure, and patriarchy.

The routinized patterns of thought referred to in the above definition may be labelled the *cultural component of social structure*. These include the norms, values, beliefs that are learned, shared and transmitted by groups of people (Udy, 1968:491). For instance, behaviour in a college classroom is almost never chaotic. Instead, activities are governed by shared ideas about such matters as the relative prestige of students versus teachers, norms about when class begins and ends, and so on. What happens there depends upon the ways of thinking and behaving that have become routinized among the particular people present that term by earlier generations of teachers and students dealing with much the same problems; and critically, though less obviously perhaps, among the hierarchy of governing bodies in school, province, and nation.

Ways of *doing* things are inextricably related

to ways of thinking referred to above. These behaviour patterns crystallize eventually into the *morphological component of social structure.* Here the sociologist has in mind the building blocks of society: statuses, stratification systems, institutions, and so on. Continuing with the same illustration, educational experiences in College X will differ somewhat from those in College Y if provincial government policy intends College X to serve students from a working-class background, and College Y to draw upper-middle-class students. Also included in the morphological aspect of social structure are such contextual variables as the spatial-temporal arrangements of individuals, and the physical size of groups (Udy, 1968:489). Student experiences will also vary with the size of the institution (800 versus 8000 students), the size of classes (20 versus 150), with the location of classes (windowless basement room versus outside lawn), with time of day (8:00 a.m. versus 8:00 p.m.), and day of the week (Monday versus Friday). [1]

Goldenberg's (1987:9) comment goes to the heart of the meaning of social structure:

[The structural view] focuses on explanatory variables that lie *outside* the individual. No reference is made to the actor's intentions, motivations, or subjective states. In fact the overall impression is more of a puppet than an actor; people are pulled and pushed, molded and constrained by forces they may well be unaware of, and that are, in a sense, beyond them. Society is seen as a complex system that existed prior to the arrival of any individual and that will exist after one's departure. Though an individual may possibly affect it, society will surely affect the person. (Emphasis in original.)

Chapter 8 analyzes gender, not as a matter of personality or face-to-face interaction, but rather as a phenomenon deeply embedded in the workings of large-scale, or macro-sociological structures. Discussion focusses upon gender stratification, as we seek to understand the extent to which gender relations stem from structural inequalities. We shall draw upon the conflict theoretical tradition in sociology that builds upon the writings of Marx (1846/47; 1859) and Engels (1902). For Marx and Engels, the core features of social structure were the relations of domination and subordination

among classes which emerged from the mode of production in society (Smelser, 1988:114). Structural analyses of the gender division of labour in the workplace and home are among this chapter's major tasks. However, the first item on the agenda is amplification of the point made above that the macro-sociological level approach of this chapter is to be regarded as a complement, rather than an alternative to the perspectives developed in the earlier chapters.

LEVELS OF EXPLANATION

The complexity of human beings is signalled by the many intellectual disciplines dedicated to their study. Biochemistry, endocrinology, psychology, history, anthropology, linguistics, political science, economics, sociology, as well as many other fields, seek to describe why people are what they are, and to explain why they do what they do. All of them offer distinctive, but perfectly legitimate, perspectives on similar research questions; hence the expression, *explanation by discipline.* The criterion for evaluating one discipline's explanation against that of another is pragmatic: which one predicts best? Given the present state of knowledge in the social sciences, it rarely happens that alternative disciplinary explanations are mutually exclusive or redundant. Generally speaking, every explanation by discipline has something to contribute to a larger mosaic. We need them all.

From the above, it follows that there exist various *levels of explanation* [2] or theoretical approaches to intellectual puzzles, including the gender concerns of this book. That is, there is a logical ordering of perspectives on human behaviour, from the basic *biological* level, to the *psychological* level, to the *social-psychological* level, to the *social-structural* level. The nature of the "beast," and the resulting disciplinary specialization described above account for the development of these several intellectual approaches. A given behaviour may sometimes reflect one level of causation, sometimes another. Most often two or more levels are implicated, because social behaviour usually has more than one cause. Before returning to gender relations, let us clarify the concept of levels of explanation through an illustration of another sort.

Take the unhappy example of suicide. The magnificent Golden Gate Bridge, which spans the entrance from the Pacific Ocean to San Francisco Bay, ranks high among the world's greatest achievements in engineering. The fiftieth birthday of the famous suspension bridge was celebrated in May 1987 with fireworks, concerts, and a parade of a quarter of a million people who strolled across it. The bridge has also gained a darker reputation as the world's most popular suicide site (Seiden and Spence, 1982). As of June 1990, the police have recorded 850 confirmed suicides, and twice as many more possible and attempted suicides.[3]

Two decades ago, the San Francisco civic government considered erecting anti-suicide barriers on the bridge. However, after $27 000 was spent on designing a model, the idea was rejected on the dual grounds of expense and aesthetics (*Calgary Herald*, October 6, 1975). The next sequence of events may well be apocryphal. Apparently someone tried to convince the San Francisco municipal government that the installation of vending machines containing chocolate bars would be just as effective as physical barriers. The reasoning: low blood sugar causes depression and suicide. A would-be suicide (presumable equipped with coins for the machines) would gulp some chocolate, feel happier and decide to go home, instead of jumping. Our concern is not with the validity of this hypothesis, but with the point that the low blood sugar hypothesis approaches suicide from the *biological level*.

Considerably more common (and plausible) is speculation concerning *psychological-level* reasons why people choose to leap from the Golden Gate Bridge. "Most jump out of desperation. Lost love, illness and financial troubles are common." Also, jumping to their death from the great bridge into the sparkling blue water impresses some people as an aesthetically pleasing romantic act. As one survivor related, "I felt absolutely at peace with myself for the first time in my life. I had the feeling that I would vanish from the face of the earth and be with God" (*Calgary Herald*, July 28, 1981). Here, causation for self-destruction appears to lie within the individual's perceptions, emotions, and experiences.

Nevertheless, when we consider the fact that would-be suicides are drawn to particular locations such as the Golden Gate Bridge (as well as Niagara Falls and the Aokigahara forest near Japan's Mount Fuji), it becomes clear that *social-structural level* variables are also at work. Norms recommend the Golden Gate Bridge as an appropriate spot for self-destruction. Suicides from the Golden Gate Bridge are prominently featured in the media. Tour bus drivers include the suicide statistics as part of their tourist litany. San Franciscans often remark that when stress gets too great, one can always "go off the Bridge." From time to time, lotteries develop where players bet on the day of the week when the next Golden Gate leap will take place. According to interviews with survivors, the bridge is regarded as a "suicide shrine," with unique meanings associated with death, grace and beauty (Seiden and Spence, 1982:36-37).

As mentioned earlier, an exhaustive explanation of a given phenomenon, such as suicide, often involves all levels of explanation. In order to make this point, we conclude this extended illustration with the case of John Thomas Doyle, who leapt from the Golden Gate Bridge in 1954, at the age of 49. Mr. Doyle left this note: "Absolutely no reason except I have a toothache" (*Calgary Herald*, May 25, 1987). Though no one really knows, it seems reasonable to speculate that this biological-level motive was accompanied by psychological pain of some sort. Mr. Doyle may have experienced some recent harsh blow to his self-esteem. Perhaps a toothache sufferer who takes himself to the parapet of a bridge rather than to the dentist's chair is mentally ill. Nonetheless, structural factors were also at work. Mr. Doyle knew where to go: after all, San Franciscans in distress can "always go off the Bridge." In sum, structural considerations interacted with psychological and biological factors to produce the demise of this gentleman.

It's time to leave behind this digression into suicide from the Golden Gate Bridge, intended to illustrate by analogy the matter of levels of explanation, and apply these ideas to gender. The notion of levels of explanation provides one useful way to organize much of the thinking that experts and laypersons do about masculinity and femininity. Indeed, this book has adopted this idea as its organizing framework. Previous chapters have discussed biological and social-psychological (socialization) explanations of gender. The present chapter approaches gender questions from the social structural level. Examples drawn from the relationships between gender and work will serve to review the theoretical perspectives of these previous chapters, and highlight the material ahead.

As we shall see later in this chapter, women and men tend to engage in distinctive work activities. Occupational gender segregation means that the incumbents of most occupations are preponderately one sex or another. Few women are found in very high-paying occupations, or in high-skill, blue-collar jobs, or at the highest level of the professions (Peitchinis, 1989). *Biological-level explanation* of occupational segregation would focus upon reproductive functions, anatomy, chromosomes, or hormones. For example, some people argue that women achieve less in the labour force because their maternal instinct channels their energy into nest-building. Others point to the emotional instability allegedly linked with menstrual cycles and menopause as excuses to bar women from positions of high responsibility. Women's smaller stature and less developed upper-body musculature have been cited as reasons to keep them out of such blue-collar occupations as firefighting. Their manual dexterity supposedly equips them for assembling tiny electronic components (but not surgery). And "men work in conditions of deafening noise, smothered with dust, exposed to the danger of fatal accidents. They are told that they are big and strong and able to 'take' it; a 'real' man doesn't cry" (Messing, 1987:351).

Although our present purpose is to communicate the meaning of levels of explanation, rather than debate their relative utility, it should be pointed out that biological-level approaches that emphasize male-female dichotomy do not take us very far in our understanding of the gender division of labour. This sentiment is nicely expressed by a feminist cartoon which shows two toddlers peering into

their underpants. The caption reads: "Oh, that explains the difference in our salaries!" In a more scholarly vein, as one consideration (among many), "the presence of at least some women in virtually every job in Canada today demonstrates that there is little biological justification for occupational segregation" (Armstrong and Armstrong, 1984:124).

Psychological-level explanation of the gender segregation of work still remains within the "skin" of the individual. "Psyche" means "mind." At this level of analysis, interest focusses upon individual characteristics, in particular on male versus female personality traits, motives, abilities, attitudes. For example, someone might argue that males' greater mathematical ability contributes to their dominance of engineering and architecture, or that females' more nurturant attitudes attract them to nursing and teaching. However, the fact that sex/gender explains so little of the variance in characteristics such as these (Chapter 3) makes professional psychologists very cautious about advancing purely individualistic arguments for the gender division of labour.

More frequent and plausible are *social-psychological level* explanations. These still focus on the individual but encompass social pressures that influence and constrain individual minds. As we have seen in previous chapters, a considerable literature suggests that early sex-typed socialization produces distinctive attitudes and abilities which, in turn, divert the occupational choices of most boys and girls along different channels. Pursuing this level of explanation, the reason women are more likely than men to end up in low-paying, dead-end jobs stems from more modest educational ambitions during adolescence. According to this argument, the occupational ambitions of young men are greater than those of their female counterparts because work has traditionally been a major ingredient of masculine self-esteem, and because males expect to spend a lifetime in the labour market. As they reach adolescence, males regard school—the avenue to the "breadwinner" role—more seriously. Society "puts real pressure on girls to postpone their identity settlements so that they may easily adapt to the requirements of the men they will marry" (Douvan, 1969). For this reason,

Sheehy (1974:65) speaks of young women's "complete-me marriages."

Feminist sociologists who approach these questions from the *social-structural perspective* identify serious limitations in social-psychological explanations that assume gendered behaviour to be fixed by early socialization (Armstrong and Armstrong, 1984:127 ff.). For instance, if, as the socialization perspective argues, wrong-headed notions are responsible for the traditional gender division of labour, the only thing required to bring about gender equality is change in the *ideas* that keep women in their place. Get rid of sexist fairytales! Abolish masculine generic pronouns! Wipe out gender stereotypes! Teach little girls to go for it! Become judges and CEOs, not mommies and secretaries! Armstrong and Armstrong (1984:134) find flaws in the extreme social-psychological level perspective which they label "idealism":

[Social-psychological level] analysis leaves unexplained the source of these ideas, the origins of changes in them, the dominance of some ideas over others, and their diversity within and between cultures....By focusing their strategy on beliefs, idealists ignore the complex manner in which they relate to and are supported by the organization of our society. By assuming beliefs about appropriate female/male behaviour to be mere vestiges of an earlier, less rational age, idealists also ignore, to a large extent, the interests served by them. Yet some interests are rationally served by these beliefs; some structures and organizations do profit from them. The adequacy of the theory is revealed by the ineffectiveness of the strategy. Little fundamental change has taken place as a result of attacks on the belief system alone.

These are the essential points: The structural approach to gender relations begins with the inescapable fact that "women get less of the material resources, social status, power, and opportunities for self-actualization than the men who share their social location—be it a location based on class, race, occupation, ethnicity, religion, education, nationality...." The most fundamental axiom of structuralism states that "this inequality results from the organization of society, not from any significant biological or personality differences between women and men" (Ritzer, 1988: 295-96). In other words, masculinity and femininity "embedded in the working of the state, of corporations, of unions, of families—quite as much as in the personality of individuals" (Carrigan et al., 1987:91).

The structural inequality inherent in gender suggests C. Wright Mills's (1959) oft-quoted distinction between "private troubles and public issues," between individual and societal inadequacies (Connelly and Christiansen-Ruffman, 1977). Sociologist Dorothy Smith (1977a:10) tells us what this distinction, as interpreted by feminism and Marxism, has meant in her personal life: "[This discovery of what oppression means] is the discovery that many aspects of my life which I had seen privately—perhaps better, experienced privately as guilt, or as pathology, or that I'd learned to view as aspects of my biological inferiority—that all these things could be seen as aspects of an objective organization of a society—as fixtures that were external to me, as they were external to other women."

Sociologists have addressed questions of inequality and power through their analysis of stratification. Discussion of the application of this central concept is the next item on our agenda.

SOCIAL STRATIFICATION AND GENDER STRATIFICATION

To pose the problem of gender is to seek to understand the disadvantaged, subordinate position of females, on the one hand, and the disproportionate control of power, prestige, and economic resources by males, on the other. The structural approach to gender relations holds that sex-based inequality is grounded in society-wide stratification.

To begin with, all societies are *differentiated* according to ascribed criteria (e.g., age, sex, family lineage, race, ethnicity, religion), as well as achieved criteria (e.g., occupation, education, earned wealth). An especially critical criterion is one's position in the division of labour that necessarily takes place in every society. It is simply impossible for individuals to supply all their own goods and services. "Rather, labor is specialized, and the results of one person's activities are exchanged with those of others" (Richardson, 1988:143). Grabb (1988:1) puts it this way: "The study of social inequality is really the study of these consequential human differences. In particular, inequality refers to differences that become socially *structured*, in the sense that they become a regular and recurring part of how people interact with one another on a daily basis." [Emphasis in original.] As we noted in Chapter 1, every known society is differentiated on the basis of sex. The development of social structure based on sex appears to be the tie between sex and reproduction and lactation discussed in Chapter 3. According to sociologists' observations, consequential differentiation is almost invariably accompanied by stratification (Eichler, 1980:71). That is, these differences are also *evaluated*. In our society, the young are valued more highly than the old, WASPs more than recent, non-white immigrants, engineers more than janitors, men more than women, and so on. A *stratification structure* consists of two or more social classes or groups of relative equals regarded as superior or inferior to one another.

Structured inequality involves a process in which groups or individuals with valued attributes "are better able than those who lack or are denied these attributes to control or shape rights and opportunities to their own ends" (Grabb, 1988:1). As a result, members of advantaged categories command a disproportionate share of wealth, power, and prestige. These resources enable them to maintain and improve their position. Specifically, people in top strata solidify and perpetuate their privilege in three inter-related ways (Grabb, 1988:9).

First, they enjoy *economic control* over others. Those who already control scarce goods can ensure that the distribution of goods and services continues to benefit themselves. Referring to Goyder's (1981) research, Brym (1989:101) says, "Match a group of Canadian men and a group of Canadian women in terms of education, occupation, amount of time worked each year, and years of job experience, and one discovers that the women earn only 63% of what the men earn."

Second, they exercise *political control*, i.e., they control other people's conduct. Just as the

privileged people are prominent in government which makes life and death decisions over the lives of the ruled, males have traditionally wielded power over females.

The third mechanism is *ideological control*. *Ideology* "refers to the set of ideas, values, and beliefs that describe, explain, or justify various aspects of the social world, including the existence of inequality" (Grabb, 1988:9). As we have already noted in the previous chapters, men act as gatekeepers in the societal institutions concerned with the production and distribution of knowledge (Smith, 1975). Beginning at an early age, through socialization agencies of family, peers, school, church, and mass media, children of both sexes receive induction into the "justice" and "rightness" of male domination.

Until the re-emergence of feminism stimulated Acker's (1973) path-blazing article on the subject, sociologists' studies of stratification excluded women almost entirely. Moreover, the omission wasn't even noticed. Researchers showed little interest in sex/gender as criterion of social differentiation, the assumption being that the family was the appropriate unit of analysis. The social position of the family was assumed to be determined exclusively by the status of the male head of the household. Women were seen to derive their status, first from their fathers, and then from their husbands. The ensuing years have seen an avalanche of publications in the area of stratification that seek to shed light on the structural position of women. Debates have ensued about whether women's class position derives from male heads of their families, or whether their own achievements need to be taken into account. (See Acker 1980, 1988; Blumberg, 1978; Boyd, 1981; Chafetz, 1984). For instance, Canadian socioeconomic indices that took into consideration employed women finally became available (Blishen and Carroll, 1978; Boyd, 1986). A complete review of the complex and controversial stratification literature would take us far beyond the scope of this book. However, two generalizations concerning the consequences of bringing females into stratification theory are in order.

First, consideration of male dominance, as a "fundamental and universal feature of social life," within the general context of social stratification was an important and creative step (Walum, 1977:141). "Evaluating social categories as better and worse, as more or less important, and rewarding them accordingly, is called *social stratification*. Defining sex-specific categories as better or worse and rewarding them accordingly" became defined as *gender stratification* (Nielsen, 1978:10). Feminists employ the concept of patriarchy to express the fact that gender stratification is a universal feature of all known societies. *Patriarchy*, which originated in the writings of Millet (1969), refers to "a hierarchical system of power in which males possess greater economic and social privilege than females" (Saunders, 1988:253). Speaking of the recent attempt by Fox (1988) to reconceptualize the concept, Armstrong and Hamilton (1988:159) state that "patriarchy refers to the production of gendered subjectivity in the context of relations of domination and subordination between the sexes." Note that usage of the concept of "patriarchy" advocated by Fox (1988) implies both morphological and cultural components of structure described at the beginning of this chapter. Stated otherwise, "gendered subjectivity" results from the ideological means of perpetuating privilege referred to above. However, socialization has been extensively dealt with in previous chapters and, therefore, the present focus will be on the *source* of ideas located in the morphological aspects of structure.

Here is the second generalization. After examining a decade and more of stratification studies that attempted to deal with females, feminist sociologists (Acker, 1980; Fox, 1989) conclude that the disadvantaged, subordinate position of women cannot be explained within the confines of androcentric stratification theories and methodologies that were initially designed to deal exclusively with males. Quantitative studies of status attainment (Cuneo and Curtis, 1975; Boyd et al. 1981; Boyd, 1985) provide a good example of this "poor fit" (Fox, 1989: 125 ff.) Because men's social status in industrialized societies is primarily determined by their occupation, stratification studies on women's status made very much the same assumption. However, even employed women are not present in the labour force in the

same way men are. Women's work efforts are affected by their family responsibilities much more than men's (Nielsen, 1979). As Fox (1989:128) notes, "a relationship to a man can be more critical than the work a woman does (although the two often go hand in hand) in determining her living standard." This does *not* mean that women's status can be equated with men's. Rather, it means that stratification theorists' models for both sexes, being too simplistic, require radical revision.

To conclude, the laudable attempts of stratification researchers to take females into account have demonstrated that models and methods originally designed by male sociologists to explain masculine stratification systems have serious inadequacies when they are stretched to apply to both sexes (Acker, 1980). Recent work that incorporates these insights has begun to produce a new and better understanding of both social stratification and gender stratification (Aker, 1988; Huber, 1990).

THREE FEMINIST EXPLANATIONS OF WOMEN'S OPPRESSION [4]

As emphasized above, the concept of patriarchy — "the totality of male domination and its pervasiveness in women's lives" (Smith, 1983:314)—is at the heart of feminist analysis of the structural disadvantages of women. Feminist attempts to understand (and to eradicate) the roots of patriarchy have, over the last two decades, produced three theoretical positions: Traditional Marxism, Radical Feminism, and Socialist Feminism (Jaggar and Rothenberg, 1984; Wilson, 1982:35-48). All three positions have been profoundly influenced by Marxian ideas about social organization. The Marxist (conflict) theoretical tradition in sociology argues that the organization of production ultimately determines social organization. Further, class is conceptualized in terms of economic control and material privilege: "In its simplest form, class stratification involves two groups...who are distinguished by their differential access to *both* the means and fruits of production" [emphasis in original] (Blumberg, 1978:15). Smith (1977a:30) expands on this definition:

Capitalism establishes a division of society into two major classes. Those two classes have been described...as those who appropriate and control the means of production, and those who must sell their labour power to those who appropriate and control the means of production. [Although] two classes don't provide a comprehensive description of the [contemporary] class structure of the society,...these two classes provide the basis on which the struggle to change the society goes on actively.

Though Marx himself had little to say about gender, feminists, in the early days of the renewed women's movement, sought theoretical understanding of gender inequality in a class analysis of women's position (Benston, 1969). According to Eichler (1985a:623), the relationship between Marxist and feminist scholarship can be described as "one of creative tension." On the one hand, "analyses within the Marxist framework continue to generate creative and valuable research.... On the other hand, scholars using this framework have criticized Marxism for its male orientation" (Eichler, 1985a:623). Attempts to apply a male-authored model, initially designed to explain male behaviour, produces inevitable difficulties. Be that as it may, Connelly and Christiansen-Ruffman (1977) among others argued the inequality of Canadian women in these structural terms:

A glance at the Canadian social structure indicates that it is men who own and control the essential resources.... Ownership of the most important resource, the means of production, is mainly in the hands of a few men who have power over almost all women as well as other men....Men also have control of the next most important resources, access to the occupational structure and control of policy making in the major areas of social life (p. 168).

For extended analysis of the claim that Canadian women are more proletarianized than men, see Cuneo (1985) and Carroll (1987). As our discussion of the three feminist positions shows, the main distinction among them is the relative importance of patriarchy versus capitalism. (For extended treatments of this debate see Armstrong et al., 1985; Burstyn and Smith, 1985).

Traditional Marxism

Orthodox Marxists claim that women's oppression originated with the introduction of private property and the resulting class system. Following Marx, irreconcilable conflict between economic classes is regarded as the key to understanding both the shape of contemporary society and the desirable direction of social change. "Ultimately, women are oppressed, not by 'sexism,' not by men, but by capitalism" (Jaggar and Rothenberg, 1984:85).

Women as a group are seen to be uniquely related to the means of production. One gender difference stems from the distinction in capitalist societies between *commodity production* (products created for exchange on the market) and the *production of use-values* (all things produced in the home). In capitalist societies, based on commodity production, housewives' unpaid efforts are not considered "real" work (Benston, 1969). Women's worth is seriously undermined by their position as "non-paid" "non-workers." Moreover, women's unpaid work in the home serves the capitalist system (Seccombe, 1974). In Fox's (1989:123) words, capitalism "requires the transformation of consumer commodities into 'use values' (e.g. meals, clean clothing), and the production and reproduction of 'labour power'(i.e., raising the next generation and maintaining people's capacity to work)." To pay women for their efforts would mean a massive redistribution of wealth.

A second gender difference in women's relationship to the means of production is their status as a reserve army in the labour force (Connelly, 1978; Simeral, 1978). *Reserve army* means that women are called into the labour force when needed (e.g., wartime) and sent home again when that need disappears. The cultural prescription that women belong in the home assures that the women will return to the home (Glazer, 1977). Moreover, capitalism employs women in low-wage sectors of the economy. Because in the past women were usually part of a family unit, capitalists continued to assume that women, as secondary earners, can "survive with less pay and disappear back into the home when they are fired or laid off" (Armstrong and Armstrong, 1978:137).

Also, the existence of this large reserve army of poorly paid women, always ready to substitute for those already in the labour force, serves to depress the wages of workers of both sexes (Fox and Fox, 1983). The dominant class, then, benefits from women's work both inside and outside the home.

Women's disadvantaged position in the capitalist system can be quickly documented. Only six percent of the members of the boards of directors—the policy-making bodies—of major Canadian corporations are female (*The Globe and Mail*, May 2, 1990:B7). Moreover, the chief executive officers of the top 500 Canadian companies in 1985 were all men (Peitchinis, 189:64). "In addition to the basic class differences between owners and workers, gender is the chief source of differences in wages and salaries, both in Canada and the United States" (Fox and Fox, 1987:375). Indeed, a pattern known as the "feminization of poverty" has been identified in this country, as well as other industrialized nations, including the United States and Great Britain. The *feminization of poverty* "is the process by which female-headed families become an increasing proportion of the low income or poverty population" (Abowitz, 1986).

In summary, the traditional Marxist argues that the division of labour by sex is an inherent aspect of capitalism. Therefore, women's liberation will come about through the overthrow of the capitalist system and its replacement with socialism. In a socialist system, women's economic dependency on men, and hence their subordination, would be abolished. Traditional Marxists assume that once women were economically independent, "remnants of the ancient prejudice against women would lose their plausibility and eventually disappear" (Jaggar and Rothenberg, 1984:86). Since capitalism is in the hands of a few men, and most men are alienated from their work, mere cogs in "impersonal machinery" (Sydie, 1983:202), most men would also benefit from capitalism's demise.

Radical Feminism

The more recent political perspective of Radical

Feminism argues that the oppression of women is the fundamental oppression, that patriarchy is not simply a derivative of capitalism. Shulamith Firestone (1971:5), for example, warns against attempts "to squeeze feminism into an orthodox Marxist framework." Women's situation of being "used, controlled, subjugated, and oppressed by men," i.e., patriarchy, "is not the unintended and secondary consequence of some other set of factors—be it biology or socialization or sex roles or the class system. It is a primary power structure sustained by strong and deliberate intention" (Ritzer, 1988:303). According to this perspective, it is no accident that it is women (not men) who are the underclass, women (not men) who are the soldiers in the reserve labour army. Women are seen to be oppressed by male domination in the private sphere, and only secondarily by class society. Indeed, radical feminists point to the oppression of women in non-capitalist societies. Radical feminists such as Hartmann (1976) argue that capitalism developed out of previously patriarchal societies, and preserved patriarchy as part of a system of control.

Radical Feminism directs attention to the role played by sexuality and reproduction in keeping women down (Mitchell, 1971). By declaring that the "personal is political," women's sexuality is seen as an aspect of the power relations between the sexes (Shulman, 1980:590). A fundamental dichotomy exists between valued male production and devalued female reproduction (O'Brien, 1981). Lipman-Blumen (1984:22) elaborates on these points:

In the private arena, the family as an institution...produces critical resources—the next generation, for one. But somehow these "means of reproduction" fail to bring women recognition, status, and power. Although women's biological contributions tend to entrap them, the resources contributed by women are still important. Otherwise, why the struggle for control over the means of reproduction—that is, women's reproductive capacity? Otherwise, why the serious policy debate about the right to contraceptive information and devices, as well as access to abortion? Otherwise, why are men willing to fight in court [and political and religious councils] to gain control over women's bodies and their sexual and reproductive functioning? In this case, folk wisdom gives us a clue to the meaning of social behavior. "Keep them barefoot and pregnant" summarizes one strategy for subordinating women.

Radical feminists are finding such recent developments in the technology of reproduction as in vitro fertilization, embryo transfer, and surrogate motherhood especially troubling (see Chapter 5).

Since Radical Feminists regard women's child-bearing function and subsequent dependence on men as the root of female oppression, in their opinion, only a biological revolution will free women (Firestone, 1971). Possibilities are extra-uterine reproduction or lesbianism. In general, Radical Feminists recommend, as a strategy of social change, separation from men in both domestic and economic spheres (Jaggar and Rothenberg, 1984:87, 219).

Socialist Feminism

The Socialist Feminist position accords with traditional Marxism that private property and class are central to an understanding of gender relations. However, the Radical Feminist insight of male dominance in the family is also incorporated into their perspective. The work of Kate Millett (1969) helped establish this view.

According to Smith (1983:316), we should "understand the inner life and work of the family and the personal relations of power between husband and wife as both situated in, and determined by, the general economic and political relations of a mode of production." She goes on (p. 323) to quote Nellie McClung's (1915/1972) account of the injustice suffered by farm women:

I remember once attending the funeral of a woman who had been doing the work for a family of six children and three hired men, and she had not even had a baby carriage to make her work lighter. When the last baby was three days old, just in threshing time, she died. Suddenly, and without warning, the power went off, and she quit without notice. The bereaved husband was the most astonished man in the world. He had never known Jane to do a thing like that before, and he could not get over it. In threshing time, too! (McClung, 1915/1972:114).

The death of the farmer's wife calls to mind the argument made by Engels (1902) that the family is the basic unit of capitalist society and of female oppression. "The modern individual family is founded on the open or concealed domestic slavery of the wife, and the modern society is a mass composed of these individual families as its molecules." Further, the first class oppression is that of the female sex by the male, "within the family, he (the man) is the bourgeois and the wife represents the proletariat" (Dunbar, 1970:486). Socialist Feminists hold that women's subordination in work in the home reinforces their subordination in the labour force. In the final analysis, "capitalism and patriarchy are mutually interdependent and reinforcing systems; women's liberation requires the abolition of both" (Jaggar and Rothenberg, 1984:89).

In general, then, feminist analysis of women's structural disadvantage concludes that patriarchy is not the result of a random concatenation of events. Vested interests benefit from its perpetuation. Corporate capitalism benefits (Smith, 1973). Individual men benefit. As Pleck (1981:235) points out, "men want power over women because it is to their rational self-interest to have it, to have the concrete benefits and privileges that power over women provides them." Nevertheless, it would be a mistake to see all men as agents of patriarchy to the same degree. The main beneficiaries of patriarchy are the white, affluent, heterosexual, well-educated males in capitalist advanced countries (Carrigan et al., 1985). "Patriarchy is a *dual* system, a system in which men oppress women, and in which men oppress themselves and each other" (Pleck, 1981:241, emphasis in original).

The implication of feminist Marxism, that all women constitute a special "proletariat" class has provoked criticism. Reed (1978), for example, argues that women, like men, are a multi-class sex. A few are part of the plutocratic class at the top; more belong to the middle class; even more belong to the proletarian layers of society. An enormous spread divides the few wealthy "society" women from the millions of poor women. She argues further that:

the notion that all women as a sex have more in common than do members of the same class with one another is false. Upper-class women are not simply bedmates of their wealthy husbands. As a rule they have more compelling ties which bind them together. They are economic, social and political bedmates, united in defense of private property, profiteering, militarism, racism—and the exploitation of other women (p. 127).

Duffy (1986) has recently cautioned against oversimplified definitions of power that lead to neglect of "the possibility that in some historical contexts, some women—as individuals, as groups or as class representatives—may exercise important power in the public domain" (p. 33). She cites cultural organizations, public morality groups, and social welfare bodies as examples of female upper-class resources.

Despite a "stormy relationship" (Marshall, 1988:208), Marxism and feminism provide a powerful intellectual approach to understanding women's structural disadvantage. Capitalism and patriarchy are so interwoven as to be one and the same system of oppression—capitalist patriarchy (Eisenstein, 1979). The emphasis of the Marxist theoretical tradition in sociology on economic production has been expanded by feminist sociologists to encompass all social production, so that "the myriad elements which reproduce and sustain social life are all included in a feminist revision of Marxism" (Berg, 1987:5). Engel's (1902) views on the family (mentioned above) have influenced feminist sociologists to understand the family to be "a key site of women's oppression" (Marshall, 1988:211). In this chapter and the next, these ideas will guide our interpretation of women's generally subordinate status vis-à-vis men in both labour force and unpaid work in home and community and in the family.

GENDER AND PAID WORK

"Gender distinctions are built into the organization of paid work..." (Acker, 1988:497). From its beginning, the discipline of sociology has understood work to be a highly significant social process, linking individuals to society and to one another. Work is a central dimension of individual lives, determining people's daily activities, the rhythm of their days, the people they meet, the relationships they form. Moreover, work largely defines people's class as status in the social structure (Feldberg and Glenn, 1979:524). However, until the re-emergence of the feminist movement, the sociology of work largely excluded women's work from its studies. Work was equated with paid work, so that the household work, child care, and volunteer activities engaged in by women (and by men as well) tended to be overlooked and/or trivialized. These very important, but unpaid activities, which sociologists now understand to be work will be dealt with later in this chapter.

Sexist assumptions also influenced pre-feminist sociological interpretations of paid work. To apply Feldberg and Glenn's (1979) apt terminology, prior to the 1970s, the *job model* was used by sociologists to explain male workers' behaviour both on and off the job. That is, the work men did automatically served as the independent variable to explain male reactions. For instance, studies of male factory workers found highly mechanized, routine, repetitive work to be associated with high levels of alienation from the job and consequent search for meaningful experiences in leisure hours. However, when sociologists studied employed women at all, they invoked the *gender model* to explain female work attitudes and behaviour. This mistaken pre-feminist analysis virtually ignored type of job, working conditions, etc. and turned to women's sex/gender characteristics and family relationships to "explain" their behaviour. For example, women in dead-end, boring jobs were seen to seek satisfaction in peer groups and family relations, not because of job characteristics (as was the case for male factory operatives), but because they were females acting out of some sort of "feminine imperative." As Kanter (1976:416) points out, "if women sometimes have lower aspirations, lesser involvement with work, and greater concern with peer group relations—so do men in positions of limited or blocked mobility."

Both models have relevance for both sexes. As the job model holds, it is important to understand the impact of such structural variables as opportunity structures, internal labour markets, sex ratios and the like upon the paid work of *both* sexes (Kanter, 1977; Northcott and Lowe, 1987). In this connection, it is especially important to incorporate gender stratification, male domination and female subordination, into analysis of work (Acher, 1990; Ferguson, 1984). Finally, we emphasize that analyses of male as well as female work benefit from some of the insights of the gender model originally reserved for women. As the rest of this chapter will show, men's and women's paid work is affected by "off the job" considerations, especially family roles, as well as actual work conditions (Feldberg and Glenn, 1979).

Changing Labour Force Participation

Toil is the lot of human beings. For centuries, the sexes lived and worked in close proximity. However, with the advent of the factory system, brought about by the Industrial Revolution, a radically new economic and social order came into existence. Now, the centralized location of the factory forced men to journey some distance to work. With industrialization, "men were expected to become the *sole* provider of their family's material needs" (Doyle, 1989: 173). Masculinity became increasingly identified with what Jessie Bernard (1981b) has called the *good-provider role*: "Men were judged as men by the level of living they provided" (Bernard, 1981b:1). Now men's major contribution to their family was their wages. The impact of industrialization upon the lives of women was equally far-reaching. Bernard (1981b:2) goes on to argue that the male good-provider role had deleterious effects for women.

Because she was not reimbursed for her contribution to the family in either products or services, a wife was stripped to a considerable extent of her access to cash-mediated markets. By discouraging labor force participation, it deprived many women, especially affluent ones, of opportunities to achieve strength and competence. It deterred young women from acquiring productive skills. They dedicated themselves instead to winning a good provider who would "take care of" them.

Examining labour participation rates over time reveals a great deal about changing gender roles in workplace and family. At the turn of the century, when the good-provider role prevailed, only 16 percent of Canadian women worked for pay (Lowe and Krahn, 1984:127). During World War II, when unprecedented numbers of women entered the labour force to replace men who had gone off to war and to fill newly created jobs, their participation rate (i.e., those women 15 years and older, either working for pay or profit, or seeking to do so) rose to the peak of 33.2 percent in 1945 (Armstrong and Armstrong, 1984:21). For the first time, large numbers of women were employed in well-paid, industrialized work (Andersen, 1988:108). When the war ended, the reserve army of working women, all along regarded as only temporary replacements for men, was sent packing from the factories. "After a decade of unemployment, World War II returned a sense of masculinity to countless men. After the war and with the economy turned around, men once again wrapped themselves in the mantle of the good-provider role" (Doyle, 1989:175). "The propaganda of the day pictured women at home and strong families as hedges against another war or as ballast in the Cold War. Economic expansion in the post-war period enabled male workers to be paid a family wage, meant to support a family" (McDaniel, 1988a:106). Married women returned home, while the unmarried ones were channelled into traditionally female occupations (Pierson, 1977:145). The Canadian government dismantled the child-care facilities and withdrew its tax concessions to working wives. Now, women could earn only $250 a year without affecting their husbands' deductions (Phillips and Phillips, 1983:31). Federal civil service regulations restricted employment of married women (Archibald, 1973:17). As historian Ruth Pierson (1986) makes clear, the assumption that the employment of women in the labour force during World War II greatly advanced the emancipation of women is mistaken. It was Canada's war effort, rather than any consideration of women's right to work, that determined the recruitment of women into the labour force. "The war's slight yet disquieting reconstruction of womanhood in the direction of equality with men was scrapped for a full-skirted and redomesticated post-war model, and for more than a decade feminism was once against sacrificed to femininity (Pierson, 1986:220).

The intensely conservative 1950s accentuated the mystique of feminine fulfillment centering on home, husband, and "baby boom" kids (Friedan, 1963). The female labour participation rate was 24.0 percent in 1951 and 29.5 percent in 1961. Since the post-war years, Canadian society has witnessed an astonishing change in labour force participation.

[As] unemployment rates rose, as wages failed to keep pace with prices, as fewer and fewer goods made in the home could be substituted for goods purchased in the market, as more money was needed to pay things like mortgages, taxes and heating oil that could not be made at home, as technology in the home made housework lighter, as more women obtained higher education, as birth rates plummeted, married women moved into the labour market to search for paid work (Armstrong, 1987:368).

The year 1980 marked the first time in Canadian history that a majority of women were in the labour force. By 1985, the participation rate for women was 54.3 percent (Labour Canada, 1987: Table I-2). Nevertheless, this statistic underestimates the true situation:

Many more women would take paid employment if the working conditions were better, if the pay increased, if childcare and housework assistance were available, if their husbands' attitudes changed, if their health improved, or if they had more or other training and education. Not only are many of those who want and need work left out of the official statistics, so are many of the women who clean houses, babysit, sew clothes, keep books, type essays, and stick labels on bottles. These women, working at home and paid in cash, are unrecorded in most statistical accounts and are unprotected by most legislation. Armstrong and Armstrong (1983:6).

Also, we must keep in mind that this rapid growth in women's labour force participation occurred "despite the fact that the rate of full-time enrollment of working-age women in educational institutions virtually doubled during the 1941-81 period" (Armstrong and Armstrong, 1984:18).

In comparison with the unprecedented

numbers of women entering paid employment, the male labour force participation rate has shown a slow, steady decline over the years. Between 1911 and 1979, the male rate dropped from 91 percent to 78.4 percent (Statistics Canada, 1974:113). By 1985, the participation rate was 76.7 percent (Labour Canada, 1987: Table I-2). The decline in the male labour force is concentrated at both ends of the male age distribution, as more young men 15-19 years remain in school and as more men 65 and older retire. These two factors have not had the same effect on women in the corresponding age categories (Calzavara, 1985:517).

So far as male-female differences are concerned, women in general are less likely to participate than men. Married women continue to bear major responsibility for the family and for the work at home, whether or not they also work outside the home (Gunderson, 1976:95). This factor can be demonstrated statistically. If we look at single people aged twenty-five to thirty-four, 85.3 percent of females and 89.0 percent of males were in the labour force in 1985. However, among the married in the same age category, 66.9 percent of the females versus 96.1 percent of the males were in the labour force in the same year (Labour Canada, 1987:Table I-9). Sex differences in part-time work also suggest the priority of women's home responsibilities. In 1985, 26.3 percent of women versus 7.6 percent of men had part-time employment (Labour Canada, 1987:Table I-12). It is important to underline the fact that much work is organized as part-time work because it is generally low-paying and offers few benefits. Also, part-time workers are easier to get rid of. Many women work part-time because those are the only jobs available to them. Nevertheless, more female married part-time employees report that they do not want full-time work than is the case for their married male counterparts (Burke, 1986:12). Though marriage and children continue to depress women's labour force participation in comparison with men's, they are weaker deterrents now than in the past. In the words of Lupri and Mills (1983:45),

...the single most dramatic and pervasive trend in the status of Canadian women since World War II has been the increase in the proportion of married women who work for pay. The five-fold increase in the proportion of married women entering the labour force has been increasing almost twice as fast as that for all women. But most important, the largest increase in labour force activity has occurred for the group generally viewed as least likely to work—mothers of preschool-age children.

In sum, household and child care responsibilities affect women's working lives far more than men (Lowe and Krahn, 1985), but the impact of these factors appears to be declining (Statistics Canada, 1985:41).

What factors account for the increase in the labour force participation of women, especially the employment of married women? Scholars have identified five interconnected reasons:

1. During the 1970s and 1980s, large numbers of married women entered the labour force, not to pick up "pin money," but because they were economically compelled to do so. First double-digit inflation, then recession has meant fewer jobs in the Canadian economy that provide for paycheques large enough to support entire families. As a result, many women have entered the labour force. Research shows that the lower the husband's income, the more likely that the wife will participate in the labour force (Calzavara, 1985:518). In Canada, "it has been estimated that poverty in husband-wife families would have increased by between 50 and 100 percent if women had not gone out to work for pay" (Armstrong and Armstrong, 1987:217).

Also, "as the standard of living in Canada rises, married women whose husbands earn low incomes must work outside the home to maintain their relative standard of living" (Connelly, 1977:25). For example, a modest Don Mills, Ontario bungalow, bought for $13 500 in 1954 cost $280 000 thirty-five years later (*The Globe and Mail Report on Business Magazine*, August 1988). It is also true that today's family has more "wants" and "needs" than the Canadian family of 30 years ago. According to *The Globe and Mail Report on Business Magazine* (Maynard, 1988), Canadians "now have more of just about everything...." Eating out and flying across the country or overseas, once viewed as budget-blowing luxuries, are

routine treats. Once only the affluent got their teeth fixed. Now nearly everyone does..." (p. 38). Nevertheless, "the National Council of Welfare estimates that the number of low-income families, 850,000 at last count in 1986, would nearly double if women in two-pay-cheque marriages stayed home" (Maynard, 1988:43).

2. The employment opportunities for women have increased. There has been a much more rapid growth in employment in service-based industries than in the goods-producing (manufacturing) sectors of the economy. The service sector (personal and community services, government services, education, and health-related services, etc.) employs a higher proportion of women (50.5 percent in 1985, compared with 23.4 percent in the goods-producing sector) (Lindsay and McKie, 1986:3-4). In addition, the economy has shifted towards clerical occupations. Among newly created jobs, casual, part-time employment has become increasingly important (Fox and Fox, 1986:2). The growing importance of service industries and white-collar work has created a demand that greatly exceeds the supply of young single women workers, once the backbone of the female labour force (Blau and Winkler, 1989:272). Loopbacks exist among these casual factors. Women's exit from the home into the labour force generated demands for new products and services. As employed women necessarily do less household work, families must either do without the traditional products of their labour or purchase them. Thus, two-earner families have provided markets for prepared food, child care, and cleaning services. These new industries and services rely on relatively large numbers of low-paid women workers (Gerstel and Gross, 1989:104).

3. The increasing education of women enhances their labour force activity. "The more educated a woman, the more likely it is that she will be in the labour force, the more likely she will be in the labour force continuously, and the more likely she will remain in the labour force over a lifetime of work" (Peitchinis, 1989:43). Indeed, the educational levels of women who work outside the home are higher than those of

male labour force participants (Gaskell, 1988:373). Educated women have both a higher salary capacity and a greater need for the stimulation available on the job.

4. Changes in family composition are also responsible for women entering and remaining in the labour force. A large and increasing proportion of women are not in husband-wife family relationships. One out of every ten Canadian families is headed by a single mother (Statistics Canada, 1985). Later marriages, postponed child-bearing, smaller family size, and higher divorce rates are additional factors encouraging women's labour force participation. However, "it is important to point out that these factors may be *consequences* as well as *causes* of the rise in women's involvement in market work" (Blau and Winkler, 1989:273, emphasis in original).

5. Societal attitudes regarding women's labour force participation have changed over the years. To take the most extreme case, in 1960 only five percent of a Canadian sample believed that women with young children should take a job. By 1982, 38 percent told the Gallup pollster that they approved of this behaviour (Boyd, 1984:46, 49). "Society no longer regards negatively the participation of women in work outside the home for pay, and although there may continue to exist some reluctance to approve without reservation their participation in all forms of employment activity—underground coal mining, flying fighter planes, working the night shift in a factory, bricklaying—the trend toward social indifference is evident" (Peitchinis, 1989:41).

Gender Segregation of Work

The sharp increase in women's labour force participation, as well as the publicity given to female pioneers in non-traditional occupations such as truck driving and construction work, convey the impression that concomitant improvements have taken place in women's work situation. In actual fact, corresponding changes have not occurred in the nature of the work most women do. The reason: the expansion of women's paid employment has occurred in a strongly gender-segregated labour market

(Ferree, 1987:325). From their analysis of census data, Canadian sociologists Pat Armstrong and Hugh Armstrong (1984:18) conclude that although the female share of the labour force has more than doubled since 1941, "[Women] are still overwhelmingly slotted into specific industries and occupations characterized by low pay, low skill requirements, low productivity, and low prospects for advancement. There is women's work and there is men's work. And women continue to be disproportionately segregated into many of the least attractive jobs." To reiterate Armstrong and Armstrong's (1984) thesis, women's disadvantaged position in the marketplace is tied to the continuing existence of "women's work" and "men's work," i.e. the *gender segregation of work*. "The division of many occupations and employments into 'male' and 'female' is a common phenomenon in all countries, regardless of political systems, levels of economic development, and social structures" (Peitchinis, 1989:73).

Industrial gender segregation refers to the fact that employed women and men are concentrated more in some industries than in others. In 1985, women were particularly likely to be found in these broad industry divisions: service (61.8 percent female); finance, insurance and real estate (60.4 percent female); trade (43.7 percent female); public administration (39.4 percent female). In the same year, men were segregated in these industry divisions: construction (89.8 percent male); primary industries besides agriculture such as forestry, mining, oil wells, fishing, trapping (88.4 percent male); transportation, communications, and other utilities (77.4 percent male); manufacturing (71.5 percent male); agriculture (70.3 percent male) (Labour Canada, 1987: Table I-5). Between 1951 and 1981, the concentration of women workers has risen in these divisions: trade; finance, insurance and real estate; community, business and personal services; and public administration (Armstrong and Armstrong, 1984). The point to be stressed here is that the industries where females are concentrated are in the low productivity, low-wage sectors. For example, in 1982, the average weekly earnings of all employees in construction, where women made up 6.6 percent of all employees, was $558.86. Contrast this earning figure with the $260.63 average weekly earnings of service sector employees, where women constituted 40.9 percent of all employees (Armstrong and Armstrong, 1984:Table 3).

Occupational gender segregation means that the incumbents of the occupation are mostly one sex/gender or the other. (The related concept, occupational sex-typing, which was introduced in Chapter 4, reflects the idea that gender-segregated jobs are quite properly women's work or men's work.) According to analysis of census data by Fox and Fox (1987:390), occupational segregation remains

at a very high level: "over 60 per cent of men or women in the labour force in 1981 would have had to change occupational categories for the two genders to have had the same occupational distributions."

Table 8.1 shows the percentages for 1975 and 1985 of female and male workers in Statistics Canada occupational categories (which are more specific than and cut across the industrial sectors discussed above). In 1985, 73.6 percent of all female employees worked in the top five occupational groupings listed in Table 8.1 (clerical, service, sales, medicine and health,

TABLE 8.1

GENDER SEGREGATION IN CANADIAN OCCUPATIONAL GROUPS, 1975 AND 1985

	Women		Men		Women as a % of total Labour Force in Occupational Category
	1975	1985	1975	1985	1985
	%	%	%	%	
Clerical	36.1	31.1	6.9	5.9	79.7
Service	16.6	18.8	9.7	10.8	56.3
Sales	10.4	9.4	11.5	8.9	43.9
Medicine and health	9.5	8.6	1.7	1.8	78.2
Teaching	7.2	5.7	2.9	2.7	60.7
Managerial, administrative	3.4	8.3	8.4	12.6	32.9
Product fabricating, assembling and repairing	5.9	4.6	11.2	10.9	23.6
Agriculture	3.0	2.6	6.8	5.7	25.2
Social sciences	1.4	2.1	1.1	1.3	55.6
Processing and machining	2.2	2.0	9.0	8.1	26.2
Artistic and recreational	1.1	1.6	1.3	1.7	40.7
Natural sciences and engineering	0.8	1.3	4.7	5.0	16.3
Materials handling	1.3	1.1	3.3	3.3	19.5
Other crafts and equipment	0.5	0.6	1.8	1.7	21.4
Transport equipment operation	0.4	0.6	6.3	6.1	6.6
Construction trades	0.1	0.3	10.9	10.0	1.9
Religion	—	0.1	0.4	0.4	55.6
Forestry and logging, fishing, hunting and trapping	—	0.1	1.1	1.5	4.9
Mining and quarrying	—	—	0.9	1.0	—
Unclassified	—	1.1	—	0.6	61.7
Total	100.0	100.0	100.0	100.0	42.6
Total employed 000's	3381	5382	5903	7257	—

SOURCE: Adapted from Labour Canada *Women in the Labour Force*, 1987, Table I-17 and Statistics Canada *Women in Canada: A Statistical Report*, 1985, Table 6.

teaching). Three in ten Canadian women work in clerical occupations. This concentration represents only a six percentage point drop from what the proportion had been a decade earlier. By contrast, these five occupational groups involve only 30 percent of male workers. Though it is true that both sexes are occupationally segregated, men are found in a greater variety of occupational groupings. (It required eight occupational categories to encompass 75 percent of male employees in 1985). That is, women are more concentrated than men in a relatively small number of occupations (Armstrong and Armstrong, 1984).

With the large influx of women into the labour force, this main trend of persisting occupational gender segregation has been eroded slightly (Fox and Fox, 1987). Occupations involving more than 90 percent female or 90 percent male have declined over time. While women remain concentrated in traditionally female jobs, they have increased their share of jobs in all occupational groupings (Statistics Canada, 1985:43). As Table 8.1 shows, the female increase in administrative and managerial occupations more than doubled. Small numbers but significant proportions of women have entered occupations such as accounting, sales supervision, and advertising management, which formerly were almost exclusively male. "At the same time, a very small percentage of men (2.6 per cent) entered occupations less than 20 per cent male in 1971" (Fox and Fox, 1987:391).

Social scientists' interest in the gender segregation of work goes beyond describing the patterns, to asking the related questions: What causes it? What can be done about it? Do men end up in "male" work and women in "female" work out of free choice or discrimination? Put another way, does gender segregation stem from individual attitudes or structural barriers? The evidence clearly demonstrates that both types of factors are involved and interactive, that an "either-or" perspective is inappropriate. For example, males "'chose' not to enter schools of nursing because nursing was not deemed appropriate for men, and the training and work environment, both within institutions and in the community at large, had female orientations" (Peitchinis 1989:73).

Since attitudes are slow to change, and corporations have not responded to voluntary directives, the federal government passed the 1986 Employment Equity Act to compel equality of opportunity for women, visible ethnic minorities, and the disabled. That Act applies to Crown corporations and federally regulated employers with more than 100 employees. The Federal Contractors Program, passed at the same time, requires that all suppliers of goods and services who have 100 or more employees and who are bidding on contracts worth more than $200 000 commit themselves to employment equity principles. Government departments and affected corporations are required to file annual reports identifying the numbers of people they employ from disadvantaged groups. Failure to comply carries a maximum $50 000 penalty. When the first mandatory reports filed under the 1986 laws showed that women remain stuck on lower work rungs (*The Globe and Mail*, October 22, 1988:A2), the Canadian Human Rights Commission, which is responsible for enforcement of this legislation, required lax corporations such as the banks, Bell Canada, and the Canadian Broadcasting Corporation to file plans for the advancement of disadvantaged groups (*The Globe and Mail*, July 10, 1989). Peitchinis (1989:162) concludes that:

The Employment Equity Act (1986) may well provide the needed impetus for desegregation. But legislation cannot establish an *ethic* of equal opportunity. Standards of ethical behaviour are set by society and enforced by social expectations. Therefore, two developments must follow: first, the law must be enforced vigorously and consistently; second, the enforcement process must evolve new standards of behaviour—it must be educative....The Employment Equity Act (1986) should be viewed as the first step in the process of desegregation. It should be followed soon with legislation applicable to the economy and society at large—to all enterprises (commercial, industrial, institutional) regardless of size. (Emphasis in original.)

Recent polls show that Canadians are not sold on the Employment Equity Act. According to a Globe and Mail-CBC News Poll, a majority of Canadians—55 percent of men and 51 percent of women—disapprove of employers giving women preference in hiring over men in order to achieve better representation for women in the workplace (*The Globe and Mail*, February 12, 1990:A10).

Related Characteristics of Women's Paid Work

The foregoing section established that a major form of gender differentiation is segregation of jobs by sex. This segregation is attended by the following important features of women's versus men's labour force experiences.

INCOME AND BENEFITS

Earnings are probably the single most important indicator of women's labour market progress (Calzavara, 1985:521). In 1911, women earned 53 cents for every dollar men earned (Calzavara, 1985:524). In the 1980s, women continue to earn considerably less than men. "All studies indicate that the earning of women in full-time, full-year employment have averaged on the aggregate (all establishments, occupations, industries, and regions) at about 60 per cent of the earnings of men" (Peitchinis, 1989:54). In 1985, the average income of married women amounted to only 46.5 percent of that of married men, whereas single, divorced or widowed women achieved 88.4 percent of the average income of unmarried men (Labour Canada, 1987:37). In the same year, women with university degrees averaged an annual income just $1861 more than that of men who had only some post-secondary education (Labour Canada, 1987:36).

The above earning gaps close somewhat after work-productivity factors (e.g., education, training, experience) are controlled. A study of men and women in the Ontario legal profession concluded that some form of structural discrimination exists. "Controlling not only for background and schooling attributes but also the area of law one practices, women are underpaid with respect to their male counterparts" (Adam and Baer, 1984:4). Canadian women who do the same work in the same company earn from 10 to 20 per cent less than

men (Calzavara, 1985:521). Gender differences in income are largely attributable to the gender segregation of work, i.e., the clustering of women in the lower ranks of low-paying occupations (Ornstein, 1983). However, discrimination is responsible for an estimated five to ten percent of the earnings gap (Calzavara, 1985:525; Peitchinis, 1989:54).

The pay differences are associated with differences in fringe benefits. According to Labour Canada (1987:85), women continue to receive lower unemployment and Canada Pension Plan/Quebec Pension Plan benefits than their male counterparts. This situation is partly explained by women's interrupted labour force participation, their low earnings levels, and greater involvement in part-time work. Not only do women receive less pension money, fewer of them are covered by any pension scheme at all. "Underpaid while they have labour force jobs, many women have even less to look forward to when they retire (Armstrong and Armstrong, 1983:248).

AUTHORITY STRUCTURES

Most women lack control over their work. "In all sectors of the economy, women tend to follow directions set down by men, and their work is often a direct response or reaction to the work of men" (Armstrong and Armstrong, 1984:51). Many women work at dead-end jobs with few opportunities for promotion. Their "chances for advancement are further restricted by the frequent failure of employers to train female workers for management positions" (Armstrong and Armstrong, 1984:55). As a result, "most women end their working lives performing much the same tasks that they performed when they began work" (Smuts, 1971, quoted in Armstrong and Armstrong [1984:55]).

Despite the foregoing, there is some truth to the new image of women in the board room (Table 8.1). These administrative positions tend to be lower- and middle-management jobs. For example, in 1987, women held 72 percent of all full-time positions in Canadian banking. However, women accounted for 38.3 percent of all middle and other management jobs, and a "minuscule 2.9 per cent of upper-level manage-ment positions" (Fife, 1989). Armstrong and Armstrong (1983:13) argue that "the much-touted promotion of women into middle man-agement positions may merely mean more work with little increase in power, more re-sponsibility but no more authority."

In general, women have made slow progress into senior management positions in industry and government service. According to Peitch-inis (1989:68), the appropriate professional education, ambition, and hard work have not been enough to carry women into these top positions. When criteria for entry into execu-tive suites remain unstructured and undefined, the old boys' networks permit mainly "old boys" to get in. Most women get just so far up the corporate ladder before hitting the "glass ceiling" where they can see, but never reach, the top. From interviews with Canadian mana-gerial women, (Symons (1986:293) concludes:

In one sense...managerial women represent a force for change, in terms of desegregating the labour market and breaking down barriers to employment opportunities based on gender. However, viewed from another perspective, these women act as a source of stability of the organization, espousing its goals, and providing continuity and dedication on the part of the personnel. For those who expect radical changes engendered by the presence of women in managerial positions, the wait may be a long one. Perhaps these changes will come about as women increase in numbers and their presence as a group is felt. At the moment, they are represented among the managerial ranks as individuals, and hence, integration into the system is the order of the day. (Emphasis in original.)

INSTABILITY OF EMPLOYMENT

Unemployment entails economic costs and psychic pain for individuals and families, re-gardless of the sex/gender of the wage earners. The traditional linking of masculinity and work means that unemployment becomes de-fined as a flaw in the individual man, not the economy (Pleck, 1981). Nevertheless, we hy-pothesize that unemployment damages the self-regard of women as well as men.

Until the late 1960s, women's unemploy-

ment rates were consistently lower than men's. From the mid-1960s, women's rates started to creep upward. Through the entire decade of the 1970s, and through part of the 1980s, women's unemployment rates were higher than men's. In 1987, women's rates, especially for people over 25 years, remained slightly higher than men's. One reason for the instability in women's work is their predominance in part-time work. Work such as retail clerking is or-ganized on a part-time basis precisely because it is easier to lay off incumbents. Another rea-son is women's increasing attachment to labour force activity. As women's wages have become more vital to families as a result of inflationary economic forces and rising divorce rates, few women have the option of returning into the household with job loss (Peitchinis, 1989:126-27). Therefore, they declare themselves unem-ployed and looking for work. In other words, contemporary women's enhanced commit-ment to work outside the home means they can no longer exclude themselves from labour market statistics by disappearing into the home when they lose their jobs.

So far, men have suffered more directly from unemployment. The reason: male dominance in industries such as construction and oil, hard hit by 1980s unemployment and women's heavy employment by the state (Armstrong and Armstrong, 1988). However, women, who are clustered in subordinate, clerical jobs and, relatively speaking, excluded from profes-sional, scientific, and technical employment, appear to be most vulnerable to the future threats of the new computer technologies:

Computer technology is increasing employment opportunities in the occupations where women are least represented; on the other hand, it is diminishing employment opportunities in the clerical occupa-tions and in the related administrative and supervi-sory positions which women were using as career ladders (Menzies, 1984:292).

At the present time, female unemployment rates are only marginally higher than those of their male counterparts (Labour Canada, 1987:31). Nevertheless, feminists worry that women's hard-won labour force victories may be in jeopardy. In Armstrong's (1987:372) words, "Women's paid jobs are threatened by the new technology, by cutbacks in public spending, by the increases in part-time employment, by their position as last hired and thus first fired and by the high unemployment rates of men."

Unionization

Over the last decade, unions have been increasingly involved in addressing many of the gender-related labour force differentials discussed above. Between 1977 and 1982, women accounted for 86.5 percent of all new union members (Edelson, 1987:1). Women's membership has more than doubled since 1962. In 1984, the Canadian Labour Congress, the powerful umbrella labour group, "expanded its executive, designating five new positions as affirmative action seats for women leaders—providing an example which has since been repeated in other organizations" (Edelson, 1987:2). Two years later, Shirley Carr was elected head of the Canadian Labour Congress. Women employed as teachers, nurses, and in public administration now have union protection (White, 1980). Although the union movement has become a central arena for feminist activities, it was slow to afford help to working women's concerns (Baker and Robeson, 1981; Marchak, 1973). The main reason was the nature of women's work. White-collar workers and part-time workers are difficult for unions to organize. In addition, blue-collar male union leaders accepted the traditional ideology that women's place is in the home. It was seen as advantageous to keep cheap female labour out of the marketplace. As well, women's double burden of home and work responsibilities sometimes discouraged extensive union participation in after-hours activities.

Union members usually have more protection and better benefits than they would if unorganized (Armstrong and Armstrong, 1983:110). Though women now constitute a greater proportion of union members than ever before, considerable struggle was often needed to make unions responsive to women's particular needs (Edelson, 1987:2). Unionization has improved women's pay and decreased the male-female earnings differential (White, 1980). Unions are now beginning to negotiate for many of the improvements women have sought—childcare, paid parental leave, affirmative action, equal pay, to name a few (Edelson, 1987). They address the issue of sexual harassment of women in the workplace (Attenborough, 1983). Unions are also involved in the battle to desegregate the workplace. Attempts by individual women to enter high-paying, non-traditional occupations got nowhere. For example, it was discovered that 10 000 women (10 percent of all applicants) had applied at Stelco over a ten-year period. None of these women were hired. Campaigns involving women and unions organized in Hamilton, Fort Erie, and Sudbury achieved modest success in placing women in non-traditional industrial jobs (Johnston, 1981; Livingstone and Luxton, 1989).

As Briskin (1983:268) emphasizes, transforming unions to meet the needs of women workers presents a formidable task:

Women activists face two kinds of resistance in the union movement. One is resistance to us as women, a reflection of the patriarchal norms and values implicit in part of every institution in capitalist society. We expect this kind of resistance. The other form of resistance is not a particular resistance to us as women. It is a resistance to our militancy: to our challenge to the leadership, to our demand that the union movement take up issues outside the narrow framework of business unionism and that it operate with more democratic and accountable structures. Simply electing women, even if they have rank and file and feminist politics, will not solve the larger problems facing women unionists and the union movement.

Julie White's (1990) analysis of women in the Canadian Union of Postal Workers sheds light on many of the issues discussed in this section.

Immigrants, Gender, and the Workplace

Newcomers to Canada often experience great difficulties in their attempts to make a living. Ethnicity, like gender and social class, is a means of organizing people in Canadian society. As Ng (1981:97) says, "ethnicity is a social construction: it exists only in, and has no other basis than, the social relations, enacted by members of society, in their everyday activities." Although immigrants of both sexes frequently encounter problems in the workplace, women's gender disadvantage multiplies their difficulties. The situation of immigrant women, whose labour force participation rate is consistently higher than that of Canadian-born women (Ng and Estable, 1987:30), received recognition in *The Report of the Royal Commission on the Status of Women in Canada* (1970:357-64).

Although these problems have less to do with the women's diverse ethnic backgrounds than with the economic and legal arrangements of Canadian society, difficulties are exacerbated for immigrant women who come from Third World countries, who are women of colour, and/or do not speak English or French well (Ng and Estable, 1987:29). These women frequently work in private domestic and janitorial services and in the lower echelons of manufacturing industries, particularly the textile and garment industries (Ng, 1988:190). Many are low-paid and without fringe benefits or the protection of labour unions.

As Cassin and Griffith (1981:119) state:

The organization of the labor force is such that "male ethnic difference" has been somewhat better accommodated than "female ethnic difference." Men have had access to unionized work in production which has provided for relatively stable employment and wages, although it is important to recognize that there is marked internal segregation along "ethnic lines" in industry (e.g. East Indian persons in the forest industry in B.C. cf. Cassin, 1977). Women inhabit the "back rooms"; as dishwashers, maids, and garment workers.

The reader is directed to these sources for more information: Arnopoulos, *Problems of Immigrant Women in the Canadian Labour Force* (1979); Gannage, *Double Day, Double Bind: Women Garment Workers* (1986); and Warren, *Vignettes of Life: Experiences and Self Perceptions of New Canadian Women* (1986).

Current Developments in the Work Men and Women Do for Pay

Newspaper human interest stories and television sitcoms often showcase gender innovations in the workplace. The reason is obvious. Female lumberjacks and male secretaries are much more interesting than male lumberjacks and female secretaries. This section inquires into the prevalence of gender pioneers at work. Is the gender segregation of work really crumbling as the media sometimes suggest?

WOMEN IN THE PROFESSIONS

Women in the elite professions are prominent in the media, depicted "as models, as the 'superwomen' who 'have it all' in the present economic structure" (Ferree, 1987:326). How realistic is this imagery? It would be surprising if the changes in the educational choices women have made in recent years, as well as the extent to which barriers to entry into educational programs have been lowered, were not having some impact on the gender segregation of the workplace:

In 1961, women constituted only 7 per cent of the university enrolment in commerce and business administration, 0.7 per cent of the enrolment in engineering and applied science, 9.8 per cent of enrolment in medicine, and 5.3 per cent of the enrolment in law....By 1984, women earned (as opposed to merely being enrolled in) 38.2 per cent of the degrees in business administration, 8.5 per cent of the degrees in engineering, 37.8 percent of the degrees in medicine, and 41.6 per cent of the degrees in law! (Peitchinis, 1989: 142-43).

Notwithstanding the fact that the number of Canadian women in the 20 highest-paid occupations quadrupled between 1971 and 1981 (Peitchinis, 1989:143), the male-female ratios in the traditional male-dominated professions remain high: physicians 5:1, dentists 11:1, architects 12:1, lawyers 6:1, university professors 3:1 (Peitchinis, 1989:Table 7.4). (These statistics are for 1981.) Keep in mind that in the past 40 years, there has been an increase of only 1.4 percentage points in the proportion of women employed in professional and technical jobs combined, and most of these have gone into the lower level technical rather than the prestigious professions (Armstrong, 1989:123). In contrast, male concentration in the professions increased between 1971 and 1981 (Armstrong, 1989:123). Only 7.4 percent of Canadian women in the labour force hold professional and managerial positions (Duffy et al., 1989:19).

Since the control of organizations and professions remains in male hands, women have so far made only limited gains in the elite professions (Robinson and McIlwee, 1989). "What women are allowed to do remains limited and barriers still restrict their mobility in the professional world. In professions that are as male-dominated today as they were a decade ago, women are still likely to be overrepresented in low-paid and low-prestige subspecialities" (Kaufman, 1989:329).

There is no doubt that women fail to advance in the professions as quickly as their male counterparts. In 1989, controversy arose over the fact that American female executives with children were especially likely to remain on the bottom rungs of corporate ladders. New York consultant Felice Schwartz argued that companies should place these women on a special lower-paid, low-pressure career track, the "mommy track." The fast track would be reserved for men and "career-primary" women who won't allow children to interfere with their ambition (*Harvard Business Review*, January-February, 1989). Feminist critics Ehrenreich and English (1989:58) replied that,

In sum, the notorious "mommy track" article is a tortured muddle of feminist perceptions and sexist assumptions, good intentions and dangerous suggestions—unsupported by any acceptable evidence at all....Bumping women—or just fertile women, or married women, or whomever—off the fast track may sound smart to cost-conscious CEOs, but eventually it is the corporate culture itself that needs to slow down to a human pace.... Work loads that are incompatible [sic] with family life are themselves a kind of toxin—to men as well as women, and ultimately to businesses as well as families.

Besides, research shows that although professional women unencumbered with family responsibilities tend to be more successful, women lag behind men regardless of their marital status and presence of children (Andersen, 1988:121). One important reason is the social organization of professions. Social control in professional life, as well as access to rewards and learning of informal norms, typically operates through a sponsorship system feminists label the "old boys' network." Within the network, sponsorship by established mentors and social relations with peers can bring access to opportunities, information, and promotion. Women professionals are often excluded from these advantages. (Epstein, 1970).

Examination of the traditional female profession of nursing reveals a great deal about the reality of women's work at the end of the twentieth century. Fifty percent of the nursing staff at most Canadian hospitals is part-time. Night and weekend shifts are routine requirements. "Many nurses work two weeks of days followed by two weeks of nights: such scheduling means most women with children are frantic about child-care arrangements, in addition to coping with disruptions in sleep cycles and family life" (Steed, 1989:D5). Eighty per cent of the entire health-care work force is female, with registered nurses making up the largest group. Ninety-eight percent of nurses are women. The work is underpaid simply because women do it. According to the Ontario Hospital Association, physicians' average gross income is well over $200 000 per year. In comparison, nurses' average yearly salary is $35 000. Toronto plumbers earn $29 an hour; Ontario nurses (paid more than most nurses in Canada) earn $18.55 after seven years. Nurses "are leaving the profession in droves reminiscent of nuns abandoning convents in the 1960s, causing chaos in a system dependent on cheap female labor, resulting in closure of beds, waiting lists for surgery, apprehension" (Steed, 1989:D5). In 1988 and 1989, large, militant nurses' unions led strikes against Saskatchewan, Alberta, Ontario, British Columbia, and Quebec hospitals. These nurses want a fairer share of provincial health budgets. They want a significant role in hospital decision-making, now monopolized by doctors and hospital administrators. They want the option of working permanent days or nights. Finally, the nurses want fundamental re-definition of a service industry, where nurses are doctors' servants, "where women's work is never done and it's never paid for" (Steed, 1989:D5).

FEMALE PIONEERS IN MALE BLUE-COLLAR PRESERVES

Truck drivers "are often glorified as highway cowboys—hard-living, hard-drinking boys who like their rigs, booze and gals in that order. But truckers may soon be packing more Vogues than Playboys and more curling irons than razors." So begins a recent newspaper story about Doreen Miller who followed her late husband into the long-distance trucking business (Livingstone, 1988). The reason shared by Ms. Miller and many other women seeking access to traditional masculine blue-collar work: the lure of decent wages. How successful have such attempts been?

Though almost every imaginable sort of work is now done by both sexes, very few women have managed so far to invade skilled trade apprenticeships and well-paying industrial jobs. According to the Canadian Council of Directors of Apprenticeship, fewer than four percent of Canadian apprentices pursuing trades such as bricklaying or carpentry are women (*The Globe and Mail*, January 10, 1990:A1). Table 8.1 shows women to be working in construction, mining, fishing, and trapping. However, this information requires interpretation. Two-thirds of the women employed in the construction industry in fact do clerical work. And more than three-fifths of the women in "fishing, hunting and trapping, and mining are typing, filing, sorting, answering phones and making coffee" (Armstrong and Armstrong, 1983:7). A large number of women are involved in factory work. However, women have not increased their share of the highly skilled and paid machining industries. Instead, most women are to be found in the lower paid jobs in labour-intensive food and clothing manufacturing industries (Armstrong and Armstrong, 1983:9). "Furthermore, the few women who have managed to capture jobs in construction, mining, quarrying, or oil drilling are increasingly facing unemployment as these sectors reduce their labour force in many regions and as women, the last hired, are the first to be fired" (Armstrong, 1989:123). Despite the

few pioneers, gender segregation remains the main pattern between and within industrial sectors. (See Harlan and O'Farrell, 1982).

Gender segregation is enforced by the biased attitudes of both company officials and workers. Westinghouse worker Stan Gray (1987) says the women "worked at more demanding jobs in terms of monotony, speed and work discipline. They got lower pay for that, were frequently laid off while junior males stayed on; they were denied chances for promotion and training at more skilled work. In their eyes, the majority of male workers were treated like privileged babies by the company and would not help them out" (p. 379). Sexism co-existed with workers' trade-union solidarity.

Leslie Martin, who did participant observation as a labourer in a Yukon lead/zinc/silver mine employing 27 women among 581 workers, describes the difficulties these women had in coping with a work culture that celebrates masculinity and devalues women. She says:

Attention to sexual differentiation is articulated daily at work: virtually every time a female voice is heard over the pit radio communications system, prolonged and squeaky kissing sounds fill the air waves. Through ever-recurring sexual banter, women are frequently reminded of their presence in a predominantly masculine work culture.... Reference is often made by the men to the women's physical appearance and bodies. One newly hired woman labourer made the unfortunate error of wearing light-coloured jeans to work one night in the mill. Dust and dirt from the milling process is impossible to avoid, and after she had sat down on some stairs to rest after a bout of vigorous shovelling, two prominent patches were highly visible on the seat of her jeans. For the rest of the shift, she was subjected to a barrage of teasing about her "nice ass" and about where she had been spending her graveyard shift: "It's real clear that you've been flat on your backside, but the big question is, who was the lucky guy on top?" In short, sexual innuendo, expressed in a way that "objectifies" women as sexual material, is a most noticeable component of work relations between the women and men (Martin, 1986:252).

Despite the foregoing, Martin concludes the other factors besides gender discrimination are equally important in understanding women's experience in jobs that are conventionally men's. Such structures as shift work, crew membership, job classifications, and seniority, which cut across gender stratification, act to transcend the masculinity of the mining environment. In other words, "women mineworkers experience work to a considerable extent in the same way that men do, as mineworkers, and not always in terms of being females in a masculine domain" (Martin, 1986:264).

Since financial remuneration, fringe benefits, authority, and adventure reward the incumbents of some (but of course, not all) of men's traditional work roles, women challenge the structural barriers of occupational segregation. Our last example concerns the male bastion of military services. According to military historians (Simpson et al., 1979:271), the sole purpose for putting Canadian women into uniform during World War II was to release men for combat duties. Women were used primarily in communication, administrative, logistic, and medical support roles. With the passing of the crisis, women were demobilized. The 1970 Royal Commission on the Status of Women sought standardization of enrollment criteria and benefits and the opening of all military occupations to women. In 1979, Canadian military colleges were opened to women. In 1987, Colonel Sheila Hellstrom, a personnel administration officer with 30 years of service, became the first female Brigadier-General in the Canadian Forces. The notion of women in combat roles aroused considerable resistance from rank-and-file soldiers. The women haven't the strength and endurance to carry heavy machine guns and ammunition across rough terrain! They would not be able to withstand strong gravitational forces during high-speed jet manoeuvres! Delicate feminine temperaments render them unsuitable for bloody combat! Besides, their presence in combat would endanger male soldiers in mixed units, who would have their attention diverted from the enemy by the need to rescue their female cohorts. Be that as it may, in 1989, the Canadian Human Rights Commission found no justification for keeping women out of any branch of the armed forces. The tribunal ruled that all combat positions, except aboard submarines where privacy is limited, must be opened to women (*The Globe and Mail*, February 22, 1989).

Although most are in non-combat roles, women now serve in artillery regiments, as pilots for CF-18 Hornet fighter jets, in military police platoons, in isolated Arctic research stations, and with peace-keeping forces (*The Globe and Mail*, March 2, 1989). Women now comprise 10 percent of Canadian Forces personnel; they serve equally as officers and non-commissioned members (*The Globe and Mail*, February 16, 1990:A9).

MALES IN FEMALE-ORIENTED WORK

For reasons that are already obvious to the reader, males are less likely than females to aspire to jobs non-traditional for their sex/gender (Marini and Brinton, 1984:200). As we have stressed, women's work brings fewer rewards and opportunities for advancement. As well, males are socialized much more strongly than females to avoid other-gender work. Men who end up in work that has been stereotyped as feminine lose status by doing so. In extreme cases, their masculinity becomes questioned. For example, sociologist Mary Dietz (1981:9) says, "The usual response when I tell people that my son is a ballet dancer is 'How nice' and a rapid change of subject." According to Dietz, the public typifies danseurs as "effeminate, and latent or overt homosexuals" (p. 26).

For the reasons enumerated above, women are more likely than men to be gender pioneers in the workplace. Nevertheless, economic forces sometimes override gender considerations. Armstrong and Armstrong (1987:218) note that high unemployment in traditionally masculine work sectors has encouraged some men to search for opportunities in "feminine" areas. For example, "more men have moved into traditional female jobs in teaching than have women into the traditional male areas of medicine, law, architecture, and engineering combined" (Armstrong, 1989: 123). Indeed, it has long been accepted for men to move into the top administrative positions in the traditionally female professions of teaching, social work, and library science (Richardson, 1988:174).

Clerical work provides our final example of

gender pioneers in the workplace. Although the turn-of-the-century office was largely a male preserve (Lowe, 1980), the contemporary office is the prototypical female job ghetto. One-third of the women in the Canadian labour force do clerical work (Armstrong, 1984). Clerical work tends to be poorly paid, non-unionized work. The work tends to be stereotypically feminine, with men giving orders and women taking them. For example, the role of the secretary shares several characteristics with that of the traditional wife. The secretary is linked with her boss in a patrimonial relationship. Like the traditional wife, the secretary serves her boss. Her status is contingent on that of her boss, whose power may determine her own. Loyalty and devotion to her employer may be the basis for her rewards (Andersen, 1988:123; Kanter, 1977).

What can we learn about male gender pioneers in the workplace from studying male secretaries? First of all, as we might expect, very few males have invaded the pink-collar ghetto of clerical work. According to *The Globe and Mail* (Motherwell, 1987), an estimated two percent of Canadian secretaries are men. Second, male secretaries get considerable firsthand experience with gender stereotypes. While women are often encouraged to enter work that was previously male-dominated, many people think there's something wrong with a man who takes on "women's work." Therefore, Guirano Toppetta, 30, who fills in at the reception desk at the Canadian Institute of Chartered Accountants, has had people mutter about having reached a wrong number, only to call again and suddenly realize that the man on the telephone is actually the switchboard operator. Sometimes, when he answers the phone, he is greeted by silence. Other callers insist on speaking with the secretary, unable to comprehend that a man could have that job (Motherwell, 1987).

Third, when men do clerical work the job undergoes redefinition. "When a woman becomes a secretary, she usually handles the phone, files and types. A male secretary does budgeting and research and is called an executive assistant. They're being assigned different components of the same job" (Locherty, 1989:10). As we saw earlier, women's work is typically dead-end work. When men enter the office, men's jobs are designed to allow upward mobility from entry level to management positions (Locherty, 1989). Interestingly, none of the male secretaries interviewed by *The Globe and Mail* (Motherwell, 1987) planned to make secretarial work a lifelong career.

Conclusions about Gender and Paid Work

Although the social science literature dealing with gender pioneers in the workplace, especially pioneers of the male variety, is not plentiful, several conclusions are in order. First, the media tend to exaggerate the number of people who challenge occupational sex-typing. Second, these innovators are more likely to be women than men. Given the unrewarding nature of "women's work," its failure to interest men is understandable. Third, professional work has been the site for innovators of both sexes. Women have used higher education as an effective conduit into the male-dominated professions. For example, women now account for 51 percent of the pharmacists in Canada (*The Globe and Mail*, March 2, 1988). Male pioneers show more interest in the better paid sorts of women's work in the helping professions, especially the administrative jobs at the top. Fourth, work often undergoes some redefinition when the sex ratio of workers shifts. Actual job descriptions may change, as seems to be the case with clerical jobs. Also, the prestige accorded the work may alter. Stereotypically feminine work taken over by males gains status, while traditionally "men's" work invaded by females loses status. In Miller's (1988:330) words, "irrespective of demonstrated value, the structural position of women's jobs itself lowers the worth attached to the work and ultimately the incumbent."

Finally, in recent years, self-employment has become an important career choice for people of both sexes (Martin, 1989). Between 900 000 and one million Canadians run their own businesses. In 1981, 20 percent of business owners were women. Between 1981 and 1986, the number of self-employed women rose by 27 percent, while the number of self-employed men increased by just 7 per cent (*The Globe and*

Mail, March 2, 1988). Although most businesses remain in male hands, a growing number of female entrepreneurs are finding alternatives to corporate gender discrimination. Says a U.S. House of Representative Small Business Committee (*Time* magazine July 4, 1988): "Women have had to work harder, wait longer, manage with fewer dollars and be content with smaller operations just to maintain their present levels of independence and business success." Despite such barriers, enterprises begun by women are having an increasingly significant impact on the economies of the United States and Canada.

Despite the very real changes that are occurring, the dominant motif remains continuity of the segregated work structures. For most, the much-heralded movement of women into the labour force has meant more of the same kind of work. "Paid or unpaid, women scrub floors, serve food, sort laundry, mind children, make coffee or clothes, answer the telephone or wait on people" (Armstrong and Armstrong, 1983:7). Although both sexes often face poor working conditions, women remain "more concentrated in the least rewarded and least rewarding work" (Armstrong and Armstrong, 1983:2). The proportion of women "with good jobs and good pay has risen only slightly over the last 40 years" (Armstrong and Armstrong, 1987:216). Andersen (1988:103) provides an apt summary of gendered work structures from the perspective of women.

[W]omen's role in economic life has been obscured by social myths about the work that women do. These myths include the idea that women who work at home as full-time housewives are not working; that women who work for wages work for extra money, not because they must; and that women's work is not as valuable as men's. As a result, women's work has been undervalued both in its objective rewards and in the ideas we have about women and work. Furthermore, because women's work has been seen as less important than men's it has not, until recently, been seriously studied.

We turn now to a discussion of the social organization of the hidden work done in the household and by volunteers.

GENDER AND UNPAID WORK

A seemingly anomalous dimension of our materialistic society is the existence of many activities of great significance to this society that are performed in the context of family life or voluntary organizations, rather than as compensated, routine occupational responsibilities (Oldham, 1979). First, volunteer work, with its less obvious gender implications, and then, household labour will be discussed in turn. As we shall see, both these types of unpaid labour are intimately connected with paid labour in our society.

Volunteer Work

"There probably isn't a job listed in the Directory of Occupations that hasn't been done somewhere by someone as a volunteer" (Barry, 1987:60). It seems odd that in a society such as ours that prizes paid labour force activity, large numbers of people of both sexes donate their time and skills to guide visitors through museums, raise funds for cancer, deliver Meals-on-Wheels, comfort the dying in hospices, operate crisis hot lines, pack groceries for food banks, take youngsters to movies as Aunts and Uncles-at-large, etc. While we cannot take time to thoroughly discuss all aspects of voluntarism, suffice it to say that individuals, as well as their communities, derive various sorts of rewards from voluntary work. Our present interest lies in the connections of volunteerism to gender, and its linkages with labour force activity.

The ties between volunteerism and the women's movements extend back into the nineteenth century, when a volunteer tradition developed among leisure-class women who worked for their own interests and the betterment of the larger society. Although the manifest function of women's voluntary associations was to do good, they constituted, in effect, surrogate and respectable careers for women bored with the loneliness and isolation of domestic life. These philanthropic organizations "gave women practice in drawing up constitutions and bylaws, in electing officers, in arranging meetings, in assigning duties, in managing funds" (Bernard, 1981a:305). Membership also contributed to women's gender consciousness, as women extended their sense of solidarity beyond kin and neighbours (Bernard, 1981b:306). Therefore, we are not surprised that such women's organizations as the Women's Christian Temperance Union played an important role in the Women's Suffrage Movement. In the 1960s, the established network of women's voluntary associations (some, but not all addressing themselves to "charity work") again played a critical role in the movement to enhance the status of women (Errington, 1988:66). In recent years, women's organizations have become "victims of their own success." "As access has opened up to government, the workplace, and the courts, women's clubs are no longer the primary path to fulfillment or power" (*Time*, May 30, 1989:73).

In view of the foregoing, it is ironical that the initial response of feminists of the 1960s and 1970s was to register "almost total condemnation of volunteer work" (Mueller, 1975:334). According to this earlier feminist opinion, volunteer work serves the interests of capitalism by keeping hardworking women from realizing cash for their efforts. In an early article, Gold (1971:552) documented that more than three-quarters of the volunteers in large American urban centres were women. She argued that the appeal of a then-popular poster proclaiming 'VOLUNTEERING IS BEAUTIFUL' "is directly bound up with one of the oldest, most subtle, most complicated ways in which women have been disengaged from the economy with their own eager cooperation ..." (p. 533). In their opinion, when women obey their traditional cultural directive to serve others, "a dizzying catalog" of vital societal tasks were handled free of charge; women, who might otherwise compete against men in the marketplace, were thereby kept busy elsewhere. A related concern was that the volunteer work done by middle-class housewives deprived poorer women of paid jobs.

Contemporary feminist interest in volunteerism reflects changing economic and social climates. Gone are the days when volunteering was the province of stay-at-home housewives. Although volunteer work attracts people of both sexes and all ages, most volunteers are middle-class women, under 60 years of age. The majority now hold full-time jobs (though homemakers still make up a substantial part of the volunteer population) (Gee and Kimball, 1987:73-74). That individual volunteers, as well as their communities, gain from these activities has become better recognized. For example, university students and housewives often look to volunteer work as a source of skills and experience that might impress future employers. After Nell Sawyer dropped out of full-time teaching for a short time to raise two small children, she joined a volunteer tutoring program for children with cancer. She says of the experience:

"The children were highly motivated, but some were very, very sick. Some days I just read aloud. Sometimes I just went in and held their hands." In addition to the emotional gratification Nell got from helping the children, she recognized that the job was "a way for me to keep my finger in the pie" (Barry, 1987:64).

The intent is not to deny volunteers' altruistic motives. See Daniels (1988) for a sympathetic sociological analysis of the service performed by full-time volunteers. Rather, our point is that previous feminist worries about the misdirection of women's energy and ambition were allayed through better understanding of the non-monetary pay-off received by people of both sexes.

Today, feminists' main concern with voluntary organizations (including those whose manifest function is philanthropy) is the role they play in buttressing the gender segregation of society. From empirical research of the American situation, McPherson and Smith-Lovin (1986:77) conclude that, "In sum, the voluntary sector tends to reflect the sex segregation in other domains of our society. It divides men and women into separate domains even more effectively than does the occupational structure."

As women have entered the labour force in large numbers, their interest has grown in the instrumental pay-off long associated with men's voluntary activities, including "networking" (a buzzword of the 1970s). One response was to start their own groups. An example is The Calgary Women's Network, which advertises that it meets for breakfast in the Westin Hotel "on the first and third Wednesday of each month to share ideas and develop friendships and business contacts." Another is the Toronto women's club, Twenty-One McGill, according to writer Martin Knelman (1986:62):

...Twenty-One McGill (now the McGill Club), according to *Saturday Night*, was viewed as a triumphantly cheeky rebuttal to male power bastions. Women who felt excluded from the snug palaces of male bonding and networking now had a place of their own to exercise, hold meetings, or, as everyone made a point of mentioning, swim nude in the pool.

Another strategy has been to challenge the sex segregation of men's organizations. Within recent years, newspaper headlines have highlighted feminists' concern about women being left out of some of the important benefits that result from meeting with others to do "good works." Business and professional women reasoned that all-male service clubs functioned as "old boys' clubs," channelling useful opportunities to their members. In response to the feminist challenge (and a shortage of male prospects), the Lions Club, Kiwanis, and Jaycees have all dropped their ban against women members. Rotary International is considering a similar move in light of a 1988 decision of the Ontario Human Rights Commission that excluding women constitutes discrimination (*The Globe and Mail*, August 14, 1987; *Calgary Herald*, July 3, 1988).

Domestic Labour

Despite the dramatic influx of women into paid employment, one-third of the married women in Canada remain full-time housewives (Duffy et al., 1989:46). Moreover, most women with paid work continue to shoulder the primary responsibility for domestic labour (Clark and Harvey, 1976; Horna and Lupri, 1987; Luxton, 1980; Meissner et al., 1975) As Fox (1988:135), among others, has emphasized, "the gender difference correspond(s) to the most significant division of work—that between unpaid, privatized and paid, socialized work..."

The tasks involved in *domestic labour* may be divided into four categories: *housework* (the household tasks performed inside and outside the home, e.g., dishwashing, vacuuming, laundry, repairs, yardwork, car maintenance); *child care* (e.g., feeding, protecting, teaching, entertaining children); *support work* (Coverman, 1989) (maintaining the emotional well-being of family members, e.g., forging and maintaining cross-household kin ties through visits, phone calls, greeting cards, organizing holiday celebrations [di Leonardo, 1987]); and *status production* (Papanek, 1979) (work that maintains and enhances the family's social standing, e.g., assisting a spouse's career through secretarial skills, home entertainment, charity activities). Discussion here will follow the lead of the empirical literature which has dealt mainly with the first two types.

The second wave of the feminist movement exposed the hidden labour performed in the household. If life is to proceed smoothly, someone has to prowl supermarket aisles in search of fresh broccoli, someone has to cook dinner, someone has to scrub toilet bowls, someone has to wipe children's runny noses. That that someone is usually the female partner in marriages and other relationships has been a major theme in the discourse of both feminist activism and scholarship. As expressed by Bem and Bem (1971:88), regardless of individual variation in talent and inclination, society consigns "a large segment of the population to the role of homemaker solely on the basis of sex [gender]."

Most of the early writings about the housewife painted a negative picture of the role. Betty Friedan's *The Feminine Mystique* (1963) publicized the plight of the post-World War II suburban housewife, who suffered from the "problem that has no name." Women socialized to "desire no greater destiny than to glory in their own femininity, afraid to ask themselves 'Is this all?'" (p. 13), were saying "I feel empty somehow...incomplete" or "I feel as if I don't exist" (p. 18). Feminist sociologists took up this negative theme. In an oft-quoted phrase, sociologist Jessie Bernard (1972:42) spoke of women "dwindling into wives." She described the housewife as "victim" and the circumstances attending her work as "pathogenic" (1974). A number of studies which focussed on housewives' attitudes towards their job reported that though aspects of it (e.g., child care, cooking) could be rewarding (Lopata, 1971), many women found the actual household work monotonous and boring (Oakley, 1984). "But unlike paid jobs that are routine, menial, and boring, domestic work is unending and uncontrollable" (Coverman, 1989:356). Women around the world would agree with this Flin Flon, Manitoba housewife: "The worst thing about cleaning this house is that it's endless. I scrub and dust and tidy and then I turn around and it's a mess again" (Luxton, 1980:151). Another key difference between labour force employment and domestic labour is the fact that many women have difficulty separating the self from the housework that "sucks you into itself as a person rather than a 'worker'" (Rowbotham, 1973: 71), so that "its space is the whole space of a woman's life" (p. 70). Naturally, there are compensations. Housewives' domestic labour differs from wage labour in that the work is usually for people who care about them.

As the focus of the work is the maintenance of the household and the people who live in it, it becomes a vehicle by which women express affection ... for their household members. Cooking a nice meal, providing clean sheets or eliminating dull, yellow floor wax become ways of expressing love (Luxton, 1980:159).

Perhaps even more important than these attitudinal studies of housewives' perceptions of their lives are the structural analyses of domestic labour referred to earlier in this chapter. This structural approach seeks to establish the linkages between the organization of the household and the organization of capitalist society, and to delineate the structural features of domestic labour. For early Canadian analyses, see Smith (1977b) and Fox (1980).

Under capitalism, women's chief productive role is relegated to the household, which is separate from the marketplace where capitalism's dominant mode of production occurs. This privatized household labour pays no wages and confers on the worker little social recognition. Instead, it is presented as a labour of love and interwoven as personal commitment to family members (Fox, 1980:12-13). Despite these sharp contrasts with wage labour, domestic labour is of immense impor-

tance to capitalism: "it not only produces the next generation, it also produces and continually reproduces the working capacity of the wage earner(s)" (p. 13).

...the worker could not return to work without the material and emotional rejuvenation he or she experiences at home, at the end of each day. Should he or she fail to recover, at home, from the daily wear and tear of work, his or her work capacity and even his or her life expectancy will shrink (Fox, 1980:13).

One of the greatest achievements of the structural perspective, inspired by the women's movement, was the elevation to visibility of unpaid domestic activities and their definition as productive *work*, to be counted as labour in the economies of family and larger society (di Leonardo, 1987; Eichler, 1978). See also Eichler, 1977; Lopata, 1971; Luxton, 1980; Oakley, 1974. Since women have traditionally been responsible for most (but not all) domestic work, feminists reasoned that: "Any attempt to upgrade the social and economic status of women requires that their major activities—housework and childcare—be acknowledged as legitimate productivity activity." (Alexander, 1979:204). Indeed, economists who responded to feminist pressure to put a dollar value on household work concluded that household work contributes more than one-third to Canada's GNP (*Canadian Social Trends*, Autumn 1986:42). If household labour had to be purchased in the marketplace, the economic costs to society would be enormous (Proulx, 1978).

The importance of pinning dollar values on domestic labour lies in the connection thus established between paid and unpaid labour. Eichler's (1985b:539) explanation of this point is worth quoting at length:

The performance of paid labour rests on a foundation of work that is currently largely unpaid but nevertheless crucial to the maintenance of a paid labour force. If people do not eat, clothe themselves, have shelter, get tended when sick, etc., they will not be able to perform paid labour. If children do not get raised, they will not be available to join the labour force as adults, resulting in a labour force totally consisting of adult immigrants. Such personal maintenance and rearing involves work on somebody's part, which is sometimes visible (e.g. when people eat in a cafeteria and pay for it, stay in hospitals in case of acute sickness, use daycare centres) and sometimes invisible (when they eat at home, are looked after at home during illness, or raise their children at home). In Marxist terms, this work process is referred to as the production and reproduction of the labour force.

Eichler (1985b:540) goes on to remark that now that the majority of wives have withdrawn from full-time housewifery, and families are buying daycare services, take-home and restaurant food, etc., the fiction that unpaid labour in the home has no economic value has been exposed.

There were several practical reasons why the women's movement sought to enhance the visibility of domestic labour and to gain societal acknowledgement that it constitutes legitimate work with economic value. One reason certainly was an attempt to enhance women's self-esteem, especially that of full-time housewives.

Second, such acknowledgment was a prerequisite for securing legal recognition of wives' contributions to the family enterprise. Until the late 1970s, most provinces had family property laws that ignored this contribution. For instance, the Supreme Court of Canada ruled that Irene Murdoch, an Alberta farm wife, "was not entitled to any share in her husband's ranching business on the grounds that she had made 'only a normal contribution as a wife to the matrimonial regime'" (Bourne, 1976, quoted in Armstrong and Armstrong, 1984:73). As a result of objections of the women's movement to the Murdoch case and others, new provincial property laws concerning the breakup of marriages now entitle the wife to an equal share in family assets. However, as Armstrong and Armstrong (1984:73) point out, "A wife can now claim half the family's property, but if her husband dies or simply disappears, a wife's housework does not qualify her for unemployment insurance of Canada/Quebec Pension, for she has not been 'employed.'"

Third, feminists argued that women's traditional responsibility for most child care and household chores has severely disadvantaged their labour force participation. As noted in previous chapters, the cultural script directing young girls' attention to marriage and family discourages preparation for satisfying, rewarding, life-long wage work. Consequently, their early career plans "appear to have been short-term, itinerant, contingent and vague..." (Duffy et al., 1989:27). As one young woman told researcher Nancy Mandell (Duffy et al., 1989:27):

"I don't know if I had any plans, really, Actually, I thought somewhere along the line I would probably get married, work for a couple of years and then stay home, like everybody else seemed to be doing. You know, with nursing you can always get a part-time job."

After marriage, the domestic responsibilities carried by women in addition to their outside employment amount to a second full-time job for many women. Remember that economic need gives most families no choice in this matter. The fact that many women carry a double work burden acts to limit their ability to commit themselves fully and continuously to their paid employment. According to Statistics Canada research (Burch, 1985:26), the "exigencies of marriage, pregnancy and child care had a major impact on the continuity of work for a majority of women, but almost no impact for men." Clearly, women's traditional double burden constitutes part of the explanation for the fact that the majority of Canadian women remain stuck in dull, repetitious, low-paid, unattractive jobs (Armstrong and Armstrong, 1984: 201). Despite the fact that young women still curtail their education in order to give precedence to being wife and mother, significant numbers end up being sole support of their children.

As Luxton (1986:33) states, "the changing patterns of paid employment are creating a crisis in the way labour is currently distributed and accomplished in the family household." This point will be pursued further in Chapter 9 in a section dealing with familial division of labour. Particular attention will then be paid to the pressure being experienced by male partners to assume a more equitable share of household work. As Coverman (1989:356) observes, because domestic labour "is essential to daily functioning, the allocation of household chores often is a subject of difficult negotiation and conflict among household members."

CONCLUSIONS

This chapter and the next complete the trilogy of perspectives on gender: the biological, the social-psychological, and the social-structural approaches. This last perspective postulates that the main source of stereotypically feminine and masculine traits and behaviour is located in males' more privileged access to power, opportunities, education, high-status occupations, financial resources, etc., and *not* in the sexes' distinctive biological makeup or socialization experiences. Although a full understanding of gender relations requires all three levels of explanation, the social structural approach is sociology's special contribution to the scholarship on gender.

After a preliminary review of the concepts of social structure, social stratification, and gender stratification, the remainder of Chapter 8 explored the inter-relationships between gender and both paid and unpaid work. If one aspect of social life can be said to dominate structural explanations of social behaviour, it is the organization of production in the labour force and in the home (Miller, 1988:327). Despite dramatic changes in the way work is accomplished, such as the massive movement of women into the labour force since World War II, and computerized technology, women remain disadvantaged in the workplace. Moreover, domestic labour remains primarily the responsibility of women. "The organization of the labour market creates and reinforces the conditions under which women are exploited as unpaid workers at home and as paid workers in the labour force" (Duffy et al., 1989:12). The inequality of the sexes in the ways in which work is organized conditions women's inequality in the other institutions of society. The next chapter pursues this analysis of structured gender inequality through examination of the family.

NOTES

1. There are a variety of approaches in sociology to the study of social structure. While social structure "nearly always includes the concepts that there are differences in social positions, that there are social relations among these positions, and that people's positions and corresponding roles influence their social relations," no consensus exists on whether it is appropriate to include the cultural dimension (Blau, 1977:27). Although Parsons distinguishes social systems from cultural systems, "his theoretical explanation of social relations and interaction is in terms of values orientations..." (Blau, 1977:27). Mayhew (1980) argues that the cultural dimension should be excluded altogether. However, Udy's (1968) usage, adopted in Chapter 8, is consistent with feminist analysis in this country. In his editorial introduction to the *Canadian Review of Sociology and Anthropology's* State of the Art issue on Sociology in Anglophone Canada, Jackson (1985:617) notes that feminist scholarship in this country incorporates both cultural and morphological aspects of structuralism. In his words, "Feminism as a paradigm rather than a category describing all and any work dealing with the condition of women, borrows from both political economy and structuralism with strong overtones of critical sociology and phenomenology." Although subjective definitions of the situation implied by the phenomenological strand of feminist sociology do not constitute social structure, ideology and patriarchy are part of what is here labelled the cultural component of structure. This dual orientation also characterizes the content of the May 1988 (volume 25:2) special issue of the *Canadian Review of Sociology and Anthropology* on feminist scholarship.

2. Nettler (1970) tells us that "explanations are manipulations of symbols performed in an attempt to satisfy curiosity" [emphasis deleted] (p. 1). Further, a distinguishing characteristic of the scientific explanation is its "self-conscious use of facts as the building blocks, the elements, of its story." Empathetic and ideological explanations, by contrast, "talk to the heart" (p. 87).

3. Source: CBC 1010 Calgary, "The Good Question," June 20, 1990.

4. Extensive use was made in the section dealing with feminist explanations of women's oppression of Jaggar and Rothenberg (1984) and Wilson (1982:35-48).

Chapter 9

A Structural Perspective on Family and Aging

Our treatment of the family as agent of gender socialization in Chapter 5 focussed on the contributions of youngsters' experiences with parents and siblings to learning to become female or male persons. From time to time, comments were made about the structural context of socialization, for instance, the section on the impact of social class upon the family as socialization agent. Chapter 9 shifts the emphasis from the individual neophyte located in social organization, to the structure itself. People's subjective response to organizational exigencies, while still important, becomes secondary.

Chapter 9 deals with the family as structural determinant of gender. Our point of reference is patriarchy, the traditional form of family organization in which men are dominant over women. Ideologies concerning the family institution, norms guiding relations among family members, and between the family and other institutions have all undergone drastic change over the past quarter century. Among the causes for this change mentioned in Chapter 5 were the entry into the labour force of large numbers of women and the rise in marital dissolution. Complete analysis of the complex reasons for, and consequences of, this revolution of the family falls within the province of the sociology of the family. As students of gender relations, our more circumscribed concern is with the manner in which the structured inequality of the family produces and reproduces gender. For more comprehensive discussion of the Canadian family, readers are invited to consult these recent sources: Baker (1990a), Eichler (1988), Lupri (1990), Mandell and Duffy (1988), Nett (1988), Ramu (1989).

Prior to the re-emergence of the feminist movement in the early 1970s, sociologists considered the family to be the domain of women and children. For that reason, most pre-1970s sociological attention to women was confined to family studies (Epstein, 1988:187). Men, on the other hand, were seldom thought about in relation to families (Wilson, 1982:32). Instead, sociologists studied males in the context of such public spheres as work and politics. The arrival of the feminist movement produced extensive revision in the accepted sociological wisdom about the roles played by both men and women, inside and outside families. Gloria Steinem (1983b:24) urged participants at a University of Manitoba conference:

We must not continue to pattern ourselves deeply into the beliefs that, as men, we cannot be loving and nurturing towards our children in the way that women can; and that, as women we cannot be competent and assertive in the world outside the home in the same way that men can.

Along with questioning the traditional role arrangements of families, feminist scholars identified the power relations underlying these arrangements. This approach to the family

...describes the relationships between men and women in the context of a structure of domination conceptualized as patriarchy, the political and social control of women by men. It is suggested that processes of control and domination come into play whenever men and women interact. Consequently, patriarchy includes an internal stratification of family life, in which men have greater power and control and receive more benefits than women (Cheal, 1989:23).

Feminists from a variety of scholarly disciplines, in conjunction with several prominent mainstream social scientists (e.g., Goode 1963, 1982), have produced a radical rethinking of the family. It is the intent of Chapter 9 to review this new structural understanding of the family.

In this chapter, we will consider first, the changing meanings of the family. Families have altered greatly in the past two or three decades as a result of the changing economic and demographic circumstances discussed in Chapter 5. The family has also been affected by criticisms registered by the feminist movement. After this discussion, the contributions of feminist scholarship to mainstream sociology's perspectives on the family will be considered. Next, we examine how the changing social structure of the family impinges differently upon women and men. This topic includes consideration of such matters as familial power, the sharing of domestic labour, parenthood, and marriage dissolution. The chapter ends with a discussion of gender and aging.

THE CHANGING MEANING OF THE CANADIAN FAMILY

— Karen Andrews, a Toronto lesbian, is waging a battle to obtain family coverage for her partner and her partner's children under the Ontario Health Insurance Plan. She is appealing an Ontario Supreme Court ruling that legally a spouse is someone of the opposite sex.
— In April 1989, a tribunal of the Canadian Human Rights Commission ruled that the Treasury Board discriminated against a civil servant when it denied him bereavement leave to attend the funeral of his male partner's father. It said gay couples may constitute a family and the couple, who have a longstanding relationship, had been discriminated against on the basis of family status (Rauhala, 1989).

The possibility that gay and lesbian couples may be family units illustrates one of many complicated situations that sociologists encounter when they attempt to establish the meaning of the contemporary family.

In 1963, Stephens provided a well-known definition of the modern family "as a social arrangement based on marriage and the marriage contract, including recognition of the rights and duties of parenthood, common residence for husband, wife, and children, and reciprocal economic obligations between husband and wife." Twenty-five years later, Eichler (1988:4) showed just how awkward Stephens' definition became when it was expanded to encompass the changing social structure of the family:

A family is a social group which may or may not include adults of both sexes (e.g., lone-parent families), may or may not include one or more children (e.g., childless couples), who may or may not have been born in their wedlock (e.g., adopted children, or children by one adult partner of a previous union). The relationship of the adults may or may not have its origin in marriage (e.g., common-law couples), they may or may not share a common residence (e.g., commuting couples). The adults may or may not cohabit sexually, and the relationship may or may not involve such socially patterned feelings as love...

Eichler goes on to observe that, unwieldy as it already is, her definition omits several structures, such as homosexual couples and group arrangements, that are regarded by the participants, but often not by outsiders, as familial groups.

One of the most important aspects of the structure of the Canadian family is its nuclear family organization (mother, father, offspring, in contrast with the extended kin group that remains important in such traditional societies as India (Lupri, 1990). Nevertheless, following Eichler's (1988) directive, we must keep in mind the many alternative family structures which co-exist with the nuclear family. As mentioned in Chapter 5, the romanticized ideal of stay-at-home mother, employed father, and two children at home now represents fewer than 10 percent of all Canadian families (Boyd, 1988:87; *Maclean's,* January 7, 1987:71). Because of the economic exigencies outlined in Chapter

8, most families are now dual-earner families. A variety of social forces, e.g., economic pressures, changing gender ideologies, liberalized divorce legislation, improved contraception, and greater life expectancies have resulted in new family forms. These include single-parent divorced families; single-parent never-married families; dual career couples who live apart; cohabitors with or without children; voluntarily childless couples; reconstituted or blended families; gay couples; post-childbearing couples; innovative familial groupings, for instance, several same-sex adults along with their offspring. This mind-boggling heterogeneity of family types is multiplied when the ethnic, social class, and regional variations of these forms are included.

As the reader will understand, exhaustive analysis of these many permutations and combinations in family structure would take us well beyond the scope of this text. Our attention must necessarily be directed to those generalizations of particular relevance to gender relations. Of paramount importance is the extent to which patriarchy characterizes old and new family structures.

THE FAMILY AS KEY SOCIAL INSTITUTION

As mentioned in Chapter 5, an overwhelming majority of Canadians acknowledge the importance of the family in their personal lives (*Maclean's*, January 5, 1987:71-72). And justly so. The modern family, heterogeneous as its structure may be, continues to be at the very centre of society. "Society's needs of the family include giving birth to new members, teaching them how to behave appropriately, inculcating ethical and moral principles shared by society, producing and/or distributing goods and services, and maintaining social order" (McDaniel, 1988a:103). From the perspective of the individual, the family provides such important benefits as physical and psychological nurturance, a sense of identity, primary bonds, and regularized sex. The location of the family at the crossroads of a network of social institutions—economic, political, educational, health, reli-

gious, and legal institutions—places it in a position to mediate between the individual and society. As Andersen (1988:148) points out, many of the strains associated with modern family life, in fact, stem from conflicts posed by the family's relationship to other social institutions.

It seems natural for most of us, as individuals, to think about and perhaps to idealize the family as a source of intimate, personal experiences. Nonetheless, the structural understanding of gender sought in this chapter demands that the family be conceptualized as a large-scale institution that is affected by, and in turn influences, other societal institutions. Especially important here is the family's relations with the economic institution. In the last chapter, we noted that feminist understanding of gender relations has been influenced by the Marxist axiom that all social relations are determined by the mode of material production. We also mentioned that Marx's colleague, Friedrich Engels (1902) viewed the monogamous family as the first expression of capitalism. As expressed by Smith (1977b:17), "the situation of women in our society must be understood in relation to the family, and the family understood in relation to the mode of production characteristic of contemporary industrial society." This way of thinking suggests that although we like to think families are about love, the realities of family life suggest otherwise. "For women, men, and children alike, the family is, and long has been, an institution based on economic dependence" (Gerstel and Gross, 1989:89). Therefore, feminist analysis of the family attends to the interpenetration of domestic and wage labour. We shall enlarge upon these ideas later on.

THE FAMILY AS TARGET OF CRITICISM

Social critics contemplating better social worlds invariably criticize existing family forms and search for alternatives. For example, Jewish immigrants from many parts of the world to the new state of Israel developed a communal family form (Spiro, 1956). The reason for social reformers' interest in the family is obvious. The institution of the family carries primary responsibility for regulating sex and reproduction and socializing the young. Moreover, the family plays an important role in linking individuals with other societal institutions.

Given that the family is the primary institution for organizing gender relations in a society, the place where the sex/gender division of labour, the regulation of sexuality and the social construction and reproduction of gender are all rooted (Glenn, 1987:348), the complaints about the patriarchal family registered by gender liberationists of both sexes are not surprising. Publication of Friedan's *The Feminine Mystique* (1963) set off fierce debates concerning women's family roles. (See also Firestone [1971]; Millet [1969]; Mitchell [1971]; Rubin [1975].) For example, Marlene Dixon (1971:170) claimed that the "institution of marriage is the chief vehicle for the perpetuation of the oppression of women; it is through the role of wife that the subjugation of women is maintained." The Royal Commission on the Status of Women in Canada (1970) offered 28 recommendations in the area of the family. Familial concerns continue to monopolize the attention of contemporary feminists. Poverty of female lone-parent families; difficulties in juggling employment and domestic labour; shortage of public childcare facilities; new reproductive technology; and abortion rights are only a few examples of this concern. However, it important to stress that feminists have not set out to destroy the family, as their political opponents often charge (Luxton and Rosenberg, 1986:12). As Eichler (1986:29) teaches, the feminist movement distinguishes between patriarchal families ("where there is exploitation, violence, abuse, incest, stifling of growth") seen as unacceptable, and families ("where there is mutual caring, support, respect, commitment and growth"), viewed as deserving of social support.

Many men, reacting to the second wave of feminism and its aftermath, have also become disillusioned with the mid-twentieth century nuclear family. In the early 1970s, they criticized the traditional family for the constraints it placed upon them to be "iron men," to live up to the "success ethic," to take total financial responsibility for the family, to make all of the

decisions (Farrell, 1974; Goldberg, 1976). "From a cynical male point of view, marriage was an arrangement through which men gave up their freedom for the dubious privilege of supporting a woman" (Ehrenreich, 1989:37).

Men's groups in th 1980s elevated the priority of the family. Some worked to improve family relationships, through closer involvement in the rearing of their children, through seeking solutions to family violence. However, fathers' rights groups, such as the Canadian group calling itself In Search of Justice (Weston, 1989), managed to get more publicity. Pointing out that Canadian law holds a natural father responsible for the financial support of a child for 18 years, they feel morally wronged by legal practices that give them more responsibilities than rights. Therefore, these groups fight for custody of their children in the divorce process and for the right to participate in abortion decisions. Men's rights groups are often associated with anti-abortion groups, and with anti-feminist ideology. In the summer of 1989, several Canadian men sought court injunctions to prevent women with whom they had previously cohabited from aborting fetuses they claimed to have fathered (*Maclean's*, July 31, 1989). A Quebec court injunction obtained by Jean-Guy Tremblay, which barred his ex-woman friend, Chantal Daigle from having an abortion, was unanimously overturned by the Supreme Court of Canada on August 8, 1989. Although the most visible masculine critique of the family emerges from conservative groups seeking to bolster patriarchy, more gender liberating goals are being pursued by coalitions among feminists, gay men, and progressive heterosexual men (Carrigan et al., 1987:187). (See Chapter 10.)

The mid-1980s saw the emergence of a social movement identifying itself as "pro-family" (Dubinsky, 1985; Eichler, 1986). This conservative movement, troubled by new societal developments it blames on the pernicious influence of feminism, calls for strengthening of the family. Members isolate society's failure to appreciate the efforts of full-time housewives, and increases in divorce, cohabiting couples, latchkey children, juvenile crime, family violence, rape, pornography, and so on as their rationale for resurrecting, what is for them, the ideal family form: the patriarchal family where women have the choice to stay at home, and the right to be supported by their husbands (Eichler, 1985a:24). This countermovement to feminism addresses itself mainly to housewives and attempts to draw together critics of the feminist movement, abortion, daycare services, and gay rights.

The concluding chapter will examine more closely the activities of the three types of social movements discussed briefly here. For the moment, the conclusion we wish to emphasize is that "the question of women's place in the family has emerged as *the* central issue for feminists and anti-feminists alike (Glenn, 1987:348, emphasis in original).

FEMINIST SOCIOLOGISTS' CONTRIBUTIONS TO FAMILY THEORY

As indicated above, the sociology of the family is the area of mainstream sociology that has been most affected by feminism (Eichler, 1985a:629). Feminist rethinking of the family involves five themes set forth below (Glenn, 1987; Thorne, 1982). Although still in a formative stage, this challenge to pre-feminist assumptions about family life in a sociology that had been shaped by masculine concerns has provided a very real contribution to the sociology of the family (Cheal, 1989).

Rejection of Biological Determination of the Family

With some exceptions (Rossi, 1984), feminists reject the assumption that family arrangements are biological in any direct or immutable way. The part played by biology is not denied. However, the *social organization* of reproduction, parenting, and the gender division of labour is stressed (Thorne, 1982:6). In Lorber's (1986) words, "Although physiological distinctions have seemed to be a natural starting place for the social construction of gender, anthropological studies suggest that the division of duties pertaining to reproduction and child rearing is more central to gender as a socially organizing principle than dichotomous repro-

ductive biology." Biological factors such as genes and hormones are downplayed, while cross-cultural and historical variations and social-economic factors shaping gender arrangements are emphasized. Whether all "real" women want to be mothers, whether the inequality between traditional husbands and wives is "natural" are questioned (Duffy, 1988:111). As Luxton and Rosenberg (1986:9) remark,

The myth that all women should be wives and mothers is used over and over to justify paying women low wages in the labour force, to exclude them from many jobs, and to discourage their participation in politics. The myth of natural maternity and domesticity is used to defend the systematic exclusion of women from power.

The more structured understanding of the family urged by feminists involves attending to linkages between family and industry, as well as family and state (Burstyn, 1985). This interest implies taking an active, critical role in shaping government policies regarding the family (Eichler, 1983:1988).

In summary, the feminist perspective takes as axiomatic that more can be learned about family dynamics by concentrating on how the work of families is organized than by assuming a "natural" division of labour and inequality stemming from biological distinctions between females and males. There is no need to reiterate the arguments presented in Chapter 3.

Criticism of the Monolithic Family

As discussed above, feminist scholars object to the idealization of the family with a male breadwinner and stay-at-home wife and children as "the normal, most healthy household arrangement" (Thorne, 1982:5). They go on to argue that when sociologists understand this nuclear family unit to be invariably responsible for a constant set of functions (procreation, socialization, residence, and so on), then wide variations in contemporary family structure either go unrecognized, or are perceived to be deviant or impaired in some way (Eichler, 1981). "Incomplete families" and "broken families" then become pejorative designations for families who depart from this "ideal." Alternative ways of living are characterized as "sad, crazy or unnatural or perhaps even dangerous" (Luxton and Rosenberg, 1986:10). In other words, the ideology of the monolithic family infuses general understanding of what *should* be (Thorne, 1982:4). Men belong in the labour force. Men have legitimate business in a variety of public settings. However, women, as anchors of the family, belong at home.

The ideology of the monolithic family also reinforces the economic exploitation of all women (Thorne, 1982:4). If it is assumed that most people live in a nuclear family, that adult women have husbands to support them, then women's lower wages and disadvantaged position in the labour force are justified by the assumption that their paid work is secondary to that of men. Similarly, believing that women are uniquely suited for domestic duties supports the gender segregation of occupations discussed in Chapter 8. Women are then confined to jobs that resemble their wife-and-mother roles: nursing, teaching and care of the young, production and selling of food and clothing, clerical work (Thorne, 1982:4).

The significance of this feminist theme is summarized by Eichler (1981). So far as sociologists are concerned, "blind adherence to the inadequate monolithic model of the family has led to a collective failure on the part of social scientists to investigate those issues which are a lived reality to a majority of people today" (p. 385). Policymakers, enthralled with a monolithic view of the family, overlook the problems of other sorts of families, such as the poverty of families headed by women and elderly women living alone, and the need for publicly supported child-care facilities.

Breakdown of the Public-private Distinction

Family sociology of the 1950s and 1960s emphasized the isolation of the contemporary nuclear family from the other societal institutions (Renzetti and Curran, 1989:135). The private sphere of family was linked with femininity and distinguished from the public, masculine worlds of work and politics (Parsons, 1955). Women were relegated to the home on the basis of their reproductive function. These views have been strongly challenged by feminist scholars. Rejecting biological causation, they argue that strict demarcation of public-private realms constitutes a false dichotomy. Family members do not experience these two spheres as separate. Moreover, to argue the automony of the family obscures the impact of other institutions, especially the economy and the state, upon the family, as well as the influence of family upon other societal institutions. In the words of Armstrong and Armstrong (1988:168), "The separation of home and work...masks the interpenetration of household and formal economy, the crucial links between what happens in the home and in the market." As noted in Chapter 8,

men and women are bound to their jobs out of the family's need for economic survival, and in many ways—evident, for example, in power relations between husbands and wives and in their use of leisure time—the nature of paid work shapes the daily experience of families. Moreover, activities in the home (housework, consumption, child care), which are mostly done by women, serve to maintain and reproduce the labor force (Thorne, 1982:16).

Feminist criticism of the public-private distinction enhances the visibility of the following dimensions of family life. First, work performed in the home is now understood to be socially and economically necessary work, not only a labour of love for family members (Luxton, 1980). That is, the inter-relationship between housework and capitalist economy can now be analyzed (Armstrong and Armstrong, 1984).

Second, the complex interweaving of men's and women's family and work roles has come to receive the scholarly attention it deserves (Lopata and Pleck, 1983; Lupri, 1990). For example, Luxton's (1980) participant observation of Flin Flon families documents the impact of men's labour force activities—shift work, strikes, wage cutbacks—on family life.

Third, adult family members of both sexes are seen to have legitimate business in the home *and* in the marketplace. Women's access to the full range of opportunities in the public sphere has been at the core of feminist movement ideology. Equality for the sexes requires that men and women share equitably the labour in and out of the home.

Lastly, the now outdated image of the home as private refuge from the stress of the larger society hid the conflict and physical abuse that frequently takes place there (Renzetti and Curran, 1989:136). The first three aspects of family will be dealt with at greater length elsewhere in this chapter. We turn now to an expanded discussion of the final issue as a major theme of feminist scholars' critique of the male-dominated sociology of the family.

Skepticism Concerning the Harmonious Family

I couldn't understand why I was being beaten. At first it was a black eye now and again or bumps and bruises that could be covered up. I started wearing tinted glasses, long-sleeved shirts and blouses, turtlenecks, and slacks. As all this was happening, I tried to figure out why. It always ended up with Bill telling me it was my fault. I began to believe him, thinking all the while that things would get better. They didn't. As time went on, I lost everything: my confidence, my self-esteem, my pride—with time, I even lost the ability to care or feel (Vallee, 1986:xi).

The abuse suffered by Jane Stafford and her children ended when this rural Nova Scotia wife was taken into custody for blowing out the brains of her husband, Billy, with a shotgun. The pre-feminist sociological image of the family as harmonious institution seems strange against the background of well-publicized cases of family violence like this one. Sociological theory of the 1950s and 1960s idealized and romanticized the family as the site of love and intimacy, the refuge of men from the stresses of the workplace. Consequently, family violence, "as an academic topic of research, remained virtually hidden until the early 1970s" (Steinmetz, 1987:725). Feminist sociologists, placing the family with its power structure into the context of the society with *its* power structures (Breines and Gordon, 1983:503), were prominent among social observers who recognized the dark side of the family, who demystified its

image as a "haven in a heartless world" (Lasch, 1979). (See Straus et al. [1980].) They argued that many families, far from being a safe refuge from the strains of other sectors of society, expose children, spouses (especially wives), and the elderly to violence. As Eichler (1981:384-85) said some years ago, "until we admit that families may exhibit the most brutalizing, abusing, dangerous and inhumane types of interaction patterns as well as loving, caring, protecting, helping, sustaining and nurturing types of relationships we will fail to understand the range of human interactions that take place within families."

Mark Liddle (1989:759) recently wrote this assessment of feminist contributions to an understanding of violence against women:

Sociological work on violence has profited in recent years from a variety of insights supplied by feminist theorists, concerning both the pervasiveness of violence against women, and the impact of this violence on the lives of individual women. On the theoretical plane the field has also been enriched by efforts to describe particular kinds of violence against women *as being linked to wider structures, and as being embedded in gendered patterns of social control* (emphasis added).

However, Liddle goes on to observe that these "contributions have been blunted by their incorporation of an implausible, one-dimensional model of male agency..." (p. 759). In other words, a full explanation of family violence requires the inclusion of other variables besides gender.[1] According to Michael Smith's (1990) survey of Toronto women, low family income is an important risk variable.

Despite variations in the amount of abuse across families, feminist thinking locates the etiology of wife battering (Breines and Gordon, 1983) and rape (Brownmiller, 1975) in the everyday fabric of the relations between the sexes in patriarchal society. (This is what Liddle (1989) means in his reference to "gendered patterns of social control.") Therefore, family violence is not viewed as a set of isolated events, confined to atypical families. Rather, abuse of family members emerges from the context of "a gendered society in which male power dominates" (Breines and Gordon, 1983:492). Individual men frequently use violence to maintain their power and privilege in the family (Dobash and Dobash, 1979). Power differentials and issues of control also enter into explanations of why women are more likely to be aggressors (but not sexual abusers) of children. Feminists have also produced much of the recent writing on incest. A noteworthy example is Canadian writer Sylvia Fraser's *My Father's House: A Memoir of Incest and of Healing* (1987). For her, the dark side of the family meant "a blasted childhood, an even worse adolescence, betrayal, divorce, craziness, professional stalemate, financial uncertainty and always, always a secret eating like dry rot at my psyche" (p. 251).

Empirical data support feminist sociologists' contention that a great many families throughout the world are places of brutality, not harmony. [2] Research "revealed that family violence occurred not only among the uneducated and poor but also among the middle class, that pregnancy is a likely time for wife-battering to occur, and that violence is not limited to psychopaths but can grow out of the normal stresses of family life" (Epstein, 1988:204). So far as Canada is concerned, MacLeod (1987) reported that one Canadian woman in eight had been battered in 1985. Lupri's (1990) national study found that over 147 000 Canadian wives or cohabiting women were beaten up by their male partners in 1986. At some time during that year, nearly 30 000 had faced a husband or cohabiting male wielding a knife or gun. Research shows that women are also capable of violence against their partners, its actual amount rivalling wife abuse (Brinkerhoff and Lupri, 1988). However, men's superior strength results in far greater injury to women. As Steinmetz (1987:749) says, husband beating would be viewed as an aberration from the perspective of radical feminist theory which explains wife beating as an example of victimization of a gender-oppressed class. For a comprehensive discussion of the many factors involved in family violence, see Steinmetz (1987).

Differentiation of Family Experiences

Feminist scholars emphasize that family is not experienced in the same way by women, men,

or by female and male children (Thorne, 1982:10). Although this observation seems self-evident in view of what we have just said about family violence, the sociology of the family has, in past years, assumed otherwise. In pre-feminist thought, women's existence was "so fused with and embedded in the family that it has been difficult to extract them as individuals— as persons acting not only within the family but also outside of it" (Glenn, 1987:349). [3]

When the sociology of the family of the 1950s and 1960s attended to gender at all, a "sex role" framework was employed. This conceptual approach masked questions of power and inequality, implying that women and men were "separate but equal" (Carrigan et al., 1987:145). These remarks need elaboration. Functionalist theory (Parsons, 1955) was the most influential approach to the study of the family 25 years ago. This perspective posited a husband-father playing the masculine, instrumental breadwinner role, and the wife-mother the feminine, expressive, domestic role. These roles meshed into an orderly "drama" which served the needs of family and society alike. As feminist critics of functionalism argued, this insistence upon the family as a unified entity overlooked the very real hierarchical divisions within families that produce different and conflicting interests among their members (Glenn, 1987:362). Put another way, feminist sociologists propose to examine the *internal* stratification of the family. This structural approach to families means that women, like men, have become, in scholars' eyes, active beings with diverse roles to play both inside and outside their families. [4]

In sum, a "major feminist contribution has been to view women as individuals within the family, rather than as mere components of it or anchors to it (Bridenthal, 1982:231). The next section elaborates upon this generalization.

So far, we have outlined the major insights contributed by feminist scholarship to a sociological understanding of family life. In review, they include these inter-related points: (1) Championing a macro-structural orientation to families, rather than biological or social-psychological perspectives; (2) Appealing to broadening the conceptualization of families beyond the model of the paternalistic nuclear family, which lives under one roof and performs these traditional functions: regulating sexuality; producing legitimate children; socializing children, etc. In this way, varieties of family that depart from this model become objects of study and social policy, rather than being viewed as deficient or impaired; (3) Arguing the case of permeability of boundaries between the private domain of the family and such public spheres as the state and the economy. Considerable light has been shed upon the family when the linkages between it and other societal institutions are examined rather than denied; (4) Substituting a conflict perspective for the received wisdom of family harmony, thereby exposing the darker side of family as site of power differences. As Lupri (1990) tells us, there is a paradox here. While the family can serve as refuge, as place of affection, comfort, and protection, it also has the potential for being a crucible of conflict and violence; (5) Challenging the unitary image of THE FAMILY to allow for the different experiences and perspectives of individual family members. This list is not exhaustive. Many of the general observations made in Chapter 1 concerning feminist theory and research apply to the family.

WOMEN'S MARRIAGE AND MEN'S MARRIAGE

Feminist scholars argue that marriage and the family have a differential impact on men and women and, further, that the family, as presently constituted, is a basic source of men's empowerment and women's subordination. Jessie Bernard (1972:15), a farsighted feminist sociologist of the family, claimed that "there are two marriages...in every marital union, his and hers." She wrote:

For there is...an objective reality in marriage. It is a reality that resides in marriage. It is a reality that resides in the cultural—legal, moral, and conventional—prescriptions and proscriptions and, hence, expectations that constitute marriage. It is the reality that is reflected in the minds of the spouses themselves. The differences between the marriages of husbands and of wives are structural realities, and it

is these structural differences that constitute the basis for the different psychological realities (Bernard, 1972:10, emphasis added.)

Canadian society has undergone many changes since Bernard's assessment was published. In the pages to follow, we consider whether current evidence supports her thesis. Note that our remarks are intended to include cohabiting, as well as legally married couples.

His and Her Priorities

The differential impact of marriage and family begins with the question of priorities. Who cares more about family, the husband or the wife? The cultural imperative that women are expected to give their families priority over alternative endeavours began with the separation of home and workplace in the last century (Cancian and Gordon, 1988:311). This ideology of feminine domesticity "originated in the nineteenth-century notion of 'true womanhood,' which argued that women are uniquely endowed with the emotional qualities necessary to oversee the private sphere and thus to safeguard society's moral fabric from the corrupting influence of industrialism" (Gerson, 1985:4). Despite women's declining fertility, their massive influx into the workforce, and the restructuring of opportunities available to them, women are still expected to find their *greatest* fulfillment within the roles of housewife and mother (Richardson, 1988:193). Women are perceived to be the specialists in loving, caring, and service to others (Cancian, 1986). Traditional norms dictate that family relationships take priority in women's lives. A recent study of metropolitan Toronto and southern Ontario women concluded that this remains so: "[U]nder patriarchy...women's family obligations are generally seen to take precedence over their employment responsibilities" (Duffy et al., 1989:12-13). Moreover, other research finds that "the compelling cultural injunction that a woman should have the love of a man has not abated" (Richardson, 1988:369). Consequently, books and articles offering advice on relationships are overwhelmingly directed to women, not men

(Cancian and Gordon, 1988: 310). "Prevailing ideas about women's lives, including the dogma of romantic love and the cult of maternalism, are so pervasive and powerful that they discourage women from exploring alternative ways of living" (Duffy, 1988:114). When both partners work, his job is considered to be the primary one, and hers, the supplementary one. Therefore, "women are expected to disrupt their work for the needs of the family, whereas men are allowed to disrupt their families because of work demands" (Richardson, 1988:195).

To summarize, evidence of various sorts indicates that men are expected to give priority to their work, while women's cultural mandate directs them to place family first. Actual behaviour has, of course, changed over the years. The contemporary implications of "her" versus "his" priorities will be explored further in the sections to follow.

Power

The intimate connections between gender and power have been a recurring theme of this volume. Contemporary research reveals that inequality continues to characterize family life, and that with great frequency, this inequality erupts into violence (Duffy, 1988:111). Psycho-analytically oriented theorists, such as Chodorow (1978) whose work was reviewed in Chapter 5, point up the influence of mothers and other female authority figures over the socialization of youngsters. Nevertheless, empirical research clearly establishes that this female power over children occurs in the shadow of the generally far greater power of husband over wife. In the words of Luxton and Rosenberg (1986:11), "Whatever the personal relations between a particular woman and her husband are, whether they are loving and intimate or fearful and cold, the structure of marriage legally, economically and normatively, subordinates women to their husbands." As Meg Luxton (1980:50) discovered from her study of Flin Flon, Manitoba housewives, being a "good wife" usually meant "doing things his way." The reasons why the woman usually ends up the less powerful partner in a relation-ship are three in number.

The first reason is economic. "The relative power of husband and wife in the family depends largely on their respective anchorage in the occupational system, since that system is the main determinant of status and privilege" (Coser and Coser, 1974:90). The twentieth-century North American economy is based on the principle of the family wage (Ehrenrich, 1983:7-8). The "breadwinner ethic" has required men to become wage earners and to share their wages with their wives and dependents. The assumption is made that when women work, they are already supported by men and can therefore be paid less than men. As a result, women have traditionally been interested in 'landing' a man, while men have resisted becoming "the lifelong support of the female unemployed" (Ehrenreich, 1983:3). Only a minority of wives are economically independent of husbands. Money being a resource, wives' generally inferior economic position renders them less powerful. Smith (1973:17-18) makes the point very clearly: "The underlying determination of the relations between men and women is this relation to the economic structure whereby the relation of wife to husband mimics the relation of husband to capitalist. She works for him because he owns the means of production upon which she depends."

Because our society values and rewards occupational achievement, husbands' status in the outside world typically spills over into the family in the form of enhanced power. The greater the discrepancy between the resources of husband and wife (occupation, income, education, worldly experience, etc.), the greater (usually) his power (Blood and Wolfe, 1960). The woman's economic dependence is increased if she is a full-time housewife, with small children.

Secondly, husbands' greater experience in the wider society has given them intellectual authority over their wives. Traditionally, they have been interpreters of the world beyond the family for their stay-at-home wives. Ng (1981:103) describes the intellectual authority of the husband of a Vancouver family that had emigrated from India.

Mrs. H. does shopping with her husband because she does not know how to get around the city very well. Sometimes she goes with relatives, but mainly with her husband. Her husband handles all the money and transactions because Mrs. H. has not learned to handle Canadian money. ...She does not go out often. She does not take the bus very much. When she must, she asks someone to write down the address on a piece of paper so that she can show the bus driver. Her husband has a car, but she doesn't know how to drive.

Although Mrs. H. is more dependent than most wives upon her husband's superior understanding of how society is organized, the broader issue is that husbands' public domain activities have traditionally given them cognitive power over their wives.

A third reason why the male partner is generally the more powerful is the ideological matter of "his" and "her" priorities raised above. Although most men also want to marry (Nordstrom, 1986), women's cultural mandate to give family top priority places the male partner in the position of "less interest." The *principle of less interest*, described in Chapter 6, holds that the partner who cares less about the equality of the relationship or whether the relationship continues at all is in an advantageous position to dominate the other party to the relationship. The husband in traditional marriages was usually the party of less interest. For one thing, marriage was at the core of his wife's life and on the periphery of his own. For another, he had alternative sources of gratification outside the family. Therefore, in all likelihood, the wife was the marital partner to make concessions, to bend her will to that of her husband.

When the Canadian wife goes out to work, her power within the household generally increases (Brown, 1978). This makes sense: a woman contributing a paycheque to a family is more likely to demand a voice in the running of the family. Wives in the labour force have less need to rely upon their husbands' interpretation of the wider society. Many employed women have been able to leave unbearable marriages (Armstrong and Armstrong, 1988:163). However, the fact that employed women usually earn considerably less than men means that male partners keep the upper hand. The gender-segregated nature of the labour market and women's household responsibilities combine to perpetuate wives' economic dependence.

Conjugal power varies over the life cycle of a marriage. In the initial stage, when the wife is usually employed and there are no children, the relationship tends to be more egalitarian. After children arrive, the wife becomes more economically, socially, and emotionally dependent. "His world is expanding while hers contracts" (Richardson, 1988:195). A childless relationship where both partners have a substantial income will remain more egalitarian.

In mid-life, the unbalanced sex ratio in the population enhances the male position as partner of less interest (Veevers, 1988). The twin facts that men die earlier, and men, but not women, may seek much younger partners combine to create a shortage of potential male partners. The relative scarcity of alternative male partners and the relative surplus of potential female partners substantially reinforces the traditional power advantage of the male. Also, as we will see at the end of this chapter, women's position is weakened further by the aging process, which takes away the traditional female assets of beauty and fecundity.

Several countervailing influences strengthen the hand of the middle-aged female partner. Whether they overrule the power that devolves upon males from their larger paycheques, their greater protection from the stigma (as opposed to the actuality) of aging, and from the higher valuation of masculinity is moot. First, greater power in relationships in mid-life is one pay-off of women's investment in education and careers. Second, the life priorities of both sexes often alter at mid-life. Men, bored with work, perhaps having failed to achieve career goals, frequently turn to their families for satisfaction. Ironically, just as husbands become more affiliative, wives, with the child-rearing behind them and renewed energy, are looking beyond the home for new goals. Stay-at-home wives may return to school; working wives who have had jobs may seek more fulfilling work. This mid-life shift may transform the wife into the partner of less interest. Third, the norm that women mate with older partners seems to be weakening somewhat. As women have more potential partners to choose from, their position should improve.

Older, retired couples enjoy the greatest equality of all (Richardson, 1988:195), a point to which we will return later in this chapter.

Domestic Labour

Another well-established difference in wives' and husbands' experience of family concerns the handling of work around the home. The inegalitarian division of household labour noted in our Chapter 8 discussion of unpaid work is linked with women's cultural mandate to give their families top priority. Traditional wisdom dictated that home and children were woman's "natural" domain, and the work involved her duty and métier. Moreover, the apportionment of household labour is intimately related to conjugal power. As Hartmann (1981:377) argued, "the time spent on housework, as well as other indicators of household labor, can be fruitfully used as a measure of power relations in the home." Once again, the permeability of boundaries between private and public spheres becomes manifest. Doing housework steals time and attention from other life interests, such as careers in the labour force. In sum, the female partner's disproportionate responsibility for housework and childcare is both consequence and reinforcement of her disadvantaged position in the larger society.

Over the years, the nature of work in the home has changed for both sexes (Armstrong, 1989: 124-25). Washers and dryers, microwave ovens, frozen foods, cake mixes, the plethora of fast-food outlets, and power lawn mowers are examples of post-war developments which have made household work easier. Also, the decline in fertility means fewer children to tend. However, other new developments have served to expand household work. A number of tasks, that were formerly sent out, such as doing the laundry are now done at home. Also, expectations concerning childcare work have been raised so that the time spent on each child has expanded. "Women spend more time keeping children's teeth, hands, and clothes clean,

driving their children around, making their beds and lunches, and worrying about the consequences of toilet-training techniques, reward systems, or salt intake" (Armstrong, 1989:125). In addition, increased life expectancy has meant a growing number of elderly relatives who cannot survive without the care of their adult children. Most significant of all is the fact that the majority of married women are now in the labour force.

How have these changed circumstances affected household work? In the initial stages of the feminist movement and women's increased labour force participation, sociologists looked ahead and predicted a new, more egalitarian family type, termed the *symmetrical family*, that would share household tasks (Young and Willmott, 1973). Later on, they also talked about "androgynous fathers" who would be anxious for heightened involvement in the lives of their children (Robinson and Barret, 1986). These predictions failed to come true (Lupri and Symons, 1982). In Epstein's (1988:210) words, "it is a ubiquitous finding that wives' employment has only a modest effect on the household division of labor in all countries." Domestic tasks, and care of children and elderly are still disproportionately shouldered by women, whether or not they also work outside the home. Studies in Halifax (Clark and Harvey, 1976), Vancouver (Meissner et al., 1975), Calgary (Horna and Lupri, 1987; Lupri and Mills, 1987), and Flin Flon (Luxon, 1986) all arrive at the assessment that "for most working women, being in the paid labor force is simply added on to their work in the family" (Andersen, 1988:165). Women continue to be responsible for "kin-keeping"— telephone calls, visits, organizing periodic family occasions (Rosenthal, 1985). Despite some assistance from male partners in the *doing* of household work, women continue to carry the responsibility for planning, remembering, and overseeing that work. In a survey cited in *Chatelaine* (February 1985), researchers found nearly one in four supermarket shoppers to be male. However, of those men who were married, three-quarters marketed with a list prepared by their wives. "The buck stops with the one who knows the mustard is used up and

Box 9.1

THE POLITICS OF HOUSEWORK

Pat Mainardi's satire illustrates the pressures experienced by a dual-career couple. The feminist wife suggests to her husband that they share the housework. His reply: "You're right. It's only fair." However, here is what he says (and how his wife interprets it) when the time actually comes to wash floors, do laundry, lug home groceries, cook meals, and scrub pots:

I don't mind sharing the housework, but I don't do it very well. We should each do the things we're best at.
Meaning: Unfortunately I'm no good at things like washing dishes or cooking. What I do best is a little light carpentry, changing light bulbs, moving furniture (*how often do you move furniture?*).
Also Meaning: I don't like the dull stupid boring jobs, so you should do them.

I don't mind sharing the work, but you'll have to show me how to do it.
Meaning: I ask a lot of questions and you'll have to show me everything everytime I do it because I don't remember so good. Also don't try to sit down and read while I'm doing my jobs because I'm going to annoy hell out of you until it's easier to do them yourself.

We used to be so happy! (Said whenever it was his turn to do something.)
Meaning: I used to be so happy.
Meaning: Life without housework is bliss. (*No quarrel here. Perfect agreement.*)

We have different standards, and why should I have to work to your standards. That's unfair.
Meaning: If I begin to get bugged by the dirt and crap I will say "This place sure is a sty" or "How can anyone live like this?" and wait for your reaction. I know that all women have a sore called "Guilt over a messy house" or "Household work is ultimately my responsibility." I know that men have caused that sore—if anyone visits and the place *is* a sty, they're not going to leave and say "He sure is a lousy housekeeper." You'll take the rap in any case. I can outwait you.
Also Meaning: I can provoke innumerable scenes over the housework issue. Eventually doing all housework yourself will be less painful to you than trying to get me to do half. Or I'll suggest we get a maid. She will do my share of the work. You will do yours. It's women's work.

I've got nothing against sharing the housework, but you can't make me do it on your schedule.
Meaning: Passive resistance. I'll do it when I damned well please, if at all. If my job is doing dishes, it's easier to do them once a week. If taking out laundry, once a month. If washing the floors, once a year. If you don't like it, do it yourself oftener, and then I won't do it at all.

I *hate* it more than you. You don't mind it so much.
Meaning: Housework is garbage work. It's the worst crap I've ever done. It's degrading and humiliating for someone of *my* intelligence to do it. But for someone of *your* intelligence...

Housework is too trivial to even talk about.
Meaning: It's even more trivial to do. Housework is beneath my status. My purpose in life is to deal with matters of significance. Yours is to deal with matters of insignificance. You should do the housework.

Source: Pat Mainardi, "The Politics of Housework," pp 447-54 in Robin Morgan (ed.), *Sisterhood is Powerful,* New York: Vintage Books (Random House), 1970.

makes the shopping list—the one who says, 'It is my job to remember'" (p. 176).

The fact that the symmetrical family has failed to materialize does *not* mean that husband-wife relations remain unchanged. As illustrated by Mainardi's satire (1970), reprinted in Box 9.1, women's entry into the labour force has altered the dynamics of family life. The paycheques and experience from the larger world have augmented women's conjugal power. As a consequence, many husbands are now under pressure to increase their share of the workload. The division of labour has become a source of conflict in many dual-worker homes (Hartmann, 1981).

Luxton's (1986) research permits us to peer through the "kitchen windows" of Flin Flon, Manitoba homes to see how large-scale societal transformations affect individual families. Luxton reports that although some women are uneasy about relinquishing their exclusive control over domestic chores (p. 18), the traditional site of female power, most, feeling the pressure of two jobs, now insist men should help out. Said one woman: "I come home from work dead tired and I still have to cook and be with the kids and clean up. And he just lies around, drinking beer, watching TV and I get so mad I could kill him" (p. 27).

Flin Flon husbands are increasing their hours of domestic labour, from an average of 10.8 hours per week in 1976 to 19.1 hours in 1981 (the year of the study). However the women with two jobs averaged 31.4 hours per week of domestic labour in 1981, only 4.3 hours less than 1976 (p. 26). Household work, like wage work, is gender segregated. For example, men change light bulbs, take responsibility for automobiles, and fix things, while women cook, clean, and change diapers. Although many women now contribute financially, disproportionate power remains in male hands. Therefore, many men are able to resist pressure to assume feminized tasks, especially unpleasant ones, so that the redistribution of work that is occurring tends to be selective. Men take on those tasks that are most clearly defined and pleasant. "Repeatedly women noted that their husbands had taken on reading the children a bedtime story and staying with them until they fell asleep, thus 'freeing' the women to wash the dishes and tidy the kitchen" (Luxton, 1986:28). As discussed in Chapter 5, one of the most significant transformations has been men's increased involvement with childcare. Nevertheless, women still remain responsible, while men "babysit" their own children. If external childcare arrangements fell through, it was the woman's problem to get time off from work (p. 29), a finding also reported by Northcott (1983).

Lupri's (1990) observations about the situation of Calgary dual-worker households are worth quoting at length:

In sum, household responsibilities continue to tax Canadian women more heavily than men, and employed mothers with young children carry the major burdens of domestic and child care tasks. Although the *relative* involvement of husbands/fathers is certainly higher, the absolute increase is small; truly androgynous men remain a distinct minority (Lupri, 1990:38, emphasis in original).

This continuing inequitable division of labour in the home carries consequences for all family members. The female partner frequently suffers from role overload. As a result of attempting to combine work and family roles, she is left "hopping on one foot and then the other" (Harper, 1985:781). Wives left to do a second shift at home after a day spent in the labour force feel frustrated and inadequate because they often cannot do justice to either job (Hochschild, 1989). Many husbands, too, feel pressured and guilty about the household division of labour. Finally, as indicated in Chapter 5, there are important socialization consequences for the children of the household: the division of labour children experience in their homes is a critical determinant of their understanding of femininity and masculinity.

Parenthood

We have already had a great deal to say about the distinctive meaning of parenthood for mothers versus fathers. To recapitulate, "the lives of individual women are always distinguished from men's by the necessity to weigh responsibilities for children against all else—in the decision whether to have children, or the daily demands of caring for them" (Fox, 1988). The more profound impact of parenting upon the lives of women begins with the *biological* fact that (at least until the advent of new reproductive technology), only women could grow babies inside them. It continues with women's traditional *cultural* mandate to take primary responsibility for nurturing and rearing their own and other people's children (Chodorow, 1978). This arbitrary association between child-bearing and child-rearing is fostered "by a powerful social belief that having children is 'natural' for women..., that mothers make the best rearers of their children" (Luxton, 1980:81). Therefore, the work associated with child-raising (motherwork) "tends to be redefined, not as unpaid labour, whether joyfully done or not, but as an extension of the natural biological process of reproduction" (McDaniel, 1988c:176). The fact that women are seen as mothers first and workers second justifies their secondary status in the labour force (McDaniel, 1988d:1).

Parenting as differential experience begins with the contemplation of a child. As discussed in Chapter 5, the "motherhood mystique" teaches that a woman must experience maternity in order to find feminine self-actualization and true happiness. Theories of maternal deprivation, "repackaged in the 1980s as bonding, have reinforced the notion that babies need mother love as much as they need food" (McDaniel, 1988d:2). Women's reproductive decisions are often complicated by the fact that the prime child-bearing years are the same years needed to establish a career. However, few men expect to sacrifice labour force advancement in order to enjoy fatherhood.

As one would expect, the actual experience of pregnancy also differs. Lips' (1983) Manitoba study of first-time expectant parents reported that the experience was a more profound one for pregnant women than for their husbands. Moreover, these mothers-to-be believed that their husbands had a stronger investment in the impending parenthood than was actually the case.

The entrance of an infant into a marriage

accentuates traditional gender roles. That is, the division of labour in the home becomes more sex segregated, especially in working-class homes (Lamb, 1978). According to the observational research of LaRossa and LaRossa (1981:57), babies are "women's work." From the start, the mother is "in charge" of the child, while the father "helps" rather than "shares" parental responsibilities. In addition to calcifying gender roles through the division of labour, parenting exacerbates women's dependency and subordination. This is especially the case for women who withdraw from the labour force with the birth of a child, and become economically, socially, and emotionally dependent upon their husbands. Of all the factors that may deter a wife from seeking paid employment, the presence of pre-school children, while less significant than it once was, remains the most important (Lowe and Krahn, 1985:3).

Several recent trends deserve special attention. In the last several years, the marked decline in the number of children born, decrease in unwanted births, delayed child-bearing, shorter time periods of active mothering, outside employment of mothers, and alternative structures for mothering such as daycare centres have all helped to shift the balance of power in women's favour (Gerson et al., 1984). As women have assumed some of men's traditional responsibility as family breadwinner, they have objected to husbands' lack of involvement in parenting. As we remarked in Chapter 5, many fathers, especially younger ones, welcome increased involvement in their children's lives (Stebbins, 1988). While androgynous fathers appear to be "exceedingly rare," fathers in dual-earner families are beginning to seek more meaningful relationships with their offspring (Lupri, 1988). We must also keep in mind that more than 17 percent of Canadian single-parent families are headed by fathers. Men in this position are quite capable of fulfilling their children's physical and psychological needs, though many worry about their ability to do so (Ambert, 1982).

Summing up, despite some redefinition of parental roles, parenthood still has a different impact on mothers and fathers. Motherhood entails more costs than fatherhood. Mother-hood also brings more rewards. When asked about fulfillment associated with the parent role, mothers are more likely than fathers to say parenthood results in a large measure of fulfill-ment (McLanahan and Adams, 1987:249).

We emphasize that parenthood and com-mitted male-female relationships need not go together. An estimated 30 percent of Canadian marriages are either voluntarily or involuntar-ily childless (McDaniel, 1988d:8). (See Veevers' [1980] pioneering work on this topic.) These issues, together with the impact of the new reproductive technologies on the meaning of parenthood, were explored in Chapter 5. Gen-der-related implications of parenting by the divorced and separated are discussed in the section to follow.

Marriage Dissolution

Most Canadians who marry intend to do so for life. Nevertheless, significant numbers of mar-riages are terminated each year through di-vorce, separation, desertion, and annulment (Peters, 1989). As Richardson (1987:164) says of divorce (the most studied type of marriage dissolution), "While divorce rates in Canada have levelled off and even abated, at least temporarily, about 70 000 divorces occur annu-ally. About half (48 percent) of these involve dependent children, which means that, each year, around 55 000 children are affected by their parents' divorce." Therefore, it is impor-tant to consider the differential effects of mar-riage dissolution on women and men. Just as there are "his" and "her" marriages, there are "his" and "her" divorces (Baker, 1984a).

Who initiates divorce? The "principle of least interest" would predict that the wife would have a greater stake than her husband in maintaining the marriage.

Since husbands have more money than wives, better jobs, more alternatives to meet persons of the other sex, and are less likely to bear total responsibility for the children if the marriage fails, we might expect that when a marriage is not satisfactory they will be more likely to be the first to suggest the possibility of divorce and then to seek it actively (Ambert, 1980:43).

Nevertheless, the data show that it is the *wife* who usually takes the first step (Ambert, 1980:44; Baker, 1984:24). According to Baker's (1983:295) interviews with separated and di-vorced people in Toronto, the women claimed to have first suggested ending the marriage "as a result of the misbehavior of their husbands."

Diane Vaughan's (1987) research on the un-coupling process, the "long goodbye," rein-forces Baker's (1983) point that identifying which partner first suggests a separation or files for divorce may not be very meaningful. Vaughan's case histories of couples—married or cohabiting, straight or gay, young or old—revealed a discernable pattern to breakups. Typically, one person wants out, while the other wants the relationship to continue. The dissatisfacted partner keeps his/her unhappi-ness secret at first, then emits subtle cues, e.g., buying inappropriate birthday gifts, making dinnertime reporting of daily events shorter and shorter. Solace is sought with sympathetic outsiders. By the time the other partner realizes the relationship is in trouble, efforts to save it are often futile (Vaughan, 1987).

Custody of the children is an area where cus-tom (but not the law) favours women. The Canadian Divorce Act of 1986 stresses the "best interests" of the child as the basis of custody decisions. Both parents "have joint financial obligation to maintain the child." Unless there is justifiable reason to the contrary, both par-ents must have access to the child (Peters, 1989:212). Nevertheless, some 85 percent of Canadian custody decisions favour the mother (McKie et al., 1983). Relatively few fathers actu-ally seek custody. Both the courts and the fa-thers themselves seem to subscribe to gender stereotypes which describe the mother as the "natural" parent. However, Richardson (1987:187) claims that when fathers "ask for or contest custody, when they have shown some prior involvement in parenting, and when they have an alternative 'mother' available to look after the children, their chances of gaining custody are relatively good."

Fathers' rights groups seek meaningful in-volvement with their children after divorce (Maynard, 1988a). As one father remarked, "It's impossible to have any sort of meaningful relationship with your children if you see them two days out of 30...You come to feel that you're the disposable parent" (Maynard, 1988a:63, 140). They object to making support payments for children they see every other weekend. They challenge what they view as the pro-mother bias of the courts, and champion the option of joint custody made available in the 1986 divorce legislation.

To reiterate the conclusion of our discussion in Chapter 5, the meaning and experience of parenthood change when couples split. The mother must often raise children virtually alone, and on diminished financial resources. The father, on the other hand, frequently has no meaningful role in his children's lives.

As suggested above, the economic implications of divorce and separation are quite different for husband and wife. The end of the marriage often spells downward economic mobility, even poverty, for the women involved (Davids, 1985; Weitzman, 1985). "Millions of women leading comfortable lives discover to their dismay that they are just a divorce...away from poverty" (Luxton and Rosenberg, 1986:11). Put numerically, single-parent families headed by women live on less than half the income of husband-wife families with children (Boyd, 1988:96). Approximately half of the single-parent families headed by females in Canada live below the poverty line (Richardson, 1987:177).

The inequitable financial circumstances of men and women after marriages end continue despite several significant changes in legislation. Among these reforms is the attempt by a growing number of provinces to collect child support payments from parents (usually fathers) who renege on court orders. As a result of efforts by provincial units to hold defaulters to account, "the percentage of fully paid-up support orders in Ontario has doubled...but that brings it only to a disgraceful 26 per cent of the 62 000 orders in the province. In Alberta, 32.5 per cent comply fully, while Quebec scores a comparatively impressive 50 per cent" (*Calgary Herald*, November 22, 1989:A4).

Equally important was the reform that finally entitled ex-wives to half the financial fruits of marriage. Prior to this change, the law failed to recognize the contribution to the marriage of the wife who chose to be a full-time

housewife or to work in a family business. The Murdoch case in the 1970s forced realization of this flaw in Canadian law. Irene Murdoch spent eight years fighting for a half interest in the Turner Valley, Alberta ranch she and her husband had built up during their marriage. In 1976, the Supreme Court of Canada awarded her 12 percent of her ex-husband's property and assets. However, in a 1978 landmark decision, the Supreme Court gave a Saskatchewan woman divorcing a farmer one-half of the farm property. Most provinces now require a 50-50 split of all assets acquired during the marriage (Peters, 1987).

There are a number of reasons why women (and children) continue to suffer economically when marriages end. For one thing, some judicial decisions may be biased in favour of men. According to Peters (1989:212), "some judges may lean toward a financial settlement which favours the principal wage earner, a value deeply rooted in the capitalist way of life and which will often be propitious for the husband." Also, as we have seen, employed women generally earn less than men. Moreover, divorced and separated women suffer from the widespread assumption that men are the chief breadwinners, and women merely secondary earners. The situation may be further exacerbated by the cost of child-care while the woman works. It is true that virtually all spousal support and child support flow from ex-husbands to their former wives (Richardson, 1987:177). However, the new divorce legislation no longer views women as "wronged" dependents, but as equal partners responsible for their own support. Therefore, fewer than 5 percent of women now receive alimony after divorce; child support payments awarded by courts are generally smaller than in the past (McDaniel, 1988a:114-15). Moreover, as Richardson (1987:177) observes, "the size of the average award is generally irrelevant because, in a large proportion of cases, fathers default on their maintenance [child support] payments." The new divorce legislation attempts to avoid gender-based assumptions and to be fair to both partners. Nevertheless, these laws, intended to be gender neutral, end up being unfair to women because they overlook "women's real wage and job prospects, as well as the demands and expense of child care" (McDaniel, 1988a:115). The older women coming out of long-standing marriages, caught in the transition between old and new marriage systems, are especially disadvantaged by no-fault divorce legislation (Wietzman, 1985).

Since three-quarters eventually remarry (McKie et al., 1983:233), most divorced people have not rejected marriage *per se*. Once again, gender makes a difference. Divorced men initiate dating more easily and are more likely than their female counterparts to describe themselves as "elated and free" after divorce (Hetherington et al., 1979). Differences also exist in the human resources available to them. As doers of the kinwork, women have available to them intimate relationships which predate the split-up. By contrast, the structure of men's lives provides access to "instant networks." While men rely less on kin and old friends, they have a wider circle of casual contacts that can be activated after the marriage dissolves (Gerstel, 1988).

Men are quicker to remarry and more of them do so (Baker, 1984). Four-fifths of divorced men versus two-thirds of divorced women, ever remarry (Ambert, 1980:189). One reason for this difference is the fact that ex-wives usually have custody of the children. However, the marriage gradient requiring women to marry someone at least their own age has been, until recently anyway, a major factor involved here, with age being a greater barrier to remarriage than dependent children. In comparison, much younger women are considered suitable marriage partners for divorced men. For example, in the summer of 1989, *Playboy Magazine* founder Hugh Hefner remarried at age 63. His 26-year-old bride, Kimberley Conrad, a former Playmate of the Year, produced a baby the next spring.

People's economic situation also influences their decisions and opportunities to remarry. Men in the lower socioeconomic strata, and women in the upper socioeconomic strata are least likely to remarry. Poor men have little to offer women seeking relief from the poverty divorce often brings. Women who are economically self-sufficient have more options (Peters, 1989:225), while women in financial need are most likely to remarry (Ambert, 1983:

Peters, 1983:297). The points made by these studies are important: people get married again for a variety of reasons; not everyone wishes to remarry.

Marriage and Psychological Distress

If the proposition of "his and her marriages" that we have been considering is valid, husbands' and wives' distinctive experiences should result in different psychological consequences. Indeed, after postulating that "there are two marriages... in every marital union, his and hers," Bernard (1972:15) remarked, *"And his... is better than hers"* (emphasis added). According to her, marriage is good for men, they need marriage more than women do; by contrast marriage damages women. Is Bernard's contention correct? The answer to this seemingly straightforward question turns out to be rather complex.

When the rates of psychological distress and disorder of women and men are compared, many studies show that on the average, women are more distressed than men (Mirowsky and Ross, 1989:83 ff.). Unmarried people (single, widowed, divorced, and separated) are, on the average, more distressed than married people (Mirowsky and Ross, 1989:90 ff.). So for both sexes, the psychological costs of being single are higher than those of marriage. When we examine gender and marital status together, the situation gets more complicated. In general, wives' rates of distress and disorder do exceed husbands' (Gove, 1978; Fox, 1980; Thoits, 1986:260). Although Bernard (1972) argued that it is *marriage* per se which makes women sicker, more recent theoretical discussions look to traditional male-female difference in the *numbers of roles* accumulated. Traditionally, married women have held fewer important social statuses. We stress the *importance* of statuses: whether one is employed versus unemployed, a partner in a committed relationship or not matters considerably more than whether one is an automobile driver, dental patient, etc. (Thoits, 1986:259). The empirical data support the hypothesis of role accumulation: those who play few societal roles—the unmarried, the unemployed, housewives, the retired, those who live alone—have a greater risk of psychological disturbance than their more socially integrated counterparts (Thoits, 1983:176). Put another way, multiple roles offer benefits that outweigh the obligations involved (Marks, 1977; Sieber, 1974). People who play many roles enjoy more social contacts and experiences, are more likely to have close, confiding relationships, and to learn a variety of skills. In addition, "multiple roles buffer the actor against the consequences of role failure or role loss; the actor has other involvements upon which to fall back" (Thoits, 1983:184). As one might suppose, there seems to be a limit to the number of statuses which add to the individual's feelings of well-being. At some point, the obligations associated with multiple roles begin to overwhelm the person. In other words, this role-accumulation is likely curvilinear (Thoits, 1983).

In general, the role-accumulation literature disproves Bernard's (1972) proposition. Although Gove (1972) and Gove and Tudor (1973) agree with Bernard that wives suffer more, the most recent literature indicates that marriage is equally beneficial for men and women (Thoits, 1986). When men and women hold the same number and types of roles, they appear to experience equivalent levels of psychological distress.

To understand married women's mental health disadvantages, we have to look closely at their work. Those who do not work outside the home are at higher risk for psychiatric symptoms than are employed women (Verbrugge, 1985:169). Employment outside the home also offers protection against suicide (Cumming et al., 1975). (This under-involvement and social isolation of housewives places them at the "low" end of the curvilinear relationships between distress and role involvement.) Nevertheless, paid work carries more mental health benefits for husbands than for wives (Mirowsky and Ross, 1989:86). For one thing, the outside work performed by employed married women typically offers less status, pay, and satisfaction than that of their male counterparts. Many studies show that working at challenging and fulfilling jobs improves mental health (Mirowsky and Ross, 1989:94). For another, the distribution of household and parenting duties between partners is usually inequitable. Consequently, women who combine marriage, parenthood, and outside work, who are forced to be Superwomen, often experience demands on their time, energies, and emotions sociologists term *role overload* (Michelson, 1985; Thoits, 1986:271). They are overwhelmed by multiple role obligations. (This places them at the "high" end of the curvilinear relationship mentioned above.)

Indeed, research shows that employed women whose husbands share the housework and childcare have lower rates of psychological distress than both full-time housewives and employed women who are also responsible for household work (Kessler and McRae, 1982; Ross et al., 1983). They and their husbands share the same low level of distress. In other words, husbands of employed wives, who approve of their wives' outside work and do their fair share of the household labour end up being happier themselves than husbands in traditional relationships with full-time housewives (Mirowsky and Ross, 1989:90).

Is it still a man's world? Or do women today "have it made"? Our attempt to untangle the complex research findings on happiness demonstrate that there are no simple answers to these seemingly straightforward questions. Family life entails somewhat different "payoffs" and "costs" for men and for women. Societal change over the past decades have altered the configuration of rewards and costs. Since women and men are heterogeneous categories, some have benefited; some have lost; and most have gained in some respects and lost in others (Gerson, 1985). Change in the organization of work and family life will continue to create new social options and new personal dilemmas for both men and women. We turn next to a discussion of how these considerations are influenced by aging.

GENDER AND AGING

In all societies, age accompanies sex/gender as major axes of social organization that shape the structure of groups and the behaviour of individuals. Gender and age are the two major dimensions of family structure in particular. Both these powerful determinants of social arrangements are social constructs erected upon a biological base. That is, there is complex interplay between the physiological processes of aging and the societal definition and evaluation of people in each age stratum. Within limits set by biology, societies have considerable leeway in deciding what old age is and how the elderly are to be treated. No consensus exists as to when people in our society pass from middle-age status to elderly. Events such as the retirement dinner, the first pension cheque, the first grandchild, or the sixty-fifth birthday all mark changes in status. However, these events do not necessarily change either personal or social identity from middle-aged to old (Matthews, 1979:58).

Although the timing of old age is sufficiently variable to keep people scrambling to hide liver spots and bald spots, the disadvantage of the elderly is exceedingly clear. Aging "generally brings with it gradual pauperization, and increases in illness and social isolation" (Penning, 1983:82). Equally important is the comcomitant loss of status associated with growing old in our society. Just as females are valued less than males, the old are valued less than the young. Beginning in the 1920s, our society has denigrated the value of experience, preferring "the potential of the young to the achievement of their elders" (Strong-Boag, 1988:179). Christopher Lasch (1979a:351) argues that old age holds special terror in Western societies today. He explains:

Obviously [people] have always feared death and longed to live forever. Yet the fear of death takes on new intensity in a society that has deprived itself of religion and shows little interest in posterity. Old age inspires apprehension, moreover, not merely because it represents the beginning of death but because the condition of old people has objectively deteriorated in modern times. Our society notoriously finds little use for the elderly. It defines them as useless, forces them to retire before they have exhausted their capacity for work, and reinforces their sense of superfluity at every opportunity....By devaluing experience and setting great store by physical strength, dexterity, adaptability, and the ability to come up with new ideas, society defines productivity in ways that automatically exclude "senior citizens" (Lasch, 1979:354).

Other cultures and historical periods accord the elderly more respect. According to Connidis (1989:3), such respect tends to be based on economic power rather than either age per se or being more loved than the elderly of today. Studies examining the relationships between aging and ethnic background conclude that the variability of cultures among Canadian ethnic groups, as well as the fact that ethnicity may be confounded with income and education, make generalizations difficult (Penning, 1983:86). Lastly, we note that for all Canadians, old age is in a different category from other stigmatizing characteristics. The fact that everyone lucky enough to survive premature death will eventually grow old means that regarding old people as "not quite human" is not as comfortable as viewing people with one leg as "not quite human" (Matthews, 1979:61).

The above paragraphs attest to the truth of Bette Davis's claim that growing old isn't for sissies. Many commentators have argued that aging is especially difficult for women. Being old and female has been labelled a "double whammy" (Posner, 1980). In other words, women are doubly jeopardized in the last stage of life. Because gender stratification and age stratification are interdependent, all the inequities that accrue to women from living in patriarchal societies seem to crystallize in old age (Abu-Laban, 1981:85-86).

In contemporary society, older women are devalued and powerless as a direct result of a wider society that oppresses all women, regardless of age, in the interests of preserving a male-dominated social order. The low status of older women represents an extension and intensification of the negative impact of sexist society, due to the added factors of age stigmatization and physical frailty (Gee and Kimball, 1987:9).

Research on the "double jeopardy" of aging women suggests that their disadvantaged situation does not translate into damage to their subjective well-being (Chappell and Havens, 1980). That is, elderly women are no less satisfied with their lives than men their age. However, on the objective level, the case for the "double whammy" seems indisputable. Sociologically speaking, females begin to age once they pass their middle twenties. As messages directed at them warn about the biological clock ticking away and the necessity for collagen creams to ward off facial lines and wrinkles, young women become aware of the double standard of aging under which their lives are lived (Bell, 1970). Although people of both sexes are becoming more body- and health-conscious, the ideology of male-dominated societies makes youth and beauty critical for women (Mackie, 1987:230-49). The billion-dollar fashion and cosmetic businesses tell women they are "monsters in disguise." Their beauty "needs lifting, shaping, dyeing, painting, curling, padding" (Stannard, 1971:192). The reason: the traditional evaluation of females in terms of their sexual and reproductive utility to men. From this perspective, postmenopausal women are judged to be "old" while men 15 to 20 years older are considered middle-aged because they retain their reproductive function. "Many middle-aged husbands have an image of themselves as vital, young, sexual, and virile men married to aging women" (Cohen, 1984:34, quoted in Gee and Kimball, 1987:99).

In recent years, people of both sexes have become more concerned about their appearance and health. Many males now show interest in fitness, body-building, fashions, and even manly cosmetics. Nevertheless, male value in the courtship "marketplace" is still heavily influenced by the power and prestige derived from their occupation and from simply being male. By comparison, many women "must rest their case largely on their bodies. Their ability to attain status in other than physical ways and to translate that status into sexual attractiveness is severely limited by the culture" (Bell, 1970:75). Until women become truly equal partners in our society, their physical appearance and the spectre of aging will continue to worry them more than they do men.

Although old age seems a time of loss for both sexes, women are the bigger losers. We consider the differential impact of aging in the passages which follow.

Loss of Spouse

Widowhood has been characterized as "an expectable life event" for women, but not for men (Matthews, 1987). Eighty-two percent of the widowed in this country are women, and their proportion is increasing. There are several reasons why losing a mate to death is experienced more frequently by women. First, there is women's greater life expectancy. For women who survive to age 65, their average life expectancy is 4.3 years longer than their male counterparts'. However, the difference in disability-free time is only 1.7 years (Dulude, 1987:328). The marriage gradient is a second reason why women are more likely to be widowed. Because of the cultural expectation that women will marry "up," husbands are, on the average, two or three years older than their wives (Gee, 1987). Widowed women are less likely than widowed men to remarry. Women's greater life expectancy results in a shortage of eligible men. The fact that the traditional direction of age differences between bride and groom is even greater with second marriages means women in second marriages face an increased probability of widowhood and a longer period of single survivorship (Abu-Laban, 1981:90).

Widowhood is the single most disruptive crisis of all the life cycle transitions (Haas-Hawkings et al., 1985). We would expect that the degree of trauma involved would depend on such variables as the happiness of the marriage, the stage of the marriage, and the manner of death. However, Guelph, Ontario widows interviewed by Anne Matthews (1987:347) indicated, without exception, that the loss of their spouse had affected them more than any other single life event. For old people, the death of a spouse often means the loss of the only person who shared one's adult history and memories. Perhaps, one begins to think of oneself as truly old when no one is left who remembers one as young. Widowhood typically means the end of living in a family. An estimated 36 percent of elderly women live alone, compared to 14 percent of men (Statistics Canada, 1984). Since spouses care for one another, marriage is also protection against institutionalization.

There are gender differences in the impact of widowhood in later years. For the male, widowhood magnifies the socio-emotional disadvantages of masculinity. He often loses his closest confidante. Both because of the nature of male friendship and the smaller number of widowed people likely to be in his circle of acquaintance, he is less likely than the widowed woman to seek emotional support from his own sex. The widowed male frequently lacks homemaking skills. Also, he is at higher risk in terms of suicide potential, morbidity, and mortality rates. The rapidity of male remarriage may indicate an "acute and devastating need for interpersonal support" (Abu-Laban, 1980b:204).

While widowed people of both sexes complain of loneliness, the second major problem for women is financial need (Matthews, 1987:350). With widowhood, women's income is reduced by as much as half (Gee and Kimball, 1987:89). Another unique difficulty faced by women is that loss of a man and movement into the company of other women may be interpreted as a drop in status (Abu-Laban, 1980a:129). Suttee, the Hindu practice of burying the widow alive with her deceased husband or burning her on his funeral pyre, was an extreme expression of the conviction that a woman without a man had no place in society (Stein, 1978).

Loss of Financial Security

Shortage of money is a very serious problem faced by the elderly in Canada. The vision of retirement as a time for couples to cultivate leisure pursuits and travel the globe is a middle-class dream available to relatively few. By conservative estimates, more than one-third of Canadian women 65 years and over live at or below the poverty line, compared with about 20 percent of aged Canadian men (Gee and Kimball, 1987:54). Shortage of money affects nearly every aspect of life, including shelter, nutrition, and health. As noted above, elderly women without husbands are especially likely to be poor.

Over 60 percent of unattached women aged 65 and over existed at or below the poverty line in 1982. The figure for unattached elderly men is high as well (48.9 percent), but there are nearly four times more unattached elderly women than men. These unattached elderly women are, for the most part, wid-

ows, and their likelihood of being poor increases with advancing age (Gee and Kimball, 1987:55).

Although homeless people are of all ages, skid row is no longer the exclusive domain of men (Harman, 1989; Ross, 1982). (See Tindale [1980] for a discussion of homeless men.)

Elderly women are poor not because they are old, but because they are women who outlived their husbands (Gee and Kimball, 1987:59). The gender-based organization of our society makes women dependent on men who control the financial resources. Older Canadian women tend to be poor because they devoted their lives to their families without pay, in the belief that would always be taken care of. "When they become widows, as they almost inevitably must under our present marriage customs, the vast majority find that the promised security does not exist" (Dulude, 1978:95). Women of earlier generations grew up in a social order which provided them with little education or job training. Those who were in the labour force worked for low pay or part-time, which gave access to low pensions, or more typically for small firms without pension plans at all (Novak, 1985:148). In the end, women's lifelong preoccupation with the family fails to pay off.

Loss of Work

Given the different meaning that work has had in men's and women's lives, gender differences in retirement experiences might be expected in a society such as ours. Specifically, since males have traditionally looked to their work as source of personal identity and social worth, one would expect retirement to represent a serious role loss for males (Blau, 1973). According to this logic, retirement should be more difficult for male workers than for their female counterparts. Surprisingly, research provides only qualified support for both the hypothesis of male retirement trauma and the hypothesis of gender differences.

According to research, most people stop working as soon as it is financially feasible to do so, and most of these "young-olds" adjust to it with little trouble (Novak, 1985:169). For instance, Atchley's (1982) sample members of both sexes found that retirement turned out to be better than they had expected. Indeed, life satisfaction improved slightly after retirement. The widespread belief that retirement increases mortality and people die shortly after retirement is not true for the majority (Parker, 1982:119). Social class is an important variable here that operates somewhat differently for men than women. Working-class men, those who do not own or control the means of production, and who have had low work satisfaction, are pleased to retire. Their life satisfaction has come from family and leisure roles and it is to these roles that they now turn. "Being the man of the house" has depended less on work outside it and more directly on being a husband and father (Hochschild, 1975). By contrast, middle-class and professional men, with control over their work, have enjoyed their work and wish to continue. However, they realign themselves to leisure occupations that resemble work. The middle-class has more resources to cope with the loss of work and their morale is higher. For all men, health and income are the factors that count in retirement adjustment (Parker, 1982).

Retirement does not emasculate or devastate. Why? These possibilities suggest themselves. Adjustment may be aided by anticipatory socialization in the last years of paid work that stresses the negative aspects of the job and the positive experiences that lie ahead. Reference group support likely operates—one's friends are also retiring and retired. Perhaps, masculine gender identity is sufficiently invested in alternate leisure and family roles. Finally, since retirement is institutionalized, expected, the "right thing" to do, the man can attribute this withdrawal from the occupational role to society, not personal failure (Riley et al., 1969:966).

With few exceptions, the retirement of women from the labour force is similar to men's. The type of work being left behind affects both sexes' attitudes (Gee and Kimball, 1987:74-75). Income and health are central to the adjustment of both (Burwell, 1984). However, being married is associated with retirement adjustment for women but not men (Atchley, 1982). And social class operates dif-

ferently. Women with lower occupational status and unmarried women plan to delay retirement for economic reasons (Atchley, 1982). Burwell (1984) cites Atchley and Corbett's (1977) intriguing finding that retirement comes for many career women before they feel they have achieved their professional goals. Such women were late-starters in careers (because of time out for child-rearing) and time ran out for them. Finally, women who have been full-time housewives do not retire in the usual sense of the term. To paraphrase the cliché, a housewife's work is never done.

Aging as Liberation from Gender Expectations

As well as the costs discussed above, growing older brings with it some gender-related benefits. McDaniel (1988b:20) suggests that both sexes can benefit from the softening of gender stereotypes that accompanies aging.

Aging....may represent a liberation from rigid gender role expectations for both women and men. Strict adherence to socially prescribed gender roles is largely a pattern of youth. With growing years and wisdom, apparently we have the good sense to realize how inhibiting and inflexible these gender roles are and to dispense with them.

With age, men become more caring (Gove et al., 1989), and women more assertive (McDaniel, 1988b:21).

Women sometimes experience gains in power and authority through the "turns of the social ferris wheel" of aging (Bart, 1969). Many people abhor the possibility that older people, especially older women, might be sexually active (Posner, 1975). While this misperception has some unfortunate implications, it can also bring advantages. Men apparently fear women's sexuality (Lipman-Blumen, 1984:86). Women's sexuality also interferes with their authority claims (the "soft body, soft mind" phenomenon [Ellmann, 1968:74]). Therefore, older women sometimes trade their *perceived* asexuality (Posner, 1975) for benefits such as power in the family, authority in professional work contexts, and physical freedom. The voice of the matriarch carries weight. The gray-haired female professor knows what she is talking about. In some countries of the world where younger women are forbidden to leave home unescorted, "older women are free to walk alone at any time of the day or night, to go to bars, to swear, and to interact freely with men" (Safilios-Rothschild, 1979:214).

Lastly, aging frees both men and women from some family responsibilities. With children grown and both partners freed of workplace responsibilities, husbands and wives in retirement-stage marriages have the opportunity to devote attention to each other (Keating and Cole, 1980). Older couples are particularly likely to be satisfied with their marriages (Connidis, 1989:20). Whether as cause or effect of this enjoyment, their sharing of work tends to become more egalitarian. Although the households of older people continue a gender-based division of labour, husbands perform an increasing number of "masculine" tasks and are less reluctant to try their hand at "feminine" jobs (Connidis, 1989:23). While it is true that most older people continue to pursue sex-linked interests established earlier in life, more possibilities are now open to organize their lives with less concern for traditional gender division of labour.

As noted earlier, elderly women are less likely to spend the last stage of their lives in marriage. The French feminist, Simone de Beauvoir (1970:543) observed that widowhood releases women from domestic responsibility: "It is for women in particular that the last age is a liberation: all their lives they were subjected to their husbands and given over to the care of their children; now at least they can look after themselves." Unfortunately, many women must "look after themselves" on precious little money.

As noted in our earlier discussion of unpaid domestic labour, it is adult daughters and daughters-in-law who take responsibility for the care of elderly parents. The role played by women in geriatric care is illustrated by the story of Claire, a 53-year-old Edmonton woman, a part-time teacher (Finlayson, 1989: 50-51).

[Claire's] father was stricken with Alzheimer's disease, and her mother's arthritis became so severe that both parents had to be placed in long-term care facilities in their hometown, an eight-hour drive away. About once every six weeks, Claire drives there and stays for a week "to do all the little things that need to be done" for her parents—the banking, making name tags for their clothing, buying underwear. In addition to the physical strain, the emotional effect of seeing her parents increasingly feeble is also wearing her down. Although she has two brothers that help out in other ways, she says "they don't do this kind of work."

Aging and Gender in the Future

The current cohort of elderly Canadians is a product of unique historical experiences. Demographic and technological developments suggest that aging in the future will be a different proposition. For example, as the baby-boomers reach old age and the proportion of the elderly in our society increases, the cult of youth should fade so that growing old will no longer be the *faux pas* it used to be (Neugarten, as interviewed by E. Hall [1980]). New economic arrangements may mean old people in the future need not contend with poverty. However, as Abu-Laban (1981:96) warns, though "the lot of older women would be improved as a comcomitant to improvements in the lot of the old in general, prophecies of 'deliverance' for older women, *as women*, are not assured" (emphasis in original). Only the disappearance of patriarchy could lift the stigma of femininity.

CONCLUSIONS

Chapter 9 continued the structural analysis of gender begun in the previous chapter. Attending to the social conditions that promote equality or inequality between the sexes directs our attention to issues of power and resources. We ask: "Who benefits from existing gender arrangements?" "What social mechanisms serve to maintain the status quo?" Men, the more powerful sex, control all the important institutions of society: government, the economy, education, religion, leisure, the justice system.

Gender and age stratification within the key institution of the family, "the cradle of gender roles" (Lipman-Blumen, 1984:97), were the concerns of Chapter 9. The enormous influence that feminism has had upon sociologists' understanding of families was discussed.

Changing family structure was a major theme of the chapter. Various social forces, among them women's changing labour force activities (Chapter 8), feminist ideology, increased prevalence of divorce, and improved contraception, have altered the structure of the Canadian family. Feminist scholars and activities argue for the legitimacy of many family types. Gloria Steinem (1983b:23), for example, says:

...we are beginning to realize that anybody who says family in the singular is talking about only one kind of *family*, and it is usually his or hers. In fact, there have always been, throughout history, many different family forms. No one kind of family is right for everyone. We are, therefore, trying to honour single-parent families, to honour extended families, to honour people who do not wish to have children, to honour chosen families. We are trying to dispense with the authoritarian structure of the family which is the model of the authoritarian state. Once we accept it at home, we are much more likely to accept it elsewhere.

Benefiting from the insights of Jessie Bernard (1972:1981a), Chapter 9 compared "his" and "her" marriages and "his" and "her" families, and concluded that both sexes encounter structural constraints. Demands and expectations emanating from the family constitute a major source, perhaps *the* major source, of women's inequality. Women experience work segregation both at home and in the labour force (Armstrong and Armstrong, 1984). Compared with men, they lack power and money. The binding of their time and energy to the demands made by traditional family has prevented women from pursuing opportunities in societal institutions beyond the family, from developing alternative bases of power and resources. The massive influx of women into the labour force since the 1960s has served to increase, not decrease, the expropriation of their energies by males. Wives, even those employed full-time, "spend about twice as much time with children and two-and-a-half times as much time on housework" (Giele, 1988:302).

Although men have been the main benefactors of patriarchal family arrangements, they too have been constrained by family. Until the 1970s, the "good-provider role" (Bernard, 1981b) held husbands-fathers responsible for the financial support of all the women and children in their lives. The good-provider role has undergone modification as a combined result of economic changes making a single income inadequate to support most families, the influx of women into the labour force, and feminist ideology. Some men have welcomed relief from sole responsibility for the burden of family support (Ehrenreich, 1983). However, many men feel bewildered, degraded, and angry about the old prerogatives they have lost and the new pressures confronting them (Bernard, 1981b:10). Wives in the labour force, with paycheques and independent experience of the world, have wrested some power away from the patriarch. Many wives demand that their partners share housework and childcare. Although employed women around the globe continue to be overloaded with a disproportionate share of household work, many male partners find "feminine" housework "demasculinizing" (Bernard, 1981b:11), and resent pressure to change. Male discomfort is understandable: the women's movement has placed many men in a "double bind." They are expected to be successful according to the traditional norms, but they are also expected to explore the new, emerging gender norms (Baker and Bakker, 1980). These new standards of achievement for males emphasize the cultivation of expressivity in their relationships with women and children.

The structural perspective on gender may convey the mistaken impression that individuals are the prisoners of social structure, sentenced to obey norms and to believe ideologies. However, the structural perspective teaches that social arrangements are somewhat arbitrary social conventions, not divinely ordained or the inevitable outcome of biology. Since they have not always and everywhere been the same, gender arrangements can be altered. Therefore, we emphasize that social structures do not perpetuate themselves. Rather, it is people who actively participate in the replication of social structures. And it is people who bring about change through skepticism and challenge. The last chapter of this book deals with the matter of bringing about change in gender relations.

NOTES

1. Gelles (1985) argues against viewing patriarchy and male domination as a single-factor explanation of family violence. According to him, research shows that the following additional factors are involved in domestic violence: the intergenerational transmission of violence; low socioeconomic status; social and structural stress; social isolation and low community embeddedness; low self-concept; personality problems and psychopathology (p. 359). See also Steinmetz (1987).
2. Family violence is a problem in many parts of the world. Identifying cross-cultural feminist movement concerns for the 1980s, Gloria Steinem (1983b:22) said, "When you tell one group of people—men—that they are superior and tell another group—women—that they are inferior, it is a lie. It can only be maintained by violence,

and thus the area in which we most reliably and intimately come together [i.e., the family] has become suffused by violence." For example, according to statistics released by the India Home Affairs Minister, in 1987, 1786 brides were murdered by their husbands for failing to bring a sufficiently generous dowry into the marriage. Demanding a dowry as a condition of marriage has been illegal in India for nearly 30 years (*The Globe and Mail Report on Business Magazine*, April 1989, p. 116). Vanaja Dhruvarajan (1989) of the University of Winnipeg emphasizes that although Indian women are equal in the eyes of the law, the Hindu family acts like a state within a state in determining women's fate.
3. At times, the sociology of the family has virtually equated families with women. Researchers encouraged wives to speak for the family as a whole (Safilios-Rothschild, 1969). Yet in other contexts, sociologists have buried women's experiences of the family through "the use of overarching, homogeneous units of analysis such as 'the household' and 'the family'" and through "the hegemony of male experiences of families..." (Thorne, 1982:11).
4. Thorne (1987) argues that since both feminist and traditional thinking in the sociology of the family remain centered around the experiences of adults, children have yet to be granted conceptual autonomy.

Chapter 10

Prospects and Avenues of Change

When people feel neglected or frustrated or mistreated by the existing social order, they sometimes band together to seek a collective solution to their problems in a social movement. A *social movement* is "a large-scale, informal effort designed to correct, supplement, overthrow, or in some fashion influence the social order" (Toch, 1965:5). Despite the worldwide historical prevalence of female disadvantage relative to males, women's collective revolt against this disadvantage has occurred only in the last century (Chafetz and Dworkin, 1986:1). [1] The first wave of feminism, the Suffrage Movement, developed in the closing decades of the nineteenth and the beginning decades of the twentieth centuries. It took place in North American, European, and other Commonwealth societies.

The end of the 1960s saw women in many parts of the world once again collectively organize to protest and improve their lot. This second wave of feminism, which continues to this day, caught most people (including such professional observers of society as sociologists) by surprise. What on earth had women to complain about? (Freeman, 1973). Since then, both continuing and newly evolved sources of female discontent have been articulated. Adamson et al. (1988:3) list the challenges and revelations of the second wave:

[I]t has challenged images of women and of femininity; the sexual division of labour in the home and the workplace; outdated laws and inadequate social services; the organization and delivery of health care to women; and the reproduction of stereotypic choices for girls and women within the education system. It has uncovered and named violence against women—sexual harassment, incest, rape, and wife abuse; it has identified the discrimination women face in the workplace, such as lack of access to the male-dominated trades, to training, or to executive promotion ladders; it has exposed the heterosexism and racism that pervade the entire social system and contribute to the double and triple oppression of lesbians, immigrants, and women of colour.

The above list is far from complete.

This chapter, as an epilogue to our discussion of the development and operation of gender, will concentrate upon the multi-faceted women's movement in Canada, its history and its changing goals. Attention will also be given to two collective responses to the second wave of feminism—the men's movement, and the conservative women's countermovement—which continue to interact with and influence feminism in this country.

HISTORICAL BACKGROUND

For centuries women have been saying much the same things they are saying today. "'Coming and going,' 'appearing and disappearing,' beginning anew virtually every fifty years and sometimes not attaining comparable insights to those who have gone before but who remain unknown...constitute[s] women's tradition" (Spender, 1982:49). Progress has been very, very slow because women's criticism of the social order has met ridicule and abuse. More often than not, feminists have been condemned "as *women* rather than responded to as writers or thinkers" (Spender, 1982:51, emphasis added).

Best known of the early feminist thinkers is Mary Wollstonecraft, whose *A Vindication of the Rights of Woman* was published in 1792 (three years after the start of the French Revolution). Wollstonecraft saw male power as the root cause of society's problems (Spender, 1982:152). Like other heirs of the Enlightenment, she believed that "reason, if properly cultivated through education, could set men and women free" (Rossi, 1973:3). Influenced by Rousseau, she wrote of her conviction that "the neglected education of my fellow-creatures is the grand source of the misery I deplore." As a result of her analysis of women's situation, Wollstonecraft was ridiculed and harassed. In her own time, she was described as a shameless woman, a "hyena in petticoats" and one of the "philosophizing serpents we have in our bosom" (Rossi, 1973:32). Twentieth-century critics have called her "an archetypal castrating female, 'God's angry woman,' a manhater whose feminist crusade was inspired by...penis envy" (Spender, 1982:154).

Mary Wollstonecraft hated men....[Her] life reads like a psychiatric case history. So, for that matter, do the lives of many later feminists....[She] was afflicted with a severe case of penis-envy...[T]hat she was an extreme neurotic of a compulsive type there can be no doubt. Out of her illness arose the ideology of feminism, which was to express the feelings of so many women in years to come (Lundberg and Farnham, 1947, quoted by Rossi, 1973:37).

In short, Wollstonecraft received personal attacks, rather than substantive criticism of her ideas.

In the centuries intervening between *A Vindication of the Rights of Woman* (1792) and the Suffrage Movement, men preserved their power monopoly; women (and some men) continued to criticize patriarchy. Contemporary feminist scholars, digging into the hidden past, have concluded that "women's meanings and values have been excluded from what have been put forward as society's meanings and values" (Spender, 1982:8). The people whose ideas counted, whose writings were preserved in our intellectual heritage were generally men (Smith, 1975).

Among these men was John Stuart Mill. His *The Subjection of Women*, published in 1869, lent the American suffrage movement prestige (Rossi, 1973:183). The beginning paragraph of his essay reads in part as follows: "The principle which regulates the existing social relations between the two sexes—the legal subordination of one sex to the other—is wrong in itself, and now one of the chief hindrances to human improvement; ...it ought to be replaced by a principle of perfect equality, admitting no power or privilege on the one side, nor disability on the other" (from Rossi, 1973:196). Another historical figure whose analysis of women's condition was influential was Friedrich Engels. His book, *The Origin of the Family, Private Property and the State* (1902), along with the work of his colleague, Karl Marx, was discussed in previous chapters.

In summary, "the meaning of female experience has been fed only rarely into the larger reservoir of valued social knowledge" (Janeway, 1980:4). Although collective feminist revolt, confined to the last hundred or so years, is a recent phenomenon on the world scene, much of the ideological underpinning of contemporary feminism is an old, old story. "When one reads the new feminists side by side with the ones from previous generations, and even centuries, one is struck by the fact that, of what is being currently said and written, very little is new: it is an ever-repeating script...[This] repetition attests to the overall lack of change that has taken place in the condition of women" (Ambert, 1976:170).

WOMEN'S SUFFRAGE IN CANADA

In a way, the suffrage movement in this country grew out of the problems of Emily Stowe. In the 1860s, Mrs. Stowe was having difficulty supporting her invalid husband and three children. By scrimping and saving part of her teaching salary, she managed to save enough to study medicine. Rejected by Canadian medical schools because of her gender, she graduated from an American school. Then she returned to Toronto as Canada's first female physician and began to work for societal reform. Because of her efforts, the University of Toronto admitted women in 1886. The vote for women was regarded by Stowe and other like-minded women as a lever to open the way to other reforms. In 1876, Dr. Stowe launched the Toronto Women's Literary Club. The word "suffrage" was avoided as too bold (Cleverdon, 1974:19-20).

The struggle for women's political rights in Canada was launched by women with strong feminist commitment, who tried to batter down the barriers against women's entrance into prestigious occupations (Bacchi, 1983:24). However, the movement also involved many people, often religiously motivated, with prior interest in other types of social reform. Supporters of the vote for women were above all else, conservative, Anglo-Protestant members of the upper-middle class, whose priority was strengthening the family through social and moral reform (Chafetz and Dworkin, 1986:118). These people were disturbed by changes in Canadian society: "The abuses of industrial capitalism, the congestion and disorder of the cities, the influx of new immigrant groups and declining fertility among the Anglo-Saxon elements of the population worried middle-class reform groups, who envisioned wholesale social degeneration" (Kealey, 1979:3-4). Although rural women in the prairie provinces did not share many of the eastern concerns with factory reform and cleaning up the cities, they did share national concerns about alcohol abuse and arrival of large numbers of immigrants (Errington, 1988:69).

Contradictory motives drove women's reform efforts (Miller, 1987). On the one hand, there were emancipatory motives to free child and female labour from terrible working conditions, to loosen the bonds of slavery (in the United States and elsewhere). Liberal, even radical, motives characterized genuine feminists who questioned women's accustomed place in all social institutions. On the other side were the repressive motives of privileged women playing their traditional role as "guardians of public morality," and protectors of home and family, displaying ladylike concern to banish drunkenness, licentiousness, and indecency from the streets of Canadian cities. For example, the Women's Christian Temperance Union (WCTU), the largest of the turn-of-the-century women's organizations, adopted prohibition as its major platform.

Drink (used as a noun), its members argued, turns "men into demons and makes women an easy prey to lust" (Mitchinson, 1979:154). The WCTU believed most women did not drink. "Where men were seemingly unable to act, then, women could and would" deal with this social ill (Mitchinson, 1979:155).

In all, feminists constituted a rather insignificant, and unpopular minority (Chafetz and Dworkin, 1986:118). In Bacchi's (1983:123) words, the Suffrage Movement in Canada "was less a 'woman's movement' than an attempt on the part of particular men and women, predominantly urban professionals and entrepreneurs, to supervise society." The WCTU, for instance, did not reject society's traditional view of women, "but argued that what made them different from men and what made them the centre of domestic life necessitated their involvement in temporal society" (Mitchinson, 1979:166). Many Suffragists regarded the vote for women as a means to an end, the key to their more pressing social reform goals (Kealey, 1979:10).[2]

The Canadian women's struggle for the vote was peaceful in comparison with the militancy of Emmeline Pankhurst's group in England, which made its point through firebrand tactics:

They cut telephone wires; broke porcelain in the British Museum; threw stones and wielded knives and hatchets; put jam and tar in mailboxes and wreaths on a statue of Joan of Arc; they set fires and planted bombs... Emily Davison hurled herself in front of the horses at the Derby and was killed [thus becoming a martyr to the movement]. The government adopted the so-called "cat and mouse" tactics to deal with hunger-strikers. They were kept in jail until they were exhausted; then they were released; after they recovered they were taken into custody again (Smith, 1957:689).

Though Canadian leaders such as Nellie McClung were thought unladylike (her motto was "Never apologize, never explain; get the job done and let them howl"), for the most part, they played by existing social rules (Kome, 1985:11).

The Suffragists here argued that it was unjust to pay taxes and obey laws without having a share in making laws. They contended that the state needed women's point of view. Failure of the male-run legislatures to pass protective laws for the women who were flooding into industry became a powerful argument for extending the franchise to women. The final argument for political equality was women's contribution to the war effort in 1914-18 (Cleverdon, 1974:10-11).

The fact that it took half a century to win the vote suggests that the males who monopolized power were not easily persuaded by the above arguments. They countered that women were too weak to participate in the excitement of elections, that since they took no share in the defence of the country they were not entitled to vote, that women did not have the mental capacity to comprehend political problems, and besides, most women did not want to vote anyway (Cleverdon, 1974:5). In the United States, "scientists argued that if women used their brains excessively, they would impair their fertility by draining off blood cells needed to support the menstrual cycle. Many genuinely believed that the dawning feminist movements threatened the survival of the race" (*Newsweek*, 18 May 1981:81).

The attention that has been given to people such as Dr. Emily Stowe, Judge Emily Murphy, Josephine Dandurand and Nellie McClung[3] invites a "great woman" approach to the Canadian Suffrage movement which is not altogether accurate. The time was one of reform, and as we noted, the issue of women's vote was associated with a wide range of social reforms relating to factory working conditions, alcoholism, poor health and diet among working people in Canada (Marsden and Harvey, 1979:190). These multiple issues explain why middle-class women's organizations such as the Women's Christian Temperance Union, the National Council of women among urban women, and the Women's Institutes among rural women played a leadership role in the Suffrage Movement. The WCTU, for example, was concerned with the problem of alcoholism among working people. Its leadership was convinced that if women obtained the vote, they would then be in a stronger position to influence liquor laws (Marsden and Harvey, 1979:191).

The first World War, women's participation in the great patriotic effort as factory workers, as well as the progressive attitudes ushered in by Canada's involvement in this global affair were instrumental in securing female suffrage (Errington, 1988:73). Women secured the federal vote in 1918, and the provincial vote between 1916 and 1922 in every province except Quebec, where women had to wait until 1940. Between 1916 and 1925, women became eligible to sit as members in the House of Commons and in all provincial legislatures, except Quebec and New Brunswick (Baines, 1988:167). Another major battle was won in 1929 when the British Privy Council amended the British North America Act to include women as legal persons. Until that time, "women under British Common Law were only considered to be persons in 'the matter of pains and penalties, but not in the matter of rights and privileges'" (Marchildon, 1981:101). The Persons case, initiated by five Alberta women in 1927, raised the issue of whether women were eligible for appointment to the Senate. The Privy Council ruled that for the purposes of Section 24 of the British North America Act, women were qualified persons and thus eligible to be summoned to the Senate (McCallum and McLellan, 1980).

In a sense, though, the Suffragists had won the battle but lost the war. "Women got the vote and achieved a measure of legal emancipation, but the real social and cultural barriers to full equality for women remained untouched" (Dixon, 1971:166). The vote was sought by a coalition of groups as a tool to further their own purposes. Once the vote was won, the coalition dissolved; the various member groups returned to their own individual interests (Kome, 1985:15). Although securing recognition of women in law as equal participants in the nation's political process was an important and necessary victory, the Suffrage Movement did not change women's place in the home, in the workplace, or alter community attitudes about the sexes (Errington, 1988:73).

From the 1920s until the 1950s, women's organizations such as the YWCA, the Canadian Federation of University Women, the Business and Professional Women's Clubs, the Women's Institutes, *L'Association féminine d'éducation et action sociale*, professional teachers' and nurses' associations, and local church groups worked quietly for various reforms (Kome, 1985:21). However, their efforts received little public attention. When the Great Depression of the "dirty thirties" fell upon the nation, women faced "increasing pressure to embrace this 'new' profession of homemaker and leave the public workplace to men, who now more than ever needed to earn a wage" (Errington, 1988:74). As mentioned in previous chapters, women participated in armed forces and factories during the Second World War. However, from the outset it was clear that their activities in the public arena were temporary measures to meet the wartime emergency. World War II was followed by the intensely conservative decade of the 1950s. Though publicly visible social movement activity diminished, some organizations and individuals continued to struggle through these decades. Events of the 1960s once again thrust feminism into the public consciousness:

The notion of a second wave catches what was happening, reminding us that in social change, as in oceans, calmer patches are followed by new and stronger peaks of activity. The second wave implies the image of a tide pouring in, each wave going further up the beach, with a continuity of organizational and individual efforts over time and a hope of progress (Black, 1988:82-83).[4]

THE RE-EMERGENCE OF THE FEMINIST MOVEMENT

The second wave of the women's movement, which developed in the late 1960s and continues to the present day, is one of the most profound political and cultural phenomena of this century. We can safely say that the lives of every Canadian woman, man, and child have been affected by its activities. For the first time ever, the tenets of patriarchy were questioned by significant numbers, as North American and European women called attention to the exploitation and oppression of women around the globe. This movement, which now exists in almost every country of the world, resists easy description:

The women's movement has a shifting, amoeba-like character; it is, and has always been, politically,

ideologically, and strategically diverse. It is not, and has never been, represented by a single organizational entity: it has no head office, no single leaders, no membership cards to sign. Indeed, much of the widespread support for women's liberation has had no organizational identification at all (Adamson et al., 1988:7).

To the extent that the Canadian segment of this worldwide movement can be talked about in organizational terms, it is made up of hundreds of groups, some small, some large, some focussed on single issues, some with complex, wide-ranging political agendas (Adamson et al., 1988:8).

The contemporary feminist movement in Canada officially began with the activities that led to the federal government's 1967 decision to establish a Royal Commission on the Status of Women in Canada (Morris, 1980). Prior to this political action, women's situation was not regarded as a social problem. A number of inter-related factors explain why women became aware in the 1960s of their disadvantaged status—a situation which had prevailed all over the world, and for most of history—and finally organized to do something about it. The post-World War II era was a time of rapid industrialization and urbanization. The tertiary sector of the economy expanded substantially, providing large numbers of new jobs in occupations long dominated by unmarried women. The result was the dramatic increase in the proportion of all women, including married middle-class women, in the labour force. Higher divorce rates and substantially reduced family size also pushed more women into the labour force. Many women became aware that they were segregated in a handful of occupations and earned less than sixty cents for every dollar earned by men. In addition, the role overload of employed married women who remained responsible for household work spurred their consciousness of the inequities of the gender system. Women's sense of deprivation in comparison with their male peers was an important cause of women's activism. Also relevant was the unprecedented numbers of females (as well as males) now being exposed to "the radicalizing force" (Lipman-Blumen, 1984:205) of higher education. The expansion of women's roles in the public sphere enhanced

the formation and spread of gender consciousness, and the amassing of personal and collective resources necessary for women to mount a
movement on their own behalf (Chafetz and
Dworkin, 1986:50-59, 220).

We should also note that the currents of intellectual thought in Canada, the United States,
and Western Europe concerning equality of
opportunity and human rights issues were ripe
for a reconsideration of women's position in
society. The second wave of the women's
movement began amidst social and political
tumult, and openness to change (Adamson et
al., 1988:260). The economically prosperous
1960s was a decade of protest: the anti-war
movement, the student movement, the American civil rights movement, the Quebec nation-
alist movement, the Red Power movement. The
combination "created a belief in, and an enthusiasm for, the possibilities of change unparal-
leled in recent history" (Adamson et al.,
1988:257). The ideology of change spilling
northward across the U.S. border through
media and personal contacts mingled with the
ideas of parallel, indigenous movements in this
country (Morris, 1980). The young women
involved in these activist movements, many of
them students and ex-students, became aware
of the subordinate position of females through
their work in organizations advocating freedom and equality for others. "Repeatedly,
women's efforts in major causes on behalf of
others opened the window to a view of their
own inequality and powerlessness" (Lipman-
Blumen, 1984:182). In the service of these
causes, women were "only asked to do the
cooking and cleaning, the licking of stamps,
and the stuffing of envelopes...but never to
advance their own ideas or become leaders
themselves" (Marsden and Harvey, 1979:195).
The Voice of Women, an organization formed
in 1960 to oppose nuclear weapons, played a
crucial role as a link between the New Left
activist groups in Canada, and the mainstream,
upper-middle-class women's organizations
(Morris, 1980). It also served as a political training ground. Also important was "the 1966 reor-
ganization of a large number of existing Quebec women's organizations into the Fédération

des femmes du Québec and the Association
féminine d'éducation et d'action sociale"
(Black, 1988:83). The establishment of a Royal
Commission on the Status of Women was the
first success of Canada's re-emerging feminist
movement.

Once again, effective leadership, this time in
the person of Laura Sabia, responded to the
zeitgeist, the spirit of the times. "Successful city
councillor in St. Catherines, Ontario, unsuccessful provincial candidate, and popular radio
talk-show host, Sabia was a charmer and a
rabble-rouser, endlessly energetic as a cam-
paigner and organizer, following in the line of
the women like Emily Murphy who energized
the first wave of Canadian feminism" (Black,
1988:86-87). As president of the Canadian Federation of University Women, Sabia invited all
established women's organizations to send
delegates to a meeting on women's status. On
May 3, 1966, women representing 32 organizations with a combined constituency of two
million women met in Toronto and created a
steering committee, headed by Sabia, to approach the government for the purpose of insti-
tuting a Royal Commission on the Status of
Women. *Chatelaine* magazine editorials were
timed to support this demand (Morris, 1980).
The Cabinet agreed to establish the Commission, thus legitimizing "the social problem
definition of the status of women" and publicly
signifying the movement's beginning (Morris,
1980).

The Commission was set up to inquire into
the situation of Canadian women, and to
"recommend what steps might be taken by the
Federal Government to ensure for women equal opportunities with men in all aspects of Canadian society" (p. vii). Its activities
intensified communication on women's issues
across the country, as hearings in 14 cities
gave women a forum to articulate their
grievances and caught media attention (Black,
1988:88). Three years later, the Commission
tabled its report, which contained 167 recommendations in the areas of the economy,
education, the family, taxation, poverty, public
life, immigration and citizenship, and criminal
law.[5]

THE BRANCHES OF CONTEMPORARY FEMINISM

Feminism is "an emancipatory project," which "aims to examine women's oppression, expose the dynamics of male domination and female subordination, and guided by that analysis, fight for women's liberation" (Maroney and Luxton, 1987a:1). As is frequently the case with complex social movements that encompass a broad set of issues (Turner and Killian, 1987), feminism does not speak with a single voice. Nonetheless, there are certain basic ideas shared by all feminists: "[A]ll believe in equal rights and opportunities for women; all recognize that women are oppressed and exploited by virtue of being women; and all feminists organize to make change" (Adamson et al., 1988:9). Within these broad parameters of commonality exist distinctive explanations of women's oppression and the strategies of change they recommend. Twenty years ago, the women were fully aware of the fact that they were initiating a new movement. However, the branches of feminism to be discussed below did not exist as such then (Adamson et al., 1988:28-29). Concern for pigeon-holing labels came later. Both feminist scholars and activists find it useful to distinguish among liberal feminism, socialist feminism, and radical feminism. (Chapter 8 discussed the last two theoretical accounts of the relations between the sexes.)

Liberal Feminism

Liberal feminists view discrimination placed on women as a group as unjust because it deprives women of equal opportunities for pursuing their own self-interest. Although existing societal arrangements will require modification to provide women with rights and opportunities equal to those enjoyed by men, the premises of society are not in question. That is, liberal feminists do *not* regard the oppression of women as a structural feature of the capitalist economic system. Therefore, unlike their more radical sisters, they do not advocate overthrowing that system. Instead, liberal feminists look to the state to bring about women's liberation through legislative measures. In addition, they are also concerned about rectifying the informal discrimination against women which grows out of the differential socialization of females and males (Jaggar, 1983:175 ff.).

Liberal feminism is one offshoot of the Western tradition of liberal political thinking (Jaggar, 1983). Liberal political theory grew out of the work of such philosophers as Thomas Hobbes (1588-1679) and John Locke (1632-1704) who argued that all members of society are free and equally participating individuals who enjoy certain rights. Though these early philosophers did not include women, "In an age when people believed that members of lower social orders should simply submit to the greater wisdom of their natural superiors and rulers, these were novel ideas" (Code, 1988:25). Mary Wollstonecraft, the Suffragists, and the coalition of women's groups which pressured the federal government to establish the Royal Commission on the Status of Women all fit into this liberal political tradition. So do such contemporary bodies as the National Action Committee on the Status of Women (an umbrella organization of women's groups that lobbies the federal government), the Canadian Advisory Council on the Status of Women, and provincial advisory councils which act as liaisons between governments and women (Hosek, 1983:7).

Because contemporary liberal feminism does not really challenge the foundations of Canadian society, but is willing to work within existing parameters, "the liberal-feminist voice is the accepted public voice of feminism" which has increased "public awareness and acceptance of feminist aspirations for change" (Adamson et al., 1988:190-91). Therefore, this branch of the women's movement has played a significant role in bringing about important reforms. For example, liberal feminists are concerned to achieve justice in the workplace (e.g., equal pay for work of equal value, equal rights training and hiring programs, maternity leave) and in the family (matrimonial property rights). They press for more daycare places, more services for abused women, pension rights. They have been influential in the passing of human rights legislation, and alterations in the educational system (Adamson et al., 1988:191).

As a final example, the federal government, responding to "agitation by native women, with the support of the women's movement and later the native movement" (Ng, 1988:201) finally, in 1985, agreed to amend the Indian Act, R.S.C. 1970, c. I-6 (amended S.C. 1985, c. 27) to remove restrictions it placed on Indian women, but not Indian men. Before this amendment, under Section 12(1)(b) of the Indian Act an Indian woman who married a non-Indian man ceased to be an Indian under Canadian law. Such a woman was required to leave her reserve upon marriage and to dispose of any reserve property she held. Her children were not recognized as Indian. She could be prevented from returning to the reserve, even if she became poverty-stricken, sick, widowed, separated, or divorced. Finally, her body could not be buried on the reserve with those of her ancestors. Indian men, on the other hand, could marry whom they pleased. Indeed, through marriage, Indian men could confer full Indian rights and status upon non-Indian wives and children (Jamieson, 1979; 1981; 1986). Bill C-31, designed to end perceived discrimination by allowing native women who married non-natives to regain full status and be eligible, along with their children, for benefits such as housing, free education, and health care ended up creating enormous difficulties. The cost of the program is estimated to exceed $1.2 billion (*Calgary Herald*, December 3, 1989). At the time of writing, the matter remains unresolved. For discussion of the complicated ramifications of this legislative change for individual natives and band councils attempting to cope with the threat to their resources by increasing membership of returning women and children, see Ponting (1986:297-300).

Because the changes enumerated above, as well as many others, constitute reforms to the existing social system, we associate them with liberal feminism. However, as Adamson et al. (1988:191) emphasize, these gains were not achieved simply through the efforts of the mainstream politics of liberal feminism. Rather, "they were the product of an overall climate of struggle generated primarily by critiques of how the system operates." These critiques came from the more radical branches of feminism to which we now turn. These branches are predicated on the assumption that alterations of existing institutions that are sexist through and through cannot fundamentally alter the power relations at the heart of patriarchy.

Socialist Feminism

The socialist-feminist branch of the renewed women's movement seeks to integrate the issues of gender and class, to unite the concepts of patriarchy and capitalism (Adamson et al., 1988:67). See Hamilton (1978), Mitchell (1971), Smith (1977a, 1977b.). Though it grounds its analysis of women's oppression in the writings of Marx and Engels, it is critical of the gender-blindness of these ideas (Sargent, 1981). Unlike middle-class liberal feminism, it targets the state/government as the site of patriarchal capitalist power (Adamson et al., 1988:112). It agrees with Marxism that the ruling class dominates, not only the economy, but the development and proliferation of knowledge (ideology) that serves to perpetuate the interest of the rulers. It extends Marxist analysis of productive activity to the gender division of labour in workplace and home, contending that "the capitalist economic system oppresses women as a group, just as it oppresses the working class as a whole" (Code, 1988:36). However, within capitalist patriarchal society, women are oppressed in additional ways:

First, within the labour force women's work is alienated labour just as men's work is: women own neither the means of production nor the products of their labour. Second, women in the labour force are commonly in positions subordinate to men whose superiority is by no means apparent: hence they are doubly alienated from realizing their own potential. Third, women who work as housewives are in a still more disadvantaged position. Their lives are characterized by servitude, their labour is accorded no material value, and they are excluded from the "public" world (Code, 1988:36-37).

As feminists, this branch opposes the traditional gender division of labour in family and labour force, and the inferior legal status of women. It struggles for women's control of reproduction, for their freedom to choose contraception and abortion. As socialists, it understands itself to be involved in the "historic struggle of working people against a system which creates poverty in the midst of wealth; alienating work in a technological society; divisions between black and white [as well as among other ethnic and racial groups], male and female, workers in this country and abroad; capitalism" (Jaggar and Rothenberg, 1984:153). In sum, the abolition of both gender and class is its goal. Socialist feminists hold that women's liberation will occur only under socialism; and socialism will only be established with the liberation of women (Adamson et al., 1988:70). Revolution is the ultimate goal. Nevertheless, pragmatism governs more immediate concerns.

The activities of the socialist feminist branch are concentrated upon various aspects of women's work (Adamson et al., 1988:71). From a different philosophical base, socialist feminists join with liberal feminists in campaigns for affirmative action programs, equal pay for work of equal value, and effective daycare (Code, 1988:31). Proposals for wages for housework have also been of considerable interest. Although socialist feminists criticize the activities of the state, they seek "to get the state to work for women rather than against them" (Adamson et al., 1988:115). Therefore, socialist feminism in Canada has found political affinity with the New Democratic Party (Adamson et al., 1988:124). Within Canadian trade unionism, which has formal alliances to the NDP, there exists "a strong, organized, and relatively successful movement of union women, heavily influenced by a socialist-feminist politic" (Adamson et al., 1988:124).

As well as advocating programs of social change that would provide alternatives to capitalistic modes of production, socialist feminists also seek alternatives to the patriarchal organization of the family. "With many other feminists, socialists see in the nuclear family a cornerstone of women's oppression" (Code, 1988:39). Their focus on the dual issues of class and gender has led them to establish alliances with immigrant women, lesbian women, and women of colour (Adamson et al., 1988:75).

Radical Feminism

Radical feminism, like socialist feminism, rejects liberal feminism's willingness to work within the basic framework of society; it, too, presents a sweeping critique of women's situation. However, radical feminism considers women's oppression to be *the* fundamental oppression (Millett, 1969).[6] Pointing out that women around the globe in a variety of economic systems live under male domination, they argue that patriarchal oppression goes deeper than class oppression. Indeed, sexism is seen to be at the root of other societal evils, such as class hatred, racism, ageism, ecological disaster, and war (Code, 1988:39). Radical feminism concentrates on "the intimate interactions of everyday life with no theory of the state" (Maroney and Luxton, 1987b:16).

Its analysis of sexism starts with human reproduction (Firestone, 1971). The gender division of labour begun with procreation extends into every aspect of human existence. Women are responsible for most of the work involved in infant care and child-rearing. As well, they are expected to tend to men's physical, emotional, and sexual needs (Jaggar, 1983:249). Radical feminism depicts a world "in which men control women's bodies and force women into motherhood or sexual slavery" (Jaggar, 1983:287). (Firestone's [1971] analysis of forced motherhood was noted in Chapter 5.) Violence against females—rape, sexual harassment, incest, pornography, domestic violence—has been its main issue (Adamson et al., 1988:71). Robin Morgan (1977:163-64) described rape as the "quintessentially patriarchal" crime and "the ultimate metaphor for domination, violence, subjugation, and possession" in patriarchal societies. While most feminists have no objection to erotica, the "passionate celebration of sex between two equal partners" (Anderson, 1984:23), they regard pornography as the antithesis of love (Manion, 1985). Pornography is viewed as hate literature against women, which society would not tolerate against Jews, Indians, or blacks. For analyses of violence against women, see Brownmiller (1975), Dworkin (1979), Clark and Lewis (1977), Griffin (1981).

Radical feminists share with socialist femi-

nists the premise that the dominant male culture promulgates a picture of reality that buttresses patriarchy and denigrates women. In
the words of MacKinnon (1983:636), "The feminist theory of knowledge is inextricable from
the feminist critique of power because the male
point of view forces itself upon the world as its
way of comprehending it." The masculine
culture is also held responsible for violence and
militarism. This linkage is expressed by author
Margaret Atwood in a letter to *The Globe and
Mail* quoted by Rosenberg (1987:515): "There
are two things that men do that women don't:
they make war and they commit rape. That's
two good reasons for working towards a future
society that derives more of its values from
women."

The conviction that male-female relations
are inevitably oppressive to women led such
radical feminists as Mary Daly (1978) to conclude that female separatism is the only answer. According to them, women "need a
womanspace, a space free from male intrusion"
where women can nurture each other, regain
control over their own bodies, and develop a
womanculture (Jaggar, 1983:270). For some,
lesbianism is the only acceptable sexual expression for women (Rich, 1980). Reproductive
freedom is at the top of their agenda.

According to Adamson et al. (1988:67), radical feminism was an important current in the
Canadian feminist movement of the 1970s. Its
teachings were influential in the establishment
of rape-crisis centres, shelters for battered
women, and campaigns against pornography.
Nevertheless, radical feminism's strategy of
withdrawal from male-dominated institutions,
as well its controversial critique of the family
and heterosexuality, do limit its appeal and
influence. Jaggar (1983:296) argues that while a
limited separatism of women from men is
healthy and necessary, a branch of feminism
whose ideology excludes the male half of the
population and all women with emotional attachments to men is "doomed to remain a small
minority."

A fine line must be drawn between appreciating the ideological and tactical distinctions
we have just made, and exaggerating the divisive forces within the Canadian women's
movement.[7] The constitutional crisis in the

early 1980s certainly provided evidence of the
ability of Canadian women, from a variety of
backgrounds, to join together to fight an important battle. When the Canadian government
moved to patriate the constitution from Great
Britain, it wished to entrench a Charter of
Rights and Freedoms in the package. A nationwide organization of women successfully over-
came the opposition of federal and provincial
politicians to strong gender equality provisions
in the Charter.

Many women were shocked to discover how hard
they had to lobby to get section 28 into the Charter.
They were astonished to find such resistance to
equality rights for women. In the midst of an historic
opportunity to make a statement about the basic
principles by which Canadian laws were to be governed, equality for women still had to be negotiated,
fought for and defended at every stage (Hosek,
1983:11).

Though the constitutional issue was a re-
formist issue, women's involvement in Canadian constitution-making in the early 1980s
was a *mass* involvement (Billings, 1983:13).
Women who believed Canadian society was
egalitarian already were drawn into the movement. Hosek (1983:11) writes, "For many, this
was a time of political awakening....There was
a sense that this was a once-in-several-lifetimes
opportunity in which one had to participate."
In 1985, four years after the equality rights
section 15 of the Charter of Rights and Freedoms came into force, the Women's Legal
Education and Action Fund (LEAF) was
founded to promote equality for women
through the litigation that became inevitable
because the Charter guarantees of 'sex equality'
do not spell out the meaning of gender equality.[8] In other words, the objective of LEAF is to
see that the Charter's guarantees are neither
restrictively interpreted nor ignored by the
Canadian courts. The fact that so few Canadian
judges are women makes LEAF's watching
brief especially important.[9]

The constitutional battle also showed the divisions within Canadian feminism. Shortly afterwards, participants and observers were eu-
phoric about the significance of the fight for the
future of the women's movement (Kome,
1983). More recent assessments are, however,

less sanguine. Commenting on the inability of the women's group to achieve consensus among Quebec and Western Canadian women, as well as the short-lived nature of the ad hoc lobbying group, Burt (1988) concludes that the episode "raises questions about the future development of the women's movement" (p. 80). During the height of the emotional Meech Lake accord negotiations in the spring of 1990, organized women's groups were strangely quiet. Although it was clear that the Meech Lake proposal (allowed to lapse by provincial governments for various other reasons) endangered women's protection under the Charter of Rights and Freedoms, there were no vociferous protestations of the accord from Canadian feminists.

We turn next to consider two organized responses to the challenge of feminism: the reactionary women's movement and the men's movements.

THE WOMEN'S COUNTERMOVEMENT TO FEMINISM

R.E.A.L. (Realistic, Equal, Active, for Life) Women of Canada, a Toronto-based group with chapters in every province, was founded in 1983. R.E.A.L. Women is the most visible organizational arm of the right-wing backlash to feminism (and to the gay liberation movement). This well-financed attempt by women to restore 1950s-style patriarchy has its roots in the anti-abortion movement and fundamentalist religion. Its ideology and efforts parallel those of turn-of-the century anti-suffrage organizations. Indeed, the American group, the Eagle Forum, led by Phyllis Schafly played a central role in the defeat of the Equal Rights Amendment to the United States Constitution which would have prohibited discrimination on the basis of sex (Marshall, 1989).[10]

At first glance, it is difficult to comprehend the virulent anti-feminism of large numbers of Canadian women. As one feminist put it, "It is as if, at the height of the civil rights movement, a large percentage of blacks had suddenly organized to say: 'Wait a minute. We don't want equal rights. We like things just the way they are.'" (English, 1982, quoted in Caplan,

1985:351). Nevertheless, this group of "generally well-educated, articulate and politically astute women" should not be dismissed as mere dupes of patriarchy (Dubinsky, 1985:4). The ideas promulgated by R.E.A.L. Women appeal to significant numbers of Canadian housewives (and a few professional women) who apparently feel belittled or threatened by feminism (Crittenden, 1988). They have needs that liberal feminism, with its emphasis on helping women to succeed in the public sphere, has neglected. Women who have remained in the home as full-time housewives and mothers are convinced that their contributions are not being properly recognized by society (Dubinsky, 1985).

What does R.E.A.L. Women stand for? This organization, and others like it, must be understood in the context of the rise of right-wing political forces in many parts of the Western world.

Calling for a return to an imaginary past when women and men were happy in clearly defined sex roles, the new right treats the women's movement as a crazy radical fringe, which the government does not need to take seriously. They have an ideal image of women as mother and helpmate to man, an ideal that has little room for lesbians, single mothers, or independent women (Adamson et al., 1988:85).

Their "separate but equal" position holds that women are uniquely suited to look after home and children, while men's domination of the public sphere is justified "by males' inherently superior aggressive, analytical, and logical abilities" (Marshall, 1989:574). Indeed, R.E.A.L. Women campaigned against the equality clause in the Canadian Charter of Rights (Eichler, 1988:419). They argue that women have equal power in the family, but a different kind of power. A spokesperson is quoted as saying, "A woman can get a man to do an awful lot if she goes about it in the right way" (McCracken, 1987). Let's look more closely at this ideology.

As mentioned in Chapter 9, R.E.A.L. Women accuse "radical" feminism of undermining "the role of the family in our society by its push for equality of women in the workplace, and easier access to abortion and divorce" (McCracken, 1987). Their own "pro-family" stance encompasses a number of inter-related issues. To them, a strong family means opposition to abortion under any circumstances. According to a position paper put out by R.E.A.L. Women, "It is repeatedly said by feminists that society over the years has oppressed women and feminism is the answer to overturning this oppression. How, then, can the genuine feminist justify, in turn, aborting her unborn son or daughter, the most deadly kind of oppression?" (Eichler, 1986:12). In general, R.E.A.L. Women present full-time housewives "as an embattled group whose status needs to be upgraded" (Eichler, 1988:417). Their "pro-family" position also implies women's right to remain at home and be supported by their husbands. In the words of a Calgary member, "Once you are a mother, your instincts tell you that raising your children is your most important role. You are not emotionally or mentally free to do anything else until that responsibility is ended" (McCracken, 1987). They sharply disagree with feminist support for universally accessible, high quality, government-subsidized daycare. R.E.A.L. Women wants government tax reform to give childcare tax credits to parents whether they use daycare or look after their children at home. Moreover, this countermovement identifies divorce "as a social evil" and opposes Canada's no fault divorce law as "the easy way out" (Eichler, 1986:20). Viewing homosexuality as a threat to marriage and family, it feels there is no need for human rights legislation to protect homosexuals from discrimination. The issue of violence against women receives no attention from this organization.

As noted above, R.E.A.L. Women affirms a "separate, but equal" doctrine which asserts that the private realm is the proper sphere for women, and the public arena is the proper sphere for men. Therefore, this countermovement to feminism rejects measures which would increase the equality of women in the public sphere (Eichler, 1988:419). Specifically, it opposes the principles of equal pay for work of equal value and affirmative action.

Canadian feminists take very seriously this anti-feminist organization that *claims* 40 000 members. Feminist sociologist Margrit Eichler is quoted as saying she has "the highest respect for the intelligence of the leaders of REAL Women. They have a great deal of political savvy" (McCracken, 1987). Several observers (e.g., Adamson et al., 1988:86) have commented on the countermovement's adept use of rhetoric to misrepresent feminism and advance its own cause. For example, its name "R.E.A.L. Women" attempts to convey the message that it is *the* authentic women's movement, representing the concerns of most women. In addition, the fact that this organization forms part of the political swing to the right enhances its threat to feminism. In the last few years, R.E.A.L. Women's lobbying efforts have achieved a hearing from the Conservative federal government. They now compete for funding with the liberal feminist organization, the National Action Committee on the Status of Women (Crittenden, 1988). Their sixth annual conference in 1989 was funded by a controversial Secretary of State grant for $21 000 (*Calgary Herald*, May 6, 1989:H3).

It is too soon to tell whether the women's countermovement will succeed in undermining the gains of feminism. Meanwhile, feminists grant that there is some truth to R.E.A.L. Women's charge that the feminist movement, in its early years, gave insufficient attention to issues pertaining to women in the home (Dubinsky, 1985:43). (See also Friedan, 1981). Nevertheless, feminists emphatically dispute R.E.A.L. Women's claim to represent the concerns of most Canadian women. "While the new right seeks to control and limit women's choices, the goal of the women's movement is for all women to have choices in all areas of our lives" (Adamson et al., 1988:86). "They are trying to turn the clock back to a time that no longer exists" (McCracken, 1987). Through feminist eyes, R.E.A.L. Women of Canada constitutes a giant step backwards. Understandably, members of this countermovement view their own goals and activities much more favourably.

THE MEN'S MOVEMENTS

Over the past 25 years, the revival of feminism has introduced many changes into the lives of Canadian men. The dissatisfaction and demands of their dating partners, wives, mothers, and work associates have required them to rethink the meaning of masculinity and their relationships with the women in their lives.

As indicated earlier, the second wave of feminism was itself, in part, a reaction to various structural developments that took place during and after the Second World War. These inter-related societal changes included the disappearance of single-paycheque jobs capable of supporting entire families; the expansion of industries which drew heavily upon female workers (e.g., personal services, finance and real estate, public administration); the massive influx of women into the labour force, and the consequent decline of the breadwinner role (Armstrong and Armstrong, 1984); more liberal divorce laws, new reproductive technology. In addition, both sexes were affected by the liberating cultural currents of the 1960s and 1970s: the civil rights, anti-war, student, women's, and gay liberation movements. In summary, much of the upheaval in men's lives that is frequently attributed to the women's movement, in reality, has other and prior causes to which the feminist movement was, itself, responding.

First of all, this section will review new challenges to traditional masculinity. Then the collective responses of men to their changing situation will be considered. The men's movements, like feminism, are not monolithic.

The Challenges to Traditional Masculinity

Change, at the heart of all social movements, renders people anxious, uncomfortable, resentful and angry. Since the late 1960s, feminists have struggled to secure greater power in their personal relationships, families, places of work, indeed, in the running of society as a whole. It is a sociological truism that those who have power resist sharing or giving it up. As gender relations specialist James Doyle (1989:302) observes, "many, it not most, men just plain enjoy having status, power, and control over women." The confusion and rage of men caught between old and new ideas about masculinity is, therefore, understandable. Although the discomfort was exacerbated for males who reached adulthood prior to the

1970s, all males have been affected by the challenge of feminism.

Let's consider some specific aspects of these changing definitions of masculinity. Traditionally, being a male meant superiority to and domination of females, success at work, providing for dependent women and children, emotional distance, even toughness, in dealing with other men, women, and children. As we have seen, definitions of masculinity vary somewhat with social class, ethnicity, and generation. However, the point being emphasized is that the economic and cultural changes of the past quarter century have seriously undermined the traditional conceptualization of masculinity.

The workplace has been an important site of changing gender definitions. The female competition encountered in school and at work has been a shock for males brought up to believe that men are naturally superior to women. Many men are angry about what they interpret to be unfair advantages being given to women through affirmative action programs. Tolson (1977:48) comments on the impact of women's massive entry into the labour force upon the complex interplay between work and masculinity:

The extent to which definitions of gender interpenetrate attitudes to 'work,' is not often fully understood. For it is not simply that [gender] enters into the division of labour, differentiating 'men's' and 'women's' jobs. Nor is it a matter merely for legislation, to be reformed by 'equal pay' and 'opportunity.' For men, definitions of masculinity enter into the way work is personally experienced, as a life-long commitment and responsibility. In some respects work itself is made palatable only through the kinds of compensations masculinity can provide....When work is unpalatable, it is often only his masculinity (his identification with the wage; 'providing for the wife and kids') that keeps a man at work day after day (Tolson, 1977:48).

See also Livingstone and Luxton (1989).

Previous chapters have emphasized the interlinkages that exist between work and family institutions. Since the majority of wives now remain in the labour force throughout their adult lives, most male egos can no longer find nourishment in being sole breadwinner. Nor

can sustenance be found in dominating dependent women. Even though the typical
woman earns far less than the typical man,
some money of her own and experience in the
public sphere increase her independence and
broaden her options. Many men are ambivalent
about women's financial contribution to the
family. Although the second paycheque is
welcomed, the consequent loss of traditional
control over wives may be resented. Also, as
discussed earlier, friction enters modern relationships when female partners pressure males
(often unsuccessfully) to share the household
work. Men often feel awkward and inadequate
when they are asked to do jobs they have never
been taught to do. Indeed, asking men to perform household tasks—diapering a baby,
cooking a meal—that contradict their conventional gender notions sometimes stimulates
deep-seated anxiety (Luxton, 1986:31). Finally,
many men are upset and confused when
women are no longer willing to serve their
needs as they did in the past. Under the influence of feminism, women "stopped thinking
about what women should do for others and
began thinking about what women wanted for
themselves" (Clio Collective, 1987:356).

Up to now, masculinity has been interpreted
as *difference* from femaleness. When women are
no longer so different, what is a man to be? The
blurring division of labour between private
and public domains, and within occupations is
sometimes accompanied by suggestions that
men *ought* to be more like women. A connection
is made between inexpressive, hard-driving,
Type A masculine personalities and heart attack statistics.

The initial and irrefutable reason for men to transform themselves was...to save their lives. No treatise
or document of men's liberation, no matter how
brief, failed to mention the bodily injuries sustained
by role-abiding men, from ulcers and accidents to the
most 'masculine' of illnesses, coronary heart disease
(Ehrenreich, 1983:140).

Middle-class men are invited to become softer,
more nurturant, to reveal their tender side, to
cry. Suggestions are made that men who have
remained emotionally distant from wives, children, and friends lose out on life's worthwhile
experiences. Nevertheless, men cannot be expected to give up their hard-driving competi-

tive behaviour and the priority attached to
work unless social rewards are provided for
androgynous behaviour that are commensu-
rate with what they already have. Status,
money, and personal power continue to be
highly valued in capitalist society. "Men may
gain better health, longer lives, more fulfilling
leisure time, and greater intimacy in relationships with men, women and children, but how
many will choose these experiences at the expense of occupational achievement and status
rewards, when their socialization has geared
them towards these goals and their society
requires them for its maintenance?" (Baker and
Bakker, 1980:558).

If some elements of feminist analysis have
left men feeling unsure about who they are,
others have instilled resentment and shame.
"For a powerful current in feminism, focusing
on sexual exploitation and violence, sees masculinity as more or less unrelieved villainy and
all men as agents of the patriarchy in more or
less the same degree" (Carrigan et al.,
1987:140). In his novel, *The Good Father* (1983:46-
47), Peter Prince describes the dismay of
Hooper, a well-meaning young Englishman, in
the early years of the women's movement,
when Janey, a fellow university student, shows
up wearing a T-shirt bearing the slogan "All
men are rapists:"

I asked her about it," said Hooper. "Did it mean: All
men are potentially rapists? Because they've got
pricks? Like: All women are murderers? Because
they could hit me on the head with a hammer if they
chose to? No, she said. It means what it says. All men
are rapists. Just that...Well, I got very angry. I mean,
if that was the case —

To state literally that all men are rapists would
be quite ridiculous. However, the important
feminist message on the T-shirt was that the
rape and battering of women are to be understood as manifestations of patriarchy, not as
aberrations of a handful of bad men. In
Kaufman's (1987b:15) words, "men's violence
against women is probably the clearest, most
straigthforward expression of relative male
and female power." [11]

Coming to terms with the reality of men's
power over women, its roots in organized patriarchal systems rather than individual per-

sonalities, has been an extremely difficult feminist lesson for men to grasp. This observation holds true for even well-educated, enlightened men of good will. The structural basis of gender is perhaps the most important of several messages about masculinity that have been conveyed to heterosexual males by the gay liberation movement.

The Challenge of Gay Liberation

The Gay Liberation Movement, like the second wave of feminism, emerged out of the social ferment of the 1960s. Gay liberation is usually dated from the 1969 Stonewall Riot in New York City (Kinsman, 1987a:112). By 1971, the first gay liberation group in Canada, the University of Toronto Homophile Association, had been formed (Adamson et al., 1988:53). In a well-publicized show of resistance in February 6, 1981, an estimated 3000 gays and their supporters demonstrated in the streets of Toronto against the arrest of 300 men on "bawdy-house" charges following police raids on gay baths (Kinsman, 1987b:13).

The assertion that "gay is just as good as straight," at the heart of gay liberation, called for gay men and lesbians to affirm their identities, and suggested that sexuality need not be solely for reproduction (Kinsman, 1987a:113-14). In 1973, as a result of movement pressure, the American Psychiatric Association re-categorized homosexuality from a mental illness to an alternative lifestyle.

Two decades later, Canadians entertain ambivalent attitudes concerning homosexuality (Rayside and Bowler, 1988). On the one hand, attitudes towards gay equality rights, e.g., job discrimination have become more liberal. On the other, the "fear and loathing of homosexuality shows no signs of abating" (Rayside and Bowler, 1988:656).[12] The AIDS epidemic, incorrectly identified by many people as a disease exclusive to gay men, has heightened moral condemnation of homosexuality among some Canadians.

Both lesbians and gay men have been involved in the organized critique of institutionalized heterosexuality: calling for pride in their sexuality, questioning the equation of homo-

sexuality with pathology, and struggling for inclusion of sexual orientation in human rights (Kinsman, 1987b:17). Given the entanglement of sexuality and gender, both have attacked traditional social constructions of gender. Indeed, because lesbians experience dual oppression as 'women' *and* as 'homosexuals,' "this has led to a broader and more diffuse social radicalization among lesbians" (Kinsman, 1987b:17). Eve Zaremba (1982:91) describes society's antagonistic response to homosexual women:

This hostile reaction on the part of the "world at large" is not surprising. Society correctly judges that any primary intensity between women must be contained or else the sexual status quo is jeopardized and with it, the whole system of male domination. Lesbian sexuality is dangerous to institutional heterosexuality and thus to every variety of patriarchy. It is basic and essential to women's liberation and vice versa. Its importance to the movement in Canada and elsewhere cannot be overestimated... The impact of the movement on our sexuality in all its diverse expressions has been no less profound.

Our present interest focusses on the connection between the impact of the gay liberation movement upon men's thinking about gender. For this reason, discussion here must be confined to gay men's challenge to hegemonic masculinity. (The interested reader is referred to Adam [1987]; Arnup [1988]; Gottlieb [1982]; Kitzinger; [1987]; and *Signs* [vol. 9, #4, 1984] devoted to "The Lesbian Issue." Also see this book's earlier discussion of the politics of lesbianism in connection with radical feminism.)

Three inter-related lessons about gender have been communicated by the gay liberation movement to those straight men who choose to attend to them. First of all, gay liberation ideology, along with the many types of gay men it encompasses who openly acknowledge their sexual orientation, challenges the necessary, invariant linkage between masculinity (gender) and heterosexuality (sex). Many males confuse their maleness (their biological sex) with personality traits, e.g., aggressiveness, toughness, competitiveness, inexpressiveness, associated with manliness in our particular culture (Kaufman, 1987a:xiv). This false equation of gender and sex explains why many straight people assume all gay men are effeminate, and all gay women are "butch" masculine types.

Over the last decade images of gay men have shifted from the effeminacy of the "gender invert" to the new macho...looks that have dominated the gay men's community. This imagery challenges the previous stereotypes of homosexuals that associated our sexuality with gender nonconformity and has asserted that we can be both homosexual and "masculine" at the same time (Kinsman, 1987a:113).

In thus challenging hegemonic masculinity, gay men provide support for feminist arguments that gender is a social construct whose content varies over history and geography. The way is open for straight men to show gentleness, sensitivity, and compassion without sacrificing their imputed heterosexuality.

Secondly, gay liberationists teach the politics of gender; that is, they underline the significance of power in constituting and maintaining hegemonic constructions of gender. From school yard to adult setting, such epithets as "queer," "fairy," "fag" are employed, usually by males, to define, encourage, and regulate the limits of "acceptable" masculinity (Kinsman, 1987a:103). Departures from "macho" masculinity are pejoratively labelled "effeminate" (female-like). In other words, denial and fear of homosexuality have served to enforce a particular type of masculinity. Similarly, power is employed to constitute females as "naturally" passive, dependent, domestic creatives, and to enforce the subservience of women to men. In short, the gay liberation movement has had a clear understanding of the hierarchy of power relations among men, and the reality of men's power over women (Carrigan et al., 1987:171, 174).

Thirdly, the gay liberation movement teaches the social-structural, systemic nature of gender relations. The penalization of gays and enforced subservience of women are linked together (Carrigan et al., 1987:171). Domination of females by males, and homosexuals by heterosexuals "is based on, and perpetuated by, a wide range of social structures, from the most intimate of sexual relations to the organization of economic and political life" (Kaufman, 1987a:xiv). Therefore, inequality between male and female, and between straight and gay are issues of power and domination that must be addressed at the level of society as a whole. Socialization measures such as encouraging boys to play with dolls, fixing up story books and advertising content will not cause centuries-old patriarchal orders to be overturned (Kaufman, 1987a:xiv).

Collective male reactions to the changing milieu, like women's reactions, have not been monolithic. Following Lyttelton (1987), two major types of men's groups may be distinguished: men's liberation and men against sexism. Both are heirs to the teachings of feminism and gay liberation that while men have something to lose in the feminist challenge to the status quo, they also have much to gain (Kaufman, 1987a:xiii). However, only Men Against Sexism takes the privilege of heterosexual males and the disempowerment of females as its starting point. Only this more radical group acknowledges the hierarchy of power among men; the domination of heterosexual, middle-class, white men over gay men, working-class men, and men of colour. After outlining these two male social movements, a third—the hostile backlash against feminism—will be discussed. This last group has much in common with the conservative women's countermovement.

The Male Liberation Movement

Male liberation emerged in the early 1970s in response to feminism and other social forces noted above. Relatively small numbers of mostly white, affluent, university-educated men in advanced capitalist countries such as the United States, England, and Canada, came together in groups modelled on feminist consciousness-raising groups (Snodgrass, 1975; Tolson, 1977). According to *The Globe and Mail* (February 25, 1989:D5), there has been a resurgence of male liberation groups across the country in the late 1980s involving some 5000 men. The article goes on to describe a Toronto gathering:

They assemble on Sunday at 6:30 p.m., their regulation meeting night. Loaded with pots and casserole dishes containing their contribution to the evening meal, they hug and greet each other, usually eight or 10 of them. After dinner, they get down to business. Tonight the topic is how this consciousness-raising group is changing them, their work, their relationships with spouses, partners, children.[13]

These groups seek "the new man." Their basic premise: males suffer from pathological aspects of the male sex-role. Male liberation groups frequently speak of being *oppressed* by sexism.[14] Lyttelton (1987:473) explains their thinking:

Men are negatively socialized—to be unemotional (except for anger), competitive, invested in the penis, etc. We have a lot to learn (or rather, steal) from women—intuitiveness, sensuality, co-operativeness—in a catchall word, nurturing. Men rely on women for emotional support and to fill our own lacks. Men must learn to give each other emotional support, learn ways of being men that are co-operative and nurturing and do not produce heart attacks.

A member of a 1980s Ontario men's support group describes learning to play rugby at school in England: "I am instructed to tackle a man behind the knees while he runs as fast as he can. I decide I'd rather run in front of a bus. Men scare men, have always scared me," he confesses (Shapiro, 1989:30). These ideas have been promoted in numerous books such as Herb Goldberg's *The Hazards of Being Male: Surviving the Myth of Masculine Privilege* (1976), Warren Farrell's, *The Liberated Man* (1974), and Marc Fasteau's *The Male Machine* (1974).

Male liberationists concentrated on "a male role, distinct from men themselves and imposed on them to their disadvantage" (Ehrenreich, 1983:125). This analysis of masculinity "implied that men could transform themselves suddenly, voluntarily and seemingly without reference to external circumstances..." (p. 126-27). A spokesman for the Toronto group mentioned above says, "The men's movement is a cultural revolution, its primary purpose to open up men to their feelings. We're denying half of our house, and that half of our house haunts us. We're manipulated by our fear of feeling" (*The Globe and Mail*, February 25, 1989:D5). (Radical feminists have an alternative explanation to the male liberationist focus on socialization gone awry. They argue that

distorted masculinity—the clogged arteries and emotional constipation—"arose from the habit of command which all men exercise over women" [Ehrenreich, 1983:124, 127].) Feminism was interpreted to "mean women breaking out of their roles [too], rather than women contesting men's power" (Carrigan et al., 1987:153).

Well-intentioned though it may be, the male liberation movement is considered by critics to be anti-feminist. Although much male liberation movement rhetoric has a pro-feminist gloss, next to nothing is said about male domination of females (or homophobia, racism, or class oppression). The movement is dangerous because it is dishonest, says Ned Lyttelton (1987:474). "It provides a way of having their cake and eating it for men who are afraid that women are going to take their cake away altogether." The male liberationists accepted "feminism in a watered-down version, hoping that men could gain something from its advent" (Carrigan et al., 1987:186-87). This viewpoint required the evasion of the issue of power, the fundamental insight of feminism, as well as any engagement with the gay liberation movement (Carrigan et al., 1987:186-87).

Men Against Sexism

Beginning in the mid-1970s, more radical men, organizing under the name "Men Against Sexism," have added their voices to male liberationists. Men Against Sexism have been sharply critical of male liberation groups for their failure to confront patriarchy and homophobia, their blindness to class and race (Carrigan et al., 1987:161). (See Snodgrass, 1977; Tolson, 1977). Like male liberation sympathizers, Men Against Sexism are predominantly white, middle-class, heterosexual men (Lyttelton, 1987:475). A similarity that these two branches of the male movement share with feminism is the diffuse nature of their enterprises. In other words, the individuals who subscribe to the beliefs and values described here are not necessarily attending meetings and conferences with like-minded people.

As noted already, Men Against Sexism acknowledge patriarchy (Doyle, 1989:308 ff.).

Their analysis borrows from feminism, rather than from the psychologizing male liberation literature. Unlike male liberationists who see contemporary men as every bit the victim of the gender status quo (e.g. Farrell, 1986), this pro-feminist men's movement argues that patriarchy harms primarily women. In contrast with the social-psychological level, "sex-role" analysis and therapeutic emphasis of male lib-erationists, Men Against Sexism attend to the social structures they believe influence men's behaviour. Patriarchal, capitalistic social systems benefit "a few privileged men (i.e., white, heterosexual, educated, and financially secure) while disadvantaging all women and most other men (i.e., nonwhite, gay, undereducated, and financially insecure)" (Doyle, 1989:309). Eradication of homophobia is essential for improving male-male relations (Doyle, 1989:310). Men's violence is an important issue. Violent men are seen, not as deviants or non-conformists, but as *over*-conformists to a culture teaching men's domination of women (Brod, 1987:270). Finally, according to Men Against Sexism, improvements in people's lives can come only through dismantling of the political, economic, and other social institutions undergirding patriarchy.

It would be hard to improve upon Kaufman's (1987a:xv) statement of this over-arching perspective:

[T]he struggle to crack the structures of patriarchy is not secondary to other economic and political changes that will make the world a better place to live. Indeed, the very possibility of creating new social orders is predicated, at least in part, on challenging the oppression of women. This is because patriarchy forms part of the cement of societies based on the domination of some humans over others and of humans over nature—forms of social organization that have led to the coexistence of abundance and poverty, to the possibility of nuclear destruction or ecological castrophe, and to countless forms of oppression based on physical, national, religious, and sexual differences.

It is important to emphasize that the men participating actively in Men Against Sexism constitute only a tiny proportion of North American males. And for good reason. Members of social movements are discontented people convinced that their situation is intolerable and seeking remedy, denied them by existing social organization, through grassroots collectivities. Such is not the case here. Since males are the powerful, prestigious sex, most do not perceive themselves as victimized by the system. Although a gender egalitarian society would widen men's available choices, improve relationships with their wives, children, and friends, and promote better health and longer lives, the costs in terms of power, status and money, all valued highly in our society, would be high (Baker and Bakker, 1980). Not many men are willing to pay the price. Indeed, American journalist Anthony Astrachan (cited in Maynard, 1988:129) has estimated that at most, 10 percent of men give women's quest for liberation their wholehearted support. Even when all the men backing feminism for pragmatic reasons are factored in, the total estimate is a modest 35 percent. "What holds men back is fear: of exposing their own weakness, of losing other men's support, and of humiliation by women" (Maynard, 1988:129).

Male Rights Groups

Time magazine (December 4, 1989:55) describes the renewed women's movement as "one of the great social revolutions of contemporary history...." One inevitable result of whatever successes the women's movement has managed to achieve so far is a backlash from those forces whose power depended on the old order (Steinem, 1983:344). Certainly, at the end of the 1980s, the most highly publicized of the Canadian men's groups are the reactionary male rights activists. Martin Dufresne, secretary of the Montreal Men Against Sexism, has been quoted as saying that the news media are mistakenly identifying men's rights activists "as a male version of feminism" (Zwarun, 1988:A3).[15] The National Action Committee on the Status of Women has also taken a public stand against men's rights activists (*Calgary Herald*, April 14, 1988:D10). Over the last few years, spokesmen for right-wing men's groups such as the Toronto-based organization, In Search of Justice, charge that feminism has gone too far (Maynard, 1988). These men are angry with women. Claiming that women get all the breaks, that anything done for women (and children) is done at the expense of men, their stated objective is to seek equality for males. Feminists, who are understandably critical of this organization, see their arguments as "based not on reason or fairness, but on corrosive anger at women" (Maynard, 1988:126).

Among the issues addressed by men's rights activists, first priority is given to family matters. (See Chapter 9.) Like R.E.A.L. Women, the movement seems to want a return to the 1950s. "It blames employed mothers for most of society's ills: drug abuse, divorce, youth suicide, teen runaways and street crime. The problem, it says, is that women have forsaken their rightful job: 'making life worth living'" (Maynard, 1988:129). The majority of the core group are divorced men who have fought their wives over child custody, access, or support. Alignments are also sought with women who have lost custody of their children, and with more moderate advocates of family law reform across Canada. Its members push for compulsory joint child custody, paternal veto on abortion, and the end to financial support of ex-wives. As mentioned in Chapter 9, men's rights groups have backed attempts by ex-boyfriends to secure court injunctions to prevent their former partners from getting abortions. Ross Virgin, head of In Search of Justice, reasons "If fathers are responsible for 18 years of child support, surely we should have a say in killing it" (Weston, 1989:C2).

Violence is another important issue. Feminists, they say, portray all men as "violent lecherous exploiters of helpless women" (Maynard, 1988:124). Therefore, these men say they seek fairer treatment of men accused of child abuse, rape, and wife assault (*Calgary Herald*, April 14, 1988). For example, they claim that children lie about abuse. They recommend that female victims' sexual history is essential for the fair trial of accused men. Accusing researchers of exaggerating the number of battered wives, men's rights activists demand more attention for battered husbands. Indeed, a Calgary group hopes to collect money through government programs and public donations for a shelter to protect men and their children from violent mates (*Calgary Herald*, January 17, 1988:C4).

Male rights group members express resentment of the presence of increasing numbers of women in the workplace. Hiring and promotion based on affirmative action are sore points. "If women want equality at work, say men's rightists, they should accept the same deal men do. That means no affirmative action, no paid maternity leave and, above all, no government programs to fatten women's paycheques" (Maynard, 1988:124).

Anti-feminist men, in Kimmel's (1989:581) opinion, yearn "nostalgically for the traditional separation of spheres that had kept women from explicitly challenging men's dominance in the public sphere. 'Get back to the home, where you belong!' might have served as the anti-feminist battle cry." The number of blatantly anti-feminist Canadian men who speak publicly appears to be small. However, their existence signals danger to the women's movement. For one thing, this small reactionary organization has forged successful coalitions with divorced men's organizations that seek improved relations with their children, with anti-abortion groups, and with the conservative women's countermovement discussed earlier in this chapter. For another, the rage they voice against women is frightening. One wonders how many silent men they speak for.

Events in the autumn of 1989 provided evidence of deep misogyny in Canadian society (Donaldson and Kymlicka, 1989). When the Canadian Federation of Students launched a campaign against date rape with the slogan "No Means No," some male students at Queen's University responded by putting up mocking slogans in the windows of their residence—"No Means Kick Her in the Teeth;" "No Means Now." At Sir Wilfrid Laurier University, "panty-raids turned ugly when male students splashed ketchup on women's underwear and hung them out for display" (Kirkey and Ibbitson, 1989).

In late December 1989, the nation was shocked that in the worst mass murder in Canadian history, the gunman had deliberately singled out women as his victims (*Maclean's*, December 18, 1989). Twenty-five-year-old

Marc Lepine shot down 14 women, and wounded 13 other people (most of them female) at the University of Montreal's Ecole Polytechnique, before shooting himself. On the second last day before Christmas vacation, Lepine burst into a computing class. He shouted, "You're all a bunch of feminists, and I hate feminists," as he asked the women to move to one side of the classroom, and ordered the men to leave. "Six of the women were shot dead. Over the course of the next 20 minutes, the young man methodically stalked the cafeteria, the classrooms and the corridors of the school, leaving a trail of death and injury in his wake" (*Maclean's*, December 18, 1989:14). Most of Lepine's victims were students of engineering, a traditionally masculine profession where, according to some men, women do not belong. His suicide note blamed feminists for ruining his life.

Two days later, an editorial advised that:

It would be rash to build too elaborate a structure of cause and effect on the fragile base of one demented mind, but the horrifying executions at the University of Montreal do emerge from a social context and cannot be disowned. The tragedy should persuade us to look intensely at the ground in which hatred takes root. It is time for men to talk with men about their continuing oppression of women. Sadly, it is still a time when women have reason to be afraid. *The Globe and Mail*, December 8, 1989).

Calgary Herald columnist William Gold (1989) added that males also need to confront fears aroused by gender: "Behind the macho doctrine of the stiff upper lip, deep fears about their place in life, indeed their very role in life, beset countless men."

THE FUTURE OF GENDER RELATIONS IN CANADA

Looking into the future of gender involves assessing what the renewed feminist movement has managed to accomplish so far, the movement's future prospects, and important tasks remaining on its agenda. Because this entire book has dealt with changing gender relations in this country, the necessarily brief remarks made in this section will focus on gender in the public arena. To paraphrase a judgment made by Penney Kome (1985:179), in gender relations, "where progress is measured in inches, women have come miles towards equality." Nevertheless, a journey of many more miles lies ahead before females and males enjoy equal power and status.

Women Legislators and Public Policy

What has been accomplished in the 20 short years since the Report of the Royal Commission on the Status of Women (1970) was tabled in the House of Commons? In contrast with the inability of the American women's movement to secure the Equal Rights Amendment to their constitution, the campaign for protection of women's rights in the new Canadian Constitution ended successfully. As mentioned earlier, LEAF, the Women's Legal Education and Action Fund, is "a voluntary women's organization whose purpose is to help support the taking of test cases to the Supreme Court of Canada on behalf of women's equality" (Hosek, 1987:513).[16]

By 1987, most of the recommendations made by the Royal Commission on the Status of Women concerning legal inequalities had been implemented at the federal level. For example, women's legal standing had been much improved in regard to family law, family property law, and law concerning sexual assault. Legal regulation of workplace access and conditions had also been ameliorated (Black, 1988a:97). An important example of changing structure in the workplace is the Employment Equity Program which concerns large organizations that bid on sizeable federal contracts. This program, a consequence of the 1983 Royal Commission on Equity in Employment, headed by Judge Rosalie S. Abella, endeavours to ensure that no one is denied employment opportunities for reasons unrelated to ability. The designated groups are women, aboriginal peoples, persons with disabilities, and visible minorities.

Since women's suffrage was the goal of the first wave of feminism, contemporary representation of women in centres of power provides a useful index of gender equality. The gains here are rather mixed. Jeanne Sauvé served as Canada's first woman Governor General from 1986 to 1990. Three women now sit on the Supreme Court of Canada: Bertha Wilson was appointed in 1982, Claire l'Heureux-Dubé in 1986, and Beverley McLachlin in 1989. Representation of women on the Supreme Court proved to be important in several key decisions concerning women made under the equality provisions of the Charter of Rights and Freedoms.

From the mid-1980s, the political parties have become considerably more interested in appealing to women as a voting group and in sponsoring female candidates in ridings where they have a reasonable chance of success. In the televised leadership debates during the 1984 and 1988 federal elections, Brian Mulroney, John Turner, and Ed Broadbent had a great deal to say about "women's" issues (Hosek, 1987:513-14). In 1989, Audrey McLaughlin of the New Democratic Party became the first woman to lead a national political party in this country. In 1990, Sheila Copps was a serious, though unsuccessful, contender for leadership of the Liberal Party of Canada.

What of the federal decision-making body, the House of Commons? In 1971, journalist Barbara Frum wrote in *Chatelaine* magazine: "There are fifty-six whooping cranes in Canada, and one female federal politician" (quoted in Kome, 1985:117). In the November 1988 federal election, 39 women were elected, giving women 13.2 percent of the seats in the House of Commons. (*The Globe and Mail*, August 10, 1989). Although the 1988 representation of women is a record high, four times the proportion of a decade ago, it will take a very long time before gender equality is reached in the House of Commons. Moreover, as Liberal MP Sheila Copps (1986:86) observes, females in politics do not necessarily work together for "women's" causes: "All too often, [the women of the House of Commons] are tied by party discipline and party labels and we can't work together in a parliamentary democracy the way we should." The fact that few women have held cabinet posts, especially outside health, education, and status of women portfolios, also reduces women's decision-making power. According to political commentator Charlotte Gray (1989), after the 1988 election, veteran women Mem-

bers of Parliament such as Flora MacDonald, Judy Erola, Pat Carney, and Lynn McDonald were replaced by mostly inexperienced women with little interest in feminist causes. Women have had considerably more success in provincial politics (five women headed provincial parties in 1989); they fare best of all at the municipal level, especially on school boards, which are seen to be a legitimate feminine domain (Kopinak, 1988).

We conclude that, "in spite of the efforts of female legislators, women's groups, and female bureaucrats, male domination of the legislatures has persisted, and women continue to press for reforms from positions that are, on the whole, outside the centres of power" (Burt, 1988:152).

The Prospects of the Women's Movement

If women remain, for the most part, outside the circle of institutionalized decision-makers, future progress toward egalitarian gender relations continues to depend on the women's movement (as well as other sympathetic social movements, such as the Gay Liberation Movement and Men Against Sexism). It is, therefore, important to examine the well-being of the women's movement. (See Adamson et al., 1988.)

The climate of Canadian opinion regarding feminism at the beginning of the 1990s defies simplistic description. On the one hand, national survey results reported by Ponting (1986) suggest strong approval of the goals of the women's movement. Seventy-four percent agreed that "There should be more laws to get rid of differences in the way women are treated, compared to men." Seventy-three percent of the national sample agreed that, "Overall, the women's movement has had more of a positive effect than a negative effect on Canadian society." However, other studies (e.g., Komarovsky, 1976) suggest that many people who support feminist goals at a general level feel otherwise about application of *general* principles to their own lives. For example, men who believe women should be free to enter traditionally masculine professions want to see their own girlfriends and wives in undemanding jobs lower in status than their own ("jobettes," to use Gloria Steinem's term).

Moreover, as previous sections have indicated, significant numbers of Canadians feel troubled and angered by feminism's challenge to the status quo. They resent the intrusion of feminism into the workplace, schoolrooms, the family, even into the most intimate relationships between women and men, into the popular discourse of TV, movies, indeed, into the very languages spoken. Many men "personally feel they are the target, although the protests are not directed against individuals but rather against the institutions, structures, norms and values that shape the oppression of women as a group" (Dumont, 1986: unpaginated). In these conservative political times, anti-feminist sentiment, both organized and unorganized, represents a serious threat to the gains achieved by the women's movement.

The women's movement is also endangered by the indifference of many young women to feminism—the "I'm not a feminist, but..." phenomenon (Dumont et al., 1987:375). Significant numbers of women, who vehemently refuse to identify themselves as feminists,[17] nonetheless take for granted the fruits of feminism: the shattering of the "feminine mystique" that defined female success only in terms of being a wife and mother, access to traditionally male occupations, the elevation of women's status in society, and so on (*Time*, December 4, 1989:56). They overlook "the realities of most women's lives: the wildly disproportionate amount of violence directed at females *because they are females*, the 'feminization of poverty' that simply means most of the poor are women and kids, the killing sexism still taken less seriously than radical or religious bias that affects men, too, the double dose of prejudice against females who are not white, not heterosexual, not able-bodied, or not young—and much, much more" (Steinem, 1987:56).

Young women take this "no, but" position out of ignorance of what life would be for women without the first and second waves of feminism; from reluctance, even fear of displeasing their male partners by openly identifying with feminist leaders, stereotyped as strident, hairy-legged man-haters; because they have not yet gone through "the four big, radi-

calizing experiences of a woman's life: joining the labour force and discovering how it treats women; getting married and discovering it is not usually an equal partnership; having children and finding out who takes care of them and who does not, and aging" (Steinem, 1983b:17). For whatever reason or combination of reasons, the complacency of women jeopardizes the outcome of the battles still being waged for gender equality.

In addition to previously mentioned external factors such as anti-feminist attitudes as part of the country's move to the political right, and the indifference of women of the younger generation, the women's movement must cope with several types of internal division. The existence of differing philosophies within feminism (liberal, socialist, and radical feminisms) was discussed earlier in this chapter.[18] The hotly contested pornography issue provides just one example of how women operating from rival theoretical positions have been seriously and very publicly divided (Burstyn, 1987). While feminists of all ideological stripes regard pornography as distasteful and humiliating to women, radical feminists and liberal feminists disagree over the censorship of pornography (McCormack, 1984).

Although Dumont's (1986:unpaginated) conclusion "that the vitality of feminism will always be measured by the diversity of its trends of thought" seems essentially correct, passionately held theoretical positions have served to divide women's energies and to reinforce men's views of women feuding ("cat-fighting") among themselves. Outsiders' difficulties in grasping just what it is that women want are exacerbated by the publicity received by counter-feminist organizations such as R.E.A.L. Women.

The energies of the feminist movement have been further fragmented by the sheer number of issues embraced by feminism (Adamson et al., 1988:259). Feminists work *for* equitable pay and pensions for women; quality, affordable daycare; control by women of their own reproduction; fair symbolic representation in the mass media and religious teaching; and *against* occupational and education barriers; violent abuse of women; compulsory heterosexuality; discrimination against women of colour, immigrant women, disabled women, old women. All these matters are of unquestioned importance. Moreover, political activity carried out under a feminist umbrella includes the peace (see *Atlantis*, Spring 1987) and environmental movements. Gender equality admittedly pales in significance in comparison with survival of our planet and species. Nevertheless, viewed from the perspective of the women's movement, women's involvement in this wide range of activities serves to undermine the unity of that movement. As Adamson et al. (1988:259) phrase it, "The problem [is] that these efforts [are] often diverse and seemingly unconnected, and the sense of movement often weak."

Also, the efforts of the women's movement are greatly complicated by the regional, ethnic and social class divisions among women in this country. Both anglophone and francophone sectors of the movement share some issues such as reproductive rights, peace, and environmental issues (Black, 1988:90). However, feminists working in Quebec and in English Canada have been isolated from one another by language barriers and by the involvement of Quebec feminists in their province's struggle for national rights within the Canadian confederation (Maroney and Luxton, 1987b:17). See also Bashevkin (1983) and Clio Collective (1987).[19] Native women and immigrant women, like francophone women, face problems not shared by other Canadian women. (See Boyd [1988].) Taking the perspective of Canadian Indian women, Jamieson (1981:131) asks "Are women all sisters under the skin?" Or "to what extent do race, culture and social class constitute a consciousness that supplants, supersedes, or prevents the development of a feminist consciousness?" Ng's (1988:202) comments regarding the relationship of immigrant women to the feminist movement are instructive:

Within the women's movement, immigrant women, together with women of colour, have begun to challenge the movement's strong middle class and racial biases. They draw attention to the fact that demands from the women's movement in the past, such as equal rights for work of equal value, were defined in terms of white middle class women's perspective

and priority. Since immigrant women's locations in society are different as a result of their unequal treatment under the law and in the labour market, their demands have been different.

Finally, as both Jamieson (1981) and Ng (1988) imply, the women's movement has from the beginning been troubled by class cleavages. The majority of feminist activists have been well-educated people from middle-class backgrounds, who have had difficulty understanding the somewhat distinctive concerns of working-class women. Moreover, "because of the educational level required by the movement's mode of communication (books, articles, and meetings), working-class women, especially the very poor ones, are not being reached" by the movement (Ambert, 1976:189). Fortunately, middle-class white feminists are becoming increasingly sensitive to the perspectives and problems of women from other social-class and cultural backgrounds. One of the most valuable lessons learned by the Canadian branch of the women's movement through the years is an appreciation of the worldwide oppression of women. Regularly scheduled world conferences held in Mexico City in 1975 (the United Nations Year of Women) and in Nairobi in 1985 are examples of these global linkages.

The Agenda of the Feminist Movement

Despite significant gains made during the relatively brief tenure of the second wave of feminism documented throughout this volume, formidable obstacles to the goal of gender equality remain. The struggles ahead concern both national and global arenas as Canadian feminists acknowledge their sisterhood with women around the globe (McCormack, 1989). Four compelling, inter-related issues that women struggled with in the 1970s and 1980s remain paramount in the 1990s.

The first issue is the feminization of poverty. In Canada and throughout the world, the poor are disproportionately women and their children. The second issue concerns work in the labour force and home. Until women have fair access to job training, employment opportunities, equal pay for work of equal value, and to affordable daycare of decent quality, they remain financially dependent on men, and subject to their authority. Many women without male financial support, especially single mothers and elderly widows, experience poverty.

As we have seen, women's status outside the home depends upon equitable division of work within the home. Women are flooding into the paid labour force. However, their presence there will not revolutionize existing gender arrangements

...if men do not flood equally into the *unpaid* labor force of child-rearing and homemaking. Women will just continue to do two jobs while men do only one, children will continue to have too much mother and too little father, and the cruel, guilt-producing impossibility of being Super Woman and Super Mom will keep on robbing the country of talent and women of peace of mind (Steinem, 1987:57).

Third, in the 1990s, women in many countries must continue the struggle for their own reproductive freedom (McLaren and McLaren, 1986; McDonnell, 1984). "Reproductive freedom" means control over all aspects of their fertility (which includes but is not limited to the right to choose abortion). Without reproductive freedom, women "can be made pregnant and there is nothing they can do about it" (Eichler et al., 1983:139). As veteran Member of Parliament, Rosemary Brown (1989) writes, "The debate about abortion, which has dogged the struggle of the liberation movement, is a recurring nightmare for feminists, a dispute less about the fetus than about power."

Finally, there is the dreadful problem of violence against women. Women throughout the world are disproportionately victims of sexual assault, domestic battering, date-rape, child abuse, ritual mutilation, and sexual harassment at work. Feminists seek to rescue victims of violence, through shelters and counselling programs, for example, and to ensure them justice under the law. Understanding violence against women to be inevitable consequences of gendered societies in which male power predominates (Breines and Gordon, 1983:493), they seek fundamental social change.

As matters now stand, men continue to control all the institutions of Canadian society.

The power to construct and transmit knowledge is still, for the most part, in male hands. Nevertheless, despite the formidable barriers to gender equality and the internal weaknesses of the women's movement discussed above, feminism offers serious opposition to male hegemony. The fact that the renewed women's movement has had access to means of word- and image-making not yet invented when the Suffragists launched their battle has enabled contemporary Western feminists to challenge masculine "knowledge-making and truth-making on a scale unprecedented in the history of rebellious movements" (Ackelsberg and Diamond, 1987:504). A defiant spirit, once unleashed upon the world, cannot be recaptured.

NOTES

1. Chafetz and Dworkin (1986:2) and Schur (1984:8-9) distinguish between the collective revolt of feminism and individual-level revolt. Chafetz and Dworkin make the important point that "much of the individual female behavior stigmatized by others as deviant are manifestations of revolt, albeit often unconscious, against gender-based inequities..., for instance, lesbianism, many behaviors defined as the manifestation of mental illness when expressed by females, and those who refuse to conform to any number of feminine gender role expectations, resulting in stigmatization as 'tomboys,' 'bitches,' 'unfeminine,' or any number of other unflattering labels" (p. 2). Individual-level female revolt has occurred in virtually every era and place. However, the social control mechanisms available within the community are sufficient to stigmatize and to discredit individual rebellion. As a consequence, change in sociocultural systems of gender inequality result, not from individual revolt, but from the collective rebellion of social movements (p. 4).

2. According to Errington (1988:70), supporters of the campaign for the women's vote did so for a variety of reasons. "For the 'club' women of the East and the cities, suffrage was merely the means to ensure the success of various reforms, particularly prohibition, protection of women in the workplace, and care of the nation's children. The female preoccupation remained the home and the family. Working women who supported the cause did so to promote the practical con-

cerns of equal pay and equality in the workplace. For the farm women of the West, though no less committed to reform, the vote was also viewed as a means to place particular regional interests on the national political agenda. And the few women of Quebec who actively campaigned for female suffrage did so cautiously because of constant pressure from the church and public opinion to abandon their cause."

3. Nellie McClung's *In Times like These*, originally published in 1915, and reissued by the University of Toronto Press, provides an interesting personal account of early twentieth-century feminist issues.

4. Penney Kome (1985:21) employs an alternative metaphor: "When feminism regained public attention in the Western world, during the 1960s and 1970s, Canada still had a deep-root system across the country that needed only a few thunderstorms for it to send up green shoots, and blossom, and spread like dandelions. Feminist ideas scattered like dandelion down, floating down onto fertile fields of active, educated, socially aware women."

5. Nemiroff (1987:535-36) observes that a decade after the Royal Commission on the Status of Women in Canada (1970) was tabled, only one-third of its recommendations had been implemented. She goes on to warn that information is a necessary, but not sufficient, condition for change. "In a world of finite power and resources, the material gain of women must cause readjustment in male ownership."

6. Robin Morgan (1977:155) differentiates radical feminism from socialist feminism by saying the former "wasn't merely a way of approaching socialist revolution; it wasn't, in fact, a wing or arm or toe of the Left—or Right—or any other male-defined, male-controlled group. It was something quite Else, something in itself, a whole new politics, an entirely different and astoundingly radical way of perceiving society, sentient matter, life itself, the universe. It was a philosophy. It was immense. It was also most decidedly a real, autonomous Movement, this feminism, with all the strengths than implied. And with all the evils, too—the familiar internecine squabbles."

7. Angela Miles (1984) who seeks dialogue among women of different political positions, suggests dissolving the hyphen from socialist-feminism to feminist feminism.

8. The sections of the Canadian Charter of Rights and Freedoms which pertain specifically to women's rights arc as follows. Section 15 reads: "(1) Every individual is equal before and under the law and has the right to the equal protection and equal benefit of th law without discrimination and, in particular, without discrimination based on race, national or ethnic origin, colour, religion, sex, age or mental or physical disability. (2) Subsection (1) does not preclude any law, program or activity that has as its object the amelioration of conditions of disadvantaged individuals or groups including those that are disadvantaged because of race, national or ethnic origin, colour, religion, sex, age or mental or physical disability." Section 12 reads: "Notwithstanding anything in this Charter, the rights and freedoms referred to in it are guaranteed equally to male and female persons."

9. Baines (1988:182) writes that "only 52 or 6 per cent of the 796 judges appointed by the federal government are women, and only 39 or 4.6 per cent of the 846 judges appointed by the provincial governments across Canada are women. The first woman to sit on the Supreme Court of Canada is Madame Justice Bertha Wilson who was appointed in 1982, just before the Charter came into effect. Madame Justice Claire l'Heureux-Dubé became the second woman to sit on the Supreme Court of Canada when she was appointed in 1987."

10. The Equal Rights Amendment, which would have amended the American Constitution to prohibit discrimination on the basis of sex, was defeated in June 1982. Ehrenreich (1983:144-45) writes: "The ERA had been a major—perhaps *the* major—goal of the American feminist movement for ten years. It would have rendered unconstitutional dozens of arcane state laws that limit women's property rights during and after marriage. It would have strengthened women's position as wage earners—helping open up higher-paying, traditionally male jobs and providing a wedge against all the subtle, informal mechanisms of wage discrimination. It would have, in symbolic fashion, finally given women recognition as full and equal citizens. Yet, in an irony that feminists and their liberal supporters have yet to fully grasp, the defeat of the ERA was celebrated by its opponents, gathered 1400-strong in the grand ballroom of Washington's Shoreham Hotel on the evening of June 30, as a 'great victory for women' and as a 'great achievement by women'."

11. According to Kaufman (1987b:2), "violence by men against women is only one corner of a triad of men's violence. The other two corners are violence against other men and violence against oneself."

12. According to national poll results published in

Maclean's magazine (January 2, 1989, p. 24), Canadian women are more sympathetic than men towards gays and lesbians. Sixty-four per cent of female respondents said that they would continue to go to a homosexual doctor or dentist, compared with only 48 percent of the men polled. Similarly, 82 percent of women said that they would continue to support a party in which a senior politician was homosexual compared with 71 per cent of men. Those with more formal education also hold more favourable attitudes.

13. The estimates, which vary from 3000 to 5000 male liberationists across Canada, should not be taken too seriously. Many figures appearing in newspapers appear to come from Ken Fisher, an Ottawa consultant selling workplace seminars called "New Men: Partners in Change" (Nicholls, 1989).

14. Feminists were quick to point out that "male oppression" is a pretentious slogan. Men have *not* been discriminated against because they are *men* (Walum, 1977:210).

15. Montreal Men Against Sexism secretary Martin Dufresne is quoted as follows: "[Men's rights activities] are quietly implementing a de facto decriminalization of every form of abuse visited by men, as men, on women and children. In the eyes of public officials, social service agencies, media and the population, they are the men's movement. Glowing media accounts of male support groups fuel their lobbying. And when they get funds to help wife-batterers, they really help them avoid prosecution...deny feminist analysis, sidetrack vital funding. It's a horror show" (Zwarun, 1988:A3).

16. Analysis of LEAF and the Canadian Advisory Council on the Status of Women showed that only 9 of 44 equality challenges under Section 15 of the Charter during the first four years of litigation were initiated by or on behalf of women. "Cases have involved issues such as drunk driving, marketing boards, regulations of airline landing fees, and manufacture of pop...cans. Some cases have challenged the few laws and programs that women have managed to secure to begin to alleviate the inequities women experience: rape shield legislation, maternity benefits and family benefits have all been attacked or threatened" (LEAF Letter #7, Summer 1989:1).

17. In the aftermath of the tragic killing of 14 women at the University of Montreal, Michele Landsberg described feminism as a "demonized" word. (CBC Morningside, December 8, 1989).

18. The National Action Committee on the Status of Women, the lobbying organization that enjoyed some success with the previous Liberal government, has since 1984 "been pushed to the margins of the political process" partly because it has "been riven by internal discord between radical feminists and social democrats" (Gray, 1989:20).

19. According to the Clio Collective (1987:367), "In 1975, feminism [in French Canada] underwent a marked transformation. All kinds of feminists began to work together. Freed from the domination of Marxism and nationalism, Francophone women leaned increasingly toward a more autonomous type of feminism. Women's liberation in Quebec no longer took second place on the political agenda; women's demands were no longer drowned in a flood of requests from unions, political parties and left-wing groups. Increasingly, feminists defined their own political strategy."

Glossary

Adult socialization. Socialization that takes place beyond the childhood and adolescence years.

Agentic orientation. A masculine orientation that stresses achievement and occupational commitment (as opposed to relationships) and is accompanied by attitudes of aggressiveness, control, and competitiveness. Also referred to as "instrumental orientation."

Aggression. Behaviour intended to hurt another.

Anal stage. Freud's second stage of personality development (18 months to three years of age) in which the child becomes preoccupied with elimination of the bowels. The superego emerges from this conflict between child and caretakers.

Andocentric. Dominated by males or masculine interests.

Androgyny. The flexible integration of positive masculine and feminine traits within individuals of both sexes.

Assigned gender. Based on the appearance of the child's external genitals, the sex/gender that parents and the rest of society believe the child to be.

Behaviourism. A methodological position that psychology should deal only with observable behaviour, and not with what goes on inside the organism.

Biological level explanation of gender relations. Emphasizes reproductive functions, anatomical distinctions, chromosomes, or hormones.

Blaming the victim. In the context of gender relations, women themselves, not the patriarchal social arrangements that bind them, are held ultimately responsible for their own oppression.

Breadwinner ethic. The traditional cultural expectation that men become wage earners and share their wages with their wives and dependants.

Castration anxiety. In Freudian theory, males' unconscious fear of losing their genital organs, as punishment for desiring their mothers.

Cognitive-developmental theory. A general psychological theory initiated by Swiss psychologist Jean Piaget which attempts to identify the systematic changes that occur over time in children's thought processes.

Commodity production. Goods and services created for exchange in the marketplace.

Communal orientation. A feminine orientation that stresses relationships (as opposed to the male agentic orientation) and is accompanied by attitudes of nurturance and dependancy. Also referred to as "expressive orientation."

Communal orientation to research. A general research style preferred by some feminists, which uses qualitative data and materials and attempts to gain understanding by seeing the world through the eyes of the people being studied.

Community of discourse. According to Tuchman (1979), the media constitute individuals into a community of discourse which "is comparable to a language; it integrates and controls; it provides common elements for strangers to use when they meet and creates strictures for what can be noticed or said."

Couvade. A practice among some preliterate societies in which the father subjects himself to various taboos associated with pregnancy and experiences labour pains and a recovery period.

Cultural component of social structure. Routinized patterns of thought shared by members of a society that include norms, values, beliefs.

Cultural universal. A certain type of behaviour found in many or most cultures, despite other variations in cultural patterns. Such behaviours are viewed as evidence for innate determination of gender relations.

Demeanour. Manner in which one conducts or presents oneself (Goffman, 1967).

Demography. The scientific study of the characteristics of human populations.

Domestic labour. Work done in the home, which may be divided into these categories: housework, childcare, emotional support work, status production (Papanek, 1979).

Drench effect. The more powerful impact upon people's gender imagery of some media versus others, or of some particular presentations versus others within the same medium (Greenberg, 1988).

Dyad. A two-person group.

Ego. The director of the Freudian personality. The ego attempts to mediate among the demands of the Id, the superego, and the external world. The ego, which encompasses the cognitive functions and the defence mechanisms, is governed by the reality principle.

Erogenous zones. In Freudian theory, the libido becomes attached to parts of the body, e.g., the mouth, the genitals, and the individual becomes preoccupied with this part as she/he moves through the developmental stages.

Ethic of care. Gilligan's (1982) feminine orientation to morality, which emphasizes concern for and connectedness with others.

Ethic of justice. Gilligan's (1982) masculine orientation to morality, which emphasizes preserving rights and upholding principles.

Explanation by discipline. Distinctive but legitimate perspectives on similar research questions characteristic of scholarly areas such as sociology, biochemistry, psychology.

Expressive orientation. See communal orientation.

Fallacy of the average. The logical pitfall of focussing on the difference in averages, e.g., between female and male aggressiveness, and ignoring the many exceptions or within-group variation (Doyle, 1989).

Feminization of poverty. "The process by which female-headed families become an increasing proportion of the low income or poverty population" (Abowitz, 1986).

Functionalists. Sociologists who view society as a system of inter-related parts that each contribute to its overall stability.

Gender. Societal definition of appropriate female and male traits and behaviours.

Gender assignment. The designation of a person as female or male at birth.

Gender constancy. The understanding developed gradually by children that a person's sex/gender is a permanent attribute of the person, regardless of changes in hair length, clothing, etc.

Gender display. "If gender be defined as the culturally established correlates of sex (whether in consequence of biology or learning), then gender display refers to conventionalized portrayals of these correlates" (Goffman, 1976).

Gender expression. The behavioural enactment of gender norms through dress, mannerisms, etc.

Gender identity. The individual's conviction of being male or female.

Gender model of work. Using women's sex/gender characteristics and family relationships to explain their work attitudes and behaviours (Feldberg and Glenn, 1979). See Job model of work.

Gender-role attitude. People's beliefs and sentiments concerning the status of the sexes and the appropriate gender division of labour in home and workplace.

Gender scripts. The details of a society's ideas about masculinity and femininity expressed in gender stereotypes and gender-role attitudes. These scripts spell out the personality characteristics and behaviours associated with one sex versus the other, the norms governing interaction of the sexes, and the relative evaluation of males and females.

Gender segregation of work. Division of occupations and employments into "women's work" and "men's work."

Gender socialization. The lifelong processes through which people learn to be feminine or masculine according to the expectations current in their society.

Gender stereotypes. Characteristics consensually assigned to females and males. For the most part, they point to beliefs about "psychological makeup."

Gender stratification. Defining sex-specific categories as better or worse and rewarding them accordingly (Nielsen, 1978).

Gender transcendance. Ideal socialization goal in which masculinity and femininity are superseded as ways of labelling and experiencing psychological traits. Boy/girl and male/female would then refer exclusively to biological distinctions.

Generalized other. The generalized standpoint of society as a whole in G. H. Mead's theory of development of the self.

Genetic sex. Male/female sex as determined by whether the 23rd pair of chromosomes is XY (male) or XX (female).

Genital sex. Male/female difference as determined by the presence of a penis or a clitoris and vagina.

Genital stage. Freud's fifth stage of personality development (adolescence) marked by a resurgence of sexual urges resulting from physiological maturation.

Gonadal sex. Female/male sex as determined by the presence of either ovaries or testes.

Good-provider role. Masculinity is identified with the level of living that men provide for their families (Bernard, 1981).

Gradient of familiarity. Stereotypes operate more powerfully at a distance. People are more likely to apply stereotypes to strangers than to friends.

Hermaphrodite. A person born with the reproductive or genital structures of both females and males.

Homogamy. The tendency for similar people to be drawn together.

Hormonal sex. Female/male difference as determined by relative levels of estrogen and testosterone.

"I". The dimension of Mead's (1934) notion of self that is active, spontaneous, creative, and unpredictable. The "I" is a component of a process, not a concrete entity.

Id. The reservoir of inborn, biological propensities in the Freudian personality structure. The selfish, impulsive id operates according to the pleasure principle.

Ideology. "The set of ideas, values, and beliefs that describe, explain, or justify various aspects of the social world, including the existence of inequality" (Grabb, 1988).

Inclusive fitness. A tenet of sociobiology that holds that individuals act so as to maximize the probability of their genes surviving. This is done by promoting their own welfare and that of relatives who share their genes.

Industrial gender segregation. Employed women and men are concentrated more in some industries than others.

Instrumental orientation. See Agentic orientation.

Job model of work. Using job type, working conditions, etc. to explain people's work attitudes and behaviours (Feldberg and Glenn, 1979). See Gender model of work.

Latency stage. Freud's fourth stage of personality development (6 to 12 years), which consolidates the achievements of the previous stages.

Lateralization. Functional specialization of left and right hemispheres of the brain.

Levels of explanation. The logical ordering of theoretical approaches to intellectual puzzles about human beings, from the basic biological level, to the psychological level, to the social-psychological level, to the social-structural level.

Liberal feminism. An offshoot of the Western tradition of liberal political thinking that recommends modification of existing social arrangements in order to provide women with equal opportunities to pursue their own self-interest. Liberal feminists look to the state to liberate women through legislative means. They criticize differential socialization of the sexes.

Libido. The inborn source of sexual energy in psychoanalytic theory.

Machismo code. Traditional definitions of masculinity imposed by boys on one another: Be first. Be tough. Defy authority. Don't be a sissy or crybaby. Keep your distance from females of all ages (Best, 1983).

Macromanipulation. Use by the less powerful of intelligence, interpersonal skill, charm, sexuality, deception, etc. to offset the control of the powerful (Lipman-Blumen, 1984).

Male bonding. Strong feelings of comradeship and loyalty among males (Tiger, 1969).

Marriage gradient. Women's traditional mandate to marry "up"; to seek a partner who is taller, older, more experienced, more occupationally successful than she is (Bernard, 1972).

Maternal deprivation. Bowlby (1952) argued that mothers who did not devote themselves full time to motherhood might well produce psychologically or socially maladjusted children.

Matrifocal. Social organization in, for example, ape societies, that develops from the mother-infant bond.

"Me". The dimension of Mead's (1934) notion of self that represents internalized societal attitudes and expectations. The "Me" is an aspect of a process, not a concrete entity.

Meta-analysis. A statistical technique that combines many studies of the same characteristic in order to arrive at conclusions about the consistency of a given sex/gender difference, and the magnitude or importance of this difference.

Micromanipulation. Use by the dominant group of the major institutions of society — law, social policy, the military — to impose its will and ensure its rule (Lipman-Blumen, 1984).

Micropolitical explanation. An explanation of gender differences in verbal and non-verbal communication that argues that the superior power of males structures communication.

Modelling. A type of learning whereby a new response is learned through observation of another's behaviour.

Monolithic family. Idealization of the family with a male breadwinner and stay-at-home wife and children, necessarily responsible for a constant set of functions, e.g., procreation, socialization, as the only normal, healthy familial arrangement.

Morphological component of social structure. Established ways of doing things in a society: statuses, stratification systems, institutions, spatial-temporal arrangements. Physical size of groups is also included.

Occupational gender segregation. The concentration of one sex in a relatively few occupations in which they greatly outnumber the other sex.

Occupational sex-typing. The societal view that certain occupations are more appropriate work for one sex than the other.

Oedipus complex. Freudian assertion that the child craves sexual possession of the other-sex parent, while viewing the same-sex parent as the rival.

Oral stage. Freud's first stage of personality development (birth to 18 months) in which the infant is preoccupied with pleasures associated with the mouth.

Particularistic expectations. The attention to individual qualities and needs that characterizes the relationship of the child with primary agents of socialization. See Universalistic expectations.

Patriarchy. Domination of women by men, as a pervasive feature of the social organization of societies (Smith, 1983).

Peer group. "An association of self-selected equals who coalesce around common interests, tastes, preferences, and beliefs" (Bensman and Rosenberg, 1979).

Phallic stage. Freud's third stage of personality development (at about four years of age), which establishes gender identity through resolution of the Oedipal conflict.

Power. The "capacity of individuals or groups to control, influence, or manipulate others' behaviour, whether these others wish to cooperate or not" (Kopinak, 1983).

Primary relationship. Relationships that involve frequent close contact and a high degree of personal involvement. They generally take place in small, informal groups.

Primary socialization. The basic induction into society that takes place in childhood and adolescence.

Principle of less interest. In a two-person relationship, the partner who cares less about the quality of the relationship, or whether the relationship continues at all, is in an advantageous position to dominate the other person (Waller, 1937).

Production of use-values. Goods and services produced in the home.

Psychological level of explanation of gender relations. Focusses upon individual characteristics, in particular, female versus male personality traits, motives, abilities, attitudes.

Radical feminism. Women's oppression is considered to be *the* fundamental oppression. Sexism is understood to be rooted in the intimate relationships of sexuality, procreation, and family life.

Reductionism. A viewpoint which "considers properties of society to be determined by intrinsic properties of individual human beings; individuals in turn are expressions of their genes" (Rossi, 1984).

Reinforcement learning. The shaping of behaviour through application of rewards for appropriate behaviour and punishments for inappropriate behaviour.

Reserve army of labour. According to Marxian theory, women constitute a flexible labour supply, drawn into the labour market when needed, and sent home when the need is past.

Resocialization. Replacement of established attitudes and behaviour patterns with new patterns.

Reverse devaluation. What is admirable in one sex is disdained in the other.

Role distance. Role player adopts a detached, humorous, or cynical attitude towards the role being enacted, rather than being a serious participant (Goffman, 1961).

Role explanation. An explanation of gender differences in verbal and non-verbal behaviour in terms of the traditional male-female division of labour.

Role-taking. "Imaginatively assuming the position or point of view of another person" (Lindesmith and Strauss, 1968).

Rooster effect. Male anger and preoccupation with their rivals in romantic relationships.

Rosenthal effect. Unwitting communication of the experimenter's expectations to the research subjects, and the consequent confounding of the reactions of the subjects.

Secondary agents of socialization. Schools, churches, clubs, business offices, unions, etc. See Secondary relationship.

Secondary relationship. Relationships that involve infrequent and impersonal contact with a low degree of personal involvement, often in large, formal organizations.

Sex. The physiological differences between females and males.

Sex-typing. The "prescription of different qualities, activities, and behaviours to females and males in the interest of socializing them for adult roles" (Williams, 1987).

Sexual dimorphism. Males and females display distinctive behaviours.

Significant other. Socialization agents who are emotionally important to the child, e.g., the parents.

Social learning theory. A general psychological theory that has attempted to identify a comprehensive set of learning principles for human beings and lower animals.

Social movement. "A large-scale, informal effort designed to correct, supplement, overthrow, or in some fashion influence the social order" (Toch, 1965).

Socialization. Complex learning process through which individuals develop selfhood and acquire the knowledge, skills, and motivations required to participate in social life.

Social-psychological level of explanation of gender relations. Explanations that focus upon the individual, but encompass social pressures that influence and constrain individuals.

Social stratification. The arrangement of social categories into hierarchical positions that are ranked unequally and rewarded (psychologically, socially, materially) accordingly.

Social structure. Routine ways of thinking and doing among societal members, that remain relatively constant over time.

Social-structural level of explanation of gender relations. A perspective that understands male-female inequality to result from the organization of society, not from biological or personality differences between the sexes.

Socialist feminism. The branch of the women's movement that seeks to integrate issues of gender and class, to unite the concepts of patriarchy and capitalism (Adamson et al., 1988).

Sociobiology. "The analysis of social behaviour as the outcome of organic evolution" (Boorman and Levitt, 1980).

Sociology of knowledge. A branch of sociology concerned with the social location of ideas.

Sociometry. A research technique for measuring the attraction and repulsion patterns in small groups.

Stereotype. Folk beliefs about the attributes characterizing a social category (the genders, ethnic groups) on which there is substantial agreement.

Superego. The Freudian conscience, or internalization of societal values and behaviour standards.

Symbol. Something that stands for something else. A red light means stop. A loonie signifies [a little] buying power.

Symbolic interactionism. Microsociological theoretical perspective inspired by G. H. Mead, C. H. Cooley, and W. I. Thomas, which emphasizes interaction, language, and the self.

Symbolic agents of socialization. Language, non-verbal communication, and the mass media.

Symmetrical family. An egalitarian family type where domestic labour is shared by male and female adult members (Young and Willmott, 1973).

Transsexuals. Individuals whose gender identity (their own conviction of being female or male) contradicts their biological sex.

Universalistic expectations. Secondary agents of socialization, e.g., teachers, attempt to judge everyone by the same objective standards. See Particularistic expectations.

Zeitgeist. The spirit of the times.

References

Abbey, Antonia
    1982   "Sex Differences in Attributions for Friendly Behavior: Do Males Misperceive Females' Friendliness?" *Journal of Personality and Social Psychology* 42: 830-38.

Abella, Judge Rosalie Silberman
    1985   *Research Studies of the Commission on Equality in Employment.* Ottawa: Supply and Services Canada.

Aberle, D., and K. Naegele
    1952   "Middle-class Fathers' Occupational Role and Attitudes Toward Children." *American Journal of Orthopsychiatry* 22: 366-78.

Abowitz, Deborah A.
    1986   "Data Indicate the Feminization of Poverty in Canada, Too." *Sociology and Social Research* 70: 209-13.

Abra, Jock
    1988   *Assaulting Parnassus: Theoretical Views of Creativity.* Lanham, Maryland: University Press of America.

Abu-Laban, Sharon
    1980a   "The Family Life of Older Canadians" in Victor W. Marshall, ed., *Aging in Canada*, pp. 125-34. Don Mills, Ontario: Fitzhenry and Whiteside.
    1980b   "Social Supports in Older Age: The Need for New Research Dimensions." *Essence* 4: 195-210.
    1981   "Women and Aging: A Futurist Perspective." *Psychology of Women Quarterly* 6: 85-98.

Achilles, Rona
    1988   "Artificial Reproduction: Hope Chest or Pandora's Box?" in Sandra Burt, Lorraine Code, and Lindsay Dorney, eds., *Changing Patterns: Women in Canada.* pp. 291-312. Toronto: McClelland and Stewart.

Ackelsberg, Martha, and Irene Diamond
    1987   "Gender and Political Life: New Directions in Political Science" in Beth B. Hess and Myra Marx Ferree, eds., *Analyzing Gender: A Handbook of Social Science Research,* pp. 504-25. Newbury Park, Calif.: Sage.

Acker, Joan
    1973   "Women and Social Stratification: A Case of Intellectual Sexism." *American Journal of Sociology* 78: 936-45.
    1980   "Women and Stratification: A Review of Recent Literature." *Contemporary Sociology* 9: 25-39.

1988   "Class, Gender and the Relations of Distribution." *Signs* 13: 473-97.
1990   "Hierarchies, Jobs, Bodies: A Theory of Gendered Organizations." *Gender & Society* 4: 139-58.

Adam, Barry D.
1986   "The Construction of a Sociological 'Homosexual' in Canadian Textbooks." *Canadian Review of Sociology and Anthropology* 23: 399-411.
1987   *The Rise of a Gay and Lesbian Movement*. Boston: Twayne.

_____ , and Douglas E. Baer
1984   "The Social Mobility of Women and Men in the Ontario Legal Profession." *Canadian Review of Sociology and Anthropology* 21: 21-46.

Adamson, Nancy, Linda Briskin, and Margaret McPhail
1988   *Feminist Organizing for Change: The Contemporary Women's Movement in Canada.* Toronto: Oxford University Press.

Alcock, J.E., D.W. Carment, and S.W. Sadava
1988   *A Textbook of Social Psychology*. Scarborough: Prentice-Hall Canada.

Alexander, Judith
1979   "Women and Unpaid Work: The Economic Consequences." *Atlantis* 4: 200-11.

Allen, Sr. Prudence
1987   "Sex Unity, Polarity, or Complementarity?" in Greta Hofmann Nemiroff, ed., *Women and Men: Interdisciplinary Readings on Gender*, pp. 3-20. Toronto: Fitzhenry & Whiteside.

Allport, Gordon W.
1961   *Pattern and Growth in Personality*. New York: Holt, Rinehart and Winston.

Ambert, Anne-Marie
1976   *Sex Structure*. 2nd ed. Don Mills, Ontario: Longman Canada.
1980   *Divorce in Canada*. Don Mills, Ontario: Longman Canada.
1982   "Differences in Children's Behavior Toward Custodial Mothers and Custodial Fathers." *Journal of Marriage and the Family* 44: 73-86.
1983   "Separated Women and Remarriage Behavior: A Comparison of Financially Secure Women and Financially Insecure Women." *Journal of Divorce* 6: 43-54.
1985   "Custodial Parents: Review and a Longitudinal Study" in Benjamin Schlesinger, ed., *The One-Parent Family in the 1980s: Perspectives and Annotated Bibliography 1978-1984*, pp. 13-34. Toronto: University of Toronto Press.
1990a   "Marriage Dissolution: Structural and Ideological Changes." in Maureen Baker, ed., *Families: Changing Trends in Canada*. 2nd ed., pp. 192-210. Toronto: McGraw-Hill Ryerson.
1990b   "The Other Perspective: Children's Effect on Parents" in Maureen Baker, ed., *Families: Changing Trends in Canada*. 2nd ed., pp. 149-65. Toronto: McGraw-Hill Ryerson.

_____ , and Gladys Symons Hitchman
1976   "A Case Study of Status Differential: Women in Academia" in Anne-Marie Ambert, *Sex Structure*. 2nd ed., pp. 113-46. Don Mills, Ontario: Longman Canada.

American Sociological Association Ad Hoc Committee on the Status of the Women in the Profession
1973   *The Status of Women in Sociology, 1968-1972*. Washington, D.C.: American Sociological Association.

Andersen, Margaret L.
1983   *Thinking About Women: Sociological and Feminist Perspectives.* New York: Macmillan.
1987   "Changing the Curriculum in Higher Education." *Signs* 12: 222-54.
1988   *Thinking About Women: Sociological Perspectives on Sex and Gender.* 2nd ed. New York: Macmillan.

Anderson, Doris
1984   "The Real Problems behind Controlling Pornography." *CAUT Bulletin* (February): 23-24.

Arcana, Judith
1979   *Our Mothers' Daughters.* Berkeley: Shameless Hussy Press.

Archer, John
1976   "Biological Explanations of Psychological Sex Differences" in Barbara Lloyd and John Archer, eds., *Exploring Sex Differences*, pp. 241-66. New York: Academic Press.

_____ , and Barbara Lloyd
1985   *Sex and Gender.* Cambridge, England: Cambridge University Press.

Archibald, Kathleen
1973   *Sex and the Public Service.* Ottawa: Information Canada.

Ardener, Edwin
1972   "Belief and the Problem of Women" in Jean La Fontaine, ed., *The Interpretation of Ritual.* London: Tavistock.

Arditti, R., and R. Duelli-Klein, and S. Minden, eds.
1984   *Test-Tube Women: What Future for Motherhood?* Boston: Pandora Press.

Argyle, M., V. Salter, H. Nicholson, M. Williams, and P. Burgess
1970   "The Communication of Inferior and Superior Attitudes by Verbal and Nonverbal Signals." *British Journal of Social and Clinical Psychology* 9: 222-31.

Aries, Elizabeth
1987   "Gender and Communication" in Phillip Shaver and Clyde Hendrick, eds., *Sex and Gender*, pp. 149-76. Newbury Park, Calif.: Sage.

Armour, Margaret Ann
1988   "The *WISEST* Approach." *New Trial* 43 (Autumn): 21-23. Edmonton: University of Alberta Alumni Association.

Armstrong, Pat
1984   *Labour Pains: Women's Work in Crisis.* Toronto: Women's Press.
1987   "Women's Work: Women's Wages" in Greta Hofmann Nemiroff, ed., *Women and Men: Interdisciplinary Readings on Gender*, pp. 354-76. Toronto: Fitzhenry & Whiteside.
1988   "Unemployment as a Women's Issue" in Lorne Tepperman and James Curtis, eds., *Readings in Sociology: An Introduction*, pp. 385-93. Toronto: McGraw-Hill Ryerson.
1989   "Work and Family Life: Changing Patterns" in G.N. Ramu, ed., *Marriage and the Family in Canada Today*, pp. 121-41 Scarborough, Ontario: Prentice-Hall.

_____ , and Hugh Armstrong
1978   *The Double Ghetto: Canadian Women and Their Segregated Work.* Toronto: McClelland and Stewart.
1983   *A Working Majority: What Women Must Do For Pay.* Ottawa: Canadian Advisory Council on the Status of Women.

1984   *The Double Ghetto: Canadian Women and Their Segregated Work.* Revised ed. Toronto: McClelland and Stewart.

1987   "Looking Ahead: The Future of Women's Work" in Heather Jon Maroney and Meg Luxton, eds., *Feminism and Political Economy: Women's Work, Women's Struggles,* pp. 213-25. Toronto: Methuen.

1988   "Women, Family and Economy" in Nancy Mandell and Ann Duffy, eds., *Reconstructing the Canadian Family: Feminist Perspectives,* pp. 143-74. Toronto: Butterworths.

_____ , Hugh Armstrong, Patricia Connelly, and Angela Miles

1985   *Feminist Marxism or Marxist Feminism: A Debate.* Toronto: Garamond Press.

_____ , and Roberta Hamilton

1988   "Introduction." *Canadian Review of Sociology and Anthropology* 25: 157-62.

Arnopoulos, Sheila McLeod

1979   *Problems of Immigrant Women in the Canadian Labour Force.* Ottawa: Canadian Advisory Council on the Status of Women.

Aronoff, Joel, and William D. Crano

1975   "A Re-examination of the Cross-cultural Principles of Task Segregation and Sex Role Differentiation in the Family." *American Sociological Review* 40: 12-20.

Arnup, Katherine

1988   "Lesbian Mothers and Child Custody" in Arlene Tigar McLaren, ed., *Gender and Society: Creating a Canadian Women's Sociology.* Toronto: Copp Clark Pitman.

Ashmore, R.D., F.K. Del Boca, and A.J. Wohlers

1986   "Gender Stereotypes" in R.D. Ashmore and F.K. Del Boca, eds., *The Social Psychology of Female-Male Relations: A Critical Analysis of Central Concepts,* pp. 69-119. Orlando, Florida: Academic Press.

Atchley, Robert C.

1982   "The Process of Retirement: Comparing Women and Men" in Maximiliane Szinovacz, ed., *Women's Retirement: Policy Implications of Recent Research,* pp. 153-68. Beverly Hills: Sage.

_____ , and S.L. Corbett

1977   "Older Women and Jobs" in L.E. Troll, J. Israel, and K. Israel, eds., *Looking Ahead: A Woman's Guide to the Problems and Joys of Growing Older.* Engelwood Cliffs, N.J.: Prentice-Hall.

Attenborough, Susan

1983   "Sexual Harassment: An Issue for Unions" in Linda Briskin and Lynda Yanz, eds., *Union Sisters: Women in the Labour Movement,* pp. 136 - 43. Toronto: Women's Press.

Atwood, Margaret

1972   *Survival: A Thematic Guide to Canadian Literature.* Toronto: Anansi Press.

1985   *The Handmaid's Tale.* Toronto: McClelland and Stewart.

1988   *Cat's Eye.* Toronto: McClelland and Stewart.

Auster, Donald

1984   "Mentors and Protegés: Power Dependent Dyads." *Sociological Inquiry* 54: 142-53.

Babchuk, Nicholas, and Alan P. Bates

1963   "The Primary Relations of Middle-class Couples: A Study in Male Dominance." *American Sociological Review* 28: 377-91.

Bacchi, Carol Lee
  1983   *Liberation Deferred? The Ideas of the English-Canadian Suffragists, 1877-1918.* Toronto: University of Toronto Press.

Baines, Beverley
  1988   "Women and the Law" in Sandra Burt, Lorraine Code, and Lindsay Dorney, eds., *Changing Patterns: Women in Canada*, pp. 157-82. Toronto: McClelland and Stewart.

Bakan, David
  1966   *The Duality of Human Existence.* Chicago: Rand McNally.

Baker, Maureen
  1983   "Divorce: Its Consequences and Meanings" in K. Ishwaran, ed., *The Canadian Family*, pp. 289-300. Toronto: Gage.
  1984a   "His and Her Divorce Research: New Theoretical Directions in Canadian and American Research." *Journal of Comparative Family Studies* 15: 17-28.
  1984b   "Male-dominated Criminology: Implications for Women in Correctional Institutions" in Jill McCalla Vickers, ed., *Taking Sex into Account: The Policy Consequences of Sexist Research*, pp. 243-55. Ottawa: Carleton University Press.
  1985   "What Will Tomorrow Bring?..." A Study of Aspirations of Adolescent Women. Ottawa: Canadian Advisory Council on the Status of Women.
  1990a   ed., *Families: Changing Trends in Canada.* 2nd ed. Toronto: McGraw-Hill Ryerson.
  1990b   "Mate Selection and Marital Dynamics" in Maureen Baker, ed., *Families: Changing Trends in Canada.* 2nd ed., pp. 41-66. Toronto: McGraw-Hill Ryerson.

_____ , and J.I. Hans Bakker
  1980   "The Double-bind of the Middle-class Male: Men's Liberation and the Male Sex Role." *Journal of Comparative Family Studies* 11: 547-61.

_____ , and Mary-Anne Robeson
  1981   "Trade Union Reactions to Women Workers and their Concerns." *Canadian Journal of Sociology* 6: 19-31.

Baker, S.W.
  1980   "Biological Influences on Human Sex and Gender." *Signs* 6: 80-96.

Bandura, A.
  1977   *Social Learning Theory.* Englewood Cliffs, N.J.: Prentice-Hall.

_____ , and R.H. Walters
  1963   *Social Learning and Personality Development.* New York: Holt, Rinehart and Winston.

Bank, Stephen P., and Michael D. Kahn
  1982   *The Sibling Bond.* New York: Basic.

Barash, D.P.
  1977   *Sociobiology and Behavior.* New York: Elsevier.
  1979   *The Whisperings Within.* Markham, Ontario: Penguin.

Bardwick, Judith M.
  1972   "The Development of Sex Differences" in Judith M. Bardwith ed., *Readings on the Psychology of Women*, pp. 1-3. New York: Harper and Row.

_____ , and Elizabeth Douvan
  1971   "Ambivalence: The Socialization of Women" in Vivian Gornick and Barbara K. Moran, eds., *Woman in Sexist Society*, pp. 225-41. New York: Signet Books.

Barfield, Ashton
1976 "Biological Influences on Sex Differences in Behaviour" in Michael S. Teitelbaum, ed., *Sex Differences: Social and Biological Perspectives*, pp. 62-121. Garden City, N.Y.: Doubleday Anchor.

Baron, Robert A., and Donn Byrne
1977 *Social Psychology.* 2nd Ed. Boston: Allyn and Bacon.

Barry, Anne
1987 "Doing Good to Feel Good." *New Woman* (December): 60-64.

Bart, Pauline B.
1969 "Why Women's Status Changes in Middle Age: The Turns of the Social Ferris Wheel." *Sociological Symposium* 3: 1-18.
1971 "Depression in Middle-aged Women" in Vivian Gornick and Barbara K. Moran, eds., *Woman in Sexist Society*, pp. 163-86. New York: Signet Books.

Bashevkin, Sylvia B.
1983 "Social Change and Political Partisanship: The Development of Women's Attitudes in Quebec, 1965-1979." *Comparative Political Studies* 16: 147-72.
1985 *Toeing the Lines: Women and Party Politics in English Canada.* Toronto: University of Toronto Press.

Basow, Susan A.
1980 *Sex-role Stereotypes. Traditions and Alternatives.* Monterey, California: Brooks/Cole.
1986 *Gender Stereotypes: Traditions and Alternatives.* 2nd ed. Monterey, Calif.: Brooks/Cole.

Batcher, Elaine
1987 "Building the Barriers: Adolescent Girls Delimit the Future: in Greta Hofmann Nemiroff, ed., *Women and Men: Interdisciplinary Readings on Gender*, pp. 150-64. Toronto: Fitzhenry & Whiteside.

Baum, Julian
1988 "Women in Pulpit Split Anglicans." *Calgary Herald* (July 23).

Becker, Gary S.
1981 *A Treatise on the Family.* Cambridge, Mass.: Harvard University Press.

Belenky, M.F., B.M. Clinchy, N.R. Goldberger, J.M. Tarule
1986 *Women's Ways of Knowing: The Development of Self, Voice, and Mind.* New York: Basic.

Bell, Alan P., Martin S. Weinberg, and Sue K. Hammersmith
1981 *Homosexualities: A Study of Diversity among Men and Women.* New York: Simon and Schuster.

Bell, Inge Powell
1970 "The Double Standard." *Trans-action 8* (November-December): 75-80.

Bell, Robert R.
1981 *Worlds of Friendship.* Beverly Hills: Sage.

Bem, Sandra L.
1974 "The Measurement of Psychological Androgyny." *Journal of Consulting and Clinical Psychology* 42: 155-62.
1976 "Probing the Promise of Androgyny" in Alexandra G. Kaplan and Joan P. Bean, eds., *Beyond Sex-role Stereotypes: Readings toward a Psychology of Androgyny*, pp. 48-62. Boston: Little, Brown.

1983   "Gender Schema Theory and its Implications for Child Development: Raising Gender-aschematic Children in a Gender-schematic Society." *Signs* 8: 598-616.

_____ , and Daryl J. Bem
1971   "Training the Woman to Know her Place: The Power of a Nonconscious Ideology: in Michele Hoffnung Garskof, ed., *Roles Women Play: Readings toward Women's Liberation*, pp. 84-96. Belmont, Calif.: Brooks/Cole.

Benbow, C.P., and J.C. Stanley
1983   "Sex Differences in Mathematical Reasoning Ability: More Facts." *Science* 222: 1029-1031.

Bensman, Joseph, and Robert Lilienfeld
1979   "Friendship and Alienation." *Psychology Today* (October): 56, 57, 59, 60, 63, 66, 114.

_____ , and Bernard Rosenberg
1979   "The Peer Group" in Peter I. Rose, ed., *Socialization and the Life Cycle*, pp. 79-96. New York: St. Martin's Press.

Benston, Margaret
1969   "The Political Economy of Women's Liberation." *Monthly Review* 21: 13-27.
1989   "Feminism and the Critique of Scientific Method" in Angela R. Miles and Geraldine Finn, eds., *Feminism in Canada: From Pressure to Politics*, 2nd ed., pp. 57-76. Montreal: Black Rose Books.

Berg, Ellen
1987   "Feminist Theory: Moving Sociology from the 'Malestream'." *American Sociological Association Footnotes* (March): 5, 11.

Berger, Brigitte, and Peter L. Berger
1984   *The War Over the Family: Capturing the Middle Ground*. Garden City, N.Y.: Doubleday Anchor.

Berger, John
1977   *Ways of Seeing*. New York: Penguin Books.

Berger, Peter L.
1963   *Invitation to Sociology: A Humanistic Perspective*. Garden City, N.Y.: Doubleday Anchor.

_____ , and Brigitte Berger
1975   *Sociology: A Biographical Approach*. 2nd ed. New York: Basic Books.

_____ , and Thomas Luckmann
1966   *The Social Construction of Reality*. Garden City, N.Y.: Doubleday Anchor.

Bernard, Jessie
1964   *Academic Women*. Cleveland, Ohio: World Publishing.
1972   *The Future of Marriage*. New York: Bantam.
1973   "My Four Revolutions: An Autobiographical History of the ASA." *American Journal of Sociology* 78: 773-91.
1974   "The Housewife: Between Two Worlds" in Phyllis L. Stewart and Muriel G. Cantor, eds., *Varieties of Work Experience*, pp. 49-66. Cambridge, Mass.: Schenkman.
1975   *Women, Wives, Mothers: Values and Options*. Chicago: Aldine.
1976   "Sex Differences: an Overview" in Alexander G. Kaplan and Joan P. Bean, eds., *Beyond Sex-role Stereotypes: Readings toward a Psychology of Androgyny*, pp. 122-33. Boston: Little, Brown.

1981a   *The Female World*. New York: Free Press.
1981b   "The Good-provider role, Its Rise and Fall." *The American Psychologist* 36: 1-12.

Berscheid, Ellen
1985   "Interpersonal Attraction" in Gardner Lindzey and Elliot Aronson, eds., *The Handbook of Social Psychology*. 3rd ed. Vol. II, pp. 413-84. New York: Random House.

_____ , and Elaine Hatfield Walster
1978   *Interpersonal Attraction*. 2nd ed. Reading, Mass.: Addison-Wesley.

Best, Raphaela
1983   *We've All Got Scars*. Bloomington, Indiana: Indiana University Press.

Beuf, Ann
1974   "Doctor, Lawyer, Household Drudge." *Journal of Communication* 24: 142- 45.

Bibby, Reginald W.
1987   *Fragmented Gods: The Poverty and Potential of Religion in Canada*. Toronto: Irwin.

_____ , and Donald C. Posterski
1985   *The Emerging Generation: An Inside Look at Canada's Teenagers*. Toronto: Irwin.

Bigelow, Brian J., and John J. La Gaipa
1980   "The Development of Friendship Values and Choice" in H.C. Foot, A.J. Chapman, and J.R. Smith, eds., *Friendship and Social Relations in Children*, pp. 15-44. New York: John Wiley & Sons.

Billings, Rosemary
1983   "Introduction" to Penney Kome, *The Taking of Twenty-Eight: Women Challenge the Constitution*. Toronto: The Women's Press.

Birdwhistell, Ray L.
1970   *Kinesics and Context*. Philadelphia: University of Pennsylvania Press.

Black, Naomi
1988   "The Second Wave" in Sandra Burt, Lorraine Code, and Lindsay Dorney, eds., *Changing Patterns: Women in Canada*, pp. 80-99. Toronto: McClelland and Stewart.
1988   "Where All the Ladders Start: A Feminist Perspective on Social Science" in Winnifred Tomm and Gordon Hamilton, eds., *Gender Bias in Scholarship: The Pervasive Prejudice*, pp. 167-89. Calgary Institute for the Humanities. Waterloo, Ont.: Wilfrid Laurier University Press.

Blau, Francine D., and Anne E. Winkler
1989   "Women in the Labor Force: An Overview" in Jo Freeman, ed., Women: A Feminist Perspective. 4th ed., pp. 265-86. Mountain View, Calif.: Mayfield.

Blau, Peter M.
1977   "A Macrosociological Theory of Social Structure." *American Journal of Sociology* 83: 26-54.

Blau, Zena Smith
1973   *Old Age in a Changing Society*. New York: New Viewpoints.

Blaubergs, Maija S.
1978   "Changing the Sexist Language: the Theory Behind the Practice." *Psychology of Women Quarterly* 2: 244-61.

Blee, Kathleen M.
  1986   "Teaching a Theory-based Sociology of Gender Course." *Teaching Sociology* 14: 162:67.

Bleier, Ruth
  1984   *Science and Gender: A Critique of Biology and Its Theories on Women.* New York: Pergamon.

Blishen, Bernard R.
  1967   "A Socio-economic Index for Occupations in Canada." *Canadian Review of Sociology and Anthropology* 4: 41-53.
  1973   "Social Class and Opportunity in Canada" in James E. Curtis and William G. Scott, eds., *Social Stratification: Canada*, pp. 162-73. Scarborough: Prentice-Hall.

_____ , and William K. Carroll
  1978   "Sex Differences in Socio-economic Index for Occupations in Canada." *Canadian Review of Sociology and Anthropology* 15: 352-371.

_____ , and Hugh A. McRoberts
  1976   "A Revised Socioeconomic Index for Occupations in Canada." *Canadian Review of Sociology and Anthropology* 13: 71-79.

Bliss, Michael
  1974   "Pure Books on Avoided Subjects: Pre-Freudian Sexual Ideas in Canada" in Michiel Horn and Ronald Sabourin, eds., *Studies in Canadian Social History*, pp. 326-46. Toronto: McClelland and Stewart.

Block, Jeanne H.
  1976   "Debatable Conclusions about Sex Differences." *Contemporary Psychology* 21: 517-22.
  1984   *Sex Role Identity and Ego Development.* San Francisco: Jossey-Bass.

Blood, Robert, and Donald Wolfe
  1960   *Husbands and Wives: The Dynamics of Married Living.* New York: Free Press.

Blumberg, Rae Lesser
  1978   *Stratification: Socioeconomic and Sexual Inequality.* Dubuque, Iowa: Wm. C. Brown.

Blumer, Herbert
  1969   *Symbolic Interactionism: Perspective and Method.* Englewood Cliffs, N.J.: Prentice-Hall.

Blumstein, Philip, and Pepper Schwartz
  1983   *American Couples.* New York: William Morrow.
  1989   "Intimate Relationships and the Creation of Sexuality" in Barbara J. Risman and Pepper Schwartz, eds., *Gender in Intimate Relationships: A Microstructural Approach,* pp. 120-29. Belmont, Calif.: Wadsworth.

Bogart, Leo
  1988   "The Multiple Meanings of Television Advertising." *Society* 25: 76-80.

Bolin, Anne
  1987   "Transsexualism and the Limits of Traditional Analysis." *American Behavioral Scientist* 31: 41-65.

Boorman, Scott, A., and Paul R. Levitt
  1980   "The Comparative Evolutionary Biology of Social Behavior." *Annual Review of Sociology* 6: 213-34.

Booth, Alan, and Elaine Hess
  1974   "Cross-sex Friendship." *Journal of Marriage and the Family*, Vol. 36: 38-47.

Boulding, Elise
    1976   *The Underside of History: A View of Women Through Time.* Boulder, Colo.: Westview Press.

Bourne, Pamela
    1976   *Women in Canadian Society.* Toronto: OISE.

Bowlby, John
    1952   *Maternal Care and Maternal Health.* Geneva: World Health Organization.

Boxer, Marilyn J.
    1982   "For and about Women: The Theory and Practice of Women's Studies in the United States." *Signs* 7: 661-95.

Boyd, Monica
    1975   "English-Canadian and French-Canadian Attitudes toward Women: Results of the Canadian Gallup Polls." *Journal of Comparative Family Studies* 6: 153-69.
    1979   *Rank and Salary Differentials in the 1970s: A Comparison of Male and Female Full-Time Teachers in Canadian Universities and Colleges.* Ottawa: Association of Universities and Colleges of Canada.
    1984   *Canadian Attitudes Toward Women: Thirty Years of Change.* Ottawa: Labour Canada.
    1985   "Educational and Occupational Attainments of Native-born Canadian Men and Women" in Monica Boyd, John Goyder, Frank E. Jones, Hugh A. McRoberts, Peter C. Pineo and John Porter, *Ascription and Achievement: Studies in Mobility and Status Attainment in Canada*, pp. 229-95. Ottawa: Carleton University Press.
    1986   "Socioeconomic Indices and Sexual Equality: A Tale of Scales." *Canadian Review of Sociology and Anthropology* 23: 457-80.
    1988   "Changing Canadian Family Forms: Issues for Women" in Nancy Mandell and Ann Duffy, eds., *Reconstructing the Canadian Family: Feminist Perspectives*, pp. 85-109. Toronto: Butterworths.

_____ , John Goyder, Hugh A. McRoberts, Frank E. Jones, Peter C. Pineo, and John Porter
    1981   "Status Attainment in Canada: Findings of the Canadian Mobility Study." *Canadian Review of Sociology and Anthropology* 18: 657-73.

_____ , and Hugh A. McRoberts
    1983   "Women, Men, and Socioeconomic Indices: An Assessment" in Mary G. Powers, ed., *Measures of Socioeconomic Status* (Current Issues). Boulder, Col.: Westview Press.

Brabant, Sarah, and Linda Mooney
    1986   "Sex Role Stereotyping in the Sunday Comics: Ten Years Later." *Sex Roles* 14: 141- 48.

Brake, Michael
    1985   *Comparative Youth Culture.* London: Routledge and Keegan Paul.

Breines, Wini, and Linda Gordon
    1983   "The New Scholarship on Family Violence." *Signs* 8: 490-531.

Brenton, Myron
    1974   *Friendship.* New York: Stein and Day.

Bridenthal, Renata
    1982   "The Family: The View from a Room of Her Own" in Barrie Thorne with Marilyn Yalom, ed., *Rethinking the Family: Some Feminist Questions*, pp. 225-39. New York: Longman.

Briggs, Sheila
  1987   "Women and Religion" in Beth B. Hess and Myra Marx Ferree, eds., *Analyzing Gender: A Handbook of Social Science Research*, pp. 408-41. Newbury Park, Calif.: Sage.

Brigham, John C.
  1986   *Social Psychology*. Boston: Little, Brown.

Brim, Orville
  1958   "Family Structure and Sex Role Learning by Children: a Further Analysis of Helen Koch's Data." *Sociometry* 21: 1-16.

Brinkerhoff, Merlin B., and Eugen Lupri
  1988   "Interspousal Violence." *Canadian Journal of Sociology* 13: 407-34.

Briskin, Linda
  1983   "Women's Challenge to Organized Labour" in Linda Briskin and Lynda Yanz, eds., *Union Sisters: Women in the Labour Movement*, pp. 259-71. Toronto: Women's Press.

Brod, Harry
  1987   "A Case for Men's Studies" in Michael S. Kimmel, ed., *Changing Men: New Directions in Research on Men and Masculinity*, pp. 263-77. Newbury Park, Calif.: Sage.

Brody, L., and L.C. Steelman
  1985   "Sibling Structure and Parental Sex-typing of Children's Household Tasks." *Journal of Marriage and the Family* 27: 265-73.

Brophy, Jere E.
  1977   *Child Development and Socialization*. Chicago: Science Research Associates.

Broverman, I.K., D.M. Broverman, F.E. Clarkson, P. Rosenkrantz, and S.R. Vogel
  1972   "Sex-role Stereotypes: a Current Appraisal." *Journal of Social Issues* 28: 59-78.

Brown, Bruce W.
  1978   "Wife-employment and the Emergence of Egalitarian Marital Role Prescriptions: 1900-1974." *Journal of Comparative Family Studies* 9: 5-17.

Brown, Rosemary
  1989   "Women Ride Roller-Coaster of Hope, Despair." *The Globe and Mail* (December 30).

Brownmiller, Susan
  1975   *Against Our Will: Men, Women and Rape*. New York: Simon and Schuster
  1984   *Femininity*. New York. Linden Press, Simon and Schuster.

Bryden, M.P.
  1979   "Evidence for Sex-related Differences in Cerebral Organization" in M.A. Wittig and A.C. Petersen, eds., *Sex-Related Differences in Cognitive Functioning: Developmental Issues*, pp. 121-43. New York: Academic Press.

Brym, Robert J. with Bonnie J. Fox
  1989   *From Culture to Power: The Sociology of English Canada*. Toronto: Oxford University Press.

Buckland, Lin
  1985   "Education and Training: Equal Opportunities or Barriers to Employment?" in Rosalie Silberman Abella, *Equality in Opportunity: A Royal Commission Report*, pp. 133-56. Ottawa: Supply and Services Canada.

Bumpass, Larry
     1984   "Some Characteristics of Children's Second Families." *American Journal of Sociology* 90:
                 608-23.
Burch, T.K.
     1985   *Family History Survey: Preliminary Findings.* Ottawa: Minister of Supply and Services.
Burke, Mary Anne
     1986   "The Growth of Part-time Work." *Canadian Social Trends, Statistics Canada.* (Autumn):
                 9-14.
Burstyn, Varda (1985)
     1987   "The Left and the Porn Wars: A Case Study in Sexual Politics" in Howard Buchbinder,
                 Varda Burstyn, Dinah Forbes, and Mercedes Steed, *Who's on Top: The Politics of Hetero-
                 sexuality*, pp. 13-46. Toronto: Garamond Press.

_____ , and Dorothy E. Smith
     1985   *Women, Class, Family and the State.* Toronto: Garamond Press.

Burt, Sandra
     1988   "The Charter of Rights and the Ad Hoc Lobby: The Limits of Success." *Atlantis* 14: 74-
                 81.

Burwell, Elinor J.
     1984   "Sexism in Social Science Research on Aging" in Jill McCalla Vickers, ed., *Taking Sex
                 Into Account*, pp. 185-208. Ottawa: Carleton University Press.

Butler, Matilda, and William Paisley
     1980   *Women and the Mass Media.* New York: Human Sciences Press.

Cahill, Spencer E.
     1980   "Directors for an Interactionist Study of Gender Development." *Symbolic Interaction* 3:
                 123-38.

Caine, Lynn
     1985   *What Did I Do Wrong? Mothers, Children, Guilt.* Toronto: Fitzhenry and Whiteside.

Caldwell, R., and L. Peplau
     1982   "Sex Differences in Same-sex Friendship." *Sex Roles* 8: 721-31.

Calzavara, Liviana
     1985   "Trends in the Employment Opportunities of Women in Canada, 1930-1980" in
                 Rosalie Silberman Abella, *Equality in Opportunity: A Royal Commission Report*, pp. 517-
                 36. Ottawa: Supply and Services Canada.

Cameron, Deborah
     1985   *Feminism and Linguistic Theory.* New York: St. Martin's Press.

Campbell, Colon
     1976   "What Happens When We Get...The Manchild Pill?" *Psychology Today* (August): 86, 88,
                 90, 91.

Campbell, Ernest Q.
     1975   *Socialization: Culture and Personality.* Dubuque, Iowa: Wm. C. Brown.

Canadian Radio-television and Telecommunications Commission
     1982   *Images of Women: Report of the Task Force on Sex-Role Stereotyping in the Broadcast Media.*
                 Hull, Quebec: Supply and Services Canada.
     1986   *Policy on Sex-role Stereotyping in the Broadcast Media.* Ottawa.

Cancian, Francesca M.
1985   "Gender Politics: Love and Power in the Private and Public Spheres" in Alice S. Rossi, ed., *Gender and the Life Course*, pp. 253 - 64. New York: Aldine.
1986   "The Feminization of Love." *Signs* 11: 692-709.

_____ , and Steven L. Gordon
1988   "Changing Emotion Norms in Marriage: Love and Anger in U.S. Women's Magazines Since 1900." *Gender and Society* 2: 308-42.

Cantor, Muriel G.
1987   "Popular Culture and the Portrayal of Women: Content and Control" in Beth B. Hess and Myra Marx Ferree, eds., *Analyzing Gender: A Handbook of Social Science Research*, pp. 190-214. Newbury Park, Calif.: Sage.
1988   "Feminism and the Media." *Society* 25 (July/August): 76-81.

Caplan, Paula J.
1985   "Anti-feminist Women." *International Journal of Women's Studies* 8: 351-55.

Caplow, Theodore
1954   *The Sociology of Work*. Minneapolis: University of Minnesota Press.

Carlson, Rae
1971   "Sex Differences in Ego Functioning: Exploratory Studies of Agency and Communion." *Journal of Consulting and Clinical Psychology* 37: 267-77.
1972   "Understanding Women: Implications for Personality Theory and Research." *Journal of Social Issues* 28: 17-32.

Carmody, Denise Lardner
1979   "Women and Religion: Where Mystery Comes to Center Stage" in Eloise C. Snyder, ed., *The Study of Women: Enlarging Perspectives of Social Reality*, pp. 262-95. New York: Harper and Row.

Carrigan, Tim, Bob Connell, and John Lee
1985   "Towards a New Sociology of Masculinity." *Theory and Society* 14: 551-604.
1987   "Hard and Heavy: Toward a New Sociology of Masculinity" in Michael Kaufman, ed., *Beyond Patriarchy: Essays by Men on Pleasure, Power, and Change*, pp. 139-92. Toronto: Oxford University Press.
1987   "Toward a New Sociology of Masculinity" in Harry Brod, ed., *The Making of Masculinities*, pp. 63-102. Boston: Allen and Unwin.

Carroll, William
1987   "Which Women are More Proletarianized? Gender, Class and Occupation in Canada." *Canadian Journal of Sociology* 24: 571-85.

Cassin, A. Marguerite
1977   "Class and Ethnicity: The Social Organization of Working Class East Indian Immigrants in Vancouver." Unpublished M.A. thesis. University of British Columbia.

_____ , and Alison I. Griffith
1981   "Class and Ethnicity: Producing the Difference that Counts." *Canadian Ethnic Studies* 13: 109-29.

Castleman, Michael
1986   "Losing it All: The Bare Facts about Balding." *Ms.* (September): 51-53, 87.

CBS Television Network
   1988   "Changes in Women's Roles on Television" in Stuart Oskamp, ed., *Television as a Social Issue*, pp. 113-17. Newbury Park, Calif.: Sage.

Chafetz, Janet Saltzman
   1974   *Masculine/Feminine or Human?* Itasca, Ill.: Peacock.
   1984   *Sex and Advantage.* Totowa, N.J.: Rowman and Allanheld.

_____ , and Anthony Gary Dworkin
   1986   *Female Revolt: Women's Movements in World and Historical Perspective.* Totowa, N.J.: Rowman and Allanheld.

Chappell, N.L., and B. Havens
   1980   "Old and Female: Testing and Double Jeopardy Hypothesis." *The Sociological Quarterly* 21: 157-71.

Cheal, David
   1989   "Theoretical Frameworks" in G.N. Ramu, ed., *Marriage and the Family in Canada Today*, pp. 19-34. Scarborough: Prentice-Hall.

Cherlin, Andrew
   1978   "Remarriage as an Incomplete Institution." *American Journal of Sociology* 84: 634-50.

_____ , and Pamela Barnhouse Walters
   1981   "Trends in United States Men's and Women's Sex-role Attitudes: 1972:1978." *American Sociological Review* 46: 453-60.

Chesler, Phyllis
   1972   *Women and Madness.* New York: Avon Books.

Chesney-Lind, Meda
   1986   "Women and Crime: The Female Offender." *Signs* 12: 78-96.

Chodorow, Nancy
   1978   *The Reproduction of Mothering: Psychoanalysis and the Sociology of Gender.* Berkeley: University of California Press.

_____ , and Susan Contratto
   1982   "The Fantasy of the Perfect Mother" in Barrie Thorne, ed., with Marilyn Yalom, *Rethinking the Family: Some Feminist Questions*, pp. 54-75. New York: Longman.

Clark, Lorenne, and Debra Lewis
   1977   *Rape: The Price of Coercive Sexuality.* Toronto: Women's Press.

Clark, Matt and David Gelman, with Mariana Gosnell, Mary Hager, and Barbara Schuler
   1987   "A User's Guide to Hormones." *Newsweek* (January 12): 50-59.

Clark, Susan, and Andrew S. Harvey
   1976   "The Sexual Division of Labour: The Case of Time." *Atlantis* 2: 46-66.

Clausen, John A.
   1968   "Perspectives on Childhood Socialization" in John A. Clausen, ed., *Socialization and Society*, pp. 130-81. Boston: Little, Brown.

Cleverdon, Catherine L.
   1974   *The Woman Suffrage Movement in Canada.* Toronto: University of Toronto Press.

Clio Collective (See also Dumont et al.)
    1987   *Quebec Women: A History.* Toronto: The Women's Press.

Code, Lorraine
    1987   "The Tyranny of Stereotypes" in Kathleen Storrie, ed., *Women: Isolation and Bonding,* pp. 195-209. Toronto: Methuen.
    1988   "Feminist Theory" in Sandra Burt, Lorraine Code, and Lindsay Dorney, eds., *Changing Patterns: Women in Canada,* pp. 18-50 Toronto: McClelland and Stewart.

Cohen, L.
    1984   *Small Expectations: Society's Betrayal of Older Women.* Toronto: McClelland and Stewart.

Coker, D.R.
    1984   "The Relationship among Concepts and Cognitive Maturity in Preschool Children." *Sex Roles* 10: 19-31.

Colby, Ann, and William Damon
    1987   "Listening to a Different Voice: A Review of Gilligan's In a Different Voice" in Mary Roth Walsh, ed., *The Psychology of Women: Ongoing Debates,* pp. 321-29. New Haven: Yale University Press.

Cole, Jonathan
    1979   *Fair Science: Women in the Scientific Community.* New York: Free Press.

Collins, H.M.
    1983   "The Sociology of Scientific Knowledge: Studies of Contemporary Science." *Annual Review of Sociology* 9: 265-85.

Collins, Monica
    1989   "Talking with Roseanne Barr: The Funniest 'Housewife' in America." *Redbook* (February): 34, 38, 40.

Coltrane, Scott
    1988   "Father-child Relationships and the Status of Women: A Cross-cultural Study." *American Journal of Sociology* 93: 1060–1095.

Colwill, Nina L.
    1982   *The New Partnership: Women and Men in Organizations.* Palo Alto, CA.: Mayfield.

Connelly, Patricia
    1977   "The Economic Context of Women's Labour Force Participation in Canada" in Patricia Marchak, ed., *The Working Sexes,* pp. 11-27. Vancouver: University of British Columbia.
    1978   *Last Hired, First Fired: Women and the Canadian Work Force.* Toronto: The Women's Press.

_____ , and Linda Christiansen-Ruffman
    1977   "Women's Problems: Private Troubles or Public Issues?" *Canadian Journal of Sociology* 2: 167-78.

Conner, J.M., and L.A. Serbin
    1978   "Children's Responses to Stories with Male and Female Characters." *Sex Roles* 4: 637-45.

Connidis, Ingrid Arnet
    1989   *Family Ties and Aging.* Toronto: Butterworths.

Cooley, Charles H.
    1902   *Human Nature and the Social Order.* New York: Scribner's.

Copps, Sheila
1986   *Nobody's Baby.* Toronto: Deneau Publishers.

Cornelius, Rudolph R., and James R. Averill
1983   "Sex Differences in Fear of Spiders." *Journal of Personality and Social Psychology* 45: 377-83.

Cosbey, Robert C.
1980   *All in Together Girls: Skipping Songs from Regina, Saskatchewan.* Regina, Canadian Plains Research Center, University of Regina.

Coser, Lewis A.
1968   "Sociology of Knowledge" in David L. Sills, ed., *International Encyclopedia of the Social Sciences*, pp. 428-35. New York: Macmillan.

_____ , with Rose Leah Coser
1974   "The Housewife and Her 'Greedy Family'" in Lewis A. Coser, *Greedy Institutions: Patterns of Undivided Commitment.* New York: Free Press.

Courtney, Alice E., and Thomas W. Whipple
1983   *Sex Stereotyping in Advertising.* Lexington, Mass.: D.C. Heath.

Coverman, Shelley W.
1989   "Women's Work is Never Done: The Division of Domestic Labor" in Jo Freeman, ed., *Women: A Feminist Perspective.* 4th ed., pp. 356 -58. Mountain View, Calif.: Mayfield.

Crane, Diana
1969   "Social Structure in a Group of Scientists: A Test of the 'Invisible College' Hypothesis." *American Sociological Review* 34: 335-52.

Crittenden, Danielle
1988   "REAL Women Don't Eat Crow." *Saturday Night* (May): 27-35.

Cumming, Elaine, Charles Lazer, and Lynne Chisholm
1975   "Suicide as an Index of Role Strain Among Employed and Not Employed Married Women in British Columbia." *Canadian Review of Sociology and Anthropology* 12, Part I: 462-70.

Cuneo, Carl
1985   "Have Women Become More Proletarianized than Men?" *Canadian Review of Sociology and Anthropology* 22: 465-95.

_____ , and James E. Curtis
1975   "Social Ascription in the Educational and Occupational Status Attainment of Urban Canadians." *Canadian Review of Sociology and Anthropology* 12: 6-24.

Curtis, James, and Ronald D. Lambert
1980   "Culture and Social Organization" in Robert Hagedorn, ed., *Sociology*, pp. 79-121. Toronto: Holt, Rinehart and Winston.

Daly, Mary
1975   "God is a Verb" in Uta West, ed., *Women in a Changing World*, pp. 153-70. New York: McGraw-Hill.
1978   *Gyn/Ecology: The Metaethics of Radical Feminism.* Boston: Beacon Press.

Daniels, Arlene Kaplan
1975   "Feminist Perspectives in Sociological Research" in Marcia Millman and Rosabeth

Moss Kanter, eds., *Another Voice: Feminist Perspectives on Social Life and Social Science*, pp. 340-80. Garden City, N.Y.: Doubleday Anchor.
1988   *Invisible Careers: Women Civic Leaders from the Volunteer World*. Chicago: University of Chicago Press.

Davids, Leo
1985   "The Lone Parent Family in Canada: The Quantitative Background" in Benjamin Schlesinger, ed., *The One-Parent Family in the 1980s: Perspectives and Annotated Bibliography 1978-1984*, pp. 1-12. Toronto: University of Toronto Press.

Davidson, L.R., and L. Duberman
1982   "Friendship: Communication and Interactional Patterns in Same-sex Dyads." *Sex Roles* 8: 809-22.

Davis, S.W.
1978   "Sex-trait Stereotypes and the Self and Peer Descriptions of Third Grade Children." Unpublished Master's Thesis, Wake Forest University.

Davison-Leong, Janis
1990   "Interest Groups and Canadian Broadcasting Regulation: An Examination of MediaWatch." Unpublished Master's Thesis, Communication Studies, The University of Calgary.

Davy, Shirley
1978   "Miss to Mrs.: Going, Going, Gone!" *Canadian Women's Studies* 1: 47-48.

Dawkins, Richard
1976   *The Selfish Gene*. London: Oxford University Press.

Deaux, Kay
1976   *The Behavior of Women and Men*. Monterey, Calif.: Brooks/Cole.
1984   "From Individual Differences to Social Categories: Analysis of a Decade's Research on Gender." *American Psychologist* 39: 105-116.
1985   "Sex and Gender." *Annual Review of Psychology* 36: 49-81.

_____, and Mary E. Kite
1987   "Thinking about Gender" in Beth B. Hess and Myra Marx Ferree, eds., *Analyzing Gender: A Handbook of Social Science Research*, pp. 92-117. Newbury Park: Sage.

_____, and Lawrence S. Wrightsman
1988   *Social Psychology*. 5th ed. Pacific Grove, Calif.: Brooks/Cole.

de Beauvoir, Simone
1952   *The Second Sex*. New York: Bantam Books.
1970   *Old Age*. Harmondsworth, England: Penguin.

Deegan, Mary Jo
1987   "Symbolic Interaction and the Study of Women: An Introduction" in Mary Jo Deegan and Michael Hill, eds., *Women and Symbolic Interaction*, pp. 3-15. Boston: Allen and Unwin.

DeKeseredy, Walter S.
1989   "Woman Abuse in Dating Relationships: An Exploratory Study." *Atlantis* 14: 55-62.

Dhruvarajan, Vanaja
1989   *Hindu Women and the Power of An Ideology*. Granby, MA.: Bergin and Garvey.

Dietz, Mary Lorenz
1981   "Managing a Deviant Identity: The Case of the Male Dancer in Ballet." Paper presented
          at the annual meeting of the Canadian Sociology and Anthropology Association, Hal-
          ifax, N.S.

di Leonardo, Micaela
1987   "The Female World of Cards and Holidays: Women, Families, and the Work of
          Kinship." *Signs* 12: 440-53.

Dinnerstein, Dorothy
1976   *The Mermaid and the Minotaur: Sexual Arrangements and Human Malaise*. New York:
          Harper and Row.

Dixon, Marlene
1971   "Why Women's Liberation" in Michele Hoffnung Garskof, ed., *Roles Women Play:
          Readings Toward Women's Liberation*, pp. 165-78. Belmont, Calif.: Brooks/Cole.

Dobash, R. Emerson, and Russell P. Dobash
1979   *Violence Against Wives: A Case Against the Patriarchy*. New York: Free Press.

Donaldson, Susan, and Will Kymlicka
1989   "No Thaw in Chilly Campus Climate." *The Globe and Mail* (November 17): A8.

Douvan, E.
1969   "Sex Differences in Adolescent Character Processes" in D. Rogers, ed., *Issues in
          Adolescent Psychology*, pp. 437-45. New York: Appleton-Century-Crofts.

Doyle, James A.
1985   *Sex and Gender: The Human Experience*. Dubuque, Iowa: Wm. C. Brown.
1989   *The Male Experience*. 2nd Ed. Dubuque, Iowa: Wm. C. Brown.

Driedger, Leo
1987   "Canadian Pluralism: Identities and Inequalities" in Leo Driedger, ed., *Ethnic Canada:
          Identities and Inequalities*, pp. 1-11. Toronto: Copp Clark Pitman.

Dubbert, Joe L.
1979   *A Man's Place: Masculinity in Transition*. Englewood Cliffs, N.J.: Prentice-Hall.

Dubinsky, Karen
1985   *Lament For a "Patriarchy Lost?": Anti-Feminism, Anti-Abortion and REAL Women in
          Canada*. Ottawa: Canadian Research Institute for the Advancement of Women.

Duffy, Ann Doris
1986   "Reformulating Power for Women." *Canadian Review of Sociology and Anthropology* 23:
          22-46.
1988   "Struggling with Power: Feminist Critiques of Family Inequality" in Nancy Mandell
          and Ann Duffy, eds., *Constructing the Canadian Family: Feminist Perspectives*, pp. 111-39.
          Toronto: Butterworths.

_____ , Nancy Mandell, and Norene Pupo
1989   *Few Choices: Women, Work and Family*. Toronto: Garamond Press.

Dulude, Louise
1978   *Women and Aging: A Report on the Rest of Our Lives*. Ottawa: Canadian Advisory Council
          on the Status of Women.
1987   "Getting Old: Men in Couples and Women Alone" in Greta Hofmann Nemiroff, ed.,

Women and Men: Inter-Disciplinary Readings on Gender, pp. 323-39. Toronto: Fitzhenry and Whiteside.

Dumont, Micheline
  1986   *The Women's Movement: Then and Now.* Ottawa: Canadian Research Institute for the Advancement of Women.

_____, Michele Jean Dumont, Marie Lavigne, Jennifer Stoddart (The Clio Collective)
  1987   *Quebec Women: A History.* Toronto: The Women's Press.

Dunbar, Roxanne
  1970   "Female Liberation as the Basis for Social Revolution" in Robin Morgan, ed., *Sisterhood is Powerful*, pp. 477-92. New York: Vintage.

Durdin-Smith, Jo, and Diane DeSimone
  1983   *Sex and the Brain.* New York: Arbor House.

Durkin, Kevin
  1986   "Sex Roles and the Mass Media." in David J. Hargreaves and Ann M. Colley, eds., *The Psychology of Sex Roles*, pp. 201-214. London, England: Harper and Row.

Dutton, D.G., and A.P. Aron
  1974   "Some Evidence for Heightened Sexual Attraction under Conditions of High Anxiety." *Journal of Personality and Social Psychology* 30: 510-17.

Dworkin, Andrea
  1979   *Pornography: Men Possessing Women.* New York: Perigee.

Eagly, Alice H.
  1987   *Sex Differences in Social Behavior: A Social-Role Interpretation.* Hilldale, N.J.: Lawrence Erlbaum.

_____, and L.L. Carli
  1981   "Sex of Researchers and Sex-typed Communications as Determinants of Sex Differences in Influencability: A Meta-analysis of Social Influence Studies." *Psychological Bulletin* 90: 1-20.

_____, and V.J. Steffen
  1984   "Gender Stereotypes Stem from the Distribution of Women and Men into Social Roles." *Journal of Personality and Social Psychology* 46: 735-54.

Eakins, Barbara Westbrook, and R. Gene Eakins
  1978   *Sex Differences in Human Communication.* Boston: Houghton Mifflin.

Eccles, Jacquelyne S., and Janis E. Jacobs
  1986   "Social Forces Shape Math Attitudes and Performance." *Signs* 11: 367-89.

Eckberg, Douglass Lee, and Lester Hill, Jr.
  1979   "The Paradigm Concept and Sociology: A Critical Review." *American Sociological Review* 44: 925-37.

Edelson, Miriam
  1987   *Challenging Unions: Feminist Process and Democracy in the Labour Movement.* Ottawa: Canadian Research Institute for the Advancement of Women.

Eder, Donna
  1985   "The Cycle of Popularity: Interpersonal Relations among Female Adolescents." *Sociology of Education* 58: 154-65.

_____ , and Maureen T. Hallinan
1978   "Sex Differences in Children's Friendships." *American Sociological Review* 43: 237-50.

Edwards, John R., and J. E. Williams
1980   "Sex-trait Stereotypes among Young Children and Young Adults: Canadian Findings and Cross-national Comparisons." *Canadian Journal of Behavioral Science* 12: 210-20.

Ehrenreich, Barbara
1983   *The Hearts of Men.* Garden City, N.Y.: Doubleday Anchor.
1989   "A Feminist's View of the New Man" in Michael S. Kimmel and Michael A. Messner, eds., *Men's Lives*, pp. 34-43. New York: Macmillan.

_____ , and Deirdre English
1978   *For Her Own Good: 150 Years of the Experts' Advice to Women.* Garden City, N.Y.: Doubleday Anchor.
1989   "Blowing the Whistle on the 'Mommy Track'." *Ms.* (July/August): 56-58.

Ehrhardt, Anke, and S.W. Baker
1978   "Fetal Androgens, Human Central Nervous System Differentiation, and Behavior Sex Differences" in R. Friedman, R.M. Richart, and R.L. Vande Wiele, eds., *Sex Differences in Behavior.* Huntington, N.Y.: Krieger.

Eichler, Margrit
1975   "Sociological Research on Women in Canada." *Canadian Review of Sociology and Anthropology* 12, Pt. I: 474-81.
1977   "The Prestige of the Occupation Housewife" in Patricia Marchak, ed., *The Working Sexes*, pp. 151-75. Vancouver: University of British Columbia.
1978   "Women's Unpaid Labour." *Atlantis* 3, Pt. 2: 52-62.
1980   *The Double Standard: A Feminist Critique of Feminist Social Science.* New York: St. Martin's Press.
1981   "The Inadequacy of the Monolithic Model of the Family." *Canadian Journal of Sociology* 6: 367-88.
1983   *Families in Canada Today.* Toronto: Gage.
1984   "Sexism in Research and its Policy Implications" in Jill McCalla Vickers, ed., *Taking Sex Into Account: The Policy Consequences of Sexist Research*, pp. 17-39. Ottawa: Carleton University Press.
1985a   "And the Work Never Ends." *Canadian Review of Sociology and Anthropology* 22: 619-44.
1985b   "The Connection Between Paid and Unpaid Labour and its Implication for Creating Equality for Women in Employment" in Rosalie Silberman Abella, *Equality in Employment: A Royal Commission Report*, pp. 537-46. Ottawa: Minister of Supply and Services Canada.
1986   *The Pro-Family Movement: Are They For or Against Families?* Ottawa: Canadian Research Institute for the Advancement of Women.
1988   *Families in Canada Today.* 2nd ed. Toronto: Gage.
1989   "Reflections on Motherhood, Apple Pie, the New Reproductive Technologies and the Role of Sociologists in Society." *Society/Société* 13: 1-5.

_____ , Deirdre English, Judy Erola, and Judith Gregory
1983   "Strategies for the Eighties" in Joan Turner and Lois Emery, eds., *Perspectives on Women in the 1980s*, pp. 136-48. Winnipeg: University of Manitoba Press.

_____ , and Jeanne Lapointe
1985   *On the Treatment of the Sexes in Research.* Ottawa: Social Sciences and Humanities Research Council of Canada.

Eisenstein, Zillah
  1979   *Capitalist Patriarchy and the Case for Socialist Feminism.* New York: Monthly Review Press.

Elkin, Frederick, and Gerald Handel
  1984   *The Child and Society: The Process of Socialization.* 4th ed. New York: Random House.

Ellis, Godfrey J.
  1983   "Youth in the Electronic Environment: An Introduction." *Youth and Society* 15: 3-12.

Ellmann, Mary
  1968   *Thinking about Women.* New York: Harcourt Brace Jovanovich.

Engels, Friedrich
  1902   *Origins of the Family, Private Property and the State.* Chicago: Charles H. Kerr.

English, Deirdre
  1982   "The War Against Choice: Inside the Anti-abortion Movement." *Mother Jones* (February/March): 16-32.

Epstein, Cynthia Fuchs
  1970   "Encountering the Male Establishment: Sex-status Limits on Women's Careers in the Professions." *American Journal of Sociology* 75: 965-82.
  1981   "Women in Sociological Analysis: New Scholarship Versus Old Paradigms" in Elizabeth Langland and Walter Gove, eds., *A Feminist Perspective in the Academy*, pp. 149-62. Chicago: University of Chicago Press.
  1988   *Deceptive Distinctions: Sex, Gender, and the Social Order.* New York: Russell Sage Foundation and Yale University Press.

Errington, Jane
  1988   "Pioneers and Suffragists" in Sandra Burt, Lorraine Code, and Lindsay Dorney, eds., *Changing Patterns: Women in Canada*, pp. 51-78. Toronto: McClelland and Stewart.

Exline, R.
  1971   "Visual Interaction: The Glances of Power and Preference" in J. Cole, ed., *Nebraska Symposium on Motivation.* Lincoln: University of Nebraska Press.

Eysenck, H.J.
  1952   "The Effects of Psychotherapy: An Evaluation." *Journal of Consulting and Clinical Psychology* 16: 319-24.
  1966   *The Effects of Psychotherapy.* New York: International Science Press.

Fagot, Beverley, I.
  1981   "Male and Female Teachers: Do They Treat Boys and Girls Differently?" *Sex Roles* 7: 263-71.
  _____ , and G.R. Patterson
  1969   "An In Vivo Analysis of Reinforcing Contingencies for Sex-role Behaviors in the Preschool Child." *Developmental Psychology* 1: 563-68.

Falbo, T., and L.A. Peplau
  1980   "Power Strategies in Intimate Relationships." *Journal of Personality and Social Psychology* 38: 618-28.

Farrell, Warren
  1974   *The Liberated Man.* New York: Random House.
  1986   *Why Men Are the Way They Are.* New York: McGraw-Hill.

Fasick, Frank A.
   1984   "Parents, Peers, Youth Culture, and Autonomy in Adolescence." *Adolescence* 19: 144-
           57.

Fasteau, Marc Feigen 1975
   1975   *The Male Machine*. New York: Dell.

Fausto-Sterling, Anne
   1985   *Myths of Gender: Biological Theories About Women and Men*. New York: Basic Books.

Fein, G.G.
   1981   "Pretend Play in Childhood: An Integrative Review." *Child Development* 52: 1095-1118.

Fein, Robert A.
   1974   "Men and Young Children" in Joseph H. Pleck and Jack Sawyer, eds., *Men and Mascu-
           linity*, pp. 54-62. Englewood Cliffs, N.J.: Prentice-Hall.

Feingold, A.
   1988   "Cognitive Gender Differences are Disappearing." *American Psychologist* 43: 95-103.

Feldberg, Roslyn L., and Evelyn Nakano Glenn
   1979   "Male and Female: Job versus Gender Models in the Sociology of Work." *Social
           Problems* 26: 524-38.

Feldman, Saul D.
   1974   *Escape from the Doll's House: Women in Graduate and Professional School Education*.
           Berkeley, Calif.: McGraw-Hill.

Feldman, S. Shirley, Sharon C. Nash, and Carolyn Cutrona
   1977   "The Influence of Age and Sex on Responsiveness to Babies." *Developmental Psychol-
           ogy* 13: 675-76.

Ferguson, Kathy E.
   1984   *The Feminist Case Against Bureaucracy*. Philadelphia: Temple University Press.

Ferguson, Marjorie
   1978   "Image and Ideology: The Cover Photographs of Traditional Women's Magazines" in
           Gaye Tuchman, Arlene Kaplan Daniels, and James Benet, eds., *Heart and Home: Images
           of Women in the Mass Media*, pp. 97-115. New York: Oxford University Press.

Ferree, Myra Marx
   1987   "She Works Hard for a Living: Gender and Class on the Job" in Beth B. Hess and Myra
           Marx Ferree, eds., *Analyzing Gender: A Handbook of Social Science Research*, pp. 322-47.
           Newbury Park, Calif.: Sage.

Fife, Sandy
   1989   "Banking Hierarchy Still Limits Women." *Calgary Herald* (March 23).

Figes, Eva
   1970   *Patriarchal Attitudes*. New York: Stein and Day.

Fine, Gary Alan
   1980   "The Natural History of Preadolescent Male Friendship Groups" in H.C. Foot, A.J.
           Chapman, and J.R. Smith, eds., *Friendship and Social Relations in Children*. New York:
           John Wiley and Sons.
   1986   "The Dirty Play of Little Boys." *Society* 24: 63-67.

Finlayson, Judith
  1989   "The Trouble with Superwoman." *Homemaker's Magazine* (October): 42-52.

Firestone, Melvin M.
  1978   "Socialization and Interaction in a Newfoundland Outport." *Urban Life* 7: 91-110.

Firestone, Shulamith
  1971   *The Dialectic of Sex: The Case for Feminist Revolution.* New York: Bantam.

Fischer, C.
  1983   "A Research Note on Friendship, Gender, and the Life Cycle." *Social Forces* 62: 124-33.

Fisher, Elaine
  1984   "Decoding Advertisements: Understanding Symbols, Language, Images and Conno-
          tation" in Women: Images, Role-Models: Proceedings of the Canadian Research
          Institute for the Advancement of Women Conference, University of Quebec, pp. 167-
          70.

Fishman, Pamela M.
  1978   "Interaction: The Work Women Do." *Social Problems* 25: 397-406.

Ford, Catherine
  1989   "Fear Takes Us Back to the Dark Ages." *Calgary Herald* (September 21).

Forgas, Joseph P., and Barbara Dobosz
  1980   "Dimensions of Romantic Involvement: Towards a Taxonomy of Heterosexual Rela-
          tionships." *Social Psychology Quarterly* 43: 290-300.

Fouts, Gregory T.
  1980   "Parents as Censors of TV Content for Their Children." *Journal of the Canadian Associa-
          tion for Young Children* 6:20-31.

Fox, Bonnie J.
  1980   "Introduction" in Bonnie Fox, ed., *Hidden in the Household: Women's Domestic Labour
          Under Capitalism*, pp. 9-23. Toronto: The Women's Press.
  1988   "Conceptualizing 'Patriarchy.'" *Canadian Review of Sociology and Anthropology* 25: 163-
          82.
  1989   "The Feminist Challenge: A Reconsideration of Social Inequality and Economic Devel-
          opment" in Robert J. Brym with Bonnie J. Fox, *From Culture to Power: The Sociology of
          English Canada*, pp. 120-67. Toronto: Oxford University Press.

_____, and John Fox
  1983   "Effect of Women's Employment on Wages." *Canadian Journal of Sociology* 8: 319-28.
  1986   "Women in the Labour Market, 1931-81: Exclusion and Competition." *Canadian Review
          of Sociology and Anthropology* 23: 1-21.
  1987   "Occupational Gender Segregation in the Canadian Labour Force, 1931-1981." *Cana-
          dian Review of Sociology and Anthropology* 24: 374-97.

Fraser, Sylvia
  1987   *My Father's House: A Memoir of Incest and of Healing.* Toronto: Doubleday.

Freeman, Jo
  1973   "The Origins of the Women's Liberation Movement." *American Journal of Sociology* 78:
          792-811.

Freire, P.
  1971   *Pedagogy of the Oppressed.* New York: Seaview.

Freud, Sigmund
   1905/1976   "Three Essays on the Theory of Sexuality" in J. Strachey, tr. and ed., *The Complete Psychological Works*. Vol. 7. New York: Norton.
   1925/1975   "Some Psychological Consequences of the Anatomical Distinction between the Sexes." Reprinted in Rhoda Kesler Unger and Florence L. Denmark, eds., *Women: Dependent or Independent Variable?* New York: Psychological Dimensions.
   1931/1976   "Female Sexuality" in J. Strachey, tr. and ed., *The Complete Psychological Works*. Vol. 21. New York: Norton.

Friday, Nancy
   1977   *My Mother, My Self*. New York: Dell.

Friedan, Betty
   1963   *The Feminine Mystique*. Harmondsworth, England: Penguin.
   1981   *The Second Stage*. New York: Summit Books.

Friedl, Ernestine
   1975   *Women and Men: An Anthropologist's View*. New York: Holt, Rinehart and Winston.

Frieze, Irene H., Jacquelynne E. Parsons, Paula B. Johnson, Diane N. Ruble, and Gail L. Zellman
   1978   *Women and Sex Roles: A Social Psychological Perspective*. New York: W.W. Norton.

Frisbie, Michael J.
   1985   "You Too Can Learn to Talk Like a Man." *McCall's* (May): 56.

Gagnon, J.H.
   1972   "The Creation of the Sexual in Early Adolescence" in J. Kagan and R. Coles, eds., *Twelve to Sixteen: Early Adolescence*. New York: Norton.

Gannage, Charlene
   1986   *Double Day, Double Bind: Women Garment Workers*. Toronto: Women's Educational Press.

Garfinkel, Harold
   1967   *Studies in Ethnomethodology*. Englewood Cliffs, N.J.: Prentice-Hall.

Garnets, Linda, and Joseph H. Pleck
   1979   "Sex Role Identity, Androgyny, and Sex Role Transcendence: A Sex Role Strain Analysis." *Psychology of Women Quarterly* 3: 270-83.

Gaskell, Jane
   1988   "The Reproduction of Family Life: Perspectives of Male and Female Adolescents" in Arlene Tigar McLaren, ed., *Gender and Society: Creating a Canadian Women's Sociology*, pp. 146 - 68. Toronto: Copp Clark Pitman.

_____, and Arlene Tigar McLaren, eds.
   1987   *Women and Education: A Canadian Perspective*. Calgary: Detselig.

_____, Arlene McLaren, and Myra Novogrodsky
   1989   *Claiming an Education: Feminism and Canadian Schools*. Toronto: Garamond.

Gecas, Viktor
   1976   "The Socialization and Child Care Roles" in F. Ivan Nye, ed., *Role Structure and Analysis of the Family*, pp. 33-59. Beverly Hills, Sage.
   1979   "The Influence of Social Class on Socialization" in W.R. Burr et al., eds., *Contemporary Theories About the Family*. Vol. 1. New York: Free Press.

Gee, Ellen M.
    1987   "Historical Change in the Family Life Course of Canadian Men and Women" in Victor W. Marshall, ed., *Aging in Canada: Social Perspectives*. 2nd ed., pp. 265-86. Toronto: Fitzhenry and Whiteside.

    _____ , and Meredith M. Kimball
    1987   *Women and Aging*. Toronto: Butterworths.

Geer, James, Julia Heiman, and Harold Leitenberg
    1984   *Human Sexuality*. Englewood Cliffs, N.J.: Prentice-Hall.

Geise, L. Ann
    1979   "The Female Role in Middle Class Women's Magazines from 1955 to 1976: A Content Analysis of Nonfiction Selections." *Sex Roles* 5: 51-62.

Gelles, Richard J.
    1985   "Family Violence." *Annual Review of Sociology* 11: 347-67.

Gerson, Judith M., and Kathy Peiss
    1985   "Boundaries, Negotiation, Consciousness: Reconceptualizing Gender Relations." *Social Problems* 32: 317-31.

Gerson, Kathleen
    1985   *Hard Choices: How Women Decide about Work, Career, and Motherhood*. Berkeley: University of California Press.

Gerson, Mary-Joan, Judith L. Alpert, and Mary Sue Richardson
    1984   "Mothering: The View from Psychological Research." *Signs* 9: 434-53.

Gerstel, Naomi
    1988   "Divorce, Gender, and Social Integration." *Gender and Society* 2: 343-67.

    _____ , and Harriet Engel Gross
    1989   "Women and the American Family: Continuity and Change" in Jo Freeman, ed., *Women: A Feminist Perspective*. 4th ed., pp. 89-120. Mountain View, Calif.: Mayfield.

Geschwind, Norman
    1979   "Specializations of the Human Brain." *Scientific American* 241 (3): 180-99.

Gibbins, Roger, J. Rick Ponting, and Gladys L. Symons
    1978   "Attitudes and Ideology: Correlates of Liberal Attitudes Towards the Role of Women." *Journal of Comparative Family Studies* 9:19-40.

Gibbs, Margaret, Doris Auerbach, and Margery Fox
    1980   "A Comparison of Male and Female Same-sex Friendships." *International Journal of Women's Studies* 3: 261-72.

Giele, Janet Z.
    1988   "Gender and Sex Roles" in Neil J. Smelser, ed., *Handbook of Sociology*, pp. 291-323. Newbury Park, Calif.: Sage.

Gilbert, Sid, and Ian Gomme
    1987   "Education in the Canadian Mosaic" in M. Michael Rosenberg, William B. Shaffir, Alan Turowetz and Morton Weinfeld, eds., *An Introduction to Sociology*, 2nd ed., pp. 197-234. Toronto: Methuen.

_____ , and Neil Guppy
1988   "Trends in Participation in Higher Education by Gender" in James Curtis, Edward
        Grabb, Neil Guppy, and Sid Gilbert, eds., *Social Inequality in Canada: Patterns, Problems,*
        Policies, pp. 163-69. Scarborough: Prentice-Hall Canada.

Gilligan, Carol
1982   *In a Different Voice.* Cambridge, Mass.: Harvard University Press.

Gillis, J.S., and W.E. Avis
1980   "The Male-taller Norm in Mate Selection." *Personality and Social Psychology Bulletin* 6:
        396-401.

Glass, G.V., B. McGraw, and M.L. Smith
1981   *Meta-Analysis in Social Research.* Beverly Hills, Calif.: Sage.

Glaxer, Nona
1977   "Housework: A Review Essay" in Nona Glazer and Helen Youngelson Waehrer, eds.,
        Woman in a Man-Made World. 2nd ed, pp. 360 - 69. Chicago: Rand McNally.

Glenn, Evelyn Nakano
1987   "Gender and the Family" in Beth B. Hess and Myra Marx Ferree, eds., *Analyzing*
        Gender: A Handbook of Social Science Research, pp. 348-80. Newbury Park, Calif.: Sage.

Goffman, Erving
1961   *Encounters.* Indianapolis: Bobbs-Merrill.
1967   *Interactional Ritual.* Garden City, N.Y.: Doubleday Anchor.
1976   *Gender Advertisements.* New York: Harper and Row.
1977   "The Arrangement between the Sexes." *Theory and Society* 4: 301-31.

Gold, Doris
1971   "Women and Voluntarism" in Vivian Gornick and Barbara K. Moran, eds., *Woman in*
        Sexist Society: Studies in Power and Powerlessness, pp. 533-54. New York: Signet.

Gold, William
1989   "Tragedy Brings Irrational Search for Excuses." *Calgary Herald* (December 12): A5.

Goldberg, Herb
1976   *The Hazards of Being Male: Surviving the Myth of Masculine Privilege.* New York: Signet.

Goldberg, Steven
1973   *The Inevitability of Patriarchy.* New York: William Morrow.

Goldenberg, Naomi
1978   "Women and the Image of God: A Psychological Perspective on the Feminist Move-
        ment in Religion." *International Journal of Women's Studies* 1: 468-74.

Goldenberg, Sheldon
1987   *Thinking Sociologically.* Belmont, Calif.: Wadsworth.

Goldsen, Rose K.
1979   Book review of Marie Winn, *The Plug-in Drug: Television, Children and the Family.* In
        American Journal of Sociology 84: 1054-56.

Goleman, Daniel
1978   "Special Abilities of the Sexes: Do They Begin in the Brain?" *Psychology Today* (Novem-
        ber): 48- 49, 51, 54-56, 58-59, 120.

Gongla, Patricia A., and Edward H. Thompson, Jr.
  1987   "Single-parent Families" in Marvin B. Sussman and Suzanne K. Steinmetz, eds., *Handbook of Marriage and the Family*, pp. 397-418. New York: Plenum Press.

Goode, William J.
  1959   "The Theoretical Importance of Love." *American Sociological Review* 24: 38-47.
  1963   *World Revolution and Family Patterns.* New York: Free Press.
  1982   "Why Men Resist" in Barrie Thorne, ed. with Marilyn Yalom, *Rethinking the Family: Some Feminist Questions*, pp. 131-50. New York: Longman.

Gornick, Vivan
  1976   "Introduction" in Erving Goffman, *Gender Advertisements*, pp. vi-ix. New York: Harper and Row.

Gottlieb, Amy
  1982   "Mothers, Sisters, Lovers, Listen" in Maureen Fitzgerald, Connie Guberman, and Margie Wolfe, eds., *Still Ain't Satisfied! Canadian Feminism Today*, pp. 224-42. Toronto: Women's Press.

Gould, Meredith
  1980   "Review Essay: The New Sociology." *Signs* 5: 459-67.

_____, and Rochelle Kern-Daniels
  1977   "Toward a Sociological Theory of Gender and Sex." *The American Sociologist* 12: 182-89.

Gove, Walter R.
  1972   "The Relationship between Sex Roles, Mental Illness, and Marital Status." *Social Forces* 51: 34-44.
  1978   "Sex Differences in Mental Illness among Adult Men and Women: An Evaluation of Four Questions Raised Regarding the Evidence on the Higher Rates of Women." *Social Science and Medicine* 12B: 187-98.

_____, Suzanne T. Orega, and Carolyn Briggs
  1989   "The Maturational and Role Perspectives on Aging and Self through the Adult Years: An Empirical Evaluation." *American Journal of Sociology* 94: 1117-45.

_____, and Jeannette F. Tudor
  1973   "Adult Sex Roles and Mental Illness." *American Journal of Sociology* 78: 812-35.

Goyder, John C.
  1981   "Income Differences between the Sexes: Findings from a National Canadian Survey." *Canadian Review of Sociology and Anthropology* 18: 321-42.

Grabb, Edward G.
  1988   "Conceptual Issues in the Study of Social Inequality" in James Curtis, Edward G. Grabb, Neil Guppy, and Sid Gilbert, eds., *Social Inequality in Canada: Patterns, Problems, Policies*, pp. 1-19. Scarborough: Prentice-Hall Canada.

Grant, Linda, Kathryn B. Ward, and Xue Lan Rong
  1987   "Is There an Association between Gender and Methods in Sociological Research?" *American Sociological Review* 52: 856 - 62.

Gray, Charlotte
  1989   "The New F-word." *Saturday Night* (April): 17-20.

Gray, Stan
    1987   "Sharing the Shop Floor" in Greta Hofmann Nemiroff, ed., *Women and Men: Interdisciplinary Readings on Gender*, pp. 377-402. Toronto: Fitzhenry and Whiteside.

Gray, Vicky A.
    1977   "The Image of Women in Psychology Textbooks." *Canadian Psychological Review* 18: 46-55.

Grayson, J. Paul
    1983   "Male Hegemony and the English Canadian Novel." *Canadian Review of Sociology and Anthropology* 20: 1-21.

Green, Maureen
    1976   *Fathering.* New York: McGraw-Hill.

Green, Richard
    1974   *Sexual Identity Conflict in Children and Adults.* Baltimore: Penguin.
    1979   *Human Sexuality.* 2nd ed. Baltimore: Williams and Wilkins.
    1987   *The "Sissy Boy Syndrome" and the Development of Homosexuality.* New Haven, Conn.: Yale University Press.

Greenberg, Bradley S.
    1988   "Some Uncommon Television Images and the Drench Hypothesis" in Stuart Oskamp, ed., *Television as a Social Issue*, pp. 88-102. Newbury Park, Calif.: Sage.

Greenberg, David F.
    1988   *The Construction of Homosexuality.* Chicago: University of Chicago Press.

Greenberger, E., and L. Steinberg
    1983   "Sex Differences in Early Labor Force Experience: Harbinger of Things to Come." *Social Forces* 62: 467-86.

Greenglass, Esther R.
    1982   *A World of Difference: Gender Roles in Perspective.* Toronto: John Wiley and Sons.

Greeno, Catherine G. and Eleanor E. Maccoby
    1986   "How Different is the 'Different Voice?'" *Signs* 11: 310-16.

Grief, E.B.
    1980   "Sex Differences in Parent-Child Conversations." *Women's Studies International Quarterly* 3: 253-58.

Griffin, Susan
    1981   *Pornography and Silence: Culture's Revenge Against Nature.* New York: Harper and Row.

Groarke, Leo
    1983   "Beyond Affirmative Action." *Atlantis* 9: 13-24.

Gruber, J.E., and L. Bjorn
    1982   "Blue-collar Blues: The Sexual Harassment of Women Auto Workers." *Work and Occupations* 9: 271-98.

Grunbaum, A.
    1984   *The Foundations of Psychoanalysis.* Berkeley, Calif.: University of California Press.

Gunderson, Morley
    1976   "Work Patterns" in Gail C.A. Cook, ed., *Opportunity for Choice: A Goal for Women in Canada*, pp. 93-142. Ottawa: Information Canada.

Guppy, Neil
  1989a   "Pay Equity in Canadian Universities, 1972-73 and 1985-86." *Canadian Review of Sociology and Anthropology* 26: 743-58.
  1989b   "Rank, Age, and Salary in Anthropology and Sociology." *Society/Société* 13 (May): 14-17.

_____ , Doug Balson, and Susan Vellutini
  1987   "Women and Higher Education in Canadian Society" in Jane S. Gaskell and Arlene Tigar McLaren, eds., *Women and Education: A Canadian Perspective*, pp. 171-92. Calgary: Detselig.

Haas, Adelaide
  1979   "Male and Female Spoken Language Differences: Stereotypes and Evidence." *Psychological Bulletin* 86: 616-26.

Haas-Hawkings, Gwen, Sandra Sangster, Michael Ziegler, and David Reid
  1985   "A Study of Relatively Immediately Adjustment to Widowhood in Later Life." *International Journal of Women's Studies* 8: 158-66.

Halberstadt, A.G., and M.B. Saitta
  1987   "Gender, Nonverbal Behavior, and Perceived Dominance: A Test of the Theory." *Journal of Personality and Social Psychology* 53: 257-72.

Hall, Edward T.
  1959   *The Silent Language*. New York: Fawcett World Library.

Hall, Elizabeth
  1980   "Acting One's Age: New Rules for Old." (Interview with Bernice Neugarten.) *Psychology Today* 13 (April): 66-80.

Hall, Judith A.
  1978   "Gender Effects in Decoding Nonverbal Cues." *Psychological Bulletin* 85: 845-75.
  1984   *Nonverbal Sex Differences: Communication Accuracy and Expressive Style.* Baltimore, MD: Johns Hopkins University Press.
  1987   "On Explaining Gender Differences: The Case of Nonverbal Communication" in Phillip Shaver and Clyde Hendrick, eds., *Sex and Gender*, pp. 177-200. Newbury Park, Calif.: Sage.

Hall, M. Ann, and Dorothy A. Richardson
  1982   *Fair Ball: Towards Sex Equality in Canadian Sport*. Ottawa: Canadian Advisory Council on the Status of Women.

Hallinan, Maureen T.
  1979   "Structural Effects on Children's Friendships and Cliques." *Social Psychology Quarterly* 42: 43-54.

Hamilton, Roberta
  1978   *The Liberation of Women: A Study of Patriarchy and Capitalism*. London: Allen and Unwin.

Handel, Gerald
  1990   "Revising Socialization Theory." *American Sociological Review* 55: 463-66.

Hanson, Shirley M.H.
  1986   "Parent-child Relationships in Single-father Families" in Robert A. Lewis and Robert E. Salt, eds., *Men in Families*, pp. 181-95. Beverly Hills, Calif.: Sage.

Haraway, Donna
1978   "Animal Sociology and a Natural Economy of the Body Politic. Part 2." *Signs* 4: 37-60.

Harding, Deborah, and Emily Nett
1984   "Women and Rock Music." *Atlantis* 10: 60-76.

Harding, Sandra
1986   *The Science Question in Feminism*. Ithaca, N.Y.: Cornell University Press.

Hargreaves, David J.
1986   "Psychological Theories of Sex-Role Stereotyping" in David J. Hargreaves and Ann M. Colley, eds., *The Psychology of Sex Roles*, pp. 27-44. London, England: Harper and Row.

Harlan, Sharon, and Brigid O'Farrell
1982   "After the Pioneers: Prospects for Women in Traditionally Male Blue Collar Jobs." *Work and Occupations* 9: 363-86.

Harlow, Harry F.
1959   "Love in Infant Monkeys." *Scientific American* 200 (June): 68-74.
1962   "The Heterosexual Affectional System in Monkeys." *American Psychologist* 17: 1-9.
1965   "Sexual Behavior in the Rhesus Monkey" in Frank A. Beach, ed., *Sex and Behavior*, pp. 234-65. New York: Wiley.

Harman, Lesley D.
1989   *When a Hostel Becomes a Home: Experiences of Women*. Toronto: Garamond Press.

Harper, Paula
1985   "The First Feminist Art Program: A View from the 1980s." *Signs* 10: 762-81.

Harris, D.A.
1974   "Androgyny: The Sexist Myth in Disguise." *Women's Studies* 2: 171-84.

Harrison, James B.
1978   "Men's Roles and Men's Lives." *Signs* 4: 324-36.

Hartley, Ruth E.
1959   "Sex-role Pressures in the Socialization of the Male Child." *Psychological Reports* 5: 457-68.

Hartmann, Heidi
1976   "Capitalism, Patriarchy, and Job Segregation by Sex." *Signs* 1, Part 2: 137-70.
1981   "The Family as the Locus of Gender, Class, and Political Struggle: The Example of Housework." *Signs* 6: 366-94.

Haskell, Molly
1988   "Hollywood Madonnas." *Ms.* (May): 84-87.

Haspiel, Erica A.
1981   "The Assignment of Expertise in Canadian Broadcasting Advertising." *Ontario Psychologist* 13: 29-34.

Haviland, Jeannette Jones, and Carol Zander Malatesta
1981   "The Development of Sex Differences in Non-verbal Signals: Fallacies, Facts, and Fantasies" in Clara Mayo and Nancy M. Henley, eds., *Gender and Nonverbal Behavior*, pp. 183-208. New York: Springer-Verlag.

Hayford, Alison
  1987   "Outlines of the Family" in Karen Anderson et al., *Family Matters: Sociology and Contemporary Canadian Families*, pp. 1-19. Toronto: Methuen.

Hays, Robert B.
  1985   "A Longitudinal Study of Friendship Development." *Journal of Personality and Social Psychology* 48: 909-24.

Hefner, R., M. Rebecca, and B. Oleshansky
  1975   "Development of Sex-role Transcendence." *Human Development* 18: 143-56.

Heinemann, Michelle
  1988   "The World Needs Science: Science Needs Women." *The University of Calgary Gazette* 18 (September 19): 5.

Henley, Nancy M.
  1977   *Body Politics: Power, Sex and Nonverbal Communication.* Englewood Cliffs, N.J.: Prentice-Hall.
  1985   "Psychology and Gender." *Signs* 11:101-19.

_____ , Mykol Hamilton, and Barrie Thorne
  1985   "Womanspeak and Manspeak: Sex Differences and Sexism in Communication, Verbal and Nonverbal" in Alice G. Sargent, ed., *Beyond Sex Roles.* 2nd ed., pp. 168-85. St. Paul, Minn.: West Publishing.

Henshel (Ambert), Anne-Marie
  1973   *Sex Structure.* Don Mills, Ont.: Longman.

Herman, Kathleen, ed.
  1986/87 *Guide to Departments: Sociology, Anthropology, Archeology in Universities and Museums in Canada.* Montreal: Canadian Sociology and Anthropology Association, Canadian Ethnology Society.

Hernadez, Donald J.
  1986   "Childhood in Sociodemographic Perspective." *Annual Review of Sociology* 12: 159-80.

Herold, Edward S.
  1984   *Sexual Behavior in Canadian Young People.* Markham, Ont.: Fitzhenry and Whiteside.

Hersley, S., and E. Werner
  1975   "Dominance in Marital Decision-making in Women's Liberation and Non-women's Liberation Families." *Family Process* 14: 223-33.

Hetherington, E.M.
  1972   "Effects of Father Absence on Personality Development in Adolescent Daughters." *Developmental Psychology* 7: 313-26.
  1979   "Divorce: A Child's Perspective." *American Psychologist* 34: 851-58.

Hetherington, E.M., M. Cox, and R. Cox
  1979   "The Aftermath of Divorce." In J.H. Stevens, Jr. and M. Matthews, eds., *Mother-Child, Father-Child Relations."* Washington, D.C.: National Association for the Education of Young Children.

Hewitt, John P.
  1984   *Self and Society: A Symbolic Interactionist Social Psychology.* 3rd ed. Boston: Allyn and Bacon.

Hewlett, Sylvia
     1986   *A Lesser Life: The Myth of Women's Liberation in America*. New York: William Morrow.

Hill, Charles T., Zuck Rubin, and Letitia Peplau
     1976   "Breakups before Marriage: The End of 103 Affairs." *Journal of Social Issues* 32: 147-68.

Hiller, Harry H.
     1979   "The Canadian Sociology Movement; Analysis and Assessment." *Canadian Journal of Sociology* 4: 125-50.
     1986   *Canadian Society: A Macro Analysis*. Scarborough, Ont.: Prentice-Hall Canada.

Himelfarb, Alexander, and James C. Richardson
     1982   *Sociology for Canadians*. Toronto: McGraw-Hill Ryerson.

Hitchman, Gladys S.
     1974   "A Report on the Reports: The Status of Women in Canadian Universities." *Canadian Sociology and Anthropology Association Bulletin* 35 (October): 11-14.

Hobart, Charles W.
     1981   "Sources of Egalitarianism in Young Unmarried Canadians."*Canadian Journal of Sociology* 6: 261-82.

Hochschild, Arlie
     1975   "The Sociology of Feeling and Emotion: Selected Possibilities" in Marcia Millman and Rosabeth Moss Kanter, eds., *Another Voice: Feminist Perspectives on Social Life and Social Science*, pp. 280-307. Garden City, N.Y.: Doubleday Anchor.
     1979   "Emotion Work, Feeling Rules, and Social Structure." *American Journal of Sociology* 85: 551-75.
     1989   *The Second Shift: Working Parents and the Revolution at Home*. New York: Viking Penguin.

Hoffman, M.L.
     1975   "Sex Differences in Moral Internalization and Values." *Journal of Personality and Social Psychology* 32: 720-29.

Hofsess, John
     1985   "The Reel Stuff: A Guide to the New Movies that Portray Women as They Really Are." *Homemaker's Magazine* (November): 16-27.

Hole, Judith, and Ellen Levine
     1971   *The Rebirth of Feminism*. New York: Quadrange Books.

Homans, George C.
     1950   *The Human Group*. New York: Harcourt, Brace.

Horna, Jarmila, and Eugen Lupri
     1987   "Fathers' Participation Work, Family Life and Leisure: A Canadian Experience" in Charlie Lewis and Margaret O'Brien, eds., *Reassessing Fatherhood: New Observations on Fathers and the Modern Family*, pp. 54-73. London, England: Sage.

Horner, Matina
     1969   "Fail: Bright Women" *Psychology Today* 3 (November): 36, 38, 62.

Horney, Karen
     1932   "The Dread of Women." *International Journal of Psycho-Analysis* 13: 348-60.

Hosek, Chaviva
     1983   "Who Women Fought for Equality." *Canadian Forum* (May): 6-14.

1987   "How Women Fought for Equality" in Greta Hofmann Nemiroff, ed., *Women and Men: Interdisciplinary Readings on Gender*, pp. 493-514. Toronto: Fitzhenry and Whiteside.

Hospital, Janette Turner
1982   *The Ivory Swing.* Toronto: Bantam Windstone.

Howe, Florence
1974   "Sexual Stereotypes and the Public Schools" in Ruth B. Kundsin, ed., *Women and Success: The Anatomy of Achievement*, pp. 123-218. New York: William Morrow.

Hsu, Francis
1980   "Margaret Mead and Psychological Anthropology." *American Anthropologist* 82: 349-53.

Hubbard, Ruth
1983   "Social Effects of Some Contemporary Myths about Women" in Marian Lowe and Ruth Hubbard, *Woman's Nature: Rationalizations of Inequality*, pp. 1-8. New York: Pergamon.
1987   "Review of Anne Fausto-Sterling, *Myths of Gender: Biological Theories about Women and Men.*" *American Journal of Sociology* 92: 1033-1035.

Huber, Joan
1976   "Toward a Socio-techonological Theory of the Women's Movement." *Social Problems* 23: 371-88.
1990   "Macro-micro Links in Gender Stratification." *American Sociological Review* 55: 1-10.

Huffhines, Kathy
1990   "Women in Film." *The Calgary Herald* (April 14): A7.

Hunter College Women's Studies Collective
1983   *Women's Realities, Women's Choices: An Introduction to Women's Studies.* New York: Oxford University Press.

Huston, Aletha C.
1983   "Sex Typing" in Paul H. Mussen, ed., *Handbook of Child Psychology*, Vol. IV., E. Mavis Hetherington, volume editor, pp. 387-467. New York: John Wiley and Sons.

Huston, Ted L., and Richard D. Ashmore
1986   "Women and Men in Personal Relationships" in Richard D. Ashmore and Frances Del Boca, eds., *The Social Psychology of Female-Male Relations*, pp. 167-210. Orlando, Florida: Academic Press.

Hyde, Janet S.
1979   *Understanding Human Sexuality.* New York: McGraw-Hill.
1981   "How Large are Cognitive Gender Differences?" *American Psychologist* 36: 892-901.

_____ , B.G. Rosenberg and J. Behrman
1977   "Tomboyism." *Psychology of Women Quarterly* 2: 73-75.

Ihlinger-Tallman, Marilyn
1988   "Research on Stepfamilies." *Annual Review of Sociology* 14: 25-48.

Inglis, J., and J. Lawson
1981   "Sex Differences in the Effects of Unilateral Brain Damage on Intelligence." *Science* 212: 693-95.

Ishwaran, K.
1979   "An Overview of Theory and Research" in K. Ishwaran, ed., *Childhood and Adolescence in Canada*, pp. 3-36. Toronto: McGraw-Hill Ryerson.

Jacklin, C.N., and E.E. Maccoby
1978   "Social Behavior at 33 Months in Same-sex and Mixed-sex Dyads." *Child Development* 49: 557-69.

Jackson, John D.
1985   "Introduction" to Special Issue on Feminist Scholarship. *Canadian Review of Sociology and Anthropology* 22: 615-18.

Jaggar, Alison M.
1983   *Feminist Politics and Human Nature.* Totowa, N.J.: Rowman and Allanheld.

_____ , and Paula S. Rothenberg
1984   *Feminist Frameworks: Alternative Theoretical Accounts of the Relations Between Women and Men.* 2nd ed. New York: McGraw-Hill.

Jamieson, Kathleen
1979   "Multiple Jeopardy: The Evolution of a Native Women's Movement." *Atlantis* 4: 157-78.
1981   "Sisters under the Skin: An Exploration of the Implications of Feminist-materialist Perspective Research." *Canadian Ethnic Studies* 13: 130 -43.
1986   "Sex Discrimination and the Indian Act" in J. Rick Ponting, ed., *Arduous Journey: Canadian Indians and Decolonization*, pp. 112-36. Toronto: McClelland and Stewart.

Janeway, Elizabeth
1974   "On 'Female Sexuality'" in J. Strouse, ed., *Women and Analysis*, pp. 57- 64. New York: Grossman.
1980   *The Powers of the Weak.* New York: Knopf.

Jhally, Sut
1987   *The Codes of Advertising.* New York: St. Martin's Press.

Johnson, Colleen Leahy
1988   *Ex Familia: Grandparents, Parents, and Children Adjust to Divorce.* New Brunswick, N.J.: Rutgers University Press.

Johnston, Wendy
1981   "Women's Struggle for Non-traditional Jobs." *Resources for Feminist Research* 10: 16-17.

Jump, Teresa L., and Linda Haas
1987   "Fathers in Transition: Dual-career Fathers Participating in Child Care" in Michael S. Kimmel, ed., *Changing Men: New Directions in Research on Men and Masculinity*, pp. 98-114. Newbury Park, Calif.: Sage.

Juteau-Lee, Danielle, and Barbara Roberts
1981   "Ethnicity and Femininity: d'après nos experiences." *Canadian Ethnic Studies* 13: 1-23.

Kagan, Jerome
1984   *The Nature of the Child.* New York: Basic.

Kalbach, Warren E.
1987   "Growth and Distribution of Canada's Ethnic Populations, 1871-1981" in Leo Driedger, ed., *Ethnic Canada: Identities and Inequalities*, pp. 82-110. Toronto: Copp Clark Pitman.

Kalin, R., J.M. Stoppard, and B. Burt
1980 "Sex-role Ideology and Sex Bias in Judgments of Occupational Suitability" in Cannie Stark-Adamec, ed., *Sex Roles: Origins, Influences, and Implications for Women*, pp. 89-99. Montreal: Eden Press.

Kando, Thomas
1973 *Sex Change: The Achievement of Gender Identity Among Feminized Transsexuals.* Springfield, Ill.: Charles C. Thomas.

Kanin, E.J., K.R. Davidson, and S.R. Scheck
1970 "A Research Note on Male-female Differentials in the Experience of Heterosexual Love." *Journal of Sex Research* 6: 64-72.

Kanter, Rosabeth Moss
1976 "The Impact of Hierarchical Structures on the Work Behavior of Women and Men." *Social Problems* 23: 415-30.
1977 "Some Effects of Proportions on Group Life: Skewed Sex Ratios and Responses to Token Women." *American Journal of Sociology* 82: 965-90.

Katz, Phillis A.
1979 "The Development of Female Identity" in Claire B. Kopp, ed., *Becoming Female: Perspectives on Development*, pp. 3-28. New York: Plenum.

Kaufman, Debra Renee
1989 "Professional Women: How Real are the Recent Gains?" in Jo Freeman, ed., *Women: A Feminist Perspective.* 4th ed., pp. 329- 46. Mountain View, Calif.: Mayfield.

Kaufman, Michael
1987a "Introduction" in Michael Kaufman, ed., *Beyond Patriarchy: Essays by Men on Pleasure, Power, and Change*, pp. xiii-xix. Toronto: Oxford University Press.
1987b "The Construction of Masculinity and the Triad of Men's Violence" in Michael Kaufman, ed., *Beyond Patriarchy: Essays by Men on Pleasure, Power, and Change*, pp 1-29. Toronto: Oxford University Press.

Kealey, Linda K.
1979 "Introduction" in Linda Kealey, ed., *A Not Unreasonable Claim: Women and Reform in Canada 1880s-1920s*, pp. 1-14. Toronto: Women's Press.

Keating, Norah C., and Priscilla Cole
1980 "What Do I Do with Him 24 Hours a Day? Changes in the Housewife Role after Retirement." *The Gerontologist* 20: 84-89.

Kerber, Linda K.
1986 "On In a Different Voice: An Interdisciplinary Forum. Some Cautionary Words for Historians" *Signs* 11: 304-10.

Kessler, Ronald C., and James A. McRae
1982 "The Effect of Wives' Employment on the Mental Health of Married Men and Women." *American Sociological Review* 47: 216-27.

Kessler, Suzanne J., and Wendy McKenna
1978 *Gender: An Ethnomethodological Approach.* New York: John Wiley and Sons.

Keywan, Zonia
1981 Pp. 38-39 in Mary Two Axe Early, Zonia Keywan, and Helen Potrebenko, "Ethnicity and Femininity as Determinants of Life Experience." *Canadian Ethnic Studies* 13: 37-42.

Kimball, Meredith M.
1986   "Television and Sex-role Attitudes" in Tannis MacBeth Williams, ed., *The Impact of Television: A Natural Experiment in Three Communities*, pp. 265-301. Orlando, Florida: Academic Press.

Kimmel, Michael S.
1989   "From Pedestals to Partners: Men's Responses to Feminism" in Jo Freeman, ed., *Women: A Feminist Perspective*, pp. 581-94. Mountain View, Calif.: Mayfield.

Kinsman, Gary
1987a   "Men Loving Men: The Challenge of Gay Liberation" in Michael Kaufman, ed., *Beyond Patriarchy: Essays by Men on Pleasure, Power, and Change*, pp. 103-19. Toronto: Oxford University Press.
1987b   *The Regulation of Desire: Sexuality in Canada*. Montreal: Black Rose.

Kirkey, Sharon, and John Ibbitson
1989   "Sexism Still Rife on Canadian Campuses." *Calgary Herald* (December 10): C2.

Kitzinger, Celia
1987   *The Social Construction of Lesbianism*. Newbury Park, Calif.: Sage.

Kohlberg, Lawrence
1963   "The Development of Children's Orientations toward a Moral Order: I. Sequence in the Development of Moral Thought." *Vita Humana* 6: 11-33.
1966   "A Cognitive-developmental Analysis of Children's Sex-role Concepts and Attitudes" in Eleanor Maccoby, ed., *The Development of Sex Differences*, pp. 82-172. Stanford, Calif.: Stanford University Press.
1981   *The Philosophy of Moral Development: Moral Stages and the Idea of Justice*. New York: Harper and Row.

_____, and D.Z. Ullian
1974   "Stages in the Development of Psychosexual Concepts and Attitudes." In R.C. Friedman, R.M. Richart, and R.L. Vande Wiele, eds., *Sex Differences in Behavior*. New York: Wiley.

_____, and Edward Zigler
1967   "The Impact of Cognitive Maturity on the Development of Sex-role Attitudes in the Years 4 to 8." *Genetic Psychology Monographs* 75: 89-165.

Kohn, Alfie
1988   "Girl Talk, Guy Talk." *Psychology Today* 22 (February): 65-66.

Kohn, Melvin L.
1977   *Class and Conformity*. 2nd ed. Chicago: University of Chicago Press.

Kollock, Peter, Philip Blumstein, and Pepper Schwartz
1985   "Sex and Power in Interaction: Conversational Privileges and Duties." *American Sociological Review* 50: 34-46.

Komarovsky, Mirra (1946 or 1964, 1973, 1976)
1946   "Cultural Contradictions and Sex Roles." *American Journal of Sociology* 52: 184-89.
1973   "Cultural Contradictions and Sex Roles: The Masculine Case." *American Journal of Sociology* 78: 873-84.
1976   *Dilemmas of Masculinity*. New York: W.W. Norton.

Kome, Penney
    1983   *The Taking of Twenty-Eight: Women Challenge the Constitution.* Toronto: Women's Press.
    1985   *Women of Influence: Canadian Women and Politics.* Toronto: Doubleday Canada.

Kopinak, Kathryn M.
    1983   "Polity" in Robert Hagedorn, ed., *Sociology.* 2nd ed., pp. 401-31. Toronto: Holt, Rinehart and Winston.
    1987   "Gender Differences in Political Ideology in Canada." *Canadian Review of Sociology and Anthropology* 24: 23-38.
    1988   "Women in Canadian Municipal Politics: Two Steps Forward, One Step Back" in Arlene Tigar McLaren, ed., *Gender and Society: Creating a Canadian Women's Sociology,* pp. 372-87. Toronto: Copp Clark Pitman.

Kostash, Myrna
    1987   *No Kidding: Inside the World of Teenage Girls.* Toronto: McClelland and Stewart.

Knelman, Martin
    1986   "Urban Lady." *Saturday Night* (December): 61-63.

Krohn, Roger
    1985   "Is Sociobiology a Political or a Research Program?" *Canadian Review of Sociology and Anthropology* 22: 227-32.

Kronenfeld, Jennie Jacobs, and Marcia Lynn Whicker
    1986   "Feminist Movements and Changes in Sex Roles: The Influence of Technology." *Sociological Focus* 19: 47-60.

Kuhn, Thomas
    1970   *The Structure of Scientific Revolutions.* 2nd ed. Chicago: University of Chicago Press.

Labour Canada
    1986   *When I Grow Up: Career Expectations and Aspirations of Canadian Schoolchildren.* Ottawa: Women's Bureau.
    1987   *Women in the Labour Force.* Ottawa: Supply and Services.

Lacasse, F.D.
    1971   *Women at Home: The Cost to the Canadian Economy of the Withdrawal from the Labour Force of a Major Proportion of the Female Population.* Studies of the Royal Commission on the Status of Women in Canada. Ottawa: Queen's Printer.

LaFrance, M.
    1985   "Does your Smile Reveal your Status?" *Social Science News Letter* 70 (Spring): 15-18.

Lakoff, Robin
    1975   *Language and Woman's Place.* New York: Harper and Row.

Lamb, M.E.
    1978   "Influence of the Child on Marital Quality and Family Interaction during the Prenatal, Natal, and Infancy Periods" in R. Lerner and G. Spanier, eds., *Child Influences on Marital and Family Interaction,* pp. 137-64. New York: Academic Press.

_____, Joseph, H. Pleck, and James A. Levine
    1986   "Effects of Increased Paternal Involvement on Children in Two-parent Families" in Robert A. Lewis and Robert E. Salt, eds., *Men in Families,* pp. 141-58. Beverly Hills: Sage.

_____ , and Brian Sutton-Smith
    1982   *Sibling Relationships Across the Life Span*. Hillside, N.J.: Lawrence Ehrlbaum.

Lamb, Theodore A.
    1981   "Nonverbal and Paraverbal Control in Dyads and Triads: Sex or Power Differences?"
            Social Psychology Quarterly 44: 49-53.

Lambert, Helen H.
    1978   "Biology and Equality: A Perspective on Sex Differences." *Signs* 4: 97-117.

Lambert, Ronald D.
    1971   *Sex Role Imagery in Children: Social Origins of Mind*. Royal Commission on the Status of
            Women in Canada, Study 6. Ottawa: Information Canada.

Lambert, W.E., A. Yackley, and R.N. Hein
    1971   "Child Training Values of English Canadian and French Canadian Parents." *Canadian
            Journal of Behavioural Science* 3: 217-36.

Lamphere, Louise
    1977   "Anthropology: Review Essay." *Signs* 2: 612-27.

Lancaster, Jane Beckman
    1976   "Sex Roles in Primate Societies" in Michael S. Teitelbaum, ed., *Sex Differences: Social and
            Biological Perspectives*, pp. 22-61. Garden City, N.Y.: Doubleday Anchor.
    1985   "Evolutionary Perspectives on Sex Differences in the Higher Primates" in Alice S.
            Rossi, ed., *Gender and the Life Course*, pp. 3-27. New York: Aldine.

Landsberg, Michele
    1982   *Women and Children First*. Markham, Ont.: Penguin.

Landy, D.
    1965   *Tropical Childhood*. New York: Harper and Row.

LaRossa, Ralph, and Maureen M. LaRossa
    1981   *Transition to Parenthood: How Infants Change Families*. Beverly Hills, Calif.: Sage.

Lasch, Christopher
    1979   *The Culture of Narcissism*. New York: W.W. Norton.
    1979   *Haven in a Heartless World*. New York: Basic.

Lauer, Jeanette, and Robert Lauer
    1985   "Marriages Made to Last." *Psychology Today* 19 (June): 22-26.

Laurence, Margaret
    1964   *The Stone Angel*. Toronto: McClelland and Stewart.

Lautmann, Rudiger
    1981   "The Pink Triangle: The Persecution of Homosexual Males in Concentration Camps in
            Nazi Germany." *Journal of Homosexuality* 6: 141-60.

Laws, Judith Long
    1979   *The Second X: Sex Role and Social Role*. New York: Elsevier North-Holland.
    _____ , and Pepper Schwartz
    1977   *Sexual Scripts: The Social Construction of Female Sexuality*. Hinsdale, Ill.: Dryden.

Leacock, Eleanor B.
   1978   "Women's Status in Egalitarian Society: Implications for Social Evolution." *Current Anthropology* 19: 247-75.
   1982   *Myths of Male Dominance.* New York: Monthly Review.

Leahy, R.L., and S.R. Shirk
   1984   "The Development of Classificatory Skills and Sex-trait Stereotypes in Children." *Sex Roles* 10: 281-92.

Lee, Deborah, and Joan Hertzberg
   1978   "Theories of Feminine Personality" in Irene H. Frieze, Jacquelynne E. Parsons, Paula B. Johnson, Diane N. Ruble, and Gail I. Zellman, eds., *Women and Sex Roles: A Social Psychological Perspective*, pp. 28-44. New York: W.W. Norton.

Leiss, William, Stephen Kline, and Sut Jhally
   1986   *Social Communication in Advertising: Persons, Products, and Images of Well-Being.* Toronto: Methuen.

Lengermann, Patricia Madoo, and Jill Niebrugge-Brantley
   1988   "Contemporary Feminist Theory" in George Ritzer, *Contemporary Sociological Theory*, pp. 282-325. Second Edition. New York: Alfred A. Knopf.

Lennards, Jos. L.
   1990   "Education" in Robert Hagedorn, ed., *Sociology.* 4th ed., pp. 399- 432. Toronto: Holt, Rinehart and Winston.

Lenski, Gerhard
   1977   "Sociology and Sociobiology: An Alternative View." *The American Sociologist* 12: 73-75.

Lerman, Hannah
   1987   "From Freud to Feminist Personality Theory: Getting Here from There" in Mary Roth Walsh, ed., *The Psychology of Women: Ongoing Debates*, pp. 39-58. New Haven, Conn.: Yale University Press.

Lever, Janet
   1976   "Sex Differences in the Games Children Play." *Social Problems* 23: 478-87.
   1978   "Sex Differences in the Complexity of Children's Play." *American Sociological Review* 43: 471-83.

Levin, Jack, and Arnold Arluke
   1985   "An Exploratory Analysis of Sex Differences in Gossip." *Sex Roles* 12: 281-86.

Levine, Helen
   1983   "The Power Politics of Motherhood" in Joan Turner and Lois Emery eds., *Perspectives on Women in the 1980s*, pp. 28-40. Winnipeg: University of Manitoba Press.

Levy, J.
   1976   "Cerebral Lateralization and Spatial Ability." *Behavior Genetics* 6: 71-78.

Lewis, Charlie
   1986   "Early Sex-role Socialization" in David J. Hargreaves and Ann M. Colley, eds., *The Psychology of Sex Roles*, pp. 95-117. London, England: Harper and Row.

Lewis, Michael
   1972   "Culture and Gender Roles: There's No Unisex in the Nursery." *Psychology Today* 5 (May): 54-57.

_____ , and Jeanne Brooks-Gunn
    1979   *Social Cognition and the Acquisition of Self.* New York: Plenum.

Liddle, A. Mark
    1989   "Feminist Contributions to an Understanding of Violence against Women — Three Steps Forward, Two Steps Back." *Canadian Review of Sociology and Anthropology* 26: 759-75.

Liebert, Robert M., and Joyce Sprafkin
    1988   *The Early Window: Effects of Television on Children and Youth.* 3rd. ed. New York: Pergamon.

Liebowitz, Lila
    1983   "Origins of the Sexual Division of Labor." In Marian Lowe and Ruth Hubbard, eds., *Woman's Nature: Rationalizations of Inequality.* New York: Pergamon.

Lightfoot, Sara Lawrence
    1977   "Family-school Interactions: The Cultural Image of Mothers and Teachers." *Signs* 3: 395-408.

Lindesmith, Alfred R., and Anselm L. Strauss
    1956   *Social Psychology.* Rev. ed. New York: Holt, Rinehart and Winston.
    1968   *Social Psychology.* 3rd ed. New York: Holt, Rinehart and Winston.

_____ , Anselm L. Strauss, and Norman K. Denzin
    1977   *Social Psychology.* 5th ed. New York: Holt, Rinehart and Winston.

Lindsay, Colin, and Craig McKie
    1986   "Annual Review of Labour Force Trends." *Canadian Social Trends* (Autumn): 2-7. Statistics Canada.

Lipman-Blumen, Jean
    1984   *Gender Roles and Power.* Englewood Cliffs, N.J.: Prentice-Hall.

Lippert, Barbara
    1988   "Send in the Wimps." *Vogue* (November): 414, 415, 456.

Lippitt, Ronald
    1968   "Improving the Socialization Process" in John A. Clausen, ed., *Socialization and Society,* pp. 321-74. Boston: Little, Brown.

Lippmann, Walter
    1922   *Public Opinion.* New York: Harcourt and Brace.

Lips, Hilary M.
    1983   "Attitudes Toward Childbearing Among Women and Men Expecting Their First Child." *International Journal of Women's Studies* 6: 119-29.

Livingstone, Barb
    1988   "Open Road Policy Lures Female Truckers." *Calgary Herald* (September 24): G1.

Livingstone, D.W., and Meg Luxton
    1989   "Gender Consciousness at Work: Modification of the Male Breadwinner Norm among Steel Workers and Their Spouses." *Canadian Review of Sociology and Anthropology* 26: 240-75.

Locherty, Lorraine
    1989   "Room at the Top." *Calgary Herald Sunday Magazine* (April 2): 6 -10.

Loewen, James W., and Samuel F. Sampson
  1986   "Getting Gender on Their Minds: A Classroom Exercise." *Teaching Sociology* 14: 185-87.

Lofland, Lyn H.
  1975   "The 'Thereness' of Women: A Selective Review of Urban Sociology" in Marcia Millman and Rosabeth Moss Kanter, eds., *Another Voice: Feminist Perspectives on Social Life and Social Science*, pp. 114-70. Garden City, N.Y.: Doubleday Anchor.

Lopata, Helena Z.
  1971   *Occupation: Housewife*. New York: Oxford University Press.
  1973   "Self-identity in Marriage and in Widowhood." *Sociological Quarterly* 14: 407-18.
  1975   "Couple-companiate Relationships in Marriage and Widowhood." In N. Glazer-Malbin, ed., *Old Family/New Family*. New York: Van Nostrand.
  1976   "Sociology: Review Essay." *Signs* 2: 165-76.
  1979   *Women as Widows*. New York: Elsevier.
  1987   "Women's Family Roles in Life Course Perspective" in Beth B. Hess and Myra Marx Ferree, eds., *Analyzing Gender: A Handbook of Social Science Research*, pp. 381-407. Newbury Park, Calif.: Sage.

_____ , and Joseph H. Pleck, eds.
  1983   *Research in the Interweave of Social Roles: Families and Jobs*. Greenwood, Conn.: JAI Press.

_____ , and Barrie Thorne
  1978   "On the Term 'Sex Roles.'" *Signs* 3: 718-21.

Lorber, Judith
  1981   "On the Reproduction of Mothering: A Methodological Debate." *Signs* 6: 482-86.
  1986   "Dismantling Noah's Ark." *Sex Roles* 14: 567-80.

Losh-Hesselbart, Susan
  1987   "Development of Gender Roles" in Marvin B. Sussman and Suzanne K. Steinmetz, eds., *Handbook of Marriage and the Family*, pp. 535-63. New York: Plenum Press.

Lott, Bernice
  1981   "A Feminist Critique of Androgyny: Toward the Elimination of Gender Attributions for Learned Behavior" in Clara Mayo and Nancy M. Henley, eds., *Gender and Non-verbal Behavior*, pp. 171-80. New York: Springer-Verlag.

Lowe, Graham S.
  1980   "Women, Work and the Office: The Feminization of Clerical Occupations in Canada, 1901-1931." *Canadian Journal of Sociology* 5: 361-81.

_____ , and Harvey J. Krahn
  1984   "Work Values and Job Satisfaction: Editors' Introduction" in Graham S. Lowe and Harvey J. Krahn, eds., *Working Canadians: Readings in the Sociology of Work and Industry*, pp. 1-3. Toronto: Methuen.
  1985   "Where Wives Work: The Relative Effects of Situational and Attitudinal Factors." *Canadian Journal of Sociology* 10: 1-22.

Lowe, Marian
  1978   "Sociobiology and Sex Differences." *Signs* 4: 118-25.
  1983   "The Dialectic of Biology and Culture" in Marian Lowe and Ruth Hubbard, eds, *Woman's Nature: Rationalizations of Inequality*, pp. 39-62. New York: Pergamon Press.

_____ , and Ruth Hubbard, eds.
  1983   *Woman's Nature: Rationalizations of Inequality*. New York: Pergamon.

Lundberg, Ferdinand, and Marynia F. Farnham
  1947   *Modern Woman; The Last Sex.* New York: Harper and Bros.

Lupri, Eugen
  1988   "Fathers in Transition: The Case of Dual-earner Families." *Zeitschrift fur sozialisations-forschung und erziehungssoziologie,* 8. Jahrgang, heft 4, 281-97.
  1990   *Reflections on Marriage and the Family in Canada: A Study in the Dialectics of Family and Work Roles.* Toronto: Holt, Rinehart and Winston.

_____ , and Donald L. Mills
  1983   "The Changing Roles of Canadian Women in Family and Work: An Overview" in Eugen Lupri, ed., *The Changing Roles of Women in Family and Society: A Cross-Cultural Comparison,* pp. 43-77. Leiden, Netherlands: E.J. Brill.
  1987   "The Household Division of Labour in Young Dual-earner Couples: The Case of Canada." *International Review of Sociology.* New Series (2): 33-54.

_____ , and Gladys Symons
  1982   "The Emerging Symmetrical Family: Fact or Fiction?" *International Journal of Comparative Sociology* 23: 166-89.

Luxton, Meg
  1980   *More Than a Labour of Love: Three Generations of Women's Work in the Home.* Toronto: Women's Press.
  1986   "Two Hands for the Clock: Changing Patterns in the Gendered Division of Labour in the Home" in Meg Luxton and Harriet Rosenberg, *Through the Kitchen Window,* pp. 17-36. Toronto: Garamond Press.

_____ , and Harriet Rosenberg
  1986   *Through the Kitchen Window.* Toronto: Garamond Press.

Lynn, David B.
  1969   *Parental and Sex Role Identification: A Theoretical Formulation.* Berkeley, Calif.: McCutchan.

Lyttelton, Ned
  1987   "Men's Liberation, Men Against Sexism and Major Dividing Lines" in Greta Hofmann Nemiroff, ed., *Women and Men: Interdisciplinary Readings on Gender,* pp. 472-77. Toronto: Fitzhenry and Whiteside.

McCallum, Sandra K., and A. Anne McLellan
  1980   "The `Persons" Case: A Beginning — Not the End." *Resources for Feminist Research* (Fall): 76-79.

McClung, Nellie L.
  1915/1972   *In Times Like These.* Toronto: University of Toronto Press.

Maccoby, Eleanor E.
  1980   *Social Development: Psychological Growth and the Parent-Child Relationship.* New York: Harcourt Brace Jovanovich.

_____ , and Carol Nagy Jacklin
  1974   *The Psychology of Sex Differences.* Stanford, Calif.: Stanford University Press.

MacCormack, Carol
  1981   "Anthropology: A Discipline with a Legacy" in Dale Spender, ed., *Men's Studies Modified: The Impact of Feminism on the Academic Disciplines,* pp. 99-110. New York: Pergamon.

McCormack, Thelma
1983 "The Androgyny Debate." *Atlantis* 9: 118-26.
1984 "Censorship May Not Be Answer to Porn." *CAUT Bulletin* (February): 27.
1985 "Becoming a Women's Studies Scholar: From Stardust to Section Fifteen." *Canadian Woman Studies* 6: 5-9.
1987 "Feminism, Women's Studies and the New Academic Freedom" in Jane Gaskell and Arlene McLaren, eds., *Women and Education: A Canadian Perspective*, pp. 289-303. Calgary: Detselig Enterprises.
1989 "Feminism and the New Crisis in Methodology" in Winnie Tomm, ed., *The Effects of Feminist Approaches on Research Methodologies*, pp. 13-30. Waterloo, Ontario: Wilfrid Laurier University Press.

McCormick, Naomi B., and Clinton J. Jesser
1983 "The Courtship Game: Power in the Sexual Encounter" in Elizabeth R. Allgeier and Naomi B. McCormack, eds., *Changing Boundaries: Gender Roles and Sexual Behavior*, pp. 64-86. Palo Alto, Calif.: Mayfield.

McCracken, Rosemary
1987 "Anti-feminist Backlash." *Calgary Herald* (January 27): A5.

McDaniel, Susan A.
1988a "The Changing Canadian Family: Women's Roles and the Impact of Feminism" in Sandra Burt, Lorraine Code, and Lindsay Dorney, eds., *Changing Patterns: Women in Canada*, pp. 103-28. Toronto: McClelland and Stewart.
1988b *Getting Older and Better: Women and Gender Assumptions in Canada's Aging Society.* Ottawa: Canadian Research Institute for the Advancement of Women.
1988c "Women's Roles and Reproduction: The Changing Picture in Canada in the 1980s." *Atlantis* 14: 1-12.
1988d "Women's Roles, Reproduction and the New Reproductive Technologies: A New Stork Rising" in Nancy Mandell and Ann Duffy, eds., *Reconstructing the Canadian Family: Feminist Perspectives*, pp. 175-206. Toronto: Butterworths.
1989 "A New Stork Rising? Women's Roles and Reproductive Changes." *Society/Société* 13: 6-14.

McDonnell, Kathleen
1984 *Not An Easy Choice: A Feminist Re-examines Abortion.* Toronto: Women's Press.

McGlone, Jeannette
1980 "Sex Differences in Human Brain Asymmetry: A Critical Survey." *Behavioral and Brain Sciences* 3: 215-63.

_____ , and A. Kertesz
1973 "Sex Differences in Cerebral Processing of Visual-spatial Tasks." *Cortex* 9: 313-20.

MacGregor, Robert M.
1989 "The Distorted Mirror: Images of Visible Minority Women in Canadian Print Advertising." *Atlantis* 15: 137-43.

McGuire, Meredith
1987 *Religion: The Social Context.* Belmont, Calif.: Wadsworth.

McKee, Lorna, and Margaret O'Brien
1982 "The Father Figure: Some Current Orientations and Historical Perspectives" in Lorna McKee and Margaret O'Brien, eds., *The Father Figure*, pp. 1-25. London, England: Tavistock.

McKie, D.C., B. Prentice, and P. Reed
    1983   *Divorce: Law and Family in Canada*. Ottawa: Statistics Canada.

Mackie, Marlene
    1973   "Arriving at `Truth' by Definition: The Case of Stereotype Inaccuracy." *Social Problems*
            20: 431- 47.
    1977   "On Congenial Truths: A Perspective on Women's Studies." *Canadian Review of Soci-
            ology and Anthropology* 14: 117-28.
    1980   "The Impact of Sex Stereotypes upon Adult Self-imagery." *Social Psychology Quarterly*
            43: 121-25.
    1985   "Female Sociologists' Productivity, Collegial Relations, and Research Style Examined
            through Journal Publications." *Sociology and Social Research* 69: 189-209.
    1986   "Women in the Profession: Collegiability and Productivity." *Society/Société* 10, #3 un-
            paginated.
    1987   *Constructing Women and Men: Gender Socialization*. Toronto: Holt, Rinehart and Win-
            ston.
    1988   "Sexism in Sociological Research" in Winnie Tomm and Gordon Hamilton, eds.,
            Gender Bias in Scholarship: The Pervasive Prejudice, pp. 1-23. Calgary Institute for the
            Humanities. Waterloo: Wilfrid Laurier University Press.
    1989   "Primary Socialization" in G.N. Ramu, ed., *Marriage and the Family in Canada Today*, pp.
            101-19. Scarborough, Ont.: Prentice-Hall.
    1990a   "Socialization" in Robert Hagedorn, ed., *Sociology*. 4th ed., pp. 61-94. Toronto: Holt,
            Rinehart and Winston.
    1990b   "Who is Laughing Now? The Role of Humour in the Social Construction of Gender."
            Atlantis 15 Spring: 11-26.

MacKinnon, Catharine A.
    1983   "Feminism, Marxism, Method, and the State: Toward Feminist Jurisprudence." *Signs*
            8: 635-58.

MacKinnon, Neil J., and Leo J. Keating
    1989   "The Structure of Emotions: Canada-United States Comparisons." *Social Psychology
            Quarterly* 52: 70-83.

Macklin, Eleanor D.
    1987   "Nontraditional Family Forms" in Marvin B. Sussman and Suzanne K. Steinmetz eds.,
            Handbook of Marriage and the Family, pp. 317-53. New York: Plenum.

McLanahan, Sara, and Julia Adams
    1987   "Parenthood and Psychological Well-being." *Annual Review of Sociology* 5: 237-57.

McLaren, Angus, and Arlene Tigar McLaren
    1986   *The Bedroom and the State: The Changing Practices and Politics of Contraception and Abortion
            in Canada, 1880-1980*. Toronto: McClelland and Stewart.

McLaren, Arlene Tigar, ed.
    1988   *Gender and Society: Creating a Canadian Women's Sociology*. Toronto: Copp Clark Pitman.

MacLeod, Linda
    1980   *Wife Battering in Canada: The Vicious Circle*. Ottawa: Advisory Council on the Status of
            Women.
    1987   *Battered But Not Beaten: Preventing Wife Battering in Canada*. Ottawa: National Council
            on the Status of Women.

McPhee, Nancy
1978   *The Book of Insults Ancient and Modern*. Toronto: Van Nostrand Reinhold.

McPherson, J. Miller, and Lynn Smith-Lovin
1986   "Sex Segregation in Voluntary Associations." *American Sociological Review* 51: 61-79.

McRoberts, Hugh A.
1985   "Mobility and Attainment in Canada: The Effects of Origin" in Monica Boyd et al., *Ascription and Achievement: Studies in Mobility and Status Attainment in Canada*, pp. 67-100. Ottawa: Carleton University Press.

Mainardi, Pat
1970   "The Politics of Housework" in Robin Morgan, ed., *Sisterhood is Powerful*, pp. 447-54. New York: Vintage (Random House).

Major, Brenda
1981   "Gender Patterns in Touching Behavior" in Clara Mayo and Nancy M. Henley, eds., *Gender and Nonverbal Behavior*, pp. 15-37. New York: Springer-Verlag.

Malamuth, Neil M., and Edward Donnerstein, eds.
1984   *Pornography and Sexual Aggression*. Orlando, Florida: Academic Press.

Malinowski, Bronislaw
1926   *Crime and Custom in Savage Society*. New York: Humanities Press.

Malmo, Cheryl
1984   "Sexism in Psychological Research" in Jill McCalla Vickers, ed., *Taking Sex Into Account: The Policy Consequences of Sexist Research*, pp. 116-32. Ottawa: Carleton University Press.

Maltz, D., and R. Borker
1982   "A Cultural Approach to Male-female Miscommunication" in J.J. Gumperz, ed., *Language and Social Identity*, pp. 196-216. New York: Cambridge University Press.

Mandell, Nancy, and Ann Duffy, eds.
1988   *Reconstructing the Canadian Family: Feminist Perspectives*. Toronto: Butterworths.

Manion, Eileen
1985   "We Objects Object: Pornography and the Women's Movement" in Marilouise and Arthur Kroker, Pamela McCallum, and Mair Verthay, eds., *Feminism Now: Theory and Practice*, pp. 65-80. Montreal: New World Paperbacks.

Manis, Jerome G., and Bernard N. Meltzer
1978   "Intellectual Antecedents and Basic Propositions of Symbolic Interactionism" in Jerome G. Manis and Bernard N. Meltzer, eds., *Symbolic Interaction: A Reader in Social Psychology*, pp. 1-9. 3rd Ed. Boston: Allyn and Bacon.

Mannheim, Karl
1936   Ideology and Utopia. New York: Harcourt, Brace and World.

Marchak, Patricia M.
1973   "Women Workers and White Collar Unions." *Canadian Review of Sociology and Anthropology* 10: 134-47.
1977   (ed.), *The Working Sexes*. Vancouver: University of British Columbia.

Marchildon, Rudy G.
    1981   "The `Persons' Controversy: The Legal Aspects of the Fight for Women Senators."
            Atlantis 6: 99-113.

Marini, Margaret Mooney, and Mary C. Brinton
    1984   "Sex Typing in Occupational Socialization" in Barbara F. Reskin, ed., *Sex Segregation
            in the Workplace*, pp. 192-232. Washington, D.C.: National Academy Press.

Marks, Stephen R.
    1977   "Multiple Roles and Role Strain: Some Notes on Human Energy, Time, and Commit-
            ment." *American Sociological Review* 42: 921-36.

Maroney, Heather Jon, and Meg Luxton
    1987a   "Editors' Introduction" in Heather Jon Maroney and Meg Luxton, eds., *Feminism and
            Political Economy: Women's Work, Women's Struggles*, pp. 1-3. Toronto: Methuen.
    1987b   "From Feminism and Political Economy to Feminist Political Economy" in Heather Jon
            Maroney and Meg Luxton, eds., *Feminism and Political Economy: Women's Work,
            Women's Struggles*, pp. 5-28. Toronto: Methuen.

Marsden, Lorna R., and Edward B. Harvey
    1979   *Fragile Federation: Social Change in Canada*. Toronto: McGraw-Hill Ryerson.

Marshall, Barbara L.
    1988   "Feminist Theory and Critical Theory." *Canadian Review of Sociology and Anthropology*
            25: 208-30.

Marshall, Katherine
    1987   *Who Are the Professional Women?* Ottawa: Statistics Canada, Cat. #99-951.

Marshall, Susan E.
    1989   "Keep Us on the Pedestal: Women against Feminism in Twentieth-century America"
            in Jo Freeman, ed., *Women: A Feminist Perspective*. 4th ed., pp. 567-80. Mountain View,
            Calif.: Mayfield.

Martel, Angeline, and Linda Peterat
    1984   "Naming the World: Consciousness in a Patriarchal Iceberg" in Jill McCalla Vickers,
            ed., *Taking Sex Into Account: The Policy Consequences of Sexist Research*, pp. 43-56. Ottawa:
            Carleton University Press.

Martin, Elaine
    1984   "Power and Authority in the Classroom: Sexist Stereotypes in Teaching Evaluations."
            Signs 9: 482-92.

Martin, Leslie E.
    1986   "Women Workers in a Masculine Domain: Jobs and Gender in a Yukon Mine" in Kath-
            erina L.P. Lundy and Barbara Warme, eds., *Work in the Canadian Context: Continuity
            Despite Change*. 2nd ed., pp. 248-80. Toronto: Butterworths.

Martin, M. Kay, and Barbara Voorhies
    1975   *Female of the Species*. Toronto: Methuen.

Martin, Tony
    1989   "Self-employment becomes Choice of a Generation." *The Globe and Mail* (August 14):
            C1.

Martyna, Wendy
    1980   "Beyond the `He/Man' Approach: The Case for Nonsexist Language." *Signs* 5: 482-93.

Marvin, C.
  1977   "Sympathy and Affection in the Peer Interaction of One Year Olds." Unpublished
          doctoral dissertation, Ohio State University.

Marx, Karl
  1846/1947   *The Poverty of Philosophy*. New York: International.
  1859/1913   *A Contribution to the Critique of Political Economy*. Chicago: Kerr.
  1904   *A Contribution to the Critique of Political Economy*. Translated from the 2nd German ed.
          by N.I. Stone. New York: International Library Publishing.

_____ , and Friedrich Engels
  1932/1947   *The German Ideology*. New York: International.

Maticka-Tyndale, Eleanor
  1989   "Impact of AIDS on Adolescent Sexuality." Unpublished Ph.D. Thesis, Department of
          Sociology, University of Calgary.

Matthews, Anne Martin
  1987   "'Widowhood as an Expectable Life Event" in Victor W. Marshall, ed., *Aging in Canada:
          Social Perspectives*. 2nd ed., pp. 343-66. Toronto: Fitzhenry and Whiteside.

Matthews, Sarah H.
  1979   *The Social World of Old Women: Management of Self-Identity*. Beverly Hills: Sage.
  1982   "Rethinking Sociology through a Feminist Perspective." *The American Sociologist* 17:
          29-35.
  1986   *Friendships Through the Life Course: Oral Biographies in Old Age*. Beverly Hills, Calif.:
          Sage.

Mayhew, Bruce H.
  1980   "Structuralism versus Individualism: Part 1, Shadowboxing in the Dark." *Social Forces*
          59: 335-75.

Maynard, Fredelle
  1988   *The Tree of Life*. Markham. Ontario: Penguin.

Maynard, Rona
  1984   "Divorced Dads: How Can We Make Them Pay Child Support?" *Chatelaine* 57 (May):
          65, 154, 156, 158, 160 - 62, 166.
  1984   "Women and Men: Is the Difference Brain-deep?" *Chatelaine* 57 (October): 76, 86, 88, 90,
          98.
  1988a   "Fathers' Rights." *Chatelaine* (November): 61-63, 140-42.
  1988b   "Were They Better off Then We Are?" *The Globe and Mail Report on Business Magazine*
          (May): 38-47.
  1988   "Why Men Are Mad as Hell." *Chatelaine* (December): 88-89, 122, 124, 126, 128-29, 131.

Mead, George Herbert
  1934   *Mind, Self and Society*. Chicago: University of Chicago Press .

Mead, Margaret
  1935   *Sex and Temperament in Three Primitive Societies*. Reprint. New York: Mentor Books.
  1949   *Male and Female*. New York: William Morrow.

Meissner, Martin, Elizabeth W. Humphreys, Scott M. Meis, William J. Scheu
  1975   "No Exit for Wives: Sexual Division of Labour and the Cumulation of Household De-
          mands." *Canadian Review of Sociology and Anthropology* 12, Part I: 424-39.

Menzies, Heather
    1981   *Women and the Chip: Case Studies of the Effect of Informatics on Employment in Canada.*
            Montreal: Institute for Research on Public Policy.
    1984   "Women and Microtechnology" in Graham S. Lowe and Harvey J. Krahn, eds.,
            Working Canadians, pp. 290-97. Toronto: Methuen.

Messing, Karen
    1987   "The Scientific Mystique: Can a White Lab Coat Guarantee Purity in the Search for
            Knowledge about the Nature of Women?" in Greta Hofmann Nemiroff, ed., *Women
            and Men: Interdisciplinary Readings on Gender*, pp. 103-16. Toronto: Fitzhenry and
            Whiteside.

Messner, Michael
    1987   "The Life of a Man's Seasons: Male Identity in the Life Course of the Jock" in Michael
            S. Kimmel, ed., *Changing Men: New Directions in Research on Men and Masculinity*, pp.
            53-67. Newbury Park, Calif.: Sage.

Miall, Charlene
    1986   "The Stigma of Involuntary Childlessness." *Social Problems* 33: 268-82.

Michelson, William
    1985   *From Sun to Sun: Daily Obligations and Community Structure in the Lives of Employed
            Women and Their Families.* Totowa, N.J.: Rowman and Allanheld.

Middlebrook, Patricia Niles
    1974   *Social Psychology and Modern Life.* New York: Alfred A. Knopf.

Miles, Angela
    1984   "Dissolving the Hyphen: From Socialist-feminism to Feminist Feminism." *Atlantis* 9:
            77-94.

_____ , and Geraldine Finn, eds.
    1982   *Feminism in Canada: From Pressure to Politics.* Montreal: Black Rose.

Mill, John Stuart
    1869   *The Subjection of Women.* Cambridge, Mass.: Massachusetts Institute of Technology
            Press (reprinted 1970).

Miller, Casey, and Kate Swift
    1977   *Words and Women.* Garden City, N.Y.: Doubleday Anchor.

Miller, Joanne
    1988   "Jobs and Work" in Neil J. Smelser, ed., *Handbook of Sociology*, pp. 327-59. Newbury
            Park, Calif.: Sage.

_____ , and Howard Garrison
    1982   "Sex Roles: The Division of Labor at Home and in the Workplace." *Annual Review of
            Sociology* 8: 237-62.

Miller, Leslie J.
    1987   "Uneasy Alliance: Women as Agents of Social Control." *Canadian Journal of Sociology*
            12: 345-61.
    1989   "Review Essay: Dorothy E. Smith, *The Everyday World as Problematic: A Feminist
            Sociology.*" *Canadian Journal of Sociology* 14: 521-30.

Miller, Neil
    1989   *In Search of Gay America: Women and Men in a Time of Change.* New York: Atlantic Monthly Press.

Millet, Kate
    1969   *Sexual Politics.* New York: Avon Books.

Millman, Marcia
    1980   *Such a Pretty Face: Being Fat in America.* New York: Berkley Books.

_____ , and Rosabeth Moss Kanter
    1975   *Another Voice: Perspectives on Social Life and Social Science.* Garden City, N.Y.: Doubleday Anchor.

Mills, C. Wright
    1959   *The Sociological Imagination.* New York: Grove Press.

Minton, C., J. Kagan, and J. Levine
    1971   "Maternal Control and Obedience in the Two-year-old Child." *Child Development* 42: 1873-94.

Minuchin, P., and E. Shapiro
    1983   "The School as a Context for Social Development" in E.M. Hetherington, ed., *Handbook of Child Psychology*, Vol. 4: *Socialization, Personality, and Social Development*, pp. 197-294. New York: Wiley.

Mirowsky, John, and Catherine E. Ross
    1989   *Social Causes of Psychological Distress.* New York: Aldine de Gruyter.

Mischel, W.
    1970   "Sex-typing and Socialization" in P.H. Mussen, ed., *Carmichael's Manual of Child Psychology*, pp. 3-72. New York: Wiley.

Mitchell, Juliet
    1971   *Woman's Estate.* Harmondsworth: Penguin.
    1974   *Psychoanalysis and Feminism.* New York: Pantheon.

Mitchinson, Wendy
    1979   "The WCTU: `For God, Home and Native Land': A Study in Nineteenth-century Feminism" in Linda Kealey, ed., *A Not Unreasonable Claim: Women and Reform in Canada 1880s-1920s*, pp. 151-67. Toronto: Women's Press.

Modleski, Tania
    1982   *Loving with a Vengeance: Mass-produced Fantasies for Women.* New York: Methuen.

Money, John, and A.A. Ehrhardt
    1972   *Man and Woman, Boy and Girl: The Differentiation and Dimorphism of Gender Identity from Conception to Maturity.* Baltimore, MD.: Johns Hopkins University Press.

_____ , and Patricia Tucker
    1975   *Sexual Signatures: On Being a Man or a Woman.* Boston: Little, Brown.

Montagu, Ashley
    1952   *The Natural Superiority of Women.* New York: P.F. Collier.

Morgan, B.S.
    1976   "Intimacy of Disclosure Topics and Sex Differences in Self-disclosure." *Sex Roles* 2: 161-66.

Morgan, Robin
1977   *Going Too Far: The Personal Chronicle of a Feminist.* New York: Random House.

Morris, Cerise
1980   "Determination and Thoroughness: The Movement for a Royal Commission on the Status of Women in Canada." *Atlantis* 5: 1-21.

Morrison, Toni
1970   *The Bluest Eye.* New York: Pocket Books.

Mortimer, John
1983   Excerpt from "Clinging to the Wreckage" in Mordecai Richler, ed., *The Best of Modern Humor*, pp. 245-58. New York: Alfred A. Knopf.

Motherwell, Cathryn
1987   "More Men Reclaiming Steno Pad and Phone." *The Globe and Mail* (May 9).

Mueller, Marnie W.
1975   "Economic Determinants of Volunteer Work by Women." *Signs* 1: 325-38.

Mullins, Nicholas C. with the assistance of Carolyn J. Mullins
1973   *Theories and Theory Groups in Contemporary American Sociology.* New York: Harper and Row.

Mura, Roberta, Meredith Kimball, and Renee Cloutier
1987   "Girls and Science Programs: Two Steps Forward, One Step Back" in Jane S. Gaskell and Arlene Tigar McLaren, eds., *Women and Education: A Canadian Perspective*, pp. 133-49. Calgary: Detselig Enterprises.

Murphy, G., L. Murphy, and T. Newcomb
1937   *Experimental Social Psychology.* New York: Harper and Row.

Mussen, Paul H.
1969   "Early Sex-role Development" in David A. Goslin, ed., *Handbook of Socialization Theory and Research*, pp. 707-31. Chicago: Rand McNally.

Myers, David G.
1990   *Social Psychology.* 3rd ed. New York: McGraw-Hill.

Nathanson, Constance
1984   "Sex Differences in Mortality." *Annual Review of Sociology* 10: 191-213.

Nelson, Geoff
1985   "Family Adaptation Following Marital Separation/Divorce: A Literature Review" in Benjamin Schlesinger, *The One-Parent Family in the 1980s: Perspectives and Annotated Bibliography 1978-1984*, pp. 97-151. Toronto: University of Toronto Press.

Nemiroff, Greta Hofmann
1987   "Introduction" in Greta Hofmann Nemiroff, ed., *Women and Men: Interdisciplinary Readings on Gender*, pp. xv-xvii. Toronto: Fitzhenry and Whiteside.
1987   "On Power and Empowerment" in Greta Hofmann Nemiroff, ed., *Women and Men: Interdisciplinary Readings on Gender*, pp, 531-42. Toronto: Fitzhenry and Whiteside.
1989   "Beyond 'Talking Heads': Towards an Empowering Pedagogy of Women's Studies." *Atlantis* 15: 1-16.

Nett, Emily M.
 1979   "Definitions of Femininity and Masculinity in Selected Canadian Textbooks: Some
        Sources and Consequences." Paper presented to Annual Meeting of Canadian Sociol-
        ogy and Anthropology Association, Saskatoon, Saskatchewan, June.
 1988   *Canadian Families: Past and Present*. Toronto: Butterworths.

Nettler, Gwynn
 1970   *Explanations*. New York: McGraw-Hill.

Newton, Esther
 1972   *Mother Camp: Female Impersonators in America*. Chicago: University of Chicago Press.

Ng, Roxana
 1981   "Constituting Ethnic Phenomenon: An Account from the Perspective of Immigrant
        Women." *Canadian Ethnic Studies* 13: 97-108.
 1988   "Immigrant Women and Institutionalized Racism" in Sandra Burt, Lorraine Code, and
        Lindsay Dorney, eds., *Changing Patterns: Women in Canada*, pp. 184-203. Toronto:
        McClelland and Stewart.

_____ , and Alma Estable
 1987   "Immigrant Women in the Labour Force: An Overview of Present Knowledge and Re-
        search." *Resources for Feminist Research* 16: 29-32.

Nicholls, Stephen
 1989   "Consultant Pushes Male Liberation." *Calgary Herald* (May 15).

Nicholson, John
 1984   *Men and Women: How Different Are They?* New York: Oxford University Press.

Nielsen, Joyce McCarl
 1978   *Sex in Society: Perspectives on Stratification*. Belmont, Calif.: Wadsworth.
 1979   "From Corrective to Creative Progress in Sex Stratification: Sociological and Anthro-
        pological Contributions." *International Journal of Women's Studies* 2: 324-39.

Nordstrom, Bruce
 1986   "Why Men Get Married: More and Less Traditional Men Compared" in Robert A.
        Lewis and Robert E. Salt, eds., *Men in Families*, pp. 31-53. Beverly Hills, Calif.: Sage.

Northcott, Herbert C.
 1983   "Who Stays Home? Working Parents and Sick Children." *International Journal of
        Women's Studies* 6: 387-94.

_____ , and Graham S. Lowe
 1987   "Job and Gender Influences in the Subjective Experience of Work." *Canadian Review of
        Sociology and Anthropology* 24: 117-31.

Novak, Mark
 1985   *Successful Aging: The Myths, Realities and Future of Aging in Canada*. Markham, Ont.:
        Penguin.

Oakley, Ann
 1972   *Sex, Gender and Society*. New York: Harper and Row.
 1974   *The Sociology of Housework*. London: Martin Robertson.
 1979   "A Case of Maternity: Paradigms of Women as Maternity Cases." *Signs* 4: 607-31.
 1980   *Women Confined: Toward a Sociology of Childbirth*. London: Martin-Robertson.
 1984   *The Captured Womb: A History of the Medical Care of Pregnant Women*. Oxford: Basil
        Blackwell.

O'Brien, Mary
1979 "Reproducing Marxist Man" in L. Clark and L. Lange, eds., *The Sexism of Social and Political Theory*, pp. 99-116. Toronto: University of Toronto Press.
1981 *The Politics of Reproduction.* London: Routledge and Kegan Paul.

O'Connell, Dorothy
1983 "Poverty: The Feminine Complaints" in Joan Turner and Lois Emery, eds., *Perspectives on Women in the 1980s*, pp. 41-65. Winnipeg: University of Manitoba Press.

O'Connell, Joanne Curry
1987 "Children of Working Mothers: What the Research Tells Us" in Mary Roth Walsh, ed., *The Psychology of Women: Ongoing Debates*, pp. 367-77. New Haven, Conn.: Yale University Press.

O'Connor, June
1989 "Rereading, Reconceiving and Reconstructing Traditions: Feminist Research in Religion." *Women's Studies* 17: 101-23.

O'Farrell, B., and S. Harlan
1982 "Craft Workers and Clerks: The Effect of Male Coworker Hostility on Women's Satisfaction with Non-traditional Jobs." *Social Problems* 29: 252-65.

O'Leary, Virginia E., Rhoda K. Unger, and Barbara S. Wallston (eds.)
1985 *Women, Gender, and Social Psychology.* Hillsdale, N.J.: Lawrence Erlbaum.

Oldham, Jack
1979 "Social Control of Voluntary Work Activity: The Gift Horse Syndrome." *Sociology of Work and Occupations* 6: 379-403.

Orbach, Susie
1978 *Fat is a Feminist Issue.* New York: Berkley.

Ornstein, Michael D.
1983 "Accounting for Gender Differentials in Job Income in Canada: Results from a 1981 Survey." Women's Bureau, Labour Canada. Ottawa: Supply and Services.

Ortner, Sherry B.
1974 "Is Female to Male as Nature is to Culture?" in Michele Zimbalist Rosaldo and Louise Lamphere, eds., *Woman, Culture, and Society*, pp. 67-87. Stanford, Calif.: Stanford University Press.

_____ , and Harriet Whitehead
1981 "Introduction: Accounting for Sexual Meanings" in Sherry B. Ortner and Harriet Whitehead, eds., *Sexual Meanings: The Cultural Construction of Gender and Sexuality*, pp. 1-27. Cambridge: Cambridge University Press.

Orwen, Patricia
1983 "Women Still Struggling for Role as Clergy." *Calgary Herald* (October 22).

Oskamp, Stuart, ed.
1988 *Television as a Social Issue.* Newbury Park, Calif.: Sage.

Osler, Margaret J.
1980 "Sex, Science, and Values: A Critique of Sociobiological Accounts of Sex Differences." *Resources for Feminist Research* (Fall, Special Publication #8): 119-24.

Ostrander, Susan A.
  1988   "Review" M.F. Belenky, B.M. Clinchy, N.R. Goldberger, and T.M. Tarule, *Women's Ways of Knowing: The Development of Self, Voice, and Mind*, in *Contemporary Sociology* 17: 745-46.

Paley, Vivian Gussin
  1984   *Boys and Girls: Superheroes in the Doll Corner*. Chicago: University of Chicago Press.

Panelas, Tom
  1983   "Adolescents and Video Games: Consumption of Leisure and the Social Construction of the Peer Group." *Youth and Society* 15: 51-65.

Papanek, Hanna
  1979   "Family Status Production: The `Work' and `Non-work' of Women." *Signs* 4: 775-81.

Parker, Stanley
  1982   *Work and Retirement*. London: George Allen and Unwin.

Parlee, Mary Brown
  1973   "The Premenstrual Syndrome." *Psychological Bulletin* 80: 454-65.
  1975   "Psychology." *Signs* 1: 119-38.
  1978   "The Sexes under Scrutiny: From Old Biases to New Theories." *Psychology Today* (November): 62-69.
  1979   "Psychology and Women." *Signs* 5: 121-33.
  1982   "Changes in Moods and Activation Levels during the Menstrual Cycle in Experimentally Naive Subjects." *Psychology of Women Quarterly* 7: 119-31.

_____ , and the Editors of Psychology Today.
  1979   "The Friendship Bond." *Psychology Today* (October): 43-45, 49, 50, 53, 54, 113.

Parsons, Talcott
  1955   "Sex Roles and Family Structure." In Talcott Parsons and Robert F. Bales, eds., *Family Socialization and Interaction Process*. Glencoe, Illinois: Free Press.
  1959   "The School as Social System." *Harvard Educational Review* 29: 297-318.

_____ , and Robert F. Bales, eds.
  1955   *Family Socialization and Interaction Process*. Glencoe, Illinois: Free Press.

Pearson, Judy Cornelia
  1985   *Gender and Communication*. Dubuque, Iowa: Wm. C. Brown.

Peitchinis, Stephen G.
  1989   *Women at Work: Discrimination and Response*. Toronto: McClelland and Stewart.

Penning, Margaret J.
  1983   "Multiple Jeopardy: Age, Sex, and Ethnic Variations." *Canadian Ethnic Studies* 15: 81-105.

Peplau, Letitia Anne
  1981   "What Homosexuals Want in Relationships." *Psychology Today* 15 (March): 28-38.
  1983   "Roles and Gender" in Harold H. Kelley et al., *Close Relationships*, pp. 220-64. New York: W.H. Freeman.

_____ , and Steven L. Gordon
  1985   "Women and Men in Love: Gender Differences in Close Heterosexual Relationships" in Virginia E. O'Leary, Rhoda Kesler Unger, and Barbara Strudler Wallston, eds., *Women, Gender, and Social Psychology*.' Hillsdale, N.J.: Lawrence Erlbaum.

_____ , and Susan Miller Campbell

1989   "The Balance of Power in Dating and Marriage" in Jo Freeman, ed., *Women*: A Feminist Perspective, 4th ed., pp. 121-37. Mountain View, Calif.: Mayfield.

Percival, Elizabeth, and Terrance Percival

1979   "Is a Woman a Person? Sex Differences in Stereotyping." *Atlantis* 4: 71-77.

Peters, John

1983   "Divorce: The Disengaging, Disengaged, and Re-engaging Process" in K. Ishwaran, ed., *The Canadian Family*, pp. 277-88. Toronto: Gage.

1987   "Changing Perspectives on Divorce" in Karen L. Anderson et al., *Family Matters: Sociology and Contemporary Canadian Families*, pp. 141-62. Toronto: Methuen.

1989   "Divorce and Remarriage" in G.N. Ramu, ed., *Marriage and the Family in Canada Today*, pp. 207-29. Scarborough: Prentice-Hall.

Peterson, Gary W., and Boyd C. Rollins

1987   "Parent-Child Socialization" in Marvin B. Sussman and Suzanne K. Steinmetz, eds., *Handbook of Marriage and the Family*, pp. 471-507. N.Y.: Plenum.

Philips, Susan U.

1980   "Sex Differences and Language." *Annual Review of Anthropology* 9: 523-44.

Phillips, E. Barbara

1978   "Magazines' Heroines: Is Ms. Just Another Member of the Family Circle?" in Gaye Tuchman, Arlene Kaplan Daniels, and James Benet, eds., *Hearth and Home: Images of Women in the Mass Media*, pp. 116-29. New York: Oxford University Press.

Phillips, Paul, and Erin Phillips

1983   *Women and Work: Inequality in the Labour Market*. Toronto: James Lorimer.

Piaget, Jean

1928   *Judgment and Reasoning in the Child*. New York: Harcourt.

1932   *The Moral Judgment of the Child*. New York: Harcourt.

Pierson, Ruth Roach

1977   "Women's Emancipation and the Recruitment of Women into the Labour Force in World War II" in Susan Mann Trofimenkoff and Alison Prentice, eds., *The Neglected Majority*, pp. 125-45. Toronto: McClelland and Stewart.

1986   *"They're Still Women After All:" The Second World War and Canadian Womanhood*. Toronto: McClelland and Stewart.

Pike, Robert M.

1988   "Problems around Educational Opportunity" in James Curtis, Edward Grabb, Neil Guppy, and Sid Gilbert, eds., *Social Inequality in Canada: Patterns, Problems, Policies*, pp. 146-62. Scarborough: Prentice-Hall.

Pleck, Joseph H.

1981   "Men's Power with Women, Other Men, and Society: A Men's Movement Analysis" in Robert A. Lewis, ed., *Men in Difficult Times*, pp. 234-44. Englewood Cliffs, N.J.: Prentice-Hall.

1987   "American Fathering in Historical Perspective" in Michael S. Kimmel, ed., *Changing Men: New Directions in Research on Men and Masculinity*, pp. 83-97. Newbury Park, Calif.: Sage.

Poelzer, Sr. Irene M.
    1980   "Feminist Theology: Implications and Significance for Women as Persons." *Resources for Feminist Research, Special Publication* 8: 36 -38.

Pogrebin, Letty Cottin
    1983   "The Secret Fear that Keeps us From Raising Free Children" in Laurel Richardson and Verta Taylor, eds., *Feminist Frontiers: Rethinking Sex, Gender, and Society*, pp. 36-39. Reading, Mass.: Addison-Wesley.

Pollack, Jack
    1967   "How Masculine or Feminine Are You?" *Teasers and Tests from Reader's Digest.* Montreal: The Reader's Digest Association (Canada) Ltd.

Ponting, J. Rick, ed.
    1986a   *Arduous Journey: Canadian Indians and Decolonization.* Toronto: McClelland and Stewart.
    1986b   "Canadian Gender-role Attitudes." Unpublished manuscript. University of Calgary.

Posner, Judith
    1975   "Dirty Old Women: Buck Brown's Cartoons." *Canadian Review of Sociology and Anthropology* 12: 471-73.
    1980   "Old and Female: The Double Whammy" in Victor W. Marshall, ed., *Aging in Canada*, pp. 80-87. Don Mills, Ont.: Fitzhenry and Whiteside.
    1987   "The Objectified Male: The New Male Image in Advertising" in Greta Hofmann Nemiroff, ed., *Women and Men: Interdisciplinary Readings on Gender*, pp. 180-89. Toronto: Fitzhenry and Whiteside.

Postman, Neil
    1982   *The Disappearance of Childhood.* New York: Penguin.

Pratt, David
    1975   "The Social Role of School Textbooks in Canada" in Elia Zureik and Robert M. Pike, eds., *Socialization and Values in Canadian Society.* Vol. 1, pp. 100-126. Toronto: McClelland and Stewart.

Prentice, A.
    1977   *The School Promoters.* Toronto: McClelland and Stewart.

Press, Andrea L.
    1986   "Ideologies of Femininity: Film and Popular Consciousness in the Postwar Era" in Sandra J. Ball-Rokeach and Muriel G. Cantor, eds., *Media, Audience, and Social Structure*, pp. 313-23. Newbury Park, Calif.: Sage.

Prince, Peter
    1983   *The Good Father.* New York: Carroll and Graf.

Proulx, Monique
    1978   *Five Million Women: A Study of the Canadian Housewife.* Ottawa: Advisory Council on the Status of Women.

Pyke, S.W.
    1975   "Children's Literature: Conceptions of Sex Roles" in Robert M. Pike and Elia Zureik, eds., *Socialization and Values in Canadian Society.* Vol. 2. pp. 51-73. Toronto: McClelland and Stewart.
    1980   "Androgyny: A Dead End or a Promise?" in Cannie Stark-Adamec, ed., *Sex Roles: Origins, Influences, and Implications for Women*, pp. 20-32. Montreal: Eden Press.

Ralston, Arthur
    1989   "She's Not Having a Baby." *Gentlemen's Quarterly* (September): 281, 284, 292, 296.

Ramu, G.N. ed.
    1989   *Marriage and the Family in Canada Today.* Scarborough: Prentice-Hall.

Rapoport, Rhona, and Robert N. Rapoport
    1977   *Dual-Career Families Re-examined.* New York: Harper and Row.

Rauhala, Ann
    1989   "Right of Gays to Be Family Unit Carries Obligations, Activists Say." *The Globe and Mail* (April 19).

Rayside, David, and Scott Bowler
    1988   "Public Opinion and Gay Rights." *Canadian Review of Sociology and Anthropology* 25: 649-60.

Reed, Evelyn
    1978   "Women: Caste, Class or Oppressed Sex?" in Alison M. Jaggar and Paula Rothenberg Struhl, eds., *Feminist Frameworks: Alternative Theoretical Accounts of the Relations between Women and Men*, pp. 119-29. New York: McGraw-Hill.

Reik, Theodor
    1954   "Men and Women Speak Different Languages." *Psychoanalysis* 2, #4: 3-15.
    1972   *A Psychologist Looks at Love.* New York: Holt, Rinehart and Winston.

Renzetti, Claire M., and Daniel J. Curran
    1989   *Women, Men, and Society: The Sociology of Gender.* Boston: Allyn and Bacon.

Restak, Richard M.
    1979   "The Sex-change Conspiracy." *Psychology Today* (December) 20:25.

Reuben, David
    1969   *Everything You Always Wanted to Know About Sex but Were Afraid to Ask.* New York: McKay.

Rheingold, Harriet, and K. Cook
    1975   "The Content of Boys' and Girls' Rooms as an Index of Parent Behavior." *Child Development* 46: 459-63.

Rich, Adrienne
    1976   *Of Woman Born, Motherhood as Experience and Institution.* New York: W. Norton.
    1980   "Compulsory Heterosexuality and Lesbian Existence." *Signs* 5: 631-60.

Richardson, C. James
    1987   "Children of Divorce" in Karen L. Anderson et. al., *Family Matters: Sociology and Contemporary Canadian Families*, pp. 163-200. Scarborough: Nelson Canada.

Richardson, Laurel
    1981   *The Dynamics of Sex and Gender.* 2nd ed. Boston: Houghton Mifflin.
    1988   "Sexual Freedom and Sexual Constraint: The Paradox for Single Women in Liaisons with Married Men." *Gender and Society* 2: 368-84. Newbury Park, Calif.: Sage Publications.
    1989   "Secrecy and Status: The Social Construction of Forbidden Relationships" in *Gender in Intimate Relationships: A Micro-Structural Approach*, pp. 108-19. Belmont, Calif.: Wadsworth.

Richer, Stephen
1979 "Sex-role Socialization and Early Schooling." *Canadian Review of Sociology and Anthropology* 16: 195-205.
1983 "Sex Role Socialization: Agents, Content, Relationships, and Emotions" in K. Ishwaran, ed., *The Canadian Family*, pp. 117-25. Toronto: Gage.
1984 "Sexual Inequality and Children's Play." *Canadian Review of Sociology and Anthropology* 21: 166-80.
1988 "Schooling and the Gendered Subject: An Exercise in Planned Social Change." *Canadian Review of Sociology and Anthropology* 25: 98-107.

Richmond-Abbott, Marie
1983 *Masculine and Feminine: Sex Roles Over the Life Cycle*. Reading, MA.: Addison-Wesley.

Riley, M.A., A. Foner, B. Hess, and M.L. Toby
1969 "Socialization for the Middle and Later Years" in David A. Goslin, ed., *Handbook of Socialization Theory and Research*, pp. 951-82. Chicago: Rand McNally.

Riordon, Michael
1990 *The First Stone: Homosexuality and the United Church*. Toronto: McClelland and Stewart.

Risman, Barbara J.
1987 "Intimate Relationships from a Micro-structural Perspective: Men Who Mother." *Gender and Society* 1: 6-32.

Risman, B., and P. Schwartz
1988 "Sociological Research on Male and Female Homosexuality." *Annual Review of Sociology* 14: 125-47.

Ritzer, George
1972 *Man and His Work: Conflict and Change*. New York: Appleton-Century-Crofts.
1975 *Sociology: A Multiple Paradigm Science*. Boston: Allyn and Bacon.
1988 *Contemporary Sociological Theory*. 2nd ed. New York: Alfred A. Knopf.

Rivlin, Lilly
1972 "Lilith: The First Woman." *Ms.* 1 (December): 92-97, 114-15.

Roberts, Donald, and Nathan Maccoby
1985 "Effects of Mass Communication" in Gardner Lindzey and Elliot Aronson, eds., *The Handbook of Social Psychology*, 3rd ed. Vol. II, pp. 539-98. New York: Random House.

Roberts, Helen, ed.
1981 *Doing Feminist Research*. London: Routledge and Kegan Paul.

Roberts, Keith A.
1984 *Religion in Sociological Perspective*. Homewood, Ill.: Dorsey Press.

Robertson, Ian
1981 *Sociology*. 2nd ed. New York: Worth.

Robinson, B.E., and Robert L. Barrett
1986 *The Developing Father: Emerging Roles in Contemporary Society*. New York: Guilford.

Robinson, Gertrude Joch
1983 "The Media and Social Change: Thirty Years of Magazine Coverage of Women and Work (1950-1977)." *Atlantis* 8: 87-111.

Robinson, J. Gregg, and Judith S. McIlwee
1989 "Women in Engineering: A Promise Unfulfilled?" *Social Problems* 36: 455-72.

Robson, R.A.H., and M. Lapointe
    1971   *A Comparison of Men's and Women's Salaries and Employment Fringe Benefits in the Academic Profession*. Royal Commission on the Status of Women in Canada, Substudy I. Ottawa: Queen's Printer.

Rodgers, Joann Ellison
    1985   "The Best Health Kick of All." *Ms.* 13 (May): 57-60, 140-141.

Rokeach, Milton
    1968   *Beliefs, Attitudes, and Values*. San Francisco: Jossey-Bass.

Rosaldo, Michelle Zimbalist
    1980   "The Use and Abuse of Anthropology: Reflections on Feminism and Cross-Cultural Understanding." *Signs* 5: 389-417.

_____ , and Louise Lamphere, eds.
    1974   *Woman, Culture, and Society*. Stanford, Calif.: Stanford University Press.

Rose, Suzanna M.
    1985   "Same- and Cross-sex Friendships and the Psychology of Homosociality." *Sex Roles* 12: 63-74.

Rosenberg, B.G., and B. Sutton-Smith
    1968   "Family Interaction Effects on Masculinity-Feminity." *Journal of Personality and Social Psychology* 8: 117-20.

Rosenberg, Dorothy Goldin
    1987   "Feminism and Peace" in Greta Hofmann Nemiroff, ed., *Women and Men: Interdisciplinary Readings on Gender*, pp. 515-30. Toronto: Fitzhenry and Whiteside.

Rosenberg, Miriam
    1976   "The Biological Basis for Sex Role Stereotypes" in Alexandra G. Kaplan and Joan P. Bean, eds., *Beyond Sex-Role Stereotypes: Readings toward a Psychology of Androgyny*, pp. 106-23. Boston: Little, Brown.

Rosenthal, Carolyn
    1985   "Kinkeeping in the Family Division of Labor." *Journal of Marriage and the Family* 47: 965-74.

Rosenthal, R., and K. Fode
    1963   "The Effect of Experimental Bias on the Performance of the Albino Rat." *Behavioral Science* 8: 183-89.

Ross, Aileen D.
    1982   *The Lost and the Lonely: Homeless Women in Montreal*. Montreal: Canadian Human Rights Foundation.

Ross, Catherine E., and John Mirowsky
    1984   "Men Who Cry." *Social Psychology Quarterly* 47: 138-46.

_____ , John Mirowsky, and Joan Huber
    1983   "Dividing Work, Sharing Work, and In-between: Marriage Patterns and Depression." *American Sociological Review* 48: 809-23.

Ross, Michael W.
    1986   "Causes of Gender Dysphoria: How Does Transsexualism Develop and Why?" in William A.W. Walters and Michael W. Ross, eds., *Transsexualism and Sex Reassignment*, pp. 16 -25. New York: Oxford University Press.

Ross, Val
    1983   "The Joys of a Bountiful Season." *Maclean's* (December 19) 40-48.

Rossi, Alice S.
    1964   "Equality between the Sexes" in Robert Jay Lifton, ed., *The Woman in America*, pp. 98-143. Boston: Houghton Mifflin.
    1965   "Naming Children in Middle-class Families." *American Sociological Review* 30: 499-513.
    1973   (ed.), *The Feminist Papers*. New York: Bantam Books.
    1984   "Gender and Parenthood." *American Sociological Review* 49:1-19.
    1985   (ed.), *Gender and the Life Course*. New York: Aldine.
    1987   "On `The Reproduction of Mothering': A Methodological Debate" in Mary Roth Walsh, ed., *The Psychology of Women: Ongoing Debates*, pp. 265-73. New Haven, Conn.: Yale University Press.

_____ , and Ann Calderwood, eds.
    1973   *Academic Women on the Move*. New York: Russell Sage Foundation.

Rowbotham, Sheila
    1973   *Woman's Consciousness, Man's World*. Harmondsworth, England: Penguin.

Rowland, Robyn
    1987   "Technology and Motherhood: Reproductive Choice Reconsidered." *Signs* 12: 512-28.

Royal Commission on the Status of Women
    1970   See Lambert, Ronald D.

Rubin, Gayle
    1975   "Traffic in Women: Notes toward a Political Economy of Sex" in Rayna Rapp Reiter, ed., *Toward an Anthropology of Women*, pp. 159-210. New York: Monthly Review Press.

Rubin, J.Z., F.J. Provenzano, and Z. Luria
    1974   "The Eye of the Beholder: Parents' Views on Sex of Newborns." *American Journal of Orthopsychiatry* 44: 512-19.

_____ , L.A. Peplau, and C.T. Hill
    1981   "Loving and Leaving: Sex Differences in Romantic Attachments." *Sex Roles* 7: 821-35.

Rubin, Lillian B.
    1985   *Just Friends: The Role of Friendship in Our Lives*. New York: Harper and Row.

Rubin, Zick
    1970   "Measurement of Romantic Love." *Journal of Personality and Social Psychology* 16: 265-73.
    1973   *Liking and Loving*. New York: Holt, Rinehart and Winston.

Ruether, Rosemary R.
    1974   *Religion and Sexism: Images of Woman in the Jewish and Christian Traditions*. New York: Simon and Schuster.
    1981   "The Feminist Critique in Religious Studies" in Elizabeth Langland and Walter Gove, eds., *A Feminist Perspective in the Academy*, pp. 52-66. Chicago: University of Chicago Press.

Rule, Jane
    1987   *Memory Board*. Toronto: Macmillan.

Russell, Susan
  1987   "The Hidden Curriculum of School: Reproducing Gender and Class Heirarchies." in Heather Jon Maroney and Meg Luxton, eds., *Feminism and Political Economy: Women's Work, Women's Stuggles*, pp. 229-45. Toronto: Methuen.

Ryan, William
  1971   *Blaming the Victim.* New York: Vintage.

Sachs, Jacqueline
  1975   "Cues to the Identification of Sex in Children's Speech" in Barrie Thorne and Nancy Henley, eds., *Language and Sex: Difference and Dominance*, pp. 152-71. Rowley, Mass.: Newbury House.

Sacks, Karen
  1979   *Sisters and Wives: The Past and Future of Sexual Equality.* Westport, Conn.: Greenwood.

Sadker, Myra, and David Sadker
  1987   "Sexism in the Schoolroom of the '80s." in E.D. Salamon and B.W. Robinson, eds., *Gender Roles: Doing What Comes Naturally*, pp. 143-47. Toronto: Methuen.

Saegert, S., and R. Hart
  1976   "The Development of Environmental Competence in Girls and Boys." In P. Burnet, ed., *Women in Society*. Chicago: Maaroufa Press.

Safilios-Rothchild, Constantina
  1969   "Family Sociology or Wives' Family Sociology: A Cross-cultural Examination of Decision-making." *Journal of Marriage and the Family* 31: 290-301.
  1979   "Sexuality, Power, and Freedom among `Older' Women" in Jon Hendricks and C. Davis Hendricks, eds., *Dimensions of Aging*, pp. 213-16. Cambridge, Mass.: Winthrop.

Sanday, Peggy Reeves
  1980   "Margaret Mead's View of Sex Roles in Her Own and Other Societies." *American Anthropologist* 82: 340-48.
  1981   *Female Power and Male Dominance: On the Origins of Sexual Inequality.* Cambridge: Cambridge University Press.

Santrock, John W.
  1984   *Adolescence.* 2nd ed. Dubuque, Iowa: Wm. C. Brown.

Sapir, E.
  1933   "Language" in *Encyclopedia of the Social Sciences*. Vol. 9, pp. 155-69. New York: Macmillan.

Sargent, Lydia, ed.
  1981   *Women and Revolution: A Discussion of the Unhappy Marriage of Marxism and Feminism.* Boston: South End Press.

Sattel, Jack W.
  1976   "Men, Inexpressiveness, and Power" in Laurel Richardson and Verta Taylor, eds., *Feminist Frontiers*, pp. 242-46. Reading, MA.: Addison-Wesley.

Saunders, Eileen
  1988   "Theoretical Approaches to the Study of Women" in James Curtis, Edward Grabb, Neil Guppy, and Sid Gilbert, eds., *Social Inequality in Canada: Patterns, Problems, Policies*, pp. 248-63. Scarborough: Prentice-Hall.

Sawchuck, Kimberly Anne
    1989   "Towards a Feminist Analysis of `Women in Rock Music': Patti Smith's `Gloria.'"
           Atlantis 14: 44-54.

Sayers, Janet
    1982   *Biological Politics: Feminist and Anti-Feminist Perspectives.* London: Tavistock.

Schecter, Stephen
    1988   "Reform Strategies for Education" in James Curtis, Edward Grabb, Neil Guppy, and
           Sid Gilbert, eds., *Social Inequality in Canada: Patterns, Problems, Policies*, pp. 170-76.
           Scarborough: Prentice-Hall.

Schlesinger, Benjamin
    1983   "Living in One-parent Families: The Children's Perspective." In K. Ishwaran, ed., *The*
           Canadian Family. Toronto: Gage.
    1985   *The One-Parent Family in the 1980s.* Toronto: University of Toronto Press.

Schneider, Frank W., and Larry M. Coutts.
    1979   "Teacher Orientations towards Masculine and Feminine: Role of Sex of Teacher and
           Sex Composition of School." *Canadian Journal of Behavioral Science* 11: 99-111.

Schneider, Joseph W., and Sally L. Hacker
    1973   "Sex Role Imagery and Use of the Generic `Man' in Introductory Texts: A Case in the
           Sociology of Sociology." *The American Sociologist* 8: 12-18.

Schudson, Michael
    1984   *Advertising, the Uneasy Persuasion.* New York: Basic Books.

Schulz, David A.
    1984   *Human Sexuality.* 2nd ed. Englewood Cliffs, N.J.: Prentice-Hall.

Schulz, Muriel R.
    1975   "The Semantic Derogation of Woman" in Barrie Thorne and Nancy Henely, eds., *Lan-*
           guage and Sex: Difference and Dominance, pp. 64-75. Rowley, MA.: Newbury House.

Schur, Edwin M.
    1984   *Labelling Women Deviant: Gender, Stigma, and Social Control.* New York: Random House.

Schutz, A.
    1967   *The Phenomenology of the Social World.* Evanston, Illinois: Northwestern University
           Press.

Schwendinger, Julia, and Herman Schwendinger
    1971   "Sociology's Founding Fathers: Sexists to a Man." *Journal of Marriage and the Family* 33:
           783-99.

Scott, Jay
    1988   "Chatelaine's Woman of the Year 1988." *Chatelaine* (January): 54, 130.

Scott, Joan Pinner
    1981   "Science Subject Choice and Achievement of Females in Canadian High Schools."
           International Journal of Women's Studies 4: 348-61.

Scully, Diana
    1980   *Men Who Control Women's Health: The Miseducation of Obstretrician-Gynecologists.* Bos-
           ton: Houghton Mifflin.

Seavey, C.A., P.A. Katz, and S.R. Zalk
    1975   "Baby X: The Effect of Gender Labels on Adult Responses to Infants." *Sex Roles* 1: 103-109.

Seccombe, Wally
    1974   "The Housewife and Her Labour under Capitalism." *New Left Review* 83: 3-24.

Secunda, Victoria
    1990   *When You and Your Mother Can't Be Friends.* New York: Delacorte Press.

Sedney, Mary Anne
    1989   "Conceptual and Methodological Sources of Controversies about Androgyny" in Rhoda K. Unger, ed., *Representations: Social Constructions of Gender*, pp. 126-44. Amityville, N.Y.: Baywood.

Seiden, Richard H., and Mary C. Spence
    1982   "A Tale of Two Bridges: Comparative Suicide Incidence on the Golden Gate and San Francisco-Oakland Bay Bridges." *Crisis* 3: 32-40.

Selman, Robert L., and Anne P. Selman
    1979   "Children's Ideas about Friendship: A New Theory." *Psychology Today* 13 (October): 71, 72, 74, 79, 80, 114.

Serbin, L., K. O'Leary, R. Kent, and I. Tonick
    1973   "A Comparison of Teacher Response to the Preacademic and Problem Behavior of Boys and Girls." *Child Development* 44: 796-804.

Sexton, Patricia
    1976   *Women in Education.* Bloomington, Indiana: Ph: Delta Kappa.

Shakin, Madeline, Debra Shakin, and Sarah H. Sternglanz
    1985   "Infant Clothing: Sex Labeling for Strangers." *Sex Roles* 12: 955-64.

Shapiro, Ivor
    1989   "The Masculine Mystique." *Saturday Night* (June): 29-31.

Shapiro, Judith
    1981   "Anthropology and the Study of Gender" in Elizabeth Langland and Walter Gove, eds., *A Feminist Perspective in the Academy*, pp. 110-29. Chicago: University of Chicago Press.

Shapiro, Laura
    1990   "Guns and Dolls." *Newsweek* (May 28, 1990): 56-62.

Shaw, Marvin, and Philip R. Costanzo
    1970   *Theories of Social Psychology.* New York: McGraw-Hill.

Sheehy, Gail
    1974   *Passages.* New York: E.P. Dutton.

Sherif, Carolyn Wood
    1979   "Bias in Psychology" in Julia A. Sherman and Evelyn Torton Beck, eds., *The Prism of Sex: Essays in the Sociology of Knowledge*, pp. 93-133. Madison: University of Wisconsin Press.
    1982   "Needed Concepts in the Study of Gender Identity." *Psychology of Women Quarterly* 6: 375-98.

Sherrod, Drury
 1987 "The Bonds of Men: Problems and Possibilities in Close Male Relationships" in Harry Brod, ed., *The Making of Masculinities*, pp. 213-39. Boston: Allen and Unwin.

Shields, Stephanie A.
 1975 "Functionalism, Darwinism and the Psychology of Women." *American Psychologist* 30: 451-64.

Shrum, Wesley, and Neil H. Cheek
 1987 "Social Structure during the School Years: Onset of the Degrouping Process." *American Sociological Review* 52: 218-23.

Shulman, Alix Kates
 1980 "Sex and Power: Sexual Bases of Radical Feminism." *Signs* 5: 590-604.

Sieber, Sam D.
 1974 "Toward a Theory of Role Accumulation." *American Sociological Review* 39: 567-78.

Simeral, Margaret H.
 1978 "Women and the Reserve Army of Labor." *Insurgent Sociologist* 8: 2-3.

Simpson, Suzanne, Doris Toole, and Cindy Player
 1979 "Women in the Canadian Forces: Past, Present and Future." *Atlantis* 4: 267-83.

Singer, Benjamin D.
 1986 *Advertising and Society*. Don Mills, Ont.: Addison-Wesley.

Singleton, C.H.
 1986 "Biological and Social Explanations of Sex-role Stereotyping" in David J. Hargreaves and Ann M. Colley, eds., *The Psychology of Sex Roles*, pp. 3-26. London, England: Harper and Row.

Smelser, Neil J.
 1988 "Social Structure" in Neil J. Smelser, ed., *Handbook of Sociology*, pp. 103 -129. Newbury Park, Calif.: Sage.

Smith, Beverley
 1988 "Fitness Fails as Schools Stress Academics." *The Globe and Mail* (May 6): A16.

Smith, C.W.
 1987 *Uncle Dad*. New York: Berkley Books.

Smith, Dorothy E.
 1973 "Women, the Family and Corporate Capitalism" in Marylee Stephenson ed., *Women in Canada*, pp. 5-35. Toronto: New Press.
 1974 "Women's Perspective as a Radical Critique of Sociology." *Sociological Inquiry* 44: 7-13.
 1975 "An Analysis of Ideological Structures and How Women Are Excluded: Considerations for Academic Women." *Canadian Review of Sociology and Anthropology* 12, Part I: 353-69.
 1977a *Feminism and Marxism — A Place to Begin, A Way to Go*. Vancouver: New Star Books.
 1977b "Women, the Family and Corporate Capitalism" in Marylee Stephenson, ed., *Women in Canada*. Rev. ed., pp. 17-48. Don Mills: General Publishing.
 1983 "Women, the Family and the Productive Process" in J. Paul Grayson ed., *Introduction to Sociology*, pp. 312-44. Toronto: Gage.
 1984 "The Renaissance of Women" in Ursula Martius Franklin et al., *Knowledge Reconsidered: A Feminist Overview*. pp. 1-14 Ottawa: Canadian Research Institute for Advancement of Women.

1987   *The Everyday World as Problematic: A Feminist Sociology.* Toronto: University of Toronto Press.

Smith, Goldwin
1957   *A History of England.* New York: Charles Scribner's Sons.

Smith, Michael D.
1990   "Sociodemographic Risk Factors in Wife Abuse: Results from a Survey of Toronto Women." *Canadian Journal of Sociology* 15: 39-58.

Smith, Peter K.
1986   "Exploration, Play and Social Development in Boys and Girls" in David J. Hargreaves and Ann M. Colley, eds., *The Psychology of Sex Roles,* pp. 118- 41. London, England: Harper and Row.

Smith, Vivian
1990   "Women of the Press." *The Globe and Mail* (March 24): D1, D8.

Smuts, Robert W.
1971   *Women and Work in America.* New York: Schochen.

Snodgrass, Jon
1975   "The Women's Liberation Movement and the Men." Paper presented to the Pacific Sociological Association meeting, Victoria, B.C.
1977   (ed.), *For Men Against Sexism.* Albion: Times Change Press.

Soley, Lawrence, and Gary Kurzbard
1986   "Sex in Advertising: A Comparison of 1964 and 1984 Magazine Advertisements." *Journal of Advertising* 15: 46-55.

Spanier, Graham B., and Frank F. Furstenberg, Jr.
1987   "Remarriage and Reconstituted Families" in Marvin B. Sussman and Suzanne K. Steinmetz, eds., *Handbook of Marriage and the Family,* pp. 419-34. New York: Plenum.

Speizer, Jeanne J.
1981   "Role Models, Mentors and Sponsors: The Elusive Concepts." *Signs* 8: 692-712.

Spence, Janet T., Kay Deaux, and Robert L. Helmreich
1985   "Sex Roles in Contemporary American Society" in Gardner Lindzey and Elliot Aronson, eds., *Handbook of Social Psychology.* 3rd. ed. vol. II, pp. 149-78. New York: Random House.

_____, and Robert L. Helmreich
1978   *Masculinity and Femininity: Their Psychological Dimensions, Correlates, and Antecedents.* Austin: University of Texas Press.

Spender, Dale
1981   (ed.), *Men's Studies Modified.* Oxford: Pergamon Press.
1982   *Women of Ideas and What Men Have Done to Them.* London: Ark Paperbacks.
1985   *Man Made Language.* 2nd ed. London: Routledge and Kegan Paul.

Spiro, Melford
1956   *Kibbutz: A Venture in Utopia.* New York: Schocken.

Sprecher, Susan
1985   "Sex Differences in Bases of Power in Dating Relationships." *Sex Roles* 12: 449-62.

Squire, Anne M.
1980   "Feminist Theology: Toward Personhood for Women." *Resources for Feminist Research,*
        Special Publication 8: 34-36.

Stacey, Judith
1983   "The New Conservative Feminism." *Feminist Studies* 9: 559-83.

_____ , and Barrie Thorne
1985   "The Missing Feminist Revolution in Sociology." *Social Problems* 32: 301-16.

Stanley, Liz, and Sue Wise
1983   *Breaking Out: Feminist Consciousness and Feminist Research.* London: Routledge and
        Kegan Paul.

Stannard, Una
1971   "The Masks of Beauty" in Vivian Gornick and Barbara K. Moran, eds., *Woman in Sexist*
        Society, pp. 187-203. New York: New American Library.

Statistics Canada
1974   *Perspective Canada I.* Ottawa: Information Canada.
1984   *Survey News.* Vol. 1, No. 2 (October-November). Ottawa: Supply and Services.
1985   *Women in Canada: A Statistical Report.* Ottawa: Minister of Supply and Services.
1987   *The Labour Force.* Ottawa: Supply and Services Canada.

Stebbins, Robert A.
1988   "Men, Husbands, and Fathers: Beyond Patriarchal Relations" in Nancy Mandell and
        Ann Duffy, eds., *Reconstructing the Canadian Family: Feminist Perspectives,* pp. 27-47.
        Toronto: Butterworths.

Steed, Judy
1989   "Nursing Ambition." *The Globe and Mail* (March 4): D5.

Steele, Phyllis L.
1987   "My Heart Was in Medicine." *New Trail* 41 (Spring): 4-5. Edmonton, Alberta: Univer-
        sity of Alberta Alumni Association.

Stein, Dorothy K.
1978   "Women to Burn: Suttee as a Normative Institution." *Signs* 4: 253-68.

Steinem, Gloria
1983   *Outrageous Acts and Everyday Rebellions.* New York: Holt, Rinehart and Winston.
1983   "Perspectives on Women in the 1980s: The Baird Poskanzer Memorial Lecture" in Joan
        Turner and Lois Emery, eds., *Perspectives on Women in the 1980s,* pp. 14-27. Winnipeg:
        University of Manitoba Press.
1987   "Looking to the Future." *Ms.* (July/August): 55-57.
1988   "Six Great Ideas that Television is Missing" in Stuart Oskamp, ed., *Television as a Social*
        Issue, pp. 18-29. Newbury Park, Calif.: Sage.

Steinmetz, Suzanne K.
1987   "Family Violence: Past, Present, and Future" in Marvin B. Sussman and Suzanne K.
        Steinmetz, eds., *Handbook of Marriage and the Family,* pp. 725 - 65. New York: Plenum.

Stephens, William
1963   *The Family in Cross-Cultural Perspective.* New York: Holt, Rinehart and Winston.

Stephenson, Marylee, ed.
1973   *Women in Canada.* Toronto: New Press.

Stets, Jan. E., and Maureen A. Pirog-Good
    1987   "Violence in Dating Relationships." *Social Psychology Quarterly* 50: 237-46.

Stier, D.S., and J.A. Hall
    1984   "Gender Differences in Touch: An Empirical and Theoretical Review." *Journal of Personality and Social Psychology* 47: 440-59.

Stockard, Jean, and Miriam M. Johnson
    1980   *Sex Roles: Sex Inequality and Sex Role Development.* Englewood Cliffs, N.J.: Prentice-Hall.

Stone, Gregory P.
    1962   "Appearance and the Self" in Arnold M. Rose, ed., *Human Behavior and Social Process*, pp. 86-118. Boston: Houghton Mifflin.

Storrie, Kathleen (ed.)
    1987   *Women: Isolation and Bonding.* Toronto: Methuen.

Strathern, Marilyn
    1987   "An Awkward Relationship: The Case of Feminism and Anthropology." *Signs* 12: 276-92.

Straus, Murray, Richard J. Gelles, and Susan K. Steinmetz
    1980   *Behind Closed Doors: Violence in the American Family.* New York: Doubleday Anchor.

Strauss, Marina
    1990   "CBC, CRTC Fail to Eradicate Sexist Beer Ads." *The Globe and Mail* (March 15).

Strobel, Margaret
    1982   "African Women." *Signs* 8: 109-31.

Strong-Boag, Veronica
    1979   "Canada's Women Doctors: Feminism Constrained" in Linda Kealey, ed., *Women and Reform in Canada*, 1880s-1920s, pp. 109-29. Toronto: Women's Press.
    1983   "Mapping Women's Studies in Canada: Some Signposts." *Journal of Educational Thought* 17: 94-111.
    1988   *The New Day Recalled: Lives of Girls and Women in English Canada*, 1919-1939. Markham, Ontario: Penguin.

Stryker, Sheldon
    1981   "Symbolic Interactionism: Themes and Variations" in Morris Rosenberg and Ralph H. Turner, eds., *Social Psychology: Sociological Perspectives*, pp. 3-29. New York: Basic Books.

Sullivan, Gary L., and P.J. O'Connor
    1988   "Women's Role Portrayals in Magazine Advertising: 1958-1983." *Sex Roles* 18: 181-88.

Surrey, J.
    1985   "Self-in-relation: A Theory of Women's Development." Unpublished manuscript. Wellesley, MA.: Stone Center for Developmental Services and Studies.

Suttles, G.D.
    1970   "Friendship as a Social Institution" in G.J. McCall, M. McCall, N.K. Denzin, G.D. Suttles, and S.B. Kurth, eds., *Social Relationships*. Chicago: Aldine.

Sutton-Smith, Brian
    1979   "The Play of Girls" in Claire B. Kopp, ed., *Becoming Female: Perspectives on Development*, pp. 229-57. New York: Plenum Press.

Swain, Scott
  1989   "Covert Intimacy: Closeness in Men's Friendships" in Barbara J. Risman and Pepper
          Schwartz, eds., *Gender in Intimate Relationships*, pp. 71-86, Belmont, Calif.: Wadsworth.

Swatos, William H.J., and Cynthia McCauley
  1984   "Working-class Sex-role Orientation." *International Journal of Women's Studies* 7: 136-
          43.

Sydie, Rosalind A.
  1980   "Women Painters in Britain: 1768-1848." *Atlantis* 5: 144-75.
  1983   "Sociology and Gender" in M. Michael Rosenberg et al., eds., *An Introduction to
          Sociology*, pp. 185-223. Toronto: Methuen.
  1987   *Natural Women, Cultured Men: A Feminist Perspective on Sociological Theory*. Toronto:
          Methuen.

Symons, Gladys L.
  1978   "Sex Status, Homophily, Sponsorship, and Professional Socialization: Doctoral Stu-
          dents." *Canadian Review of Sociology and Anthropology* 15: 384-93.
  1986   "Careers and Self-Concepts: Managerial Women in French and English Canada" in
          Katherina L.P. Lundy and Barbara Warme, eds., *Work in the Canadian Context: Continu-
          ity Despite Change*. 2nd ed., pp. 282-94. Toronto: Butterworths.

Szekely, Eva
  1988   *Never Too Thin*. Toronto: The Women's Press.

Tancred-Sheriff, Peta
  1985   "Women's Experience, Women's Knowledge and the Power of Knowledge." *Atlantis*
          10: 106-17.

Task Force on Child Care
  1986   *Report of the Task Force on Child Care*. (Dr. Katie Cooke, Chair.) Ottawa: Supply and
          Services.

Tauer, Carol A.
  1979   "Freud and Female Inferiority." *International Journal of Women's Studies* 2: 287-304.

Tavris, Carol, and Carole Offir
  1977   *The Longest War: Sex Differences in Perspective*. New York: Harcourt, Brace, Jovanovich.

_____ , and Carole Wade
  1984   *The Longest War: Sex Differences in Perspective*. 2nd ed. San Diego: Harcourt, Brace,
          Jovanovich.

Taylor, W.
  1985a   "Super Athletes Made to Order." *Psychology Today* (May): 62-66.
  1985b   *Hormonal Manipulation: A New Era of Monstrous Athletes*. Jefferson, N.C.: McFarland.

Temerlin, Maurice K.
  1975   "My Daughter Lucy." *Psychology Today* 9 (November): 59-62, 103.

Tesson, Geoffrey
  1987   "Socialization and Parenting" in Karen L. Anderson et. al., *Family Matters: Sociology and
          Contemporary Canadian Families*, pp. 87-111. Toronto: Methuen.

Thibault, Gisele
  1988   "Women and Education: On Being Female in Male Places" in Winnifred Tomm and
          Gordon Hamilton, eds., *Gender Bias in Scholarship: The Pervasive Prejudice*, pp. 63-98.
          The Calgary Institute for the Humanities. Waterloo: Wilfrid Laurier University Press.

Thoits, Peggy A.
  1983   "Multiple Identities and Psychological Well-being: A Reformulation and Test of the
          Social Isolation Hypothesis." *American Sociological Review* 48: 174-87.
  1986   "Multiple Identities: Examining Gender and Marital Status Differences in Distress."
          American Sociological Review 51: 259-72.

Thom, Mary
  1988   "Dilemmas of the New Birth Technologies." *Ms.* (May): 70-72.

Thomas, Audrey
  1984   *Intertidal Life*. New York: Beaufort Books.

Thompson, H.L., and D.R. Richardson
  1983   "The Rooster Effect: Same Sex Rivalry and Inequality as Factors in Retaliatory Aggres-
          sion." *Personality and Social Psychology Bulletin* 9: 415-25.

Thorne, Barrie
  1987   "Re-visioning Women and Social Change: Where Are the Children?" *Gender and
          Society* 1: 85-109.

_____, with Marilyn Yalom, ed.
  1982   *Rethinking the Family: Some Feminist Questions*. New York: Longman.

_____, and Nancy Henley
  1975   "Difference and Dominance: An Overview of Language, Gender, and Society" in
          Barrie Thorne and Nancy Henley, eds., *Language and Sex: Difference and Dominance*, pp.
          5-42. Rowley, MA.: Newbury House.

_____, and Zella Luria
  1986   "Sexuality and Gender in Children's Daily Worlds." *Social Problems* 33: 176-90.

_____, Cheris Kramarae, and Nancy Henley
  1983   "Feminist Transformation of Language" in Barrie Thorne, Cheris Kramarae, and
          Nancy Henley, eds., *Language, Gender, and Society*. Rowley, Mass.: Newbury House.

Thornton, Arland, Duane F. Alwin, and Donald Camburn
  1983   "Causes and Consequences of Sex-role Attitudes and Attitude Change." *American
          Sociological Review* 48: 211-27.

Tiger, Lionel
  1969   *Men in Groups*. New York: Random House.

Tindale, Joseph
  1980   "Identity Maintenance Processes of Old Poor Men" in Victor W. Marshall, ed., *Aging
          in Canada*, pp. 88-94. Don Mills, Ont.: Fitzhenry and Whiteside.

Toch, Hans
  1965   *The Social Psychology of Social Movements*. Indianapolis: Bobbs-Merrill.

Tolson, Andrew
  1977   *The Limits of Masculinity*. London: Tavistock.

Tousley, Nancy
    1985   "Little Mermaid Graces Terrace." *The Calgary Herald* (November 3): E3.

Treiman, Susan
    1988   "Sex-typing Tough to Escape." *The Calgary Herald,* January 7, 1988:D10.

Tresemer, David W.
    1975   "Assumptions Made about Gender Roles" in Marcia Millman and Rosabeth Moss Kanter, eds., *Another Voice: Feminist Perspectives on Social Life and Social Science,* pp. 308-39. Garden City, N.Y.: Doubleday Anchor.
    1977   *Fear of Success.* New York: Plenum.

Trivers, R.L.
    1972   "Parental Investment and Sexual Selection." In B. Campbell, ed., *Sexual Selection and the Descent of Man 1871-1971.* Chicago: Aldine.

Tronto: Joan C.
    1987   "Beyond Gender Difference to a Theory of Care." *Signs* 12: 644-63.

Tuchman, Gaye
    1975   "Women and the Creation of Culture" in Marcia Millman and Rosabeth Moss Kanter, eds., *Another Voice: Feminist Perspectives on Social Life and Social Science,* pp. 171-202. Garden City, N.Y.: Doubleday Anchor.
    1978   "Introduction: The symbolic Annihilation of Women by the Mass Media" in Gaye Tuchman, Arlene Kaplan Daniels, and James Benet, eds., *Hearth and Home: Images of Women in the Mass Media,* pp. 3-38. New York: Oxford University Press.
    1979   "Women's Depiction by the Mass Media." *Signs* 4: 528-42.

_____ , and Nina E. Fortin
    1984   "Fame and Misfortune: Edging Women out of the Great Literary Tradition." *American Journal of Sociology* 90: 72-96.

Turkle, Sherry
    1984   *The Second Self: Computers and the Human Spirit.* New York: Simon and Schuster.

Turner, Ralph H.
    1970   *Family Interaction.* New York: John Wiley and Sons.
    1978   "The Role and the Person." *American Journal of Sociology* 84: 1-23.

_____ , and Lewis M. Killian
    1987   *Collective Behavior.* 3rd ed. Englewood Cliffs, N.J.: Prentice-Hall.

Turrittin, Anton H., Paul Anisef, and Neil J. Mackinnon
    1983   "Gender Differences in Educational Achievement: A Study of Social Inequality." *Canadian Journal of Sociology* 8: 395-419.

Udy, Stanley, H., Jr.
    1968   "Social Structural Analysis." International Encyclopedia of the Social Sciences 14: 489-95. New York: Macmillan and Free Press.

Umiker-Sebeok, Jean
    1981   "The Seven Ages of Woman: A View from American Magazine Advertisements" in Clara Mayo and Nancy M. Henley, eds., *Gender and Nonverbal Behavior,* pp. 209-52. New York: Springer-Verlag.

Unger, Rhoda Kesler
1978   "The Politics of Gender: A Review of Relevant Literature" in Julia A. Sherman and
        Florence L. Denmark, eds., *The Psychology of Women: Future Directions in Research*. New
        York: Psychological Dimensions.

_____, and Florence L. Denmark, eds.
1975   *Women: Dependent or Independent Variable?* New York: Psychological Dimensions, Inc.

Vallee, Brian
1986   *Life with Billy*. Toronto: McClelland-Bantam.

Vandell, Deborah L., and Edward C. Mueller
1980   "Peer Play and Friendships during the First Two Years" in H.C. Foot, A.J. Chapman,
        and J.R. Smith, eds., *Friendship and Social Relations in Children*, pp. 181-208. New York:
        John Wiley and Sons.

van den Berghe, Pierre L.
1975   *Man in Society: A Biosocial View*. New York: Elsevier.
1977   "Response to Lee Ellis' `The Decline and Fall of Sociology.'" *The American Sociologist* 12:
        75-76.

Van Gelder, Lindsy
1985   "Help for Technophobes: Think of Your Computer as Just Another Appliance." *Ms.* 13
        (January): 89-91.

Van Herk, Aritha
1987   *No Fixed Address: An Amorous Journey*. Toronto: McClelland-Bantam.

Vaughan, Diane
1987   *Uncoupling: Turning Points in Intimate Relationships*. New York: Oxford University
        Press.

Veevers, Jean E.
1980   *Childless by Choice*. Toronto: Butterworths.
1988   "The `Real' Marriage Squeeze: Mate Selection, Mortality, and the Mating Gradient."
        Sociological Perspectives 31: 169-89.

Verbrugge, Lois M.
1977   "The Structure of Adult Friendship Choices." *Social Forces* 56: 576-97.
1985   "Gender and Health: An Update on Hypotheses and Evidence." *Journal of Health and
        Social Behavior* 26: 156-82.

Vickers, Jill McCalla
1976   "Women in the Universities" in Gwen Matheson, ed., *Women in the Canadian Mosaic*,
        pp. 199-240. Toronto: Peter Martin Associates.
1984   (ed.), *Taking Sex Into Account: The Policy Consequences of Sexist Research*. Ottawa:
        Carleton University Press.

_____, and June Adam
1977   *But Can You Type?* Toronto: Clarke, Irwin in association with the Canadian Association
        of University Teachers.

Waddington, C.H.
1977   *Tools for Thought*. London: Jonathan Cape.

Wakil, S. Parvez, C.M. Siddique, and F.A. Wakil
    1981   "Between Two Cultures: A Study in Socialization of Children of Immigrants." *Journal of Marriage and the Family* 43: 929-40.

Walker, L.
    1984   "Sex Differences in Development of Moral Reasoning: A Critical Review." *Child Development* 55: 677-91.

Wallace, Cecelia
    1976   "Changes in the Churches" in Gwen Matheson, ed., *Women in the Canadian Mosaic*, pp. 93-128. Toronto: Peter Martin Associates.

Waller, W.
    1937   "The Rating and Dating Complex." *American Sociological Review* 2: 727-34.

Walsh, Mary Roth
    1987   "Is Psychoanalytic Theory Relevant to the Psychology of Women?" in Mary Roth Walsh, ed., The *Psychology of Women: Ongoing Debates*. New Haven, Connecticut: Yale University Press.

Walster, E., G.W. Galster, J. Piliavin, and L. Schmidt
    1973   "Playing Hard-to-Get: Understanding an Elusive Phenomenon." *Journal of Personality and Social Psychology* 26: 113-21.

_____ , and G. William Walster
    1978   *A New Look at Love.* Reading, Mass.: Addison-Wesley.

Walters, William A.W., and Michael W. Ross, eds.
    1986   Transsexualism and Sex Reassignment. Toronto: Oxford University Press.

Walum, Laurel Richardson
    1977   *The Dynamics of Sex and Gender: A Sociological Perspective.* Chicago: Rand McNally.

Ward, Kathryn B., and Linda Grant
    1985   "The Feminist Critique and a Decade of Published Research in Sociology Journals." *Sociological Quarterly* 26: 139-57.

Warren, Catharine E.
    1986   *Vignettes of Life: Experiences and Self Perceptions of New Canadian Women.* Calgary: Detselig Enterprises.

Weeks, Wendy
    1984   "Part-time Work: The Business View on Second-class Jobs for Housewives and Mothers" in Graham S. Lowe and Harvey J. Krahn, eds., *Working Canadians: Readings in the Sociology of Work and Industry*, pp. 137-46. Toronto: Methuen.

Weiner, Nella Fermi
    1979   "Lilith: First Woman, First Feminist." *International Journal of Women's Studies* 2: 551-59.

Weiss, Robert S.
    1982   "Attachment in Adult Life" in Colin Murray Parkes and Joan Stevenson-Hinde, eds., *The Place of Attachment in Human Behavior*, pp. 171-84. New York: Basic Books.

Weisstein, Naomi
    1971   "Psychology Constructs the Female, or the Fantasy Life of the Male Psychologist" in Michele Hoffnung Garskof, ed., *Roles Women Play: Readings toward Women's Liberation*, pp. 60-83. Belmont, Calif.: Brooks/Cole.
    1982   "Tired of Arguing about Biological Inferiority?" *Ms.* (November): 41-46, 85-86.

Weitz, Shirley
1977 *Sex Roles: Biological, Psychological, and Social Foundations.* New York: Oxford University Press.

Weitzman, Lenore
1985 *The Divorce Revolution: The Unexpected Social and Economic Consequences for Women and Children in America.* New York: Free Press.

West, Candace, and Don H. Zimmerman
1977 "Women's Place in Everyday Talk: Reflections on Parent-child Interactions." *Social Problems* 24: 521-28.
1987 "Doing Gender." *Gender and Society* 1: 125-51.

Weston, Greg
1988 *Reign of Error: The Inside Story of John Turner's Troubled Leadership.* Toronto: McGraw-Hill Ryerson.
1989 "Courts Tackle `Fathers' Rights.'" *Calgary Herald* (July 30): C2.

Weston, Julia
1989 "Girls as Capable as Boys in Math..." *University Affairs* 30, #9, 5-6.

Weyant, Robert G.
1979 "The Relationship between Psychology and Women." *International Journal of Women's Studies* 2: 358-85.

White, Burton L.
1987 "Should you Stay Home with Your Baby?" in Mary Roth Walsh, ed., *The Psychology of Women: Ongoing Debates*, pp. 358-66. New Haven, Conn.: Yale University Press.

White, G.L.
1981 "Some Correlates of Romantic Jealousy." *Journal of Personality* 49: 129-47.

White, Julie
1980 *Women and Unions.* Ottawa: Advisory Council on the Status of Women.
1990 *Mail and Female: Women and the Canadian Union of Postal Workers:* Toronto. Thompson Educational Publishing.

White, Lynn K., and David B. Brinkerhoff
1981 "The Sexual Division of Labor: Evidence from Childhood." *Social Forces* 60: 170-81.

Whitehurst, Robert N.
1984 "The Future of Marriage and the Nuclear Family." In Maureen Baker, ed., *The Family: Changing Trends in Canada.* Toronto: McGraw-Hill Ryerson.

_____ , and G.V. Booth
1980 *The Sexes: Changing Relationships in a Pluralistic Society.* Toronto: Gage.

Whiting, B.B., and C.P. Edwards
1973 "A Cross-cultural Analysis of Sex Differences in the Behavior of Children Aged Three Through 11." *Journal of Personality and Social Psychology* 91: 171-88.

Whorf, B.
1949 *Four Articles on Metalinguistics.* Washington, D.C.: Foreign Service Institute, Department of State.

Wilkinson, Sue, ed.
1986 *Feminist Social Psychology: Developing Theory and Practice.* Philadelphia: Open University Press.

Williams, John E., and Deborah L. Best
    1982   *Measuring Sex Stereotypes: A Thirty-Nation Study*. Beverly Hills: Sage.

Williams, Juanita H.
    1978   "*Woman: Myth and Stereotype*." International Journal of Women's Studies 1: 221- 47.
    1983   *Psychology of Women*. 2nd ed. New York: Norton.
    1987   *Psychology of Women: Behavior in a Biosocial Context*. 3rd ed. New York: W.W. Norton.

Williams, Tannis MacBeth, ed.
    1986   *The Impact of Television: A Natural Experiment in Three Communities*. Orlando, Florida: Academic Press.

Williamson, Nancy
    1976   "Sex Preferences, Sex Control, and the Status of Women." *Signs* 4: 847-62.

Wilson, Edward O.
    1975   *Sociobiology: The New Synthesis*. Cambridge: Harvard University Press.
    1978   *On Human Nature*. Cambridge, Mass.: Harvard University Press.

Wilson, Susannah J.
    1981   "The Image of Women in Canadian Magazines." in Elihu Katz and Tamas Szeckso, eds., *Mass Media and Social Change*, pp. 231-45. Beverly Hills, Calif.: Sage.
    1982   *Women, the Family and the Economy*. Toronto: McGraw-Hill Ryerson.
    1986   *Women, the Family and the Economy*. 2nd ed. Toronto: McGraw-Hill Ryerson.

Winn, Marie
    1977   *The Plug-in Drug: Television, Children and the Family*. New York: Viking.
    1983   *Children without Childhood*. New York: Pantheon.

Wolfenstein, Martha
    1968   "Children's Humor: Sex, Names, and Double Meanings" in Toby Talbot, ed., *The World of the Child*, pp. 266-84. Garden City, N.Y.: Doubleday Anchor.

Wollstonecraft, Mary
    1792   *A Vindication of the Rights of Woman*. New York: W.W. Norton, 1967.

Woodward, Kenneth L.
    1990   "Young Beyond Their Years." *Newsweek, Special Issue on 'The 21st Century Families.'* Winter/Spring: 54, 55, 57, 60.

Woolf, Virginia
    1938   *Three Guineas*. New York: Harcourt Brace.

Woollett, A., D. White, and L. Lyon
    1982   "Observations of Fathers at Birth." In N. Beail and J. McGuire, eds., *Fathers: Psychological Perspectives*. London: Junction.

Woolsey, Lorette K.
    1987a   "Bonds Between Women and Between Men, Part I: A Review of Theory." *Atlantis* 13: 116-24.
    1987b   "Bonds Between Women and Between Men, Part II: A Review of Research." *Atlantis* 13: 125-36.

Wright, Paul H.
    1982   "Men's Friendships, Women's Friendships and the Alleged Inferiority of the Latter." *Sex Roles* 8: 1-20.

Wrightsman, Lawrence S., and Kay Deaux
1981   *Social Psychology in the 80s.* 3rd ed. Belmont, Calif.: Wadsworth.

Wylie, Philip
1942   *Generation of Vipers.* New York: Rinehart Pocket Books.

Yoels, William C., and David A. Karp
1978   "A Social Psychological Critique of `over-socialization': Dennis Wrong Revisited." *Sociological Symposium* 24: 27-39.

Young, Bert
1987   "Looking for Lonely Men" in Greta Hofmann Nemiroff, ed., *Women and Men: Interdisciplinary Readings on Gender*, pp. 303-15. Toronto: Fitzhenry and Whiteside.

Young, Michael, and Peter Willmott
1973   *The Symmetrical Family: A Study of Work and Leisure in the London Region.* London: Routledge and Kegan Paul.

Zaremba, Eve
1982   "Shades of Lavender: Lesbian Sex and Sexuality" in Maureen Fitzgerald, Connie Guberman, and Margie Wolfe, eds., *Still Ain't Satisfied! Canadian Feminism Today*, pp. 85-92. Toronto: Women's Press.

Zellman, Gail L., and Jacqueline D. Goodchilds
1983   "Becoming Sexual in Adolescence" in Elizabeth R. Allgeier and Naomi B. McCormick, eds., *Changing Boundaries: Gender Roles and Sexual Behavior*, pp. 49-63. Palo Alto, Calif.: Mayfield.

Zuckerman, Diana M., and Donald H. Sayre
1982   "Cultural Sex Role Expectations and Children's Sex-role Concepts." *Sex Roles* 8: 853-62.

Zwarun, Suzanne (1984, 1987, 1989)
1988   "Male Lobby Undermines Progress." *Calgary Herald* (July 25): A3.
1989   "Women Forced to Smile." *Calgary Herald* (January 30): A3.

Index

Authority, and means of production, 57

B

Bakan, David, 28
Baker, Maureen, 84
Barash, D.P., 58, 59
Bardwick, Judith M., 47
Bart, Pauline, 111
Batcher, Elaine, 89, 147
Belenky, M.F., 163-64, 191 n3
Bem, Sandra, 77, 96
Benston, Margaret, 17
Berger, Brigitte, 6, 18, 76, 182, 190, 193
Berger, John, 26
Berger, Peter, 6, 13, 18, 76, 182, 190, 193
Bernard, Jessie, 8, 12, 17, 26, 32, 33, 214, 218, 219, 233, 242, 249
    stag effect, 11
Best, Raphaela, 130, 136, 137, 138, 140, 159
Birth control, 57, 118
Birth rate, declining, 105
Blainey, Justine, 85
Bleier, Ruth, 33, 45, 52, 68, 70
Block, Jeanne H., 98-99
Bonaparte, Napoleon, 26
Boyd, Monica, 29, 31
Boys, as first child, preference for, 5
Brain controversy, 32
Brain lateralization, 69-70
Broverman, L.K., 29
Brownmiller, Susan, 5, 81, 231, 259
Brym, Robert, 198

C

Canadian Charter of Rights and Freedoms, 260, 261, 271
    women's rights sections, 275 n8
Canadian Labour Congress, 212
Canadian Newsletter of Research on Women, 8
Canadian Research Institute for the Advancement of Women, 8
Canadian Sociology and Anthropology Association, 8
Capitalism
    and radical feminism, 201-202
    and socialist feminism, 202-203
    women's relationship to means of production, 200-201
Carr, Shirley, 212
Chafetz, Janet, 6, 131, 134, 143, 144
Childcare, 239-40. *See also* Daycare.
Child-rearing, sex/gender differences in, 80
Children's books, gender imagery in, 180-81
Chodorow, Nancy, 111, 116, 142, 239
Chromosomes, 35
Circumcision accident, 69

Clerical work, 216-17
Cognitive-developmental theory, 95-97
    conservation of physical properties, 95
Comic strips, gender images in, 181
Communal mode
    as feminine orientation, 28
    of sociological research, 17
Communication
    changing sexist forms of, 190
    micropolitical explanation of gender differences, 189
    role explanation of gender differences, 189
    sociolinguistic gender subcultures, 189-90
Communication, non-verbal, 156, 187-89
    demeanor, 188
    gaze, 187
    importance of, 182-83
    personal space, 188-89
    smiling, 187-88
    touching, 188
Communication, verbal
    as gender socialization agent, 182
Complaints of female sociologists, 10-14
    androcentric nature of sociology, 12-14
    women's status in academia, 10-12
Contraceptives, legalization of, 118
Cooley, Charles Horton, 94
Copps, Sheila, 271
Coser, Lewis, 13
Couvade, 54, 72 n4
COWDUNG, 42
Creativity, 39
Cross-sex relationships, 142-53
    platonic friendships, 143-45
    romantic relationships, 145-53
Cultural universals, 52
    division of labour, 52
    male dominance, 52-53
    in sociobiology, 58
Custody of children, 240, 242

D

Daigle, Chantal, 228
Daly, Mary, 260
Darwin, Charles, 58
Dawkins, Richard, 58
Daycare, 262
    need for, 114
Deaux, Kay, 34, 37, 38, 39, 40, 41, 78
Differentiation of sexes, 4-5
Division of labour
    bases of, 55-56
    as cultural universal, 52
    during gender socialization, 82
    familial, instrumental vs. expressive specialists, 29

Hormone theory of gender *(continued)*
  and animal studies, 60
  brain lateralization, 69-70
  gender-related emotions, 66-67
  psychosexual abnormalities, 67-69
Horney, Karen, 61
Housework, 220-23, *see also* Work, unpaid.
  politics of, 237
Huston, Aletha, 78, 79, 82, 85, 86, 87, 88, 90, 93, 95, 96, 97, 109, 112, 113, 120, 121, 159

I

Incest, 232
Incest taboo, animal vs. human, 51
Inclusive fitness, maximizing, 58
Indian Act, amendments to, 258
Infertility, 119
In Search of Justice, 228, 268-69
Instrumental specialists, men as, 29
Intellectual abilities, sex differences in, 37-39
  creativity, 39
  IQ, 37
  mathematical ability, 38
  spatial skills, 38
  verbal abilities, 37-38

J

Jacklin, Carol N., 34, 38, 39, 40, 41, 66, 67
Jealousy, male, 143
Joint custody, 240

K

Kanter, Rosabeth, 11, 203, 204
Keywan, Zonia, 124
Kimball, Meredith, 182, 244, 245, 246, 247
Kin-keeping, 236
Kohlberg, Lawrence, 95-97
Kome, Penney, 254, 255, 260, 270, 271, 275 n4
Kostash, Myrna, 89, 91, 144, 185

L

Labour force participation, 204-207
  of men, 205
  reasons for increase, 206-207
  of women, 204-205
Lambert, Helen H., 58
Lambert, W.E., 2, 125
Lancaster, Jane, 48, 49, 50, 51
Landsberg, Michele, 104
lang, k.d., 76, 181
Language
  euphemisms, 184
  gender differences in structure and content, 183-84
    definition by gender, 183-84

evaluation by sex, 184
exclusion of women, 184
importance of, 182-83
linguistic usage and conversational style, 185-86
male-constructed, 183
reverse devaluation, 184
sexist, 184, 190, 192 n7
Lepine, Marc, 270
Lesbians, *see also* Homosexuals.
  dual oppression of, 265
Lewis, Charles, 87
Lewis, Michael, 79, 80, 90, 94
Liberal feminism, 257-58
Lipman-Blumen, Jean, 2, 4, 5, 6, 7, 25, 157, 163, 189, 201-202, 247, 249, 255, 256
Lynn, David, 100

M

McClung, Nellie, 202, 253, 275 n3
McDaniel, Susan, 118, 119, 204, 227, 239, 240, 242, 247
Maccoby, Eleanor, 34, 38, 39, 40, 41, 66, 67
  IQ scores, 37
Machismo, in agentic research, 17
Macho code, 136, 137, 140
Macromanipulation vs. micromanipulation, 7, 56-57
Magazines
  as gender socialization agent, 178-80
  for homemakers, 178-79
  for working women, 179
Male bonding, 132-33
Male dominance
  and authority, 57
  basis of, 56-57
  as cultural universal, 52-53
Male-female differences, *see* Sex differences; Sex/gender differences.
Male liberation, 266-67
Male sex role literature, 10
Malmo, Cheryl, 33
Man-the-Hunter theory, 52, 55
Marriage
  dissolution, 240-42
  and domestic labour, 236, 238
  gradient, 148
  his and her priorities, 233-34
  and oppression of women, 228
  and parenthood, 238-40
  and power, 234-36
  and psychological distress, 242-43
  women's, and men's, 233-43
Marxism
  influence on feminism, 199-200, 203
  traditional, 200-201
Masculinity
  as agentic orientation, 28

Sociobiology *(continued)*
  inclusive fitness, 58
  parental investment, 58-59
  and sexual double standard, 59
Sociology
  agentic mode of research, 17
  communal mode of research, 17
  complaints of female sociologists, 10-14
  of gender relations, history of, 7-10
  methodology, 16-18
  pre-feminist, 13-14
  research topics, 14-15
  teaching, 18-19
  theory, sexism in, 15-16
Sociology of knowledge perspective, 13
Sociometryl, 154 n3
Spatial skills, 38
Spender, Dale, 16, 17, 192 n7, 251, 252
Steele, Phyllis, 160
Steinem, Gloria, 1, 152, 225, 249, 250 n2, 268, 272, 274
Stereotype, defined, 27
Stone, Gregory, 81
Stowe, Emily, 252-53
Stratification, internal, 232
Stratification structure, 198
Strong-Boag, Veronica, 9, 19, 157, 244
Structural barriers in academia, 11
Suffrage Movement, 251, 252
Suicide, levels of explanation for, 195
Surnames, changing, 183
Suttee, 246
Symbolic interactionism, 92-94
  generalized other, 94
  language, role of, 93
  role-taking, 92
  self-concept, 92
  significant other, 92

T
Task Force on Sex-role Stereotyping in the Broadcast Media, 173
Tavris, Carol, 24, 26, 36, 38, 39, 40-41, 46, 48, 58, 60, 67
Tchambuli, 54-55, 57
Teachers
  banker, 163-64
  as gender socialization agents, 158-59
  midwife, 163-64
Television, as gender socialization agent, 174-75
Temerlin, Maurice, 50-51
Terms of address, 183
Tesson, Geoffrey, 120, 130
Testosterone, 35, 50
  and aggression, 53, 67
Textbooks, gender depiction in, 161-62
Theoretical orientation, defined, 21 n4
Theory, defined, 21 n4

Thomas, Audrey, 113
Tiger, Lionel, 131, 132-33
Transsexual, 2, 46, 75
  Agnes, 73-75
Tremblay, Jean-Guy, 228
Tuchman, Gaye, 25, 39, 172

U
Unemployment, 211-12, 216

V
Vallee, Brian, 6-7
van Leeuwenhock, 33
Vaughan, Diane, 240
Verbal abilities, sex differences in, 37-38
Vickers, Jill, 10, 11, 12, 16, 18
Violence, 269
  against women, 274
  as expression of power, 6-7
  familial, 231-32, 250 n1
  in romantic relationships, 152
Voice of Women, The, 256

W
Wade, Carol, 24, 26, 36, 38, 39, 40-41, 46, 48, 58, 60, 67
Wakil, S.P., 123-24
Walum, L.R., 199
Weisstein, Naomi, 45, 50, 55
Whitehurst, R.N., 7
Widowhood, 245-46
Williams, John G., 27, 77, 86-87
  international study of stereotypes, 27-29
Wilson, Edward O., 57
Wollstonecraft, Mary, 252, 257
Women
  in academia, status of, 10-12
  folk theories about, 24-31
  myths of, 25-26
   as insignificant non-person, 26
   as mother nature, 25
   as saint, 25
   as sex object, 25-26
   as terrifying enchantress, 25
  resistance to male power, 7
Women's Christian Temperance Union (WCTU), 253, 254
Women's Legal Education and Action Fund (LEAF), 260, 270
Women's movement, *see also* Feminism.
  agenda of, 273-74
  history, 251-52
  prospects of, 271-73
  re-emergence of, 255-56
  suffrage in Canada, 252-55
  vote, support for, 274-75 n2
Women's studies, and sociology of gender, 9

Woolley, Helen, 32
Work, paid
  authority structures, 210-11
  conclusions about gender and, 217-18
  current developments, 213-17
  and gender, 203-18
  gender model, 203
  gender segregation of, 207-210
  immigrant women, 212-13
  income and benefits, 210
  instability of employment, 211-12
  job model, 203

men in female-oriented work, 216-17
part-time, 205, 206
pre-feminist interpretations of, 203
professional women, 213-15
unionization, 212
women in blue-collar preserves, 215-16
Work, unpaid
  domestic labour, 220-23
  gender and, 218-23
  volunteer work, 218-20
Wylie, Philip, 111